MW01200559

Read this book online today:

With SAP PRESS BooksOnline we offer you online access to knowledge from the leading SAP experts. Whether you use it as a beneficial supplement or as an alternative to the printed book, with SAP PRESS BooksOnline you can:

• Access your book anywhere, at any time. All you need is an Internet connection.
• Perform full text searches on your book and on the entire SAP PRESS library.
• Build your own personalized SAP library.

The SAP PRESS customer advantage:

Register this book today at *www.sap-press.com* and obtain exclusive free trial access to its online version. If you like it (and we think you will), you can choose to purchase permanent, unrestricted access to the online edition at a very special price!

Here's how to get started:

1. Visit *www.sap-press.com*.
2. Click on the link for SAP PRESS BooksOnline and login (or create an account).
3. Enter your free trial license key, shown below in the corner of the page.
4. Try out your online book with full, unrestricted access for a limited time!

Your personal free trial **license key** for this online book is:

w7rk-hmu9-epiv-82bs

SAP® Extended Warehouse Management:
Processes, Functionality, and Configuration

 PRESS

SAP PRESS is a joint initiative of SAP and Galileo Press. The know-how offered by SAP specialists combined with the expertise of the Galileo Press publishing house offers the reader expert books in the field. SAP PRESS features first-hand information and expert advice, and provides useful skills for professional decision-making.

SAP PRESS offers a variety of books on technical and business related topics for the SAP user. For further information, please visit our website: *www.sap-press.com*.

Varun Uppuleti
Customizing Extended Warehouse Management with SAP ERP
2009, 226pp., hardcover
978-1-59229-286-8

Martin Murray
Maximize your Warehouse Operations with SAP ERP
2010, 303pp., hardcover
978-1-59229-309-4

Martin Murray
Warehouse Management with SAP ERP: Functionality and Technical Configuration (Second Edition)
2012, 579pp., hardcover
978-1-59229-409-1

M. Brian Carter, Joerg Lange, Frank-Peter Bauer,
Christoph Persich, Tim Dalm

SAP® Extended Warehouse Management:
Processes, Functionality, and Configuration

Galileo Press

Bonn • Boston

Galileo Press is named after the Italian physicist, mathematician and philosopher Galileo Galilei (1564–1642). He is known as one of the founders of modern science and an advocate of our contemporary, heliocentric worldview. His words *Eppur si muove* (And yet it moves) have become legendary. The Galileo Press logo depicts Jupiter orbited by the four Galilean moons, which were discovered by Galileo in 1610.

Editor Erik Herman
Copyeditor Mike Beady
Cover Design Jill Winitzer
Photo Credit Image Copyright Volyntsev Andrey. Used under license from Shutterstock.com
Layout Design Vera Brauner
Production Editor Kelly O'Callaghan
Assistant Production Editor Graham Geary
Typesetting Publishers' Design and Production Services, Inc.
Printed and bound in Canada

ISBN 978-1-59229-304-9

© 2012 by Galileo Press Inc., Boston (MA)

1st edition 2010; 1st reprint, with corrections, 2012

Library of Congress Cataloging-in-Publication Data
SAP Extended Warehouse Management: Processes, Functionality, and Configuration / M. Brian Carter ... [et al.].-- 1st ed.
p. cm.
Includes bibliographical references and index.
ISBN-13: 978-1-59229-304-9 (alk. paper)
ISBN-10: 1-59229-304-2 (alk. paper)
1. Warehouses--Management--Computer programs. 2. Business logistics--Computer programs. 3. Inventory control--Computer programs. 4. SAP EWM. I. Carter, M. Brian.
HF5485.E97 2010
658.7'85028553--dc22
2009053213

Contents at a Glance

Contents

Acknowledgments

The authors would like to thank their colleagues in the SAP development, suite solution management, and consulting teams for providing first-hand knowledge and valuable feedback for this text. In particular, the authors would like to thank the development team of Bernd Ernesti and Thomas Griesser, in particular, Stefan Grabowski, Andreas Daum, Bernhard Hauser, and Jan Kappallo for their individual contributions. While the authors thank these individuals and the additional ones listed below for their assistance, the authors themselves are solely responsible for the content of the text and any omissions from it.

We would also like to thank Jenifer Niles, Erik Herman, and the editing team at SAP PRESS for their time, effort, and patience in the construction of this text.

M. Brian Carter

I would like to thank my friends and colleagues at SAP, especially the many people who encouraged me to go forward with the project, for their support on the creation of this text. In particular, I would like to thank my co-authors as well as Richard Kirker and Madhu Madhavan for their active involvement and valuable insights for my own contributions. I would also like to thank my management teams at SAP, especially Bryan Charnock and Kerstin Geiger, for supporting the project and my participation in it. And finally, I would especially like to thank my friends and family for their love and support – especially my wife, Teresa, and two children, Evan and Meredith, who had to endure many hours of absence during the construction of this text.

Joerg Lange

I would like to thank my colleagues within SAP Consulting Industrial Manufacturing in Ratingen for their detailed reviews and feedback, especially Markus Plessmann, Stefan Kalms and Stefan Reichert. I would also like to thank my wife Rebecca for her outstanding support throughout the writing for this text.

Frank-Peter Bauer

Many thanks to my wife for her understanding during the construction phase. And many thanks to colleagues of EWM standard development mentioned above and also to Gunther Sanchez from EWM solution consulting for their support.

Christoph Persich

I would like to thank my friends and colleagues for their support during the creation of this text. Special thanks go to Matthias Schilka from EWM Solution Consulting for his exceptional support.

Tim Dalm

I would like to additionally thank Harald Breitling for his valuable input.

The SAP® Extended Warehouse Management (EWM) application provides functionality for managing complex scenarios for high-volume distribution operations.

1 Introduction to SAP Extended Warehouse Management

This text provides you with the information you need to understand the SAP EWM solution, including the functions that it supports, how to set up those functions, and how to get started with a project that will utilize those functions to support your warehouse operations. In this chapter, we will start by providing some background and history on SAP's warehousing applications, tell you how SAP EWM evolved, inform you about the variations of the EWM brand, and tell you who this text is for and how to use it. We hope that the text serves to inform and educate you and help you make the right decisions regarding your EWM implementation.

1.1 Background and History

In the past few decades, warehouses have evolved from simple receiving, storage, and shipping facilities to full-scale, high-volume, flow-through distribution operations. Global competition has driven businesses to hold less inventory and to get their products to market both faster and with more precise timing than in the past. Competition has also driven both local and global corporations to become leaner and more efficient and to react faster to both changes in the marketplace and in the internal business environment. Constantly shifting business priorities, increasing seasonality of products, faster business cycles, and more frequent mergers and acquisitions are just some of the market conditions that lead to intense pressure on warehouses to increase efficiency while still providing flexibility to the business to allow it to react to changing demands.

At the same time, disproportionate increases in costs of labor, raw materials, and real estate threaten to drive warehousing costs higher, impeding companies' ability to make a profit. For some companies, this pressure to perform effective logistics operations is too great or comes at too great a cost, and they are increasingly turning to outsourced solutions, such as third-party logistics providers, to cost-effectively handle the volumes of products and ever-changing business requirements. However, this just shifts the burden to a whole new group of people, upon whom the pressures are even more intensified by the need to not only maintain flexibility for a single organization, but to maintain flexibility across multiple organizations. To top it off, those organizations often have very different products, processes, business requirements, and management styles.

This increase in pressure on warehouses to do more with less has led to a corresponding increase in the complexity of business processes. In turn, this increasing complexity of business processes then requires both an increase in talent of warehouse managers and an increase in capabilities of the systems that help those managers run their businesses.

The evolution of the warehouse management system (WMS) software industry has run parallel to the changes in the warehousing and distribution marketplace, with ever-increasing business process capabilities supported by more and more capable WMSs delivered by companies who specialize in standardized software. However, there are still companies who prefer to run their own bespoke systems filled with functionality specific to their own businesses and supported by armies of programmers. But more and more, those companies are realizing the benefits in the total cost of ownership (TCO) of using standard software solutions that also meet their business needs. And those companies are turning to software vendors like SAP for their software solutions.

Since 1972, SAP has specialized in providing standard software solutions for common business processes. Since the first release of R/1 a year after the company's founding, SAP has constantly evolved their products to expand into new markets or to match the changing business needs of their customer base. Through the R/2 days in the late 1970s and 1980s, SAP delivered software to not only meet the needs of back-office functions like finance and purchasing, but began to move more and more to the front lines of managing the product manufacturing, sales, and distribution. In the early 1990s, SAP delivered its flagship client-server product, SAP R/3, and it has continued to enhance that application throughout its life-cycle. The SAP R/3 product evolved in the early 2000s into what is today known as SAP ERP. In the meantime, starting in the late 1990s, SAP began to deliver, in addition to its core ERP functions, specialized functions for Customer Relationship Management (CRM), Supply Chain Management (SCM), and Business Warehousing (BW). The collective release of these products was dubbed the "New Dimension" products, representing a new dimension in enterprise software.

In the 2000s, SAP continued to refine and expand those products, delivering release after release of new and revised functionality. As part of this wave of new and expanded functionality, SAP delivered the first release of SAP EWM in 2005. At the time, EWM was part of the SAP SCM solution and could not be delivered separately. Since then, SAP has delivered the capability to deploy EWM as an add-on to SAP ERP, allowing EWM to break free from its SCM roots and enjoy its own product naming and branding — SAP EWM.

In this text, we will discuss SAP EWM, including its history, configuration, implementation, utilization for solving common business problems, and extension to solve implementations specific business problem. We will discuss the functionality of the latest release, SAP EWM 7.0. Unless otherwise specified, all screenshots and product descriptions are specific to the SAP EWM 7.0 solution.

1.2   The Evolution of SAP WMS

Even as early as release R/2, SAP contained functionality for locating products in the warehouse. At the time, it was a basic locator system, but it provided the baseline for SAP's foray into the warehouse management (WM) world. In 1993, SAP released R/3 Release 2.0 and with it, its first warehousing application on the client server framework. Back then, SAP WM only covered the basics of a warehousing application, namely to track product in multiple bins in the warehouse and assign pallet identification labels, or pallet IDs, to the product in the bin. In SAP parlance, these pallet IDs were known as storage units.

Since its initial releases, SAP has extended its WM application with additional functionality including:

- integration to SAP R/3 Production Planning, Quality Management, and Logistics Information Systems (in SAP R/3 Release 3.0 and 3.1)

- wave picking, warehouse monitoring, and integration to SAP R/3 Human Resources (HR) (in SAP R/3 Release 4.0)

- decentralized WM and radio frequency support (in SAP R/3 Release 4.5)

- support for handling unit (HU) management (an Inventory Management–level method for tracking pallet IDs across plants, storage locations, and warehouses) and packing station capabilities (in SAP R/3 Release 4.6)

- task and resource management for handling multistep movements that could be performed by multiple resources (in SAP R/3 Enterprise (4.7) Extension Set 1.1)

- support for yard management, cross-docking, and value-added services (VAS) (in SAP R/3 Enterprise (4.7) Extension Set 2.0)

In parallel, businesses around the world started to use the SAP WM system to manage more and more complex warehouses and distribution centers. As the product grew, the customer base grew with it, and today, SAP WM is deployed by more than 5,000 SAP customers worldwide.

In 2005, SAP released version 5.0 of its SCM software, and with it, released the first version of its SAP SCM EWM software. This version of the WM software was completely separate architecturally from the SAP WM from ERP. Although they shared some common themes in terms of capabilities, the SAP EWM was designed from the ground up with the needs of complex, highly automated, high-volume distribution centers in mind.

The design of the solution was based on a coordinated effort between the industry, solution, and development experts at SAP and a set of development partners who brought extensive business expertise on high-volume planning, order fulfillment, and distribution operations. SAP worked together with its development partners in a strategic development project that lasted over three years to design and deploy a standard software solution that would compete in the marketplace with the most advanced WMS. SAP and the development partners engaged in this effort to build a complete set of software solutions to manage their complex, high-volume service parts operations — not just a WMS, but also a planning and fulfillment system that would coordinate together perfectly to manage entire operations. Today, those applications, including SAP CRM, SAP ERP, and SAP SCM, including the Service Parts Planning and EWM applications, are marketed together in the SAP Service and Asset Management industry solution. The components of the industry solution used for service parts are often collectively referred to as "the SAP solution for service parts management."

Even though the development partners of SAP intended to use the solution to manage distribution centers full of service parts, and the solution was delivered along with other applications specific to service parts, the SAP EWM solution was built with the intent that it could be used across multiple industries. For instance, the first release of EWM (as part of SAP SCM 5.0) delivered functionality to support the needs of complex, high-volume distribution centers, including:

- slotting
- deconsolidation
- cross-docking
- yard management
- complex internal routing
- kitting
- VAS

In EWM 2007 (also called EWM 5.1), SAP added support for:

- Labor Management (LM)
- Radio Frequency Identification (RFID) enablement for internal warehouse processes
- kit-to-stock
- additional goods receipt functions
- catch weight support
- capabilities for direct connection to automated material handling equipment, or Material Flow Systems (MFS)
- enhancements for batch management
- enhancements for serial number handling
- manual creation of outbound deliveries

In more recent years, SAP has added additional functionality to SAP EWM to support the needs of consumer products and retail companies, and today, the solution is marketed and sold to all industries that require complex WMSs. Specifically, in EWM 7.0, SAP added support for:

- graphical warehouse layouts
- additional resource management features, including:
  - task interleaving
  - execution constraints
  - support for semi-system guided work
- additional cross-docking support, including:
  - opportunistic cross-docking
  - retail merchandise distribution
  - production cross-docking
- support for production supply from an EWM-managed warehouse

Following Release EWM 7.0, SAP will convert the SCM platform, including EWM, to the enhancement package model for deploying new functionality. This model has already been employed on ERP following the release of SAP ERP 2005 (or what is now known as SAP ERP 6.0), and now the same model will be utilized for SCM, CRM, and the other major SAP business applications. The enhancement package model allows SAP to deliver enhanced functionality through regular updates between major releases. The updates can be activated as needed via business functions.

The business functions contain a set of similar or related functions, allowing you to decide which business functions to activate without requiring you to activate all of the functionality delivered with the enhancement package at once. This can save you considerable time in testing the application of the enhancement package, because you only have to test the functions that are affected by the activated business functions. In turn, the business functions allow you to deploy the functionality to your end users faster. And the enhancement package model allows SAP to bring new functionality to market faster, making it a win-win for everyone.

The first enhancement package for SAP EWM is scheduled to be released in mid-2010. The functions will be delivered in separate business functions, which will allow you to install the enhancement pack and then activate one or all (or none) of the business functions and test your solution accordingly. In the coming years, SAP will continue to add additional features to the EWM 7.0 release through enhancement packages.

1.3   The EWM Brand

When SAP released its SAP R/3 Enterprise Extension Set 2.0 functionality to support yard management, cross-docking, and VAS, it assigned the informal name Extended Warehouse Management to this collection of new functions. Though you wouldn't find this name anywhere in the system, the features were collectively referred to using this moniker so that SAP employees and partners could effectively discuss the new features with their customers.

One common point of confusion is that the EWM brand, as it applies to ERP WM, does not include the function Task and Resource Management (TRM). TRM was released with SAP R/3 Enterprise Extension Set 1.1, whereas the EWM naming only applies as of R/3 Enterprise Extension Set 2.0.

What is also sometimes confusing is that the EWM naming does not even apply to all of the features that were delivered for SAP ERP WM with Extension Set 2.0. For example, dynamic cycle counting, the functionality that lets the user walk up to a storage bin in the warehouse with a Radio Frequency device and initiate an ad hoc cycle count, was introduced with Extension Set 2.0, but it is not included in the EWM features. The only three functions that are included in the EWM brand as it applies to SAP ERP WM include cross-docking, yard management, and VAS.

When SAP delivered SAP SCM 5.0 in 2005, it also delivered EWM. As mentioned previously, this version of EWM was related to SAP ERP EWM in name only. The SAP SCM EWM was delivered on the SCM platform, completely separate from SAP ERP and without any direct link to SAP ERP WM or SAP ERP EWM. It uses different tables, different structures, and different program from the ERP application. In some ways, it uses the same concepts and paradigms, but in other ways, it is significantly different and even performs the same functions in uniquely different ways. To hopefully make it more clear, Figure 1.1 provides a visual diagram of the functions to which the EWM is used to refer. However, in this text, we will focus on the right-hand side of the diagram — the SCM EWM.

In 2007, SAP decoupled EWM from the SCM Basis layer so that the company could prepare to deploy the solution as an add-on to ERP. An add-on is a product that can be deployed on top of another application platform without being coupled to or dependent on the underlying software technology architecture. Allowing the EWM to be deployed as an add-on would mean that businesses of all sizes that did not necessarily have the skills, manpower, or funding to deploy an SCM server could deploy EWM on their ERP server and enjoy the benefits of the latest warehousing applications.

As briefly mentioned earlier, in 2005, SAP announced that it would migrate its ERP application to the Enhancement Pack model and that the ERP 2005 release (which it later renamed ERP 6.0) would be the "go to" release for the next several years. This Enhancement Pack model allows SAP to deliver new functions in a quicker way and allows customers to implement those new functions more quickly and easily by giving customers the freedom to choose which business functions to activate after implementing the enhancement pack.

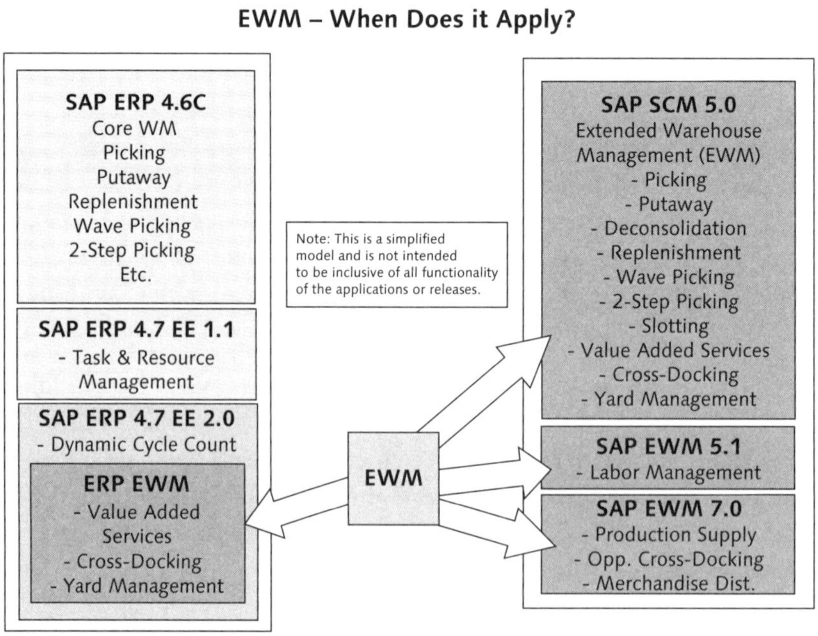

EWM – When Does it Apply?

SAP ERP 4.6C
Core WM
Picking
Putaway
Replenishment
Wave Picking
2-Step Picking
Etc.

Note: This is a simplified model and is not intended to be inclusive of all functionality of the applications or releases.

SAP ERP 4.7 EE 1.1
- Task & Resource Management

SAP ERP 4.7 EE 2.0
- Dynamic Cycle Count

ERP EWM
- Value Added Services
- Cross-Docking
- Yard Management

EWM

SAP SCM 5.0
Extended Warehouse Management (EWM)
- Picking
- Putaway
- Deconsolidation
- Replenishment
- Wave Picking
- 2-Step Picking
- Slotting
- Value Added Services
- Cross-Docking
- Yard Management

SAP EWM 5.1
- Labor Management

SAP EWM 7.0
- Production Supply
- Opp. Cross-Docking
- Merchandise Dist.

Figure 1.1 The EWM name can be applied to functionality of ERP and SCM. In this text, we will focus on the functionality on the right side.

When SAP delivered its second Enhancement Pack for ERP, SAP ERP 2005 Enhancement Pack 2, in 2007, it made good on its promise to allow EWM to be deployed as an add-on to ERP. Now customers have the choice of whether to deploy EWM on the SCM platform or on their existing ERP platform, giving them the freedom to provide all of the functionality on the right-hand side in Figure 1.1 on the ERP platform. In Chapter 26, Deploying EWM, we will further discuss the option of deploying EWM as an add-on to ERP.

1.4   Target Audience

In this text, we intend to provide knowledge, information, and reference material for project leads, implementation consultants, project team members, business analysts, and business users who are responsible for implementing, maintaining, or problem solving for the SAP EWM solution. Key decision makers who need to understand the application well enough to decide how and where to deploy EWM may also find the text useful in their decision-making processes. The text will cover an overview of the capabilities of the EWM solution, the configuration elements available in the standard solution, the methods used to solve common business process problems, plus the possibilities to extend the solution to meet more complex or unique business requirements. The text will provide both detailed system configuration and setup instructions, and descriptions of and solutions to common business concerns for complex high-volume distribution operations.

Following the introduction, the second section of the text will cover the basic warehouse setup, including the warehouse structure, warehouse master data, stock management, and warehouse document types. This section will provide a baseline for understanding the remaining sections and will also provide a reference for users who are getting started with an EWM implementation.

The third section will cover configuration and setup for basic warehousing processes, including inbound processing, outbound processing, internal movements (including replenishment and rearrangement), and physical inventory.

The fourth section will cover special cross-topics such as cross-docking, yard management, VAS, and data capture (including mobile data entry using radio frequency–enabled devices and RFID).

The final section and the appendix will provide conclusions, a list of common abbreviations, and the index. If you are not familiar with the SAP warehousing terms already, you may want to check the index or the online glossary (available in the SAP Online Help at *http://help.sap.com/saphelp_glossary/en/*) before you continue, or you may find it helpful to refer to them periodically as you read through the chapters.

Whether you read the text cover to cover or place it on your desk to use as a handy reference during your implementation (or both), we think that you will enjoy the text and find it both interesting and useful.

1.5   Summary

In this chapter, we introduced SAP EWM and described the contents of this text. Hopefully, this gives you an idea of what this text is about and how to use it. In the next chapters, we will describe the organizational structure and master data for EWM.

The organizational structure in ERP provides the basis for moving material in Inventory Management (IM), and it should generally model the operating environment of your company.

2   Organizational Structure

The first step in modeling the warehouse structure is to model the organizational structure of the supply chain and set up the warehouses that will be run using Extended Warehouse Management (EWM). The organizational structure is set up in the SAP ERP system. The typical structure looks somewhat like a pyramid (see Figure 2.1), with the company codes at the top level, the plants on the next level, storage locations on the next level, and then warehouses on the next level. The example provides here is strictly an example. However, the pyramid can sometimes look like it has an unstable base, as it tends to only get larger down to the storage location level, and the number of warehouses can be smaller than the number of storage locations. Your organization structure will look somewhat different than our example — the example here is strictly for illustrative purposes.

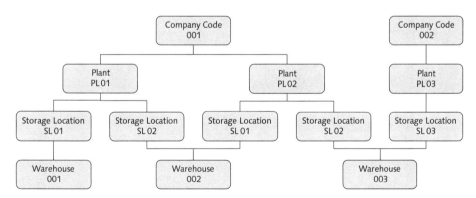

Figure 2.1   Typical Organizational Structure

At the top level of the pyramid is the company code. The company code is typically a financial structure, because the roll-up of the company's financial picture is usually performed at the company code level. You may often hear the company level of the organization referred to in common parlance as divisions or regions.

Each company code should contain one or more plants. Typical reasons to have separate company codes include:

▶ having locations in multiple countries

▶ having multiple divisions with different products or different lines of business

▶ other fiscal concerns that may drive a separate accounting for different locations and products

In the example provided in Figure 2.1, we show multiple company codes to illustrate how a single warehouse could be tied to multiple plants even if the plants are assigned to multiple company codes.

Frequently in this book, we will refer to the Implementation Guide (IMG). To access the IMG from any SAP system, use Transaction code SPRO or, from the SAP menu, follow the menu path TOOLS • CUSTOMIZING • IMG • EXECUTE PROJECT. Transaction codes can be entered in the transaction code box in the top left portion of the SAP Graphical User Interface (GUI), as shown in Figure 2.2. Menu items can be selected by using the standard SAP menu after logging on to the system. The standard SAP menu can be accessed by selecting the SAP MENU button from the button bar (also seen in Figure 2.2).

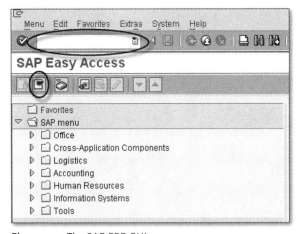

Figure 2.2 The SAP ERP GUI

To create the company codes in the ERP system, in the IMG, follow the menu path ENTERPRISE STRUCTURE • DEFINITION • FINANCIAL ACCOUNTING • EDIT, COPY, DELETE, CHECK COMPANY CODE • EDIT COMPANY CODE DATA.

In the case of the company codes, it is also possible to use a special function to copy the company code plus related tables together in one transaction. To access this transaction in the ERP IMG, follow the ENTERPRISE STRUCTURE • DEFINITION • FINANCIAL ACCOUNTING • EDIT, COPY, DELETE, CHECK COMPANY CODE • COPY, DELETE, CHECK COMPANY CODE menu path and use the relevant functions there.

The company code data is often set up by the financial accountants or the group within the implementation team responsible for that activity. We recommend to coordinate with the financial accounting team before making any changes to the company code level data, as the changes could have far reaching consequences.

2.1 Plants

At the next level of the pyramid are the plants. Each plant must be assigned to a single company code, but may contain one or multiple storage locations. The plants are typically used to segregate inventory into geographic or logical locations. The inventory which is located in these plants is valued in its respective plant and that inventory value rolls up to the company code level for financial tracking.

There are many reasons to have multiple plants, but geographic segregation is the most common one. Another reason may be to segregate inventory for financial tracking without affecting the financial consolidation at the company code level. And yet one more reason may be to segregate inventory for purposes of the sales teams. For example, one sales team may want to hold inventory for a group of customers and this inventory may be segregated into a separate logical plant, but it may still be physically held in the same locations. While the focus of this book is not on the organizational structure or the setup and configuration of SAP Financials (FI) or SAP Materials Management (MM), we discuss these reasons here because they may impact the setup of the organizational structure for the warehouse.

To create the plants in the ERP system, in the IMG, follow menu path ENTERPRISE STRUCTURE • DEFINITION • LOGISTICS GENERAL • DEFINE, COPY, DELETE, CHECK PLANT • DEFINE PLANT. To assign the plants to the relevant company codes, in the IMG, follow menu path ENTERPRISE STRUCTURE • ASSIGNMENT • LOGISTICS – GENERAL • ASSIGN PLANT TO COMPANY CODE.

There are additional settings that must be made to enable transactions to occur within a plant assigned to the company code, but we provide this information just to give you an idea regarding the organizational structure, which will allow you to make decisions about how to model your own organization using the SAP organizational structure.

2.2 Storage Locations

The next level of the pyramid is the storage location. Each storage location must be assigned to a single plant, but there may be more than one storage location assigned to each plant (as seen in Figure 2.1). One reason to segregate the inventory into multiple storage locations is due to physical segregation. For example, the inventory can be held in multiple buildings in a single geographic location where the buildings are close to each other, making it simple to transfer inventory from one location to another without requiring extensive transportation or documentation.

When the buildings are far enough away to require transportation between the buildings, the stocks are often transferred using stock transport orders. Using a stock transport order allows you to execute the request using an outbound delivery, which can in turn be used to provide the necessary shipping documentation. It also allows an inbound delivery to be created.

To create the storage locations, follow the menu path ENTERPRISE STRUCTURE • DEFINITION • MATERIALS MANAGEMENT • MAINTAIN STORAGE LOCATION.

The storage locations are plant specific and therefore no additional assignment of the storage locations to the plants is necessary. The storage locations database table (table T001L) key includes both the plant and the storage location in the key. Therefore, the name of the storage location can be the same for multiple plants. This allows the same storage location names, Available for Sale (AFS) and Received on Dock (ROD), to be used for all EWM-managed plants.

However, a more simplistic organizational structure than the one described in Figure 2.1 is also possible. In Figure 2.3, you see the most simplistic organizational structure possible, with a single company code, a single plant, a single storage location, and a single warehouse.

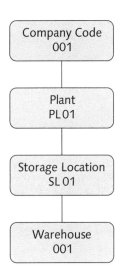

Figure 2.3 Simplest Organizational Structure Including a Warehouse

While it is possible to use this simple organizational structure for an EWM-managed warehouse, it is also possible to use a function in EWM that causes the typical organizational structure for an EWM-managed warehouse to be at least somewhat more complex. Many warehouse managers prefer to segregate inventory when it is received into a location that is not yet available for picking, even at the IM level. In other words, when the stock is received, it is updated in IM, is reflected in FI, and the vendor can be paid (if the receipt was related to an external purchase order). However, the inventory is in a storage location that can be configured such that it does not allow the inventory to be promised to customer orders or committed to outbound deliveries. In the standard delivered configuration, this storage location is named ROD ("Received on Dock"), as reflected in Figure 2.4.

When the product is put into the warehouse, it is automatically transferred by the EWM system to the storage location that is available for picking. In the standard delivered configuration, this storage location is named AFS ("Available For Sale"), as reflected in Figure 2.4. In this book, we will refer to the ROD and AFS storage locations, but you can name them anything you like. The AFS storage location can be configured to allow the inventory to be promised to customer orders and committed to outbound deliveries, making the AFS storage location a "pickable" storage location.

In Chapter 4, Product Master Data, we will discuss how the stock types in EWM are mapped to these storage locations, allowing full control and flexibility regarding the storage location assignment of the products in the warehouse. But now, let's take a look at how the warehouse is created in ERP and EWM.

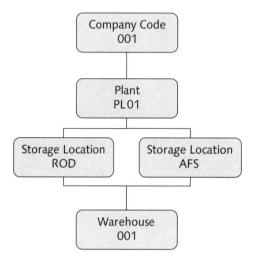

Figure 2.4 Organizational Structure for a Typical EWM Warehouse

2.3 Warehouses

Once the plants and storage locations are created and assigned, the final steps to complete the organizational structure in ERP are to:

▶ create the warehouses

▶ assign the warehouses to the plant and storage location

▶ specify how the warehouse will be managed

2.3.1 Defining the Warehouse Numbers

Before creating and assigning the warehouses, you must decide how the warehouses will be assigned. Before you make those decisions, there are a few concepts that you should understand.

First, it is possible to assign multiple storage locations to a single warehouse. This is required to allow the multiple storage location paradigm described earlier, which allows you to separate the inventory between pickable and non-pickable inventory, by storage locations. It also allows logical division of inventory using storage locations, even when the product belongs to the same plant. When the same plant owns the inventory, it allows you to manage the product with logical separations using IM without impacting financial accounting.

Second, these storage locations are not required to belong to the same plant. While it was true in early releases of SAP Warehouse Management software that the warehouse could only be assigned to storage locations of the same plant (and only a single storage location before SAP R/3 version 4.0A), the single plant restriction has not been a constraint for the last several years and doesn't affect anyone implementing SAP ERP today. Allowing the product to belong to multiple plants provides the flexibility to manage the stock in the same physical space while keeping them logically separate for financial accounting purposes.

And, finally, the plants to which the warehouses are assigned are not required to be assigned to the same company code. This allows you to store product from multiple business divisions (which can be managed as separate company codes) within the same warehouse, and even allows the same product to belong to different business divisions and stored in the same warehouse — even in the same bin.

Let's review the figure from the beginning of this chapter again. In Figure 2.5, you can see that the concepts discussed previously are reflected in the example organizational structure that we introduced.

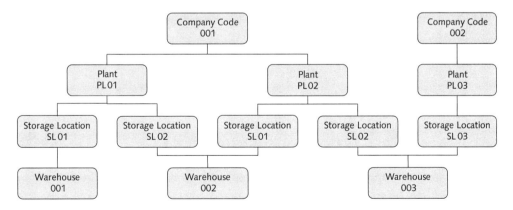

Figure 2.5 Example Organizational Structure with Warehouses Assigned to Multiple Storage Locations

The ability to store the products in the same physical space while still keeping them logically separate is enabled by the method used to track the stock in the warehouse. All stock is tracked down to the bin level and the stock data contains information regarding which plant and storage location owns the stock. This information is contained within the database record for the stock, which is known in SAP as the "quant." In Chapter 6, Warehouse Stock Management, we will further discuss the quants and provide more details on how they are used.

Once you have decided how many warehouses to create, how to assign them, and how to manage them, you can begin the process of configuring the warehouse in the organizational structure of ERP. To start, create the warehouse in the IMG of the ERP system by following the menu path ENTERPRISE STRUCTURE • DEFINITION • LOGISTICS EXECUTION • DEFINE, COPY, DELETE, CHECK WAREHOUSE NUMBER • DEFINE WAREHOUSE NUMBER. In Figure 2.6, you can see that the transaction includes the ability to create, change, copy, or delete the warehouse number. Note that the warehouse number for the ERP warehouse is only 3 characters, and the description is 25 characters.

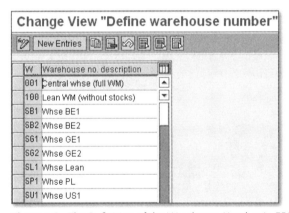

Figure 2.6 The Definition of the Warehouse Number in ERP

You can also use a special transaction to copy the warehouse and related tables, but this transaction is not usually necessary in the case of EWM, because the additional tables copied with this special transaction are only relevant to ERP Warehouse Management. This transaction could be accessed via the menu path ENTERPRISE STRUCTURE • DEFINITION • LOGISTICS EXECUTION • DEFINE, COPY, DELETE, CHECK WAREHOUSE NUMBER • COPY/DELETE/CHECK WAREHOUSE NUMBER.

Next, you will assign the warehouse to the plants and storage locations. To make the assignment in the IMG, follow the menu path ENTERPRISE STRUCTURE • ASSIGN-MENT • LOGISTICS EXECUTION • ASSIGN WAREHOUSE NUMBER TO PLANT/STORAGE LOCA-TION. Simply enter the plant, storage location, and the warehouse number to the table, as seen in Figure 2.7.

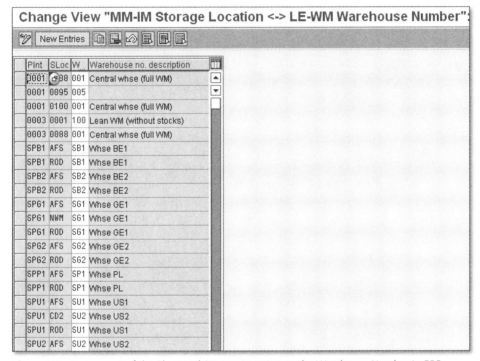

Figure 2.7 Assignment of the Plant and Storage Location to the Warehouse Number in ERP

Note

In this book, we will assume that you are using the two storage locations, ROD and AFS, to distinguish between unavailable stock and available stock. Furthermore, we will assume, unless otherwise stated, that you are using a simple structure with a warehouse assigned to a single plant and a single company code.

2.3.2 Integrating to DWM and EWM

Once you make the assignment of the warehouse to the plant/storage location combination, the ERP system will be able to determine which warehouse is relevant for IM transactions and deliveries. Every IM transaction created in the ERP system must have a plant and storage location assigned to the line item of the transaction (table MSEG). When an IM transaction is performed for a plant and storage location that is assigned to a warehouse, the relevant warehouse number is assigned to the line item. If the warehouse is managed by Decentralized Warehouse Management (DWM) or EWM, the transaction is interfaced to the relevant system.

Likewise, when inbound deliveries or outbound deliveries are created, each line item is assigned to a plant and storage location. Based on the plant and storage location assigned at the line item level, the warehouse is determined and assigned to the line item. When the warehouse determined is managed by DWM or EWM, the delivery is integrated to the relevant system.

2.3.3   Specifying the Warehouse Management Methodology

Once the warehouse is defined, you can specify how the warehouse will be managed. That is, whether you will use ERP Warehouse Management (ERP WM), DWM, or EWM to manage the warehouse. If you use ERP WM, there is nothing more to do — you can start setting up the warehouse in ERP. If you use DWM or EWM, there are a couple of more steps before you can start setting up the rest of the warehouse structure.

DWM is essentially a second ERP system that is configured in a slightly different way to allow you to distribute the deliveries to the external ERP system and manage only the warehouse functions on that ERP system. If you want to set up a DWM system, in the IMG, you would follow the menu path LOGISTICS EXECUTION • DECENTRALIZED WMS INTEGRATION • CENTRAL PROCESSING • APPLICATION • ACTIVATE DECENTRALIZED WMS. As you can see in Figure 2.8, not every warehouse in the system will be displayed in this table. If you want to activate DWM, you will need to create a new entry in the table.

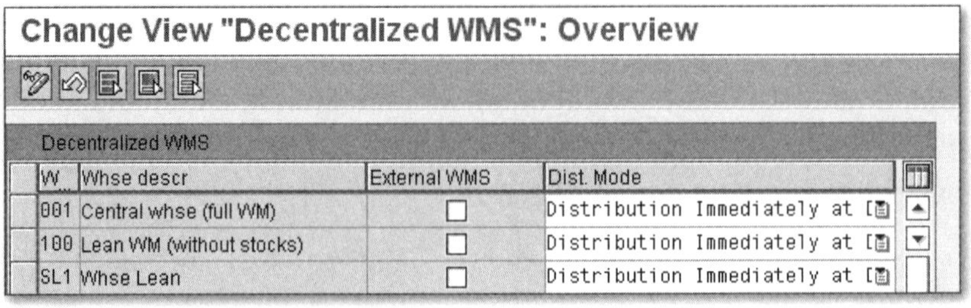

W	Whse descr	External WMS	Dist. Mode	
001	Central whse (full WM)	☐	Distribution Immediately at ▢	▲
100	Lean WM (without stocks)	☐	Distribution Immediately at ▢	▼
SL1	Whse Lean	☐	Distribution Immediately at ▢	

Change View "Decentralized WMS": Overview

Decentralized WMS

Figure 2.8   Activation of DWM

> **Note**
>
> Unless you will use DWM for one of your warehouses, it is not necessary to configure the preceding setting. We include the discussion here just to point out the differences between the setup for DWM and EWM.

To activate the warehouse for EWM, first assign the warehouse number in ERP to the warehouse number in EWM by following the ERP IMG menu path INTEGRATION WITH OTHER MYSAP.COM COMPONENTS • EXTENDED WAREHOUSE MANAGEMENT • ASSIGN WAREHOUSE NUMBER TO WAREHOUSE NUMBER OF DECENTRALIZED SCM SYSTEM. In Figure 2.9, you can see that the assignment is a simple one-to-one assignment between the ERP warehouse number and the EWM warehouse number.

Change View "Assign Warehouse No.

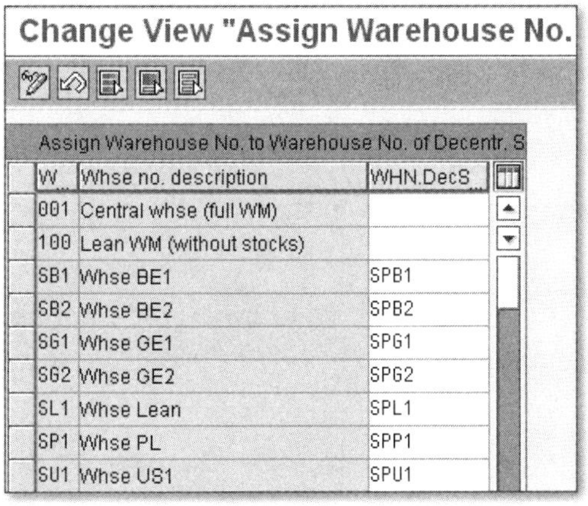

W	Whse no. description	WHN.DecS
001	Central whse (full WM)	
100	Lean WM (without stocks)	
SB1	Whse BE1	SPB1
SB2	Whse BE2	SPB2
S61	Whse GE1	SPG1
S62	Whse GE2	SPG2
SL1	Whse Lean	SPL1
SP1	Whse PL	SPP1
SU1	Whse US1	SPU1

Figure 2.9 Assignment of the EWM Warehouse Number to the ERP Warehouse

Note that the ERP system does not read the SCM tables directly in this transaction, so there will be no validation of the EWM warehouse number entered in the table. Every warehouse will be visible in this table, so only enter the EWM warehouse numbers for the relevant ERP warehouses.

In addition to making the warehouse number assignment, you must also activate the warehouse for EWM and set the additional EWM-related parameters in table T340D (as seen in figure 2.10). To make the settings in the ERP IMG, follow the menu path LOGISTICS EXECUTION • SERVICE PARTS MANAGEMENT (SPM) • INTEGRATE SPM WITH OTHER COMPONENTS • MAINTAIN EXTENDED WM-SPECIFIC PARAMETERS.

> **Note**
>
> Even though the menu path to the settings for the activation of EWM reference the Service Parts Management solution, the EWM is relevant across multiple industries. However, this menu path must be used to access the settings regardless of the industry for which the EWM is used.

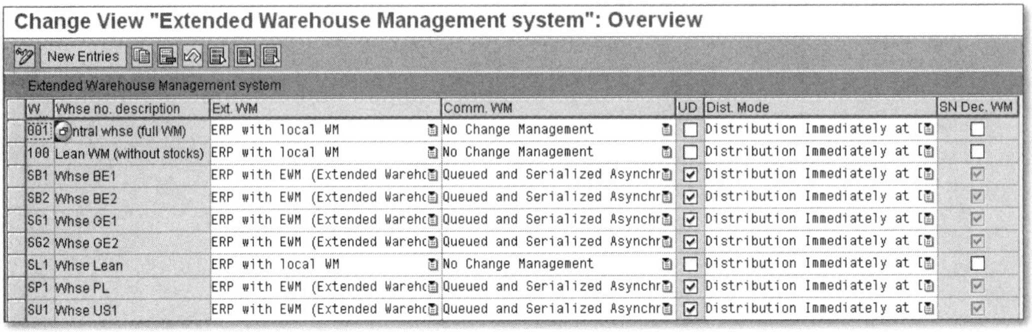

Change View "Extended Warehouse Management system": Overview

New Entries 🗐 🗐 🗐 🖉 🗐 🗐 🗐

Extended Warehouse Management system

W.	Whse no. description	Ext. WM	Comm. WM	UD	Dist. Mode	SN Dec. WM
001	Central whse (full WM)	ERP with local WM	No Change Management	☐	Distribution Immediately at	☐
100	Lean WM (without stocks)	ERP with local WM	No Change Management	☐	Distribution Immediately at	☐
SB1	Whse BE1	ERP with EWM (Extended Wareho	Queued and Serialized Asynchr	☑	Distribution Immediately at	☑
SB2	Whse BE2	ERP with EWM (Extended Wareho	Queued and Serialized Asynchr	☑	Distribution Immediately at	☑
SG1	Whse GE1	ERP with EWM (Extended Wareho	Queued and Serialized Asynchr	☑	Distribution Immediately at	☑
SG2	Whse GE2	ERP with EWM (Extended Wareho	Queued and Serialized Asynchr	☑	Distribution Immediately at	☑
SL1	Whse Lean	ERP with local WM	No Change Management	☐	Distribution Immediately at	☐
SP1	Whse PL	ERP with EWM (Extended Wareho	Queued and Serialized Asynchr	☑	Distribution Immediately at	☑
SU1	Whse US1	ERP with EWM (Extended Wareho	Queued and Serialized Asynchr	☑	Distribution Immediately at	☑

Figure 2.10 Activation of Extended Warehouse Management in ERP

In Figure 2.10, you can see the parameters of the table related to the activation of EWM, including:

▸ External Warehouse Management: The REFERENCE TO EXTERNAL WAREHOUSE MANAGEMENT indicator should be set to the value ERP WITH EWM (EXTENDED WAREHOUSE MANAGEMENT) for all EWM-related warehouses.

▸ Communication with Warehouse Management: The COMMUNICATION WITH THE WAREHOUSE SYSTEM indicator should be set to the value QUEUED AND SERIALIZED ASYNCHRONOUS RFC for all EWM-related warehouses.

▸ Unchecked Deliveries: The DISTRIBUTE UNCHECKED DELIVERIES TO WAREHOUSE indicator determines whether unchecked deliveries are distributed to the warehouse. If you use SAP Customer Relationship Management (CRM) for order management and if the Direct Delivery Scenario is activated (which indicates that an unchecked delivery is created in ERP in place of sales order replication from CRM), an unchecked delivery is created in ERP when the sales order is saved in CRM. If you also want to distribute these unchecked deliveries to EWM when they are saved in ERP, then select this indicator. Sending the unchecked deliveries to EWM gives the warehouse management team a preview of the orders that will be delivered to them in the future, providing them visibility to the workload for staff planning purposes. In Chapter 8, Integration from ERP to Extended Warehouse Management, we will further discuss the integration of outbound deliveries, including the checked delivery concept.

► Distribution Mode: The DISTRIBUTION MODE FOR THE DELIVERY indicator controls when the delivery is distributed to the DWM or EWM once the delivery is created in ERP. In most cases, you will set the value to Distribution Immediately at Document Creation, but in some cases, you may need to make changes to the delivery information after it is created in ERP but before it is submitted to the warehouse. In those cases, set the value to Stop Distribution.

► Serial Numbers in DWM: The ALLOW SERIAL NUMBERS IN DECENTRALIZED WAREHOUSE MANAGEMENT indicator controls how serial numbers are controlled in the DWM or EWM. For EWM-managed warehouses, it should always be set to allow serial numbers.

2.3.4 Delivery Split Indicators

To ensure that the delivery is properly integrated to the relevant systems, the configuration must be set to allow the delivery to be split according to the warehouse assignment. If the settings which control the delivery split are not set accordingly, the deliveries will not be sent to the warehouse management systems. To set the delivery split indicator at the delivery type level in the IMG of the ERP system, follow the menu path LOGISTICS EXECUTION • SHIPPING • DELIVERIES • DEFINE SPLIT CRITERIA FOR DELIVERIES • DELIVERY SPLIT BY WAREHOUSE NUMBER • DEFINE DELIVERY SPLIT PER DELIVERY TYPE. As you can see in Figure 2.11, you should activate the setting for each delivery type that you expect to be distributed to EWM.

Delivery Split for Warehouse Number per Delivery Type		
Del. type	Description	Delivry Split - WhNo
SV	Cash Sales	☐
CEM		☐
DIG	Inb.Deliv.Gds Mvmnt	☑
DOG	Outb.Deliv.Gds Mvmnt	☑
DTR	Central Postng Chnge	☑
EG	Rough GR	☑
EL	Inbound Delivery	☑
GPLF	Delivery for SW mtn.	☐
HID	Inbnd Dlv. HU Mvmnt	☐
HOD	Outb.Deliv.GI Mvmnt	☑

Figure 2.11 Delivery Split by Delivery Type

To activate the settings per warehouse, follow the menu path LOGISTICS EXECUTION • SHIPPING • DELIVERIES • DEFINE SPLIT CRITERIA FOR DELIVERIES • DELIVERY SPLIT BY WAREHOUSE NUMBER • DETERMINE DELIVERY SPLIT PER WAREHOUSE NUMBER. As you can see in Figure 2.12, you should activate the setting for each warehouse that you will manage using EWM.

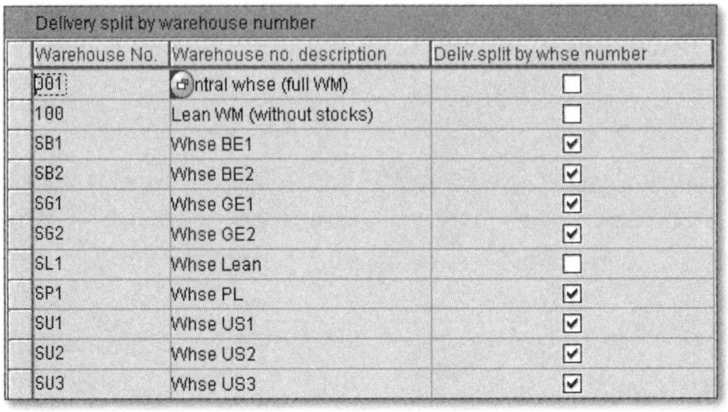

Warehouse No.	Warehouse no. description	Deliv.split by whse number
001	Central whse (full WM)	☐
100	Lean WM (without stocks)	☐
SB1	Whse BE1	☑
SB2	Whse BE2	☑
SG1	Whse GE1	☑
SG2	Whse GE2	☑
SL1	Whse Lean	☐
SP1	Whse PL	☑
SU1	Whse US1	☑
SU2	Whse US2	☑
SU3	Whse US3	☑

Figure 2.12 Delivery Split by ERP Warehouse Number

2.3.5 Connecting ERP to EWM

Now that you have created the warehouse, assigned the warehouse, specified how the warehouse will be managed, and properly set the delivery split indicators, the IM transactions and deliveries will be set to be distributed from the ERP system to the relevant warehouse management system when they are created.

The next step to setting up the connection between ERP and EWM is to set up the Application Link Enablement (ALE) layer. In Chapter 8, Integration from ERP to EWM, we will discuss the setup of the ALE and the rest of the steps necessary for integration between ERP and EWM. In the meantime, we will continue the discussion in the next section with the EWM settings related to the warehouse structure.

2.3.6 Defining the Warehouse in EWM

The final steps for connecting ERP and EWM are to create the warehouse in the EWM system and make the link between the ERP warehouse number and the EWM warehouse number. The ERP warehouse number is restricted to three characters, whereas the EWM warehouse number allows four characters. The additional character was added to the EWM warehouse number to allow additional flexibility for such options as assigning a single EWM instance to multiple ERP instances.

To create the warehouse number in the IMG of the EWM system, follow the menu path EXTENDED WAREHOUSE MANAGEMENT • MASTER DATA • DEFINE WAREHOUSE NUMBERS. As you can see in Figure 2.13, the warehouse number is four characters in EWM and the description is forty characters. As previously mentioned, this allows the flexibility to connect EWM to multiple ERP systems without worrying about having the same warehouse numbers in the two systems. The additional characters in the warehouse description also allow you to add additional descriptors to the text. Note that there is also a detailed view to this table table view, which you can access by double-clicking on the line or selecting a line and choosing the DETAILS button, but the detailed view does not contain any additional data, so we do not include it here.

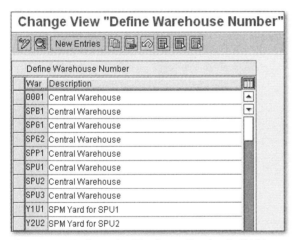

Figure 2.13 Defining the Warehouse Number in EWM

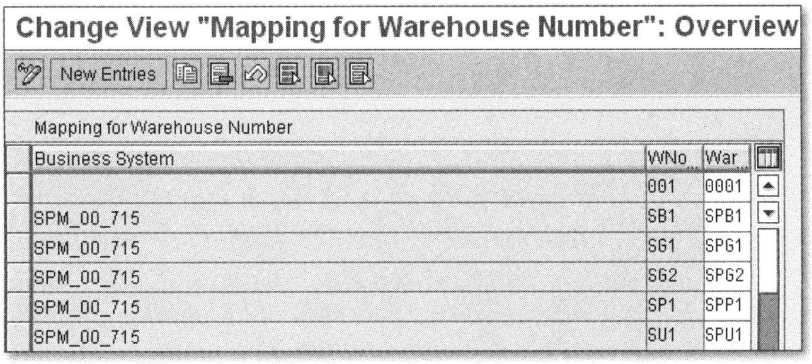

Change View "Mapping for Warehouse Number": Overview

Mapping for Warehouse Number

Business System	WNo	War
	001	0001
SPM_00_715	SB1	SPB1
SPM_00_715	S61	SP61
SPM_00_715	S62	SP62
SPM_00_715	SP1	SPP1
SPM_00_715	SU1	SPU1

Figure 2.14 Assigning the Warehouse in ERP to the Warehouse in EWM

2.3.7 Assigning the Warehouse in EWM to the ERP Warehouse

To assign the EWM warehouse number to the corresponding ERP warehouse number in the IMG of the EWM system, follow the menu path EXTENDED WARE-HOUSE MANAGEMENT • INTERFACES • ERP INTEGRATION • GENERAL SETTINGS • MAP WAREHOUSE NUMBERS FROM ERP SYSTEM TO EWM. Figure 2.14 shows the mapping, which can also include the business system. Because the business system is included here, you should perform this step after the basic technical integration is set up between the ERP and EWM systems, as described in Chapter 8.

2.3.8 Assigning Business Partners and Supply Chain Units

After completing the configuration for the warehouse, you must also assign some master data attributes to the warehouse, including the supply chain units and the business partners. We will further discuss business partners and supply chain units in Chapter 5, Other Warehouse Master Data. To assign the business partners and supply chain unit to the warehouse, in the SAP Easy Access menu of EWM, follow the EXTENDED WAREHOUSE MANAGEMENT • SETTINGS • ASSIGNMENTS: WAREHOUSE NUMBERS/BUSINESS PARTNERS menu path, or use Transaction code /SCWM/LGNBP. Figure 2.15 shows the assignment of the business partners and supply chain unit to the warehouse.

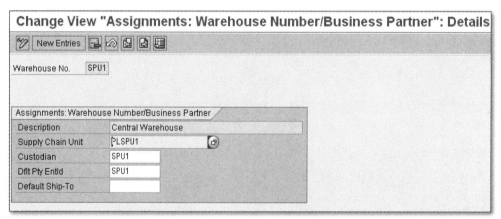

Figure 2.15 Assignment of the Supply Chain Unit and Business Partners to the Warehouse

2.4   Summary

In this chapter, we described the organization structure necessary to support EWM. Part of the organizational structure is set up in ERP and part in EWM. You should now be able to create your own organizational structure from scratch and link an ERP warehouse number to an EWM warehouse. Once that is complete, you can continue the setup of the warehouse in the EWM system. In the following chapters, we will describe the setup of the master data necessary to support the business processes, and then we will begin to describe the setup of the warehouse.

The SAP Extended Warehouse Management (EWM) warehouse structure is designed to allow you to model your physical warehouse into the warehouse management system and provides the flexibility for you to closely model the software functions to your warehouse business process.

3   The Warehouse Structure

Once you have set up the organizational structure, linked the warehouse to the plant and storage locations in ERP, and linked the warehouse in EWM to the ERP warehouse as described in Chapter 2, Organizational Structure, you can begin the setup of the warehouse structure in the EWM system.

The warehouse structure provides the baseline for modeling warehouse processes. The breakdown of the warehouse into areas and subdividing those areas allows for a flexible structure that can be used to model those processes.

From years of experience in warehousing and distribution, our observation is that, despite even the most seasoned expert's desires or efforts to replicate warehouses with consistent processes, inevitably the individual warehouses will take on a character of their own. Each warehouse will start to adjust its structure and its processes to match the activities that it must perform and even warehouses that start out exactly the same can start to operate very differently. Warehouse managers and supervisors bring in their own experiences and adjust the processes. Industrial engineers learn from their experiences and make adjustments to the layout and structure. Warehouse workers themselves even learn better ways to do things and share and adjust on the fly, often affecting the standard operating procedures by making suggestions based on what really happens on the warehouse floor.

Sometimes these adjustments take place as early as the blueprinting process, with engineers and warehouse managers learning as they roll out a template across a region or across the world. Sometimes local practices are adopted and adjustments to the buildings are made accordingly. Sometimes costs of land and building affect the building envelope. Sometimes labor costs will drive more or less automation to be employed. Sometimes customers will change their ordering patterns or entire industries will change and cause the warehouse processes to change to remain in sync. Whatever the cause, the end result is that even warehouses that start out the same end up being unique in some significant way.

For this reason, it is important to accurately model the structure of the warehouse into the warehouse management system that will control it. Because no two warehouses look the same, any software company would be ill advised to design a warehouse management system that does not have the ability to be modeled differently for different warehouses. All top-tier warehouse management systems have this ability, and the SAP Warehouse Management systems are no different.

The parameters assigned to each area in the warehouse and the assignment of the warehouse bins to those areas defines how the product will be moved into and out of those areas and warehouse bins. In this book, we often refer to those parameters assigned to the different warehouse elements as the *configuration*. When we configure an element, we assign the values to the parameters that drive the behaviors of the program that read and process the data.

In this chapter, we will discuss the configuration of the warehouse structures. We will define the structures, describe how they are used, and discuss how to create and configure them to allow you to model your warehouse in the SAP EWM system.

3.1 Storage Types

Storage types are the highest level of organization within the warehouse (as seen in Figure 3.1). The most basic definition of a storage type is a group of warehouse bins with similar characteristics. A warehouse bin is a discrete area in the warehouse where a product or group of products is stored, usually represented by a set of numbers or characters that are arranged in a sequence, which makes the warehouse bin easy to find for warehouse operators.

Usually, the bins in a storage type are grouped together in a single area. The bins do not necessarily need to be the same size or have the same capacity, because we will define this at a lower level when we set up the storage bins. While technically, they represent a difference in the method or type of storage to be used in a particular area, in actual practice, you can use them to devise strategies to help you optimize the flexibility and efficiency of the warehouse operations.

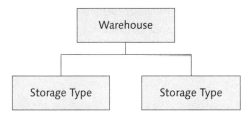

Figure 3.1   Relationship between Warehouse and Storage Types

Some examples of commonly used storage types include:

▶ fixed bin areas, also called primary pick areas; fixed bin areas may be:

   ▶ lower level(s) of high-rack storage, accessible by order pickers on floor level equipment

   ▶ pallet flow racks (often used for case picking)

   ▶ case flow racks (often used for case, inner pack, or each picking)

▶ high-rack areas, commonly for overstock or general storage

▶ floor storage areas, commonly for overstock or general storage

▶ bulk storage areas, commonly for overstock or general storage

▶ push back racks, commonly used for overstock or general storage

▶ special storage areas, for example, for hazardous materials

▶ automated storage and retrieval areas

In addition, you can create storage types to control:

▶ interim bins for inbound and outbound movements

▶ pick points

▶ identification points

▶ staging areas

▶ work centers

▶ doors

▶ yard bins (for inbound and outbound trailers)

We will be discussing each of these additional topics in later chapters, so we will not cover them in detail here.

Several parameters are assigned to the storage type level, including placement and removal strategies, indicators for handling unit (HU) management (a method for unique pallet identification, which we will describe further in Chapter 4, Product Master Data), and other settings that control how the product is placed into, removed from, or stored within the bins that are assigned to the storage type. To configure the storage types in the Implementation Guide (IMG) of the EWM system, follow the menu path EXTENDED WAREHOUSE MANAGEMENT • MASTER DATA • DEFINE STORAGE TYPE. Because the parameters assigned to the storage type provide the basis for how product is stored in your warehouse, in the following sections we'll describe each of these parameters and how they are used to control the product movements and storage of product in the bins of the storage type.

Note that some of the settings in the storage type configuration are dependent on one another. If a field value does not match the allowed values according to a cross-checked dependent field value, you will receive an error message when you try to update the field. In this case, you will need to either update the field value again or update the cross-checked field value to continue with the update and save the settings.

> **Note**
>
> Note that each of these settings is made for each storage type, so you will have to make these decisions for each of the areas in your warehouse. These are some of the most important settings in your warehouse and you should consider them carefully. Understanding these settings and knowing how to use them is important in helping to determine how many and which types of storage types you will create in your warehouse. Therefore, it is important to understand each of these settings in detail.
>
> Remember that the objective is to model your warehouse business processes using the warehouse management system. You should let the system help you work the way that you want to work, and not let the system dictate how you should work.

3.1.1 General

The GENERAL section controls the general settings for the storage type that are not related to the type of movement (i.e., placement, removal, replenishment). In Figure 3.2, you can see the parameters assigned to the GENERAL section.

Storage Type Role

The STORAGE TYPE ROLE is used to define how the storage type is used. Most of the storage types used to store products in the warehouse will have the parameter

assigned as a blank value (or space). This value has the text description STANDARD
STORAGE TYPE. Other values can be assigned to indicate that the storage type is
being used for some special purpose, such as for pick points, work centers, production supply, or other purposes. Use the dropdown selection to choose from the
available list of storage type roles.

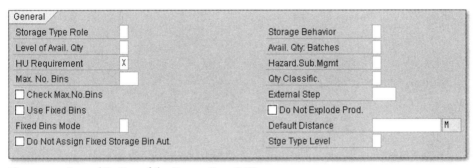

Figure 3.2 General Section of the Storage Type Settings

Level of Available Quantity

The LEVEL OF AVAIL. QTY determines how the available quantity is determined
during a stock removal. The only two options are STORAGE BIN and HIGHEST-LEVEL
HU. If the available quantity is determined at the storage bin level, then no HU
will be assigned to the warehouse task when it is created. This would allow the
warehouse operator to select the stock from any available HU while performing
the stock removal. For example, the available quantity should be set to the storage bin level for bulk storage types. This would allow the warehouse operator to
remove the product from any HU that he can access, rather than potentially being
told to remove the stock from an inaccessible HU.

If the available quantity is determined at the highest-level HU, then the HU is
assigned to the warehouse task when it is created, and the warehouse operator
would not have flexibility to specify a different HU during the stock removal. The
available quantity should be set to the highest-level HU when the HU must be
specified in the warehouse task, such as for staging areas, packing stations, deconsolidation stations, and counting stations.

HU Requirement

In EWM, the utilization of HUs is much different than in ERP Warehouse Management (ERP WM). In EWM, it is possible to store products both with HUs and with-

out HUs within the same warehouse, the same storage type, or even within the same storage bin. In Chapter 4, we will discuss HU management in more detail.

At the storage type level, the HU REQUIREMENT field is used to specify how HUs should be used for managing the stock in the storage type. The choices include:

- ▶ HUs allowed but not required
- ▶ HUs required
- ▶ HUs not allowed

Maximum Number of Bins

MAX. NO. BINS indicates the maximum number of bins that can be allowed per product within the storage type. This parameter lets you ensure that a single product does not overfill the storage type. Additional product of the same product number received into the warehouse would have to be stored in a different storage type. This field is especially pertinent to fixed bin storage types where the number of fixed bins is constrained and multiple products compete for space in the fixed bin area.

It is also possible to set the maximum number of bins per storage type on a product-specific basis by specifying the maximum number of bins in the product master. If the maximum number of bins is specified in the product master, this value overrides the value specified in the storage type. In either case, the maximum number of bins is only checked if the CHECK MAX.NO.BINS field is selected.

Check Maximum Number of Bins

This indicator controls whether the field indicating the maximum number of bins in a storage type for an individual product is checked, either on the storage type settings or on the product master. If the field is not selected, no check is performed.

Use Fixed Bins

Each storage type can only utilize either fixed bins or dynamic bins. If fixed bins are used in the storage type, this indicator should be selected.

Fixed Bins Mode

If the USE FIXED BINS indicator is specified, the fixed bins mode controls how the stock will be put away to the fixed bins. If the indicator is set to only put away to optimum fixed bins (value blank or space), then only those fixed bins that have been determined by the putaway algorithm, together with slotting, are considered relevant for use for that material in that storage type (and bins marked as improvable will not be used). If the indicator is set to prefer to put away to optimum fixed bins, then the putaway algorithm will first try to put the stock away into the optimum fixed bins and then try other bins in the storage type (which could include the improvable bins).

The optimal fixed bins are determined by the slotting algorithm. If slotting determines that the product should be moved to a different fixed bin (or set of fixed bins), the new bins will be assigned to the product and the previously assigned bins, if they contain stock at the time, will be marked as IMPROVABLE (in the STORAGE BIN IMPROVABLE field) in the fixed bin assignment table. The fixed bin assignments can be reviewed in the SAP Easy Access menu by following the EXTENDED WAREHOUSE MANAGEMENT • MASTER DATA • STORAGE BIN • MAINTAIN FIXED STORAGE BIN menu path, or using Transaction code /SCWM/BINMAT. We will discuss slotting and assignment of fixed bins further in Chapter 7, Warehouse Document Types.

Do Not Assign Fixed Storage Bin Automatically

During the putaway bin determination, the system can assign a bin for putaway that is not already assigned as a fixed bin for the material, either because there are no fixed bins assigned or because there are not enough fix bins assigned and all of the fixed bins are full. In this case, if the DO NOT ASSIGN FIXED STORAGE BIN AUT. indicator is set, putaway bins which are selected for putaway during the putaway bin determination will not be automatically assigned as fixed bins for the material. Otherwise, if the indicator is not set, then the bin will be assigned as a fixed bin on the fixed bin assignment table (which can be accessed as described earlier). As mentioned previously, we'll discuss slotting and assignment of fixed bins further in Chapter 7.

Storage Behavior

STORAGE BEHAVIOR defines how pallets will be managed in the storage type. Options include:

► **Standard warehouse**

In high-rack storage or general storage areas, the parameter will be set to STANDARD WAREHOUSE, which specifies no special behaviors of the stock.

► **Pallet storage**

In pallet storage areas, identical sub-bins will be created during the initial put-away. Sub-bins are portions of bins that are created to store an individual unit of material. For example, if you can fit two U.S. pallets or three Euro pallets into the bin, either two or three sub-bins will be created, depending on whether you add stock to the bin on U.S. pallets or Euro pallets.

► **Bulk storage**

For bulk warehouses (for example, a floor area where multiple pallets of the same product are stacked one atop another in the same warehouse bin, sometimes multiple pallets deep into the bin), this storage behavior supports putting away multiple pallets into the same warehouse storage bin.

Available Quantity: Batches

This parameter controls the management of batch data at the bin level. If there are multiple batches in the bin, you have the option to control the batches discretely or to manage only the total quantity of the products in the bin without regard to the actual batches stored there. This concept is similar to the *documentary batch* concept available in ERP, where the total quantity of the material is tracked while the batch information is only captured during certain activities, such as receiving or shipping.

If you want to specify certain batches in the warehouse request (which could be triggered by a sales order and delivery or production supply request or other activity), or if you want to perform batch determination in the warehouse for specifying the batch to pick in the warehouse task, then you should manage the available quantity of the batches in a batch-specific manner (value blank or space). If you do not have such requirements and instead want to allow the warehouse operator to flexibly determine the batch for picking, then you may opt to manage the available quantity of the batches in a batch-neutral manner (value "1").

Hazardous Substance Management

You can use HAZARD.SUB.MGMT to check whether certain stocks can be mixed in an area according to the hazardous substance rules. If you want to perform a hazardous substance check during the putaway of the products in the storage type, you should set this parameter to perform the check at the storage type level (value "1") or the storage type and storage section level (value "2"). If you leave the field blank, then no hazardous substance check will be performed.

Quantity Classification

The QUANTITY CLASSIFICATION is used together with the *packaging specifications* (pack spec) to determine the correct location for removal of a product based on the quantity of that product being requested — for example, whether the requested quantity is a partial case, full case, or full pallet (or combination thereof). Specifically, it is used in the following ways:

▸ During the storage type determination for stock removal or stock putaway, the pack spec is read based on the the requested quantity for the product. The quantity classification is derived from the level within the pack spec that matches the requested quantity. Then the storage type search sequence determination is read based on the determined quantity classification. In case of small/large quantity strategy assignment in the storage type, the cascading effect is triggered according to the quantity classification of the respective storage types.

▸ From the pack spec level (as determined previously), the assigned operative unit of measure is adopted as the alternative unit of measure for the warehouse tasks, and the HU type of the pack spec level is adopted to the warehouse task as well.

▸ Depending on the settings for the rounding, the quantity of the warehouse task may be rounded according to the assigned quantity per HU type from the pack spec.

The allowed values for the quantity classification can be specified in the IMG by following the menu path EXTENDED WAREHOUSE MANAGEMENT • CROSS-PROCESS SETTINGS • WAREHOUSE TASK • DEFINE QUANTITY CLASSIFICATIONS.

External Step

The EXTERNAL STEP assigned to the storage type is only used if the HU moved into the storage type has not yet achieved the assigned step within the routing profile from the process-oriented storage control (POSC). In that case, the step assigned to the storage type would replace the last completed external step assigned to the

HU. In the case of storage types for work centers, the process step assigned to the work center is compared instead of the one assigned at the storage type level. The POSC and assignment of the external process steps to the HU will be discussed in Chapter 13, Configuring Multistep Warehouse Movements.

Do Not Explode Product

Products can be moved on their own in the warehouse as part of a product warehouse task, or an HU can be moved using an HU warehouse task. If an HU warehouse task is used, you can choose whether you want to individually track the warehouse movements of the products associated with the HU or whether it is sufficient just to track the HU moves by maintaining this parameter. If the parameter is selected, then the HU is not exploded into a separate tracking table during a warehouse task confirmation. In this case, you would not be able to see the warehouse transfers of the product by selecting warehouse tasks by product in the warehouse monitor. If the parameter is left blank, then both the HU transfer and the associated product transfers are tracked and can be later monitored using the warehouse monitor.

Tracking the product transfers in addition to the HU transfer requires additional system overhead (i.e., performance of the confirmation of the HU tasks will be slower). However, if you want to track the product movements after the fact for inventory reconciliation or investigation of inventory differences, then you should leave the DO NOT EXPLODE PROD. parameter blank.

Default Distance

When Labor Management (LM) is activated, the system always determines the travel path from bin to bin using the coordinates of the bin and the travel paths determined by LM (we will cover LM in detail in Chapter 19, Labor Management). However, if you confirm the warehouse task using the desktop transaction (Transaction /SCWM/TO_CONF) instead of the radio frequency–based transaction, the system cannot determine where the operator was last located. In that case, this parameter is used to determine the distance to get to the first bin of the warehouse order. The distance between the remaining bins is calculated using the standard method from LM, because the system can then tell the current and subsequent bin for the movement of the warehouse operator. If the mobile data entry transactions are used, the last bin is known at the start of the confirmation of the warehouse order, and this parameter would not be used in that case.

Storage Type Level

The STGE TYPE LEVEL is used by the graphical warehouse layout to depict multiple storage level, such as a mezzanine. The storage type level is one of the selection criteria when calling the graphical warehouse layout. If it is not maintained, all storage types are assumed to be at the same level. However, if any one storage type has the storage type level assigned, you must enter the appropriate level when calling the graphical warehouse layout. The STGE TYPE LEVEL parameter is only one character and it only allows a numeric entry.

3.1.2 Putaway Control

The PUTAWAY CONTROL section includes parameters associated with inbound movement or putaway into the storage type. Putaway, in this context, does not necessarily mean that the product is being moved from the goods receiving dock. In this case, putaway could be any movement into the storage type from any storage type (including another bin in the same storage type). We will discuss putaway in greater detail in Chapter 7. In Figure 3.3, you can see the parameters assigned to the PUTAWAY CONTROL section.

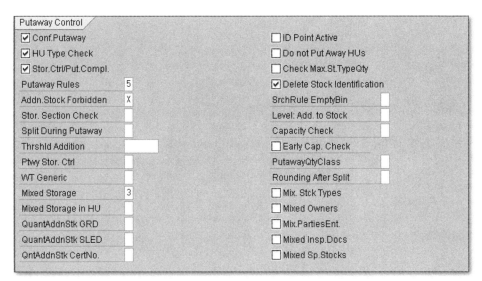

Figure 3.3 Putaway Control Section of the Storage Type Settings

Confirm Putaway

The CONF.PUTAWAY indicator controls whether the warehouse task must be confirmed for putaway into this storage type. If the source storage type does not require confirmation for removal and the destination storage type does not require confirmation for putaway, then the warehouse task need not be confirmed and the stock will be immediately transferred when the warehouse task is created. However, if either the source requires confirmation for removal or the destination requires confirmation for putaway, then the task can be confirmed and the stock will not be transferred until the task is confirmed. We will discuss confirmation of tasks further in Chapter 5, Other Warehouse Master Data, and Chapter 20, Kitting.

HU Type Check

If this parameter is selected, and if the warehouse task is created using a HU assignment, the system will check whether the HU type associated with the HU is allowed in the storage type. The allowed HUs for the storage type are configured in the EWM IMG by following the menu path EXTERNAL WAREHOUSE MANAGEMENT • CROSS-PROCESS SETTINGS • HANDLING UNITS • BASICS • DEFINE HU TYPES FOR EACH STORAGE TYPE.

If the HU TYPE CHECK is activated for the storage type, all bins created for the storage type are required to have the STORAGE BIN TYPE assigned to the bin.

Storage Control/Putaway Completed

The STOR.CTRL/PUT.COMPL. parameter determines that this storage type should be a final destination for products for determining the POSC. The storage types that represent physical warehouse bins for storage should have this parameter selected, and should include pick point and ID point storage types and scrapping zones. Interim storage types, including storage types used for work centers, deconsolidation, packing, counting, and quality inspection should not have this parameter selected.

Putaway Rules

PUTAWAY RULES are used to determine the logic that will be used by the system to determine the destination bin during putaway into the warehouse. The options include:

▶ **Addition to Existing Stock/Empty Bin**

The system first attempts to add stock to bins that already contain stock, according to the other rules of the storage type (e.g., mixed storage, mixed stock types, splitting rules, etc.). If it does not find an acceptable bin that already contains stock, then it searches for the next available empty bin.

▶ **Consolidation Group**

Storage bins within the storage type are assigned to consolidation groups and only stock from that consolidation group can be placed in the bin. You may want to use this setting, for example, in the packaging areas to ensure that stocks are collected in a single bin by consolidation group. We will discuss consolidation groups further in Chapter 8, Integration from ERP to EWM.

▶ **General Storage Area**

General storage areas are used to control stock in interim storage bins (packing areas, goods receipt and goods issue areas, deconsolidation, quality inspection, scrapping areas, and interim zones for two-step picking). Generally, in these storage areas, a single bin is created in each storage section and the storage type is set to allow addition to existing storage and mixed storage so that putaways into the bin are not precluded.

▶ **Empty Bin**

Stock is only put away to empty bins within the storage type. No additional stock is added to a bin that already contains stock.

Addition to Stock Forbidden

The ADDN. STOCK FORBIDDEN parameter determines whether additional stock may be added to the bin once the bin already contains stock. The possible values include:

▶ Addition to existing stock permitted

This value permits additional stock to be added to the bin.

▶ Addition to existing stock generally not permitted

This value precludes stock from being added to the bin.

▶ Product putaway profile decides

If this option is selected, then the product putaway profile is used to determine whether new stock can be added to the existing stock.

> **Note**
>
> The product putaway profile can be accessed in the IMG via the menu path EXTENDED WAREHOUSE MANAGEMENT • GOODS RECEIPT PROCESS • STRATEGIES • DEFINE PRODUCT PUT-AWAY PROFILE. The relevant product putaway profile is determined from the putaway control indicator assigned to the product in the product master. The settings for the putaway control indicator can be accessed in the IMG via the menu path EXTENDED WAREHOUSE MANAGEMENT • GOODS RECEIPT PROCESS • STRATEGIES • STORAGE TYPE SEARCH • DEFINE PUTAWAY CONTROL INDICATOR.
>
> We will reference the product putaway profile several times for other storage type parameter settings in the following sections.

Storage Section Check

The STOR. SECTION CHECK parameter controls the storage section determination and check function. Storage section determination is the process of determining the possible storage sections for putaway during the automatic putaway bin determination, according to the configuration of the storage section determination. We will discuss this function in more detail in Chapter 7. Storage section check is the process of determining the allowed storage sections for putaway during a manual storage bin specification.

The possible values include:

- No storage section determination or check
- Storage section determination and check
- Storage section determination, no check

Split During Putaway

This parameter controls whether the quantity being put away can be split into multiple bins if the entire quantity cannot fit into the initial bin. The possible values include:

- Do not split during putaway
- Split during putaway
- Product master decides

In the final case, the product master is checked and the SPLIT DURING PUTAWAY value in the product master on the storage type data view controls whether the split will occur.

Threshold Addition

This value is assigned in terms of percent of the storage capacity of the bin. If the SPLIT DURING PUTAWAY is determined to be relevant, this indicator is checked. A split is only performed if the available capacity of the bin exceeds the value of the THRSHLD ADDITION parameter. This lets you control the size of the split quantities, ensuring that the system does not direct the operator to put a small quantity into the bin with existing stock and then place the rest in another bin, as this reduces the operational efficiency.

> **Example**
>
> If the bin holds 100 widgets and the value of the THRSHLD ADDITION is set to 10 percent, then a putaway split will only be performed if the bin already contains less than 90 widgets.

Putaway Storage Control

If you are using POSC to determine the putaway path, the PTWY STOR. CTRL indicator is used to determine which type of warehouse task will be created (i.e., product warehouse task or HU warehouse task). The options include:

- **Storage Control: Dynamically Evaluated**

  The control of creation of the warehouse tasks is determined based on the setting for the PUTAWAY WTS or HU PICK-WTS field assigned to the external storage process step within the storage process definition (found in the IMG via the following menu path EXTENDED WAREHOUSE MANAGEMENT • CROSS-PROCESS SETTINGS • WAREHOUSE TASK • DEFINE PROCESS-ORIENTED STORAGE CONTROL • STORAGE PROCESS – DEFINITION • ASSIGN STORAGE PROCESS STEP)

- **Storage Control: Putaway with HU WT**

  The system always uses an HU warehouse task for the putaway, regardless of the number of putaway tasks for the HU.

- **Storage Control: Putaway with Product WT**

  The system always uses a product warehouse task for putaway.

If you are not using POSC, you simply specify the setting at the warehouse process type level in the SELECT HU W/O WAREHOUSE STORAGE PROCESS field.

WT Generic

The WT GENERIC (warehouse task generic) parameter controls which destination data will be determined as part of the warehouse task during the task creation.

Options include:

▶ Not Generic (Storage Type, Storage Section, and Storage Bin)

▶ Storage Type and Storage Section

▶ Only Storage Type

> **Example**
>
> When the warehouse task is created for putaway to the packing station (and if the consolidation group should not be used to determine the storage bin for putaway at the packing station), it is possible to determine only the storage type (or the storage type and storage section) during the creation of the warehouse task. Then, when the warehouse task is confirmed by the warehouse operator, the operator can specify the storage bin for putaway based on the physical availability of the bin.

Mixed Storage

The MIXED STORAGE parameter indicates how product can be mixed in the bin.

Options include:

▶ **Mixed Storage without Limitations**

You can mix products in the bin without checking to see whether the storage bin allows mixed products or mixed batches; mixing of products and batches within an HU is controlled by the MIXED STORAGE IN HU indicator.

▶ **Several Non-Mixed HUs with the Same Product/Batch**

You can place multiple HUs of the same product and batch into the same storage bin.

▶ **Several HUs with Different Batches of the Same Product**

You can place multiple HUs into the storage bin with different batch numbers, but they must all be the same product.

▶ **One HU Allowed per Bin**

You can only place a single HU into the bin; determination of whether the HU may contain mixed products is controlled by the MIXED STORAGE IN HU indicator.

Mixed Storage in HU

The MIXED STORAGE IN HU parameter indicates how product can be mixed in the HU while it is put away into the storage type.

Options include:

▶ **Mixed Storage Not Allowed**

You can't mix products or batches on the HU; product in the HU must be same product and the same batch number.

▶ **Several Batches of the Same Product per HU**

You can mix batches on the HU, but they must be the same product.

▶ **Mixed Storage without Limitations in HU**

You can mix products and batches in the HU without checking to see whether the HU allows mixed products or mixed batches.

Quant Addition to Stock Goods Receipt Date

If the storage type allows addition to existing stock, it may be possible to receive stock and add it to the same storage bin or HU even though the new stock has a different goods receipt date than the original stock. Because there is only one Goods Receipt Date field on the quant, the QUANTADDNSTK GRD indicator controls whether it is possible to add additional stock with a different goods receipt date and it specifies how the goods receipt date is handled if stock can be added.

Options include:

▶ **Allowed — Most Recent Date Dominant**

Allows addition to existing stock and updates the goods receipt date to the most recent goods receipt date of the different stocks.

▶ **Allowed — Earliest Date Dominant**

Allows addition to existing stock and updates the goods receipt date to the earliest (i.e., the oldest) goods receipt date of the different stocks.

▶ **Not Allowed**

Does not allow the new stock to be added to the existing stock if the goods receipt dates are different.

▶ **Product Putaway Profile Decides**

If this option is selected, then the relevant field setting in the Product Putaway

Profile is used to determine whether new stock can be added to the existing stock.

Quant Addition to Stock Shelf-Life Expiration Date (SLED)

If the storage type allows addition to existing stock, it may be possible to receive stock and add it to the same storage bin or HU even though the new stock has a different SLED than the original stock. Because there is only one SLED field on the quant, the QUANTADDNSTK SLED indicator controls whether it is possible to add additional stock with a different SLED date and it specifies how the SLED date is handled if stock can be added.

Options include:

▶ **Allowed — Most Recent Date Dominant**

Allows addition to existing stock and updates the SLED date to the most recent SLED date of the different stocks.

▶ **Allowed — Earliest Date Dominant**

Allows addition to existing stock and updates the SLED date to the earliest (i.e., the oldest) SLED date of the different stocks.

▶ **Not Allowed**

Does not allow the new stock to be added to the existing stock if the SLED dates are different.

▶ **Product Putaway Profile Decides**

If this option is selected, then the relevant field setting in the Product Putaway Profile is used to determine whether new stock can be added to the existing stock.

Quant Addition to Stock Certificate Number

If the storage type allows addition to existing stock, it may be possible to receive stock and add it to the same storage bin or HU even though the new stock has a different CERTIFICATE NUMBER than the original stock. Because there is only one CERTIFICATE NUMBER field on the quant, the QNTADDNSTK CERTNO. indicator controls whether it is possible to add additional stock with a different Certificate Number and it specifies how the CERTIFICATE NUMBER is handled if stock can be added.

Options include:

▸ **Allowed — Delete**

Allows stock with a different CERTIFICATE NUMBER to be added to the storage bin or HU and deletes the CERTIFICATE NUMBER from the quant.

▸ **Not Allowed**

Does not allow stock with different CERTIFICATE NUMBERS to be put away into the same storage bin or HU.

▸ **Product Putaway Profile Decides**

If this option is selected, then the relevant field setting in the PRODUCT PUTAWAY PROFILE is used to determine the system behavior with regard to the CERTIFICATE NUMBER in the quant.

ID Point Active

An *identification point* (ID point) is a location where product is temporarily placed to be identified before putaway or temporarily stored until an operator or the proper equipment is available to perform the putaway. An ID point is also called a pick-up and drop-off point. If this parameter is selected, then an ID point is active for the storage type and putaways to the storage type are directed, according to the layout-oriented storage control (LOSC), to be moved into the ID point before finally being put away into the destination storage type. The LOSC can be accessed in the IMG via the menu path EXTENDED WAREHOUSE MANAGEMENT • CROSS-PROCESS SETTINGS • WAREHOUSE TASK • DEFINE LAYOUT-ORIENTED STORAGE PROCESS CONTROL.

Do Not Put Away HUs

If this parameter is selected, HUs are not allowed to be put away into the storage type. If an HU is used to manage the stock during the putaway process, when this parameter is selected, a product warehouse task is created to move the product from the HU on the resource to the final destination bin at confirmation of the putaway warehouse task.

Check Maximum Stock Type Quantity

The CHECK MAX.ST.TYPEQTY parameter controls whether the maximum storage type quantity in the storage type view of the product master (table /SAPAPO/MATLWHST) is checked during the task creation. If the parameter is selected and the putaway into the storage type would cause the total quantity of the same product in the storage type to exceed maximum quantity, then the putaway will not be allowed and the next storage type in the putaway sequence would be checked (we will discuss the putaway strategies in further detail in Chapter 8).

Delete Stock Identification

DELETE STOCK IDENTIFICATION (Stock ID) is a unique indicator that is assigned to the group of products being moved within the warehouse. We will discuss the Stock ID further in Chapter 5. This parameter controls whether the Stock ID is deleted when the task is confirmed and the product is put away into the bin. If it is no longer necessary or desired to maintain the unique identifier upon putaway, you should select this indicator. Note that it is necessary to select this indicator on all storage types used for storage in the warehouse. If it is not selected, an error message will result when updating the storage type settings.

> **Example**
>
> If you are using the Stock ID to execute and track the movements of small containers of parts into the storage bin and you no longer need to maintain the Stock ID after the product is put away, then you should select the DELETE STOCK IDENTIFICATION indicator for the destination storage type of the putaway.

Search Rule Empty Bin

If the search strategy calls for putting the product away into an empty bin, the SRCHRULE EMPTYBIN indicator controls how the bins are sorting during the search. Options include:

▶ **Sorting According to Definition**

The bins are sorted according to the sort field specified on the storage bin master data.

▶ **Near To Fixed Bin**

The bins are sorted according to proximity to the fixed picking bin for the product.

▶ **Product Decides**

The SORT RULE FOR EMPTY STORAGE BIN SEARCH field (the field name is displayed as EMP.STORBIN SCH on the screen) on the STORAGE TYPE view of the product master is used to determine how the empty bins should be sorted.

Level: Addition to Stock

If you allow addition to existing stock in the storage type, the LEVEL: ADD. TO STOCK parameter controls at which level the stock is added during the creation of the warehouse task. Options include:

▸ **Addition to Stock at Bin Level**

Even if HUs already exist in the storage bin, when this option is specified, no destination HU is specified during the creation of the warehouse task; the warehouse operator must specify the destination HU when he confirms the warehouse task. It is appropriate to select this option when the operator requires operational flexibility to specify the HU based on the physical accessibility of that HU at the time of putaway.

▸ **Addition to Stock at Highest HU Level**

When this option is specified, the system determines the destination HU during warehouse task creation. It is appropriate to select this option when you are certain that the operator can access the designated HU.

Capacity Check

This indicator determines whether a capacity check is performed for the bin according to the dimensionless capacity specified in the storage bin master data (or alternatively, it can be specified in the bin type settings, which can be accessed in the IMG via the menu path EXTENDED WAREHOUSE MANAGEMENT • MASTER DATA • STORAGE BINS • DEFINE STORAGE BIN TYPES).

Options include:

▸ **No Check According to Key Figure**

No check is performed against the TOTAL CAPACITY assigned to the storage bin or bin type.

▸ **Check Acc. to Key Figure Product**

A check is performed against the TOTAL CAPACITY of the bin according to the dimensionless capacity consumption indicator assigned to the unit of measure in the UNITS OF MEASURE tab of the product master.

▸ **Check Acc. to Key Figure HU Type**

A check is performed against the TOTAL CAPACITY of the bin according to the capacity utilization of the HU, as determined by the capacity of the packaging material for the HU according to the UNIT OF MEASURE tab of the product master for the packaging material.

▶ **Check Acc. to Key Figures Product and HU Type**

A check is performed against the Total Capacity of the bin according to both the product master and the HU type data, as described previously. If either calculation exceeds the TOTAL CAPACITY, then the putaway would not be allowed.

▶ **No Check Against Key Figure, Weight, and Volume**

If this option is selected, then no check will be made against either the dimensionless capacity indicator or against the specified maximum weight and volume. This option should be selected for storage types for which the bins have no inherent capacity (such as interim storage types), and it should also be used for storage types that contain work centers.

> **Note**
>
> Unless the NO CHECK AGAINST KEY FIGURE, WEIGHT, AND VOLUME option is chosen, the system will always perform a weight and volume capacity check during putaway as long as a weight and volume are specified in the master data for the storage bin.
>
> For both functional and performance reasons, you should avoid checking capacity for interim storage types, or, in most instances, even work centers, where the capacity of the bin is not subject to physical limitations.

Early Capacity Check

The EARLY CAP. CHECK indicator triggers a check of the capacity of the bin types before checking the capacity of the individual bins within the storage, and causes the system to remove all bins from the search whose bin type does not exceed the required capacity. It may not be relevant to activate in all cases, but can significantly increase the performance of the putaway bin determination if you use bin types with varying capacities.

Putaway Quantity Class

The PUTAWAYQTYCLASS indicator is used during the capacity check of the destination bin. During the putaway bin determination, the system reads the relevant packaging specification level correlating to the assigned PUTAWAY QUANTITY CLASSIFICATION for the storage type (or the storage type view in the product master) and checks the capacity of the bin according to the assigned quantity in the packaging specification level. Together with rounding, you could, for example, specify that only full cases of the product are to be stored in a given storage type by assigning the appropriate putaway quantity classification that correlates to case quantities on the packaging specifications for the products.

The possible values for the quantity classification are set in table /SCWM/TQUAN-CLA, which can be accessed in the IMG via the menu path EXTENDED WAREHOUSE MANAGEMENT • CROSS-PROCESS SETTINGS • WAREHOUSE TASK • DEFINE QUANTITY CLASSIFICATIONS.

Rounding after Split

If the putaway task is split according to the splitting rules (see the previous section, Split during Putaway), the ROUNDING AFTER SPLIT parameter controls how the split quantity is rounded after the split is calculated. Options include:

▶ **No Rounding**

The split quantity is not rounded after being calculated.

▶ **Round Down WT Quantity to a Multiple of a Unit**

The warehouse task is rounded down to a multiple of a unit, according to the PUTAWAY QUANTITY CLASSIFICATION assigned earlier.

> **Example**
>
> If the SPLIT DURING PUTAWAY rule defines that the split should occur for a putaway and if the capacity of the bin within the storage type that already contains stock is enough to add three additional cases and five eaches, then the ROUNDING AFTER SPLIT rule is checked to determine whether the actual quantity to be put away into the bin should be rounding down to a multiple of a unit. If the ROUNDING AFTER SPLIT rule is specified to round down the warehouse task and the PUTAWAY QUANTITY CLASS is specified as Cases, then the warehouse task for putaway will be rounded to put away three full cases to the storage bin and the remaining five will be put away to a different bin.

Mixed Stock Type

The MIX. STCK TYPES indicator controls whether different stock types can be mixed in the bin. When mixed stock types are placed into the bin, the stock being added to the bin would be tracked using a different quant number, to allow the stocks of the different stock types to be tracked separately.

Mixed Owners

All stock in the EWM warehouse is assigned to an *owner*. As described in Chapter 6, Warehouse Stock Management, the owner "represents the party of the organization that *owns* the stock" (see Chapter 6 for more details on how the owner is used). The owner is stored on the quant data and is an additional factor used to determine whether the same quant number can be used when new stock is added to existing stock (i.e., the same product of the same batch added to the same bin but with different owners would require a new quant number for tracking). The MIXED OWNERS indicator specifies whether the new stock can be added to the bin in the case where the owner is not the same as the existing quant. If the checkbox is selected, then mixed owners will *not* be allowed for the products in the same bin. We will discuss the concept of the stock owner further in Chapter 5.

Mixed Parties Entitled

All stock in the EWM warehouse is also assigned to a *party entitled to dispose*. The party entitled to dispose is defined as the "plant or organization who is entitled to dispose of stock," and further "[u]sually this is the plant in which the stocks are planned, and which the ATP check is performed." In many cases (outside of a logistics service provider case), the entitled to dispose would be the same as the plant that owns the stock. Like the owner, the party entitled to dispose is stored on the quant data and is an additional factor used to determine whether the same quant number can be used when new stock is added to existing stock (i.e., the same product of the same batch added to the same bin but with a different party entitled to dispose would require a new quant number for tracking). The MIX.PARTIESENT. indicator specifies whether the new stock can be added to the bin in the case where the party entitled to dispose is not the same as the existing quant. If the checkbox is selected, then mixed parties entitled to dispose will *not* be allowed for the products in the same bin. We will further discuss the concept of the party entitled to dispose in Chapter 5.

Mixed Inspection Documents

If the stock in the bin is in inspection stock (as a result of being assigned to a quality inspection document), the MIXED INSP. DOCS indicator determines whether multiple groups of products assigned to different inspection documents can be placed into the same storage bin. If the indicator is selected, then multiple groups of material assigned to different inspection documents are *not* allowed to be placed in the same bin. Adding stock with a different inspection document to the bin will cause a separate quant number to be created.

Mixed Special Stocks

Special stocks are stocks that are assigned to some special purpose, for example, for sales order stock or project stock. The purpose and a reference number are assigned to the quant so that the special stock is tracked throughout the warehouse. If the MIXED SP.STOCKS indicator is selected, multiple groups of material assigned different special stock indicators are *not* allowed to be placed in the same bin, nor would stock assigned to the same special stock indicator but different special stock reference numbers. If the indicator is not selected, adding stock with a different special stock indicator or special stock reference number to the bin will cause a separate quant number to be created.

3.1.3   Stock Removal Control

The STOCK REMOVAL CONTROL section includes parameters associated with outbound movements or stock removals from the storage type. Stock removal is not necessarily restricted to picks for customer orders, stock transport orders, or production supply. Stock removal, in this context, applies to any outbound movement from the bins in the storage type to another bin, including bins in the same storage type and any other storage type, such as interim storage types. We will discuss stock removal in more detail in Chapter 8. In Figure 3.4, you can see the parameters assigned to the STOCK REMOVAL CONTROL section.

Figure 3.4 Stock Removal Control Section of the Storage Type Settings

Confirm Removal

If this indicator is selected, removals from the storage bin in the storage type will require confirmation. If the source storage type does not require confirmation for removal and the destination storage type does not require confirmation for putaway, then the warehouse task need not be confirmed and the stock will be immediately transferred when the warehouse task is created. However, if either the source requires confirmation for removal or the destination requires confirmation for putaway, then the task can be confirmed and the stock will not be transferred until the task is confirmed. We will discuss confirmation of tasks further in Chapter 7 and Chapter 22, Data Capture and Resource Optimization.

Stock on Resource

If this indicator is selected, then the stock on the relevant resources, or material handling equipment, will be considered during the storage type search. For example, for a storage type with a connected *pick point* (or P&D area), you may want to consider the stock for removal that has been picked from the storage type and is on the resource on its way to the pick point. This way, you would not overlook the stock simply because it's in transit between the storage type and its assigned pick point.

Negative Stock

This parameter controls whether negative stock is allowed in a storage bin. The options include:

▶ **Negative Stocks Not Allowed**

Negative stock is not allowed in the storage bin; only the available stock in the bin may be selected for removal.

▶ **Negative Available Quantity Allowed**

When creating a task for removal, the task is allowed to remove stock from the bin even when the available stock is not sufficient to fulfill the requested quantity as long as the total stock exceeds the available quantity; the total stock represents the available stock that is currently in the bin plus the stock scheduled for putaway into the bin (for example, for a putaway or replenishment task). However, the operator will not be allowed to confirm the task until sufficient stock has been placed into the bin.

▶ **Negative Stocks Allowed**

When creating a task for removal, the task can schedule removal of stock from the bin even when the total stock (available stock plus stock for putaway) is not sufficient to fulfill the requested quantity. The task will also be allowed to be confirmed, even though the stock is negative after the confirmation.

When the strategy for picking suggests that the picking should always occur from the primary picking bin, regardless of where else the stock is stored in the warehouse, the warehouse tasks for removal should be created with this primary picking bin as the source bin and the replenishments should be scheduled accordingly (or the picker-directed replenishment technique should be used). To enable this strategy, the NEGATIVE STOCK indicator should be set to allow negative stock, so that the picking task can be generated regardless of the replenishment situation.

If you want to ensure that the stock is always selected from the bin without regard to the available stock in the bin or the stock planned for putaway into the bin, then you should set the indicator to always allow negative stock. However, this strategy runs the risk that the operator may be directed to go to the picking bin even when no stock is available there and none is planned for putaway.

HU Picking Control

The HU PICKING CTRL indicator controls how the HU should be affected if a full homogeneous pallet (i.e., containing only a single quant with the entire quantity having the same stock data) will be removed from the bin. Options include:

▶ **Adopt Source HU with Lower-Level HUs into Pick-HU**

The source HU is adopted as a lower level HU onto the destination pick HU during the task confirmation.

▶ **Propose Source HU as Destination HU**

The source HU is adopted as the destination HU during the task confirmation.

▶ **Warehouse Process Type Controls Proposal for Destination HU**

The settings in the storage process control the proposal for the destination HU. The storage process control settings can be accessed in the IMG by following the menu path EXTENDED WAREHOUSE MANAGEMENT • CROSS-PROCESS SETTINGS • WAREHOUSE TASK • DEFINE WAREHOUSE PROCESS TYPE. For the assigned storage process of the warehouse task, the CONTROL FOR HU PICK indicator is used to determine the destination HU proposal.

▶ **Only Adopt Contents (Prod. and Lower-Level HUs) into Pick-HU**

Only the contents (the products or the lower level HUs) of the source HU are adopted to the destination pick HU.

> **Note**
>
> This indicator only controls the default selection on the destination screen of the warehouse task. The operator can override the default selections if circumstances warrant different values to be entered.

Pick Point Active

If this indicator is selected, a *pick point* is active for the storage type. A pick point is a work center within a storage type that is used during the stock removal to remove a partial HU from the source storage bin. If a partial quantity is required, the operator is directed to drop the HU down to the pick point, remove the destination quantity at the pick point, then place the partial HU back into a destination storage type. If a destination storage type is not specified, the putaway strategy is used to determine the destination storage type.

Use for Rough Bin Determination

If you set this indicator, then the storage type will be assigned to the outbound delivery line during the rough bin determination even if there is not sufficient product in the storage type to satisfy the requirements. This way, you can use the order-related replenishment (which reads the rough bin data from the delivery) to drive replenishment into the storage type for later picking for the delivery. Subsequently, when the warehouse task is created for picking, there would be enough stock in the bin (available, or stock for putaway, depending on the timing of the task creation relative to the replenishment task execution) to satisfy the pick request.

Stock Removal Rule

The STOCK REMOVAL RULE defines how the stock quants will be sorted when selecting which quant should be assigned to the warehouse task for stock removal (e.g., for specifying first-in first-out (FIFO), last-in first-out (LIFO), first-expiring first-out (FEFO), best before data (BBD), etc.). The possible entries are configured on table /SCWM/T334RR, which can be accessed in the IMG via the menu path EXTENDED WAREHOUSE MANAGEMENT • GOODS ISSUE PROCESS • STRATEGIES • SPECIFY STOCK REMOVAL RULE. The storage type is the last of the multiple places checked for determination of the stock removal rule. Before the storage type rule is checked, the storage type search sequence and storage type group are checked for assignment of a stock removal rule.

Round Whole Units

Storage types in the warehouse can be designated for a specific purpose, such as full pallet picking (e.g., bulk), case picking (e.g., floor level (or "A" level) picking, pallet flow, or case picking to conveyor scenarios), or each picking (case flow or bin picking). If you use the storage type for picking in whole units, you may specify that the quantities to be picked in the storage type should be rounded appropriately. The options include:

▶ **No Rounding**

No rounding occurs for the quantities removed from the storage type.

▶ **Round Down WT Quantity to Single Unit**

Quantities for each warehouse task are rounded down to a single unit; this is especially useful for creating separate warehouse tasks for full pallet picks when a total of more than one pallet is required.

▶ **Round Down WT Quantity to a Multiple of a Unit**

Quantities for each warehouse task are rounded down to a multiple of a single unit; especially useful for rounding down quantities to full case or full pallet quantities, where the remainder will be picked from another storage type.

▶ **Round Up WT Quantity to a Multiple of a Unit**

Quantities for each warehouse task are rounded up to a multiple of a single unit; especially useful if the quantities will be removed to a pick point where they can be split into the required quantity and a remainder quantity to be put back into stock (perhaps in another location appropriate to the remainder quantity).

3.1.4 Goods Movement Control

The GOODS MOVEMENT CONTROL section includes parameters that control various aspects of how products are moved into and out of the storage type. In Figure 3.5, you can see the parameters assigned to the GOODS MOVEMENT CONTROL section.

Goods Movement Control			
Availability Group	002	☑ Mandatory	
Non-Dep. Stock Type		☑ No GI	
Post.Change Bin		Stock Type Role	

Figure 3.5 Goods Movement Control Section of the Storage Type Settings

Availability Group

The AVAILABILITY GROUP assigned to the storage type controls the availability of stock within the storage type, according to SAP Advanced Planning and Optimization (APO), for the purposes of the global available-to-promise (gATP), by controlling which storage location the stock is stored within the ERP Inventory Management (IM). The AVAILABILITY GROUP is mapped to the corresponding IM storage locations within the IMG by following the menu path EXTENDED WAREHOUSE MANAGEMENT • INTERFACES • ERP INTEGRATION • GOODS MOVEMENTS • MAP STORAGE LOCATIONS FROM ERP SYSTEM TO EWM. For more details and examples regarding the use of the availability group, see Chapter 6.

Non-Dependent Stock Type

The NON-DEP. STOCK TYPE defines the quality status of the stock (i.e., unrestricted, quality inspection, blocked stock). If the storage type is to be used solely for storing stock of a particular Non-Dependent Stock Type, this indicator should be set to the relevant value. Options include:

- Unrestricted-use stock
- Quality inspection stock
- Blocked stock
- Returns blocked stock

> **Note**
>
> Returns blocked stock is non-valuated and is not visible to APO for gATP. It is used for returned stock that has not been inspected. Because the disposition has not been made, it should not be made available for sale or valuated in inventory.

Posting Change Bin

If a posting change is performed for the stock in the storage bin to change the stock from one stock type to another, the POST.CHANGE BIN indicator controls whether the product will remain in the same storage bin or be moved to another storage bin. The options include:

- **Posting Change Always in Storage Bin**

    Posting changes are always performed for the stock in the same storage bin and the stock is not moved as a result of the posting change, regardless of the mixed storage settings from earlier (even if only a partial quantity is changed).

▶ **Posting Change According to Mixed Storage Setting**

Posting changes are performed for the stock in the same storage bin as long as the change does not conflict with the mixed storage settings for the storage type; if the change conflicts with the settings, the changed stock will be moved to another appropriate bin via a warehouse task.

▶ **Posting Change Never in Storage Bin (Create Transfer Order)**

Posting changes always result in the stock being moved to a different storage bin from the original bin via a warehouse task.

Mandatory

If this indicator is selected, then only stocks from the assigned availability group for the storage type will be allowed into the storage type. If you place stock already assigned to a different availability group into the storage type, then the system automatically posts the stock to the new availability group of the destination storage type and posts the relevant storage location transfer to ERP IM, if applicable.

No GI (Goods Issue)

If the No GI indicator is selected, GIs may not be directly posted from the bins in the storage type. This indicator is often selected for warehouse bins used for storage, but should not be set for interim storage types or exception handling storage types.

Stock Type Role

If the storage type is to be used solely for storing stock of a particular stock type (normal stock, stock to be scrapped, or customs blocked stock), this indicator should be set to the relevant stock type. Options include:

▶ Customs Blocked Stock

▶ Scrapping Stock

▶ Normal Stock

When stock of a different stock type is moved into a bin within the storage type, it is automatically moved to the stock type assigned as the STOCK TYPE ROLE for the storage type. For example, you can create a storage type specifically for holding stock that is ready to be scrapped or stock that should be in stock type CUSTOMS

BLOCKED STOCK. In that case, as soon as the stock is moved into the storage type, it is automatically moved to the new stock type.

3.1.5 Replenishment

The REPLENISHMENT section includes parameters associated with replenishing products into the storage type from other warehouse storage bins. We will discuss replenishment further in Chapter 10, Outbound Processing. In Figure 3.6, you can see the parameters assigned to the REPLENISHMENT section.

Figure 3.6   Replenishment Section of the Storage Type Settings

Replenishment Level

The replenishment level determines at what level the stocks will be read during a replenishment run (i.e., when the replenishment tasks are created). Options include:

▶ **Storage Bin Level for Fixed Bins**

   The stock levels will be read for the individual fixed bins and the replenishment quantities will be calculated based on the stocks available in the bin compared to the required quantities.

▶ **Storage Type Level**

   The stock levels will be read for the entire storage type and the replenishment quantities will be calculated based on the stocks available in the entire storage type compared to the required quantities.

> **Note**
>
> The calculation for the required quantities depends on which type of replenishment is executed. We will discuss the replenishment strategies further in Chapter 11, Production Supply.

Tolerance

TOLERANCE is used during the replenishment and is checked to determine whether the replenishment quantity is sufficient to consider the replenishment request completed. The tolerance is defined as a percentage. If the actual replenished quantity is delivered with less quantity that requested (i.e., underdelivered), but the quantity is within the specified percentage of the requested quantity, then the request will be considered fulfilled and no further replenishment tasks will be created.

3.2   Storage Sections

A storage section is a subdivision of a storage type (as seen in Figure 3.7) and represents a group of bins that generally have some sort of like attribute. For example, you can subdivide the storage type by type of product stored (large bulk items versus standard size pallets) or by velocity of the products (fast moving versus slow moving). You can have any number of storage sections within a storage type, up to the theoretical maximum according to the field size. Because the field size is four characters and allows alphanumeric entry, theoretically you can have almost 1.7 million storage sections per storage type. However, when deciding on how many storage sections to create, you should carefully consider the purpose in segregating the bins and your strategies for putaway.

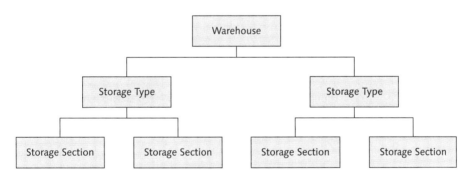

Figure 3.7   Relationship between the Warehouse, Storage Type, and Storage Section

Storage sections are only used in EWM for determining the putaway storage bin. You are no longer (as of EWM version 5.1) required to create any storage sections for a storage type — even the putaway bin determination can be used without them. For example, for interim storage types, it might make sense to avoid creating storage sections altogether, as they may not serve a purpose for some storage types.

To create the storage sections, in the EWM IMG follow the menu path EXTENDED WAREHOUSE MANAGEMENT • MASTER DATA • DEFINE STORAGE SECTION. Figure 3.8 displays the transaction for creating and naming the storage sections.

In Chapter 8, we will discuss how to use the storage sections during the putaway strategy to determine where to place the products in the warehouse for storage.

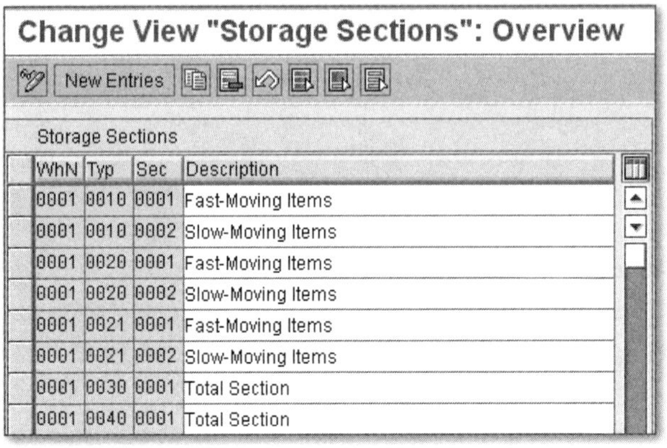

Change View "Storage Sections": Overview

WhN	Typ	Sec	Description
0001	0010	0001	Fast-Moving Items
0001	0010	0002	Slow-Moving Items
0001	0020	0001	Fast-Moving Items
0001	0020	0002	Slow-Moving Items
0001	0021	0001	Fast-Moving Items
0001	0021	0002	Slow-Moving Items
0001	0030	0001	Total Section
0001	0040	0001	Total Section

Figure 3.8 Creating the Storage Sections

3.3 Storage Bins

The storage bin represents the physical location or storage space where the products are stored in the warehouse. As seen in figure 3.9, each storage bin is assigned to a warehouse, storage type, and storage section. Storage bins are generally named within the warehouse according to a grid pattern and the grid coordinates are generally used to signify the location of the storage bin. This grid may be subdivided into aisles, racks, stacks, sections, levels, etc. For example, in a high-rack storage area, the bin location that can be found in the second aisle in the third section on the fourth level could be referred to as bin 02-03-04 or 02-06-D (in cases where the sections are numbered alternately on opposite sides of the aisle).

Naming the bins in the warehouse is an art unto itself and deciding how to name the areas of the warehouse is best left to the industrial engineers and warehouse managers, who often have strong opinions about what works "best" under given conditions. Whatever you decide to name your bins, the EWM system should be able to accommodate your naming conventions, as long as you stay within the parameters. The storage bin length is 18 characters (as opposed to the storage bin length in ERP WM, which is only 10 characters), so you have some flexibility in naming (for example, you can decide to include dashes in the bin names for readability — just keep in mind that the system operators will have to hand key those dashes every time they have to do a manual entry).

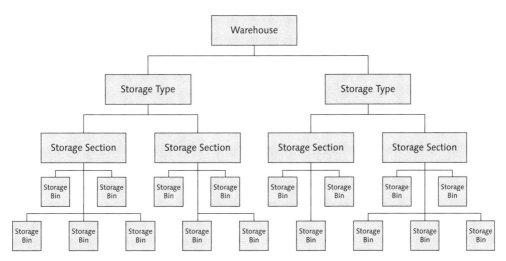

Figure 3.9 The Storage Bins Are Assigned to a Warehouse, Storage Type, and Storage Section

> **Note**
>
> The storage bins are not configurations, they are master data. This allows the end users greater control over creating the storage bins as needed to maximize operational effectiveness and minimize administrative overhead. Control over who is allowed to create the storage bins is managed using the authorization concept, which will be discussed further in Chapter 25, Authorizations and Roles and Data Archiving.

3.3.1 Creating Storage Bins

To create a bin, from the SAP Easy Access Menu, follow the EXTENDED WAREHOUSE MANAGEMENT • MASTER DATA • STORAGE BIN • CREATE STORAGE BIN menu path, or use Transaction code /SCWM/LS01. In Figure 3.10, you can see the bin creation transaction.

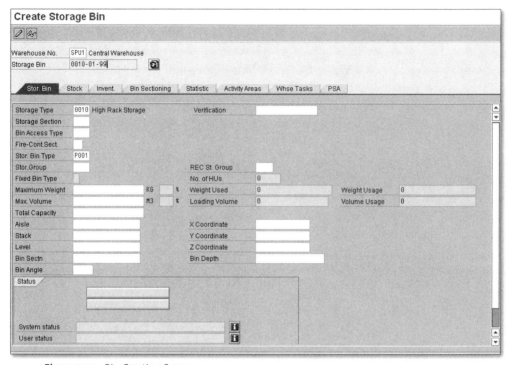

Figure 3.10 Bin Creation Screen

To create a bin, you must enter, at a minimum, the warehouse number, storage bin name, and storage type. Unlike in ERP WM, the storage bin names in EWM are unique and may not be duplicated across storage types. This also applies to interim storage types and storage types that can be used for large, generic storage areas. In addition to the warehouse, storage bin, and storage type, the following information may be optionally assigned to the storage bin:

▶ **Storage section (though it is optional)**

The Storage section was described previously and is used in the storage section search strategy (discussed in Chapter 9, Inbound Processing) during putaway.

▶ **Bin access type**

The bin access type is used by resource management in determining the execution priorities of tasks. To maintain bin access types in the IMG, follow the menu path EXTENDED WAREHOUSE MANAGEMENT • MASTER DATA • STORAGE BINS • DEFINE BIN ACCESS TYPES. To maintain execution priorities related to the bin access types, in the Easy Access Menu, follow the EXTENDED WAREHOUSE MAN-

AGEMENT • MASTER DATA • RESOURCE MANAGEMENT • MAINTAIN EXECUTION PRI-
ORITIES menu path, or use Transaction code /SCWM/EXECPR.

▸ **Fire containment section**

The fire containment section is used to identify areas in the warehouse that are within certain fire containment zones and can be used to create reports, for example, of which hazardous materials may be contained within each fire containment section.

▸ **Storage bin type**

The storage bin type can be used to divide the storage type into groups according to the size or conditions of the storage bins. For example, you can segregate the storage bins by size. The storage bin type is used in the determination of allowed HU types. To create the storage bin types in the IMG, follow the menu path EXTENDED WAREHOUSE MANAGEMENT • MASTER DATA • STORAGE BINS • DEFINE STORAGE BIN TYPES. To assign the allowed HU types per storage bin type in the IMG, follow the menu path EXTENDED WAREHOUSE MANAGEMENT • GOODS RECEIPT PROCESS • STRATEGIES • STORAGE BIN DETERMINATION • HU TYPES • DEFINE HU TYPES FOR EACH STORAGE BIN TYPE.

> **Note**
>
> If the HU TYPE CHECK is activated in the warehouse storage type, the storage bin type becomes a required field.

▸ **Storage group**

The storage group can be used to further subdivide the storage type for determining the intermediate storage type during the LOSC (which we'll discuss further in Chapter 12, Internal Warehouse Movements). To create the possible entries for the storage group in the IMG, follow the menu path EXTENDED WAREHOUSE MANAGEMENT • CROSS-PROCESS SETTINGS • WAREHOUSE TASK • DEFINE STORAGE GROUPS FOR LAYOUT-ORIENTED STORAGE CONTROL. To define the intermediate storage type based on the combination of source and destination storage types and storage groups in the IMG, follow the menu path EXTENDED WAREHOUSE MANAGEMENT • CROSS-PROCESS SETTINGS • WAREHOUSE TASK • DEFINE LAYOUT-ORIENTED STORAGE PROCESS CONTROL.

▸ **Resource Execution Constraint storage group**

The RESOURCE EXECUTION CONSTRAINT (REC) STORAGE group is used to group bins together for the REC checks. The REC is used to determine how many resources can be working in an area of the warehouse at the same time and is designed to let you optimize the efficiency of the warehouse workers by preventing congestion. To define the possible entries for the REC storage group in the IMG, follow the menu path EXTENDED WAREHOUSE MANAGEMENT • CROSS-PROCESS SETTINGS • RESOURCE MANAGEMENT • CONTROL DATA • ASSIGN RESOURCE EXECUTION CONSTRAINTS TO REC STORAGE GROUP (note that you should first create the ID to Group Resource Types, discussed further in Chapter 5). To activate the REC per REC storage group in the SAP Easy Access Menu, follow the menu path EXTENDED WAREHOUSE MANAGEMENT • MASTER DATA • RESOURCE MANAGEMENT • ACTIVATE RESOURCE EXECUTION CONTROL FOR STORAGE GROUPS. In Chapter 5, we will discuss in detail how to create and assign the RECs.

▶ **Capacity information**

You define the maximum weight, volume, and total capacity (in dimensionless units) of the bin that is checked during the putaway for determination. As soon as you maintain the weight and volume information on the storage bin, the total weight and volume of the products in the bin will be checked against the maximum weight and volume, and if either is exceeded, the putaway would not be allowed. The only exception occurs if you specify in the storage type that the weight and volume should not be checked (see the Storage Types section of this chapter for more details). The weights, volumes, and product capacities are specified in the product master on the Units of measure tab for each relevant unit of measure.

▶ **XYZ coordinates**

The X, Y, and Z coordinates specify the location of the bin in the warehouse and are used in the travel path calculations for labor management. The naming comes from the XYZ coordinates of a three-dimensional map. You can determine the XYZ coordinates of your warehouse storage bins by overlaying your warehouse diagram onto a map and measuring the location of the storage bins according to the XYZ coordinates of the map.

▶ **Information about the storage bin used for visualization, such as aisle, stack, level, bin section, bin depth, and bin angle**

This information is used in the graphical warehouse layout to determine certain parameters of the bin used in visualizing the warehouse layout. It can also be used to provide additional information to the warehouse worker about the bin location or can be used in analytical reporting.

> **Note**
>
> A common question from practitioners who are first implementing labor management is how they should determine where to place the origin (the 0,0,0 point) in their warehouse. Because the distance calculations are based on relative differences between the points, it doesn't really matter where the origin is located. However, it makes it easier for most people to understand where the locations are relative to one another if the origin is placed in the bottom left part of the map when looking at it in its most common orientation. This allows all of the numbers to be on the positive scale in all three dimensions. Just remember that your yard locations can also be assigned XYZ coordinates, so you may want to consider that as well when determining your origin.
>
> Another common question is what unit of measure should be used. Again, it doesn't really matter. You only have to account for the constraints of the relevant fields when making that decision. The field is a decimal field type and allows 10 numerals before the decimal and 3 after. Therefore, common units of measure used in the assignment are feet, yards, or meters.

▶ **System status**

The system status field provides information about certain system status codes that are currently assigned to the bin. For example, the putaway block and stock removal block will be reflected here if they are activated. The status codes are only four-digit codes, but if you want to get more details on the codes, press the INFORMATION button to the right of the SYSTEM STATUS field (as seen in Figure 3.10).

▶ **User status**

The user status field provides information about user status codes that are currently assigned to the bin. These user statuses can be assigned to the bins manually, or they can be assigned using business transactions. You can create your own user status profiles and user status codes for the profiles in the IMG by following the menu path EXTENDED WAREHOUSE MANAGEMENT • MASTER DATA • STORAGE BINS • DEFINE USER STATUS PROFILE.

You can also assign user status codes to a group of bins in the SAP Easy Access Menu by following the EXTENDED WAREHOUSE MANAGEMENT • MASTER DATA • STORAGE BIN • ADD USER STATUS FOR STORAGE BINS menu path, or using Transaction code /SCWM/BINSTAT. A prerequisite to being able to assign user statuses to the bin is that the status profile must be assigned to the warehouse number via the warehouse number control. To access the warehouse number control in the IMG, follow the menu path EXTENDED WAREHOUSE MANAGEMENT • MASTER DATA • DEFINE WAREHOUSE NUMBER CONTROL.

A major advantage of creating and assigning user statuses for the bins is that each bin can be blocked for multiple reasons, and any single reason is sufficient to block the bin for putaway. Therefore, you can block the bin for multiple reasons, and then remove each blocking reason as the situation is resolved, without unblocking the bin completely, because the other blocking reasons are still intact. This allows you to track and maintain all of the different reasons that a bin can be blocked simultaneously, which you would have to do manually if you only had one blocking reason code.

▶ **Verification field**

The verification field is used during the mobile data entry transactions to verify that the user is at the correct bin. The verification field should match the barcode that is physically located at the bin. You can use a simple technique of making the verification field the same as the bin name, you can use check digits at the end of the bin (to ensure that the user correctly keyed the bin), or you can use a scheme of random bin verification fields if you prefer a "blind" confirmation and want to ensure that the operator always scans the bin. You can enter the verification field manually in the bin if you create the bins one by one, or you can use the method described in Section 3.3.6, Creating Verification Fields.

If you want to change an existing storage bin, use the Extended Warehouse Management • Master Data • Storage Bin • Change Storage Bin menu path, or Transaction code /SCWM/LS02. To display an existing storage bin, use the Extended Warehouse Management • Master Data • Storage Bin • Display Storage Bin menu path, or Transaction code /SCWM/LS03.

3.3.2 Generating Storage Bins Using Storage Bin Structures

To facilitate the process of initially creating storage bins or adding a large group of storage bins, SAP provides a tool that lets you specify a structure for the bin naming, assign parameters, and create the storage bins *en masse* based on the structures. To create the storage bin structures in the IMG, follow the menu path Extended Warehouse Management • Master Data • Storage Bins • Define Storage Bin Structure.

Before creating the bin structures, you should maintain the storage bin identifiers for the bin structures. These allow you to specify which parts of the bin structure are used to relate to the aisle, stack, level, subdivision, and depth. To create the storage bin identifiers in the IMG, follow the menu path EXTENDED WAREHOUSE MANAGEMENT • MASTER DATA • STORAGE BINS • DEFINE STORAGE BIN IDENTIFIERS FOR STORAGE BIN STRUCTURES.

For the most part, the bin structures are fairly self-explanatory. You create a group with begin and end bin names, tell the system what the increments should be between the bins, and assign the parameters for the group, including storage type, storage bin type, storage section, fire containment section, bin access type, and storage group. If any of these parameters change, then you should create another sequence to create the bins with the different parameters (or if there are just a few that are different from the rest, you could decide to change them later). However, there a couple of concepts worth explaining in more detail, namely the template, structure, and increments.

Storage Bin Structure — Template

The template is used to define the structure of the bin name itself, sort of the metadata for the bin name. There are three characters used to define the structure:

- ▶ N stands for a numeric character (i.e., 0 to 9)
- ▶ A stands for alphabetic character
- ▶ C stands for a constant (i.e., every bin name in this sequence will have the same value in that position)

When you combine these characters together in a sequence, you define the format of the bin name.

> **Example**
>
> To create a bin structure for a group of bins that range from A01A to A99D, you would specify the structure to be CNNACCCCCCCCCCCCC. Note that the empty characters at the end of the bin name should be filled with C to specify that it is a constant. The structure defines that the first character is a constant (i.e., it is always A within this sequence), the second and third characters are numeric, the fourth character is an alphabetic character, and the rest are constant (blanks).

Note that if you have two or more characters in a row that need to be incremented together as a group, for example from 001 to 999 or AAA to CCC, these items should be grouped together side by side and should be given the same bin template character.

Storage Bin Structure — Structure

Next, you define the structure of the bin. This is where you define which of the groups of characters are used as the aisle, stack, level, subdivision, and depth. Note that the indicators that you use here are the ones that you defined earlier as the storage bin identifiers.

Example

Using the same bin sequence used previously, A01A to A99D, the storage bin structure would be defined as ASSL (if A is defined in the storage bin identifiers for the aisles, S is defined for the stacks, and L is defined for the levels). The rest of the field would be left blank.

Storage Bin Structure — Increments

Once the template and structure are assigned, you then define the storage bin structure increments. You should only define increments for those portions of the bin template that will increase in between the start value and the end value. Also, note that you can increment the values in single value increments (ex. 01, 02, or 03), or you can increment the values in multiple value increments (ex. 01, 03, 05). Also, you can increment the values of single characters independently or you can increment the value of a group of characters together.

Example

For the example provided earlier, A01A to A99D, the increment would be straightfor- wardly assigned as " 011" (note the blank at the beginning of the value, which is used to indicate that the first character is not incremented). If, on the other hand, you only wanted to create odd values (ex. A01A, A03A, A05A, etc.), you would specify the incre- ment as " 021" (meaning that the second and third values are grouped together and are incremented by two each time).

To give another example, let's assume that the bin stacks only go to 06, by even num- bers, and then start over again (ex. 02, 04, 06, 12, 14, 16, 22, 24, 26, etc.). In this case you would keep the same template and structure, but be sure to make the start value begin with an even number and then increment the third character by two. Also, you would increment the second character and the third character independently, because there is a break in the sequence. The values would therefore be:

Start value: A02A

End value: A26D

Increment: " 121" (shown in quotes only to reiterate the blank character at the beginning)

The increment is defined this way because the second character should be incremented by two, the third character by two, and the fourth character by one. This would allow the sequence of bins to be created as A02A, A02B, A02C, A02D, A04A, A04B, A04C, A04D, A06A, A06B, A06C, A06D, then A12A, A12B, A12C, A12D, A14A, A14B, etc.

Generating the Storage Bins

Once the structures are configured, you can then use the structures to generate the storage bins. To generate the bins, you must use the separate transaction for bin generation in the SAP Easy Access Menu by following the EXTENDED WAREHOUSE MANAGEMENT • MASTER DATA • STORAGE BIN • GENERATE STORAGE BINS menu path, or using Transaction code /SCWM/LS10. Even though the Create Bins button is available in the structures when you access them via the IMG, you cannot use this button while you are in the configuration transaction. From within the bin generation transaction from the SAP Easy Access Menu, simply double-click on the line that represents the sequence that you want to create, select the CREATE BINS button, verify that the bins listed are the ones that you want to create, then select the CREATE button.

> **Note**
>
> You can also use this transaction to change a group of bins to match the parameters currently set for the storage bin sequence. Even though the bins are already created, you still use the CREATE BIN button to access the list of generated bins that will then be changed when you execute the transaction from within the list.

When you access the transaction, you will only be shown the bin sequences for the warehouse that is currently defined as your default warehouse. If you have never set a default warehouse by running a transaction that requires one or by specifying parameters within your OWN DATA for your user profile (which can be accessed from any transaction by following the menu path SYSTEM • USER PROFILE • OWN DATA), then you will be requested to enter the warehouse number when you first call the transaction.

> **Note**
>
> If you enter the bin generation transaction and want to change the default warehouse, follow the menu path TABLE VIEW • OTHER VIEW. Thereafter, the warehouse number is stored in the parameter ID /SCWM/LGN and will not need to be entered again for any transactions that use the parameter ID to determine the default warehouse number.

3.3.3 Mass Change to Bins

Once you have created the storage bins, you can change several of the parameters for the existing storage bins at one time. To access the mass bin change transaction, from the EWM Easy Access menu follow the EXTENDED WAREHOUSE MANAGEMENT • MASTER DATA • STORAGE BIN • MASS CHANGE TO STORAGE BINS menu path, or use Transaction code /SCWM/LS11. On the selection screen, enter selection criteria to select a range of bins to view the work list. From the work list (as seen in Figure 3.11), you can select a bin or bins that you want to update, then select the STORAGE BINS button (circled in the figure), enter the new data in the pop-up screen for the fields that you want to change, and press ⌈Enter⌉ (or select the green checkmark). If you want to clear the field for all selected entries, select the Reset checkbox to the right of the respective field. Once any data for the field is changed, an asterisk will appear in the BIN CHGED field in the table. When you save the transaction, the data will be written to the database and the bins will be changed. Note that if you exit without saving, you will not get a pop-up message, but the data will not be written to the database, so don't forget to save the data before you exit.

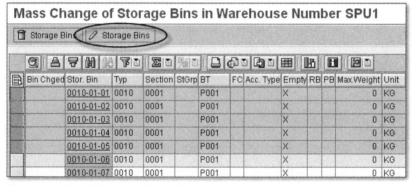

Figure 3.11 Mass Change to Storage Bin

3.3.4 Setting Up Storage Bin Sorting

In order for the warehouse tasks to be sorted according to your wishes, you must create the bin sorting for each warehouse, activity area, and activity combination. To create the bin sorting sequence in the SAP Easy Access Menu, follow the EXTENDED WAREHOUSE MANAGEMENT • MASTER DATA • STORAGE BIN • SORT STORAGE BINS menu path, or use Transaction code /SCWM/SBST. Enter the warehouse number and optionally the activity area and activity. If you leave the activity area or the activity blank, then the system will determine all possible entries and create each combination. The resulting list is simply a simulation to show you the expected results (as seen in Figure 3.12), and you must select the EXECUTE button to actually generate the bin sorting.

Simulation of Bin Sorting

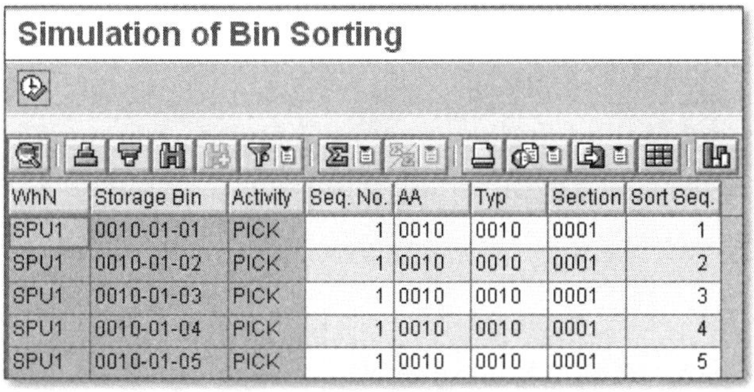

WhN	Storage Bin	Activity	Seq. No.	AA	Typ	Section	Sort Seq.
SPU1	0010-01-01	PICK	1	0010	0010	0001	1
SPU1	0010-01-02	PICK	1	0010	0010	0001	2
SPU1	0010-01-03	PICK	1	0010	0010	0001	3
SPU1	0010-01-04	PICK	1	0010	0010	0001	4
SPU1	0010-01-05	PICK	1	0010	0010	0001	5

Figure 3.12 Simulation of Bin Sorting

> **Note**
>
> The storage bin sorting must be created in order for the system to find the correct source storage bin during the warehouse task creation. If the storage bin sorting is not created for a bin or group of bins, then those bins will be skipped during the warehouse bin determination. For this reason, if you create new bins, activity areas, or activities, you must regenerate the bin sorting in order for the task creation to function properly.

3.3.5 Fixed Bin Assignments

To use the fixed bin picking technique (which will be described further in Chapter 9), you will need to assign fixed bins within the fixed bin storage type. To assign the fixed bins manually in the SAP Easy Access Menu, follow the EXTENDED WAREHOUSE MANAGEMENT • MASTER DATA • STORAGE BIN • MAINTAIN FIXED STORAGE BIN menu path, or use Transaction code /SCWM/BINMAT. In Figure 3.13, you can see the existing assignment of several materials to fixed storage bins.

To assign a new material to a fixed bin, switch to change mode by pressing the Display/Change button, and then press the APPEND ROW button (circled in Figure 3.13). This will result in a new row being created at the top and you can enter the data manually.

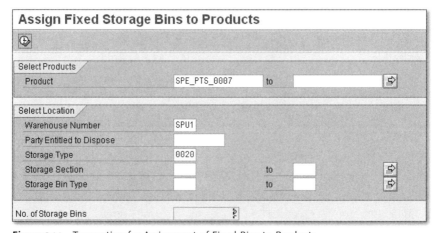

Warehouse Number SPU1: Maintain Fixed Storage Bin

WhN	Ent.toDisp	Storage Bin	Typ	Product	StBinImp	Changed On	Max.Qty	DisplayUoM	Min. Qty	DisplayUoM
SPU1	SPU1	0050-01-01-B	0050	SPE_PTS_0001		07.09.2006	0,000		0,000	
SPU1	SPU1	0020-01-03-C	0020	SPE_PTS_0002	B	15.11.2006	0,000		0,000	
SPU1	SPU1	0020-01-03-D	0020	SPE_PTS_0002	B	15.11.2006	0,000		0,000	
SPU1	SPU1	0020-01-02-A	0020	SPE_PTS_0007		25.02.2009	0,000		0,000	
SPU1	SPU1	0050-01-02-A	0050	SPE_PTS_0008		23.09.2007	0,000		0,000	
SPU1	SPU1	FLOW-30-01-01-1	FLOW	SPE_SFS_0001		15.09.2006	250,000		55,000	
SPU1	SPU1	FLOW-30-01-01-2	FLOW	SPE_SFS_0009		15.09.2006	250,000		55,000	

Figure 3.13 Existing Assignment of Products to Fixed Storage Bins, in Change Mode

To have the system automatically assign fixed bins based on the available bins in the storage type, in the SAP Easy Access Menu, follow the menu path EXTENDED WAREHOUSE MANAGEMENT • MASTER DATA • STORAGE BIN • ASSIGN FIXED STORAGE BINS TO PRODUCTS. As you can see in Figure 3.14, you must enter the product(s), warehouse number, storage type, and the number of storage bins to be assigned. The system will then automatically determine the available bins and assign them to the product, and then the information bar will indicate the number of fixed bins assigned (or the number of errors).

Assign Fixed Storage Bins to Products

Select Products
Product   SPE_PTS_0007   to

Select Location
Warehouse Number   SPU1
Party Entitled to Dispose
Storage Type   0020
Storage Section   to
Storage Bin Type   to

No. of Storage Bins

Figure 3.14 Transaction for Assignment of Fixed Bins to Products

To delete fixed bin assignments in the SAP Easy Access Menu, follow the EXTENDED WAREHOUSE MANAGEMENT • MASTER DATA • STORAGE BIN • DELETE FIXED STORAGE

Bin Assignment menu path, or use Transaction code /SCWM/FBINDEL. The system will delete any fixed bin assignments made for the parameters specified.

3.3.6 Creating Verification Fields

In addition to the possibility described earlier for manually entering the verification field for the bin, you can also automatically create the verification fields for several bins at once, as long as they follow a describable pattern. To assign the verification fields, in the SAP Easy Access Menu, follow the Extended Warehouse Management • Master Data • Storage Bin • Maintain Verification Field menu path, or enter Transaction code /SCWM/LX45. In Figure 3.15, you can see the selection screen for creating the bin verification fields.

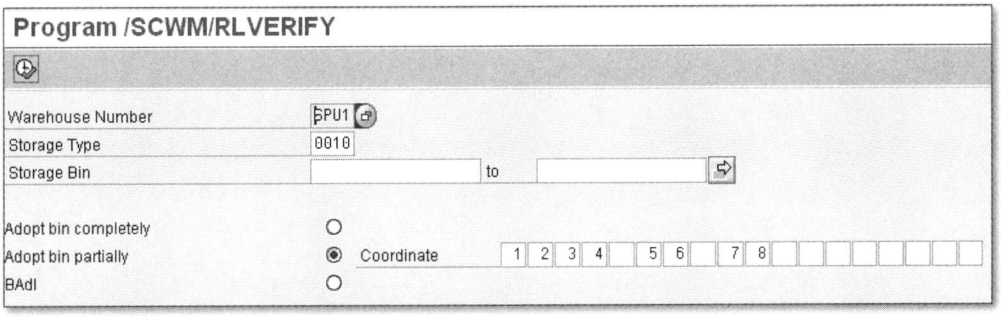

Figure 3.15 Selection Screen for Maintaining Verification Fields

On the selection screen, aside from the selection criteria for warehouse number, storage type, and storage bin, you also specify how the verification field for each bin should be constructed. The options include:

▶ **Adopt bin completely**

The entire bin name is directly taken over as the verification field.

▶ **Adopt bin partially**

Only certain characters of the bin are taken over as the verification field. You can use this option to remove the dashes from the bin name, common leading characters, or any other characters from the bin name. To specify that the character should be included in the verification field, simply enter a two-digit number into the corresponding position of the Coordinate fields that correspond to the position of the character in the verification field (see Figure 3.16 for the corresponding results from the selections specified in Figure 3.15).

▶ **BAdI**

You can use a Business Add-In (BAdI) to otherwise manipulate the storage bin name to determine the verification field, add a check digit to the end of the storage bin name, create a random but unique verification field, or use any other scheme to determine the appropriate verification field.

Once you specify the selections and the storage bin name adoption criteria, execute the transaction and you will see the simulation results on the following screen (as in Figure 3.16). Once you have reviewed the simulation results, select the UPDATE button to update the storage bin table (/SCWM/LAGP) with the verification fields.

Program /SCWM/RLVERIFY

⊕ Update

Warehouse Number   SPU1
Storage Type   0010

Storage Bin	Verifier	
0010-01-01	00100101	
0010-01-02	00100102	
0010-01-03	00100103	
0010-01-04	00100104	

Figure 3.16 Simulation of Verification Fields Based on Entries on the Selection Screen

3.3.7 Printing Labels for Storage Bins

In order for the warehouse workers to identify the warehouse storage bins, the bins should be labeled with the bin names. The labels on the storage bins should match the system both in terms of readable bin name and the verification field, which is often printed as a barcode on the bin label. You can print the bins from the SAP Easy Access Menu by following the EXTENDED WAREHOUSE MANAGEMENT • MASTER DATA • STORAGE BIN • PRINT STORAGE BIN LABEL menu path, or by using Transaction code /SCWM/PRBIN. In Figure 3.17, you can see the selection screen for printing the bin labels. The standard Smartform /SCWM/BIN_LABEL is provided for printing the bin labels. If you would like to enhance the form, you can create your own using Transaction SMARTFORMS and assign it as the form name within the transaction.

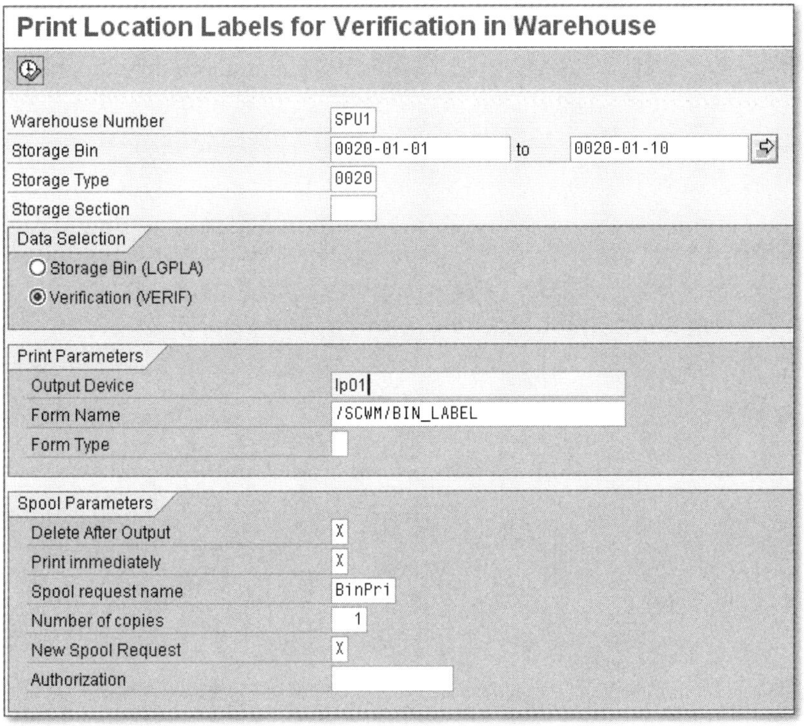

Figure 3.17 Transaction for Printing Storage Bin Location Labels

When printing the labels for storage bins that are assigned as fixed bins for materials, it can often make sense to also print the product identification on the bin label as well. Therefore, EWM also provides a transaction and standard form for printing fixed bin storage labels. To print the fixed bin labels, from the SAP Easy Access Menu, follow the EXTENDED WAREHOUSE MANAGEMENT • MASTER DATA • STORAGE BIN • PRINT STORAGE BIN LABEL menu path, or call Transaction /SCWM/ PRFIXBIN. Figure 3.18 shows the selection screen for printing the fixed bin labels. The standard Smartform /SCWM/FIXBIN_LABEL is provided for printing the fixed bin labels. If you would like to enhance the form, you can create your own using Transaction SMARTFORMS and assign it as the form name within the transaction.

For both bin label printing transactions, when you execute the transaction, a pop-up box like the one in Figure 3.19 will appear. Specify the output device and the other spool request data and select the PRINT or PRINT PREVIEW buttons to continue.

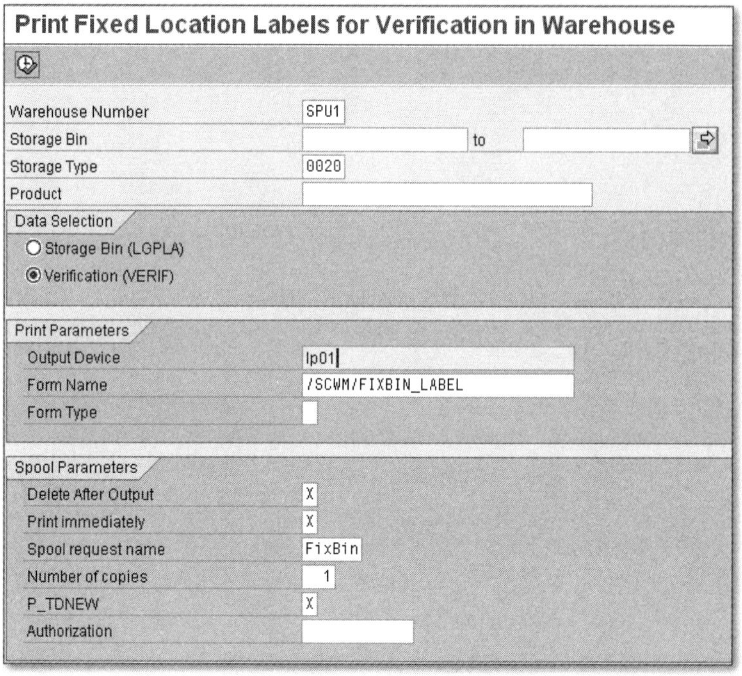

Print Fixed Location Labels for Verification in Warehouse

Warehouse Number	SPU1
Storage Bin	to
Storage Type	0020
Product	

Data Selection

○ Storage Bin (LGPLA)
◉ Verification (VERIF)

Print Parameters

Output Device	lp01
Form Name	/SCWM/FIXBIN_LABEL
Form Type	

Spool Parameters

Delete After Output	X
Print immediately	X
Spool request name	FixBin
Number of copies	1
P_TDNEW	X
Authorization	

Figure 3.18 Transaction for Printing Storage Fixed Bin Location Labels

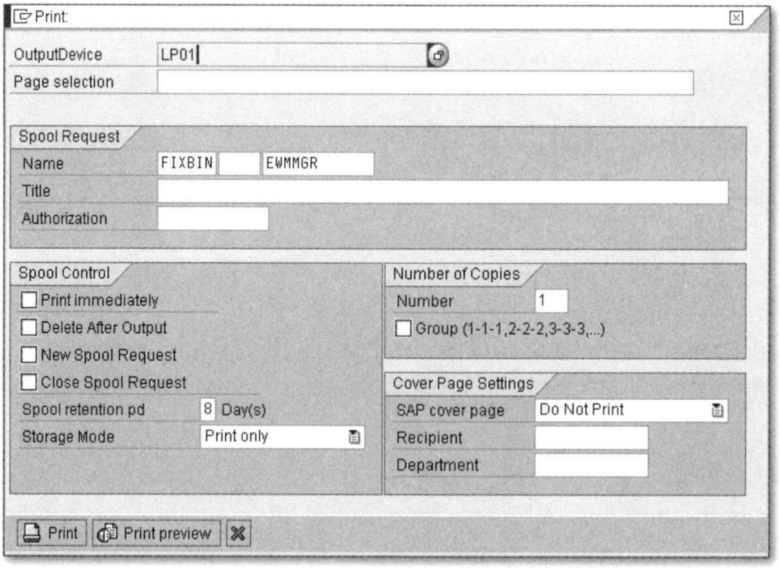

Print:

OutputDevice	LP01
Page selection	

Spool Request

Name	FIXBIN	EWMMGR
Title		
Authorization		

Spool Control

☐ Print immediately
☐ Delete After Output
☐ New Spool Request
☐ Close Spool Request

Spool retention pd	8 Day(s)
Storage Mode	Print only

Number of Copies

Number	1

☐ Group (1-1-1,2-2-2,3-3-3,...)

Cover Page Settings

SAP cover page	Do Not Print
Recipient	
Department	

🖨 Print | 🖨 Print preview | ✖

Figure 3.19 Print Output Pop-up That Appears Following the Selection Screen for the Bin Label Printing Transactions

3.4   Activity Areas

Activity areas are a new structure for EWM (i.e., they did not exist in ERP WM). The activity area represents a group of storage bins that are grouped together for creating warehouse orders related to particular activities, such as picking, putaway, or physical inventory. The activity area is used to define the bin sorting, by activity, as described previously in the Bin Sorting section. Figure 3.20 describes the relationship between the warehouse, storage types, storage sections, storage bins, and activity areas. Note, as shown in the figure, that you can assign the same bin to multiple activity areas.

To create the activity areas in the IMG, follow the menu path EXTENDED WARE-HOUSE MANAGEMENT • MASTER DATA • ACTIVITY AREAS • DEFINE ACTIVITY AREA. As you can see in Figure 3.21, the creation of the activity areas is straightforward — you simply enter the warehouse, storage type, activity area, and text description. The additional field JOINED is used to indicate that the activity area is a higher level activity area for using the *Pick, Pack, and Pass* rule. After setting the join indicator, to join the activity areas together in the EWM IMG, follow the menu path EXTENDED WAREHOUSE MANAGEMENT • CROSS-PROCESS SETTINGS • WAREHOUSE ORDER • JOIN ACTIVITY AREAS TOGETHER.

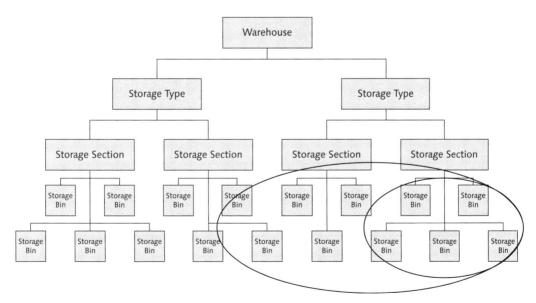

Figure 3.20   Activity Areas Can Be Comprised of Bins from Multiple Storage Types and the Same Bin Can Be Assigned to Multiple Activity Areas

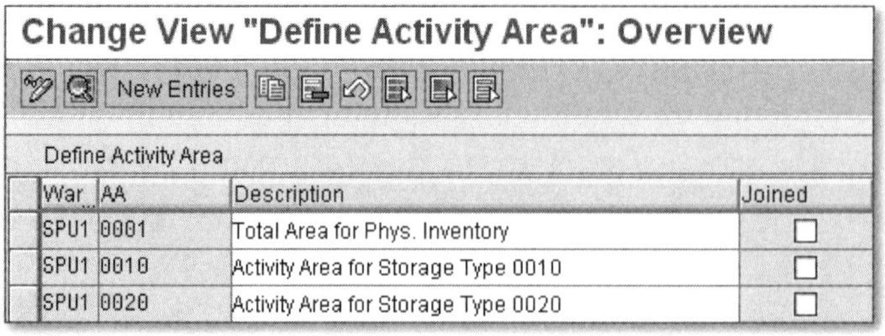

Change View "Define Activity Area": Overview

Define Activity Area

War	AA	Description	Joined
SPU1	0001	Total Area for Phys. Inventory	☐
SPU1	0010	Activity Area for Storage Type 0010	☐
SPU1	0020	Activity Area for Storage Type 0020	☐

Figure 3.21 Defining the Activity Areas

To automatically create activity areas from your defined storage types in the EWM IMG, follow the menu path EXTENDED WAREHOUSE MANAGEMENT • MASTER DATA • ACTIVITY AREAS • GENERATE ACTIVITY AREA FROM STORAGE TYPE. Enter the warehouse number, storage type, and activity, if relevant (or leave it blank to create the activity areas for all activities), execute the transaction, and the activity areas will be automatically created.

After creating the activity areas, you must assign the bins to the activity areas. To assign the bins in the IMG, follow the menu path EXTENDED WAREHOUSE MANAGEMENT • MASTER DATA • ACTIVITY AREAS • ASSIGN STORAGE BINS TO ACTIVITY AREAS. In the most straightforward example, you can simply create an activity area for each storage type using the implicit assignment (as shown in Figure 3.22), that is, this method implies that all of the bins of the storage type belong to the activity area. You can also choose to explicitly assign bins by ranges of bin components (i.e., aisle, stack, level, bin section). You can use multiple sequence numbers to create multiple ranges within a storage type, keeping in mind, as indicated previously, that you can even assign the same bin to multiple activity areas (the bins can be assigned to different activity areas for different activities via Transaction /SCWM/SBST).

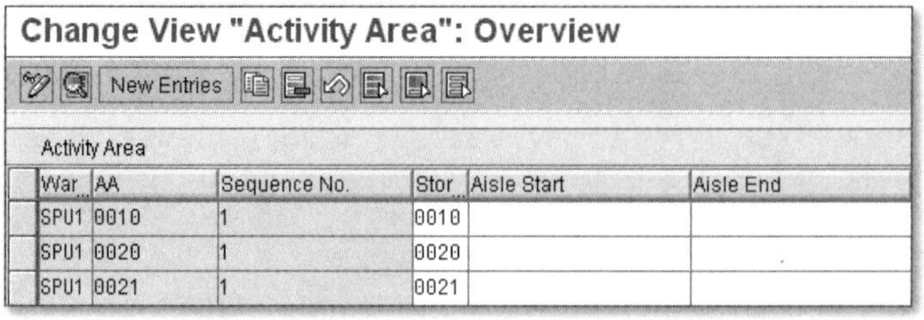

Change View "Activity Area": Overview

Activity Area

War	AA	Sequence No.	Stor	Aisle Start	Aisle End
SPU1	0010	1	0010		
SPU1	0020	1	0020		
SPU1	0021	1	0021		

Figure 3.22 Implicit Assignment of Bins per Storage Type to the Activity Area

The activity areas are used to determine how the warehouse tasks are grouped together into warehouse orders. In Chapter 7, we will describe the warehouse order in detail and provide more information on how the activity areas are used during warehouse order creation.

3.5 Doors and Staging Areas

Warehouse doors are the locations at which the loading and unloading activities occur for movements into and out of the warehouse. Many warehouses have multiple doors, and the doors are generally given a name or number for ease of communication in the warehouse. The staging areas are generally physical areas within the warehouse near the doors where product is staged temporarily before the loading process or after the unloading process. The activities, together with the activities in the yard, are collectively known in EWM as the Shipping and Receiving (S&R) processes.

Warehouse Doors

The doors in EWM represent an organizational unit that can be used to direct activities to the location in the warehouse where the physical loading and unloading processes will occur. To create the warehouse doors in the IMG (as shown in Figure 3.23), follow the menu path EXTENDED WAREHOUSE MANAGEMENT • MASTER DATA • WAREHOUSE DOOR • DEFINE WAREHOUSE DOOR.

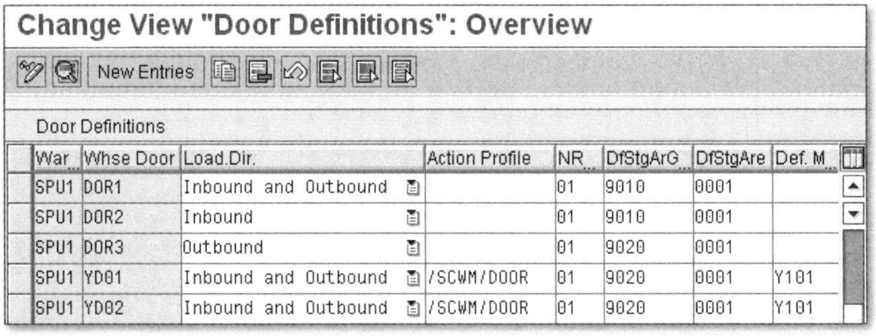

Change View "Door Definitions": Overview

New Entries

Door Definitions

War	Whse Door	Load.Dir.		Action Profile	NR	DfStgArG	DfStgAre	Def. M
SPU1	DOR1	Inbound and Outbound			01	9010	0001	
SPU1	DOR2	Inbound			01	9010	0001	
SPU1	DOR3	Outbound			01	9020	0001	
SPU1	YD01	Inbound and Outbound		/SCWM/DOOR	01	9020	0001	Y101
SPU1	YD02	Inbound and Outbound		/SCWM/DOOR	01	9020	0001	Y101

Figure 3.23 Creating the Warehouse Doors

For each door, you can specify that the direction is either inbound, outbound, or both (although this is, at the moment, only used for informational purposes). The action profile is used to determine relevant Post-Processing Framework (PPF) actions for printing, for example, to print requests to move an empty trailer from the yard to a door for loading. We will describe the PPF actions further in Chapter 24, Post-Processing Framework and Form Printing. The default staging area group and default staging area are the values to be used if the system cannot determine a staging area via the following configuration, and the same is true for the default means of transport.

Warehouse Staging Areas

To create the staging areas in the IMG, follow the menu path EXTENDED WARE-HOUSE MANAGEMENT • MASTER DATA • STAGING AREAS • DEFINE STAGING AREAS. You can see the table view for the creation of the warehouse staging area and its related parameters in Figure 3.24.

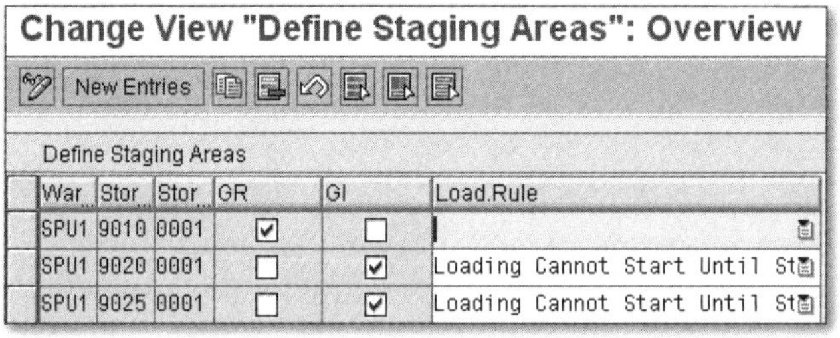

Change View "Define Staging Areas": Overview

New Entries

Define Staging Areas

War	Stor	Stor	GR	GI	Load.Rule
SPU1	9010	0001	☑	☐	
SPU1	9020	0001	☐	☑	Loading Cannot Start Until St
SPU1	9025	0001	☐	☑	Loading Cannot Start Until St

Figure 3.24 Creation of the Warehouse Staging Areas

In this view, you create the staging area, specify whether the staging area is relevant for goods receipt, goods issue, or both, and specify the loading rule for the staging area. The options for the loading rule include:

▶ Loading can start when the first HU arrives

▶ Loading cannot start until staging has been completed

▶ Loading cannot start until 24 hours wait time have passed

> **Note**
>
> The staging area is technically just another storage section in the staging type, but one that is used for the special purpose of staging. You can reuse the single storage section typically created for an interim storage type (as seen in Figure 3.24), or you can create additional storage sections to be used specifically for staging. However, if you want to use additional storage sections as staging areas, you must first create them in table /SCWM/T302 (as described previously in the section above regarding Storage Sections).

To assign the STAGING AREA/DOOR DETERMINATION GROUP to the warehouse products for use in the staging area and door determination, you must first create the determination groups in customizing. To create the determination groups in the IMG, follow the menu path EXTENDED WAREHOUSE MANAGEMENT • MASTER DATA • STAGING AREAS • DEFINE STAGING AREA AND DOOR DETERMINATION GROUPS.

Assigning Staging Areas to Doors

Following the creation of the warehouse doors, staging areas, and determination groups, you can maintain the rules for determining which STAGING AREA/DOOR DETERMINATION GROUPS are allowed for a warehouse door. This determination group is assigned to the product and can therefore be used to determine which doors are relevant for which products (for example, bulk goods versus palletized goods or frozen goods versus goods at ambient temperature). In Figure 3.25, you can see the table used to maintain the allowed STAGING AREA/DOOR DETERMINATION GROUP.

Also, following the warehouse door and staging area creation, you can assign the staging area group and staging area to the warehouse door (see Figure 3.26).

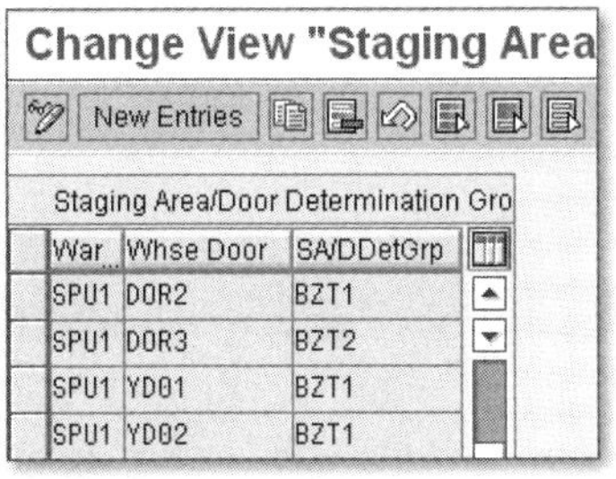

Figure 3.25 Determination of Allowed Staging Area/Door Determination Groups for Warehouse Doors

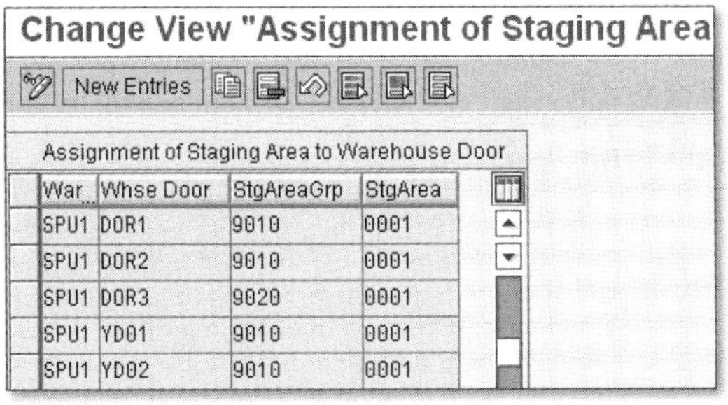

Figure 3.26 Assigning Staging Areas to the Warehouse Doors

3.6   Work Centers

Work centers are locations in the warehouse where special processes occur, including packing, deconsolidation, value-added services (VASs), counting, quality inspection, identification point or pick point activities, and other activities (each of these special processes will be discussed further in later chapters). The work center can be referenced individually, or they can be grouped together into work center groups. For example, a work center can be specified as the destination location for a warehouse task, or the warehouse task can specify that the operator should take the product or HU to a work center group (technically identified by EWM as a storage section), in which case the final work center would only be determined when the task is being confirmed. This allows the determination of the relevant work center only at the last moment, providing for the best possibility to take into account available capacity at the work centers.

3.6.1   Work Center Layout

The same user interface is used for all work centers, but the available functions of the user interface are defined by the work center layout. The work center layout can be specified in the IMG by following the menu path EXTENDED WAREHOUSE MANAGEMENT • MASTER DATA • WORK CENTER • SPECIFY WORK CENTER LAYOUT. Because the warehouse layout is specified when you create the work centers, you should verify or create the warehouse layout before you start creating the work centers.

There are several parameters assigned to the warehouse layout that controls which tree structures or buttons are available, which functions are allowed, which BAdIs are called, and which tab pages are shown. The options are fairly self-explanatory and don't require full explanations for each here, but if you have questions about the effects of settings certain parameters, you may want to set up an example work center in a sandbox environment (a dedicated system landscape often set up as part of an implementation project for the express purpose of testing and trying different system options) and try the different settings. Layouts are delivered for several common work center functions, and you may be able to use the existing layouts in many cases.

3.6.2 Creating Work Centers

To create the work centers in the IMG, follow the menu path EXTENDED WAREHOUSE MANAGEMENT • MASTER DATA • WORK CENTER • DEFINE WORK CENTER. In Figure 3.27, you can see the work centers created for our example warehouse, including new work centers created for outbound pack stations and quality inspection.

Change View "Define Work Center": Overview

Define Work Center

War	Work Cntr.	Description	Step	Stor	ISec	OSec	Repack	Layout
SPU1	DEKO	Deconsolidation in Goods Receipt	IB02	8010	INBD	OUTB	3040	DKMX
SPU1	PAK1	Pack in Goods Issue	OB02	8030	INBD	OUTB	3040	VPMX
SPU1	QINS	Quality Inspection Station	QM01	8020			3040	QI
SPU1	SCRP	Repack for Scrapping		8040			3040	VPMX
SPU1	STAG	Packing in Staging Area	OB03	9025	INBD	OUTB	3040	VPMX
SPU1	VERP	Pack in Goods Issue	OB02	8030	INBD	OUTB	3040	VPMX
SPU1	WV01	Vas - Outbound Packing w/Vas	VSPK	8030			3040	VAS1
SPU1	WVI1	VAS Oil Station	VS01	8050	VI11	VI10	3040	VAS1

Figure 3.27 Defining Work Centers

For each work center, the following settings are assigned, aside from the warehouse, work center name, and description:

▶ **Step**

Defines the external storage process step assigned to the work center. As described in the section above regarding storage types, when an HU is moved into a storage type, and if the HU is relevant for POSC, the system compares the external step of the storage type to the latest external step of the HU and replaces it if the external step of the storage type is greater than (i.e., later in the routing) the external step currently assigned to the HU. In the case of a storage type used for work centers, this check is performed at the work center level, because each work center could have a separate external step assigned.

▶ **Storage Type**

Specifies the Storage Type of the work center. The role assigned to the specified storage type must be one of:

▶ E — Work Center

▶ B — Pick Point

- ▸ I — Work Center in Staging Area Group

- ▸ C — Identification Point

▸ **Inbound Section**

The Inbound Section is a storage section that is used to store the products waiting to be processed at the work center.

▸ **Outbound Section**

The OUTBOUND SECTION is a storage section that is used to store the products that have already been processed at the work center.

▸ **Repack Warehouse Process Type**

The warehouse process type used for repacking at the storage type. If no process type is specified, the default process type for repacking (e.g., 3040) would be used.

▸ **Layout**

The layout used for the user interface for activities performed at the work center, as defined in the previous section.

▸ **RF: HU Ready for Input**

This field determines whether the HU IDENTIFICATION field is displayed on the mobile data entry ("Radio Frequency") transactions. If the field is enabled, the warehouse operator can create a new HU with an external HU number or use an existing HU in the packing transaction.

▸ **Print Determination Procedure**

The Print Determination Procedure is the procedure used to determine factors associated with the printing of the HU labels.

▸ **Process**

The Process is the process type used for return transfer from the pick point, if the work center is used for processing the quantities at the pick point (we will discuss pick points in detail in Chapter 9).

▸ **Return Storage Type**

The RETURN STORAGE TYPE is the storage type used for the putaway of unused material from the pick point, if the work center is used for processing the quantities at the pick point.

▶ **Return Storage Section**

The RETURN STORAGE SECTION is the storage section used for the putaway of unused material from the pick point, if the work center is used for processing the quantities at the pick point.

▶ **HU From PP**

This field defines the warehouse process type used for HU warehouse task created to move the HU back from the pick point to the return storage type, if the work center is used for processing the quantities at the pick point.

▶ **Activity**

The activity defines the activity used to determine the text displays used within the work center.

▶ **Plan Activity Area**

This field defines the default activity area used by Labor Management.

▶ **Save**

If this field is selected, the system will automatically save the data after each action is performed in the warehouse. Using this action could be a performance detriment to the system, but could save the user significant time if the transaction is interrupted before the user saves. The default value for the delivered work centers is that this field is activated.

▶ **Exclusive Lock When Repacking**

This field determines whether an exclusive lock is set on the source HU during the repacking process. If the field is selected, then the exclusive lock is used. Unless you need to have multiple operators unpacking an HU at the same time, you should activate the exclusive lock. Failure to do so could result in the operator not being able to update header information on the HU while repacking (due to the fact that the exclusive lock can no longer be set once a shared lock is activated).

▶ **Check When Repacking According to Consolidation Group**

This field determines whether a check is performed on the consolidation group via the available BAdI when repacking. The options include:

  ▶ No check

  ▶ Check while repacking products

  ▶ Check while repacking HUs and products

▶ **Check When Repacking According to Stop on Route**

This field determines whether a check is performed according to the stop on the route via the available BAdI when repacking. The options include:

  ▶ No check

  ▶ Check while repacking products

  ▶ Check while repacking HUs and products

▶ **Repack Active Warehouse Tasks**

The parameter is checked to determine whether products or HUs on active warehouse tasks can be repacked. The options include:

  ▶ Repacking Active WT Not Allowed

  ▶ Repacking Active WT Allowed

▶ **Measuring Catch Weight Quantity in Work Center Possible**

This parameter determines whether the operator is allowed to capture the actual catch weight quantity at the work center using scales. If it is not allowed at the work center, then the system completely ignores the catch weight profile of the product.

3.6.3 Optimizing Work Center Determination

The settings are used to determine which fields will be used in what sequence to determine the work center during the work center determination, with the goal of reducing the number of entries necessary in the work center determination table.

As you can see in Figure 3.28, the WORK CENTER DETERMINATION IN GOODS ISSUE can include the ROUTE, ACTIVITY AREA, and CONSOLIDATION GROUP. As such, the number of possible entries for determining the work center could be very large. To access the work center determination table, in the SAP Easy Access Menu, follow the EXTENDED WAREHOUSE MANAGEMENT • MASTER DATA • WORK CENTER • DETERMINE WORK CENTER IN GOODS ISSUE menu path, or use Transaction code /SCWM/PACKSTDT.

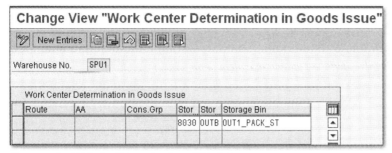

Figure 3.28 Table for Determination of Work Center

To speed up the access and to only check for relevant entries, the system first selects entries from the work center determination table that meet all criteria (or a "fully qualified entry"). If it cannot find a fully qualified entry, it then uses the access optimization table, progresses through the sequences, determines whether a qualified entry matches the necessary criteria, and selects the first match that it finds. In Figure 3.29, you can see the access optimization table, which allows you to select which entries are relevant, and which sequence should be used to check the entry combinations.

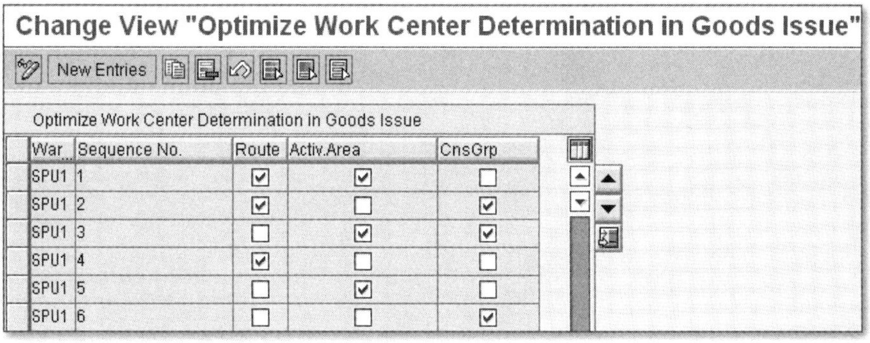

Figure 3.29 Access Optimization for Work Center Determination

3.7 Summary

In this chapter, we described the warehouse structure and its elements, including details on how to configure them. You should now have a good sense of how to set up storage types, storage sections, activity areas, doors and staging areas, and work centers. Now that you have an understanding of how to set up the warehouse structure, we can now begin to describe the master data and the transactional processes. On several occasions throughout the text, we will refer back to this chapter rather than describe again how to set up the organizational elements of the warehouse. If you have trouble finding the appropriate sections, we suggest you refer to the table of contents or the index to locate the specific topic that we reference.

Effective master data management is critical to the success of any SAP implementation, and it helps to maximize the value of the application to the organization.

4   Product Master Data

Good master data is often considered one of the most important aspects of a successful system implementation, and SAP Extended Warehouse Management (EWM) is no different in that regard. The master data of the system, together with the configuration, is used to control the processes that are performed in the system. The difference between the two is that the master data is under the direct control of the end users of the system. For that reason, it is important for the implementation team to understand and clearly communicate to the end users exactly how the master data should be maintained to allow the system to run effectively. In this chapter, we'll discuss the master data associated with products in both ERP and EWM.

4.1   The ERP Material Master

The material master, or product master, as it is called in EWM, is perhaps the most important master data in the system. Every warehouse operation involves a product and every aspect of that operation — what steps are involved, how it flows, what bins are involved, etc. — is decided based on the information stored in the product master.

The product master of EWM is derived from, or integrated with, the material master data of ERP. ERP is the master in this master-slave relationship, in that the materials are created in ERP and then distributed via the ERP-EWM interface to EWM using the core interface (CIF) technology. Once the ERP data is interfaced to EWM, the additional EWM data can be added to the product master to control the warehouse processes for that product.

In addition to providing the baseline for the product master data of EWM, the ERP material master contains important data in its own right for controlling the processes of ERP (e.g., availability checking rules, planning for purchasing and production). In this section, we will not cover every view or every field of the ERP material master — there are plenty of sources you can go to for that. However, we will discuss the primary fields that are relevant to the EWM activities and describe the proper way to use those fields to control the behavior of EWM.

To display an existing material in ERP, from the Easy Access menu, follow the LOGISTICS • MATERIALS MANAGEMENT • MATERIAL MASTER • MATERIAL • DISPLAY • DISPLAY CURRENT menu path, or use Transaction code MM03 (or for change, use Transaction code MM02, and for creation, use Transaction code MM01). There are also options for creating materials of particular material types or scheduling and activating changes, but we will not cover those details here. When you enter the transaction, select the relevant views for the material and enter the appropriate organizational data that correlates to the warehouse for which you want to process the data.

Not every bit of data on every material master view is relevant for every process in ERP. Likewise, not every field from the ERP material master is relevant for EWM (in fact, only data from six of the tabs, or views, in the material master are distributed to EWM, assuming that you are using the non-industry-specific material master). Therefore, only a subset of the data is sent from ERP to EWM to facilitate the EWM processes. Once that data arrives in EWM, it needs to be augmented with additional data that is only relevant to EWM. We'll take a look at the EWM product master in a moment, but first let's look into the views and data fields of the ERP material master. We won't cover every view or every field, but we will focus on those that are relevant to EWM processes.

> **Note**
>
> In the following sections and throughout the book, we may make general comments regarding materials and products, even though in industry-specific applications, the same data may be referred to using the industry or application-specific terms such as articles. Unless otherwise specified, the information should also apply to the industry or application-specific variants on the terms.

4.1.1 Existing Views of the ERP Material Master

Several views of the ERP Material Master contain information that should be passed to EWM, aside from the new views that are added. The existing views that we describe in Table 4.1 include:

▶ Basic data

▶ Units of measure

▶ Sales: general/plant

▶ Plant data/storage 1

Table 4.1 is a list of the fields from these veiws that should be passed to EWM during the standard CIF transfer.

ERP View	ERP Field	EWM View	EWM Field
All Views	Material Number	All Views	Product Number
All Views	Material Description	All Views	Product Description
Basic Data	Material Group	Properties	Material Group
Basic Data	Product Hierarchy	Properties	Product Hierarchy
Basic Data	General Item Category Group	Storage	Item Category Group
Basic Data	Material Group: Packaging Materials	Packaging Data	Packing Group
Units of Measure	Denominator	Units of Measure	Denominator
Units of Measure	Alternate Unit	Units of Measure	Alternate Unit
Units of Measure	Numerator	Units of Measure	Numerator
Units of Measure	Base Unit	Units of Measure	Base Unit
Units of Measure	EAN/UPC	Units of Measure	EAN/UPC
Units of Measure	EAN Category	Units of Measure	EAN Category
Units of Measure	Length/Width/Height	Units of Measure	Length/Width/Height
Units of Measure	Unit of Dimension	Units of Measure	Unit of Dimension
Units of Measure	Volume	Units of Measure	Volume
Units of Measure	Volume Unit	Units of Measure	Volume Unit
Units of Measure	Gross Weight	Units of Measure	Gross Weight
Units of Measure	Net Weight	Units of Measure	Net Weight
Units of Measure	Weight Unit	Units of Measure	Unit of Weight

Table 4.1 Fields from the Existing Views of the ERP Material Master That Are Transferred to EWM

ERP View	ERP Field	EWM View	EWM Field
Units of Measure	Remaining Volume after Nesting	Units of Measure	Remaining Volume after Nesting
Units of Measure	Maximum Stacking Factor	Units of Measure	Maximum Stacking Factor
Units of Measure	Capacity	Units of Measure	Capacity Consumption
Units of Measure	Category of Unit of Measure	Units of Measure	UoM Category
Sales: General/ Plant	Transportation Group	Properties	Transportation Group
Sales: General/ Plant (and Basic Data)	Packaging Material Type	Packaging Data	Packaging Material Type
Sales: General/ Plant	Allowed Package Weight	Packaging Data	Maximum Weight
Sales: General/ Plant	Excess Weight Tolerance	Packaging Data	Excess Weight Tolerance
Sales: General/ Plant	Allowed Package Volume	Packaging Data	Maximum Volume
Sales: General/ Plant	Allowed Volume Tolerance	Packaging Data	Allowed Volume Tolerance
Sales: General/ Plant	Closed	Packaging Data	Closed Packaging
Plant Data/Storage 1	Batch Management	Properties	Batch Management Required
Plant Data/Storage 1	Minimum Remaining Shelf Life	Properties	Required Minumum Shelf Life
Plant Data/Storage 1	Total Shelf Life	Properties	Shelf Life
Plant Data/Storage 1	Rounding Rule SLED	Properties	Rounding Rule
Plant Data/Storage 1	Storage Percentage	Properties	% Remaining Shelf Life

Table 4.1 Fields from the Existing Views of the ERP Material Master That Are Transferred to EWM (Cont.)

4.1.2 WM Execution

The Warehouse Management Execution view was added specifically for integration with EWM and several of the EWM-relevant fields are visible there, including the fields in the following sections (and seen in Figure 4.1).

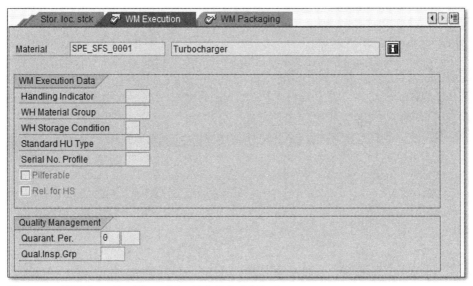

Figure 4.1 WM Execution View of the ERP Material Master

Handling Indicator

The HANDLING INDICATOR is used to determine how the product should be handled when moving from one location to another (e.g., fragile, no clamp). To specify the entries for the HANDLING INDICATOR in the ERP Implementation Guide (IMG), follow the menu path INTEGRATION WITH OTHER mySAP.com COMPONENTS • EXTENDED WAREHOUSE MANAGEMENT • ADDITIONAL MATERIAL ATTRIBUTES • ATTRIBUTE VALUES FOR ADDITIONAL MATERIAL MASTER FIELDS • DEFINE HANDLING INDICATOR.

Warehouse Material Group

The WH MATERIAL GROUP is transferred to the WAREHOUSE PRODUCT GROUP field on the STORAGE view of the EWM product master. It is used to group materials together to determine certain processes in the warehouse. To specify the entries for the WAREHOUSE MATERIAL GROUP in the ERP IMG, follow the menu path INTEGRATION WITH OTHER mySAP.com COMPONENTS • EXTENDED WAREHOUSE MANAGEMENT • ADDITIONAL MATERIAL ATTRIBUTES • ATTRIBUTE VALUES FOR ADDITIONAL MATERIAL MASTER FIELDS • DEFINE WAREHOUSE MATERIAL GROUP.

Warehouse Storage Condition

The WH STORAGE CONDITION is used to specify that the product must be stored under certain conditions (e.g., dry, cool, freezer). To specify the possible entries for the WAREHOUSE STORAGE CONDITION in the ERP IMG, follow the menu path INTEGRATION WITH OTHER mySAP.com COMPONENTS • EXTENDED WAREHOUSE MANAGEMENT • ADDITIONAL MATERIAL ATTRIBUTES • ATTRIBUTE VALUES FOR ADDITIONAL MATERIAL MASTER FIELDS • DEFINE WAREHOUSE STORAGE CONDITION.

Standard Handling Unit (HU) Type

The STANDARD HU TYPE identifies the HU type that should be used for the mixed products, in which case packing instructions are not necessary. To specify the entries for the STANDARD HU TYPE in the ERP IMG, follow the menu path INTEGRATION WITH OTHER mySAP.com COMPONENTS • EXTENDED WAREHOUSE MANAGEMENT • ADDITIONAL MATERIAL ATTRIBUTES • ATTRIBUTE VALUES FOR ADDITIONAL MATERIAL MASTER FIELDS • DEFINE HANDLING UNIT TYPE.

Serial Number Profile

The SERIAL NO. PROFILE is used to specify how serial numbers should be managed in the warehouse. For example, you can specify within the serialization profile and related procedures whether serialization is required, optional, or not relevant for a business transaction, whether the serial number should be attached to equipment, whether the serial number master record must exist before it can be used in transactions, and so on. We'll discuss serial numbers further in Chapter 6, Warehouse Stock Management. To create the entries and specify the related parameters in the ERP IMG, follow the menu path INTEGRATION WITH OTHER MYSAP.COM COMPONENTS • EXTENDED WAREHOUSE MANAGEMENT • ADDITIONAL MATERIAL ATTRIBUTES • ATTRIBUTE VALUES FOR ADDITIONAL MATERIAL MASTER FIELDS • DEFINE SERIAL NUMBER PROFILE.

Pilferable

The PILFERABLE indicator is used to indicate materials that have a high likelihood of pilferage (or shrinkage, or theft).

Relevant for Hazardous Substances

The REL. FOR HS indicator lets you indicate that the system should read the *hazardous substance* data to determine additional data relevant to storing the product in the warehouse. The data is transferred to the HAZARDOUS SUBSTANCE STORAGE-RELEVANT field of the EWM product master (on the Storage view).

Quarantine Period

The QUARANT. PER. is the time that the product must remain in the warehouse before it can be shipped to the customer.

Quality Inspection Group

The QUAL.INSP.GRP can be used to group together materials to determine quality inspection. To create the possible entries for the Quality Inspection Group in the ERP IMG, follow the menu path INTEGRATION WITH OTHER MYSAP.COM COMPONENTS • EXTENDED WAREHOUSE MANAGEMENT • ADDITIONAL MATERIAL ATTRIBUTES • ATTRIBUTE VALUES FOR ADDITIONAL MATERIAL MASTER FIELDS • DEFINE QUALITY INSPECTION GROUP.

> **Note**
>
> The catch weight–relevant fields described in the following text are not shown on the screenshot of the WM EXECUTION tab in Figure 4.1. The fields only appear if catch weight is activated in ERP. For detailed information on catch weight, see Chapter 6.

Logistics Unit of Measure

The LOGISTICS UNIT OF MEASURE is the unit of measure used to move a catch weight–managed product in the warehouse. It is separate from the base unit of measure, which is used for valuation of the material in ERP. For catch weight–managed products, all transactions must be entered in terms of both the base unit of measure and the logistics unit of measure.

Catch Weight Relevant

The CATCH WEIGHT RELEVANT indicator is used to identify that the product is managed using catch weight. The indicator is transferred to the CATCH WEIGHT PRODUCT field on the STORAGE view of the EWM product master.

Catch Weight Profile for Catch Weight Quantity

The CATCH WEIGHT PROFILE FOR CATCH WEIGHT QUANTITY specifies how the quantities are to be entered for catch weight–managed products. It is transferred to the CATCH WEIGHT PROFILE field on the STORAGE view of the EWM product master. To create the entries for the CATCH WEIGHT PROFILE for CATCH WEIGHT QUANTITY in the ERP IMG, follow the menu path INTEGRATION WITH OTHER MYSAP. COM COMPONENTS • EXTENDED WAREHOUSE MANAGEMENT • ADDITIONAL MATERIAL ATTRIBUTES • ATTRIBUTE VALUES FOR ADDITIONAL MATERIAL MASTER FIELDS • DEFINE CATCH WEIGHT INPUT CONTROL.

Catch Weight Tolerance Group

The CATCH WEIGHT TOLERANCE GROUP specifies the tolerances above and below the planned catch weight conversion values that are allowed before the system will provide a warning message or an error message. To create the possible entries for the CATCH WEIGHT TOLERANCE GROUP in the ERP IMG, follow the menu path INTEGRATION WITH OTHER MYSAP.COM COMPONENTS • EXTENDED WAREHOUSE MANAGEMENT • ADDITIONAL MATERIAL ATTRIBUTES • ATTRIBUTE VALUES FOR ADDITIONAL MATERIAL MASTER FIELDS • DEFINE CATCH WEIGHT TOLERANCE GROUPS.

4.1.3   WM Packaging

The WM PACKAGING view was also added specifically for integration with EWM and several of the EWM-relevant fields are visible there, including the fields in the following text (and seen in Figure 4.2).

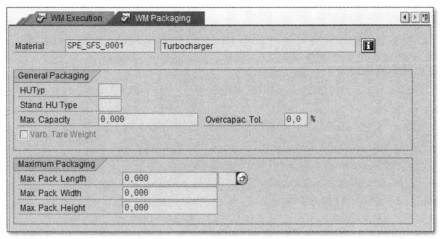

Figure 4.2 WM Packaging View of the ERP Material Master

HU Type

The HUTyp field specifies the default HU type used if the product is used as a packaging material for creating an HU. To create the possible entries for the HU Type in the ERP IMG, follow the menu path Integration with Other mySAP.com Components • Extended Warehouse Management • Additional Material Attributes • Attribute Values for Additional Material Master Fields • Define Handling Unit Type.

Standard HU Type

The Stand. HU Type field from the WM Packaging view is the same as the field from the WM Execution view. See the previous section for the field description.

Maximum Capacity

The Max.Capacity indicates the maximum capacity that can be used by products packed within the packaging material, according to the unitless Capacity indicator from the Units of Measure view.

Overcapacity Tolerance

At times, the Max.Capacity may not specify the absolute maximum capacity utilization of products that can be packed inside the HU. In this case, you can use the Overcapac. Tol. to specify the percent tolerance above the Maximum Capacity that can be allowed if the warehouse operator deems it appropriate. The data is transferred to the EXCESS CAPACITY TOLERANCE field on the PACKAGING tab of the EWM product master.

Variable Tare Weight

The VARB. TARE WEIGHT checkbox is used to indicate that the tare weight of the packaging material is variable (i.e., not fixed). The indicator is transferred to the TARE WEIGHT VARIABLE field on the PACKAGING tab of the EWM product master.

Maximum Packaging Length/Width/Height

These parameters specify the maximum length, width, and height of the products that can be packed inside

Unit of Measure for Maximum Packaging

This unit of measure applies to the MAX. PACK. LENGTH, WIDTH, and HEIGHT fields.

4.1.4   Integrating the ERP Material Master to EWM

Once the material master is updated in ERP and saved, the data must be transferred to EWM. The data is transferred using the CIF. The CIF is the method used to exchange all master data between EWM and SAP ERP. The CIF is an integrated part of SAP ERP as of SAP ECC 6.0 (otherwise known as SAP ERP 6.0, and formerly known as SAP ERP 2005). To use CIF together with earlier releases of SAP ERP (or SAP R/3), you can apply the relevant R/3 plug-in to the ERP or R/3 application, if available, or you can use the intermediate document (IDoc) method for integrating the master data. We will explain the IDOC method in a moment, but first, let's take a look at the CIF method for interfacing with the master data.

Integrating Master Data via the CIF

To transfer data via the CIF, you must first create a CIF integration model, which specifies which data is transferred and to which target system the data should be transferred. The CIF interface is the same one used for transfer of data to Advanced Planning and Optimization (APO), therefore the menu path used to access the transaction for creating and managing the CIF model is the same as for APO. To access the transaction in ERP, from the SAP Easy Access menu, follow the LOGISTICS • CENTRAL FUNCTIONS • SUPPLY CHAIN PLANNING INTERFACE • CORE INTERFACE ADVANCED PLANNER AND OPTIMIZER • INTEGRATION MODEL • CREATE menu path, or use Transaction code CFM1. You can use this transaction to create the integration model based on given parameters.

Because you should avoid having the same data included in multiple models, the most effective way to generate integration models is to decide which data should be included in which model and create variants for the selection screen to create those integration models. There are more detailed strategies for managing master and transactional data that we will not go into in this book, but master data management can be very straightforward if a simple approach is used. For example, in the screen shown in Figure 4.3, you can see that the materials, plant, customers, and vendors that follow a basic pattern are selected to be sent to the EWM system.

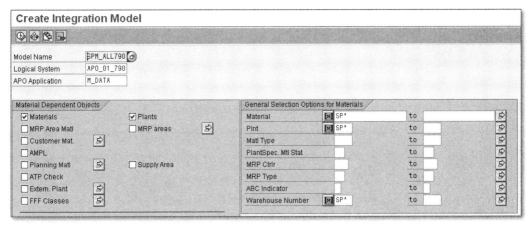

Figure 4.3   CIF Integration Model for Sending Master Data to EWM

> **Note**
>
> Before creating the CIF integration model, you must first specify the location of your EWM system by creating the remote function call (RFC) destination and the logical system. Once the communication to the EWM system is established, the logical system can be specified during the creation and activation of the CIF integration model. For help establishing communication between your ERP and EWM systems, you should employ the assistance of your SAP NetWeaver consultant or your system administration team (especially if you don't have authorization to do it on your own anyway).

You can also specify additional parameters in the selection by selecting the additional entries arrow next to the individual data elements, as seen for customers and vendors in Figure 4.4. The relevant selection criteria will subsequently appear in the right pane, and those criteria will be included in the variant as well when you save it.

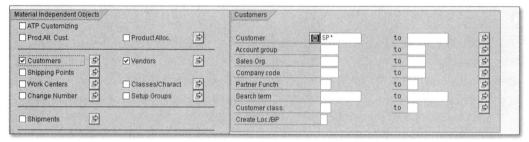

Figure 4.4 Additional Selection Criteria for Creating CIF Integration Models

Once you enter the selection criteria and save the selection criteria as a variant (or selected an existing variant for selection), you must execute the transaction to select the relevant data for inclusion into the integration model. On the display screen, you can drill down into the data to check which data has been selected by simply single-clicking on the number, or you can create the integration model by selecting the GENERATE IM button as indicated in Figure 4.5.

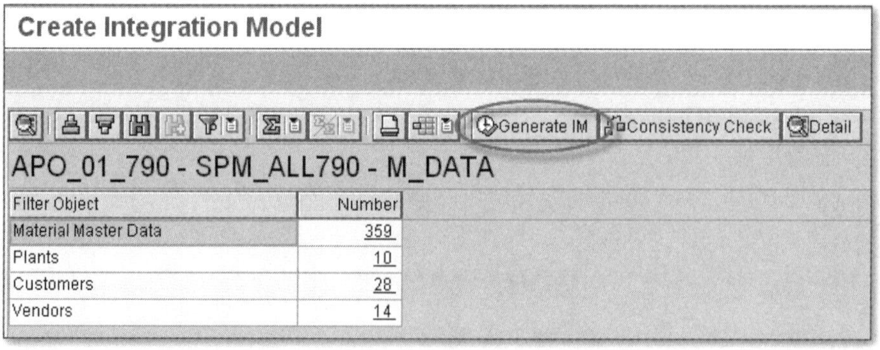

Create Integration Model

⟨Generate IM⟩ Consistency Check Detail

APO_01_790 - SPM_ALL790 - M_DATA

Filter Object	Number
Material Master Data	359
Plants	10
Customers	28
Vendors	14

Figure 4.5 Results Screen for Data Selection during Creation of the CIF Integration Model

Once the integration model is created, it needs to be activated to gather the data and send it to the EWM system. To activate the integration model, from the ERP Easy Access menu, follow the menu path LOGISTICS • CENTRAL FUNCTIONS • SUPPLY CHAIN PLANNING INTERFACE • CORE INTERFACE ADVANCED PLANNER AND OPTIMIZER • INTEGRATION MODEL • ACTIVATE. To activate the integration model, you should specify the same selection criteria in the MODEL, LOGICAL SYSTEM, and APO APPLI-

CATION fields as you did when you created the integration model (this data can also be saved into a variant for easy access later), as seen in Figure 4.6.

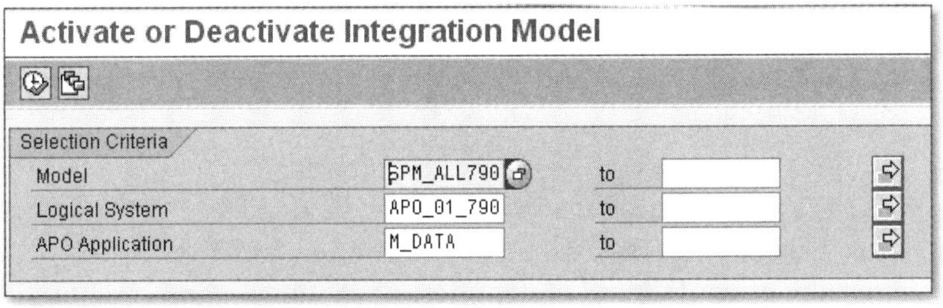

Activate or Deactivate Integration Model

Selection Criteria			
Model	SPM_ALL790	to	
Logical System	APO_01_790	to	
APO Application	M_DATA	to	

Figure 4.6 Selection Screen for Activation of the CIF Integration Model

If a new integration model has been created and needs to be activated, it can be accessed by selecting the application data indicator on the left side. The view on the right pane should then look something similar to Figure 4.7. To activate the new model, one method is to simply single click on the red X in the NEW STATUS column, which will turn the red X into a checkmark. Then, when you select the START button, the new model will be activated.

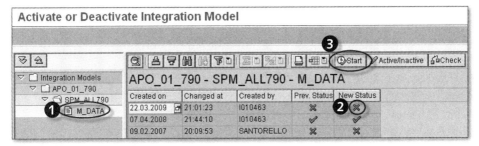

Figure 4.7 Activation of the CIF Integration Model

Once the CIF integration model is activated, changes to data elements (materials, customers, vendors, or other master or transactional data as specified in the model) will be redistributed to the target system via the CIF. If new data elements are added (e.g., new materials), the CIF model must be recreated and reactivated. For environments where new additions occur frequently, these activities can be scheduled as a system administration activity and would typically be administered and monitored by the systems operations team.

Once you have created and activated the CIF model, the ERP material master data should be available in the EWM system. The next step is to create the warehousing-relevant data in the EWM system, which will then allow the product to be managed in the warehouse.

Integrating Master Data via IDocs

When integrating EWM to older versions of ERP (before ERP 6.0, previously known as ERP 2005), you may need to use the IDoc method of integrating transactional data and possibly even master data (if the R/3 add-in for CIF is not relevant or has not been implemented). In this case, you should become familiar with the IDoc method for replicating master data. This is the same method used to transfer data to a Decentralized Warehouse Management (DWM) system from ERP. This method has been detailed in various sources and is not widely used for EWM implementations today, so we will not cover it in detail in this text.

4.2   The EWM Product Master

Once the material master data is distributed from ERP via the CIF (or IDocs), the product master (as it is known on the EWM side) must be extended to include the data for warehousing. At the very least, you must create the warehouse view of the product master to use the product in any warehousing transactions. To create the warehouse data for the product master, from the SAP Easy Access menu of EWM, follow the EXTENDED WAREHOUSE MANAGEMENT • MASTER DATA • PRODUCT • MAINTAIN WAREHOUSE PRODUCT menu path, or use Transaction /SCWM/MAT1.

> **Note**
>
> For EWM transaction codes that begin with a slash (/), because the SAP system will not allow you to use a transaction that begins with a slash directly, you must precede the transaction code with a slash n (/n), which is normally used to end an existing transaction and call a new one. Therefore, to call Transaction /SCWM/MAT1, you must enter /n/SCWM/MAT1 into the transaction code box. This is one more reason to use Favorites to call your most frequently used transactions, as you can save a few keystrokes per transaction.

On the initial screen of the warehouse product master creation (as seen in Figure 4.8), you must specify the product number, the warehouse number, and the entitled to dispose. As we also discussed in Chapter 3, the Warehouse Structure, the entitled to dispose is defined as the "plant or organization who is entitled to dispose of stock," and further "[u]sually this is the plant in which the stocks are planned, and which the ATP check is performed." In many cases (outside of a logistics service provider case), the entitled to dispose would be the same as the plant that owns the stock.

Once you enter the data on the selection screen, press Enter, and (assuming that the product did not already exist for the warehouse) save the transaction. The relevant entry is created on table /SAPAPO/MATEXEC. This is the minimum data necessary to perform most warehouse transactions in EWM.

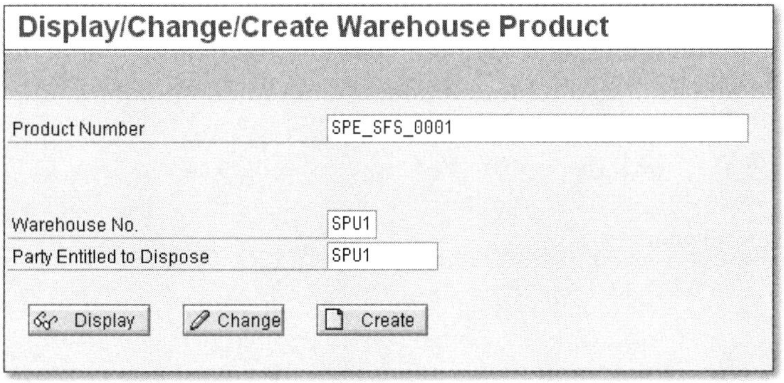

Figure 4.8 Initial Screen for Creation, Change, or Display of a Warehouse Product

However, if you want to further specify parameters that affect the transactions in various ways, you should review and update the data on the views, or tabs, of the warehouse product master. In the following sections, we will review the data on each view and discuss how the data is used to affect the warehouse transactions and therefore the product and process flows in the warehouse.

Note that not all of the data on the various views is actually relevant to the warehouse processes. Because the same "header" views are displayed in both the EWM and APO product views (a separate transaction is available to access the APO views), not all of the data there will be relevant to the warehouse. In some cases, the data is only provided for informational purposes. However, you should be aware that if you change this data, and if APO processes are being performed in the same system and client as the EWM processes, then you could also be affecting the APO processes. Therefore, caution should be taken when changing any existing data there.

> **Note**
>
> When a user changes a field on the ERP material master after a change to the same field on the EWM system, the change is overwritten, however, in some cases, if the user changes another field on the material master, the change doesn't overwrite the changed value with the original one from ERP. For fields that you have concerns about warehouse changes being overwritten by the ERP values, you should test your proposed master data update processes during your implementation project.

4.2.1 General

The general information about the product includes the product number itself, the product description, the organizational information, and the base unit of measure. You can see the general data in Figure 4.9. This general data is always displayed at the top of the product master maintenance screen, and the individual tabs are below the general data.

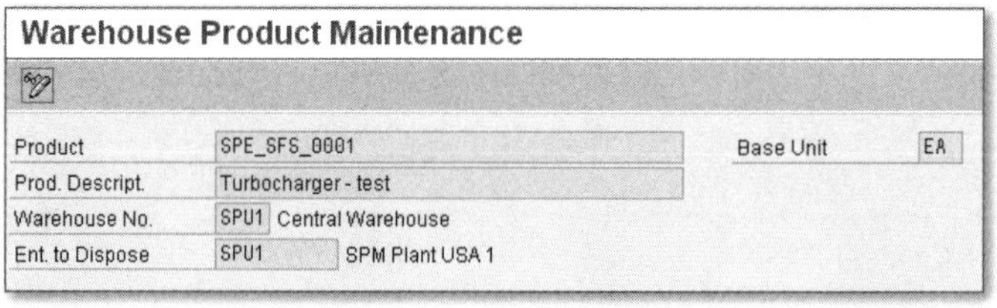

Figure 4.9 General Data about the Product on the EWM Product Master

The product number is up to 40 characters long and therefore supports the long material number (or LAMA) function of ERP, which was originally created for the automotive industry but is now used in multiple industries. The product number is the first entry in the key of all relevant tables, so you can't change the product number on the EWM system.

The description is up to 60 characters long, and is interfaced from ERP together with the other relevant material information as part of the CIF interface described earlier. It can be changed in EWM, if, for example, you want to store additional information to let warehouse operators more easily distinguish one product from another. If you change other data on the ERP material master, the changed data is redistributed from ERP to EWM. However, not all of the data that has been changed on the EWM side will be overwritten. For example, the product description is not overwritten if you change it on EWM and then later some other field on the ERP material master, even after the distribution of that data to EWM.

In addition to the product and description, you can also see the organizational data on the general part of the product master, namely the warehouse number and entitled to dispose. These fields were entered on the initial screen for the product master selection.

4.2.2   Properties

The PROPERTIES tab of the EWM product master stores data related to the general properties of the material. The data can be seen in Figure 4.10, and includes the fields described in the following sections.

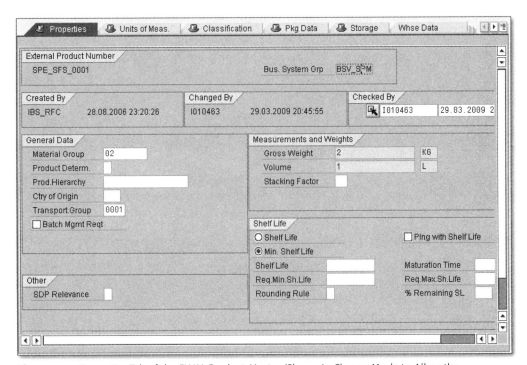

Figure 4.10   Properties Tab of the EWM Product Master (Shown in Change Mode to Allow the "Checked By" Indicator to Be Shown)

External Product Number

The EXTERNAL PRODUCT NUMBER is the number that is used for the product in the source system. This is stored in case the EWM product number differs from the ERP material number (or the material number in whatever source system is used; we'll discuss additional options further in Chapter 26, Deploying Extended Warehouse Management). There are various reasons why the product number may differ in the source and target system, but the most likely reason is if some suffix is added via the available Business Add-In (BAdI) for enhancing the product number. This is used, for example, when the EWM has multiple potential source systems, especially if there's a possibility that the material numbers on the multiple source system may overlap.

Business System Group

The Bus. System Grp identifies the business system group assigned to the source system of the material. The business system groups can be created in the EWM IMG by following the SCM Basis • Integration • Basic Settings for Creating the System Landscape • Maintain Business System Group menu path, and are assigned at the menu path SCM Basis • Integration • Basic Settings for Creating the System Landscape • Assign Logical System and Queue Type.

Created By

The CREATED BY field indicates the username of the product creator and the date and time that it was created. The username will often be the system user that is used in the interface from ERP.

Changed By

The CHANGED BY field indicates the username of the person who last changed the product and the date and time that it was changed. This field is updated when the user initially extends the product master with the warehousing-relevant views as described earlier and during each subsequent change to the product master.

Checked By

These fields specify the username of the person who checked the material and the date and time of the check. The fields are updated in change mode when the user clicks the SET TO CHECKED button (to the left of the CHECKED BY username in Figure 4.10). You can use this method to verify which materials have been checked by an administrator familiar with the warehouse operations. Note that you can only set the CHECKED BY username once for each material and once the CHECKED BY username is set, the SET TO CHECKED button no longer appears for any other user in change mode for the product. The button continues to appear for the same user, and the user can update the date and time of the check by selecting the button again, but no other user can update it. Also, when the operator clicks the SET TO CHECKED button, he can change the username assigned to the check, however, this does not impact which operator can still access the SET TO CHECKED button (i.e., if one operator sets the checked-by data and sets the username to a second operator's username, the SET TO CHECKED button still only appears for the first operator and not for the second).

Material Group

The MATERIAL GROUP is an identifier that can be assigned to multiple materials and can be used to group them together for analysis and reporting, or for selecting material using the dropdown selection boxes for material numbers in ERP. Even though the MATERIAL GROUP is not used in EWM for the standard dropdown selection box, you can, as part of your implementation project, create custom tabs in the product selection dropdown box that allow you to use MATERIAL GROUP or other parameters from the product master in the selection.

Product Determination

The PRODUCT DETERM. field is used by Supplier Network Collaboration (SNC) to determine supplier products when ordering from suppliers. It is not used by EWM.

Product Hierarchy

The PROD. HIERARCHY is another method of grouping materials, similar to the material group. However, the product hierarchy is also used in pricing determination, profitability analysis, and other reporting tools. The PRODUCT HIERARCHY can be assigned in ERP using a hierarchical selection method.

Note that, although you could change the product hierarchy assignment in EWM, EWM does not access the product hierarchy configuration from ERP, so you cannot use the drilldown selection in the same way. In fact, the levels of the product hierarchy are not known to EWM — only the assigned value is stored there. It is primarily stored there for reporting or printing documents that may require the product hierarchy.

Country of Origin

The CTRY OF ORIGIN is typically the country where the product was manufactured or from which it was originally sourced. It is used, for example, to print on certain import and export documentation. Note that the Country of Origin field of the EWM product master is *not* sourced from the Country of Origin field of the ERP material master FOREIGN TRADE: EXPORT DATA view. It is also separate from the COUNTRY OF ORIGIN field of the batch master record, which can be integrated directly to the ERP batch master characteristics. You should discuss and decide how your organization will use the country of origin data, what is the best location for storing country of origin data, and which forms or output will include country of origin data from which source.

Transportation Group

The TRANSPORT. GROUP is used to group materials that are similar in routing and transportation requirements. It is used by CRM, ERP, and EWM to determine the route assignment for deliveries.

Batch Management Requirement

The BATCH MGMT REQT checkbox indicates whether or not a material is managed in batches (if the checkbox is activated, the material is handled in batches). Depending on whether batches are determined at the company level, material level, or material and plant level, the indicator can be stored on different tables in ERP (but is still displayed in the same field on the screen). For example, if the batches are determined on the material level, the batch indicator is stored on the ERP MARA table, whereas if batches are determined on a material and plant level, the batch indicator is stored on the ERP MARC table. Note that when the data is passed to EWM, EWM does not similarly distinguish how it stores the BATCH MANAGEMENT REQUIREMENT checkbox.

Gross Weight

The GROSS WEIGHT is the total weight of the product and the packaging when the product is packaged according to the specified unit of measure.

Volume

The VOLUME of the container in which the product is stored when using the specified unit of measure (or consumed by the product itself if it is not in a container) is stored per unit of measure.

Stacking Factor

The STACKING FACTOR is used to specify how many pallets can be stacked on top of one another. This factor is used, for example, in the transportation planning functions of SCM to determine how many pallets can fit into a transportation unit (TU). However, this factor is *not* used in EWM for the determination of the number of pallets that can be stacked in a bulk bin location. Likewise, because this factor applies at the pallet level, it is not used in the determination of how many items can be stored in a container when packing. Instead, those determinations are made using the packaging specifications (pack specs). This STACKING FACTOR field is *not* derived from the STACKING FACTOR field in the SALES: GENERAL/PLANT view of the ERP material master.

SDP Relevance

This field is used to determine the relevance of the product in Demand Planning (DP) and Supply Network Planning (SNP). It is not used in EWM.

Shelf Life (Radio Button)

This radio button is used to specify that the product is managed in EWM according to the shelf life. It is derived from the MARA-SLED_BBD field from ERP.

Minimum Shelf Life (Radio Button)

This radio button is used to indicate that the product is relevant to the minimum remaining shelf life check, if it is configured for the document category (and document and item type, if relevant).

Planning with Shelf Life

This indicator is used by APO to determine whether the maturity and shelf life of products currently in inventory should be taken into account when planning the product.

Shelf Life

The SHELF LIFE is the time that a product can be kept in the warehouse or used. It is used in EWM to calculate the shelf life expiration date based on the date of manufacture or the goods receipt date (if the date of manufacture is not known). The data is interfaced from the TOTAL SHELF LIFE field from the PLANT DATA/STORAGE 1 view of the ERP material master. In EWM, this field is only known in days, so it is converted if it is stored in weeks or months in ERP (see the previous note in the ERP material master section).

Required Minimum Shelf Life

The REQ.MIN. SH.LIFE specifies the number of days of shelf life that must be remaining in order for the product to be used on delivery. It is checked according to the settings for the minimum remaining shelf life, which is made in the EWM IMG via the menu path EXTENDED WAREHOUSE MANAGEMENT • CROSS-PROCESS SETTINGS • BATCH MANAGEMENT • MAKE SETTING FOR DELIVERY. The value is derived from the MINIMUM REMAINING SHELF LIFE field of the GENERAL PLANT DATA/STORAGE 1 view of the ERP material master.

Specifying a required minimum shelf life affects the calculation of the latest delivery date of the stock, which is managed for shelf life. In the warehouse monitor, the latest delivery date for products that have a required minimum shelf life is calculated as the best before date minus the required minimum shelf life (otherwise, the latest delivery date is calculated as the best before date minus the product of shelf life multiplied by the percent of remaining shelf life).

On goods receipt, a tolerance check for the minimum remaining shelf life is performed if both the configuration specified earlier is activated and the minimum remaining shelf life is populated in the product master.

Rounding Rule

The ROUNDING RULE can be used to specify that a different date other than the goods receipt should be used in determining the shelf life expiration date. Example rules include START OF WEEK, START OF FOLLOWING WEEK, and START OF MONTH, and there are several more. This rule can be used, for instance, if there is commonly some duration between the manufacture date and the goods receipt date into the warehouse and the actual manufacture date is not known. The rounding rule is not used by EWM at this time, however, you can use it in a BAdI during the calculation of the BBD/shelf life expiration date (SLED).

Maturation Time

The MATURATION TIME is the time that must pass after the product is manufactured before it can be shipped to the customer. This requirement is common in food industries or pharmaceuticals, where the product must be kept for some period of time to allow for proper testing or if the product must be kept under certain conditions (e.g., in a refrigerator or freezer) for a period of time before it can be shipped to ensure that the entire product is at the correct temperature for long-term storage or transportation. The maturation time is included in the total shelf life of the product, and it must be taken into account in planning. It is not used in EWM.

Required Maximum Shelf Life

The REQ.MAX.SH.LIFE is the maximum shelf life of products which can be taken into account for planning. The field is not used by EWM.

Percent Remaining Shelf Life

This field is used to determine the percent of the total shelf life that must be remaining for the product for internal transfers (e.g., from one site to another).

4.2.3   Units of Measure

Just like the UNITS OF MEASURE view on the ERP material master, the UNITS OF MEAS. tab of the EWM product master (as seen in Figure 4.11) defines the conversion from alternate units of measure to the base unit of measure (e.g., cases to eaches, pallets to eaches, gaylords to gallons, sacks to kilograms, etc.), and it is also used to define the parameters associated with the alternate unit, which can be different from the base unit (e.g., length, width, height, capacity, etc.). As also mentioned previously, it can be especially useful to define the dimensions and capacity of the alternate units if the result is not a simple calculation of the base unit times the number of base units per alternate unit.

Most of the fields on the UNIT OF MEAS. tab of the EWM product master are exactly the same as the ones already described previously for the material master, and the data is taken directly from ERP to EWM via the CIF interface. So rather than take the time and space to describe every field, we will only describe the ones that vary in naming or in existence.

Denominator

This field represents the Denominator used when converting from base unit of measure to an alternate unit of measure. It is represented in the ERP material master with the simple field description of X.

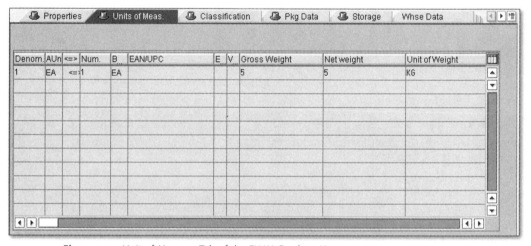

Figure 4.11 Unit of Measure Tab of the EWM Product Master

Alternate Unit

The Alternate Unit is the unit of measure to which all of the values on the line apply.

Numerator

This field represents the Numerator used when converting from the base unit of measure to an alternate unit of measure. It is represented in the ERP material master with the simple field description of Y.

Base Unit

The BASE UNIT is the unit of measure to which all transactions are converted for storing inventory and financial data.

> **Example**
>
> If a goods receipt is entered in cases and 3 cases are received, and if the number of eaches per case is 40, then the number of cases is multiplied by 40 and divided by 1 to determine the number of eaches in inventory (120, in this case) and the number of eaches valuated in Financial Accounting (FI).

EAN/UPC

The international article number (EAN) or universal product code (UPC) for the material can be stored by unit of measure. Often, the EAN or UPC for an alternate unit (e.g., case or pallet) of product can differ from the EAN or UPC for an individual unit, or "each," so that the system can differentiate between the two when a barcode of the EAN or UPC code from the product is scanned by a barcode scanner.

EAN Category

As described previously, the EAN CATEGORY relates to the EAN/UPC field and is used to define the category of the EAN/UPC code and whether the EAN/UPC number is externally assigned or internally assigned. Note that, on EWM, the EAN CATEGORY field doesn't include a check table assignment, and therefore does not include a dropdown selection for possible entries — the entries should only be made in ERP. It is only provided on EWM for information purposes. In EWM, the field name is completely spelled out in the table header, whereas in ERP, the field name is abbreviated to CT.

Variant GTIN

This field is used to describe the variant for the global trade identification number (GTIN). The GTIN variant is used for communication to SAP Auto ID Infrastructure (AII) for support of processes using radio frequency identification (RFID) technologies. The field only exists on the EWM product master (i.e., it does not exist on the ERP material master).

Gross Weight

The GROSS WEIGHT is the total weight of the product and the packaging when the product is packaged according to the specified unit of measure.

Net Weight

The NET WEIGHT is typically the product weight (not including the packaging) when the product is packaged according to the specified unit of measure. For example, the net weight of a carton of a product that is packaged 12 per carton would generally be calculated as the net weight of the product, not including the packaging (external, internal, or both depending on your organization's or industry's use of the term "net weight").

Unit of Weight

The field that defines the unit which the weight is defined in is described on the EWM product master as UNIT OF WEIGHT and on the ERP material master as WEIGHT UNIT.

Unit of Volume

The field that defines the unit the volume is defined in is described on the EWM product master as UNIT OF VOLUME and on the ERP material master as VOLUME UNIT.

Capacity Consumption

The unitless CAPACITY CONSUMPTION indicator described previously is indicated in the table header on the EWM product master as CAPACITY CONSUMPTION and on the ERP material master as the abbreviation CAPA.

Length/Width/Height

The LENGTH, WIDTH, and HEIGHT of the container the product is stored in when using the specified unit of measure are stored per unit of measure.

Unit of Dimension

The UNIT OF DIMENSION field applies to the LENGTH, WIDTH, and HEIGHT. The unit of dimension is important to get correct, as the units must be converted if the units of dimension of the product or unit of measure and the object that it is being checked against are different.

In EWM, the length, width, and height can be used in slotting and in the capacity determination of a warehouse storage bin. During slotting, the capacity utilization is determined based on the determination rule, which allows for either simple dimension checks, dimension checks using rotation on a Z-axis, or dimension checks using rotation and tilt (meaning a three-dimensional rotation of the product to check how it can best fit into the bin).

Maximum Stacking Factor

The MAXIMUM STACKING FACTOR is transferred from ERP, but it is not used in the standard capacity determination in EWM. However, you can use it in the available BAdIs for capacity checking, for example, during putaway or during loading. The field is abbreviated in the table header of the EWM product master as MAX.STACK FACTOR and in the ERP material master (Unit of Measure view) as MAX. STACK.

Remaining Volume after Nesting

The REMAINING VOLUME AFTER NESTING specifies the volume remaining in one item when another of the same item is stacked inside it. The value is specified in terms of percent of total volume, and is used in the capacity determination for the product and unit of measure to which it is specified. This may apply to stackable items like cups, chairs, certain type of ladders, or other similar items. If no value is specified, then the item is not considered nested for capacity determination.

The indicator that specifies the REMAINING VOLUME AFTER NESTING is abbreviated in the table header of the EWM product master as REM.VOL.AFTERNESTG and in the ERP material master as REMVOLNEST.

Unit of Measure Category

The UNIT OF MEASURE CATEGORY used in the determination of parallel units of measure for catch weight management is abbreviated in the table header of the EWM product master as UoM CATEGORY and in the ERP material master as CATEGORY OF UNIT OF.

4.2.4   Classification

The CLASSIFICATION tab provides information related to the reference products and classes assigned to configurable products. Additional classification assignments (e.g., material class, batch class) are not displayed here.

4.2.5 Packaging Data

The PKG DATA tab of the product master provides information related to the packaging of products within HUs. You can see in Figure 4.12 that the view is broken into three areas. The BASIC DATA: PACK section includes information related to the products that go inside a packaging material and is therefore relevant for the salable or shippable items in the warehouse.

Each packaging material used in the warehouse is also designated by a product number, and the BASIC DATA: PACKAGING MATERIAL section is relevant for those packaging materials. Under certain circumstances, only certain packaging materials are allowed for certain products, and the data on the products and the packaging materials is used to help determine which packaging materials are relevant for which products.

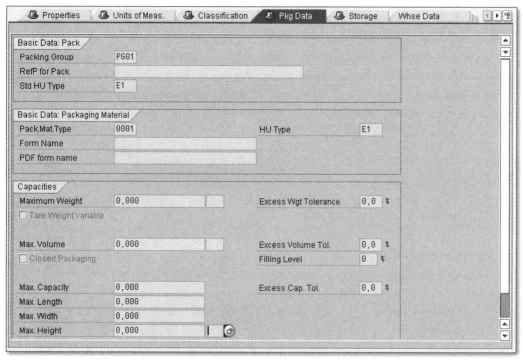

Figure 4.12 Packaging Data Tab of the EWM Product Master

The CAPACITIES section is also only relevant for the packaging materials and is used to determine the capacity of the packaging material, which defines how many of the individual products can fit a single unit of the packaging material.

The fields from the three previous sections include the fields described in the following sections.

Packing Group

The PACKING GROUP field is used to group together materials that require similar packaging materials. For example, liquids may need to be packed into jugs or waterproof containers, whereas certain hazardous materials may be required to be packed into special containers designed to contain spills or leaks. This data is transferred from the ERP MATERIAL GROUP: PACKAGING MATERIALS field to EWM. In EWM, the data is used to determine allowed packaging materials via the allowed packaging material types.

To configure the allowed packing groups in the EWM IMG, follow the menu path EXTENDED WAREHOUSE MANAGEMENT • CROSS-PROCESS SETTINGS • HANDLING UNITS • BASICS • DEFINE PACKING GROUPS FOR PRODUCTS. The values should coincide with the allowed values in the ERP system for the MATERIAL GROUP: PACKAGING MATERIALS field (or at least the values that will be used in EWM).

Reference Product for Packing

The REFP FOR PACK. field can be used to simplify the determination of pack specs in EWM. When EWM determines a pack spec for a product, for example, for automatic packing or for putaway, you can use the REFERENCE PRODUCT FOR PACKING field to maintain a pack spec only for this Reference Product.

For example, if you create product PROD01 and maintain a pack spec for the product in EWM, then you can create product PROD02 and assign PROD01 as the reference product for packing. You can then set up the condition record for pack spec determination in EWM based on reference products, which will find the pack spec of product PROD01 for product PROD02.

Standard HU Type

The STD HU TYPE identifies the HU type that should be used for the mixed products if packing instructions are not relevant. The allowed HU types can be configured in the EWM IMG by following the menu path EXTENDED WAREHOUSE MANAGE-

MENT • CROSS-PROCESS SETTINGS • HANDLING UNITS • BASICS • DEFINE HU TYPES. The data is transferred from the STANDARD HU TYPE field on the WM PACKAGING view of the ERP material master.

Packaging Material Type

The PACK.MAT.TYPE identifies the material type of the packaging material and is used in the determination of the allowed packaging materials, both in ERP and in EWM. The field can be found in the ERP material master on both the BASIC DATA 1 and SALES: GENERAL/PLANT views. You can configure the allowed values in the EWM IMG by following the EXTENDED WAREHOUSE MANAGEMENT • CROSS-PROCESS SETTINGS • HANDLING UNITS • BASICS • DEFINE PACKAGING MATERIAL TYPES menu path, and the values should generally be synchronized with the allowed entries for the related field in ERP.

To configure the allowed packaging material types, follow the menu path EXTENDED WAREHOUSE MANAGEMENT • CROSS-PROCESS SETTINGS • HANDLING UNITS • BASICS • MAINTAIN ALLOWED PACKAGING MATERIAL TYPES FOR PACKING GROUP.

HU Type

The HU TYPE field specifies the default HU type used if the product is used as a packaging material for creating an HU. The allowed HU types can be specified in the EWM IMG by following the menu path EXTENDED WAREHOUSE MANAGEMENT • CROSS-PROCESS SETTINGS • HANDLING UNITS • BASICS • DEFINE HU TYPES. The data is transferred from the HU TYPE field on the WM PACKAGING view of the ERP material master.

Form Name

The FORM NAME specifies the Smart Form to be used for printing HU labels for HUs that use the product as a packaging material. The labels can be specified as an auxiliary packing material in the pack specs, and then the labels will be printed together with packaging instructions from the packaging work center. We'll discuss pack specs later in this chapter.

PDF form name

The PDF FORM NAME specifies the form name for the PDF Form, if it is used. It is only used if a Smart Form name is not assigned — if a Smart Form name is specified in the FORM NAME field, the Smart Form name is used for printing by default.

Maximum Weight

The MAXIMUM WEIGHT specifies the maximum loading weight of products that can be packed within an HU that uses the product as a packaging material. The Maximum Weight is derived from the ERP ALLOWED PACKAGE WEIGHT field from the SALES: GENERAL/PLANT view.

Excess Weight Tolerance

At times, the MAXIMUM WEIGHT may not specify the absolute maximum weight that can be packed inside the HU. In this case, you can use the EXCESS WGT TOLERANCE to specify the percent tolerance above the MAXIMUM WEIGHT which can be allowed if the warehouse operator deems it appropriate. The EXCESS WGT TOLERANCE field is derived from the similarly named field on the SALES: GENERAL/PLANT view of the ERP material master.

Tare Weight Variable

The TARE WEIGHT VARIABLE checkbox is used to indicate that the tare weight of the packaging material is variable (i.e., not fixed). If you have more confidence in the product weights than in the tare weight of the packaging material, you should choose this option. In that case, the tare weight would be calculated as the total weight of the HU subtracting the sum of the product weights. If this option is not selected, the total weight is calculated as the sum of the product weights plus the tare weight of the packaging material. An example of a packaging material you would select the TARE WEIGHT VARIABLE indicator would be custom wooden crates. The flag is transferred from the VARIABLE TARE WEIGHT field on the WM PACKAGING view of the ERP material master.

Maximum Volume

The MAX. VOLUME specifies the maximum loading volume of products that can be packed within an HU that uses the product as a packaging material. The MAX. VOLUME is derived from the ERP ALLOWED PACKAGE VOLUME field from the SALES: GENERAL/PLANT view.

Excess Volume Tolerance

At times, the MAX. VOLUME may not specify the absolute maximum volume that can be packed inside the HU. In this case, you can use the EXCESS VOLUME TOL. to specify the percent tolerance above the MAX. VOLUME that can be allowed if the warehouse operator deems it appropriate. The EXCESS VOLUME TOL. field is derived from the similarly named field on the SALES: GENERAL/PLANT view of the ERP material master.

Closed Packaging

The CLOSED PACKAGING indicator specifies that the packaging material is a closed container. If the indicator is set, the total volume is not increased past loading volume of the materials contained within the package. For example, a box with a lid would be considered a closed container, and its volume does not change whether it is empty, half filled, or completely filled. On the other hand, a pallet would not be a closed container, and its volume does change depending on how completely it is packed. The CLOSED PACKAGING indicator is derived from the CLOSED indicator from the SALES: GENERAL/PLANT view of the ERP material master for packaging materials.

Filling Level

The FILLING LEVEL specifies the maximum percentage of the total volume that should be filled within the packaging material. The FILLING LEVEL is provided for informational purposes only, but can be used in custom transactions of custom checks, for example, in a BAdI.

Maximum Capacity

The MAX. CAPACITY indicates the maximum capacity that can be used by products packed within the packaging material, according to the unitless Capacity indicator from the UNITS OF MEASURE tab. The data is transferred from the MAXIMUM CAPACITY field on the WM PACKAGING view of the ERP material master.

Excess Capacity Tolerance

At times, the MAX CAPACITY may not specify the absolute maximum capacity utilization of products that can be packed inside the HU. In this case, you can use the EXCESS CAP TOL to specify the percent tolerance above the MAX CAPACITY that can be allowed if the warehouse operator deems it appropriate. The data is transferred from the OVERCAPACITY TOLERANCE field on the WM PACKAGING view of the ERP material master.

Maximum Length

The MAX. LENGTH specifies the maximum length of products that can be packed inside the packaging material. This may differ from the length of a unit of the packaging material for multiple reasons. First, the length, width, and height assignments within the unit of measure view of the product master for the packaging material can be used to indicate the parameters of the packaging material in its shippable form (e.g., cardboard boxes that are "broken down" or in their disassembled form for shipment). Second, the length, width, and height of the area inside the container may be different than the length, width, and height of the outside of the container, especially if the container has thick walls (e.g., plastic gaylords, or steel containers for shipping liquids). The data is transferred from the MAXIMUM PACKAGING length field on the WM PACKAGING view of the ERP material master.

Maximum Width

The MAX. WIDTH specifies the maximum width of products that can be packed inside the packaging material. This may differ from the length of a unit of the packaging material, for the same reasons as provided above. The data is transferred from the MAXIMUM PACKAGING WIDTH field on the WM PACKAGING view of the ERP material master.

Maximum Height

The MAX. HEIGHT specifies the maximum height of products that can be packed inside the packaging material. This may differ from the length of a unit of the packaging material, for the same reasons as provided earlier. The data is transferred from the MAXIMUM PACKAGING HEIGHT field on the WM PACKAGING view of the ERP material master.

Unit of Measure for Maximum Packing Length/Width/Height

The UNIT OF MEASURE field (seen in Figure 4.12 to the right of the MAX. HEIGHT field) applies to the MAX. LENGTH, MAX. WIDTH, and MAX. HEIGHT fields. The data is transferred from the similar UNIT OF MEASURE field on the WM PACKAGING view of the ERP material master.

4.2.6   Storage

The STORAGE tab (as seen in Figure 4.13) provides information on how the product should be stored, including grouping information, serial number profiles, catch weight information, and hazardous or dangerous material data. The fields of the STORAGE tab are described in the following sections below.

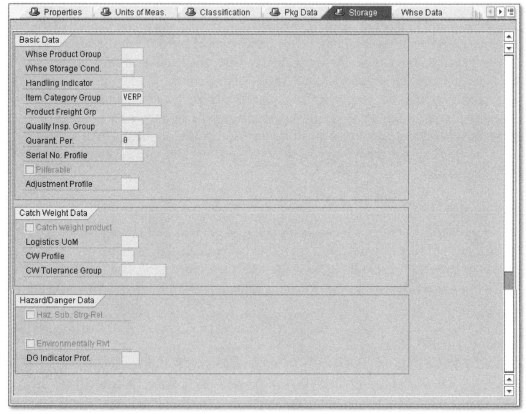

Figure 4.13   Storage View of EWM Product Master

Warehouse Product Group

The WHSE PRODUCT GROUP is used to group materials together for determining certain processes in the warehouse. In particular, the WHSE PRODUCT GROUP is used in the determination of the existence check for packspecs (table /SCWM/ TPSMGR) and is also used in the determination of the deletion indicator for fixed bin assignment (table /SCWM/TFBIN_UNAS). To specify the determination of the deletion indicator for fixed bin assignment in the EWM IMG, follow the menu path EXTENDED WAREHOUSE MANAGEMENT • GOODS RECEIPT PROCESS • STRATEGIES • DELETE FIXED BIN ASSIGNMENT. To create the possible entries for the WHSE PRODUCT GROUP in the EWM IMG, follow the menu path EXTENDED WAREHOUSE MANAGEMENT • MASTER DATA • PRODUCT • DEFINE WAREHOUSE PRODUCT GROUP.

Warehouse Storage Condition

The WHSE STORAGE COND. is used to specify that the product must be stored under certain conditions (e.g., dry, cool, freezer). To create the possible entries in the EWM IMG, follow the menu path EXTENDED WAREHOUSE MANAGEMENT • MASTER DATA • PRODUCT • DEFINE WAREHOUSE STORAGE CONDITION. The data is transferred from the WAREHOUSE STORAGE CONDITION field on the WM EXECUTION view of the ERP material master.

Handling Indicator

The HANDLING INDICATOR is used to determine how the product should be handled when moving from one location to another (e.g., fragile, no clamp). To specify the possible entries for the HANDLING INDICATOR in the EWM IMG, follow the menu path EXTENDED WAREHOUSE MANAGEMENT • MASTER DATA • PRODUCT • DEFINE HANDLING INDICATOR. The data is transferred from the HANDLING INDICATOR field on the WM EXECUTION view of the ERP material master.

Item Category Group

The ITEM CATEGORY GROUP is adopted from the General Item Category Group field on the Basic Data 1 view of the ERP material master. It does not include check tables for possible entries in EWM, and it is not used for any specific purpose in EWM. It is provided in the product master for informational purposes only (or possibly for customized use by BAdIs or other custom coding).

Product Freight Group

The PRODUCT FREIGHT GRP is used in the determination within Freight Order Management of appropriate freight codes and freight order classes. To create the possible entries for the PRODUCT FREIGHT GRP in the EWM IMG, follow the menu path EXTENDED WAREHOUSE MANAGEMENT • GOODS ISSUE PROCESS • TRANSPORTATION MANAGEMENT • BASICS • DEFINE PRODUCT FREIGHT GROUPS.

Quality Inspection Group

The QUALITY INSP. GROUP can be used to group together materials for determination of quality inspection relevance. To create the possible entries for the QUALITY INSP. GROUP in the EWM IMG, follow the menu path EXTENDED WAREHOUSE MANAGEMENT • CROSS-PROCESS SETTINGS • QUALITY MANAGEMENT • SETTINGS FOR INSPECTION RULES • DEFINE QUALITY INSPECTION GROUP.

The QUALITY INSP. GROUP is also used in the determination of the value interval for counting, which can be accessed in the EWM IMG by following the menu path EXTENDED WAREHOUSE MANAGEMENT • CROSS-PROCESS SETTINGS • QUALITY MANAGEMENT • SETTINGS FOR INSPECTION RULES • MAINTAIN VALUE INTERVAL FOR COUNTING. And it is used to specify the forbidden goods movements from inspection stock, which can be accessed in the EWM IMG via the menu path EXTENDED WAREHOUSE MANAGEMENT • CROSS-PROCESS SETTINGS • QUALITY MANAGEMENT • FORBID GOODS MOVEMENTS OF INSPECTION STOCKS.

Quarantine Period

The QUARANT. PER. is the time that the product must remain in the warehouse before it can be shipped to the customer. This is especially useful for products that require a quarantine period but are not managed in batches (and therefore cannot use batch statuses for the same effect). For product managed in batch, the batch management functionality is generally a more robust and effective method of managing the quarantine period. The field to the right of the quantity field (as seen in Figure 4.13) is the unit of measure relevant to the quantity for the quarantine period (e.g. days, weeks).

Serial Number Profile

The SERIAL NO. PROFILE is used to specify how to manage the serial numbers in the warehouse (we'll discuss serial numbers further in Chapter 6). The SERIAL NO. PROFILE is derived from the SERIAL NUMBER PROFILE field on the WM EXECUTION view of the ERP material master (not the GENERAL PLANT DATA/STORAGE 2 view). To create the possible entries for the SERIAL NUMBER PROFILE in the EWM IMG, follow the menu path EXTENDED WAREHOUSE MANAGEMENT • MASTER DATA • PRODUCT • DEFINE SERIAL NUMBER PROFILES (SIC) • DEFINE WAREHOUSE NUMBER-INDEPENDENT SERIAL NUMBER PROFILES.

You can also specify warehouse-dependent settings for the profiles by following the menu path EXTENDED WAREHOUSE MANAGEMENT • MASTER DATA • PRODUCT • DEFINE SERIAL NUMBER PROFILES (SIC) • DEFINE WAREHOUSE NUMBER DEPENDENT SERIAL NUMBER PROFILES, but the profiles must first be set up in the warehouse number independent section.

Pilferable

The PILFERABLE indicator is used to indicate materials that have a high likelihood of pilferage (shrinkage, or theft). It is not currently used in any determination of putaway strategies, but may be used in the available BAdIs to determine the relevant putaway storage type, section, or bin.

Adjustment Profile

The ADJUSTMENT PROFILE is used by Merchandise Distribution (a specific cross-docking function used by the retail industry, which will be described in Chapter 17, Cross-Docking) to define how the inbound products are allocated to outbound orders. To create the Adjustment Profiles in the EWM IMG, follow the menu path EXTENDED WAREHOUSE MANAGEMENT • CROSS-PROCESS SETTINGS • CROSS-DOCKING (CD) • PLANNED CROSS-DOCKING • MERCHANDISE DISTRIBUTION • DEFINE ADJUSTMENT PROFILE. Note that there is also an ADJUSTMENT PROFILE field on the WAREHOUSE DATA tab that is relevant at the warehouse level (and they use the same field help, and therefore the same configuration node, to create possible entries). If the adjustment profile is set at the product level, the data should also be populated in the adjustment profile of the ERP article master (MARA-ADPROF), and then it will be used for all warehouses.

Catch Weight Product

The CATCH WEIGHT PRODUCT indicator is used to make sure that the product is managed using catch weight (which will be described further in Chapter 6). The indicator is derived from the CATCH WEIGHT RELEVANT field on the WM EXECUTION view of the ERP material master.

Logistics Unit of Measure

The LOGISTICS UoM is the unit of measure used to move a catch weight–managed product in the warehouse. It is separate from the base unit of measure, which is used for valuation of the material in ERP. For catch weight–managed products, all transactions must be entered in terms of both the base unit of measure and the logistics unit of measure. It is also derived from the WM EXECUTION view of the ERP material master.

Catch Weight Profile

The CW PROFILE specifies how the quantities are to be entered for catch weight–managed products. To create the possible entries for the Catch Weight Profile in the EWM IMG, follow the menu path EXTENDED WAREHOUSE MANAGEMENT • MASTER DATA • PRODUCT • CATCH WEIGHT • DEFINE CATCH WEIGHT PROFILE FOR CATCH WEIGHT QUANTITIES. The field is derived from the CATCH WEIGHT PROFILE FOR CATCH WEIGHT QUANTITY field on the WM EXECUTION view of the ERP material master.

Catch Weight Tolerance Group

The CW TOLERANCE GROUP specifies the tolerances above and below the planned catch weight conversion values that are allowed before the system will provide a warning message or an error message (separate values are provided for warning and error messages). To create the possible values for the CATCH WEIGHT TOLERANCE GROUP in the EWM IMG, follow the menu path EXTENDED WAREHOUSE MANAGEMENT • MASTER DATA • PRODUCT • CATCH WEIGHT • DEFINE CATCH WEIGHT TOLERANCE GROUPS.

Hazardous Substance Storage-Relevant

The HAZ. SUB. STRG-REL. indicator lets you indicate that the system should read the hazardous substance data to determine additional data relevant to storing the product in the warehouse. We'll discuss how the hazardous substance data is stored in Chapter 23, Integration with Other SAP Applications. The field is derived from the RELEVANT FOR HAZARDOUS SUBSTANCE indicator on the WM EXECUTION view of the ERP material master.

Environmentally Relevant

The ENVIRONMENTALLY RLVT indicator specifies that the product is potentially impactful to the environment.

Dangerous Goods Indicator Profile

The DG INDICATOR PROF. specifies whether the product is relevant to certain dangerous goods processes, checks, and documents. It is transferred from the DANGEROUS GOODS profile of the BASIC DATA 2 view of the ERP material master (the field is only relevant for certain material types).

4.2.7 Warehouse Data

The WHSE DATA tab (as seen in Figure 4.14) provides information related to the storage of product in the warehouse, including process-related parameters, cycle count indicators, stock putaway, and stock removal control indicators. The fields of the WHSE DATA tab are described in the following sections.

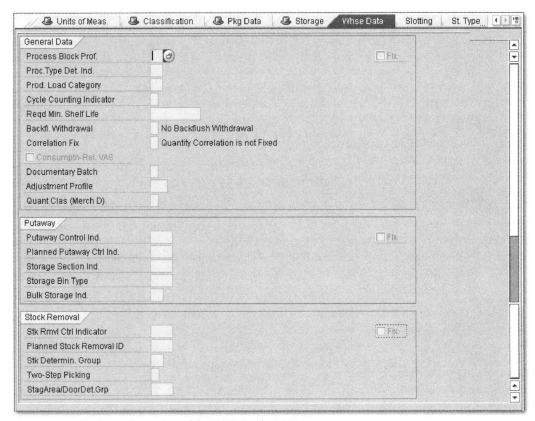

Figure 4.14 Warehouse Data View of the EWM Product Master

Process Block Profile

The PROCESS BLOCK PROF. allows you to trigger a warning or error message when certain warehouse processes (e.g., warehouse task creation or confirmation, goods issue, goods receipt, physical inventory) are performed in the warehouse. To create possible entries for the PROCESS BLOCK PROFILE in the EWM IMG, follow the menu path EXTENDED WAREHOUSE MANAGEMENT • MASTER DATA • PRODUCT • DEFINE PROCESS BLOCK PROFILE.

Process Type Determination Indicator

The PROC. TYPE DET. IND. is used to determine the relevant process type for warehouse activities. To create the possible entries for the WAREHOUSE PROCESS TYPE DETERMINATION INDICATORS in the EWM IMG, follow the menu path EXTENDED WAREHOUSE MANAGEMENT • CROSS-PROCESS SETTINGS • WAREHOUSE TASK • DEFINE CONTROL INDICATORS FOR DETERMINING WAREHOUSE PROCESS TYPES. To determine the process types based on the PROCESS TYPE DETERMINATION INDICATOR in the EWM IMG, follow the menu path EXTENDED WAREHOUSE MANAGEMENT • CROSS-PROCESS SETTINGS • WAREHOUSE TASK • DEFINE CONTROL INDICATORS FOR DETERMINING WAREHOUSE PROCESS TYPES.

Product Load Category

The PROD. LOAD CATEGORY is used to determine the workload for Labor Management (LM) for activities involving the product (which will be discussed further in Chapter 21, Labor Management). To specify the allowed entries for the PRODUCT LOAD CATEGORY in the EWM IMG, follow the menu path EXTENDED WAREHOUSE MANAGEMENT • CROSS-PROCESS SETTINGS • WAREHOUSE TASK • DEFINE EXTRACT TIME DETERMINATION • DEFINE PRODUCT LOAD CATEGORIES. To determine the workload from the PRODUCT LOAD CATEGORY in the EWM IMG, follow the menu path EXTENDED WAREHOUSE MANAGEMENT • CROSS-PROCESS SETTINGS • WAREHOUSE TASK • DEFINE EXTRACT TIME DETERMINATION • DEFINE EXTRACT TIME CALCULATION.

Cycle Count Indicator

The CYCLE COUNT INDICATOR (often referred to as the ABC indicator) is used to determine the frequency of cycle counting of the product in the warehouse. To create the possible entries for the CYCLE COUNT INDICATOR in the EWM IMG, follow the menu path EXTENDED WAREHOUSE MANAGEMENT • INTERNAL WAREHOUSE

Processes • Physical Inventory • Warehouse-Number-Specific Settings • Configure Cycle Counting. (There is no check table assigned to the domain for the field of the structure, but there is a search help assigned.) You also specify the interval between cycle counts and the buffer time (both in workdays) on the same table. You can also transfer the Cycle Count indicator from APO from the EWM Easy Access menu by following the Extended Warehouse Management • Master Data • Product • Transfer Cycle Counting Indicator from SAP APO menu path, or using Transaction code /SCWM/CCIND_MAINTAIN.

The Fix checkbox (seen in the top right in Figure 4.14) indicates the Cycle Count Indicator is fixed and should not be automatically changed by the slotting function. If the Fix indicator is not set, the Cycle Count Indicator can be evaluated during slotting.

Required Minimum Shelf Life

This value for the Reqd Min. Shelf Life determines the number of days of remaining shelf life required for the product during the goods receipt, if the Remaining Shelf Life Check is activated (in the EWM IMG at the node: Extended Warehouse Management • Goods Receipt Process • Inbound Delivery • Batch Management and Remaining Shelf Life Check in the Inbound Delivery). BAdI /CWM/EX_DLV_BT_VAL_DATE_WE can be used to influence the date determination for comparison.

Backflush Withdrawal

The Backfl. Withdrawal indicator is used in the production supply process to specify that the material is to be backflushed (i.e., goods issued automatically at the time of confirmation of the production order).

Correlation Fix

The Correlation Fix indicator defines whether the quantity of the components of a kit are fixed to the header quantity when using value-added service (VAS) orders. If the quantity correlation is fixed, the quantity of items on the kit is automatically adjusted when the quantity on the header is changed. There are two possible entries for the value — one indicating that the quantity correlation is fixed and one indicating that the quantity correlation is not fixed (value blank, which is also the default value).

Consumption-Relevant for VAS

The CONSUMPTN-REL. VAS checkbox is used for auxiliary products (which we'll discuss further in Chapter 19, Value-Added Services) to indicate that the auxiliary products should be consumed during the VAS order execution.

Documentary Batch

The DOCUMENTARY BATCH field is used to indicate whether products are tracked using documentary batches, which allows batches to be captured at the point of goods receipt or goods issue without having to manage the batches throughout the complete processes. The only valid values for the field indicate either DOCUMENTARY BATCH or NO DOCUMENTARY BATCH. We will discuss documentary batches further in Chapter 6.

Adjustment Profile

The ADJUSTMENT PROFILE is used by Merchandise Distribution (a specific cross-docking function used by the retail industry, which will be described further in Chapter 17) to define how the inbound products are allocated to outbound orders. To create the ADJUSTMENT PROFILES in the EWM IMG, follow the menu path EXTENDED WAREHOUSE MANAGEMENT • CROSS-PROCESS SETTINGS • CROSS-DOCKING (CD) • PLANNED CROSS-DOCKING • MERCHANDISE DISTRIBUTION • DEFINE ADJUSTMENT PROFILE. Note that there is also an ADJUSTMENT PROFILE field on the STORAGE tab that is relevant at the product level (and they use the same field help, and therefore the same configuration node, to create possible entries). If the adjustment profile is set at the warehouse level, it will only be used per warehouse.

Quantity Classification (for Merchandise Distribution)

The QUANT CLAS (MERCH D) field is used in Merchandise Distribution to determine in which quantities the product is handled (e.g., eaches, cases, pallets).

Putaway Control Indicator

The PUTAWAY CONTROL IND. is used to specify how the product should be put away in the warehouse. Specifically, it is used to determine the search sequence indicator during the storage type determination within the putaway strategy (which will be described further in Chapter 9). To create the possible entries for the PUTAWAY CONTROL Indicator within the EWM IMG, follow the menu path EXTENDED WAREHOUSE MANAGEMENT • GOODS RECEIPT PROCESS • SLOTTING • MASTER DATA •

DEFINE PUTAWAY CONTROL INDICATOR. To use the Putaway Control Indicator to determine the Storage Type Search Sequence, in the EWM IMG, follow the menu path EXTENDED WAREHOUSE MANAGEMENT • GOODS RECEIPT PROCESS • STRATEGIES • STORAGE TYPE SEARCH • SPECIFY STORAGE TYPE SEARCH SEQUENCE FOR PUTAWAY.

The FIX checkbox to the right of the PUTAWAY CONTROL INDICATOR is used to indicate that the PUTAWAY CONTROL INDICATOR is fixed and should not be automatically changed by the slotting function. If the FIX indicator is not set, the PUTAWAY CONTROL INDICATOR can be evaluated during slotting.

Planned Putaway Control Indicator

The PLANNED PUTAWAY CTRL IND. is the value that is set during slotting if the option to SAVE RESULTS is used during the execution of the slotting program. In this case, the data is saved in the PLANNED… field until the slotting run is activated. Once the slotting run is activated, the PLANNED PUTAWAY CONTROL INDICATOR data will be moved to the active PUTAWAY CONTROL INDICATOR field and the planned field will be cleared.

Storage Section Indicator

The STORAGE SECTION IND. is used to determine the relevant storage section for putaway during the putaway bin determination. To create the possible entries for the storage section indicator in the EWM IMG, follow the menu path EXTENDED WAREHOUSE MANAGEMENT • GOODS RECEIPT PROCESS • STRATEGIES • STORAGE SECTION SEARCH • CREATE STORAGE SECTION INDICATORS. To check how the Storage Section Indicator is used during the putaway bin determination, in the EWM IMG, follow the menu path EXTENDED WAREHOUSE MANAGEMENT • GOODS RECEIPT PROCESS • STRATEGIES • STORAGE SECTION SEARCH • MAINTAIN STORAGE SECTION SEARCH SEQUENCE.

> **Note**
>
> The STORAGE SECTION INDICATOR is found on both the WAREHOUSE DATA and STORAGE TYPE DATA views. If a STORAGE SECTION INDICATOR is found on the STORAGE TYPE DATA view for the relevant storage type, then that STORAGE SECTION INDICATOR is used in the bin determination. If not, then the indicator found on the WAREHOUSE DATA view is used. Likewise, the STORAGE SECTION INDICATOR determined during slotting only affects the STORAGE TYPE DATA view and not the warehouse data view (therefore, you can manually specify a default STORAGE SECTION INDICATOR in the WAREHOUSE DATA view without affecting the results determined during slotting).

Storage Bin Type

The STORAGE BIN TYPE indicator is used to determine the relevant storage bin type for putaway during the putaway bin determination if no bin is found that matches the optimum bin type specified on the WAREHOUSE STORAGE TYPE view. To create the possible entries for the STORAGE BIN TYPE in the EWM IMG, follow the menu path EXTENDED WAREHOUSE MANAGEMENT • GOODS RECEIPT PROCESS • STRATEGIES • STORAGE BIN DETERMINATION • DEFINE STORAGE BIN TYPES. To check how the STORAGE BIN TYPE is used during the putaway bin determination, in the EWM IMG, follow the menu path EXTENDED WAREHOUSE MANAGEMENT • GOODS RECEIPT PROCESS • STRATEGIES • STORAGE BIN DETERMINATION • ALTERNATIVE STORAGE BIN TYPE SEQUENCE.

> **Note**
>
> The comments regarding the STORAGE SECTION INDICATOR also apply for the STORAGE BIN TYPE indicator. In addition, if an alternate storage bin type sequence is not specified in the IMG node as indicated previously, then only storage bins of the specified optimum bin type would be found during the bin type search. Finally, this configuration only applies in cases where the HU type is not used to determine the relevant bin type sequence.

Bulk Storage Indicator

Bulk storage bins are typically floor storage bins (i.e., without racks) that can hold multiple units (often pallets or other large storage containers) of a product. The BULK STORAGE IND. is used to specify how the products can be stacked in the bulk storage bin. In particular, the bulk storage indicator determines how many pallets can be stored in the bin (as determined by the combination of the bulk storage indicator assigned to the material and the bin type assigned to the bin). To specify the possible entries for the BULK STORAGE INDICATOR in the EWM IMG, follow the menu path EXTENDED WAREHOUSE MANAGEMENT • GOODS RECEIPT PROCESS • STRATEGIES • PUTAWAY RULES • STORAGE BEHAVIOR: BULK STORAGE • DEFINE BULK STORAGE INDICATORS. To check how the Bulk Storage Indicators are used to determine how many units can fit into the bin, in the EWM IMG, follow the menu path EXTENDED WAREHOUSE MANAGEMENT • GOODS RECEIPT PROCESS • STRATEGIES • PUTAWAY RULES • STORAGE BEHAVIOR: BULK STORAGE • DEFINE BULK STRUCTURES.

Stock Removal Control Indicator

The STK RMVL CTRL INDICATOR is used to specify how the product should be picked in the warehouse. Specifically, it is used to determine the search sequence indicator during the storage type determination within the removal strategy (which will be described further in Chapter 10, Outbound Processing). To create the possible entries for the STOCK REMOVAL CONTROL INDICATOR within the EWM IMG, follow the menu path EXTENDED WAREHOUSE MANAGEMENT • GOODS ISSUE PROCESS • STRATEGIES • DEFINE STOCK REMOVAL CONTROL INDICATOR. To use the STOCK REMOVAL CONTROL INDICATOR to determine the STORAGE TYPE SEARCH SEQUENCE, in the EWM IMG, follow the menu path EXTENDED WAREHOUSE MANAGEMENT • GOODS ISSUE PROCESS • STRATEGIES • DETERMINE STORAGE TYPE SEARCH SEQUENCE FOR STOCK REMOVAL. To optimize the access strategies (i.e., to specify which fields are used in which sequence for the determination) for selecting the storage type determination search sequence, in the EWM IMG, follow the menu path EXTENDED WAREHOUSE MANAGEMENT • GOODS ISSUE PROCESS • STRATEGIES • OPTIMIZATION OF ACCESS STRATEGIES FOR STOR. TYPE DETERMINATION IN STCK RMVL.

The FIX checkbox to the right of the STK RMVL CTRL INDICATOR is used to indicate that the STOCK REMOVAL CONTROL INDICATOR is fixed and should not be automatically changed by the slotting function. If the FIX indicator is not set, the STOCK REMOVAL CONTROL INDICATOR can be evaluated during slotting.

Planned Stock Removal ID

The PLANNED STOCK REMOVAL ID is the value that is set during slotting if the option to SAVE RESULTS is used during the execution of the slotting program. In this case, the data is saved in the PLANNED… field until the slotting run is activated. Once the slotting run is activated, the PLANNED STOCK REMOVAL ID data will be moved to the active STK RMVL CTRL INDICATOR field and the planned field will be cleared.

Stock Determination Group

Stock determination is the method of determining the relevance and relative prioritization of stocks in the warehouse for a certain process. You can take into account stock ownership, stock type, and the process type for determining when stocks of certain types or belonging to certain owners should be used for certain processes. For example, you can determine the relative sequence of picking of stocks owned by certain parties for selecting subcontracting stocks for picking, or you can include quality stocks in replenishment activities but not allow them to be selected for picking. The Stk Determin. Group lets you group materials for inclusion in the stock determination. To specify the allowed entries for the Stock Determination Group in the EWM IMG, follow the menu path Extended Warehouse Management • Cross-Process Settings • Stock Determination • Maintain Stock Determination Groups. To check how the Stock Determination Group is used in the stock determination in the EWM IMG, follow menu path Extended Warehouse Management • Cross-Process Settings • Stock Determination • Configure Stock Determination.

Two-Step Picking

Two-step picking is the process of consolidating requirements (for example, in a wave), removing the consolidated required quantities of stock from a source storage bin to a deconsolidation area, then splitting the relevant quantities to the individual requirements. The Two-Step Picking indicator of the EWM product master is used to specify which materials are relevant for using the two-step picking method. If the indicator is set to 2, then the product is relevant for two-step picking. If the indicator is blank, then the product is not relevant for two-step picking.

Staging Area/Door Determination Group

The StagArea/DoorDet.Grp is used to determine the staging area or door during both loading and unloading processes. To specify the possible entries for the Staging Area/Door Determination Group in the EWM IMG, follow the menu path Extended Warehouse Management • Master Data • Staging Areas • Define Staging Area and Door Determination Groups. To assign the Staging Area/ Door Determination Groups to doors in the EWM IMG, follow the menu path Extended Warehouse Management • Master Data • Warehouse Door • Assign Staging Area/Door Determination Group to Door.

To use the Staging Area / Door Determination Group in the staging area and door determination for inbound receipts, in the EWM Easy Access menu, follow the Extended Warehouse Management • Settings • Shipping and Receiving • Staging Area and Door Determination (Inbound) menu path, or use Transaction code /SCWM/STADET_IN. To use the Staging Area/Door Determination Group in the staging area and door determination for outbound shipments, in the EWM Easy Access menu, follow the Extended Warehouse Management • Settings •

SHIPPING AND RECEIVING • STAGING AREA AND DOOR DETERMINATION (OUTBOUND) menu path, or use Transaction code /SCWM/STADET_OUT. To specify the access sequence for the staging area and door determination, in the EWM Easy Access menu, follow the EXTENDED WAREHOUSE MANAGEMENT • SETTINGS • SHIPPING AND RECEIVING • ACCESS SEQUENCE TO STAGING AREAS AND DOOR DETERMINATION menu path, or use Transaction code /SCWM/STADET_ASS.

4.2.8 Slotting

The SLOTTING tab (shown in Figure 4.15) contains information related to the slotting of the product (which will be discussed further in Chapter 9), including the status, demand data, and indicators related to the product dimensions. The fields on the SLOTTING tab are described in the following sections.

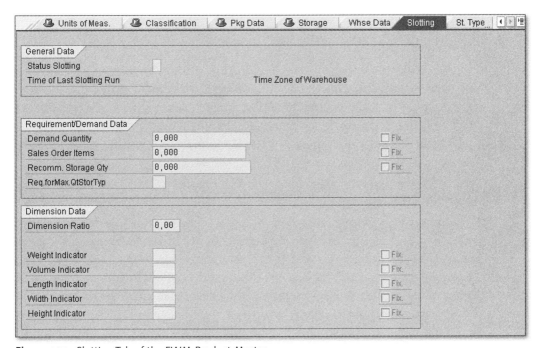

Figure 4.15 Slotting Tab of the EWM Product Master

> **Note**
>
> The Fix flags to the right of the fields generally indicate that the data is fixed and should not be updated during slotting.

Status Slotting

The STATUS SLOTTING indicator specifies the current status of slotting and whether or not the slotting can be reevaluated (or whether reslotting is allowed). The possible values include:

- ▶ Product not yet slotted/slotting allowed
- ▶ Product not yet slotted/slotting not allowed
- ▶ Product already slotted/reslotting allowed
- ▶ Product already slotted/reslotting not allowed

Time of Last Slotting Run

This read-only indicator specifies the date and time that the last slotting run was performed.

Demand Quantity

The DEMAND QUANTITY field is used during the slotting run to determine the total quantity that must be shipped from the warehouse during a given time frame. It can be stored on and read from the EWM product master, or it can be read directly from APO during the slotting run (and can be stored on the EWM product master during the slotting run, if the parameter is specified appropriately on the slotting run selection screen).

Sales Order Items

The SALES ORDER ITEMS field is used during the slotting run to determine the total number of sales order items to be shipped from the warehouse during a given time frame. It can be stored on and read from the EWM product master, or it can be read directly from APO during the slotting run (and can be stored on the EWM product master during the slotting run, if the parameter is specified appropriately on the slotting run selection screen).

Recommended Storage Quantity

The RECOMM. STORAGE QTY field is used during the slotting run to determine the recommended storage quantity for the product within the given warehouse. It can be stored on and read from the EWM product master, or it can be read directly from APO during the slotting run (and can be stored on the EWM product master during the slotting run, if the parameter is specified appropriately on the slotting run selection screen).

Request for Calculation of Maximum Quantity in Storage Type

This indicator is used to determine which field is used in determining the maximum quantity in the storage type (which is a parameter stored on the storage type view of the product master) during the slotting run. The possible values include:

- Demand Quantity
- Number of Order Items
- Recommended Warehouse Stock

Dimension Ratio

The DIMENSION RATIO is used during bin type determination (the ones that include dimensional checks). If the calculated ratio between length, width, and height exceeds the assigned dimension ratio for the product, then the orientation for which the ratio was calculated is not allowed. For more information on the bin type determination, see Chapter 9.

Weight/Volume/Length/Width/Height Indicators

These indicators are used to group together like products in terms of weight, volume, length, width, and height. They can be determined during slotting and can be used in the bin type determination during the putaway bin determination.

4.2.9 Storage Type Data

The STORAGE TYPES view of the EWM product master (as seen in Figure 4.16) includes information related to the placement and removal of stock from the specified storage type. Note that there may be more than one storage type for a product. If so, the multiple storage types will be shown on the left-hand pane of the STORAGE TYPES view. To create a new storage type view, in change mode, select the CREATE icon (circled in Figure 4.16), enter the data on the screen, then click the ADOPT DATA button (to the left of the CREATE button). To display or change data for a particular storage type, simply select the storage type on the left pane with a single left mouse-click.

The fields on the storage type view are described in the following sections.

> **Note**
>
> The FIX flags to the right of the fields generally indicate that the data is fixed and should not be updated during slotting.

Storage Type

The STORAGE TYPE field indicates which storage type the data displayed on the view applies to. You can create new data for a storage type by clicking the CREATE button (the one circled in Figure 4.16), entering the storage type and the other relevant data on the screen, and then clicking the ADOPT DATA button at the top of the screen (as shown in Figure 4.16). Once the storage type data is created, the storage type is displayed in the list on the left side of the screen. To display or change the data related to the storage type, simply single-click on the storage type in the list.

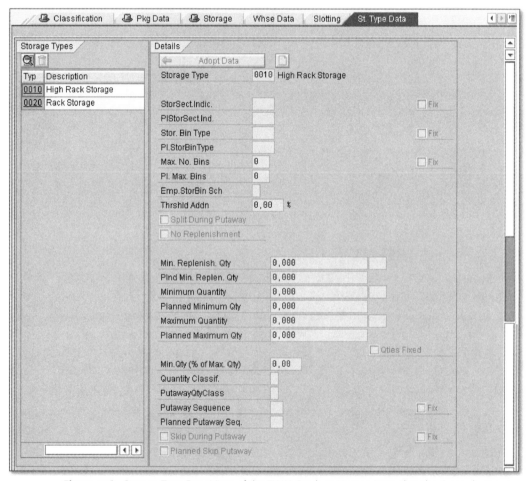

Figure 4.16 Storage Type Data View of the EWM Product Master. Note that the Create button is only active in change mode.

Storage Section Indicator

The STOR. SECT. INDIC is used to assign groups of products to storage section search sequences, which is in turn used to determine the sequence of storage sections to be used during the storage section search during putaway. To create possible entries for the STORAGE SECTION INDICATOR in the EWM IMG, follow the menu path EXTENDED WAREHOUSE MANAGEMENT • GOODS RECEIPT PROCESS • STRATEGIES • STORAGE SECTION SEARCH • CREATE STORAGE SECTION INDICATORS. To check the storage section search sequence that is assigned to each storage type and Storage Section Indicator in the EWM IMG, follow the menu path EXTENDED WAREHOUSE MANAGEMENT • GOODS RECEIPT PROCESS • STRATEGIES • STORAGE SECTION SEARCH • MAINTAIN STORAGE SECTION SEARCH SEQUENCE. And finally, to specify which storage types are relevant to storage section determination and storage section check in the EWM IMG, follow the menu path EXTENDED WAREHOUSE MANAGEMENT • GOODS RECEIPT PROCESS • STRATEGIES • STORAGE SECTION SEARCH • STORAGE SECTION CHECK. We'll discuss the STORAGE SECTION INDICATOR further when we discuss putaway strategies in Chapter 9.

> **Note**
>
> As described earlier, the STORAGE SECTION INDICATOR is found on both the WAREHOUSE DATA and STORAGE TYPE DATA views. See the previous note for more details.

Planned Storage Section Indicator

The PL STOR SECT.IND. is the value that is set during slotting if the option to Save Results is used during the execution of the slotting program. In this case, the data is saved in the PLANNED… field until the slotting run is activated. Once the slotting run is activated, the PLANNED STORAGE SECTION INDICATOR data will be moved to the active STORAGE SECTION INDICATOR field and the planned field will be cleared.

Storage Bin Type

The STOR. BIN TYPE indicator is used to determine the relevant storage bin type for putaway during the putaway bin determination if no bin is found that matches the optimum bin type specified on the Warehouse . view. To create the possible entries for the STOR. BIN TYPE in the EWM IMG, follow the menu path EXTENDED WAREHOUSE MANAGEMENT • GOODS RECEIPT PROCESS • STRATEGIES • STORAGE BIN DETERMINATION • DEFINE STORAGE BIN TYPES. To check how the STOR. BIN TYPE is used during the putaway bin determination, in the EWM IMG, follow the menu path Extended Warehouse Management • Goods Receipt Process • Strategies • Storage Bin Determination • Alternative Storage Bin Type Sequence.

> **Note**
>
> The comments regarding the Storage Section Indicator also apply to the Storage Bin Type indicator. In addition, if an alternate storage bin type sequence is not specified in the IMG node as indicated earlier, then only storage bins of the specified optimum bin type would be found during the bin type search. Finally, this configuration only applies in cases where the HU type is not used to determine the relevant bin type sequence.

Planned Storage Bin Type

The Planned Storage Bin Type indicator is the value that is set during slotting if the option to Save Results is used during the execution of the slotting program. In this case, the data is saved in the Planned... field until the slotting run is activated. Once the slotting run is activated, the Planned Bin Type indicator will be moved to the active Storage Bin Type field and the planned field will be cleared.

Maximum Number of Bins

The Max. No. Bins field specifies the maximum number of fixed picking bins that should be assigned within the specified storage type. It can be specified manually or it can be determined during the slotting execution.

Planned Maximum Number of Bins

The Pl. Max. Bins indicator is the value that is set during slotting if the option to Save Results is used during the execution of the slotting program. In this case, the data is saved in the Planned... field until the slotting run is activated. Once the slotting run is activated, the Planned Maximum Number of Bins indicator will be moved to the active Maximum Number of Bins field and the planned field will be cleared.

Empty Storage Bin Search

The Emp. StorBin Sch indicator specified the sort rule that is to be used if the putaway storage bin search finally determines that an empty bin should be found within the specified storage type (e.g., if the Addition to Existing Stock/Empty Bin or Empty Bin putaway rules are assigned to the storage type in the EWM IMG). Possible entries for the Empty Storage Bin Search include:

▶ **Sorting According to Definition**

The storage bins are sorted according to the bin sortation for putaway (Transaction /SCWM/SBST).

▶ **Near To Fixed Bin**

The system attempts to place the product in an empty bin as close to the fixed bin as possible.

▶ **Product Decides**

This option is intended for use when specifying the rule at the storage type level — if you specify the bin search rule for the storage type such that the product decides, then on the product, you should specify one of the rules above.

Threshold Addition

The THRSHLD ADDN parameter is checked if the SPLIT DURING PUTAWAY is active. In this case, stock is only added to the bin (and therefore the split can only occur) if the available remaining capacity of the bin exceeds the Threshold Addition indicator. You therefore use the THRESHOLD ADDITION indicator to ensure that the system is not sending operators to several bins just to fill up small available capacities of the bins.

The SPLIT DURING PUTAWAY can be activated in one of two ways. Either the SPLIT DURING PUTAWAY indicator of the Storage Type configuration settings in the IMG is set to the value SPLIT DURING PUTAWAY, or the indicator is set to PRODUCT MASTER DECIDES and the SPLIT DURING PUTAWAY indicator on the STORAGE TYPE view of the product master is activated.

Example

Bin A contains 8 pieces of product X, which utilizes 80% of the available capacity of the bin (i.e., 10 pieces will fit into the bin). If an additional putaway for product X is performed for 5 pieces, and the SPLIT DURING PUTAWAY is also activated (as described earlier), the system will first attempt to add as much stock as possible to bin A before finding an additional bin for the stock. But first, it much check whether the available capacity exceeds the THRESHOLD ADDITION indicator for the specific storage type for the product. If the THRESHOLD ADDITION is set to 10%, which is less than the available capacity of 20%, then 2 pieces of the stock would be added to bin A and the rest to an additional bin. On the other hand, if the THRESHOLD ADDITION is set to 30%, which exceeds the available capacity, then the system will skip this bin and continue to find another available bin.

Split During Putaway

If the configuration setting SPLIT DURING PUTAWAY on the storage type settings in the IMG for the putaway storage type is set to PRODUCT MASTER DECIDES, then the SPLIT DURING PUTAWAY indicator on the storage type view of the product master controls whether the system will attempt to split the putaway quantity on multiple bins during the putaway bin determination. See the explanation and example from the description of the THRESHOLD ADDITION indicator for a detailed description of how the SPLIT DURING PUTAWAY indicator and the THRESHOLD ADDITION parameter are used together.

No Replenishment

The NO REPLENISHMENT indicator controls whether the replenishment program will attempt to refill the bins for the material in the specified storage type during the replenishment run. You can use this indicator to specify that certain materials are not relevant for replenishment even though other materials in the same storage type may be relevant.

Minimum Replenishment Quantity

The MIN. REPLENISH. QTY specifies the minimum quantity to be moved during the replenishment for the product in the specified storage type. For example, you can specify that only a full case or full pallet should be moved at one time, even if the requested replenishment quantity is less than the full case or full pallet. This helps to minimize the number of replenishments being performed and also reduces the effort to execute the replenishment by ensuring operators are not being forced to break full containers during the replenishment activity. The field to the right of the MINIMUM REPLENISHMENT QUANTITY represents the UNIT OF MEASURE in which the parameter is specified.

Planned Minimum Replenishment Quantity

The PLND MIN. REPLEN. QTY is the value that is set during slotting if the option to SAVE RESULTS is used during the execution of the slotting program. In this case, the data is saved in the PLANNED… field until the slotting run is activated. Once the slotting run is activated, the PLANNED MINIMUM REPLENISHMENT QUANTITY field will be moved to the active MIN. REPLENISH. QTY field and the planned field will be cleared. The Unit of Measure field to the right of the MIN. REPLENISH. QTY also applies to the PLANNED MINIMUM REPLENISHMENT QUANTITY.

Minimum Quantity

The MINIMUM QUANTITY specifies the minimum quantity of the product that should be stored in the storage type. It is used during the planned replenishment (i.e., if the PLANNED REPLENISHMENT option is selected when executing the replenishment program, which can be accessed in the SAP Easy Access menu via the EXTENDED WAREHOUSE MANAGEMENT • WORK SCHEDULING • SCHEDULE REPLENISHMENT menu path, or by using Transaction code /SCWM/REPL). The field to the right of the MINIMUM QUANTITY represents the unit of measure in which the parameter is specified.

Planned Minimum Quantity

The PLANNED MINIMUM QTY is the value that is set during slotting if the option to SAVE RESULTS is used during the execution of the slotting program. In this case, the data is saved in the PLANNED field until the slotting run is activated. Once the slotting run is activated, the PLANNED MINIMUM QTY field will be moved to the active MINIMUM QUANTITY field and the planned field will be cleared. The UNIT OF MEASURE field to the right of the MINIMUM QUANTITY also applies to the PLANNED MINIMUM QUANTITY.

Maximum Quantity

The MAXIMUM QUANTITY specifies the maximum quantity of the product that should be stored in the storage type. It is used during the planned replenishment (which can be accessed as described previously). The field to the right of the MAXIMUM QUANTITY represents the UNIT OF MEASURE in which the parameter is specified.

Planned Maximum Qty

The PLANNED MAXIMUM QTY is the value that is set during slotting if the option to SAVE RESULTS is used during the execution of the slotting program. In this case, the data is saved in the PLANNED... field until the slotting run is activated. Once the slotting run is activated, the PLANNED MAXIMUM QTY field will be moved to the active MAXIMUM QUANTITY field and the planned field will be cleared. The UNIT OF MEASURE field to the right of the MAXIMUM QUANTITY also applies to the PLANNED MINIMUM QTY.

Quantities Fixed

The QTIES FIXED flag applies to the minimum and maximum quantities described previously. It is used to indicate that the quantities are fixed and should not be automatically changed by the slotting function. If the FIX checkbox is not set, the quantities can be evaluated during slotting.

Minimum Quantity (as Percentage of Maximum Quantity)

This parameter provides an alternate method of specifying the MINIMUM QUANTITY. If you specify a number in this field (between 0 and 100), the MINIMUM QUANTITY is calculated as the specified percentage of the MAXIMUM QUANTITY.

Quantity Classification

The QUANTITY CLASSIF. in the STORAGE TYPE view of the product master is used to determine the operative unit of measure for the pack spec if the quantity classification is not specified in the storage type configuration setting for the storage type.

Putaway Quantity Classification

The PUTAWAYQTYCLASS is used for the capacity check of the destination bin. When validating the capacity of a storage bin during the bin determination for putaway, if the PUTAWAY QUANTITY CLASSIFICATION is assigned for the storage type on the product master, then the capacity of the bin is checked based on the capacity utilization according to the pack spec level with the assigned quantity classification.

Putaway Sequence

The PUTAWAY SEQUENCE is used to sort the storage types within a storage type group during the putaway bin determination. It can be set by slotting, or manually specified in the product master.

The FIX checkbox to the right of the PUTAWAY SEQUENCE field is used to indicate that the PUTAWAY SEQUENCE is fixed and should not be automatically changed by the slotting function. If the FIX checkbox is not set, the PUTAWAY SEQUENCE can be evaluated during slotting.

Planned Putaway Sequence

The PLANNED PUTAWAY SEQ. indicator is the value that is set during slotting if the option to SAVE RESULTS is used during the execution of the slotting program. In this case, the data is saved in the PLANNED... field until the slotting run is activated. Once the slotting run is activated, the PLANNED PUTAWAY SEQ. indicator will be moved to the active PUTAWAY SEQUENCE field and the planned field will be cleared.

Skip During Putaway

The SKIP DURING PUTAWAY indicator is used to specify that the specified storage type should be skipped during the determination of the destination storage bin during the putaway bin determination. It can be set during slotting or manually.

Planned Skip Putaway

The PLANNED SKIP PUTAWAY indicator is the value that is set during slotting if the option to Save Results is used during the execution of the slotting program. In this case, the data is saved in the PLANNED... field until the slotting run is activated. Once the slotting run is activated, the PLANNED SKIP PUTAWAY indicator will be moved to the active SKIP DURING PUTAWAY field and the planned field will be cleared.

4.3   Summary

In this chapter, we described the relevant product master fields on both ERP and EWM. You should now have a good understanding of how to set up the data for your products in ERP, transfer the data to EWM, and set up the additional necessary data in EWM. In the next chapter, we will describe the additional EWM master data (business partners, supply chain units, packaging, transportation, production, resources, and other master data). This knowledge will provide a baseline for understanding how to set up your data to support your business processes, which will be described in later chapters.

In addition to the product master data, other important master data is critical to the success of the Extended Warehouse Management (EWM) implementation.

5   Other Warehouse Master Data

Aside from the product master data, there are several other important master data that must be maintained in the EWM system to ensure successful processing of the transactional data. In particular, these include:

- Business partner (BP) data
- Supply chain units
- Packaging materials
- Packaging specifications (pack specs)
- Transportation routes
- Production master data
- Resources

Each of these data are important to execute for certain business processes in the system, and each are explained in detail, together with the business processes to which they are important, in the following sections.

5.1   Business Partner Data

BPs are entities outside of your own (both internal and external to your organization) that you do business with and which are therefore important to various business processes. Each of these business entities must be represented in the EWM system to ensure that their relevance to various business processes is understood and accurately tracked throughout the business process. BPs may include:

- Customers
- Vendors

- ▸ Third-party suppliers
- ▸ Carriers
- ▸ Freight forwarders
- ▸ Plants
- ▸ Employees

Each of these BPs must contain different details within the BP data and can be integrated into EWM from different sources, however, they are all maintained or displayed within EWM using the same data structures and the same transaction. To access the BP data for any BPs from the SAP Easy Access Menu, follow the EXTENDED WAREHOUSE MANAGEMENT • MASTER DATA • MAINTAIN BUSINESS PARTNER menu path, or use Transaction code BP.

Each of the BPs can be classified as a person, organization, or group. If you are creating a BP from scratch in the EWM system, you must choose one of these options by selecting the appropriate button from the button bar (or the appropriate menu path from the menu bar). Figure 5.1 shows the BUSINESS PARTNER transaction as it is initially displayed.

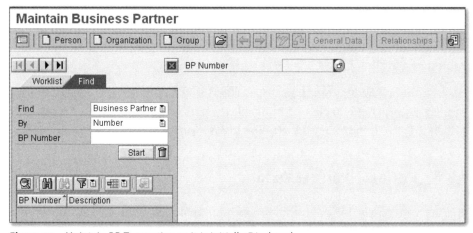

Figure 5.1 Maintain BP Transaction as it is Initially Displayed

On the left side of the transaction, you can use the FIND tab to find one or more BPs of any type (or of a specific type) by entering the relevant criteria in the FIND and BY selection dropdown boxes and then the relevant data. Note that the selection criteria will be different based on the entries that you select in the FIND and

By dropdown boxes. You can use an asterisk (*) as a wild card to perform the selection. For example, if you set FIND equal to ORGANIZATIONS and BY equal to NUMBER, then you can enter SPU* in the BP NUMBER selection criteria and click the START button to find all of the organizations (e.g., customers, vendors) that start with the letters SPU (as seen in Figure 5.2).

You can also find a list of all BPs of a certain type (or even all types), by specifying the FIND and BY criteria, leaving the additional selection criteria blank, and clicking the START button.

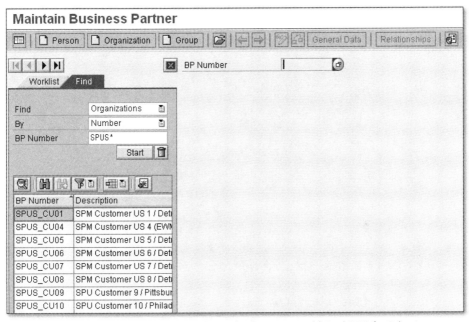

Figure 5.2 Selection of Organizations in the Find Tab Using a Wild Card ("*") for Selection

Double-clicking on the results in the list will display the detailed data for that BP. To switch to the maintenance view, select the SWITCH BETWEEN DISPLAY AND CHANGE button from the button bar (circled in Figure 5.3), or press F6.

If you click the TRASH CAN button within the FIND tab (also circled in Figure 5.3), it will delete the selection criteria that you entered (it will not delete all of the BPs that match your selection criteria).

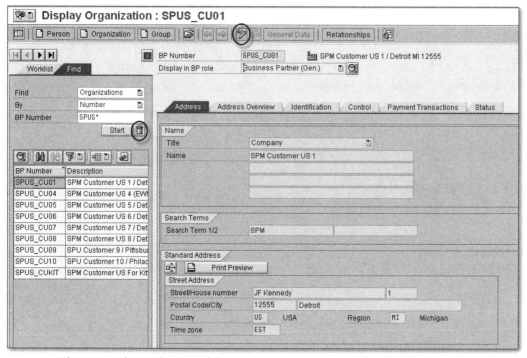

Figure 5.3 The Display View of the BP after Selecting the Entry from the Find Tab

Note also the DISPLAY IN BP ROLE selection dropdown box just below the BP number. Each BP can be maintained for multiple roles, and the valid roles will depend on the type of BP. For example, a customer may be relevant for a general BP role (used to define the general data for the customer), a financial services BP (used to define the data of the customer as a payor), and a sold-to BP (used to define the data of the customer as a party to which products are sold). There may also be customers that are created strictly as a ship-to party, which would require them to only have the general data and ship-to party data. Note that some of the data will be replicated across the various role views, while other data may be specific to a particular role. If the data is replicated from a source system, such as SAP ERP, the relevant roles can be automatically created during the interface.

To create an additional view of the BP, switch to the change mode by selecting the SWITCH BETWEEN DISPLAY AND CHANGE button (as seen in Figure 5.3), then select an additional BP role in the CHANGE IN BP ROLE dropdown selection box. If any roles aside from the BUSINESS PARTNER (GEN.) role and the FINANCIAL SERVICES BP

role are already maintained, they will be marked in the dropdown selection with
(MAINTAINED) to the right of the role name (as seen in Figure 5.4).

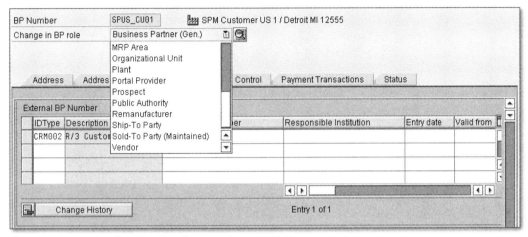

Figure 5.4 Creation of a New BP Role in Maintenance Mode

Aside from the identification numbers on the IDENTIFICATION tab, the warehouse
administrator will not have reason to frequently update the master data of the BP
directly. Rather, the BP data is most often under the ownership of the source system for the data (e.g., SAP ERP) and the administrators who are responsible for
maintaining the data in those systems.

The following sections describe the different types of BP data, how they are typically created, and which data is most relevant to the EWM business processes.

5.1.1 Customers

The customer master data is interfaced with EWM from ERP via the core interface
(CIF). It can be created initially in ERP, or it may have been created in the Customer
Relationship Management (CRM) system and interfaced with ERP.

The customer master data includes the basic details of the customer, including the
customer name, addresses, various communication information, and various data
that are not usually relevant to warehouse operations (but may be useful nonetheless under certain circumstances), such as tax classification, payment details, and
status information.

The details that are relevant to warehouse processes include address information (which must be printed on shipping documentation and other forms, and is also used, for example, in route determination), identification numbers (as seen in Figure 5.4), and business hours of the customer (as seen in Figure 5.5 and may have been used, for example, in the determination of the expected goods issue dates and times of the outbound deliveries).

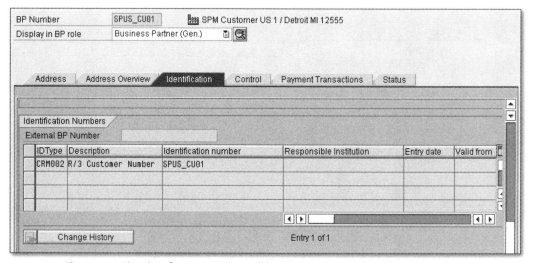

Figure 5.5 The Identification Numbers of the BP, Which Can Be Used for Determining BP Data for Certain Warehouse Documents

Maintaining the identification numbers is important because they are used to determine the relevant BP data to be used for certain warehouse documents, based on the BP assigned to the source document. For example, the identification CRM002 is used to determine the customer number for the outbound delivery notification (ODN) (and subsequent outbound delivery order (ODO) and outbound delivery (OD)) based on the ship-to partner assigned to the outbound delivery in ERP. In other words, the partner is not taken directly from the outbound delivery document from ERP into the ODN within EWM, but the BP data maintained in EWM is used to determine the relevant partner information. In the case shown in Figure 5.4, the identification number is the same as the BP number. This assignment is made for simplicity and it will often be this way as well for your own implementation, but it may not always be the case. For instance, in a third-party logistics environment, the BP number from the source system for outbound deliveries may be different than the numbers used in the warehouse for the relevant BPs.

In display mode, you can select the relevant business hours of the customer on the CONTROL tab. Selecting the relevant button from the BUSINESS HOURS section of the CONTROL tab will result in the pop-up box being displayed, as seen in Figure 5.6. Note that the relevant selections will be marked on the right side of the button with the text "have been maintained" (hidden by the pop-up in Figure 5.6) and will not be grayed out.

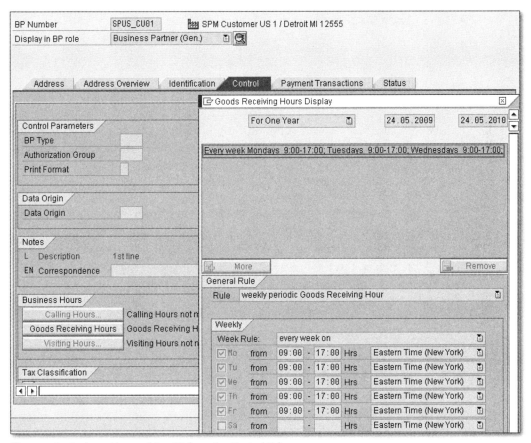

Figure 5.6 Business Hours of the BP from the Control Tab

The typical roles of a customer BP that also act as a sold-to and ship-to party include BUSINESS PARTNER (GEN.), FINANCIAL SERVICES BP, and SOLD-TO PARTY.

> **Note**
>
> If the customer is both a sold-to party and ship-to party, the SHIP-TO PARTY business party role does *not* need to be created in addition to the SOLD-TO PARTY business party role. It is sufficient for the SOLD-TO PARTY role (which should be created automatically during the Business Party creation during the interface).

5.1.2 Vendors

The vendor master data is also interfaced with EWM from ERP via the CIF. It can be created initially in ERP, or it may have been created in the CRM system and interfaced with ERP.

The vendor master data includes the basic details of the vendor, including the vendor name, addresses, various communication information, and various data that are not usually relevant to the warehouse operations (but can be useful nonetheless under certain circumstances), such as tax classification, payment details (e.g., for return payments), and status information.

The structure of the vendor business party data is very similar to the customer business party data, with a couple of key exceptions. First, the identification numbers in the IDENTIFICATION tab must include the IDType CRM004 (R/3 Vendor Number). Second, the typical business party roles include BUSINESS PARTNER (GEN.), FINANCIAL SERVICES BP, and VENDOR.

There is less data available for the VENDOR BP role on the IDENTIFICATION tab, the INDUSTRIES and TAX NUMBERS sections are no longer relevant.

5.1.3 Employees

The employee master data can also be interfaced with EWM from ERP via the CIF. It can be initially created in ERP, or it may have been created in the CRM system and interfaced with ERP.

The employee master data includes the basic details of the employees, including the name, addresses, various communications information, and other data. You do not need to assign identification numbers to the employee BP. The typical business party roles include BUSINESS PARTNER (GEN.), FINANCIAL SERVICES BP, and Employee. On the EMPLOYEE BP role, the PERSONNEL NUMBER and the USER NAME can be assigned to the employee. This information is used for interfacing the Labor

Management (LM) performance data to the Human Resources (HR) application. To do this, the processor role should be created for the employee, either via the generic BP transaction or in the dedicated processor creation transaction discussed in Chapter 21, Labor Management.

5.1.4 Plants

Plants are distributed from ERP to EWM via the CIF and create BPs in EWM with relevant role assignments so that they can be used as BPs for transfers between plants and for other activities. Plants should be created with the BUSINESS PARTNER (GEN.), FINANCIAL SERVICES BP, and SOLD-TO PARTY BP roles. The BP should have the ID types for customer (CRM002), vendor (CRM004), and plant (CRM011) assigned if it will be used for those respective roles.

5.1.5 Other Business Partner Roles

Other BPs can also be created in EWM and some are necessary to support certain business processes. The list of possible BP roles is the same as in the CRM or ERP system, but several of those are not relevant for EWM. The ones most relevant to EWM, aside from those already discussed, include:

- Carrier
- Consolidator
- Customs BP
- Customs Office
- Foreign Trade Organizational Unit
- Material Resource Planning Area
- Remanufacturer

Each of these BPs can be created as an organization (using the Create Organization button as seen in Figure 5.1) with the relevant data assigned to each BP role. Each BP should include at least the BUSINESS PARTNER (GEN.) role, FINANCIAL SERVICES BP role, and the relevant role matching the type of organization. Throughout this book, we will discuss creation of the BPs for each business transaction.

5.2   Supply Chain Units (SCUs)

SCUs represent physical locations or organizational elements that are used by EWM to model the supply chain of your organization. Examples of SCUs include:

- Plants
- Customers
- Vendors
- Shipping points
- Material Requirements Planning (MRP) Areas
- Warehouses
- Warehouse doors
- Shipping zones
- Transportation service providers
- Terminals or ports

5.2.1   Maintaining SCUs

Each SCU contains data about its geographical location, BP assignment, time zone, address, and business attributes. The business attributes (also called business character) identify how the SCU is used, for example, whether the SCU is a warehouse, shipping office, door, ship-to location, zone, or other type of SCU.

In Figure 5.7, you can see the business attribute assignments for the SCU. To access the maintenance transaction for the SCUs from the SAP Easy Access menu, follow the EXTENDED WAREHOUSE MANAGEMENT • MASTER DATA • MAINTAIN SUPPLY CHAIN UNIT menu path, or use Transaction code /SCMB/SCUMAIN.

The SCUs are often used to make assignments of locations in transactions that need to refer to the geographical location of the entities. For example, routes are created using SCUs to refer to locations such as warehouses, vendors, and customers. However, this is generally limited to the setup of the configuration and master data and the SCUs are generally known to or used by general workers in the warehouse (with a potential exception being an administrator who is responsible for creating transportation routes).

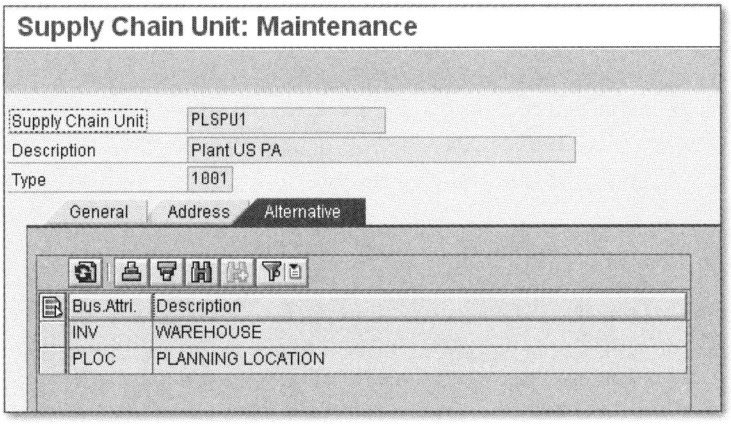

Supply Chain Unit: Maintenance

Supply Chain Unit	PLSPU1
Description	Plant US PA
Type	1001

General | Address | Alternative

	Bus.Attri.	Description
	INV	WAREHOUSE
	PLOC	PLANNING LOCATION

Figure 5.7 Business Attributes of the SCU

5.2.2 Assigning SCUs to the Warehouse

Each warehouse is assigned an SCU. The relevant BPs and the SCU are assigned to the warehouse in the SAP Easy Access Menu of EWM by following the EXTENDED WAREHOUSE MANAGEMENT • SETTINGS • ASSIGNMENTS: WAREHOUSE NUMBERS/BUSINESS PARTNERS menu path, or using Transaction code /SCWM/LGNBP. Figure 5.8 shows the transaction where the BPs and SCU are assigned to the warehouse (as also discussed in Chapter 2, Organizational Structure).

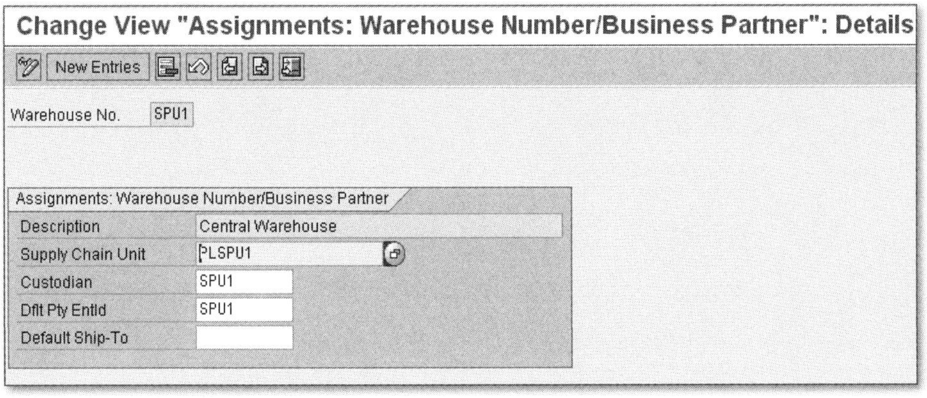

Change View "Assignments: Warehouse Number/Business Partner": Details

New Entries

Warehouse No. SPU1

Assignments: Warehouse Number/Business Partner

Description	Central Warehouse
Supply Chain Unit	PLSPU1
Custodian	SPU1
Dflt Pty Entld	SPU1
Default Ship-To	

Figure 5.8 Assignment of the SCU and BPs to the Warehouse

5.2.3 Using SCUs in Transportation

SCUs are also used in the various shipping and receiving entities of EWM. For example, the SCUs are referenced when creating transportation lanes, zones, routes, and carrier profiles. We will discuss these transportation elements in more detail in Section 5.3, Master Data for Transportation.

5.2.4 Assigning Calendars to SCUs

You can assign a calendar to each SCU. This can be important, for example, in determining the shipping calendar of the entity, and is used to determine expected delivery dates as part of the route determination. To assign a calendar to the SCU from the EWM Easy Access menu, follow the EXTENDED WAREHOUSE MANAGEMENT • MASTER DATA • SHIPPING AND RECEIVING • ROUTE DETERMINATION • ASSIGN CALENDAR TO SUPPLY CHAIN UNIT menu path, or use Transaction code /SCTM/DEPCAL. Note that you can create a new departure calendar via the transaction by assigning a name in the CALENDAR section and selecting the CREATE button next to it. To assign an existing calendar (or calendars), select the APPEND ROW button (which also looks like a CREATE button) in the table at the bottom. Figure 5.9 shows the calendar assignment transaction.

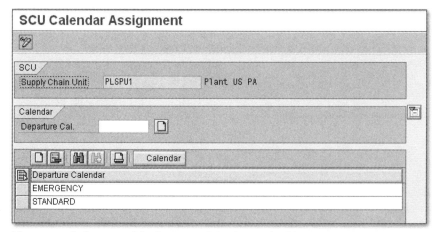

Figure 5.9 Assignment of the Departure Calendars to the SCU

5.3 Master Data for Transportation

The master data used for managing transportation within EWM is primarily used to support route determination. The routing guide engine (RGE) from Advanced Planning and Optimization (APO) is leveraged by EWM in route determination, and therefore the same elements used by the RGE are also used by EWM, including the elements described next. We will discuss route determination and its impacts on processing deliveries further in Chapter 9, Inbound Processing, and Chapter 10, Outbound Processing.

5.3.1 Prerequisite Configuration

Certain configuration elements must be configured to support the transportation master data. In particular, transportation modes, mode of transport categories (for dangerous goods), means of transport, request types, shipping conditions, and transportation groups are required.

To create transportation modes in the EWM Implementation Guide (IMG), follow the SCM BASIS • MASTER DATA • TRANSPORTATION LANE • MAINTAIN TRANSPORTATION MODE menu path.

To create a mode of transport categories for dangerous goods (if you need to assign one to the means of transport) in the EWM IMG, follow the menu path SCM BASIS • EH&S SERVICES • DANGEROUS GOODS MANAGEMENT • SPECIFY MODE-OF-TRANSPORT CATEGORIES.

To create a means of transport in the EWM IMG, follow the menu path SCM BASIS • MASTER DATA • TRANSPORTATION LANE • MAINTAIN MEANS OF TRANSPORT.

To create request types in the EWM IMG, follow the menu path SCM BASIS • ROUTING GUIDE • DEFINE REQUEST TYPES FOR ROUTING GUIDE.

To create shipping conditions in the EWM IMG, follow the menu path EXTENDED WAREHOUSE MANAGEMENT • CROSS-PROCESS SETTINGS • DELIVERY PROCESSING • GENERAL SETTINGS • DEFINE SHIPPING CONDITIONS.

To create transportation groups in the EWM IMG, follow the menu path SCM BASIS • MASTER DATA • PRODUCT • MAINTAIN TRANSPORTATION GROUP.

In addition, to maintain the compatibility between transportation groups and means of transport in the EWM IMG, follow the menu path EXTENDED WARE-

HOUSE MANAGEMENT • CROSS-PROCESS SETTINGS • SHIPPING AND RECEIVING • GENERAL SETTINGS • DEFINE COMPATIBILITY OF MEANS OF TRANSPORT AND TRANSPORTATION GROUP.

5.3.2 Transportation Hierarchy

To create the transportation routes, you must first create a transportation hierarchy. To create the transportation hierarchy in the EWM Easy Access menu, follow the ADVANCED PLANNING AND OPTIMIZATION • MASTER DATA • HIERARCHY • MAINTAIN HIERARCHY menu path, or use Transaction code /SAPAPO/RELHSHOW. When creating the transportation hierarchy, you should assign object type 7 (Transportation Zone) and structure category 4 (Extended Hierarchy). Figure 5.10 shows what the transportation hierarchy should look like. Note that it is not necessary to complete the hierarchy; it is only necessary that one is created.

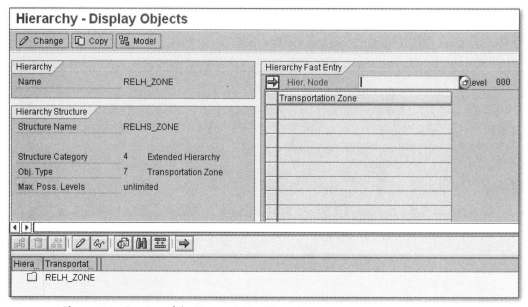

Figure 5.10 Creation of the Transportation Hierarchy

5.3.3 Transportation Lanes

A transportation lane is a direct link for transportation between two locations, whether they are internal plants, customers, or vendors. Transportation lanes are used to define which products can be shipped between locations and which means of transport can be used for the given transportation lane. The products and the available means of transport are assigned directly to the transportation lane within the system responsible for transportation. In EWM, the transportation lanes are relevant for the determination of the valid routes and are used during the route determination.

To maintain the transportation lanes (as seen in figure 5.11) from the SAP Easy Access menu, follow the EXTENDED WAREHOUSE MANAGEMENT • MASTER DATA • SHIPPING AND RECEIVING • ROUTE DETERMINATION • TRANSPORTATION LANE menu path, or use Transaction code /SAPAPO/SCC_TL1.

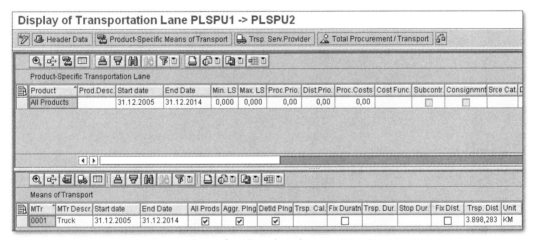

Figure 5.11 A Transportation Lane, Relevant for All Products between Two Given Locations Transferred via Truck

5.3.4 Transportation Zones

When a route or route leg is created, a corresponding transportation zone is created for the route or route leg. The transportation zone can be used to group locations together and is used to reduce master data entry by transferring properties of the transportation zone to its locations. Transportation zones are assigned types, which can include postal code zones, direct zones, region zones, and mixed zones. The type specifies how locations are determined to be relevant for the transportation zone. For instance, a postal code zone specifies relevance using ranges of postal codes, direct zones use direct specification of individual locations, and region zones use country and regions. For region zones, if you want specify that all regions of a country are relevant, simply specify the country on the ZONE-REGION tab. Transportation zones that have criteria entered for multiple zones are known as mixed zones.

> **Note**
>
> Once you have entered selection criteria for a transportation zone on multiple tabs, it is defined henceforth as a mixed zone, and this setting cannot be undone, so use caution when entering relevant specification criteria.

The transportation zone transaction can be used to determine which locations are linked by the transportation zone and can also be used to determine which routes are utilizing the route leg by selecting the appropriate tab on the bottom pane (as shown in Figure 5.12).

To maintain the transportation zones from the SAP EWM Easy Access menu, follow the EXTENDED WAREHOUSE MANAGEMENT • MASTER DATA • SHIPPING AND RECEIVING • ROUTE DETERMINATION • MAINTAIN ZONES FOR ROUTES menu path, or use Transaction code /SCTM/ZONE.

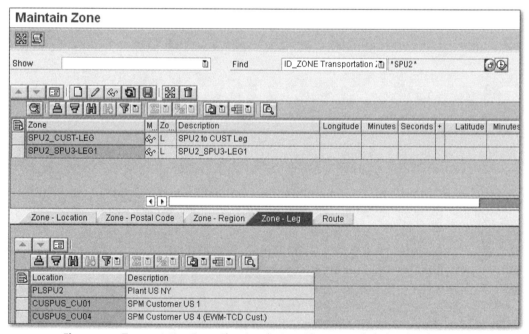

Figure 5.12 Transportation Zone, Showing the Legs That Are Included within the Transportation Zones.

5.3.5   Transportation Routes

Transportation routes are used to describe the characteristics of transportation between two locations along a particular route using a particular mode of transportation. The information in EWM should therefore reflect the characteristics of the physical route used to transport goods. The transportation routes are read during route determination to determine the most relevant route for transporting the goods from one location to another, and the resultant route is then used to determine other characteristics of the ODOs, such as the latest ship date and goods issue date allowed in order for the goods to arrive at the destination location according to the requested time. To maintain the transportation routes in the SAP EWM Easy Access menu, follow the EXTENDED WAREHOUSE MANAGEMENT • MASTER DATA • SHIPPING AND RECEIVING • ROUTE DETERMINATION • MAINTAIN ROUTE menu path, or use Transaction code /SCTM/ROUTE. Figure 5.13 shows the header of the route.

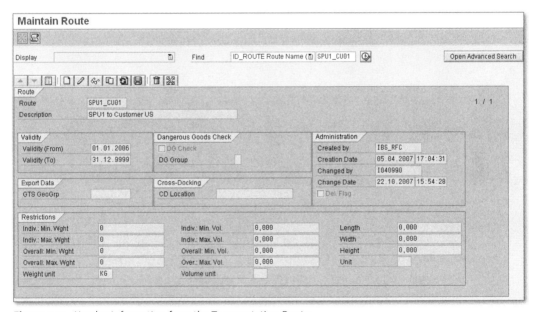

Figure 5.13   Header Information from the Transportation Route

In the header of the transportation route, you can also add information related to the validity dates, global trade relevance, dangerous good relevance, cross-docking locations (for cross-docking route, which we will discuss further in Chapter 17,

Cross-Docking), and restrictions on weight, volume, and dimensions. This information is also used in route determination to determine whether the route is relevant for the goods being shipped.

For each route, you also assign the following characteristics via the tabs at the bottom of the transactions (as seen in Figure 5.14):

▶ LEGS, including source and destination location (via the respective SCUs) and means of transport

▶ CD ROUTES, which are used to assign the inbound and outbound routes for a cross-docking route

▶ REQUEST TYPES, which indicate the request type of ODOs relevant to the route

▶ LEAD TIMES, which specify lead times necessary for particular request types

▶ SHIPPING CONDITIONS, which reflect the allowed shipping conditions of ODOs relevant to the route

▶ TRANSP. GROUPS, which reflect the allowed transportations groups of ODOs relevant To the route

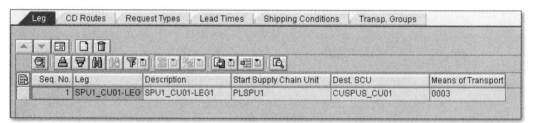

Figure 5.14 Legs and Other Conditions Assigned to the Transportation Route

We will discuss transportation routes and route determination further in Chapter 10, when we discuss outbound processing, and in Chapter 9, when we discuss inbound processing, as transportation routes are relevant in both the inbound and outbound direction. In addition, routes are used in determining relevance for loading handling units (HUs) onto transportation units (TUs) assigned to particular routes and in other shipping and transportation activities.

5.3.6 Carriers as Business Partners

In ERP, carriers are created as vendors with special characteristics. Likewise, when the carrier information is distributed to EWM, it is stored in EWM as a BP. To access the BP transaction from the SAP EWM Easy Access menu, follow the EXTENDED WAREHOUSE MANAGEMENT • MASTER DATA • MAINTAIN BUSINESS PARTNER menu path, or use Transaction code BP.

The carrier will include BP role CRM010 (Carrier). The carrier's standard carrier alpha code (SCAC) is typically stored on the IDENTIFICATION tab of the BP as ID Type BUP006 (Standard Carrier Alpha Code), in addition to the R/3 Vendor Number, which is stored in ID Type CRM004 (R/3 Vendor Number).

5.3.7 Carrier Profiles

Additional data related to the carrier that is only relevant to EWM is stored in the carrier profile (as seen in Figure 5.15), including:

▶ communication data: The communication data includes mailing address, telephone number, fax number, and email address.

▶ administrative data: Administrative data includes data related to the creation and change of the carrier profile data in EWM.

▶ geographical information and means of transport: The geographical information relevant to the carrier profile includes the leg and means of transport assigned for the profile. These are used in the route determination to determine the relevant carrier profiles for the route. Note that the means of transport can belong to a hierarchy, and the route determination will take into account leg zones and means of transport, which are equivalent to or superior to the means of transport assigned to the leg.

▶ freight code sets: Freight codes are used for communication with freight forwarders and other service providers, and freight code sets are used to group individual freight codes. Assigning freight code sets to the carrier profile defines the allowed frieght code sets (and therefore freight codes) that are relevant to the carrier. To create allowed entries for freight code sets and freight codes in the EWM IMG, follow the menu path EXTENDED WAREHOUSE MANAGEMENT • GOODS ISSUE PROCESS • TRANSPORTATION MANAGEMENT • BASICS • DEFINE FREIGHT CODE SETS, FREIGHT CODES, AND DETERMINATION.

► transportation group and product freight sets: The TRANSP. GROUPS and PROD-FREIGHT SET assigned to the carrier profile indicate the allowed values and are compared to the assigned values (TRANSP. GROUPS and PRODFREIGHT SET) for the materials of the ODO during the route determination.

► transportation costs: Transportation costs can be calculated based on the carrier profile using the sum of the fixed transportation costs and the dimension costs, which is a variable cost dependent on factors such as distance traveled, duration traveled, quantity (e.g., number of pallets), or number of stops (however, the system does not currently provide a standard method for determining this for the purposes of freight calculation).

To maintain the carrier profiles for route determination in the SAP EWM Easy Access menu, follow the EXTENDED WAREHOUSE MANAGEMENT • MASTER DATA • SHIPPING AND RECEIVING • ROUTE DETERMINATION • CARRIER PROFILE FOR ROUTING GUIDE menu path, or use Transaction code /SCTM/TSPP.

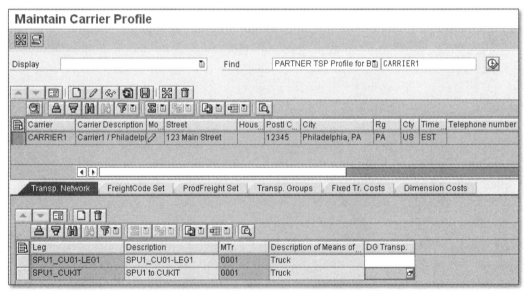

Figure 5.15 Carrier Profile Data

5.4 Packaging Materials

Packaging materials are any materials used to collect or contain materials for storage within the warehouse or for transportation. Auxiliary packaging materials are materials generally added during the preparation for transportation for protecting the materials in transit (e.g., to cushion or to prevent shifting or other movement in transit; also commonly called "dunnage").

Packaging materials in EWM are created as products with specific characteristics. The leading system for the creation of the product, like other products in EWM, is ERP, where the packaging material is created as a material of an appropriate material type (similar to the standard packaging material type, VERP). In Chapter 4, Product Master Data, we specifically discussed the fields that are relevant to packaging materials in the EWM product master, including specific values or requirements for:

▶ Units of measure capacity information

▶ Packaging material type

▶ Allowed package weight

▶ Allowed package volume

▶ Closed

▶ Packaging material type

▶ HU type

▶ Form name

▶ PDF form name

▶ Capacity information and the TARE WEIGHT VARIABLE and CLOSED PACKAGING indicators in the PACKAGING DATA view, CAPACITIES section (as seen in Figure 5.16).

Packaging materials are assigned at a work center (e.g., deconsolidation, packaging, value-added services (VAS), etc.) when creating an HU and the relevant items are assigned to the HU to indicate which items are contained within the physical package. *Auxiliary packaging materials* can be added to the HU at one of the work centers and can be consumed during the VAS execution. We will discuss packaging materials and auxiliary packaging materials further in Chapter 19, Value-Added Services.

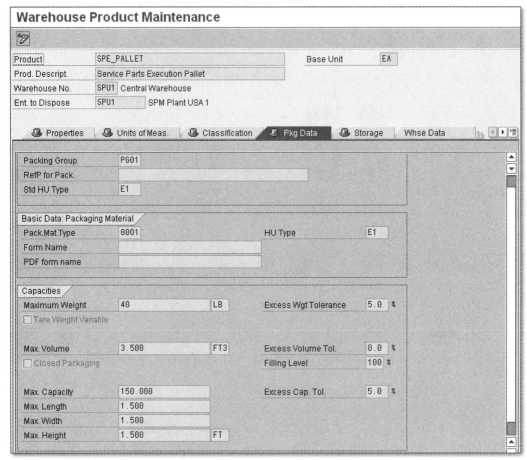

Figure 5.16 Capacity Information for Packaging Materials on the Packaging Data View of the EWM Product Master

5.5 Packaging Specifications

Pack specs are master data that is designed to provide information to the system to determine how products should be grouped together in an HU and to provide information to users on which activities should be performed while grouping those products together. Pack specs leverage the Integrated Product and Process Engineering (iPPE) engine, which is used by Supplier Network Collaboration (SNC) and APO, and EWM.

5.5.1 Structure of the Packaging Specification

In Figure 5.17, you can see the structure of the pack spec, which is comprised of the HEADER, CONTENTS, LEVELS, ELEMENT GROUPS, ELEMENTS, STEPS, and PACKAGING MATERIALS. These components are described further in the following section.

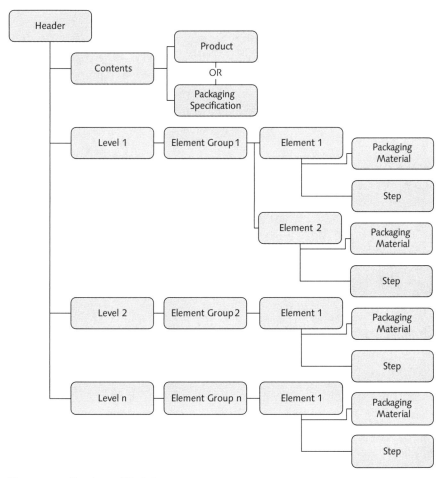

Figure 5.17 Structure of Pack Specs

As seen in Figure 5.17, the pack spec is comprised of the following components:

▶ HEADER: The header contains the name (or number) of the pack spec, change number, status, description, pack spec group, level set assignment, other administrative information (e.g., creation user name, date, time, source system, etc.), rounding data, and links to documents assigned via the document management system (if relevant). While viewing the header record, you can also access the determination conditions, which are used to determine the relevance of the pack spec.

▶ CONTENTS: The contents can specify either a product or products or another pack spec.

▶ LEVELS: The levels represent the different groupings within the pack spec (not to be confused with the physical layers of products within the package, which can be defined within the level). Within the level, you can define the relevant level type, the target quantity, minimum quantity, and quantity per layer. For each level, the target quantity that you assign indicates the number of units of the previous packaging level that is targeted to be packed into the current level.

Example

If a product is generally packaged 24 units per pallet when it is stored in the warehouse and 6 units per layer (with 4 layers), then you can create a pack spec and assign the contents quantity as 1 each, the target quantity for the layer as 24 units, and the number of layers quantity as 6. The total quantity will be automatically calculated as 24 eaches, and the number of layers will be automatically calculated as 4 layers (note that these quantities match the screenshot shown in Figure 5.18).

To configure the level types, which may be optionally assigned to the pack spec level, in the EWM IMG, follow the menu path SCM BASIS • PACK • PACKAGING SPECIFICATION • MAINTAIN STRUCTURE OF PACKAGING SPECIFICATION • DEFINE LEVEL TYPE.

▶ ELEMENT GROUPS: Element groups can be used to simplify the process of creating new pack specs by letting you assign an existing element group to the pack spec rather than creating the elements individually. When you assign elements to a pack spec manually, the system automatically creates an element group and assigns the element group a number. This element group can, in turn, be assigned to subsequent pack specs by choosing the ASSIGN ELEMENT GROUP option in the pack spec maintenanace, and the corresponding elements will be automatically assigned.

You should assign a number range for the element groups in the EWM IMG by following the menu path SCM BASIS • PACK • PACKAGING SPECIFICATION • DEFINE GENERAL PACKAGING SPECIFICATION PARAMETERS.

▶ ELEMENTS: For each level, you assign the elements that are relevant to the level, including the packaging material and the work step. As described previously, when you define a new set of elements manually, a element group will be auto matically created, which you can then use when defining elements in further pack specs. To assign an element group (and the corresponding elements) to a pack spec, simply enter the element group number and the corresponding elements will be assigned. If you enter the elements manually, you can assign the element type; the packaging material and quantity for the packaging material; HU relevance; work step assignment; weight, volume, and dimension data; quantity classification assignment (used for rounding the pack spec); HU type; operative unit of measure; external step; rounding parameters; and long text for the element (which can be printed on packaging labels at the packaging work centers).

To create the allowed entries for the element type and specify the relevant parameters for the element type in the EWM IMG, follow the menu path SCM BASIS • PACK • PACKAGING SPECIFICATION • MAINTAIN STRUCTURE OF PACKAGING SPECIFICATION • DEFINE ELEMENT TYPE.

To create work steps that can be assigned to the element, from the SAP Easy Access menu, follow the EXTENDED WAREHOUSE MANAGEMENT • MASTER DATA • PACKAGING SPECIFICATION • MAINTAIN PACKAGING WORK STEP menu path or use Transaction code /SCWM/PSWORKSTEP. When creating the work step, you can specify the work step description and long text that will act as the work instructions for the worker performing the packaging operation. If there are additional back-up documents, they can be linked to the work step via the document management system.

5.5.2 Creating a Packaging Specification

To create a pack spec or maintain existing pack specs, from the SAP Easy Access menu, follow the EXTENDED WAREHOUSE MANAGEMENT • MASTER DATA • PACKAGING SPECIFICATION • MAINTAIN PACKAGING SPECIFICATION menu path, or use Transaction code /SCWM/PACKSPEC. From the main screen, select an existing pack spec, or select the option to create a new one, and you should see the maintenance screen, as shown in Figure 5.18. The pack spec shown in the figure is a simple example for packaging materials at goods receipt for putaway. Note that the quantity to be packed per HU is assigned to the level and not to the contents (as described in the example from the previous section).

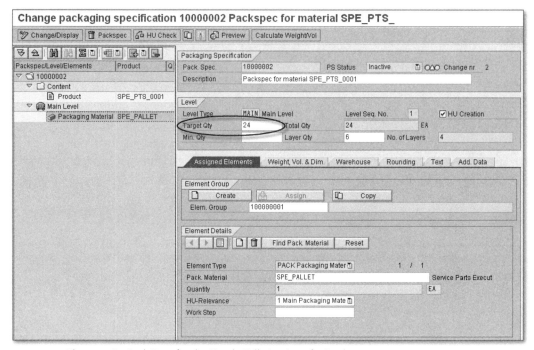

Figure 5.18 Pack Spec for the Simple Palletization of a Product

To create pack specs, you need to create and assign number ranges and define the general pack spec parameters. To create the number ranges from the EWM IMG, follow the menu path SCM BASIS • PACK • PACKAGING SPECIFICATION • DEFINE NUMBER RANGE FOR PACKAGING SPECIFICATION. To define the general parameters from the EWM IMG, follow the menu path SCM BASIS • PACK • PACKAGING SPECIFICATION • DEFINE GENERAL PACKAGING SPECIFICATION PARAMETERS.

In addition, you can choose to create pack spec groups. These groups allow you to assign parameters and predefined structures for specific purposes. For example, for processes such as kitting or VASs, or simply to change the default parameters for the default pack spec group. To define the pack spec groups from the EWM IMG, follow the menu path SCM BASIS • PACK • PACKAGING SPECIFICATION • DEFINE PACKAGING SPECIFICATION GROUP.

5.5.3 Activating the Packaging Specification

Once you have created the pack spec, you must activate it before it can be used by the system. To activate the pack spec, from within the pack spec maintenance, select the ACTIVATE button. Alternatively, from the PACKAGING SPECIFICATION OVER-VIEW screen, you can choose the pack spec and select the Activate button (or the Activate Packspec option from the dropdown menu selection next to the Activate button).

> **Note**
>
> Depending on the changes that you have made while maintaining the specification, the system may not allow you to successfully activate the pack spec from within the detailed maintenance view. If this occurs, simply save the pack spec on the maintenance view and return to the PACKAGING SPECIFICATION OVERVIEW screen and activate it from there.

Once you have activated the pack spec, you will not be able to change the active version. If you want to make a change, you will need to create a new version of the pack spec and then activate the new version. To create a new version, from the PACKAGING SPECIFICATION OVERVIEW screen, select the relevant pack spec, and click the CREATE 2ND VERSION button. Once you have created the new version, you can maintain the new version while the old version remains active. Once you have updated the new version, you can activate the new version and then the old version will no longer be active — only one version can be active at a time. If you don't want the system to use any other pack spec while you are updating the pack spec, you can deactivate the original version by selecting the DEACTIVATE PACKSPEC option from the dropdown menu next to the ACTIVATE button, however, even if you deactivate the original, you must still create a new version to edit it.

5.5.4 Distributing Packaging Specifications

It's possible to maintain the pack specs in one system and distribute them to the other systems, allowing you to reduce the amount of manual maintenance and ensure that the pack specs are consistent for different warehouses and even for different applications. For example, you can choose to maintain the pack specs in a single warehouse and then distribute the pack specs to the other warehouses, or you can even choose to maintain the pack specs in a centralized system, such as the Service Parts Planning (SPP) system (because the pack specs are created in the SCM basis layer), and distribute the pack specs from there to the warehouses. Because the pack specs are not created specifically for a single warehouse, if you have multiple warehouses using the same client within a single instance, you do not have to distribute the pack specs from one warehouse to another within the same client in the same instance. However, if you maintain multiple clients or multiple instances, you will need to either maintain the pack specs separately or set up the pack spec distribution to synchronize the pack specs.

To set up the distribution, you must first connect the systems via remote function call (RFC) connections. Your technical support team will generally be responsible for setting up the basic technical connection between the systems. Once the RFC connections are established, you will need to specify the RFC connections for distribution in the source system for pack spec creation. To specify the relevant RFC connections, from the EWM IMG, follow the menu path; SCM BASIS • PACK • PACKAGING SPECIFICATION • DEFINE RFC CONNECTION FOR PACKAGING SPECIFICATION DISTRIBUTION. Once you set up the RFC destination for the pack specs, there is nothing more to set up to trigger the distribution (i.e., there are no batch programs to schedule). However, there is a program available (/SCWM/PS_DISTRIBUTION) if you need to redistribute the pack specs manually.

5.5.5 Determination of Packaging Specifications

Pack specs are used during various processes within EWM, including:

- Automatic packing in the inbound delivery (ID)
- Packaging material determination during warehouse order (WO) creation
- Packaging material determination in the outbound delivery (OD)
- Packaging material determination during deconsolidation
- Packaging material determination when packing in the packing station, including for outbound deliveries, posting changes, and stock transfers
- Slotting
- Internal warehouse processes (for palletization data or determination of the operative unit of measure)

The determination of the pack spec uses the familiar condition technique. To configure the condition tables, access sequences, condition types, and determination procedures, from the EWM IMG, access the nodes beneath the menu path SCM BASIS • MASTER DATA LAYER • PACK • PACKAGING SPECIFICATION • DETERMINATION OF PACKAGING SPECIFICATIONS.

To create the condition records for the determination of the pack specs, you must go to the pack spec maintenance (as described in the previous sections), select a pack spec and enter the change mode for the pack spec. If the pack spec is already active, you must create a new version, update the new version, and activate the new version, as also described in the previous sections. Within the pack spec maintenance, at the header level, select the DETERMINATION tab. On the DETERMINATION tab, in the CONDITION type column, enter a new condition type, specify the condition key combination from the resulting pop-up box, if relevant, and enter the relevant determination characteristics for the condition key. Once you have created the condition records, the records will be read during the relevant processes according to the configuration for the pack spec determination, and the packaging will be performed accordingly.

5.6   Production Master Data

To support the process of picking and staging materials for production supply (which will be described further in Chapter 11, Production Supply), there are several master data elements that must be created in both ERP and EWM. In ERP, the traditional master data to support production supply must be created, including:

▶ Materials

▶ Bills of materials (BoM)

▶ Routings

▶ Work centers

▶ Production supply areas (PSAs)

In addition, in EWM, the following data must be created and linked to the ERP master data:

▶ Materials

▶ PSAs

▶ Bins within the PSAs

We already discussed creation and updating of the materials in Chapter 4. In the following sections, we will discuss the possible methods for creating the PSAs and bins in EWM.

5.6.1   Creating Production Supply Areas

PSAs represent the area where the product is stored until it is immediately needed in the production area. Often, the PSA is a physical area in the warehouse that is also near the production area. The various methods for working with PSAs will be covered in Chapter 11. The PSAs can be created by integrating the data from ERP (as the PSAs are also created in ERP), or they can be created directly in EWM. Both options are described in the following sections.

Integrating Production Supply Areas from ERP

PSAs can be created in EWM by integrating the supply area data from ERP. This method actually uses a "pull" mechanism using a report generated in the EWM system. To execute the report from the SAP EWM Easy Access Menu, follow the EXTENDED WAREHOUSE MANAGEMENT • INTERFACES • ERP INTEGRATION • REPLICATE PRODUCTION SUPPLY AREA (PSA) menu path, or use Transaction code /SCWM/ PSA_REPLICATE. The selection screen for the transaction will look like the screen shown in Figure 5.19.

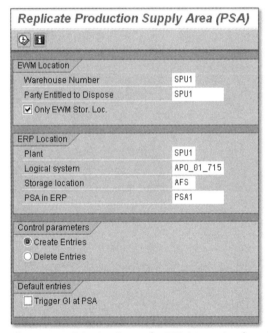

Figure 5.19　Selection Screen for PSA Integration from ERP to EWM

The TRIGGER GI AT PSA checkbox controls whether the indicator by the same name is set in the PSA in EWM. If so, the goods issue for the stock will be triggered as soon as it is delivered to the PSA. Note that if this option is selected, you must also define the settings for automatic goods issue in the EWM IMG

(which can be accessed in the EWM IMG via the menu path EXTENDED WARE-
HOUSE MANAGEMENT • GOODS ISSUE PROCESS • OUTBOUND DELIVERY • PRODUCTION
SUPPLY • MAINTAIN SETTINGS FOR AUT. GOODS ISSUE FOR PRODUCTION SUPPLY).

Creating Production Supply Areas Directly in EWM

You can also create the PSAs directly in EWM from the Easy Access menu by following the EXTENDED WAREHOUSE MANAGEMENT • MASTER DATA • PRODUCTION
SUPPLY AREA (PSA) • DEFINE PSA menu path, or using Transaction code /SCWM/
PSA. On the warehouse selection screen (if required), enter the warehouse number. On the table maintenance screen, select the NEW ENTRIES button, and then
enter the data about the PSA, as shown in Figure 5.20.

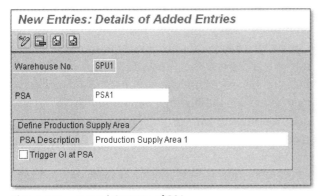

Figure 5.20 Manual Creation of PSA

Note that the TRIGGER GI AT PSA checkbox is the same as the one described in the
previous section.

5.6.2 Mapping Production Supply Areas

Once the PSAs are created in EWM, they must be mapped to the PSAs in ERP to
ensure the proper transactional integration for the production supply process. To
map the PSAs, from the EWM Easy Access menu, follow the EXTENDED WARE-
HOUSE MANAGEMENT • INTERFACES • ERP INTEGRATION • MAP PRODUCTION SUPPLY
AREA (PSA) menu path, or use Transaction code /SCWM/PSAMAP. On the table
maintenance view, click the NEW ENTRIES button to map a new PSA, as seen in
Figure 5.21 (note that the PSA must already exist in EWM and can be created using
the steps described previously).

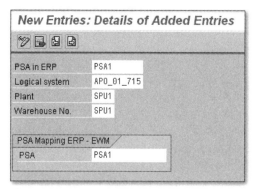

Figure 5.21 Mapping EWM PSAs to ERP PSAs

5.6.3 Assigning Bins for Production Supply

The staging area for transferring products from the warehouse to production supply is represented by a bin in the warehouse, and this bin is assigned according to the PSA, product or product group, and entitled to dispose. To maintain the assigned bin, you can use one of two transactions that allow entry of the assignment in slightly different ways. To enter the PSA, product or product group, and entitled to dispose for each entry individually, from the EWM Easy Access menu, follow the EXTENDED WAREHOUSE MANAGEMENT • MASTER DATA • PRODUCTION SUPPLY AREA (PSA) • ASSIGN BIN TO PSA/PRODUCT/ENTITLED IN WAREHOUSE NUMBER menu path, or use Transaction code /SCWM/PSASTAGE. If the warehouse is not already specified as a default, you need to specify the warehouse and then the table (as seen in Figure 5.22) will be displayed.

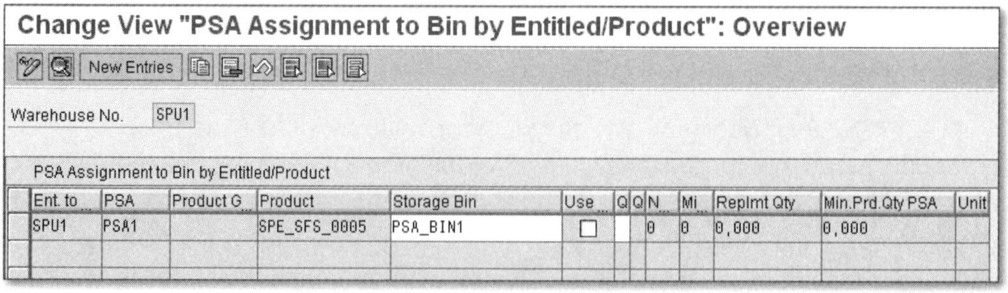

Change View "PSA Assignment to Bin by Entitled/Product": Overview

Warehouse No.   SPU1

PSA Assignment to Bin by Entitled/Product

Ent. to	PSA	Product G	Product	Storage Bin	Use	Q	Q	N	Mi	Replmt Qty	Min.Prd.Qty PSA	Unit
SPU1	PSA1		SPE_SFS_0005	PSA_BIN1	☐			0	0	0,000	0,000	

Figure 5.22 Assignment of a Bin within the PSA According to Party Entitled and Product (or Product Group)

To create a new entry in the table, select the NEW ENTRIES button. The recorded entry will look like the screen shown in Figure 5.23.

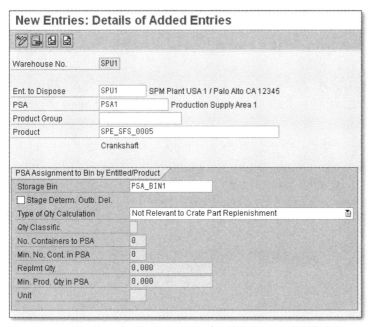

Figure 5.23 Creation of a Bin Assignment for PSAs By Party Entitled

When creating the bin assignment for a PSA by party entitled and product, there are some options within the assignment that control the execution of the production supply and determination of the storage bin or staging area. First, you can choose to assign either a product or a group of products to the PSA by specifying either the product number of the product group (but not both). This way, you can reduce the amount of master data creation necessary by grouping the assignments by product group. Second, you can choose to either enter a storage bin statically, or you can have the system determine the bin according to the staging area determination. To do so, select the STAGE DETERM. OUTB. DEL. checkbox (just below the STORAGE BIN assignment in Figure 5.23). If you select this option, you must maintain the staging area determination for the outbound process from the SAP Easy Access menu by following the EXTENDED WAREHOUSE MANAGEMENT • SETTINGS • SHIPPING AND RECEIVING • STAGING AREA AND DOOR DETERMINATION (OUTBOUND) menu path, or using Transaction code /SCWM/STADET_OUT. You should either maintain this setting or the static bin assignment (but not both). Third, you can specify the method of quantity calculation in the case of crate part replenishment (which will be further explained in Chapter 11). The options for the crate part replenishment quantity method include:

- ▶ Not Relevant to Crate Part Replenishment: No additional entries are required if this option is selected.

- ▶ Crate Part Replenishment Based on Packaging Specification: The QTY CLASSIFIC., NO. CONTAINERS TO PSA, and MIN. NO. CONT. IN PSA fields will open for entry if this option is selected (after you press Enter) and the relevant data should be entered to these fields.

- ▶ Quantity-based Crate Part Replenishment: The REPLMT QTY, MIN. PROD. QTY IN PSA, and UNIT fields will become available for entry if this option is selected (after you press Enter) and the relevant data should be entered into these fields.

You can also maintain the PSA bin assignment in the SAP Easy Access menu by following the EXTENDED WAREHOUSE MANAGEMENT • MASTER DATA • PRODUCTION SUPPLY AREA (PSA) • ASSIGN BIN TO PRODUCT/ENTITLED IN PSA menu path, or using Transaction code /SCWM/PSASTAGE2. This transaction provides another view to the same data (from table /SCWM/TPSASTAGE), but lets you refine the view to only show the entries for a single party entitled and PSA (as seen in Figure 5.24). These data (warehouse, party entitled, and PSA) must be entered on the initial selection screen to see the table as shown in Figure 5.24.

> **Note**
>
> Creating a new entry or drilling down into the entry for display or change uses the same view as seen in Figure 5.23.

Change View "PSA Assignment to Bin by Entitled/Product": Overview
New Entries
Warehouse No. SPU1
Ent. to Dispose SPU1
PSA PSA1 Production Supply Area 1
PSA Assignment to Bin by Entitled/Product
Product Group
Product
Storage Bin
Stag. Det.
Q
Q
N
Mi
Replmt Qty
Min.Prd.Qty PSA
Unit
SPE_SFS_0005
PSA_BIN1
0
0
0,000
0,000

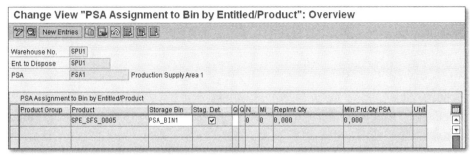

Figure 5.24 A Different View of the PSA Bin Assignment, Using Transaction /SCWM/PSASTAGE2, which Shows the Same Data Using a Different Refinement Method

5.7 Resources

A resource is an entity within the warehouse that performs work by executing warehouse tasks. A resource can be a worker or a piece of equipment, such as a manually operated forklift, automatic guided vehicle, conveyor, or other type of automated equipment that moves products from one place in the warehouse to another.

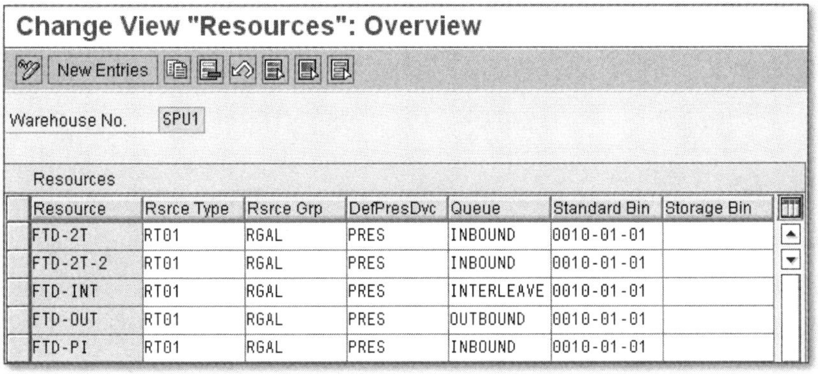

Change View "Resources": Overview
New Entries
Warehouse No. SPU1
Resources
Resource
Rsrce Type
Rsrce Grp
DefPresDvc
Queue
Standard Bin
Storage Bin
FTD-2T RT01 RGAL PRES INBOUND 0010-01-01
FTD-2T-2 RT01 RGAL PRES INBOUND 0010-01-01
FTD-INT RT01 RGAL PRES INTERLEAVE 0010-01-01
FTD-OUT RT01 RGAL PRES OUTBOUND 0010-01-01
FTD-PI RT01 RGAL PRES INBOUND 0010-01-01

Figure 5.25 Maintenance of Resources and Their Associated Attributes

The resources are created in a simple table that allows assignment of a resource name and the associated resources type, resource group, presentation device, queue, and standard bin (or start bin). You can also see in the table (as seen in Figure 5.25) the current storage bin of the resource. These fields and their use are described in the following sections. To access the resource maintenance from the SAP Easy Access Menu, follow the EXTENDED WAREHOUSE MANAGEMENT • MASTER

DATA • RESOURCE MANAGEMENT • MAINTAIN RESOURCE menu path, or use Transaction code /SCWM/RSRC.

5.7.1 Resource Types

A resource type is a grouping of resources that have similar attributes. Each resource is assigned a resource type, and the resource type of the resource is used to determine which types of bins the resource can access and which HU types the resource can transport. Resource types are considered configuration and are therefore transportable to destination systems. To access the resource types (as seen in Figure 5.26) via the SAP EWM IMG, follow the menu path EXTENDED WAREHOUSE MANAGEMENT • CROSS-PROCESS SETTINGS • RESOURCE MANAGEMENT • DEFINE RESOURCE TYPES.

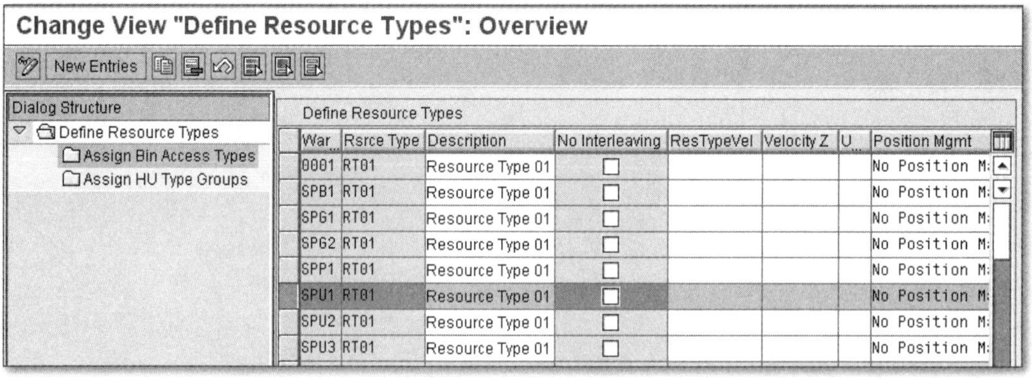

Change View "Define Resource Types": Overview

New Entries

Dialog Structure
- Define Resource Types
  - Assign Bin Access Types
  - Assign HU Type Groups

Define Resource Types

War	Rsrce Type	Description	No Interleaving	ResTypeVel	Velocity Z	U	Position Mgmt	
0001	RT01	Resource Type 01	☐				No Position M:	
SPB1	RT01	Resource Type 01	☐				No Position M:	
SPG1	RT01	Resource Type 01	☐				No Position M:	
SPG2	RT01	Resource Type 01	☐				No Position M:	
SPP1	RT01	Resource Type 01	☐				No Position M:	
SPU1	RT01	Resource Type 01	☐				No Position M:	
SPU2	RT01	Resource Type 01	☐				No Position M:	
SPU3	RT01	Resource Type 01	☐				No Position M:	

Figure 5.26 Creation of Resource Types and Assignment of Allowed Bin Access Types and HU Type Groups

Note

The NO INTERLEAVING checkbox, velocity assignment (horizontal and vertical), and position management assignment are also assigned to the resource type, not to individual resources. Therefore, resources that may have other similar characteristics, but which travel at different speeds, or which have different settings for interleaving or position management will require creation of an additional resource type.

Once you have created the resource types, you can assign the allowed bin type and HU types by selecting the resource type and the double-clicking on ASSIGN BIN ACCESS TYPES or ASSIGN HU TYPE GROUPS from the tree structure on the left side (also shown in Figure 5.26). Here, you simply enter the allowed bin types. Priorities used in WO selection are assigned as master data.

5.7.2 Execution Priorities

After creating the resource type and assigning the allowed bin access types and HU types, you can assign the execution priorities for the bin access types and HU types. To assign the priorities from the Easy Access menu, follow the Extended Warehouse Management • Master Data • Resource Management • Maintain Execution Priorities menu path, or use Transaction code /SCWM/EXECPR. After entering the warehouse number in the work area selection screen, on the Define Resource Types folder, select the resource type and then double-click on either the Maintain Bin Access Type Priority Value (as selected in Figure 5.27) or Maintain HU Type Grp Priority Value folder to access the priority assignment for the bin access type and HU type group.

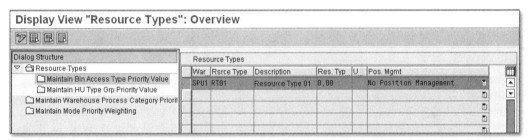

Figure 5.27 Selection of the Resource Type for Assignment of the Allowed Bin Access Types and HU Types

> **Note**
>
> In change mode, the New Entries button may appear, however, you cannot create new entries for the resource types, the allowed bin access types, or HU type groups. These must be added in the configuration element described previously.

Once you select, for instance, the folder for assignment for access of the bin access type, you can specify the priority for each allowed bin access type (as shown in Figure 5.28). The priority is used in determining the WOs, which are selected by warehouse operators during the WO selection. The priorities are assigned a two-character numeric value, with larger numbers increasing the probability that the WO with the assigned bin access type will be selected. The reason for assigning the priorities is related to the WO selection. The bin access type, HU type, and warehouse process category are used together in a formula for calculating the total priority of the WO, which also takes into account the weightings of the individual factors according to the assigned mode. We will discuss WO prioritization further in Chapter 22, Data Capture and Resource Optimization.

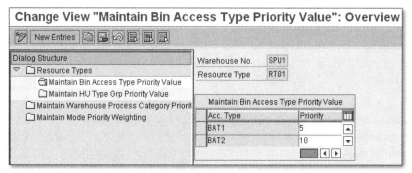

Figure 5.28 Assigning Bin Access Types and Priorities to the Resource Type

Assignment of the prioritization for the HU types per resource type works in a similar way and looks similar to the priority assignment for the bin access types.

5.7.3 Resource Groups

Resource groups are groups of resources for managing the queue assignments for the resources (see the sections later in this chapter for more information on queues and queue sequences). To maintain the resource groups from the Easy Access menu, follow the EXTENDED WAREHOUSE MANAGEMENT • MASTER DATA • RESOURCE MANAGEMENT • MAINTAIN RESOURCE GROUP menu path, or use Transaction code /SCWM/RGRP. The view is a simple table entry with just the resource group name (four characters) and the description (which, like most descriptions, is language specific), as seen in Figure 5.29.

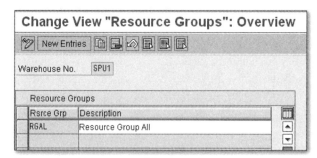

Figure 5.29 Maintenance of Resource Groups

5.7.4 Queues

Queues are used to manage the assignment of WOs in the warehouse. Each WO is assigned to a queue, and each warehouse resource group is assigned to a sequence of queues, from which WOs may be assigned to the resource that is part of the resource group.

> **Note**
>
> WOs can also be manually assigned to resources, but this is much less efficient than the automated methods available and is generally only used on an exception basis.

To define the queues WOs can be assigned to in the EWM IMG, follow the menu path EXTENDED WAREHOUSE MANAGEMENT • CROSS-PROCESS SETTINGS • RESOURCE MANAGEMENT • DEFINE QUEUES. From here, the following activities can be selected.

Define Queues

With this view (seen in Figure 5.30), you can define the queues and provide the description, and assign the queue type, operating environment, and specify whether semisystem guided processing is allowed for the WOs assigned to the queue (semisystem guided processing is described further in Chapter 9). The operating environment assignment specifies whether the queue is to be used in an RF environment, non-RF environment, or for a material flow system (MFS).

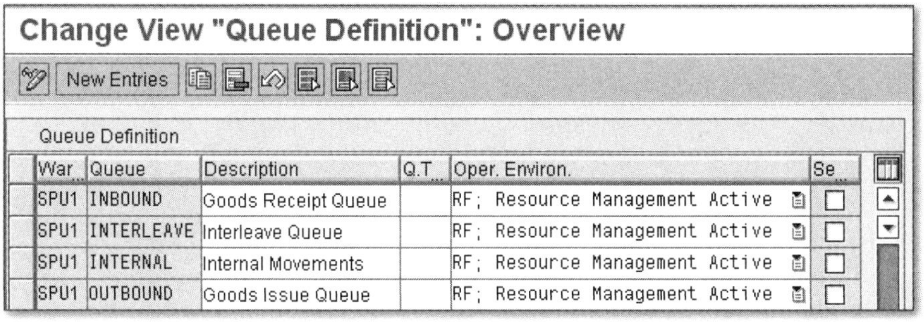

Change View "Queue Definition": Overview

New Entries

Queue Definition

War	Queue	Description	Q.T	Oper. Environ.	Se
SPU1	INBOUND	Goods Receipt Queue		RF; Resource Management Active	☐
SPU1	INTERLEAVE	Interleave Queue		RF; Resource Management Active	☐
SPU1	INTERNAL	Internal Movements		RF; Resource Management Active	☐
SPU1	OUTBOUND	Goods Issue Queue		RF; Resource Management Active	☐

Figure 5.30 Definition of the Queues

Define Queue Determination Criteria

Once the queues are defined, you can next define the criteria to determine which queue should be assigned to the WOs. Note that the queue determination is first performed for the warehouse task (therefore the data used in the determination comes from the warehouse task), then when the WOs are created from the warehouse tasks, one of the split criteria is the queue assignment — warehouse tasks assigned to different queues will be assigned to different WOs, therefore the queue assignment only needs to be stored on the database at the WO level.

The parameters used in the queue determination (as seen in Figure 5.31) include:

- Source activity area
- Destination activity area
- Bin access type
- Warehouse process type
- Activity

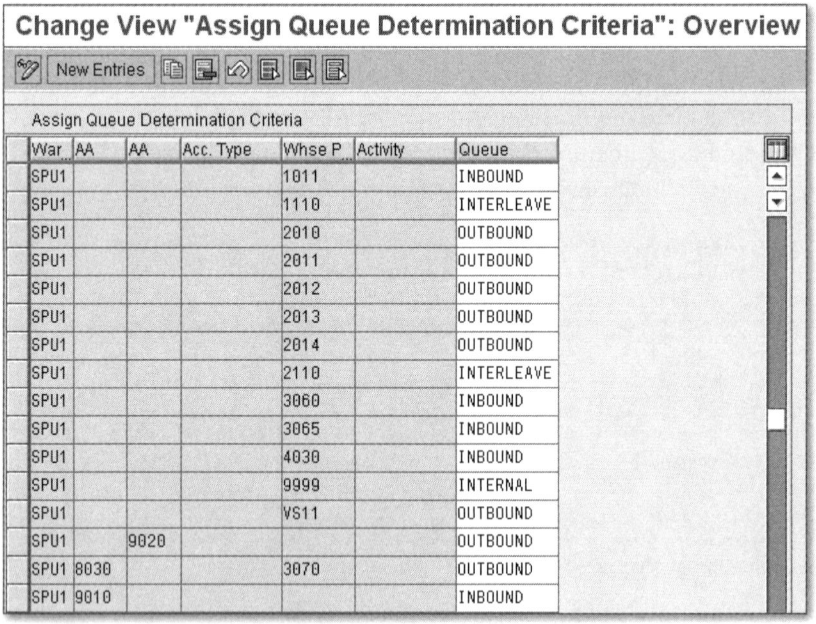

Change View "Assign Queue Determination Criteria": Overview

New Entries

Assign Queue Determination Criteria

War	AA	AA	Acc. Type	Whse P.	Activity	Queue
SPU1				1011		INBOUND
SPU1				1110		INTERLEAVE
SPU1				2010		OUTBOUND
SPU1				2011		OUTBOUND
SPU1				2012		OUTBOUND
SPU1				2013		OUTBOUND
SPU1				2014		OUTBOUND
SPU1				2110		INTERLEAVE
SPU1				3060		INBOUND
SPU1				3065		INBOUND
SPU1				4030		INBOUND
SPU1				9999		INTERNAL
SPU1				VS11		OUTBOUND
SPU1		9020				OUTBOUND
SPU1	8030			3070		OUTBOUND
SPU1	9010					INBOUND

Figure 5.31 Queue Determination Criteria

Define Queue Access Sequences

To increase the efficiency of the queue determination in the case of large queue determination tables and to establish prioritization of which determination table record is selected if multiple entries may be applicable for a warehouse task, a queue determination access sequence is established (as seen in Figure 5.32), which specifies which field combinations should be checked and in what sequence. For example, you can specify that the system should check the combination of activity areas and warehouse process type, and if an entry is not found based on that criterion, then the system should check for an entry based solely on the process type.

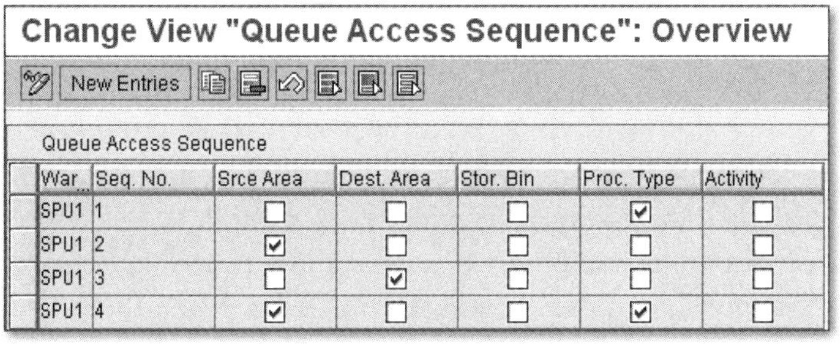

Change View "Queue Access Sequence": Overview						

New Entries

Queue Access Sequence

War	Seq. No.	Srce Area	Dest. Area	Stor. Bin	Proc. Type	Activity
SPU1	1	☐	☐	☐	☑	☐
SPU1	2	☑	☐	☐	☐	☐
SPU1	3	☐	☑	☐	☐	☐
SPU1	4	☑	☐	☐	☑	☐

Figure 5.32 Specification of the Queue Access Sequence, the Sequence in which the Fields Are to Be Checked for the Queue Determination

5.7.5 Queue Sequences

Queue sequences are assigned to resource groups and are used in the determination of the WOs to be assigned to a resource during WO selection when using system-guided processing (system guided processing is described further in Chapter 22). WOs assigned to the first queue in the sequence would have priority over WOs assigned to the second queue in the sequence, and so on. To create the queue sequence (as seen in Figure 5.33) from the EWM Easy Access menu, follow the EXTENDED WAREHOUSE MANAGEMENT • MASTER DATA • RESOURCE MANAGEMENT • MAINTAIN QUEUE SEQUENCE FOR RESOURCE GROUP menu path, or use Transaction /SCWM/QSEQ.

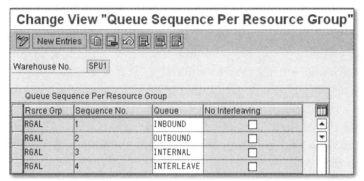

Figure 5.33 Assignment of the Queue Sequence to the Resource Group

5.7.6 Queue Types

Queue types are groups of queues that are used during task interleaving to identify which queues should be the next ones considered for selection of the next WO for execution. Queue types are assigned to the queues during the queue maintenance as described previously (and seen in Figure 5.30). To create the queue types (as seen in Figure 5.34) in the EWM IMG, follow the menu path EXTENDED WAREHOUSE MANAGEMENT • CROSS-PROCESS SETTINGS • RESOURCE MANAGEMENT • DEFINE QUEUE TYPES.

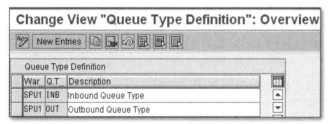

Figure 5.34 Queue Type Definition

> **Note**
>
> Queue types are optional. If you will not implement interleaving, it's not necessary to set up queue types or queue type sequences.

5.7.7 Queue Type Sequences

The queue type sequence specified the order the queue types are to be selected during the interleaving process (interleaving is discussed further in Chapter 22).

Figure 5.35 shows the assignment of the queue types according to the warehouse and resource group and with a specified sequence number.

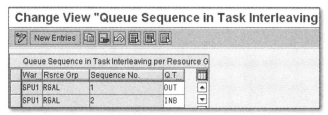

Figure 5.35 Specifying the Queue Sequence for Task Interleaving, by Warehouse and Resource Group

5.7.8 Standard Bin (or "Start Bin")

The Standard Bin (or Start Bin) assigned to the resource (as shown previously in Figure 5.25) is the bin that is used by LM to determine the current location of the resource if the last storage bin is not currently known, for example, when the user has just logged on to the resource and is ready to begin the workday. The bin is used to determine the distance from the start bin of the next WO and can be used both in the WO selection and in the determination of the travel time and distance for the execution of the warehouse task.

5.7.9 Tracking the Current Storage Bin

The STORAGE BIN field (shown previously in Figure 5.25) is used to store the last bin that the resource visited and is used to track the resources current location. There are known limitations with this method of tracking the current locations of resources, but short of implementing GPS and tracking the resources actual physical location in the warehouse, this method is relatively accurate and is a generally accepted practice in the industry.

> **Note**
>
> Even though the STORAGE BIN field is open for entry during the resource maintenance, you should not maintain it there, because it will be overwritten during the WO execution by the resource. You should instead only maintain the Standard Bin as described previously, as the STANDARD BIN is never overwritten by the system, and it is used to determine the current location of the resource if the STORAGE BIN field is not filled.

5.7.10 Maintaining Users

Maintaining the users lets you specify default parameters for logon to the RF Transaction (/SCWM/RFUI) based on system user ID (as seen in Figure 5.36). Note that it is not necessary to specify the default entries for a user, but it will limit the data entry required on the RF menu start screen if the entries are defaulted. Also, if you want to specify a personalization profile for the user (other than the standard **) to personalize their experience with the RF screens, you need to create an entry in the user table (personalization will be described in more detail in Chapter 22). In addition, if you want the user to be logged directly into the RF menu without having to enter the additional information on the RF start screen, you can create an entry for the user and specify that the AUTO LOGON is active by selecting the checkbox for the user. This requires that all of the necessary data is entered in the default data for the user. If, for example, the warehouse or resource is not specified in the default entry, the RF start screen will still appear for the user.

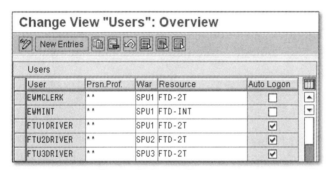

Figure 5.36 Specifying Default Data for RF Device Users

5.7.11 Resource Execution Constraints (RECs)

RECs are used to alleviate congestion in areas of the warehouse that may be prone to congestion or negatively affected by it by specifying the number of resources that can operate in the area at a given time. As seen in Figure 5.37, when the system is determining which WOs are relevant for a resource during the system-guided WO determination, it takes into account which WOs are already assigned to other resources and in which areas they are working. If there are too many resources already working in a given area (as determined by reading the table shown in Figure 5.38), the system will not assign the WOs for that area to the resource, but will instead assign the resource to the highest priority WO in another area of the warehouse.

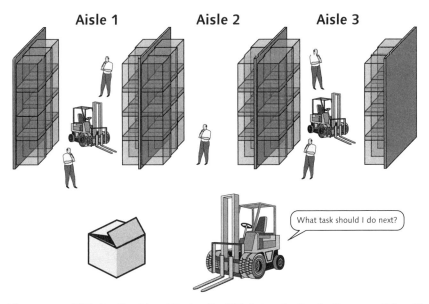

Figure 5.37 RECs Are Considered During the WO Determination for Resources When They Use System-Guided Determination

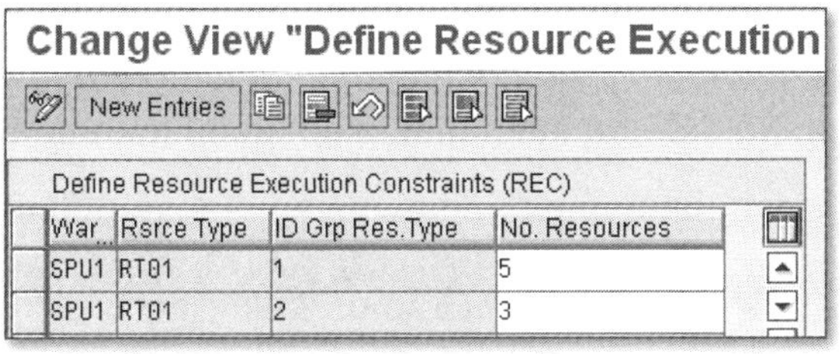

Change View "Define Resource Execution

	War	Rsrce Type	ID Grp Res.Type	No. Resources	
	SPU1	RT01	1	5	
	SPU1	RT01	2	3	

New Entries

Define Resource Execution Constraints (REC)

Figure 5.38 Defining the RECs, Including Creation of the ID to Group Resource Types and Assignment of the Number of Resources Allowed in the Work Area

> **Note**
>
> If the data to support the travel time and distance calculation are available in the system, the system actually determines the time that it will take for the resource to arrive at the source bin of the warehouse task, and if it determines that one of the resources currently working in the area will complete its work and depart the area before the new resource arrives, then it will determine that the WO is still potentially relevant for the resource.

To enable the RECs, you must group the resources, group the storage bins, and set how many resources of each type can enter the area of grouped storage bins. To do so, you must define the RECs, assign the RECs to REC storage groups, assign the REC storage groups to bins, and activate the REC check for the REC storage groups.

Defining RECs

To allow the system to determine the number of resources that should be allowed within an area, you must first group the resources. These groups are indicated by the identification number called ID GRP RES. TYPE. In the table (see Figure 5.38), you assign for each warehouse and resource type, one or more of these identification numbers, and for each one, you specify the number of resources that can be used for this group. Later you will assign these IDs to REC storage groups and the storage groups to bins, thus completing the assignment. To create the ID GRP RES. TYPE from the EWM IMG, follow the menu path EXTENDED WAREHOUSE MANAGEMENT • CROSS-PROCESS SETTINGS • RESOURCE MANAGEMENT • CONTROL DATA • DEFINE RESOURCE EXECUTION CONSTRAINTS (REC).

Assigning RECs to REC Storage Groups

Once you have created the ID to group resource types, you can then create the REC staging groups and assign the ID to group resource types to the REC staging group (as seen in Figure 5.39). From the EWM IMG, follow the menu path EXTENDED WAREHOUSE MANAGEMENT • CROSS-PROCESS SETTINGS • RESOURCE MANAGEMENT • CONTROL DATA • ASSIGN RESOURCE EXECUTION CONSTRAINTS TO REC STORAGE GROUP.

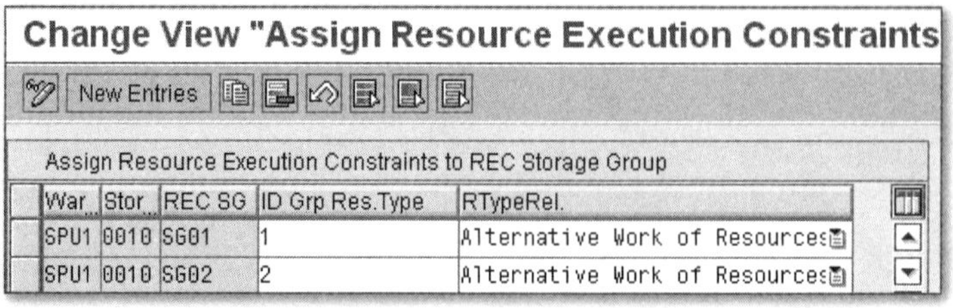

Figure 5.39 Assigning the RECs According to the Combination of the REC Staging Group and the ID to Group Resource Types

Assigning REC Storage Groups to Warehouse Storage Bins

Once you have created the REC staging groups, you can assign the REC staging groups to the warehouse bins. In Chapter 3, The Warehouse Structure, we described in detail the warehouse storage bin maintenance. To access the storage bin change transaction, from the EWM Easy Access menu, follow the Extended Warehouse Management • Master Data • Storage Bin • Change Storage Bin menu path, or use Transaction code /SCWM/LS02. If you have already created the storage bins and you want to assign the REC storage groups to several bins at once, you can use the mass change transaction for bins (described in detail in Chapter 3). To access the mass change for storage bins, from the EWM Easy Access menu, follow the Extended Warehouse Management • Master Data • Storage Bin • Mass Change to Storage Bins menu path, or use Transaction code /SCWM/LS11.

Activating REC for REC Storage Groups

Once you have created the REC storage groups, you can activate the checks for the REC (as seen in Figure 5.40) from the EWM IMG by following the Extended Warehouse Management • Master Data • Resource Management • Activate Resource Execution Control for Storage Groups menu path, or using Transaction code /SCWM/REC_ACTIVATE. Simply activate the checkbox for each REC storage group you would like the system to check.

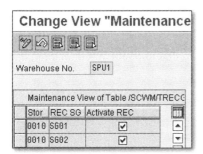

Figure 5.40 Activating the REC per REC Storage Group

5.7.12 Processors

Processors are a particular type of BP that represents an employee in LM. Processors are used to store data related to the employees' labor activities, such as labor factors, warehouse relevance, performance expectations per activity, and default parameters for the employee. To create a processor, from the EWM Easy Access menu, follow the Extended Warehouse Management • Master Data • Resource Management • Processor • Create Processor menu path, or use Transaction code /SCMB/PRR1.

> **Note**
>
> The BP roles must be properly created and assigned in order for the processor creation transaction to start. If the transaction will not start, see the following section on creating and assigning BP role categories and BP roles.

When creating the processor, you should assign the relevant data on the ADDRESS and ADDRESS OVERVIEW tabs, then on the IDENTIFICATION tab (as seen in Figure 5.41), you should assign the users SAP EWM User Name. This allows the employee to be correlated by their logon ID to the processor. In addition, you can assign a personnel number, which should correlate to the employee's personnel number from the SAP HCM system (formerly known as SAP HR), and an external BP number, which correlates to the employee's employee or BP number from other external systems.

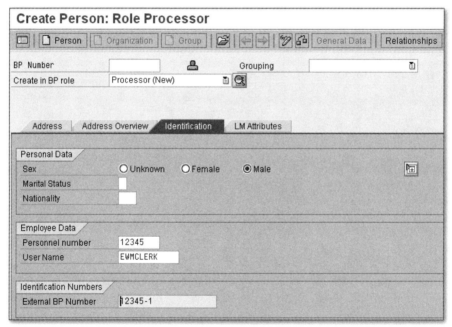

Figure 5.41 Assigning the User Name and Employee Number on the Identification Tab of the Processor BP

In addition to assigning the user's identification information, you can also assign certain parameters used by the calculations within LM (which will be discussed further in Chapter 21). For example (as seen in figure 5.42), you can assign:

▶ the user's labor factor (which can be used by a Business Add-in (BAdI) to calculate cost information)

▶ the relevant business system for HR (for exchanging labor data with HR for performance management)

▶ the warehouse relevance

▶ for each warehouse, certain default parameters

▶ for each warehouse activity, performance levels (if any are less than 100%), which can be used in planning reports to take into account that a user may not be working at 100% of the engineered standard for any reason (e.g., the employee is training on the process, the employee is injured or otherwise restricted, or the employee generally does not meet the standard for some other reason)

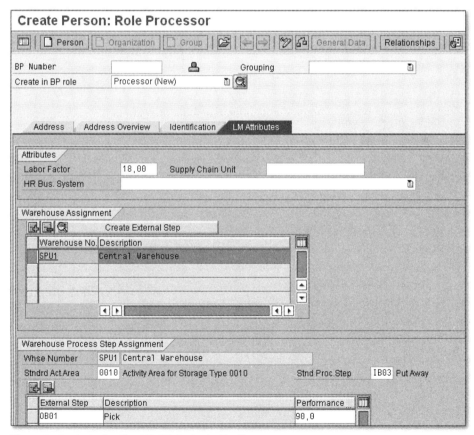

Figure 5.42 Assigning the LM Attributes to the Processor

Note

To enter the step assignment details and external steps, after entering the warehouse number in the WAREHOUSE ASSIGNMENT section, you must select the warehouse and then click the CREATE EXTERNAL STEP button.

Once you save the processor, a BP number will be assigned (assuming that you are using internal number assignment for the BP role).

Creating BP Roles for Processors

Before you create a processor, you must ensure that the BP role PROCESSOR already exists in your system. Until the BP role exists, you will not be able to start the processor creation transaction. If the BP role does not exist, you must create the BP ROLE CATEGORY and BP ROLE. To create the BR ROLE CATEGORY and BP ROLE, from the EWM IMG, follow the menu path CROSS-APPLICATION COMPONENTS • SAP BUSINESS PARTNER • BUSINESS PARTNER • BASIC SETTINGS • BUSINESS PARTNER ROLES • DEFINE BP ROLES. First, you should create the BP ROLE CATEGORY, similar to the one in Figure 5.43.

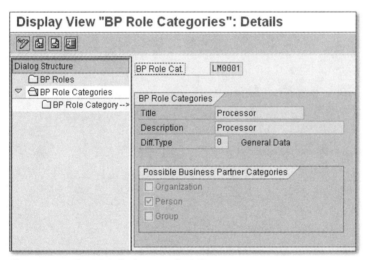

Figure 5.43   The BP Role Category for LM

Once you have created the BP ROLE CATEGORY, you can create the BP ROLE, similar to the one in Figure 5.44.

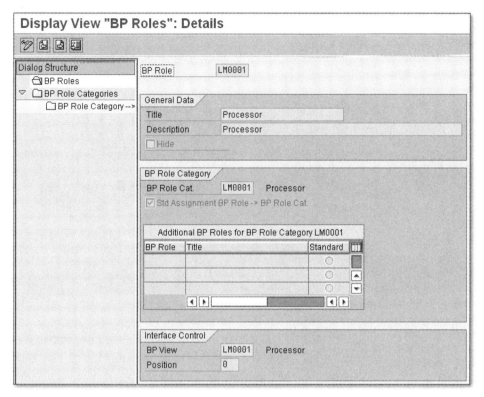

Figure 5.44 The BP Role for Processors, to Be Used in LM

Defining the Application Transaction for Processor Maintenance

Once you have created the BUSINESS PARTNER ROLE CATEGORY and BP ROLE, you must ensure that the BP ROLE is assigned to the processor maintenance transactions. To assign the BP ROLE CATEGORY and BP ROLE to the transactions, from the EWM IMG, follow the menu path CROSS-APPLICATION COMPONENTS • SAP BUSINESS PARTNER • BUSINESS PARTNER • BASIC SETTINGS • BUSINESS PARTNER ROLES • DEFINE APPLICATION TRANSACTIONS. In the table, for the create, change, and display Transactions (/SCMB/PRR1, /SCMB/PRR2, and /SCMB/PRR3, respectively), ensure that either the BP ROLE CATEGORY or the BP ROLE for processors is assigned, as in Figure 5.45.

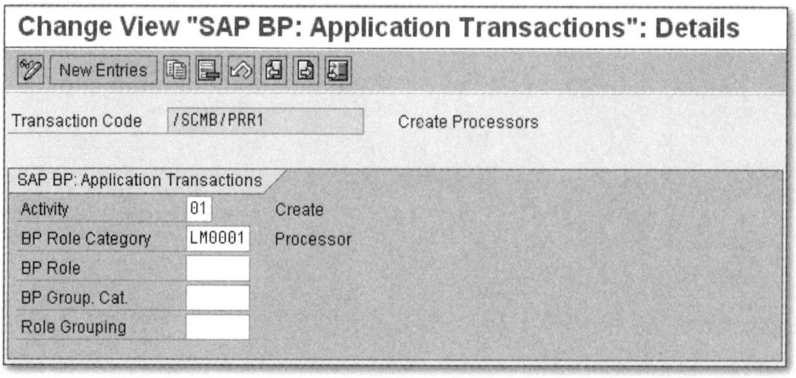

Figure 5.45 Assignment of BP Role Category (or BP Role) to the Application Transaction for Creating Processors

5.7.13 Presentation Devices

In order for the warehouse workers to use RF-enabled mobile data entry devices (which will be discussed further in Chapter 22), the device types must be set up in the EWM system as Presentation Devices. To create the Presentation Devices from the EWM Easy Access menu, follow the EXTENDED WAREHOUSE MANAGEMENT • MASTER DATA • MAINTAIN PRESENTATION DEVICES menu path, or use Transaction code /SCWM/PRDVC. On the table, you can specify the following criteria for the presentation device:

▶ Presentation device name and description

▶ Display profile: This profile is used by the RF screen manager to determine which customized presentation screens should be used, if any. If the default screens are used, assign the value **.

▶ Presentation device type: This one-character field is used for informational purposes and does not drive any standard functionality in the system.

▶ Data entry type: This one-character field is used for informational purposes and does not drive any standard functionality in the system.

▶ Function key quantity: The function key quantity refers to the profile that defines, based on the number of function keys available, how the function key layout should be defined on the RF screen. For more details on the function key quantity profile, see Chapter 22.

- Clear all: If this indicator is set, the CLEAR ALL function will be enabled, which allows the user to click the CLEAR button on the screen a second time to clear all of the input fields on the screen.

- Shortcut: If this indicator is set, the SHORTCUT field is displayed on the screen if it is enabled for the relevant function code profile, which allows the user to enter the shortcut key in the shortcut field instead of pressing the relevant function key.

- Default: If this indicator is set, the corresponding presentation device is set as the default presentation device for users when they log on to the mobile data entry Transaction (/SCWM/RFUI). Only one entry should be set as the default.

- Sound for information, error, warning, and success messages: If sound is enabled for the RF device, you can use this field to send a signal for the sound to be generated when a message is generated to the user.

- Resource: You can assign a resource to the presentation device for informational purposes, however, this does not preclude other resources from using the presentation device, nor does it preclude the assigned resource from using other presentation devices.

Once the presentation device is created, you can specify the presentation device when you log on to the mobile data entry Transaction (/SCWM/RFUI), using either the SAP GUI, SAP Console, or Mobile Internet transaction server (ITS).

> **Note**
>
> Unlike the resource numbers for equipment (which can't be used by multiple warehouse operators at the same time), you don't need to create new presentation devices for every piece of RF-enabled equipment, because they can be reused. Therefore, a practical method for creating presentation devices is to create a presentation device for each type of presentation device (rather than each one individually). If any of the significant parameters change from device to device, you will need to create a new presentation device in EWM, but if this is not the case, you can significantly reduce the amount of data creation and maintenance by simply creating a device for each device type.

5.8   Summary

In this chapter, we described the additional master data used by EWM (aside from the product master data, which was covered in Chapter 4). You should now have a good idea of how to set up your own master data to support your warehouse business processes. In the coming chapters, we will begin to describe the stock management and document concepts that you need to understand before you begin setting up those processes in EWM.

In this chapter, we'll discuss the different types of stock and methods for managing stock using Extended Warehouse Management (EWM). Special care will be taken to distinguish between the features of ERP, which may share the same name as the features of EWM, and how they are integrated with each other.

6   Warehouse Stock Management

A core competence of EWM is the functionality it provides for handling different types of stock. In this chapter, we'll discuss the different methods for managing stock. We'll start with an introduction about what quants are and how they build up the warehouse stock. We'll also explain how EWM manages stock in bins; on resources, such as forklift trucks and picking carts; and on transportation units (TUs).

Afterward, we'll talk about the organizational model of stock ownership: EWM manages stock by assigning a party entitled to dispose, an owner, and a custodian. This is important if you want to manage stock for multiple plants or consignment stock with EWM.

Batch management is fully integrated in EWM. We'll describe how batch management can be used and how documentary batches work. We'll also explain, in detail, how serial numbers can be flexibly handled by EWM. You can set up EWM to only use serial numbers for a delivery item, but in a way where the serial number is a stock attribute with full transparency of where the serial number is at every moment.

We'll also describe how HU management is integrated into warehouse management and give a short introduction on TUs. We'll also explain the concept of stock identification (stock ID). Stock IDs are particularly useful if you manage more than one warehouse with EWM and use stock transfer orders (STOs) from one warehouse to another. Then we'll look at shelf life expiration date (SLED) control and best-before dates.

EWM can store catch weight–managed products. This applies to industries where weights can vary from piece to piece, either due to biological variations or because of weight changes during storage. This variability should not be lost by using fixed conversion factors — EWM is flexible in this respect.

We'll explain how stock with different countries of origin can be tracked. You can use the same product number, and EWM still captures where the product originally came from. Then we will introduce stock determination and valuation in EWM. Finally, we'll describe the handling of special stocks, such as sales order stock and project stock.

6.1 Quants

A *quant* is a stock segment of a specific quantity of a product with the same characteristics in one location.

6.1.1 Definition of a Quant

A quant can only be created and deleted by a warehouse movement, such as a warehouse task (WT) or a posting change. The quantity of a quant can be increased by moving stock of the same product with the same characteristics (i.e., stock type, batch number, owner, party entitled) to the location of the quant. It can be reduced by moving a partial quantity of the quant to another location or by changing one of the other quant attributes via a posting change, for example, from available stock to blocked stock.

When you put a product away into an empty bin, the system generates a quant in this storage bin. When you remove the quantity from storage, the system automatically deletes the quant.

In the quant record, the system manages the data for the products collected together in the quant. This data includes:

▸ Location of the quant (storage bin, HU, resource or TU)
▸ Product and quantity
▸ Stock type
▸ Stock usage
▸ Batch number

6.1.2 Adding To Existing Quants

For some of the quant properties, you can configure how the system should react if a new quant arrives in the same location with different properties than the existing quant. The compared characteristics include the goods receipt date, the SLED, and the certificate number. In Figure 6.1, you can see these configuration elements on the storage type configuration table.

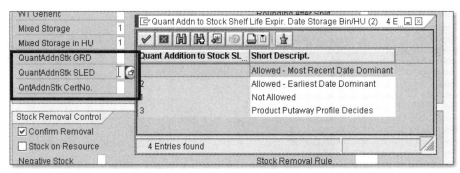

Figure 6.1 Configuration for Storage Type to Allow Addition to Stock for Different Characteristic

6.1.3 Displaying Quants

A quant can be displayed using the EWM monitor from the SAP Easy Access menu, via the EXTENDED WAREHOUSE MANAGEMENT • MONITORING • WAREHOUSE MANAGEMENT MONITOR menu path, or by using Transaction /SCWM/MON. The monitor node to display the quant is: STOCK AND BIN • PHYSICAL STOCK (see Figure 6.2).

Some special attributes of a quant can be changed directly, without creating a WT or a posting change, including the following:

▸ Goods receipt date and time

▸ SLED

▸ Country of origin (COO)

▸ Certificate number

You can change these attributes by selecting the CHANGE ATTRIBUTES dropdown menu from the MORE METHODS button in the PHYSICAL STOCK view in Figure 6.3.

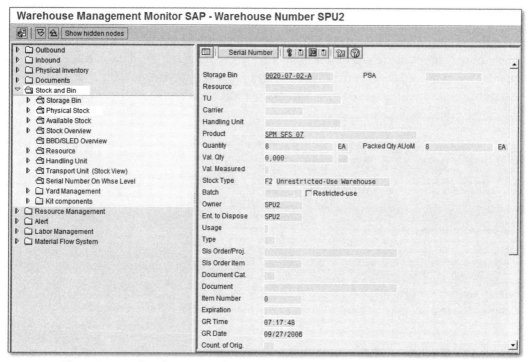

Figure 6.2 Display of a Quant in the EWM Monitor

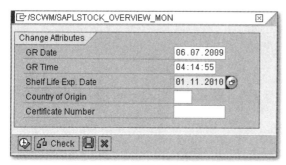

Figure 6.3 Changing the SLED in the Warehouse Monitor

The COUNTRY OF ORIGIN and the SLED can only be changed on the quant if batch management is not used. In the following sections, we'll describe how to manage the COO and SLED in EWM.

6.1.4 Stock Visibility on Storage Bins, Resources, and Transportation Units

In SAP EWM, stock can be placed not only on storage bins, but also on resources (such as forklift trucks, picking carts, etc.) and on TUs. In the following sections, we will describe each of these objects in more detail:

Stock on Storage Bins

Most of the time, EWM will store stock on a storage bin. This includes stock in final storage types (such as rack storage, block storage, and general storage areas), in interim storage types (such as staging areas), and in work centers (such as a packing work center or quality inspection (QI) work center).

Stock on Resources

For some radio frequency (RF) transactions, once an HU is scanned using one of the EWM RF transactions, the stock may be posted onto the resource. Not all RF transactions result in movement of the stock to the resource — it depends on the transaction and on the expected duration of the activity. For example, when a user scans two HUs for distributed putaway, the stock is moved to the resource. Putaway of an HU is a process that typically takes a longer period of time, and it makes sense to have correct stock visibility of the resource during the physical operation. So in this case, as soon as the user scans an HU for putaway, EWM automatically posts the HU on the resource (see Figure 6.4).

Figure 6.4 Stock Placed onto a Resource when Scanning the HU Number in an EWM RF Transaction

Stock is posted onto resources if the resource management is set to ACTIVE for the respective queue in the following Implementation Guide (IMG) path: EXTENDED

WAREHOUSE MANAGEMENT • CROSS-PROCESS SETTINGS • RESOURCE MANAGEMENT • DEFINE QUEUES • DEFINE QUEUES (as seen in Figure 6.5).

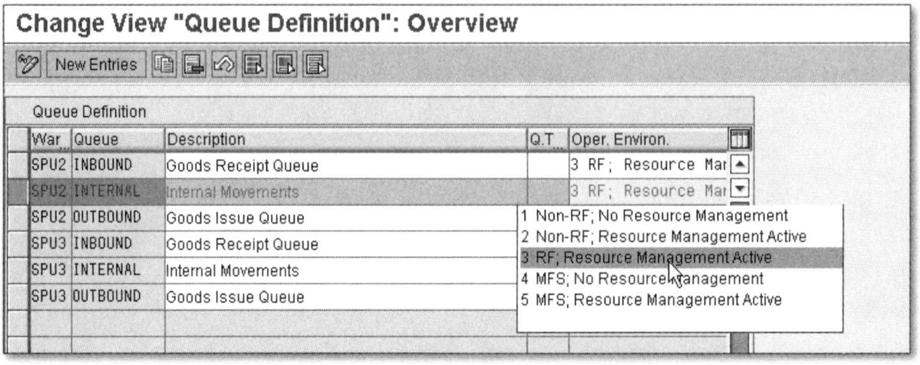

Figure 6.5 Stock Posted onto Resources in EWM if Resource Management is Set to Active

Stock on Transportation Units

For the inbound process in EWM, deliveries and HUs can be assigned to TUs. If the delivery is assigned to a TU, and the goods receipt is posted for the TU, the stock is posted onto the TU instead of onto the storage bin. To enable the posting of the stock to the TU in the EWM IMG, follow the menu path EXTENDED WAREHOUSE MANAGEMENT • CROSS-PROCESS SETTINGS • SHIPPING AND RECEIVING • GENERAL SETTINGS • SET UP CONTROL OF GOODS MOVEMENTS. In Figure 6.6, you can see the configuration table for the assignment of posting of goods movement to the TU.

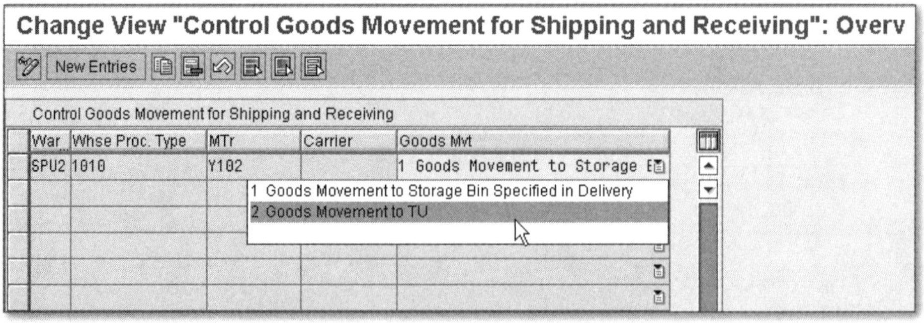

Figure 6.6 Configuration Table for the Assignment of Posting of Goods Movement

For the outbound process in EWM, stock is placed onto a TU if there is an active TU assigned to the outbound delivery and the loading is done via the Loading step of the process-oriented storage control (POSC). The destination of the loading WT is the TU.

Monitoring Of Stock

Stock on all of the three levels (bins, resources, and TUs) can be selected and displayed by the EWM monitor. On the bottom of each of the selection screens for the stock display are three checkboxes to exclude selection for stock on bins, resources, or TUs. For performance reasons, only the EXCLUDE STORAGE BIN checkbox is deselected by default. If you want to see stocks on resources, you have to uncheck the respective box. Figure 6.7 shows how you can select only stock on resources.

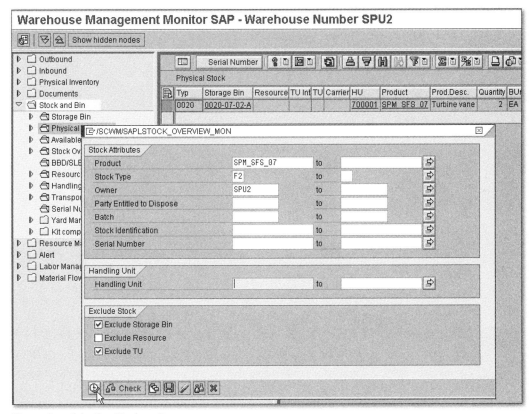

Figure 6.7 Selecting Stock on Resources

6.1.5 Physical Stock and Available Stock, Incoming and Outgoing Stock

EWM distinguishes between physical stock (stock currently physically on the bin) and available stock (stock that is available for creating WTs). You can use the Stock Overview to monitor the incoming and outgoing stock of a bin.

Physical Stock and Available Stock

Physical and available stock can be displayed using the EWM monitor (nodes Stock and Bin • Physical Stock and Stock and Bin • Available Stock). The display of physical stock shows the stock that is physically available at the respective location. Technically speaking, the display of physical stock shows every quant individually.

The available stock shows the stock that can be used to create WTs. Available stock is not reserved yet by other WTs. Outgoing stock in open WTs is not considered available. Incoming stock in open WTs is not yet considered available stock until the WT is confirmed.

In the EWM IMG, you can specify if you want to aggregate the available stock as:

▶ Either on the level of the top HU (highest level HU) or on the storage bin level

▶ Either per batch number or batch neutral

Figure 6.8 shows a storage type that keeps the level of available stock on the top HU level and batch specific. To access the customizing settings in the EWM IMG, follow the menu path Extended Warehouse Management • Master Data • Define Storage Type.

The desired removal process determines which level of available stock you should choose for a storage type. If you want the EWM system to tell the warehouse employee which HU to pick, you set the level of available quantity on HU level. If you want the system to only show the quantity and the warehouse employee selects the best HU manually, then you set the level of available quantity on bin level. This is typically the case in block (or bulk) storage, where pallets or containers of the same product are placed on top and beside each other in one bin. Then, the warehouse employee, and not the system, manually selects the next best pallet.

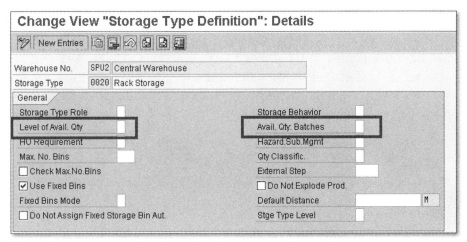

Figure 6.8 Customizing of the Level of Available Stock per Storage Type

The available stock for batches works similarly. If you specify batch-specific available stock, then the system already proposes the batch during WT creation. If you set batch-neutral available stock, then the warehouse employee decides which batch to select during the WT confirmation.

In Figure 6.9, we have created an example in the system for a bulk storage type, where the level of available stock is the storage bin. For this reason, the physical quantity of the three quants in HUs 700000, 700001, and 700002 is aggregated on the storage bin level. If we create a WT from this bin, we don't need to specify an HU yet — we only need to specify the HU during confirmation of the WT.

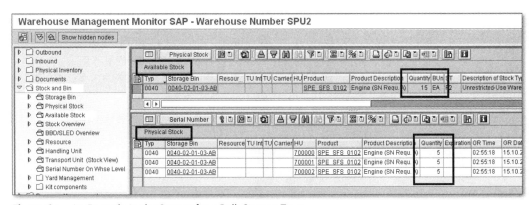

Figure 6.9 An Example in the System for a Bulk Storage Type

Incoming and Outgoing Stock

In the stock overview in the EWM monitor, you can display the incoming and outgoing stock for every bin. This represents the quantities in the open WTs that are scheduled to be added to or removed from the bin. In the EWM monitor, use the node STOCK AND BIN • STOCK OVERVIEW. In Figure 6.10, you can see an example of the incoming and outgoing stock display.

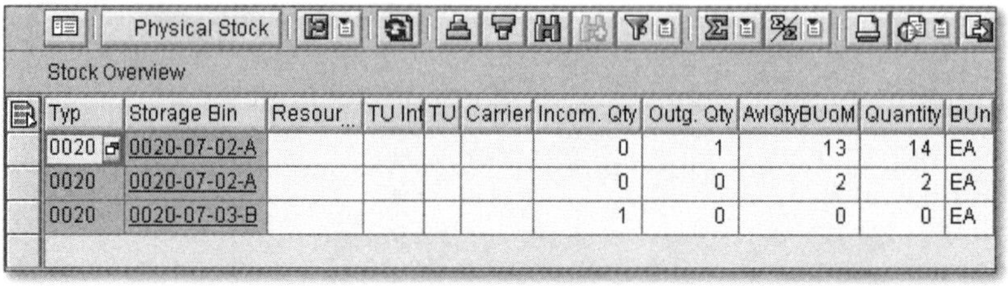

Typ	Storage Bin	Resour	TU Int	TU	Carrier	Incom. Qty	Outg. Qty	AvlQtyBUoM	Quantity	BUn
0020	0020-07-02-A					0	1	13	14	EA
0020	0020-07-02-A					0	0	2	2	EA
0020	0020-07-03-B					1	0	0	0	EA

Figure 6.10 Stock Overview Showing Stock Outgoing from Bin 0020-07-02-A and Incoming to Bin 0020-07-03-B

6.1.6 Logistics Inventory Management Engine (LIME)

To store the warehouse stocks, EWM makes use of the LIME. The LIME is an engine for the near-real-time and highly flexible management of inventory quantities. As an engine, the LIME is an independent set of coding and is designed to be used by multiple applications. One of these applications is SAP EWM, but there are others, including ERP Catch Weight Management.

The LIME consists of an extremely powerful framework of more than 100 database tables, many classes, and function modules. It provides queries to read the current stock and historical stock in an efficient way. The main tables of the LIME are /LIME/NTREE, which contains the stock hierarchy in a tree structure (there is a root node (type "R"), under which there are locations nodes (type "L") and HU nodes (type "H")), and /LIME/NQUAN, which contains the quantities for stock item nodes (type "S"). In addition, there are index tables (starting with /SCWM/ STOCK_, /SCWM/HU_ and /SCWM/LOC_) and shadow tables for stock, HUs, and locations, respectively. It is also possible to interface LIME stocks with SAP Netweaver Business Warehouse (BW).

In addition to the LIME tables, EWM stores additional stock information in two EWM tables. Table /SCWM/QUAN stores the additional data not stored on the LIME tables, including goods receipt date, SLED, and other information. Table

/SCWM/AQUA contains the aggregated available quantities and is used by many parts of EWM that deal with location determination.

6.2 Stock Types

In EWM, you can subdivide different stocks by stock types. They typically give an indication of a product's usability, for example, whether the stock is available, if it is blocked, or if it is in a quality inspection state.

Table 6.1 lists the standard delivered stock types that exist in EWM.

Stock Type	Description
B5	Blocked in Putaway
B6	Blocked Warehouse
C1	Customs — Free in Putaway
C2	Customs — Unrstrctd-Use Ptaway
C3	Customs — Quality in Putaway
C4	Customs — Quality in Warehouse
C5	Customs — Blocked in Putaway
C6	Customs — Blocked in Warehouse
D1	Free for Cross-Docking
F1	Unrestricted-Use in Putaway
F2	Unrestricted-Use Warehouse
Q3	Stock in QI in Putaway
Q4	Stock in QI in Warehouse
S5	Scrapping from Putaway
S6	Scrapping from Warehouse

Table 6.1 Standard Delivered Stock Types in EWM

Most of the stock types in EWM exist as a pair — one type for stock in putaway and one for stock in the warehouse. For example, F1 is the stock type for unrestricted stock in putaway, and F2 is the stock type for unrestricted stock in the warehouse. The reason for these stock type pairs is that a stock type in EWM is linked to a combination of a storage location and a particular stock category in

ERP. In the preceding example, stock type F1 is linked to storage location received on deck (ROD) and stock type F2 to storage location available for sale (AFS), both with the stock category (blank), which represents free stock. The same applies to other stock types as well, as shown in Figure 6.11. The stock types are defined in the EWM IMG via the menu path SCM BASIS • LOGISTICS INVENTORY MANAGEMENT ENGINE (LIME) • BASIC SETTINGS • APPLICATION-SPECIFIC SETTINGS • DETERMINE STOCK TYPE.

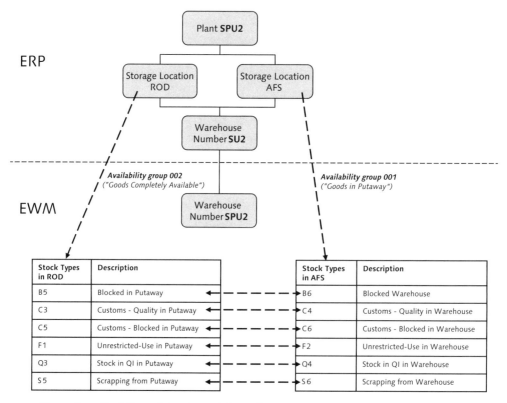

Figure 6.11 Stock Types Belonging to ROD and AFS Storage Locations

Availability Groups

Stock types in EWM and plants/storage locations in ERP are linked via *availability groups*. To access the mapping table in the EWM IMG, follow the EXTENDED WAREHOUSE MANAGEMENT • INTERFACES • ERP INTEGRATION • GOODS MOVEMENTS • MAP STORAGE LOCATIONS FROM ERP SYSTEM TO EWM menu path, as shown in Figure 6.12.

Change View "Customizing Mapping Table for ERP Plant Storage Location"

New Entries

Customizing Mapping Table for ERP Plant Storage Location

Plnt	SLoc	Logical sys	War	AGr	Description	Ent. to Disp	Desc.Person Ent. to Dispose of	
SPU2	AFS	SPM_00_715	SPU2	002	Goods Completely Availab	SPU2	SPM Plant USA 2 / New York NY	▲
SPU2	ROD	SPM_00_715	SPU2	001	Goods in Putaway	SPU2	SPM Plant USA 2 / New York NY	▼

Figure 6.12 Mapping of Availability Groups (AGr) to ERP Storage Locations

The EWM stock type is linked to one of the defined availability groups in the EWM IMG via the EXTENDED WAREHOUSE MANAGEMENT • GOODS RECEIPT PROCESS • CONFIGURE AVAILABILITY GROUP FOR PUTAWAY menu path, as seen in Figure 6.13. In the table, the ninth column (N...) is called the *location-independent stock type*, which is equivalent to the stock category in ERP. The last column (R.) is the stock type role.

Customizing View - EWM Stock Types

War	ST	D	S	S	D	AGr	Description	N	Description	R.	
SPU2	F1	Unre				001	Goods in Putaway	FF	Unrestricted-Use Stock	N Normal Stock	▲
SPU2	F2	Unre				002	Goods Completely Ava	FF	Unrestricted-Use Stock	N Normal Stock	▼
SPU2	Q3	Stoc				001	Goods in Putaway	QQ	Quality Inspection Stock	N Normal Stock	
SPU2	Q4	Stoc				002	Goods Completely Ava	QQ	Quality Inspection Stock	N Normal Stock	
SPU2	S5	Scra				001	Goods in Putaway	BB	Blocked Stock	S Scrapping St	
SPU2	S6	Scra				002	Goods Completely Ava	BB	Blocked Stock	S Scrapping St	
SPU3	B5	Bloc				001	Goods in Putaway	BB	Blocked Stock	N Normal Stock	
SPU3	B6	Bloc				002	Goods Completely Ava	BB	Blocked Stock	N Normal Stock	
SPU3	C1	Cust				001	Goods in Putaway	FF	Unrestricted-Use Stock	C Customs Bloc	
SPU3	C2	Cust				002	Goods Completely Ava	FF	Unrestricted-Use Stock	C Customs Bloc	

Figure 6.13 Mapping of Availability Groups (AGr) to Stock Types (ST)

Available Stock

Available stock doesn't have any restrictions with regards to its use. The stock is also called *unrestricted stock* or *unrestricted use stock*; it is meant to be picked, put away, and moved freely within the warehouse. Standard delivered EWM stock types for available stock are F1 for unrestricted use in putaway (storage location ROD, availability group 001) and F2 for unrestricted use in the warehouse (storage location AFS, availability group 002).

Blocked Stock

When stock is damaged or otherwise unusable, it can be posted into blocked stock. Normal documents searching for available stock can't pick or use blocked stock. Standard delivered EWM stock types for blocked stock are B5 for blocked in putaway (storage location ROD, availability group 001) and B6 for blocked in warehouse (storage location AFS, availability group 002).

Quality Inspection Stock

Stock that is to be inspected (for example, stock being received from external suppliers) is posted into QI stock. A QI document is created for the inbound delivery (ID) item, and upon goods receipt, the stock is posted into QI stock. During the physical QI, for example, in a work center, you can post the quality stock to available stock or to blocked stock for scrapping. You can also post stock into QI stock using an ad hoc QI. Standard delivered EWM stock types for QI stock are Q3 for QI stock in putaway (storage location ROD, availability group 001) and Q4 for QI stock in warehouse (storage location AFS, availability group 002).

Link between Stock Types and Storage Types

You can configure a storage type such that stock is always posted into a specific availability group when a WT is confirmed into this storage type. EWM makes use of this possibility for all final storage types. The stock is posted into the corresponding stock type of availability group 002 (corresponds to ERP storage location AFS) when a putaway WT is confirmed. For example, when stock comes in with stock type B5 (for blocked in putaway), it is posted to stock type B6 (for blocked in warehouse) when it is put away into the final storage type. In Figure 6.14, you can see the fields that control this posting change. The availability group, 002, control the availability group that the stock will be posted to when the product is put away to the storage type. Note that the MANDATORY checkbox is also checked, which indicates that only the assigned availability group is allowed, therefore if any stock from another availability group is moved to the storage type, it is automatically posted to the new availability group via a transfer posting. To access these settings in the EWM IMG, follow the menu path EXTENDED WAREHOUSE MANAGEMENT • MASTER DATA • DEFINE STORAGE TYPE.

Figure 6.14 Goods Movement Control within Storage Type Customizing

Setting Up New Stock Types in Customizing

A common task during an implementation of EWM at a customer is to create new stock types. To create and use a new stock type to map to a new ERP storage location, you should:

1. Create a new storage location in ERP for a plant and assign the plant/storage location to the warehouse number

2. Create a new availability group in EWM — for example, availability group Z02 — in the EWM IMG via the menu path EXTENDED WAREHOUSE MANAGEMENT • GOODS RECEIPT PROCESS • CONFIGURE AVAILABILITY GROUP FOR PUTAWAY • DEFINE AVAILABILITY GROUP.

3. Create a new stock type in the customizing for LIME — for example, Z2 — in the EWM IMG by following the menu path SCM BASIS • LOGISTICS INVENTORY MANAGEMENT ENGINE (LIME) • BASIC SETTINGS • APPLICATION-SPECIFIC SETTINGS • DETERMINE STOCK TYPE. In EWM, you can only use stock types that have been defined in the LIME.

4. Create a new stock type in EWM with the same name as the LIME stock type — Z2 in our example — and assign the availability group (Z02) to it. To configure the EWM stock type in the EWM IMG, follow the menu path EXTENDED WAREHOUSE MANAGEMENT • GOODS RECEIPT PROCESS • CONFIGURE AVAILABILITY GROUP FOR PUTAWAY • CONFIGURE STOCK TYPE.

5. Create an interface mapping entry for your new ERP plant and storage location combination and assign your EWM availability group (Z02) to it, via EWM IMG the menu path EXTENDED WAREHOUSE MANAGEMENT • INTERFACES • ERP INTEGRATION • GOODS MOVEMENTS • MAP STORAGE LOCATIONS FROM ERP SYSTEM TO EWM.

6. Optionally, if you want the stock moved into a certain storage type to be automatically posted into your new stock type, assign the availability group Z02 to it and check the MANDATORY checkbox. To configure the storage type settings in the EWM IMG, follow the menu path EXTENDED WAREHOUSE MANAGEMENT • MASTER DATA • DEFINE STORAGE TYPE.

> **Note**
>
> In the ERP system, the availability of a product is managed in the ERP system by using different *stock categories*. There are stock categories for free (unrestricted), blocked, and quality stock. In EWM, you use *stock types* to distinguish the inventory — an EWM stock type is a combination of the ERP stock category and ERP storage location. For example, standard delivered stock type B5 may refer to blocked stock (stock category "S") in storage location ROD, whereas B6 may refer to blocked stock in storage location AFS.

6.3 Owner

In EWM, the *owner* is a business partner (BP) that represents the party of the organization that *owns* the stock. Assigning an owner to the stock in EWM allows EWM to support vendor consignment. When you order from an external vendor, you can track the stock as *vendor consignment stock* in your plant. The goods then remain the property of the external vendor and do not belong to your valuated stock. You can always change this stock from the consignment stock to your own stock using posting changes. However, you can also pick and ship vendor consignment stock for outbound deliveries. In the case of vendor consignment stocks, the owner is the BP of the external vendor that owns the stock. Otherwise, the owner is the BP of the ERP plant. As this is the most common scenario, the BP of the plant is also called the "default owner."

Next, we'll show you an example of an inbound process for vendor consignment stock in the EWM system. In the ERP system, we created a purchasing document and an inbound deliveryusing special stock indicator K (vendor consignment stock). The inbound deliveryis replicated to EWM. In Figure 6.15, you can see that the delivery item has usage C (CONSIGNMENT STOCK) and a special owner. Note that the OWNER and ENT. TO DISPOSE are different. The OWNER in this case is SPE_VND0, who is a vendor in the ERP system and in EWM a BP with partner role BBP000 and identification type CRM004 maintained. The maintenance of those fields in the EWM BP happens automatically during the core interface (CIF) (as described in detail in Chapter 4, Product Master Data).

When the putaway WTs are created for the ID, the stock usage and the owner are copied to the task. You can determine a specific storage type search sequence for consignment stock based on the stock usage C. Once the WT is confirmed, the stock on the final bin also contains stock usage and owner, as seen in Figure 6.16.

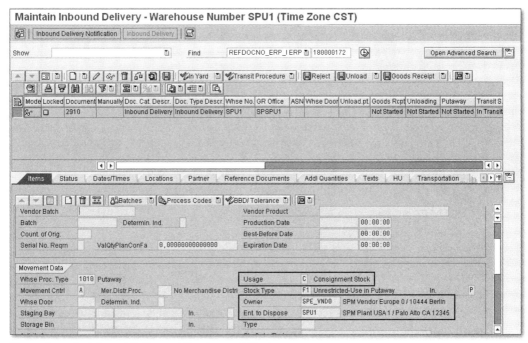

Figure 6.15 An Inbound Delivery of Consignment Stock

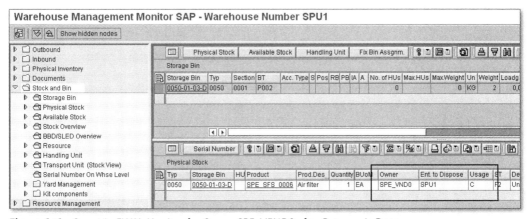

Figure 6.16 Quant in EWM Monitor for Owner SPE_VEND0 after Putaway Is Done

In the ERP system, the goods receipt posting and the transfer posting from storage location ROD to AFS are performed using the special stock indicator K (Consignment (vendor)), as seen in Figure 6.17.

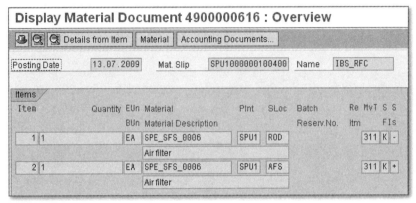

Figure 6.17 Postings in ERP Have Special Stock Indicator K

6.4   Party Entitled to Dispose

In EWM, the *party entitled to dispose* is a BP that represents the party or the organization that is entitled to dispose of the warehouse stock. Usually, this is the BP of the plant in which the stock is placed and in which the ATP check is performed. If you want to manage stocks from several plants in one warehouse, you can use multiple parties entitled to dispose to track the stocks. The entitled party can be entered in all transactions in EWM that deal with inventory management, for example, for selecting stocks in the EWM monitor, as seen in Figure 6.18.

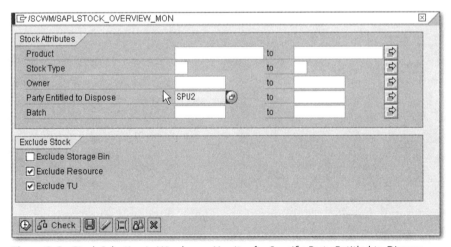

Figure 6.18 Stock Selection in Warehouse Monitor for Specific Party Entitled to Dispose

In delivery processing, the party entitled to dispose comes from the ERP plant that was assigned to the delivery. If you create the delivery in EWM manually, you have to maintain the party entitled to dispose in the default values for the delivery user interface, as seen in Figure 6.19. This rule applies to both inbound deliveriess and ODOs.

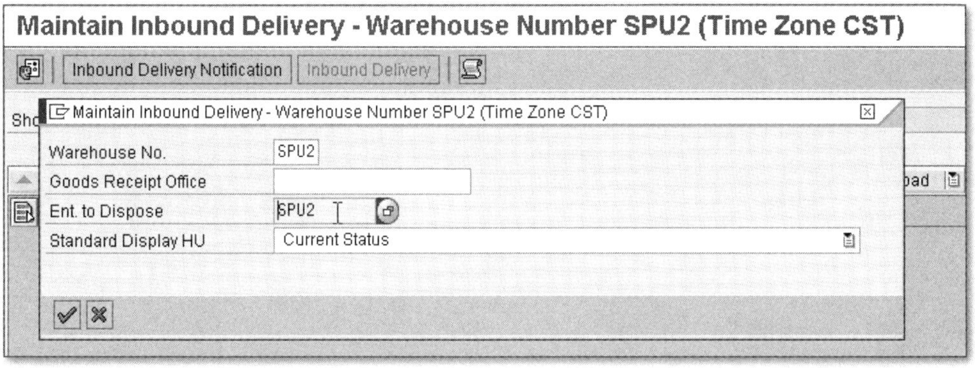

Figure 6.19 Maintaining Default Party Entitled to Dispose for Delivery Processing

The warehouse-specific product master data in Transaction /SCWM/MAT1 maintains different views per entitled party, as seen in Figure 6.20. This makes it possible to, for example, have a different putaway location determination strategy for different entitled parties, or a different storage process with a value-added service (VAS) step for the goods issue process.

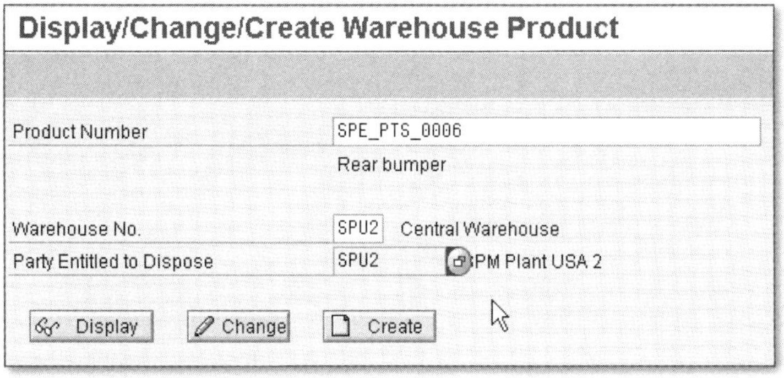

Figure 6.20 Selection of Warehouse Product Master Views Based on Organizational Element Party Entitled to Dispose

6.4.1 Stocks from a Single Plant in One Warehouse

In the simple case, where EWM stores stock for only one plant, there is only one PARTY ENTITLED TO DISPOSE, as seen in the example in Figure 6.21.

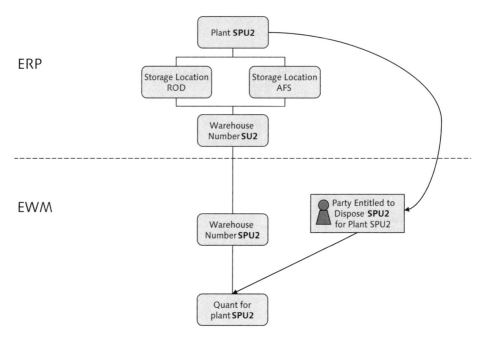

Figure 6.21 Organizational Structure for a Warehouse with a Single Party Entitled to Dispose

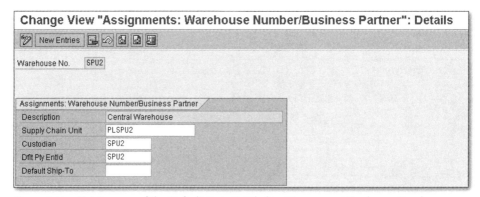

Figure 6.22 Maintenance of the Default Party Entitled to Dispose per Warehouse Number

In this case, it is recommended that you maintain the respective party entitled to dispose in the customizing of the EWM warehouse number in the EWM IMG via the EXTENDED WAREHOUSE MANAGEMENT • MASTER DATA • ASSIGN WAREHOUSE NUMBERS menu path, as seen in Figure 6.22. When you maintain the party entitled there, then you do not need to maintain a party entitled to dispose manually in the transactions where inventory data is entered. The default entitled is also set as a default for maintaining warehouse-specific product master data in Transaction /SCWM/MAT1.

6.4.2 Stocks from Several Plants in One Warehouse

In some industries, especially for logistics service providers, it is common practice to store stocks for more than one plant in the same warehouse number. For example, the organizational structure in ERP and EWM may look like the one shown in Figure 6.23. In this case, stock for the two plants, SP1A and SP1B, are managed in the same warehouse number. Every time inventory is updated, the respective PARTY ENTITLED TO DISPOSE has to be specified by the user.

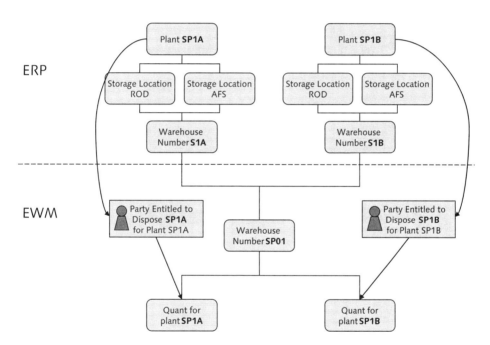

Figure 6.23 Stocks for Two Parties Entitled to Dispose in One Warehouse

If you have multiple parties entitled to dispose assigned to the warehouse, you have to assign a *custodian* to the warehouse number as well. The custodian is the BP that stores, manages, or further processes stock for another BP, but without transfer of title. Therefore, the custodian is usually the owner of the warehouse. The custodian only maintains effective possession of the stock, whereas the owner maintains legal possession. The custodian should not be confused with the owner.

The custodian is the *owner of the warehouse*, whereas the party entitled to dispose is the *owner of the stocks*. (The custodian may also be referred to as the "holder" of the stocks.)

> **Note**
>
> Although it has a high business importance, the custodian is not visible on any of the EWM user interfaces. Instead, you specify the custodian using the warehouse number. Technically, the custodian is used in the LIME, where some of the index tables of the stocks have the CUSTODIAN as a key field.

6.4.3   Background on the Party Entitled to Dispose

For each plant in SAP ERP, there is a BP available in EWM. In the standard setup, this BP has the same name as the plant. It can be displayed and maintained in Transaction BP. Every plant BP must have an identification entry with the identification type CRM011, as shown in Figure 6.24, and the identification number that matches the ERP plant. This BP is then one of the available parties entitled to dispose.

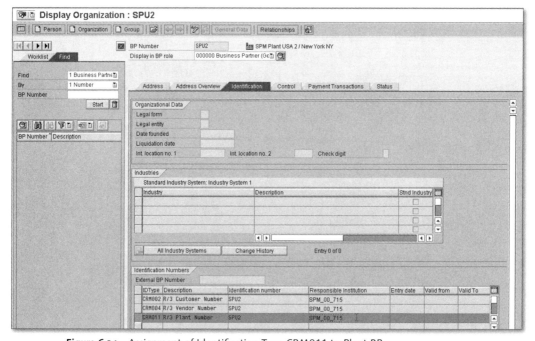

Figure 6.24   Assignment of Identification Type CRM011 to Plant BP

6.4.4 Link between Custodian, Party Entitled to Dispose, and Owner

To help you understand the concept of EWM using custodian, party entitled to dispose, and owner, and to clearly show the links and the differences between these three objects, we will provide an example. In this example, the custodian is the owner of the warehouse A. There is always *only one custodian*. In EWM, you need to create a BP (Transaction BP) for company A and assign it as a warehouse attribute.

To simplify the maintenance, usually the BP of the plant is chosen as the custodian. So, even if the owner of the warehouse is company A, and the plant is called PL01, then you use BP PL01 as the custodian. This saves you the step of creating an additional BP. However, when you use stock for multiple plants within the same warehouse, you can't do this, and you assign company A as custodian.

You have one party entitled to dispose for every plant, for which you manage stock. If you manage stock for only one plant (for example, PL01) in your EWM warehouse number, then you only have one party entitled to dispose. Then, you can make use of the DEFAULT PARTY ENTITLED TO DISPOSE attribute of the warehouse number and set it to PL01, so you dont' have to enter this value all of the time. If you want to manage stock for multiple plants (for example, PL01 and PL02), you have multiple parties entitled to dispose, one per plant. Then, it doesn't make sense to assign a DEFAULT PARTY ENTITLED TO DISPOSE to the warehouse number, so you leave this field empty.

The *owner* is the party that owns the stock, which is normally the ERP plant for the stock. If you manage stock for two plants in your warehouse number, for example, for plants PL01 and PL02, the owner will always be either PL01 or PL02. If you use vendor consignment stocks, the real owner is still the vendor — until you consume the stock. If you have, for example, stock for vendor VEND01 in plant PL01, then the owner is VEND01. The ERP plant is still the party entitled to dispose of the stock, but the vendor (consignment stock owner) is the owner.

6.5 Batch Management

Batches are used in many industry sectors, such as pharmaceutical, chemical, and manufacturing to differentiate products by characteristics. You can capture technical, physical, or chemical properties of stock via the batch and use these characteristics in warehouse processing.

If you have a product, for example, a lacquer, it can be characterized by the proper-ties color, viscosity, and expiration date. You can create a product master that you can enable batch management from. First, you assign a batch class with the three characteristics. Then, during inbound processing, you can set a batch and maintain the characteristics for it. For outbound processing, if you get a customer order to ship a green lacquer with a certain viscosity requirement, EWM will then suggest the best batch for the customer's needs.

Using batch management in EWM, you can work with the following functions:

▶ **Handling of batch master data in EWM**

Batch master data can be distributed by ERP, created manually in EWM, or cre-ated automatically on the fly during creation of an inbound delivery.

▶ **Batch determination in outbound processing**

You can set and display the selection criteria for each outbound delivery order (ODO) and, based on them, you can determine batches in the picking process. When creating a WT, the system only selects the batches that correspond to these criteria.

▶ **Predetermined batches**

If you specify batches in the outbound delivery, the system uses the batches that you specified.

▶ **Batch status management**

Batches in EWM can have the characteristics *unrestricted* and *restricted*. When a batch is set to restricted, you can specify that no movements are allowed for this batch. You can also stop them from being posted for goods issue or goods receipt.

▶ **Monitoring**

In the EWM monitor, you can select stock using batch characteristics.

▶ **Documentary batch**

Documentary Batches are not managed in inventory in the system. You can use them to store additional information and to do follow-ups in the ERP system. For more information about documentary batches, see Chapter 7, Warehouse Document Types.

In the following sections, we'll will explain these functions in more detail.

6.5.1 Batch Management in EWM

If you want to use batches in EWM, you need to enable batch management in ERP as well. Batches are managed centrally in the ERP system — as the "master data system" for batches. From ERP, batches and classes/characteristics can be distributed to all connected EWM systems via the CIF. You can create or change batches in EWM. When you create or change batches in EWM, the batch data is transferred to the ERP system, and ERP distributes the batch data to all of the other connected EWM systems.

> **Note**
>
> If you want to use batches in EWM with connection to ERP, you have to set up unique batch names at the *material level*. To specify the batch level in the ERP IMG, follow the menu path LOGISTICS - GENERAL • BATCH MANAGEMENT • SPECIFY BATCH LEVEL AND ACTI- VATE STATUS MANAGEMENT • BATCH LEVEL. Communication between ERP and EWM does not support other batch levels, for example, batches on the plant level.

In addition, you need to make the following general customizing settings in EWM:

▶ You must define number ranges for batches in EWM. This number range is used when EWM creates batches, for example, automatically at the creation of the inbound delivery. To define the number ranges in the EWM IMG, follow the menu path EXTENDED WAREHOUSE MANAGEMENT • CROSS-PROCESS SETTINGS • BATCH MANAGEMENT • DEFINE NUMBER RANGE FOR BATCH.

▶ You must set up the *update control* for batches, in the EWM IMG, via the EXTENDED WAREHOUSE MANAGEMENT • CROSS-PROCESS SETTINGS • BATCH MAN- AGEMENT • SET UPDATE CONTROL (CENTRALIZED, DECENTRALIZED) menu path, as seen in Figure 6.25.

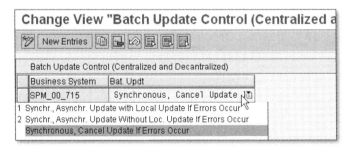

Figure 6.25 Setup Update Control for Batches

When EWM creates or changes batches, it attempts to call the ERP system synchronously to inform it about the change. If you use the default update control (blank), then the system triggers an error message if there is an error in the call (for example, if the ERP system is temporarily offline or the batch is locked). For update control values 1 and 2, EWM won't display a direct error message and will attempt to update the batch asynchronously later. This lets you continue to work in EWM without interruption.

To enable batch management for a product, you must set the corresponding checkbox in the material master in ERP. Then, you assign a batch class of the class type 023. While assigning the batch class, you may also assign the object characteristics LOBM_HERKL (COO), LOBM_VFDAT (SLED, minimum shelf life), and LOBM_ZUSTD (batch status) to the batch class. These three characteristics (COO, expiration date, and batch status) represent stock attributes in EWM. Once you post goods receipt for stocks using a batch with these fields, the assigned values for the characteristics are automatically transferred to the corresponding stock fields. These values then influence processes in EWM, such as WT creation.

You can edit and create batches in EWM from the EWM Easy Access menu by following the EXTENDED WAREHOUSE MANAGEMENT • MASTER DATA • PRODUCT • MAINTAIN BATCHES FOR PRODUCT menu path, or using Transaction /SCWM/WM_BATCH_MAINT. With this transaction, you can change the characteristics of a batch, as seen in Figure 6.26.

The *batch status*, which is one of the characteristics of the batch, can be used to prevent goods receipt or goods issue for delivery items with batches of status *restricted* or to prevent WT creation for stock with batches of status *restricted*. To control the batch status management from the EWM IMG, follow the menu path EXTENDED WAREHOUSE MANAGEMENT • CROSS-PROCESS SETTINGS • BATCH MANAGEMENT • BATCH STATUS MANAGEMENT.

6.5.2 Batches in the Goods Receipt Process

When creating an inbound delivery in the ERP system, the batch number is distributed as part of the delivery item to EWM. If the batch is already available in EWM with a master data record, you can create the putaway task and the batch number will be placed in stock. If the batch in not yet available in EWM with a master data record, then you can create the batch either "in foreground" via the inbound delivery or automatically during creation of the inbound delivery. If no batch number is available, the system determines a new number from the defined number range (as described previously). If EWM creates the batch master, the values of the delivery are copied into the new batch, including COO, expiration date, SLED, and production date.

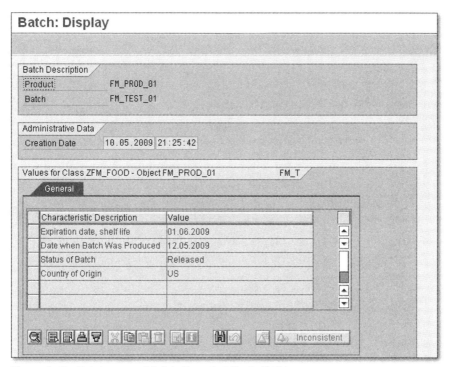

Figure 6.26 Maintenance of Batch Characteristics in EWM

Note

To transfer additional valuations into the batch master during creation, you can implement the available Business Add-Ins (BAdIs), including BAdI /SCWM/DLV_BATCH_VAL and /SCWM/DLV_BATCH_CHAR.

6.5.3 Batches in Goods Issue Process

Starting from the ERP system, you can assign batch selection criteria for outbound deliveries and distribute them to EWM together with the delivery. When creating the picking WT, the specified selection criteria are taken into consideration when searching for suitable batches. If the quantity of a batch is insufficient to fill the required quantity, the system determines multiple batches that fit the selection criteria.

You can display the selection criteria in EWM by pressing the Selection button on the Items tab of the ODO in Transaction /SCWM/PRDI.

If you enter a batch number directly in the outbound delivery, the system then uses the batch that you specify. You can also manually specify the batch number during WT creation instead of letting EWM determine the batch numbers. If you specify the batches manually, the EWM system will check whether the batch you have entered meets the selection criteria (you can control this in the EMWM IMG via the menu path Extended Warehouse Management • Cross-Process Settings • Batch Management • Make Setting for Delivery).

During WT creation, you can also select available batches by letting EWM display a list of available stocks for a particular product based on the batch selection criteria and then distributing the requested quantity manually among the displayed batches. If you pick multiple batches for an ODO, EWM will perform a batch split in the delivery item, and you can visualize the batch split within the delivery processing transaction by selecting the item and pressing the Batch Split button.

6.6 Documentary Batch Management

A *documentary batch* is a special kind of batch that is not inventory managed. This means you can guarantee the traceability of a product with documentary batches, but you don't have to perform inventory management for the product. In Table 6.2, you can see the main differences between standard batch management and documentary batch management.

Functionality	Standard Batch Management	Documentary Batch Management
Batch master	Available	Not available
Where-used list	Yes	Only in ERP system
Batch status management	Possible	Not Possible
Batch search	Possible	Not Possible
Batch stock	Yes	No
Class assignment	Possible	Not Possible

Table 6.2 Functionality of Different Batch Management Techniques

Documentary batch management is enabled by setting the DOCUMENTARY BATCH indicator of the EWM product master to 1, as you can see in Figure 6.27. You can either manually maintain this field, or use a report to distribute this setting from the ERP system. In the next section, we'll discuss the distribution of the documentary batch settings in more detail.

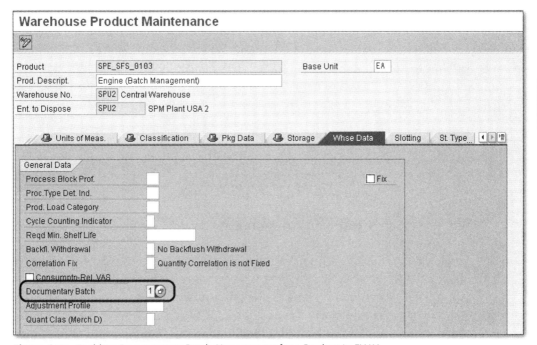

Figure 6.27 Enabling Documentary Batch Management for a Product in EWM

When you have set the DOCUMENTARY BATCH indicator, you can maintain a documentary batch number in the items for inbound deliveries and ODOs. When creating WTs, you can also specify the documentary batch number. In goods receipt, when you confirm a WT for putaway, you must record the documentary batch when confirming a WT. The documentary batch will not be posted into the stock, as documentary batches are not inventory managed. You can specify for every *delivery item type* if the documentary batch must be specified, or if it is only optional. To specify the settings for the delivery item type in the EWM IMG, follow the menu path EXTENDED WAREHOUSE MANAGEMENT • CROSS-PROCESS SETTINGS • BATCH MANAGEMENT • SET DOCUMENTARY BATCH.

6.6.1 Distribute Documentary Batch Management Settings to EWM

In Figure 6.27, you can see that you enable documentary batch management in EWM by setting the respective indicator in the EWM product master to 1. Usually, you would set this parameter from the ERP system. However, this function is not handled by the CIF. Therefore, you can distribute the ERP settings regarding the documentary batches by using a report in the EWM system. To start the distribution from the EWM Easy Access menu, follow the EXTENDED WAREHOUSE MANAGEMENT • MASTER DATA • PRODUCT • SYNCHRONIZE ERP/EWM SETTINGS FOR DOCUMENTATION BATCHES menu path, or use Transaction /SCWM/DBATCHSYNC. This distribution report can be scheduled to run periodically in the background. It reads the ERP system and sets the DOCUMENTARY BATCH box in EWM to 1.

> **Note**
>
> In ERP, you can also enable documentary batch management by using a BAdI. The distribution report in EWM will also transfer the settings that were initiated in the BadI.

6.7 Serial Number Management

Serial number management in EWM is used to uniquely trace and identify a product in your warehouse, from goods receipt to goods issue. With serial numbers, you can determine who has moved the product where and when, what date you received it from a vendor or from another warehouse, and who performed the QI. You can also see when you have shipped the product to a customer, who packed the product, and when the packing was done, and other relevant data about the transactions in the warehouse.

Serial number management provides you with complete transparency about everything that happens with your stock. However, for the system to know where your product is at all times, there is additional administrative work involved. For example, users always have to specify the serial number when they handle stock. For this reason, serial numbers are typically only used for important products, either expensive ones or ones where transparency is required by other parties (for example, by your customers). If stock gets lost in your warehouse, you know exactly which serial numbers were lost and who moved it last from what bin. If a pallet gets lost at your carrier, you still know exactly which serial numbers were on that pallet. If a customer returns stock to your warehouse, you can check if he really got the specified serial number from you and when.

In EWM, there are three different levels of serial number requirements. This is very important, as each level is different in terms of how much stock transparency you have, but also how much administrative work is required by the users. The options for the serial number control include:

1. **Serial Number Requirement A: Serial Numbers for Document Items**

   This serial number requirement lets you enter serial numbers for an inbound delivery item before goods receipt, or for an outbound delivery item before goods issue. As a result, you can check which delivery was used for inbound and outbound processing. However, you can't see what products are currently in the warehouse. You do not have any stock visibility for a unique product.

   You can specify on the item type level if serial numbers are obligatory or optional. After the goods receipt posting, you work with the product inside the warehouse as if it were not serial number managed.

   This serial number requirement is typically used to check whether a product left your warehouse and on which delivery to which customer. This enables you to validate whether the product a customer is complaining about really is the same product that was delivered to him.

2. **Serial Number Requirement B: Serial Numbers at Warehouse-Number Level**

   This serial number requirement forces you to enter serial numbers in goods issue and goods receipt. Based on these entries, the system is always able to give you an overview about which serial numbers you have in the warehouse. However, after the goods receipt posting you work with the product inside the warehouse as if it were not serial number managed. Therefore, you do not have any stock visibility on the storage bin level for a product.

   With this serial number requirement, the system knows that a certain serial number is in your warehouse, but it does not know *where* (i.e., in which bin) the serial number is located. Therefore, this serial number requirement is named "on warehouse level."

3. **Serial Number Requirement C: Serial Numbers in Inventory Management**

   This serial number requirement allows you to trace a serial number in your warehouse stock, even down to the bin level. This requirement is the most detailed one, as you always know where a product is. To track the serial number to the detailed level, the serial number becomes a quant attribute, and the serial number must be entered during every warehouse transaction. Therefore, you have a complete stock visibility on the quant level. The downside is that most of the administrative work is required by the warehouse operators to accommodate the serial number tracking.

Figure 6.28 provides an overview to the serial number requirement methods and the consequences for each.

	Serial Number Requirement "A – on Document Level"	Serial Number Requirement "B – on Warehouse Level"	Serial Number Requirement "C – on Inventory Level"
Serial Numbers in inbound delivery item	Can be entered (depending on delivery item type mandatory or optional)	Must be entered before goods receipt (or at putaway in case of provisional serial numbers)	Must be entered before goods receipt (or at putaway in case of provisional serial numbers)
Serial Numbers in outbound delivery item	Can be entered (depending on delivery item type mandatory or optional)	Must be entered before goods issue	Must be entered before goods issue
Serial Numbers in warehouse tasks	Generally, serial numbers can not be entered. Exception: picking warehouse tasks.	Generally, serial numbers can not be entered. Exception: picking warehouse tasks.	Serial numbers have to be entered for every movement
	⬇	⬇	⬇
Stock Visibility and Control	None. But control of serial numbers possible, e.g. in customer returns process	Information, which serial numbers are available in the warehouse	Exact information where every serial number is located in the warehouse

Figure 6.28 Overview of EWM Serial Number Requirements

> **Note**
>
> A serial number is always unique in conjunction with a product. That means the same serial number can be used for two different products, but not for the same product at the same point of time (in other words, the same serial number for the same product cannot be entered twice in the warehouse at the same time, as the serial number/product combination should be unique). For example, you can post goods receipt for products MAT_4711 and MAT_4712, where both have the same serial number ENGINE_A701. You are not allowed to subsequently post goods receipt afterward for product MAT_4711 and serial number ENGINE_A701 until you have removed this serial number from your warehouse (e.g., by goods issue, by physical inventory, or by scrapping).

Serial number management affects all areas in EWM that work with inventory, including:

▸ Product Master

▸ EWM Processes, both desktop (or GUI) and mobile data transactions

▸ Delivery Processing

▸ Processing at work centers (for example, Packing or QI)

▸ Physical Inventory (PI)

▸ Warehouse Monitor

▸ Integration with SAP ERP

In the following sections, we will describe the implications of serial number management in EWM in more detail. First, we will explain how you activate serial numbers by maintaining a serial number profile for a product. We will explain all of the fields on the serial number profile in detail. Then, we will explain how serial numbers are used in delivery processing and in WT processing. And, finally, we'll describe some general settings that you need to check, before you start working with serial numbers.

6.7.1   Setting Up Serial Number Profiles

If you work with serial numbers in conjunction with SAP ERP, you need to maintain two independent serial number profiles. One is the old profile on the SALES: GENERAL/PLANT view of the material master. This enables the logistical documents, such as deliveries, to work with serial numbers. We'll refer to this profile as the *LES Serial Number profile*.

In addition, there is a *new* profile on the WM EXECUTION view of the material master. This profile is only relevant in combination with EWM. It needs to be maintained the same way in the ERP and EWM system. We will refer to this profile as the *EWM Serial Number profile*. In the following two subsections, we'll describe both of these profiles.

Serial Number Profile in ERP

The LES SERIAL NUMBER PROFILE on the SALES: GENERAL/PLANT view of the ERP material master needs to be maintained to work with serial numbers in ERP. This profile can be defined in the ERP IMG via the menu path Logistics Execution • Shipping • Basic Shipping Functions • Serial Numbers • Determine Serial Number Profiles. When you set up this LES serial number profile, it is recommended to disable the stock check in Customizing, because goods movement postings originating from EWM do not register serial numbers in the ERP system. In Figure 6.29, you can see the relevant part of the ERP material master maintenance, where this serial number profile can be assigned.

Figure 6.29 LES Serial Number Profile on the Sales: General/Plant View of ERP Material Master

The EWM Serial Number Profile on the WM Execution view of the material master needs to be maintained to work with serial numbers in combination with EWM. When you transfer the material master to the EWM system via the CIF, this field is transferred into the warehouse product master of EWM. In Figure 6.30, you can see the WM Execution view in the ERP material master, where the EWM serial number profile can be assigned.

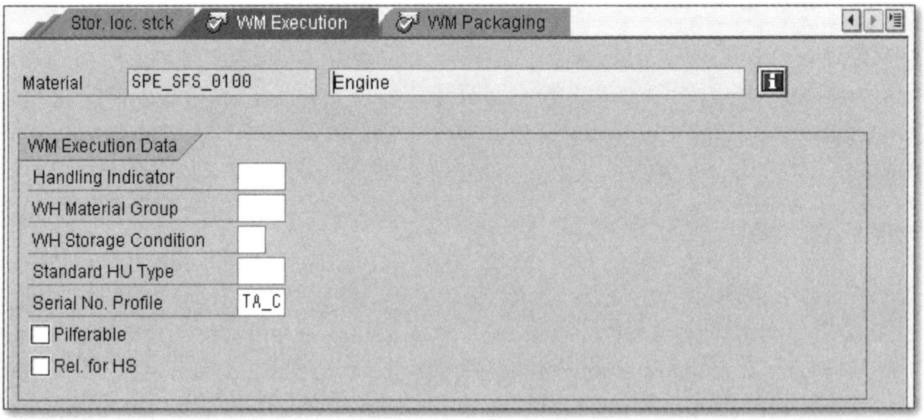

Figure 6.30 EWM Serial Number Profile in the WM Execution View of ERP Material Master

This EWM-related serial number profile can be defined in the ERP IMG via the Integration with Other mySAP.com Components • Extended Warehouse Management • Additional Material Attributes • Attribute Values for Additional Material Master Fields • Define Serial Number Profile menu path. This customizing table looks exactly the same as the customizing table in EWM, and you should manually synchronize the settings on the tables in ERP and EWM.

Serial Number Profile in EWM

In EWM, you define the serial number profile in the customizing via the IMG menu path EXTENDED WAREHOUSE MANAGEMENT • MASTER DATA • PRODUCT • DEFINE SERIAL NUMBER PROFILES • DEFINE WAREHOUSE NUMBER-INDEPENDENT SERIAL NUMBER PROFILES. Note that this table is a mirror of the table in the ERP system. Normally, you maintain this field in the ERP material master and the data is transferred to EWM — therefore, the check table must be maintained in both places and synchronized manually. In addition to this warehouse number–independent serial number profile, there is also a warehouse number–dependent serial number profile. We'll explain the difference between these two profiles later in this section. In Figure 6.31, you can see the definition of the warehouse number–independent serial number profile.

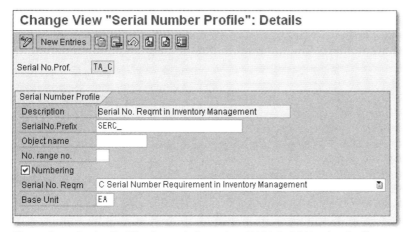

Figure 6.31 Setting Up Warehouse-Independent EWM Serial Number Profile

The serial number profile contains the following information:

▸ **Description**

This is a short description of the profile. You can see it when maintaining or displaying a warehouse product master next to the entered serial number profile. You can also see it in the input help (F4 help) when entering a new serial number profile. It's a good idea to mention in the serial number profile what level of serial number requirement the user can expect (as in the example in Figure 6.31).

► **Serial Number Prefix**

When you let EWM automatically assign serial numbers for your inbound delivery, you can use this field to add a prefix to every serial number. If the prefix is, for example, SERC_, and the number range interval is at number 610000610, you will get serial numbers such as SERC_610000611, SERC_610000612, etc. It makes sense to maintain a prefix (e.g., ENGINE_) if you create a serial number profile specifically for a product or a product range.

► **Object Name and No. range no**

You can use these two fields to enable automatic creation of serial numbers for your products. You can specify the name of a number range object and a number range interval within that object. This will be used to fetch the next serial number for automatic numbering. You can create number range objects and intervals using Transaction SERNO. If the serial number prefix is maintained (as described earlier in this chapter), it will always be added in front of the number of this number range.

> **Note**
>
> If you do not maintain a number range object and interval, you can still use automatic numbering. To do so, the NUMBERING checkbox (described in the next bullet) must be set.

► **Numbering**

If you do not maintain a number range object and interval, you can set the AUTOMATIC NUMBERING checkbox. In this case, the numbering starts with 1 for every product. The last number for every product is stored in the LSERD field of SAP table /SCWM/SERH. It is increased by 1 for every new serial number created. If the serial number prefix is maintained (as described previously), it will be always be added as a prefix to the determined number from the number range.

> **Note**
>
> If you maintain a number range object and interval, the serial number is generated from the number range interval, even if you have set the NUMBERING checkbox.

If you do *not* maintain a number range object and interval but have set the NUMBERING checkbox, the automatic numbering from table /SCWM/SERH is used.

If you do *not* maintain a number range object and interval and have *not* set the NUMBERING checkbox, you can't use automatic numbering.

▶ **Serial Number Requirement**

In this field, you specify the serial number requirement for the serial number profile. The possible input options include:

- ▶ A — Serial Number Requirement for Document Item
- ▶ B — Serial Number Requirement on Warehouse Number Level
- ▶ C — Serial Number Requirement in Inventory Management
- ▶ D — No Serial Number Requirement

We have already described serial number requirements A - C earlier in this section. You can use serial number requirement D in conjunction with the warehouse number dependent serial number profile (as described later in this section) to work in one warehouse number without serial numbers.

▶ **Base Unit**

Here, you specify the base unit of measure for the serial numbers. Often, this is at the unit level — for example, the unit of measure EA or PC.

Warehouse Number–Dependent Serial Number Profiles

In the material master maintenance in the ERP system, you assign a serial number profile that is valid for all warehouse numbers (i.e., it is *warehouse-number independent*). In EWM, you can *overrule* the serial number profile coming from the ERP system by assigning a *warehouse number dependent* serial number profile.

When processing a product, EWM searches for the warehouse number–dependent serial number profile first. If it is not maintained on the product master, EWM uses the warehouse number–independent one. This way, you can make a product require a serial number in one warehouse and not require one in another. Another good example is that you can assign a warehouse number–independent profile with serial number requirement A. For one specific warehouse you can then overwrite this requirement by assigning a warehouse number–dependent profile with serial number requirement C. In customizing in EWM, you define the warehouse number dependent serial number profile via the IMG menu path EXTENDED WAREHOUSE MANAGEMENT • MASTER DATA • PRODUCT • DEFINE SERIAL NUMBER PROFILES • DEFINE WAREHOUSE NUMBER-DEPENDENT SERIAL NUMBER PROFILES.

In the following sections, we'll describe how EWM uses serial numbers with illustrations about all relevant process steps. Most of the time, we'll refer implicitly to serial number requirement C because this is the most complex and has most constraints. We'll briefly mention certain steps that are not necessary for the other two serial number requirements.

6.7.2 Serial Numbers in Delivery Processing

In this section, we'll describe how EWM uses serial numbers in delivery processing. First, we'll discuss inbound deliveries, then outbound deliveries. In both cases, we'll explain the integration with the ERP system.

Serial Numbers for Inbound Delivery Processing

In an inbound delivery, the serial numbers can be specified within the notification from the supplier (via electronic data interchange (EDI), Supplier Network Collaboration (SNC), or other integration method), specified in the inbound delivery in ERP (manually entered, scanned, or created automatically), or specified in the inbound delivery in EWM (manually entered, scanned, or created automatically). In Figure 6.32, you can see the ERP Create Inbound Delivery transaction (Transaction VL31N). To enter serial numbers in the ERP delivery, choose menu item EXTRAS • SERIAL NUMBERS from the menu. A pop-up window opens where you can enter the serial numbers for the delivery item (see Figure 6.32).

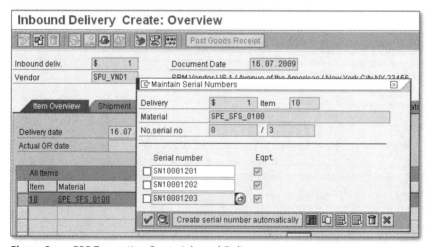

Figure 6.32 ERP Transaction Create Inbound Delivery

In ERP, it's also possible to assign serial numbers for HU items. In Transaction VL31N, you can use the PACK button (or menu function EDIT • PACK) to jump to the HU overview. In the HU overview, there is a TTL CONTENT tab, that contains a SERIAL NOS. button for assigning serial numbers (as seen in Figure 6.33).

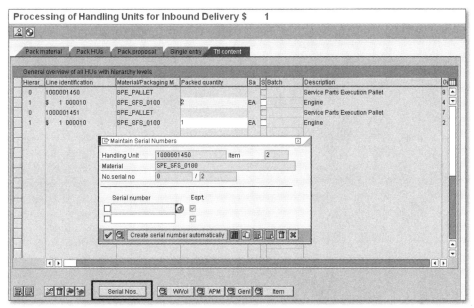

Figure 6.33 Assigning Serial Numbers per HU Item in the ERP Inbound Delivery

In addition to Transaction VL31N, you can also use Transaction VL60 (which offers advanced features in conjunction with EWM) to create inbound deliveries. Transaction VL60 only allows assigning serial numbers to delivery items (as seen in Figure 6.34), not to HU items.

If you work with serial numbers created in the ERP system in an inbound delivery, you can manually overwrite these serial numbers in EWM. In EWM, based on the inbound delivery in ERP, an IDN is created (see Chapter 7, Warehouse Document Types, for more information). While the notification is created, the serial number profile from the product master is evaluated and the serial number requirement determined. The serial number requirement is then visible on the IDN item (Transaction /SCWM/IDN) and on the inbound delivery item (Transaction /SCWM/PRDI), as seen in Figure 6.35.

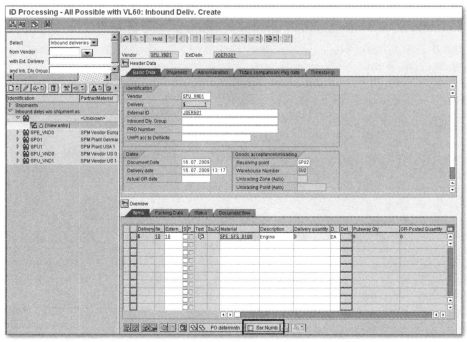

Figure 6.34 Button to Enter Serial Numbers in Transaction VL60

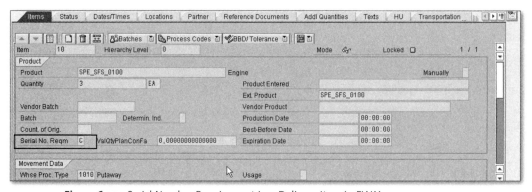

Figure 6.35 Serial Number Requirement in a Delivery Item in EWM

In EWM, you can always see the serial numbers under the SERIAL NUMBERS tab of the delivery item (as seen in Figure 6.36), whether they were assigned to a delivery item or to an HU item in ERP. This makes it easier to get an overview about all serial numbers. If you didn't receive any serial numbers from the ERP system, the tab strip will be empty.

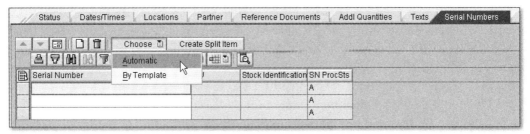

Figure 6.36 Serial Numbers Tab of an EWM Inbound Delivery Item

In this tab, you can either enter the serial numbers manually, in the leftmost column of the table. Alternatively, you can use one of the two functions of the CHOOSE button to create serial numbers automatically (CHOOSE • AUTOMATIC) or use a template (CHOOSE • BY TEMPLATE), as also seen in Figure 6.36. Choosing the *automatic serial number creation function* results in a pop-up window where you can specify how many serial numbers shall be created (as seen in Figure 6.37). Instead of entering a number, you can set the TOTAL QUANTITY checkbox, to create serial numbers for the entire quantity of the delivery item.

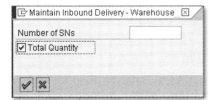

Figure 6.37 Pop-up Box in Inbound Delivery for Automatic Serial Number Creation

If you confirm this dialogue by pressing on the left (checkmark) button, serial numbers are generated based on the settings in your serial number profile (including the prefix as described earlier, if relevant).

If you choose the *serial number creation by template,* a different pop-up window will result, as seen in Figure 6.38.

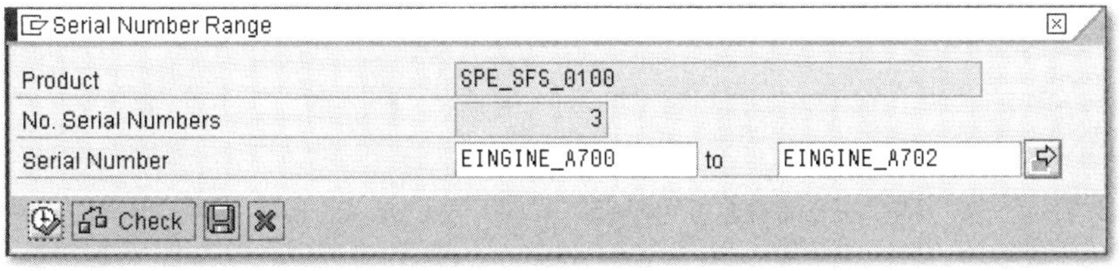

🖸 Serial Number Range				⊠
Product	SPE_SFS_0100			
No. Serial Numbers	3			
Serial Number	EINGINE_A700	to	EINGINE_A702	⇨

🔾 🔒 Check 💾 ✖

Figure 6.38 Serial Number Creation by Template in ID

269

In the SERIAL NUMBER field selection option, you enter a starting and ending serial number string and EWM will automatically determine how many and which serial numbers need to be created. EWM will split the starting and ending serial number into a prefix part and a numeric (suffix) part. Generating serial numbers is only possible if the prefix part is identical and the numeric part of the ending serial number is higher than the one of the starting serial number. In the example from Figure 6.38, serial numbers ENGINE_A700, ENGINE_A701, and ENGINE_A702 would be created.

Goods Receipt for Inbound Delivery

If you use serial number requirement B or C, you can only post goods receipt if you have specified the required serial numbers *or* if you enabled use of provisional serial numbers (described in the next section). If you use serial number requirement A, you can post the goods receipt without serial numbers. This means that for this serial number requirement, serial numbers are not enforced. At goods receipt, the serial numbers are sent back from EWM to ERP. In the ERP system, you can see the serial numbers in the material document (follow the GOTO • SERIAL NUMBER menu path on the material document item) and on the inbound delivery item (via the menu path EXTRAS • SERIAL NUMBERS).

Serial Numbers for Outbound Delivery Processing

Similar to the inbound process, you can specify serial numbers in the ERP system as part of the ERP outbound delivery item (via the menu path EXTRAS • SERIAL NUMBERS). This may be used, for example, if the customer orders a specific serial number. The serial numbers in this process are also called *predetermined serial numbers*. If you use serial number requirement C, EWM needs this data to create the picking WTs. You have to pick this specific serial number or deny the picking (execute a pick denial exception).

In any case, you can't assign or change any serial numbers in the EWM outbound delivery. Instead, they are assigned by confirming the picking WTs. If the user confirms a picking WT in EWM, he is required to specify the serial numbers. The serial numbers are then copied from the WT to the outbound delivery item. For more details on assignment of serial numbers to the WT, refer to Section 6.7.4, Serial Numbers in Warehouse Tasks.

Goods Issue for Outbound Delivery

If you use serial number requirement B or C, you can only post goods issue if you have specified the required serial numbers. On the other hand, if you use serial number requirement A, you can post the goods issue without serial numbers (meaning that serial numbers are not enforced for this requirement level). At goods issue for the outbound delivery, the serial numbers are sent back from EWM to ERP. In the ERP system, you can see the serial numbers in the material document (via menu option GOTO • SERIAL NUMBER on a material document item) and on the outbound delivery item (via the menu path EXTRAS • SERIAL NUMBERS).

6.7.3 Provisional Serial Numbers

If you haven't entered any serial numbers before goods receipt posting, EWM can assign a *provisional serial number*. The provisional serial number will be replaced by the "real" serial number in one of the subsequent steps of the inbound process — at the latest, at confirmation of the putaway WT. To enable provisional serial numbers in the EWM IMG, follow the menu path EXTENDED WAREHOUSE MANAGEMENT • MASTER DATA • PRODUCT • DEFINE SERIAL NUMBER PROFILES • SERIAL NUMBERS: SETTINGS FOR WAREHOUSE NUMBER.

A provisional serial number always begins with $ and has 30 characters (e.g., $20 09072017560537900000000001). EWM stores them internally, assigned to the delivery and in stock — however, it doesn't display them on any UI.

EWM uses provisional serial numbers for serial numbers at the warehouse number level or for serial numbers in inventory management (serial number requirements B and C). Usually, for both of these serial number requirements, you can only post goods receipt or goods issue if you have specified the required serial number. If you work with provisional serial numbers, the system lets you post the goods receipt, but you must replace them with valid serial numbers before confirming the putaway WT to the final storage bin.

> **Note**
>
> If you want to track information about serial numbers in the ERP system, don't use provisional serial numbers. As soon as you use provisional serial numbers and replace them with your own serial numbers at a later point in time, EWM no longer reports these serial numbers to the ERP system. The consequence is that the ERP system doesn't have updated information regarding the status of the serial numbers in EWM.

6.7.4 Serial Numbers in Warehouse Tasks

If you use serial number requirement C, the system always needs to know which serial numbers you move. For serial number requirements A and B you generally can't specify a serial number during WT confirmation. Only when picking can you specify the serial number. For more information regarding the assignment of serial numbers in picking WTs, see the following section, Serial Numbers in Picking Warehouse Tasks.

If you confirm a WT and find a stock discrepancy, you need to specify which of the serial numbers is missing. Similarly, when you repack stock in a work center, if you repack a partial quantity, you need to specify which serial numbers you repack. Only when you put away without discrepancies, or repack a full HU, does the system already know the serial numbers and does not ask again.

Serial Numbers in Putaway Warehouse Tasks

Serial numbers assigned to the putaway WT are visible on the SERIAL NUMBER tab for each item of the WT, as you can see in Figure 6.39. In the following example, we will provide more information on the process flow when a user reports a discrepancy in the serial numbers during the putaway task confirmation.

As you can see in Figure 6.39, in the table on the bottom of the screen, you enter the serial numbers for WT confirmation. There you also have three columns with checkboxes, where you can indicate if the line contains a serial number that exists (ACTUAL) or is missing (DIFF). You can also enter differences for a WT by using the SERIAL NUMBERS DIFF button. If you select this function, EWM attempts to determine possible predetermined serial numbers and displays them in an input help. When specifying the serial numbers during the *low stock check* at picking (described further in Chapter 10, Outbound Processing), you can use the SERIAL NUMBERS LS (low stock) button in the detail view for the item, or set the LS (low stock) checkbox for each serial number. If you used provisional serial numbers, you have to enter the actual serial numbers at putaway WT confirmation.

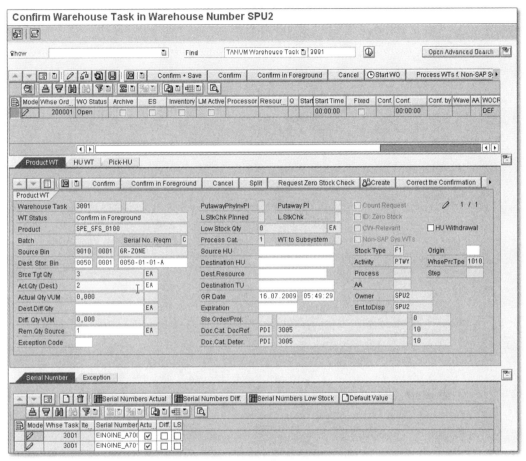

Figure 6.39 Serial Numbers Specified In the Case of Differences at Putaway

Serial Numbers in Picking Warehouse Tasks

For picking WTs, you need to manually specify the serial numbers you want to pick. This is required if you use serial number requirement C. You need to tell the system which of the serial numbers from the bin you have picked. In Figure 6.40, you can see the RF picking transaction. After the source data (source bin, source HU, product, quantity) have been validated, a new screen comes up that asks for the serial numbers. In the example in Figure 6.40, you can see that two serial numbers are required for entry.

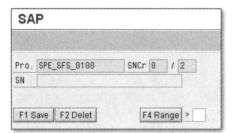

Figure 6.40 Serial Number Entry for Picking WT in Mobile Data Entry Transaction

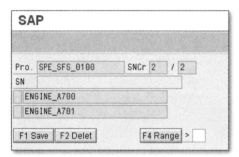

Figure 6.41 Multiple Serial Numbers Specified in Mobile Data Entry Transaction for Picking WT

Once the two serial numbers have been scanned, the screen displays the selected serial numbers in a list (as you can see in Figure 6.41). If several serial numbers have been entered, you may need to scroll up and down to see them all. Once all of the serial numbers have been entered, you can press ⌈Enter⌋ to continue confirming the serial number assignment and continue to the next screen.

> **Note**
>
> You can also specify serial numbers at picking if you use serial number requirement A or B. In this case, the serial numbers are assigned to the outbound delivery item at WT confirmation. During picking, you can see and handle the individual products, making it simpler to enter the serial number.

6.7.5 Serial Numbers in the Warehouse Management Monitor

In the warehouse monitor, you can see serial number details of the stock in the warehouse on the STOCK AND BIN • PHYSICAL STOCK • SERIAL NUMBER node if serial number requirement C is assigned. You can see in Figure 6.42 that the system knows the exact location of each serial number (in which bin, resource, or TU the serial number is located).

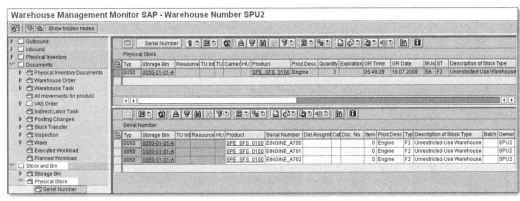

Figure 6.42 Serial Numbers in EWM Monitor of Serial Number Requirement C

Also, in the warehouse monitor, if you assigned serial number requirement B, you can see the serial numbers on the STOCK AND BIN • SERIAL NUMBER ON WHSE LEVEL node, as seen in Figure 6.43. In this case, you can see that the system only knows that the serial number is *in* the warehouse, but it doesn't know *where* exactly.

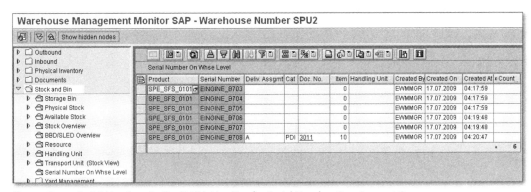

Figure 6.43 Serial Numbers in the EWM Monitor for Serial Number Requirement B

6.7.6 General Settings for Using Serial Numbers in EWM

To use serial numbers in EWM, you need to check the settings for the serial number length, and the serialization for delivery item types, as described in the following sections.

Serial Number Length

In addition to assigning the profiles to your products, you need to specify general settings per warehouse number. You can assign the maximum length of the serial number, and you can allow or disallow provisional serial numbers. To specify these settings, as seen in Figure 6.44, in the EWM IMG follow the menu path EXTENDED WAREHOUSE MANAGEMENT • MASTER DATA • PRODUCT • DEFINE SERIAL NUMBER PROFILES • SERIAL NUMBERS: SETTINGS FOR WAREHOUSE NUMBER.

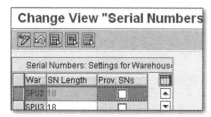

Figure 6.44   Specifying the Attributes for Serial Numbers for the Warehouse

> **Note**
>
> Serial numbers in EWM can be up 30 characters long. However, if you want to use data records for master data in the ERP system, the serial number in EWM can only have 18 characters. If necessary, you can use a BAdI (/SCWM/EX_ERP_SN) for mapping the serial number between the ERP system and EWM, which could allow you to work with serial numbers in EWM up to 30 characters.

Serialization for Delivery Item Types

To use serial numbers for serial number requirement A, you must check the SERIALIZATION checkbox on the relevant delivery item type. If this checkbox is set for an item type, you can only post a goods receipt or goods issue if you have entered serial numbers for the *complete quantity* of the delivery item. If the checkbox is not set, you can enter fewer serial numbers, but the system would not provide an error messages during the execution. To specify the setting in the EWM IMG, follow the menu path EXTENDED WAREHOUSE MANAGEMENT • GOODS RECEIPT PROCESS • INBOUND DELIVERY • MANUAL SETTINGS • DEFINE ITEM TYPES FOR THE INBOUND DELIVERY PROCESS.

6.8   Handling Unit Management

In the past, SAP has defined an HU as a physical unit consisting of packaging materials and the goods contained on/in it, and an HU was always a combination of products and packaging materials. The interesting point in this definition is that SAP *usually* only processes HUs with content — which means that SAP can't work with empty HUs.

For EWM, this is no longer true: You can create empty HUs. You can empty a full HU by moving out the stock and it still exists. HU management is completely integrated into EWM — by design. All processes work with HUs. Some processes are dependent on the existence of HUs, for example, the multistep inbound and outbound processing (using the POSC and LOSC). And HUs can be nested into each other, making up a hierarchy of HUs, as described in detail in the next section.

> **Note**
>
> To use HUs in stock in EWM, you don't need to switch on HU management within the Logistics Execution System (LES) component of the ERP system. LES HU management involves a complex setup with so-called *partner storage locations*, which is not required in conjunction with EWM. You can still use Pick/Ship HUs coming from EWM in the outbound delivery and work with planned HUs in the inbound delivery, even if LES HU management is not activated.

6.8.1   Structure of an HU Hierarchy

An HU consists of an HU header and possibly HU items. The HU header data of an HU contains data including the packaging material, weight, volume and dimensional data, HU type, and the status (both system status and user status). The HU items can consist of products, auxiliary packaging materials, and other HUs. If an HU item is a nested HU, this can hold items within it as well. In Figure 6.45, you can see a couple of examples of nested HUs in EWM. The example on the left contains a pallet that holds a carton. Both pallet and carton are modeled as HUs and both have an assigned HU number (HU 100 and 101). The example on the right consists of a pallet, HU 102, and on the pallet, there are three small cartons (HU 103, 104, and 105), material 4712 (directly on the pallet, without nesting) and an auxiliary packing material 4713 (in this case, a band that holds the three cartons together).

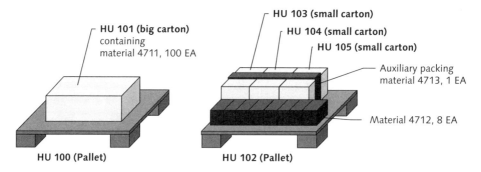

Figure 6.45   Examples of Nested HUs in EWM

Note

EWM also uses the object HU internally for storage bins, resources and TUs. However, this is hidden from the user; you won't see any of this on the user interfaces. The effect is that EWM always internally packs stock items on HUs, even when moving stock from one bin to another.

6.8.2   Packaging Materials

A packaging material is a product that is used as a container for other material to be packaging in or on it to create an HU (where the HU is the packaging material plus the products contained within it). As the packaging material is also a product, there is certain master data associated with it that controls, for example, the capacity of the HU, tare weight, tare volume, and other data about the HU when the product is used as the packaging material for the HU. Examples of packaging materials include pallets, cartons, and containers. You can find more information about packaging materials in Chapter 5, Other Warehouse Master Data.

6.8.3   Empty HUs in EWM

When the last product of the pallet in a rack is removed by a picker, the pallet becomes empty. In EWM, you can configure, per packaging material type, whether you want EWM to continue tracking the empty HU on the bin, or if you want the HU to disappear. To specify the settings in the EWM IMG, follow the menu path EXTENDED WAREHOUSE MANAGEMENT • CROSS-PROCESS SETTINGS • HANDLING UNITS • BASICS • DEFINE PACKAGING MATERIAL TYPES. You can see the configuration settings in Figure 6.46.

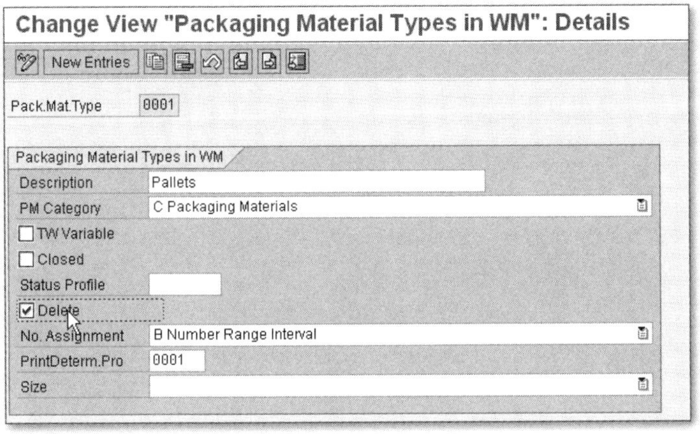

Figure 6.46 Settings on the Packaging Material Type

6.8.4 Printing HUs

You can print documents for HU documents out of EWM. You can set up EWM to automatically print a list or a label when you create an HU or when it arrives at a certain process step in your warehouse, but you can also manually trigger the printing, for example, from a work center. HU documents can contain information about the HU itself, such as HU number and barcode, weight, consolidation group, packing material, but also information about the contents such as materials, dangerous goods, destination, owner, and other information.

HU printing in EWM is based on Adobe Forms technology or on SAP Smart Forms technology. In the following description, we will focus our explanations on the Smart Forms technology, as this is the most widely used method for printing with EWM.

When you save HUs or confirm a WT, the system calls the Post-Processing Framework (PPF) (see Chapter 24 for more details about the PPF) and attempts to print the relevant documents. If there is a condition record for the PPF action definition, the PPF triggers the printing.

6.8.5 Smart Forms Available in EWM Standard for Printing HUs

In the standard EWM solution, there are several Smart Forms for HU printing that are delivered standard, including those in Table 6.3.

Smart Form	Description	PPF Action Definition
/SCWM/HU_LABEL	Print HU label	HU_LABEL
/SCWM/HU_SHPLABEL	Print shipping label	HU_SHPLABEL
/SCWM/HU_TO	Print HU warehouse tasks	HU_TO
/SCWM/HU_CONTENT	Print HU contents document with serial numbers	HU_CONTENT
/SCWM/HU_EXPRESS	Print express shipping label	HU_EXPRESS
/SCWM/HU_SERIAL	Print HU with serial number label	HU_SERIAL
/SCWM/HU_HAZARD	Print dangerous goods label	HU_HAZARD

Table 6.3 Smart Forms in EWM Standard for Printing HUs

You can also define your own Smart Forms by copying the forms in Table 6.3 from SAP standard into the customer namespace. Then, you can modify the form as you want. Or you can create your own forms from scratch. Typically, in SAP implementation projects, the layout and the content of the standard forms is changed, as companies often have specific requirements that are unique to their business.

6.8.6   PPF Framework and Condition Maintenance for HU Printing

As already discussed, printing HUs in EWM is controlled by the PPF. For more information on setting up the PPF and creating the necessary condition records, see Chapter 24.

> **Note**
>
> A very common issue when setting up printing is that EWM will show an error in the determination log such as NO CONDITION RECORD FOUND, even though the condition records have been created and the customizing is correct. The reason for this issue is that EWM often searches for the condition record for printing at the creation of an object and then saves the number into a buffer table (search for /SCWM/*PPF). This also applies for HUs. The condition record is already written into table /SCWM/HU_PPF and is not redetermined every time the HU is requested to be reprinted. When you set up printing in EWM, we suggest that you always test by creating new HUs, not by using existing HUs.

Also, the PPF can write a determination and a processing log during printing. You can switch these logs on by defining user parameter /SCWM/HU_PRT_PROT as X. Note that the logs can get very large over time, so make sure you only switch on logging when it is required, such as when you are problem-solving issues with the form printing.

6.8.7 Status Management

HUs also utilize the general status management capabilities of EWM. This enables you to document the various physical statuses (such as planned or realized) and other attributes (for example, blocked for movements or customs block) for an HU. General status management works with *system statuses* and *user statuses*. System statuses are used by SAP Standard and cannot be changed. By using a *user status profile*, you can create and assign your own statuses and use them to document various attributes and to react on them, for example, by printing them out triggering a follow-up action via a BAdI. To create a user status profile in the EWM IMG (as seen in Figure 6.47), follow the menu path EXTENDED WAREHOUSE MANAGEMENT • CROSS-PROCESS SETTINGS • HANDLING UNITS • BASICS • DEFINE USER STATUS PROFILE.

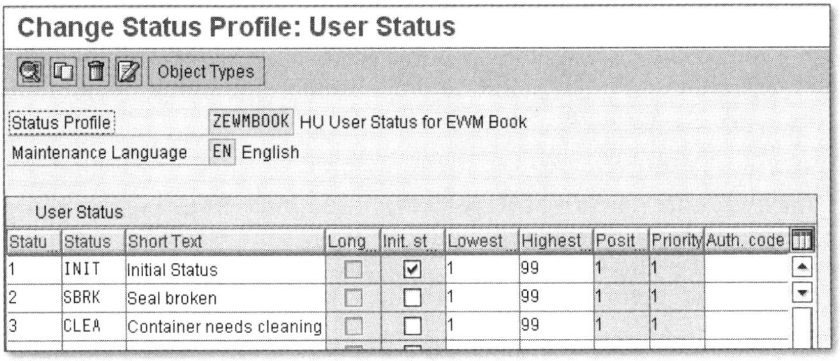

Figure 6.47 Creation of an HU User Status Profile

Once you have created the HU USER STATUS PROFILE, you can assign the status profile to the packing material type in the EWM IMG, via the menu path EXTENDED WAREHOUSE MANAGEMENT • CROSS-PROCESS SETTINGS • HANDLING UNITS • BASICS • DEFINE PACKAGING MATERIAL TYPES. Once this is complete, the user status profile is enabled. When you create a new HU, it will get the appropriate user status profile assigned, as seen in Figure 6.48.

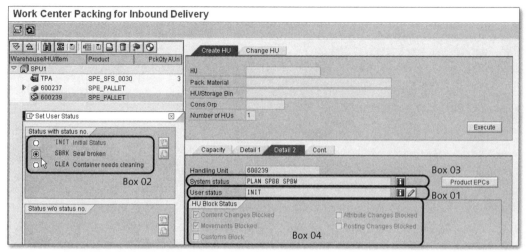

Figure 6.48 System Status and User Status for an HU in the Packaging Work Center

As you can see in Box 01 in Figure 6.48, the HU has a user status INIT assigned. This is the default user status. By clicking on the small CHANGE pencil button on the right side of Box 01, you get the pop-up window that is displayed on the left. There, you can specify the user statuses (Box 02). In Box 03, you can see the system statuses. Some statuses can be set with the checkboxes on the bottom of the screen (as seen in Box 04). The status SPBW, for example, corresponds to the MOVEMENTS BLOCKED checkbox.

6.8.8 Unique Identification of HUs Using Serialized Shipping Container Code (SSCC) Numbers

Each HU must be uniquely identifiable within an EWM system. Within a client, this uniqueness can be ensured by using a number range object (which is the standard delivered or normal setting). If you need to guarantee uniqueness across systems, you can use number range intervals that do not overlap, or by assigning an SSCC18 number.

Due to global networking between different parties of a supply chain, communication is becoming more important. The basis of efficient processing is a common numbering standard, which is defined by international standardization organizations (UCC, EAN International). The UCC/EAN128 and one of its subcomponents, the SSCC/Number of the Shipping Unit (NSU), are defined as a part of these standards, and they can be used to identify HUs. For more information, see the IMG documentation in the EWM IMG for the nodes under the menu path EXTENDED WAREHOUSE MANAGEMENT • CROSS-PROCESS SETTINGS • HANDLING UNITS • EXTERNAL IDENTIFICATION • SSCC NUMBER ASSIGNMENT ACCORDING TO EAN128 • MAINTAIN SSCC GENERATION FOR EACH WAREHOUSE NUMBER.

> **Note**
>
> Before you can work with the EAN128 functions, you must request the basic international location number (ILN) 2 from either the UCC or EAN International.
>
> If you have an existing implementation of a software solution which uses the same ILN number, be sure when you implement SAP EWM that you do not overlap number ranges for the HUs with the existing solution, as this would make it more difficult to manage and track individual HUs that were shipped by your organization.

6.9 Transportation Units

A TU in EWM is the smallest loadable unit of a vehicle that is used to transport goods. For trains, TUs are typically the stage cars; for trucks, the trailers or the truck itself — if it can also hold stock.

TUs can be assigned to *vehicles*. A vehicle is a means of transport, for example, the train engine or the truck engine. Vehicles can hold one or more TUs.

For stock management, it is important to know that TUs can hold stock in EWM — they are key fields of the quant table, very similar to a storage bin. For more details, see Section 6.1.4, Stock Visibility on Storage Bins, Resources, and TUs. For more details regarding TUs and vehicles, see Chapter 18, Yard Management.

6.10 Stock Identification

The stock ID is a unique number that you can use to identify stock with all of its attributes such as quantity, batch, or stock type. A stock ID is typically generated at picking. It can be used to simplify further processing of the stock, for example, at packing.

However, the greatest benefit comes from using STOs in ERP to ship products from one EWM-managed warehouse to another. In this case, the stock ID is transferred from the shipping EWM into ERP system and from ERP into the receiving EWM. This means you can print the stock ID on the picking/shipping label in the sending warehouse, for example, as a barcode. At the receiving warehouse, you can then simply scan the number and the system knows what stock you are handling. In the receiving EWM warehouse, you can use the stock ID throughout the receiving process, for example, for inbound counting, deconsolidation, packing and putaway.

> **Note**
>
> In the ERP system, the stock ID is saved as part of the HU item in the VEPO-SPE_ID-PLATE field. This means that the stock ID only works when you also use HUs on the delivery for the STO.

6.10.1 Creation of Stock Identification

A stock ID is created when a WT is created, typically when creating a WT for picking. You define if a new stock ID should be created in the warehouse process type (WPT) of the WT, as seen in Figure 6.49. To access the WPT configuration in the EWM IMG, follow the menu path EXTENDED WAREHOUSE MANAGEMENT • CROSS-PROCESS SETTINGS • WAREHOUSE TASK • DEFINE WAREHOUSE PROCESS TYPE.

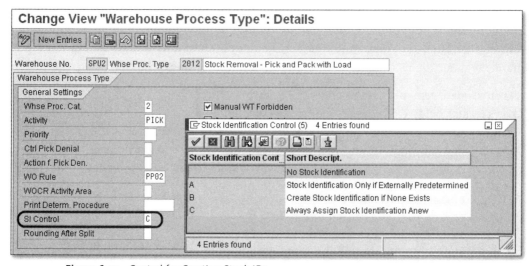

Figure 6.49 Control for Creation Stock IDs

The possible values for Stock ID control are:

► **(blank) — No Stock Identification**

EWM doesn't use stock ID for this WT. An existing stock ID will be deleted.

▶ **A —Stock Identification Only if Externally Predetermined**

EWM uses the stock ID provided by the ERP system (coming from the sending warehouse). If no stock ID is provided, it will not create one.

▶ **B —Create Stock Identification if None Exists**

EWM uses the stock ID provided by the ERP system (coming from the sending warehouse). If no stock ID is provided, it will create one.

▶ **C —Always Assign Stock Identification Anew**

EWM creates a new stock ID, even if another stock ID already exists for the stock.

When a stock ID is created, the number of the stock ID is set by default as the name of the warehouse number plus the WT number (e.g., SPU2000000341457). If you want to specify your own numbering for the stock ID, you can utilize BAdI /SCWM/EX_CORE_CR_STOCK_ID).

6.10.2 Deletion of a Stock Identification

A stock ID is deleted when a WT is confirmed into a storage type that has the DELETE STOCK IDENTIFICATION checkbox activated. Typically, all final storage types have this checkbox set, whereas all interim storage types (such as staging areas, doors, work centers, etc.) don't have it set (see Figure 6.50).

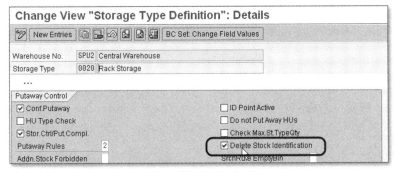

Figure 6.50 Settings for Deletion of Stock IDs for Storage Type

6.10.3 Use of Stock Identification

In the inbound process, you can use the stock ID in the receiving process, for example, for inbound counting, deconsolidation, packing, and putaway. Some of the RF transactions also support stock ID. If this is the case, the input field is often labeled with SI (however, in some cases the stock ID may be used in place of the material, even though the field is not labeled as such). In the warehouse monitor, you can search for open and confirmed WTs by the stock ID (via node DOCUMENTS • WAREHOUSE TASK), and you can also search for stock by stock ID (via node STOCK AND BIN • PHYSICAL STOCK).

6.10.4 Splitting a Stock Identification

When you confirm a WT with a partial quantity, a WT split occurs. In this case, EWM needs two stock IDs — one for the remaining quantity and one for the split quantity. Because stock IDs have to be unique, EWM will create and assign a new stock ID to the split quantity. The remaining quantity with keep the original stock ID — even if its quantity is now reduced. The same happens when repacking partial quantities. The remaining quantity keeps the original stock ID, and the repacked (split) quantity gets a new stock ID.

6.11 Shelf-Life Expiration Date Control

SLED controls how long a material can be retained in storage and remain acceptable for use. It is often used for perishable products or products that must not be used after some period of time due to legal requirements. SLED control has influence on several EWM functions, including:

▶ **Master Data Maintenance**

You maintain in the EWM product master the total shelf life and the required minimum shelf life.

▶ **Goods Receipt Process**

During goods receipt, EWM can check the remaining shelf life and compare it to the required minimum shelf life of the product master. SLED works with and without batches. When you let EWM create a batch, the expiration date and the production date of the inbound delivery are written in the corresponding batch characteristics.

▶ **Goods Issue Process**

You can use SLED in your picking strategy, by sorting stock for picking by the SLED. When using SLED with batches, you can use search characteristics (LOBM_RLZ) for batch determination.

▶ **Monitoring**

You can monitor stocks with SLED in the EWM monitor via node STOCK AND BIN • BBD/SLED OVERVIEW.

▶ **Printing**

You can print the SLED on HU documents or warehouse shipping documents.

> **Note**
>
> In conjunction with SLED functions in EWM, you will sometimes find the term best-before date (BBD). BBD is basically a synonym for SLED. The two terms can best be explained by their different origin. BBD originally comes from the food industry, and SLED originally comes from the pharmaceutical industry.
>
> In EWM stock and WT tables, you will only find the VFDAT field — this handles both SLED *and* BBD. The same applies to most of the user interfaces — with one notable exception. The EWM delivery transactions distinguish and provide two fields (one for BBD and one for SLED) — but there is no functional difference within EWM.

6.11.1   Master Data for SLED Control

There are some master data fields for SLED control, both in the ERP and EWM material master. In Figure 6.51, you can see the relevant fields from the SHELF LIFE tab of the EWM product master.

In the ERP and EWM material master, you can set up whether the expiration date should be handled as SLED or as BBD. In Figure 6.51, the product is set up to use BBD (MIN. SHELF LIFE checkbox). The other checkbox (SHELF LIFE) means that the expiration date is handled as a SLED.

The PLNG WITH SHELF LIFE checkbox is not relevant in conjunction with EWM. In the SHELF LIFE field, you maintain the *total shelf life* of the product. This is the time period that the product can be kept or used starting from the date of receipt or production until its expiration date. The REQ.MIN.SH.LIFE is the minimum amount of time the material must have left compared to its expiration date for goods receipt to be accepted by the system.

The MATURATION TIME is the time period required by a product after production before it can be used. The % REMAINING SL defines necessary remaining percentage of the total shelf life of the product that must not yet have expired if the product is sent from one plant to another (for example, it is used in the SAP Retail functions).

Material:
Total shelf life: 50
Required minimum shelf life: 20

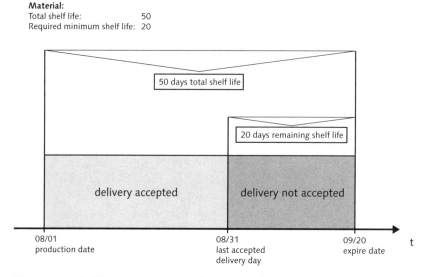

Figure 6.51 Shelf Life Master Data on the EWM Product Master

6.11.2 SLED Control in Goods Receipt Process

During goods receipt process, EWM can check the SLED date. If you specify the required minimum shelf life in a product master, EWM checks the SLED date of the delivery item with the required minimum shelf life, as shown in Figure 6.52.

Material:
Total shelf life: 50
Required minimum shelf life: 20

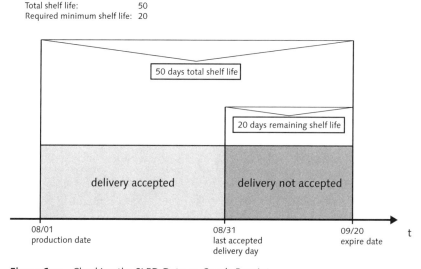

Figure 6.52 Checking the SLED Data on Goods Receipt

288

The delivery is accepted if the calculated remaining shelf life is bigger than the required minimum shelf life. On the other hand, the delivery item is locked (status "red"), if the calculated remaining shelf life is shorter than the required minimum shelf life. If EWM has not blocked a delivery item, you can post a partial or complete goods receipt. You can set up how EWM should check the remaining shelf life of stock during goods receipt in the EWM IMG via the EXTENDED WAREHOUSE MANAGEMENT • EXTENDED WAREHOUSE MANAGEMENT • CROSS-PROCESS SETTINGS • BATCH MANAGEMENT • MAKE SETTINGS FOR DELIVERY menu path, as shown in Figure 6.53.

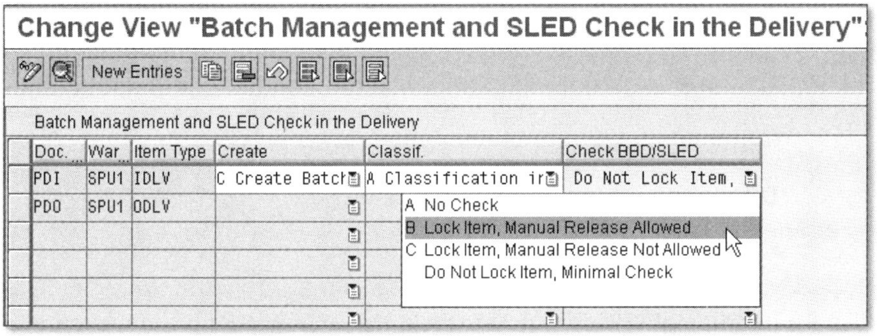

Figure 6.53 Control for Checking the BBD/SLED in the Identification

To lock the delivery item, you need to activate a specific status type in EWM customizing via the IMG menu path EXTENDED WAREHOUSE MANAGEMENT • EXTENDED WAREHOUSE MANAGEMENT • CROSS-PROCESS SETTINGS • DELIVERY PROCESSING • STATUS MANAGEMENT • DEFINE STATUS PROFILES. In the status profile of the inbound delivery item (/SCDL/INB_PRD_DLV_STANDARD), you can activate Status type DSL (called CK REMAINING SHLIF). If the shelf life does not correspond with the required minimum remaining shelf life from the product master, the delivery item will be locked.

You can manually approve or reset the check of the SLED/BBD within the inbound delivery by using a pull down menu of the inbound delivery item, as you can see in Figure 6.54. If you manually approve the check, EWM sets the status for the check to OK, MANUALLY. You can then post the goods receipt.

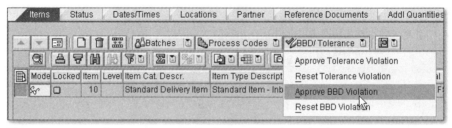

Figure 6.54 Manually Approving a BBD Violation of an Inbound Delivery Item

If the product is not handled with batches, you update the SLED of the stock during goods receipt and before confirmation of the WT. If the product is handled with batches, you can change the SLED attribute for the existing batch. Based on the batch attribute change, EWM changes the batch in the stock and in the inbound delivery. EWM also updates the SLED corresponding to the batch characteristic.

6.11.3 SLED Control in Goods Issue Process

EWM uses *stock removal strategies* to determine where the system should search for stock. The stock removal strategy defines the storage types in which the system should search and how to sort the stock. One of the possible stock removal strategies is SLED. In this case, you sort the stock by the VFDAT field. To specify the stock removal rule in the EWM IMG, follow the menu path EXTENDED WAREHOUSE MANAGEMENT • GOODS ISSUE PROCESS • STRATEGIES • SPECIFY STOCK REMOVAL RULE.

If you use products with SLED *and* batch management, you can also use the batch determination to search stock with a certain minimum requested shelf life. Using the batch determination, you create a selection class that contains characteristics and assigned values. This is done in the ERP system and passed to EWM. This way, you can search for stock of batches that fulfill the required characteristic values that are assigned to the selection class. By using the LOBM_RLZ field (which stores the remaining shelf life), you can search for batches with a minimum amount of remaining shelf life (for example, with remaining shelf life greater than or equal to 60 days).

6.11.4 Monitoring SLED of Warehouse Stock

You can display stock whose BBD or SLED is expired (and therefore can no longer be used). In the EWM monitor node STOCK AND BIN • BBD/SLED OVERVIEW, you can specify either a BBD or a SLED as a reference date. EWM then displays all stock that does not meet the BBD/SLED requirement. By using the CHANGE STOCK TYPE method on the top of the monitor table, you can change the stock type of the selected stock (for example, to stock for scrapping).

6.12   Catch Weight Management

Catch Weight Management (CWM) applies mainly to the meat/dairy industry, where the weights of products can vary from piece to piece, either due to biological variations or because of weight changes during storage. This variability should not be lost by using fixed conversion factors, because this would mean that many business processes (especially billing) would be based on incorrect values.

With CWM, a distinction between a logistic unit of measure and a valuation unit of measure can be made. While the logistic unit is the leading unit for all processes in operative logistics (including EWM), the valuation takes place on the basis of the valuation unit of measure. As a logistic unit of measure, pieces, cases, or eaches are often used. For the valuation unit of measure, typically weight units such as kilogram or pound are used.

One of the consequences of using CWM is that you have complete stock transparency in ERP and EWM on *two independent units of measure*. In the ERP system, you create a material and define the base unit of measure (for example, EA). Then, you activate CWM for this material by adding a parallel unit of measure (for example, KG). When you do that, you also decide whether the base unit of measure or the parallel unit of measure is the valuation unit of measure. The logistic unit of measure is always the base unit of measure.

EWM is capable of managing catch weight information by keeping stock records for products in the two independent units of measure. Both units of measure are of equal status. CWM affects several areas in EWM, including:

▶ Product Master
▶ EWM Processes, including both desktop and mobile data transactions
▶ Delivery Processing
▶ EWM Quality Inspection
▶ Physical Inventory
▶ Warehouse Management Monitor
▶ Integration with SAP ERP

> **Note**
>
> The recommended approach to using CWM in EWM is to connect it to an SAP ERP system with CWM activated. However, you can also use catch weight for some products in EWM only. This could make sense for customers, for example, who can't or don't want to switch on CWM in ERP. This can be executed by maintaining a parallel unit of measure in the product master. EWM then behaves the same way, just as if CWM is switched on in ERP. The difference is that during the interfacing of goods movements to ERP, ERP cannot handle the parallel units that come from a EWM goods movement. The ERP-EWM interface detects this and acts accordingly — in the case of goods movement for deliveries, the delivery items in ERP get the correct weight from the EWM interface.

6.12.1 Activating CWM per Product

CWM is activated per product in the EWM product master (Transaction /SCWM/MAT1) by maintaining a parallel unit of measure in the product master, as seen in Figure 6.55.

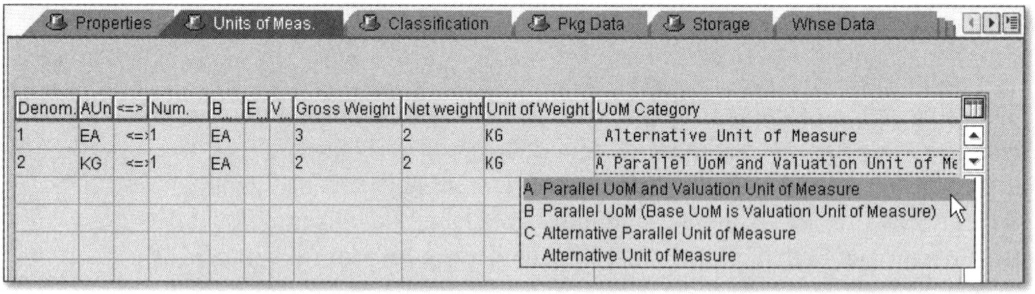

						Gross Weight	Net weight	Unit of Weight	UoM Category	
Denom.	AUn	<=>	Num.	B	E	V				
1	EA	<=>	1	EA			3	2	KG	Alternative Unit of Measure
2	KG	<=>	1	EA			2	2	KG	A Parallel UoM and Valuation Unit of Me

Properties / Units of Meas. / Classification / Pkg Data / Storage / Whse Data

A Parallel UoM and Valuation Unit of Measure
B Parallel UoM (Base UoM is Valuation Unit of Measure)
C Alternative Parallel Unit of Measure
Alternative Unit of Measure

Figure 6.55 Activating CWM for a Product in the EWM Product Master

The maintenance of the units of measure is typically done in the ERP system and transferred to EWM using the CIF. CWM is activated by choosing UoM CATEGORY A or B.

It's possible to assign a CW PROFILE and a CW TOLERANCE GROUP to the product, as in Figure 6.56, however, this step is not necessary for CWM to work. These fields are available on the product master (Transaction /SCWM/MAT1) on the STORAGE tab.

Figure 6.56 Additional Catch Weight Parameters on the Storage Tab of EWM Product Master

The CW PROFILE controls which steps you must enter the parallel quantity in for CWM (for example, at goods receipt, at goods issue, and at the work center).

The CW TOLERANCE GROUP allows the system to check whether a user has entered acceptable values for the logistic quantity and parallel quantity — in other words, if the entered value lies inside the allowed tolerances. You can help minimize errors during data input by using the CW tolerance group. To configure the possible entries for the catch weight tolerance groups in the EWM IMG, follow the menu path EXTENDED WAREHOUSE MANAGEMENT • MASTER DATA • PRODUCT • CATCH WEIGHT • DEFINE CATCH WEIGHT TOLERANCE GROUPS.

6.12.2 Integration of CWM into the EWM Processes

You can control if the user is forced to enter a parallel quantity upon confirmation of a WT with the VAL. QTY INPUT REQ checkbox on the warehouse process type as seen in Figure 6.57. To configure the warehouse process types in the EWM IMG, follow the menu path EXTENDED WAREHOUSE MANAGEMENT • CROSS-PROCESS SETTINGS • WAREHOUSE TASK • DEFINE WAREHOUSE PROCESS TYPE.

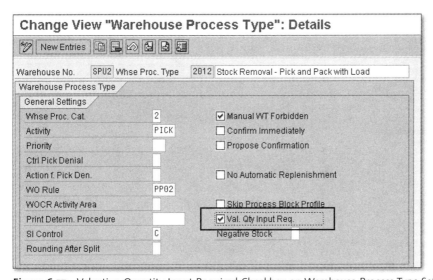

Figure 6.57 Valuation Quantity Input Required Checkbox on Warehouse Process Type Settings

The VAL. QTY INPUT REQ checkbox forces the user to input the quantity, however, even if the checkbox is not set, the user *can* enter a parallel quantity during WT confirmation (Transaction /SCWM/TO_CONF), as seen in Figure 6.58.

In the stock nodes of the EWM monitor, you can see the parallel quantity and the VAL. MEASURED field, which controls if the parallel quantity has been measured or not. The valuation quantity is measured, for example, if the user enters the parallel quantity before goods receipt or during the WT confirmation and the exact parallel quantity is known by the system and the VAL. MEASURED field is set to A (Valuation quantity is measured). If the user confirms a WT without entering the parallel quantity, the stocks on the source and destination bin get the VAL. MEASURED field set to the value B (Valuation quantity is not measured).

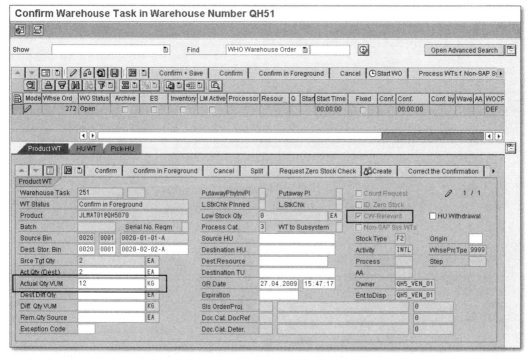

Figure 6.58 WT Confirmation with Parallel Quantity Specified for the Catch Weight Product

6.12.3 Integration of CWM into the EWM Delivery Process

During the inbound delivery processing, you can change the parallel quantity before posting goods receipt. This means that you can enter a quantity that may differ from the notified delivery quantity. The system always corrects the delivery quantity during the actual goods receipt posting.

When you have an inbound delivery without HUs, you can change the parallel quantity on the ADDL QUANTITIES tab of the delivery item. When you press the

VALUATION QUANTITY on this tab, the pop-up screen for the valuation quantity appears, as shown in Figure 6.60.

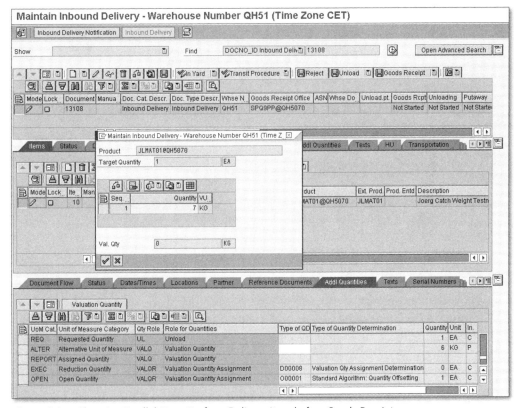

Figure 6.59 CWM Stock in the EWM Monitor

Figure 6.60 Changing Parallel Quantity for a Delivery Item before Goods Receipt

When you are using HUs, you can change the parallel quantity in the packing user interface for the inbound delivery in Transaction /SCWM/PRDI, as seen in Figure 6.61. You can see that the parallel quantity can be changed. The original parallel quantity, in this case, 6 KG, is either the notified quantity or the planned quantity (from the product master). Once the valuation quantities are specified, either in the inbound delivery or in the EWM processing steps, the parallel quantity in the inbound delivery is updated.

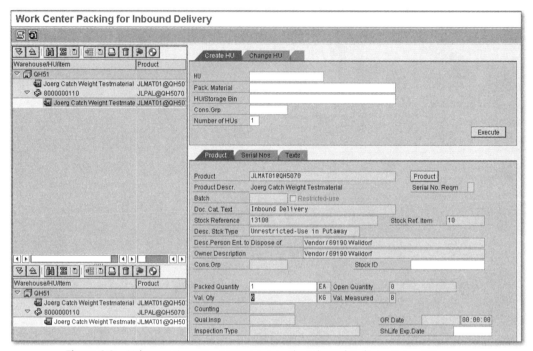

Figure 6.61 Valuation Quantity Assignment on the Inbound Delivery Using HUs

6.12.4 Integration of CWM to Physical Inventory

The creation of a PI document for catch weight–managed products is the same as for standard products. The process becomes different when executing the counting for the PI document, as seen in Figure 6.62. The logistics and parallel quantities can both be entered for catch weight products. The system displays the book inventory quantity in both the logistics unit of measure and the parallel unit of measure, as seen in the quantities on the right side of the count entry in Figure 6.62.

You can specify in customizing that the user must not enter the catch weight quantity manually. In this case, only the logistics quantity can be entered for the PI and the system determines the corresponding parallel quantity automatically in the background using the conversion factors from the product master. This setting is based on the reason code that you enter at the creation of the PI document, which you can configure in the EWM IMG via the menu path EXTENDED WAREHOUSE MANAGEMENT • INTERNAL WAREHOUSE PROCESSES • PHYSICAL INVENTORY • WAREHOUSE-NUMBER-SPECIFIC SETTINGS • REASON AND PRIORITY • DEFINE REASON FOR PHYSICAL INVENTORY.

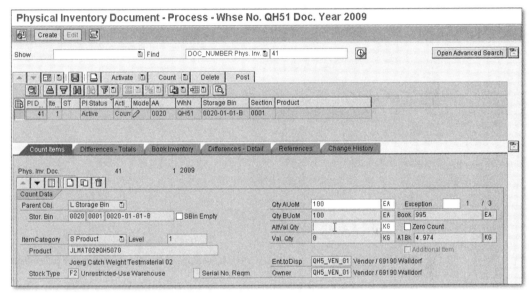

Figure 6.62 Counting CWM Items during PI

To continue the example shown previously, we finally counted 1000 EA and 5100 KG, which results in a difference of 5 EA and 126 KG. After posting the PI document, the difference is moved to the difference area and can be visualized in the difference analyzer, as seen in Figure 6.63.

The displayed difference value (-252 EUR) is shown based on the valuation unit of measure. For products that are not catch weight managed, this value would relate to the logistics unit of measure. The product valuation is integrated from ERP as described in Chapter 14, Physical Inventory, and Chapter 23, Integration with Other SAP Applications.

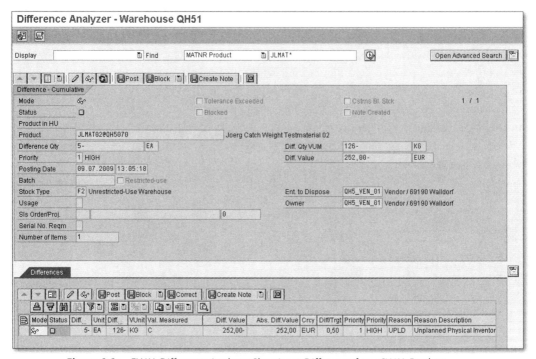

Figure 6.63 EWM Difference Analyzer Showing a Difference for a CWM Product

6.13 Tracking Country of Origin

The Country of Origin (COO) is the country in which goods were originally derived or manufactured. The COO and the rules to determine a COO are covered under various national laws and international treaties. For warehouse management, it is important to distinguish between different COOs, particularly for bonded warehouses or in industries where customers want or have to only order certain COOs for a certain product. For more information on these features and integration with global trade services, see Chapter 23.

SAP EWM allows goods tracking in the warehouse with respect to their COO. You can, for example, have one product number with stock in the warehouse from different countries of origin (e.g., U.S. and China). COO works with and without batches. In the following two sections, we will describe how COO works, first without batch management, then with it.

6.13.1   Country of Origin without Batch Management

If you want to use COO without batches, you can specify the COO before goods receipt in the delivery item. Then, when you create a WT for putaway, the COO will be taken over from the delivery item into the WT. During confirmation of the WT, you can once again change the COO, if necessary or relevant (for example, if the COO is only known after the package is opened during putaway).

The COO is then visible in stock, in the quant. For example, you can see the COO in the warehouse monitor via the STOCK AND BIN • PHYSICAL STOCK node. By using the CHANGE ATTRIBUTES monitor method, you can also change the COO after putaway.

In the standard EWM, the COO is not used in outbound processing. The system doesn't take the COO into consideration when selecting stock for picking. If you need to consider the COO during the WT creation, you can implement it in the available BAdIs for the WT creation.

> **Note**
>
> Using COO *without batches* provides only limited functionality. For example, without using batches, the COO can be overwritten if you add to existing stock and you add stock of one COO to the existing stock of another COO, as the COO is not a "quant splitting" attribute. In addition, you can't use COO during outbound processing without batches (without a BAdI). Therefore, if you need to track COO, we recommend using batches.

6.13.2   Country of Origin with Batch Management

You can also use COO with batches. In this case, you must assign a batch class of the class type 023 to the product master in SAP ERP. You must also assign the object characteristics LOBM_HERKL, which allows you to specify the COO field as a batch characteristic. The COO will still remain a stock attribute and an attribute of the delivery item simultaneously.

It's possible to adopt the COO of the inbound delivery in the corresponding batch characteristic automatically. This already happens in the ERP system. The ERP system transfers the batch with the inbound delivery to the EWM system. When the batch master is created in EWM, EWM can copy over the COO. If a product is batch managed and it is relevant to *customs warehousing*, you must specify a COO in the delivery for goods receipt posting.

In goods receipt, you can only change existing batches for a stock. If you change this, you must also specify an exception code. EWM changes the batch in the stock and in the inbound delivery. EWM also updates the COO, corresponding to the batch characteristic of the new batch.

Outbound deliveries behave similar to inbound deliveries. When confirming the picking WT, the stock and the batch get assigned to the delivery item and the COO, as a batch characteristic, and is also copied over. The customer can specify a COO already in the outbound delivery by using batch selection fields.

6.14 Stock Determination and Valuation

In this section, we will describe the stock determination and the valuation for products in EWM.

6.14.1 Stock Determination

By using stock determination, you can influence how EWM determines in which sequence and from which storage type for every product removed from the requested stock. Stock determination is executed during the creation of WTs. In particular, you can use it to group and sequence stocks by *owner* or by *stock type*. For example, you can specify that EWM first takes into consideration your own stocks and then *consignment stocks* for the same product. In the case of internal movements, you can specify that EWM also takes into consideration different stock types when it can't fulfill the requested quantity by the original stock type.

To use stock determination, you must maintain a STOCK DETERMINATION GROUP in customizing. You assign this group to the product master. Then, for every group, you specify how EWM should determine stock. To maintain the STOCK DETERMINATION GROUPS in the EWM IMG (as seen in Figure 6.64), follow the menu path EXTENDED WAREHOUSE MANAGEMENT • CROSS-PROCESS SETTINGS • STOCK DETERMINATION • MAINTAIN STOCK DETERMINATION GROUPS.

In the stock determination group, you specify the parameter WM HANDLING, which is used to control the determination of the relevant stock for removal during the WT creation. The options for WM HANDLING include:

► **WM has priority**

This means that EWM will use the standard stock removal strategies (for example, first-in/first-out (FIFO) with priority. Within those, EWM will use the owner or stock types you assign to the STOCK DETERMINATION GROUP. For example, you may want to use your own stock and consignment stock for partners 001 and 002 for your product with equal importantance, but respect FIFO across the stock type.

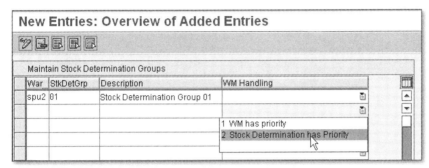

Figure 6.64 Setup of Stock Determination Group

▶ **Stock determination has priority**

This means that priority is given to the stock determination customizing and its sequence. For example, you may want to first pick your own stock (using FIFO) and then consignment stock of partner 001 (using FIFO) and then consignment stock of partner 002 (using FIFO), without regard to managing FIFO across the stock types.

You assign the STOCK DETERMINATION GROUP in the STOCK REMOVAL section of the WAREHOUSE DATA tab on the EWM product master, as seen in Figure 6.65.

Figure 6.65 Stock Determination Group in the EWM Product Master

After you have created and assigned the stock determination group, you must assign either different stock types or owners to the assigned stock determination group. To specify the settings for the stock determination in the EWM IMG, follow the menu path EXTENDED WAREHOUSE MANAGEMENT • CROSS-PROCESS SETTINGS • STOCK DETERMINATION • CONFIGURE STOCK DETERMINATION. In the example provided in Figure 6.66, for WTs with the ACTIVITY PICK and STOCK DETERMINATION GROUP 01, EWM will also take into consideration stock type F1 if stock type F2 was originally requested.

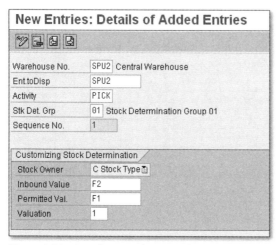

Figure 6.66 Specification of Settings for Stock Determination

As another example, imagine that you have the setup in warehouse SPU2 for stock determination for different owners as described in Table 6.4.

Stock Determination Group	Characteristic	Inbound Value	Permitted Value	Valuation
01	Owner	SPU2	SPU2	10
01	Owner	SPU2	Partner_001	1

Table 6.4 Simplified Example for Stock Determination

In this case, if you use the stock determination has priority strategy, EWM first only searches the warehouse (according to the assigned valuation 10) for your own stock. Within your own stock, it uses the normal stock removal strategy, for example, FIFO. If EWM can't fill the required quantity for the WT, it also searches for the consignment stock of Partner_001 (valuation 1), to fulfill the required quantity. Within this stock, it uses the normal stock removal strategy, for example, FIFO.

If you use the WM has priority strategy, EWM searches for stock from your own warehouse *and* (at the same time) for consignment stock of owner Partner_001. It then combines all found stock and respects the normal stock removal strategy, for example, FIFO. Note that this also means that the *valuation* is not important for the WM has priority strategy.

6.14.2 Stock Valuation

In general, EWM doesn't store or use any valuation data for products. EWM is a logistics module, all financial accounting and controlling is done in the underlying ERP system. However, it is required to have the costs of a material available in EWM for the posting stock differences in the EWM difference analyzer (and especially for tolerance checks of the difference posting), and for counting during inbound processing (you can set up EWM to route a certain product to a counting work center or to force counting during putaway based on the value of the product).

To determine the costs of products from the ERP system and store them in EWM in the EWM Easy Access menu, following the EXTENDED WAREHOUSE MANAGEMENT • PHYSICAL INVENTORY • PERIODIC PROCESSING • DETERMINE AND SET PRICES FROM ERP menu path, or use Transaction code /SCWM/VALUATION_SET. Figure 6.67 shows the results of execution of the valuation set transaction. After you transfer the values to EWM, they are stored there in table /SCWM/T_VALUATE.

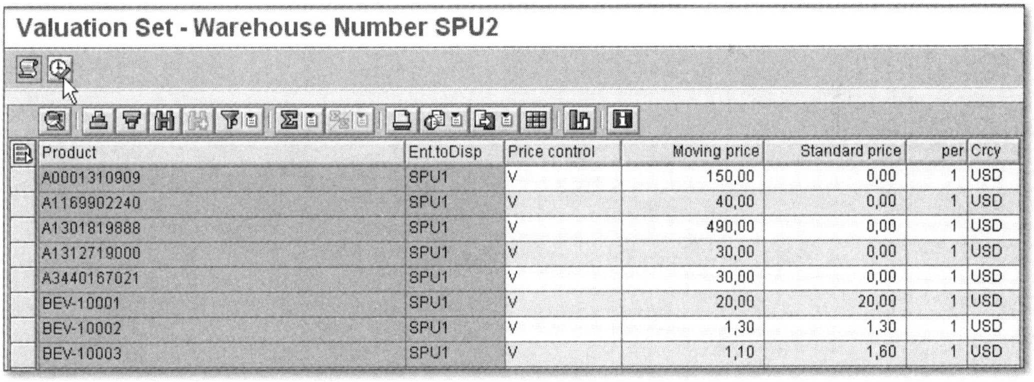

Valuation Set - Warehouse Number SPU2

Product	Ent.toDisp	Price control	Moving price	Standard price	per	Crcy
A0001310909	SPU1	V	150,00	0,00	1	USD
A1169902240	SPU1	V	40,00	0,00	1	USD
A1301819888	SPU1	V	490,00	0,00	1	USD
A1312719000	SPU1	V	30,00	0,00	1	USD
A3440167021	SPU1	V	30,00	0,00	1	USD
BEV-10001	SPU1	V	20,00	20,00	1	USD
BEV-10002	SPU1	V	1,30	1,30	1	USD
BEV-10003	SPU1	V	1,10	1,60	1	USD

Figure 6.67 Importing Stock Valuations from ERP to EWM

6.15 Special Stocks

Special stock is stock that is separated from regular stock, because it is reserved either for a specific sales order item or for project stock. Both options have their own type and number in EWM, which makes it possible that these stocks are only used for their respective purpose. When special stock exists in the warehouse, it can be visualized, together with its respective special stock type and special stock number assignment in the EWM monitor, for example, in the PHYSICAL STOCK node. You can post stock into a special stock type using goods movements for deliveries or posting changes (see the example in the next section).

6.15.1   Sales Order Stock

Stock for individual customers is managed by the special stock type Sales Order Stock (SOS). You can post stock to SOS, for example, using a posting change, as seen in Figure 6.68. You can also receive stock directly to SOS, if the stock is ordered from a vendor specifically for fulfilling a sales order. In the latter case, the special stock type and special stock number are specified in the purchase order and inbound delivery used for processing in EWM.

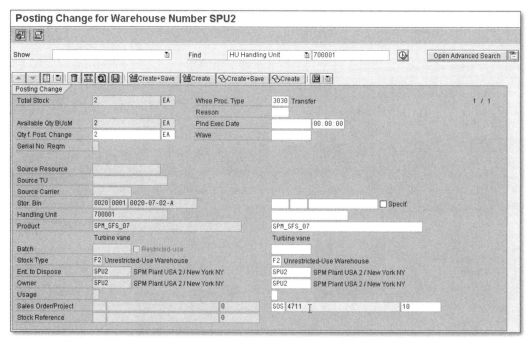

Figure 6.68   Creating a Posting Change to Post Stock onto Sales Order Stock

After the posting change, the special stock type, the sales order number, and sales order item number are assigned a quant, as seen in Figure 6.69.

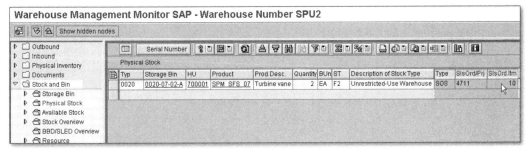

Figure 6.69 Physical Stock (Quant) in Warehouse for SOS

6.15.2 Project Stock

Project stock is stock managed in the warehouse for a specific Work Breakdown Structure element (WBS element) of a project that is defined in the Project System (PS). The components can only be withdrawn for the WBS element. This stock can be seen in the EWM monitor similar to the SOS. Project stock uses the special stock type PJS.

6.16 Summary

In this chapter, we described the many functions and methods that are used in EWM to manage the stocks in the warehouse. This should give you a basis for understanding the functions that utilize these stock management techniques to segregate and differentiate the stocks so that you always have knowledge and visibility to the stocks in your warehouse and the ability to process them. In the coming chapters, we will further enhance your understanding of the basic concepts of EWM by describing the warehouse document types and the methods for integration to ERP, then we will begin to describe the functions in the warehouse that make use of these basic concepts.

In this chapter, we'll introduce the different warehouse document types and explain their meaning and use.

7   Warehouse Document Types

In the following sections, we'll describe the most important document types in Extended Warehouse Management (EWM). We'll start with the document types for inbound delivery and outbound delivery processing. After that, we will explain the *warehouse task (WT)*, which is a single movement of one product or handling unit (HU), and the *warehouse order (WO)*, which is a combination of warehouse tasks. Then we will show how EWM combines the outbound delivery items into *waves*. Wave management is very flexible in EWM and significantly enhanced compared to ERP Warehouse Management.

After that, we will discuss *physical inventory (PI) documents*, which are used to manage PI processes. Next, we'll cover the *value-added service (VAS) order*, which is a special document type for managing activities for VASs, for example, packaging, oiling, or repainting of a product.

Then, we'll look at *stock transfer documents* and *posting change documents*. Stock transfers are created to plan movements within the warehouse from one bin to another, whereas posting changes are created to plan movements within the warehouse from one stock type to another. And, finally, we'll explain the *quality inspection documents* in EWM.

7.1   Inbound Delivery Documents

The inbound process in EWM usually starts within the ERP system. In ERP, an inbound delivery document is created with reference to a purchase order or a scheduling agreement, either manually or based on receipt from an Advanced Shipping Notice (ASN) via Electronic Data Interchange (EDI) or within the Supplier Network Collaboration (SNC) solution. Upon saving the inbound delivery document, ERP checks to see if the delivery belongs to an EWM-managed warehouse number. If the inbound delivery is EWM managed, the document is transferred to the EWM system. A delivery is EWM managed if the combination of plant and storage location used in the delivery item belongs to an EWM warehouse number. The settings for the inbound delivery type in ERP must be set correctly with regard to the split of the deliveries by warehouse number in order for the documents to be correctly distributed to EWM.

When the inbound delivery document is received in EWM from ERP, a document called the *inbound delivery notification* (IDN) is created in EWM. This document contains all of the information from the inbound delivery sent by ERP.

The IDN is a document that exists mainly in the background. You don't usually work actively with an IDN — it is meant to be an interim document. There are no meaningful follow-up functions with an IDN, such as warehouse task creation. The only possible actions are either to activate or reject the IDN with two pushbuttons above the header data, as seen in Figure 7.1. The primary role of the IDN is to hold the original inbound delivery information from ERP and to act as an interim document for the creation of the EWM inbound delivery (inbound delivery; as described later) if, for example, you need to specify some split criteria for the creation of the ID documents.

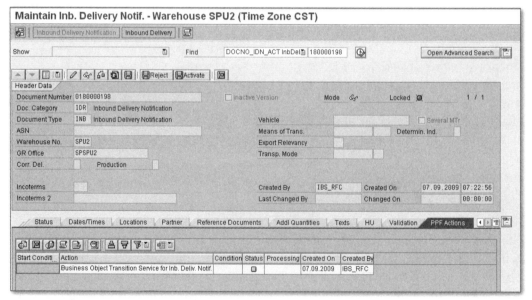

Figure 7.1 IDN in EWM with Post-Processing Framework (PPF) Action for Activation

There are two possible actions for the IDN once it is created — you can reject the IDN, or you can activate it. Rejecting an IDN means to set the delivery quantity to zero in EWM and in ERP. You can use this function, for example, if you learn from the vendor that the product will not actually arrive in the warehouse or if an administrator in ERP made a mistake in creating the inbound delivery. Activating an IDN, on the other hand, will result in the creation of the subsequent document in EWM — the inbound delivery. The activation of the IDN is normally set to be created in the background (see the following note), so if you create an inbound delivery document in the ERP system, you get the inbound delivery created in EWM. The EWM inbound delivery then acts as the main document for further inbound processing.

> **Note**
>
> In EWM Standard, the activation of an IDN happens automatically. However, the activation is configurable. In the PPF the Processing Time is set to 3 — IMMEDIATE PROCESSING for action definition /SCDL/IDR_TRANSFER of action profile /SCDL/IDR and application /SCDL/DELIVERY.
>
> To switch the automatic activation off, you can set the processing time to 1 — PROCESSING USING SELECTION REPORT. For more information about the PPF, see Chapter 24, Post-Processing Framework and Form Printing.

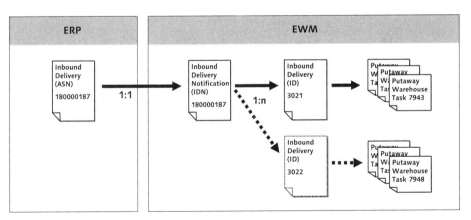

Figure 7.2 Documents in inbound deliveries Processing

In Figure 7.2, you can see a diagram of how the ERP inbound delivery document is linked to the EWM IDN and the EWM inbound delivery. In the simple process, you have one ERP inbound delivery, one EWM IDN, and one EWM inbound delivery. However, EWM also allows multiple inbound deliveries for one IDN. This makes sense in some business scenarios, for example, when you determine during goods receipt that a delivery item (product) will arrive later. In this case, you can split off this delivery line from the current inbound delivery and let EWM create another inbound delivery with a new number. Both inbound deliveries have the same IDN as a reference.

For more information about inbound delivery processing, see Chapter 9, Inbound Processing.

7.2   Outbound Delivery Documents

The outbound process in EWM is usually initiated from the ERP system. In ERP, an outbound delivery document is created, usually with reference to a customer sales order (from ERP or Customer Relationship Management (CRM)) or a stock transport order. Upon saving the outbound delivery document, ERP determines if the combination of plant and storage location used in the delivery item belongs to a warehouse that is managed by EWM. If the delivery is EWM managed, the document is transferred to EWM. Like the inbound delivery processing, the settings for the outbound delivery type in ERP must be set correctly with regard to the split of the deliveries by warehouse number in order for the documents to be correctly distributed to EWM.

When the ERP outbound delivery document is received in EWM, a document called the *outbound delivery request* (ODR) is created. This document contains all of the information sent from ERP on the outbound delivery document. The ODR is a document that exists mainly in the background. You don't usually work actively with an ODR, it is meant to be an interim document. There are no meaningful follow-up functions with an ODR, such as warehouse task creation. The primary role of the ODR is to hold the original outbound delivery information from ERP and to act as an interim document for the creation of the *outbound delivery order* (ODO) (described next) if, for instance, you need to specify some split criteria for the creation of the ODOs.

There are two possible actions for the ODR once it is created — you can reject the ODR, or you can activate it. Rejecting an ODR will result in setting the delivery quantity to zero in EWM and in ERP. On the other hand, activating an ODR will result in the creation of the subsequent document in EWM — the ODO. The activation normally happens in the background (similar to the previous note regarding the inbound delivery documents), so if you create an outbound delivery document in the ERP system, you get the EWM ODO. The ODO acts as the main document for outbound processing in EWM.

Upon posting goods issue for the ODO, EWM creates a third document — the EWM outbound delivery, which is sometimes called the *final delivery* (FD). The illustration in Figure 7.3 shows how the documents in EWM outbound processing are linked to each other. In the simplest case, you have one ERP outbound delivery, one EWM ODR, one EWM ODO, and one EWM outbound delivery (i.e., a 1:1 relationship between the documents). EWM also allows multiple ODOs for one ODR and multiple outbound deliveries for one ODR (i.e., a 1:n relationship, where one document can have multiple follow-up documents).

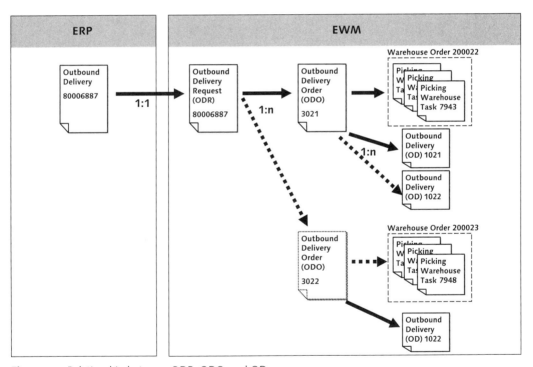

Figure 7.3 Relationship between ODR, ODO, and OD

For more information about outbound processing, see Chapter 10, Outbound Processing.

7.3   Warehouse Tasks

The WT document is used to represent both physical movements and posting changes in the warehouse. There are two types of WTs in the warehouse. For physical movements, EWM distinguishes between WTs for stock (also called *product warehouse tasks*) and WTs for an HU (also called *handling unit WTs* or simply *HU WTs*).

For posting changes, WTs are used to document the change of a stock value (e.g., owner or stock type) on the database. WTs for posting changes typically have two items (one item for the original data and a second item for the changed data). They have a special WT category and number range, so it is easy to distinguish them from physical movements.

The categories for warehouse tasks in EWM include:

- ▶ 1 — Putaway
- ▶ 2 — Stock Removal
- ▶ 3 — Internal Warehouse Movement
- ▶ 4 — Posting Change

> **Note**
>
> To create WTs, you must define and assign two number range intervals (for example, 01 for physical movements and 02 for posting changes). To create the number ranges in the EWM Implementation Guide (IMG), follow the menu path EXTENDED WAREHOUSE MANAGEMENT • MASTER DATA • DEFINE NUMBER RANGES • DEFINE NUMBER RANGES FOR WAREHOUSE TASKS/WAREHOUSE DOCUMENTS. To assign the number range intervals to the warehouse in the EWM IMG, select the activity ASSIGN NUMBER RANGE INTERVALS TO WAREHOUSE NUMBER from the preceding IMG path.

The processing status of the warehouse tasks is tracked for each WT according to its status. The possible statuses for the WTs include:

- ▶ (blank) — Open
- ▶ A — Cancelled
- ▶ B — Waiting
- ▶ C — Confirmed

When you create a WT, it is usually created with the initial status OPEN, which indicates that you can work with the WT by confirming or cancelling it. Once a WT is confirmed or canceled (status A or C), you cannot change it or revert the status back to OPEN. Status B (Waiting, also referred to as Inactive) is assigned to WTs that are part of EWMs multistep storage control (which is further described in Chapter 13, Configuring Multistep Warehouse Movements). This status indicates that another WT must be confirmed before the Waiting WT can be executed. Confirmation of the dependent WT will automatically update the Waiting WT and update the status to OPEN when appropriate.

In addition to product WTs and HU WTs, there is also a third variant — yard WTs. In the following subsections, we will explain each of these three WT variants in more detail.

7.3.1 Product Warehouse Tasks

Product WTs are movements of stock within the warehouse. A product WT always contains a product number, quantity, and source and destination location (storage bin or a resource). Product WTs are normally used for picking, putaway, and internal movements (there are some exceptions). For these processes, the product WT is generally created initially to determine the original source and destination bins, and then the storage control functions (process-oriented storage control (POSC) and layout-oriented storage control (LOSC)), if they are relevant, are used to determine the interim steps for multistep movements. When this occurs, the first WT generated according to the storage control (which contains the first interim location as the destination bin) is activated while the product WT (which maintains the final location as the destination bin) is in status WAITING (as described previously). The product WT remains in status WAITING until it can be activated for the final movement into the destination bin.

Product WTs for internal movements may also be created from the EWM Easy Access menu by following the EXTENDED WAREHOUSE MANAGEMENT • WORK SCHEDULING • CREATE WAREHOUSE TASK WITHOUT REFERENCE • MOVE PRODUCT menu path, or using Transaction code /SCWM/ADPROD.

7.3.2 Handling Unit Warehouse Tasks

An HU WT is used to move an entire HU in the warehouse — including its content. An HU WT always contains an HU number and a source and destination location. It does not contain any product number or quantity, but is linked implicitly to the contents of the HU via the HU number. The POSC is only relevant in the case of full HU movement, and therefore the interim tasks described previously are always HU tasks. For more information about configuring multistep warehouse movements, see Chapter 13.

In addition to the HU WTs created for inbound and outbound processes, you can also create ad hoc WTs for internal movements from the EWM Easy Access menu by following the EXTENDED WAREHOUSE MANAGEMENT • WORK SCHEDULING • CREATE WAREHOUSE TASK WITHOUT REFERENCE • MOVE HANDLING UNIT menu path, or using Transaction code /SCWM/ADHU. Because it also possible to create and track empty HUs in EWM, you can move the empty HUs by creating an HU WT.

7.3.3 Yard Warehouse Tasks

Yard WTs are only used to move transportation units and vehicles in the yard of an EWM warehouse. The source and destination of a yard WT are yard bins, doors, or checkpoints. You can only create yard WTs by following the EXTENDED WAREHOUSE MANAGEMENT • SHIPPING AND RECEIVING • YARD MANAGEMENT • CREATE WAREHOUSE TASK IN YARD menu path, or using Transaction code /SCWM/YMOVE. For more information about yard movements, see Chapter 18, Yard Management.

7.4 Warehouse Orders

EWM uses WO documents to bundle one or more WT documents into work packages, with the intent that a warehouse employee can execute the WT within a reasonable time period (as defined by your warehouse operations). Every WT in EWM is assigned to a WO. However, they are most useful in creating work packages that let you use system-driven processing, allowing the EWM system to propose the next suitable work package to the user for processing.

In the next three sections, we will explain the WO concept in more detail, explain the rules for WO creation, and describe how the WO document is also used to group PI documents.

7.4.1 The Warehouse Order Concept

When creating the WTs, EWM first searches for stock and creates one or more WTs for each item. Then EWM passes the created WTs to a function called WAREHOUSE ORDER CREATION (as seen in Figure 7.4). This function creates the WOs and assigns the WTs to the WOs, based on certain rules, limits, filters, and profiles (determined according to the *warehouse order creation rule* (WOCR) determination). A warehouse employee receives this WO as a work package to execute the movements (for example, picks for an ODO). By appropriately using the WOCR and creating well-formed WOs, you can optimize the efficiency of your employees and resources in the warehouse.

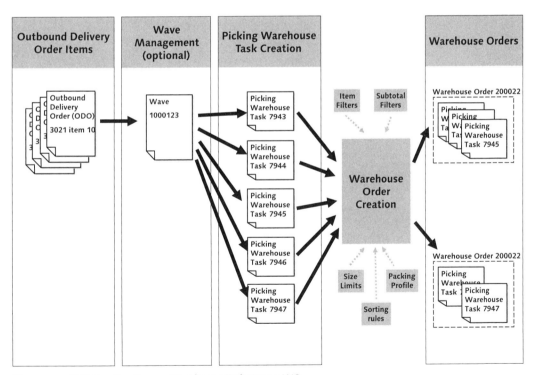

Figure 7.4 WO Creation Groups Warehouse Tasks into a WO

You can use WO creation together with wave management to effectively manage your outbound processes. *Waves* are documents used to group delivery items together before the WT creation to process the items at the same time. You can create picking WTs for all delivery items in the wave together, and the WO creation will then process all of the WTs together to create more efficient WOs.

You can print WO documents using the PPF or within the EWM Warehouse Monitor (Transaction /SCWM/MON) via the DOCUMENTS • WAREHOUSE ORDER node, however the most common method for executing WOs in large or high-volume distribution centers is using the mobile data entry transactions.

The possible statuses for the WOs once they have been generated include:

▸ (Blank) — Open

▸ A — Cancelled

▸ B — Locked

▸ C — Confirmed

▸ D — In Process

When a WO is created, it is usually assigned to the OPEN status. If you use wave management and choose the wave release method "release locked"; the WO will get status B (Locked) and you must *unlock* the WO before you can execute it (for example, via the EWM Warehouse Monitor node: DOCUMENTS • WAREHOUSE ORDER). When a warehouse employee is working on a WO, the status changes from Open to D (In Process). When all WTs of a WO are confirmed, the WO is assigned to status C (Confirmed).

Note

EWM starts the WO creation once an *active* WTs is created or once an inactive WT is activated. Inactive WTs (status B) are not yet assigned to a WO.

7.4.2 Warehouse Order Creation Rules

When WTs are passed to the WO creation, they are processed according to the defined WOCR. The sequence of events within the WO creation progresses as follows:

1. All WTs are grouped by activity area (AA) and queue. Every group of WTs with the same AA and queue is passed independently to the next step.
   Note: You can set up in the Warehouse Process Type (WPT) if the AA should be based on the source bin or on the destination bin of the WT.

2. EWM customizing is read to determine which WOCRs exist for the AA. You can set up multiple WOCRs per AA and bring them into a sequence. EWM starts with the first WOCR and passes all WTs to it.
   Note: If no WOCR is set up, EWM uses a default WOCR called DEF.

3. EWM applies an item filter and a subtotal filter to WTs. You can use these filters to filter out tasks that do not meet certain conditions, for example, all tasks with more than a specific weight. The subtotal filter is used to filter WTs that do not fulfill certain criteria by consolidation group (the criteria for "subtotal" is always the consolidation group). For example, you can filter out all WTs for a specific consolidation group if there are not at least *x* WTs processed.

4. All WTs that did not pass the filters of the WOCR are passed on to the next WOCR in the sequence, according to the customizing settings.
   Note: If there are no WOCRs left in the sequence for the AA, EWM assigns a default WOCR called UNDE (meaning Undetermined).

5. The WTs that passed the filters are now sorted. The sorting at this step is called *inbound sorting*. You can configure the criteria for which the sorting will take place. For example, the sequence number of the bin can be used if you want to pick according to the pick path defined by the bin sequence.

6. The sorted WTs are next checked according to the *limits*. You can configure limits per WOCR, for example, a maximum of 10 tasks per WO. The limits do not change the WOCR, they only impact on the size of the individual WOs.

7. Another sorting function, called *pack sorting*, occurs next. Pack sorting allows you to sort the WTs, for example, by descending volume.

8. Next, the packing profile is applied to each WO. Packing materials can be assigned to the WO based on weight, volume, or dimensional data. Pick HUs can be created and assigned to the WO based on the determined packing materials. If the WTs do not fit completely in one Pick HU according to the capacity of the packaging material, they can be split into multiple HUs.

9. Finally, a last sort is executed, called *WT sorting*. Using WT sorting, you can sort the WTs once again, for example, by pick path. This lets you sort the tasks for picking within the WO (as opposed to the previous sorts that occur before the splitting of the WOs and therefore are used primarily for determining which items are included within each WO).

At the end, the created WOs (and the associated WTs that were grouped into the WO) are saved to the database and, assuming they are created in an open status, can then be executed by the warehouse employees.

7.4.3 Warehouse Orders for Physical Inventory Documents

WOs are also used to group PI documents to assign work packages to the warehouse employees who execute the counting. For more information about PI counting, see Chapter 14, Physical Inventory.

7.5 Waves

Wave documents are used to group delivery items and to create WTs and WOs for the group of delivery items at the same time. This allows optimization of the picking efficiency and also eases monitoring and tracking of the outbound process.

Waves can be created automatically or manually. To facilitate the automatic creation of waves, you can use *wave templates*. Attributes such as lock time, planned pick and release time, calendar, and capacity data are determined from the wave templates. To create the wave templates from the Easy Access menu, follow the EXTENDED WAREHOUSE MANAGEMENT • WORK SCHEDULING • WAVE MANAGEMENT • MAINTAIN WAVE TEMPLATES menu path, or use Transaction code /SCWM/WAVETMP. Determination of the relevant wave template is based on the condition technique. To specify the conditions for wave template determination from the EWM Easy Access menu, follow the EXTENDED WAREHOUSE MANAGEMENT • WORK SCHEDULING • WAVE MANAGEMENT • MAINTAIN CONDITIONS FOR DETERMINING WAVE TEMPLATES menu path, or use Transaction code /SCWM/WDGCM.

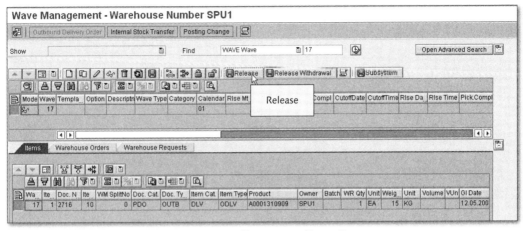

Figure 7.5 Processing Existing Wave Using Wave Management Transaction

If you want to manually create a new wave or change or display an existing wave, EWM provides a single transaction (seen in Figure 7.5) that combines all of the important activities for wave processing. To access the wave processing transaction from the SAP Easy Access menu, follow the EXTENDED WAREHOUSE MANAGEMENT • WORK SCHEDULING • WAVE MANAGEMENT • MAINTAIN WAVES menu path, or use Transaction /SCWM/WAVE. For more information about wave management for outbound processing, see Chapter 10.

7.6   Physical Inventory Documents

PI documents are the basis for the PI process. They are used to plan the PI, perform the counting, record the count data, and post the differences that can occur during count. To create PI documents from the SAP Easy Access menu, follow the EXTENDED WAREHOUSE MANAGEMENT • PHYSICAL INVENTORY • CREATE PHYSICAL INVENTORY DOCUMENT menu path, or use Transaction code /SCWM/PI_CREATE. To process existing PI documents (as seen in Figure 7.6) from the Easy Access menu, follow the EXTENDED WAREHOUSE MANAGEMENT • PHYSICAL INVENTORY • PROCESS PHYSICAL INVENTORY DOCUMENT menu path, or use Transaction code /SCWM/PI_PROGRESS.

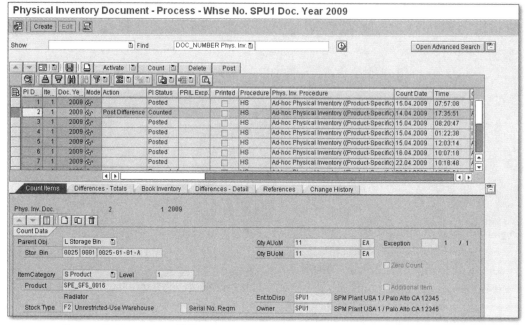

Figure 7.6 Processing a PI Document

When processing PI documents, you can perform the following functions:

▶ Activate/Deactivate: An inactive PI document is not yet assigned to a WO and therefore cannot be processed by a resource. To count and print PI documents, you must first activate them.

▶ Count: While counting the PI document, you can enter data such as counter, count date, product, batch, and quantity of the stock.

▶ Recount: If you have doubts about a count result (or if the difference in the count from the book quantity exceeds the allowed tolerance), you can trigger a recount. In this case, the system automatically creates a new PI document with reference to the original PI document, and the new count document can again be executed in the warehouse.

▶ Delete: You can delete PI documents if they have the status Active, Inactive, or Counted. If the count results have been posted, you can no longer delete the PI document.

▸ Post: When you post the PI document, you complete the PI document and trigger the posting of relevant stock differences to the bin (with the differences posted to the difference area to be evaluated by the Difference Analyzer).

▸ Print: You can print a PI document if you want the counters to document the count results on paper and an administrator to subsequently enter the counts into the documents within EWM. The printed document is also called the *PI count document*.

For more information about PI counting, see Chapter 14.

7.7 Value-Added Service Orders

VAS orders are documents that contain information related to the execution of VASs in the warehouse. Typical VAS activities include labeling, oiling, packing products (according to customer requirements or internal requirements), or kitting. The VAS order is used to inform warehouse employees about the work they have to perform when executing the VAS, and which products should be processed with the VAS (including products, packaging material, and auxiliary packaging materials). The VAS order can be printed, displayed in the VAS maintenance transaction (as seen in Figure 7.7), or displayed at the VAS work center.

A VAS order consists of the following components:

▸ VAS Order Header: The header contains (besides other fields) an overall status and the packaging specification used for creating the order.

▸ VAS Activities: VAS activities contain (besides other fields) a product (e.g., a packing material), the quantity, an activity status field, the duration, the work center in which the activity is performed, and the step of the internal routing.

▸ Warehouse Request Items: The warehouse request items contain the product and the quantity on which the VAS Activities should be performed.

▸ Auxiliary Products: Auxiliary products can be used to document consumption of other products (for example, oil).

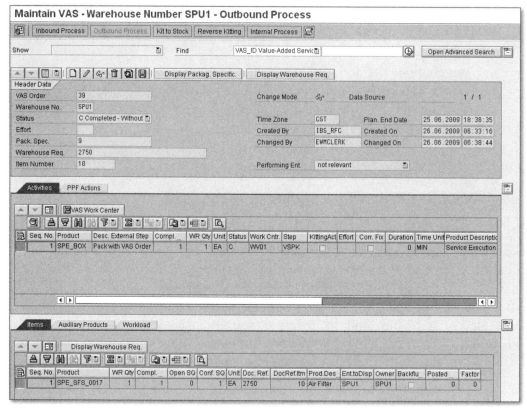

Figure 7.7 Maintenance of a VAS Order

VAS orders are always related to a delivery item and to a packaging specification, which is the primary master data used for generating a VAS activity. For more information about VASs, see Chapter 19, Value-Added Services.

7.8 Stock Transfers and Posting Changes

EWM distinguishes between the terms *stock transfer* and *posting change*. A stock transfer refers to a movement of stock from one location to another within the warehouse. On the other hand, a posting change is used if the stock attributes, such as the stock type, need to be changed (and often involves a transfer of data to ERP about the change in stock attributes, depending on the mapping to the ERP stock categories).

To create stock transfers or posting changes in EWM, you can either create the WTs directly, or you can first create a warehouse request (WR) and then create the WTs with reference to the WRs.

To directly create a WT for a stock transfer from the EWM Easy Access menu, follow the EXTENDED WAREHOUSE MANAGEMENT • WORK SCHEDULING • CREATE WAREHOUSE TASK WITHOUT REFERENCE • MOVE PRODUCT menu path, or use Transaction /SCWM/ADPROD (or for HUs, you can also use Transaction /SCWM/ADHU) and select the CREATE WAREHOUSE TASK button. To first create a WR, use the same transaction, but select the CREATE WAREHOUSE REQUEST (or CREATE + SAVE WAREHOUSE REQUEST) button. When you generate a WR this way, an EWM internal delivery document is created, which you can then use for further processing. This allows you, for example, to create multiple WRs for stock transfer, combine them into a wave, then release the wave to optimize the picking of the stock.

To create a posting change (for example, to change the stock type) from the EWM Easy Access menu, follow the EXTENDED WAREHOUSE MANAGEMENT • WORK SCHEDULING • MAKE POSTING CHANGE FOR PRODUCT menu path, or use Transaction /SCWM/POST, and click on the CREATE POSTING CHANGE button. Alternatively, if you want to first create the WR, use the same transaction, but select the CREATE WAREHOUSE REQUEST (or CREATE + SAVE WAREHOUSE REQUEST) button (as seen in Figure 7.8).

You can also create WRs for stock transfers from the EWM Easy Access menu by following the EXTENDED WAREHOUSE MANAGEMENT • DELIVERY PROCESSING • MAINTAIN INTERNAL STOCK TRANSFER menu path, or using Transaction code /SCWM/IM_ST. And you can create WRs for posting changes from the EWM Easy Access menu by following the EXTENDED WAREHOUSE MANAGEMENT • DELIVERY PROCESSING • POSTING CHANGE • MAINTAIN POSTING CHANGE menu path, or using Transaction code /SCWM/IM_PC.

For more information about internal movements, including stock transfers and posting changes, see Chapter 12, Internal Warehouse Movements.

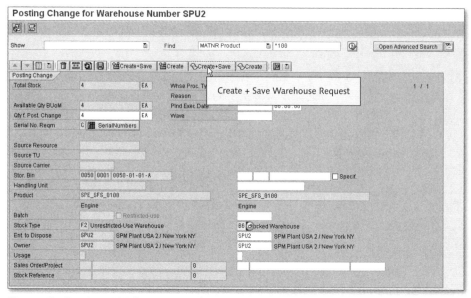

Figure 7.8 Creating a WR for a Posting Change to Change the Stock Type

7.9 Quality Inspection Documents

Quality Inspection (QI) documents in EWM are used to store information about the stocks that are to be quality checked and the findings and results from the inspection. In Figure 7.9, you can see the EWM transaction for processing QI documents. For more information about QI during inbound processing, see Chapter 9, Inbound Processing.

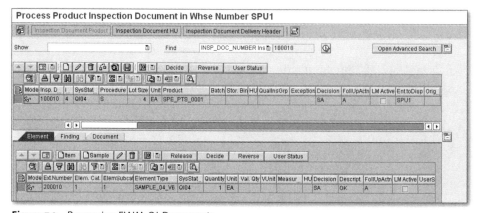

Figure 7.9 Processing EWM QI Documents

7.10   Summary

In this chapter, we described the main document types used by EWM and briefly, how to use them. You should now have a good basis for understanding the basic architecture of the EWM solution. In the following chapter, we will describe the integration between ERP and EWM, and then in the next chapters we begin to describe the features and functions of EWM in detail.

In this chapter, we will discuss the basic setup of the integration between ERP and Extended Warehouse Management (EWM) for both master data and transactional data.

8   Integration from ERP to EWM

One of the first steps in the realization phase of an SAP project is the setup of the system landscape. In this chapter, we will explain the specific steps required to install a system environment consisting of an SAP ERP and an EWM instance. Usually, EWM is installed on a separate system or instance, connected to an ERP system via remote function calls (RFCs). EWM is technically based on the SAP Supply Chain Management (SCM) basis. This means, EWM is a decentralized system by design and there are interfaces that have to be set up to integrate the solution to ERP.

The decision to design EWM in a decentralized way was based partially on the experiences with ERP warehouse management. ERP warehouse management provides the option to manage the Warehouse Management module within the central ERP system (so on the same system where Finance (FI), Controlling (CO), Sales and Distribution (SD), Production Planning (PP), Materials Management (MM), and other applications run). However, it is also possible to manage the Warehouse Management module decentralized on a separate ERP system that is entirely reserved for warehouse management. The latter has a lot of business benefits. Even if the central ERP is down for maintenance, the work in the warehouse can continue. Also, from a performance perspective, the warehouse management system can be sized and upgraded independently, and the warehouse management hardware can be physically located close to the warehouse itself leading to faster response times. The same advantages also hold true for deploying EWM on the SCM platform, which is decentralized, or segregated from ERP, by design.

In addition to the option to deploy EWM on the SCM platform, SAP now also provides the option to install EWM as an add-on to an SAP ERP system. The benefit to implementing the EWM add-on is that you have one less system to purchase and maintain, and users would be able to use both ERP and EWM via a single menu and a single logon. However, from an integration standpoint, the EWM add-on solution works the same as if it was deployed on the SCM platform — you still have to configure the RFC interfaces for the communication between ERP and EWM, but the interfaces are recursive, meaning that the system is basically interfacing with itself. The advantage to this design is that SAP (and you) doesn't have to maintain two separate interface methods, depending on the deployment option — the same interfaces are used for both. In this chapter, we will focus on the SCM deployment option, but the comments, in most cases, will apply to both solutions.

The interfaces between the ERP and EWM systems are using queued RFC (qRFC) technology for communication, for both master data (which uses a special implementation of the qRFC known as the SAP Advanced Planning and Optimization (APO) core interface (CIF) and application data. In Figure 8.1, you can see an example of the qRFC integration to support a specific business process, in this case, to support the integration of inbound deliveries.

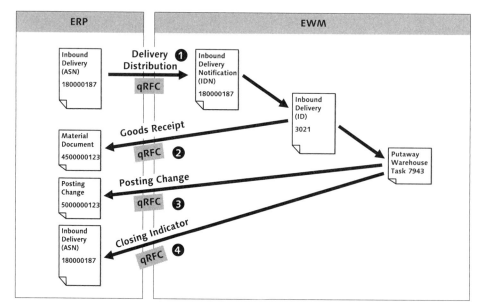

Figure 8.1 Integration between EWM and ERP Works via qRFC

For releases of SAP ERP earlier than ERP 2005, intermediate documents (IDocs) may be used to interface delivery documents between ERP and EWM. The IDoc interface is based on the interface that already existed for connecting ERP to a decentralized warehouse management (DWM) system. While the IDoc interface supports the basic processes of EWM, this interface method doesn't support every EWM business processes. Because the IDoc interface is not the primary interface method and will be implemented on a limited basis, we will not describe it in detail in this text, but for a little more information about the IDoc interface, see Chapter 23, Integration to Other Applications.

8.1 Basic System Setup

After the ERP and EWM systems are installed from an SAP basis perspective, you can start to connect ERP and EWM from a business process point of view. To begin the process, you need to consider the following steps during the basic setup (among others):

- Create an RFC user in ERP/EWM
- Name the logical systems and assign them to clients
- Define the RFC destinations in ERP
- Set the target system and queue type
- Maintain qRFC monitor settings in ERP
- Set user parameters for data transfer
- Activate additional material master screens and additional screen sequences
- Maintain number ranges
- Activate enhancements for service parts management (SPM)
- Define a separate business system
- Set up control for qRFC
- Set control parameters for ERP version control in EWM

More details about these steps can be found in the SAP *EWM-ERP Integration-Guides*, which can be found in the SAP Solution Manager. To access the guides within the SAP Solution Manager from the SAP Easy Access menu, follow the Tools • SAP Solution Manager • Configuration menu path, or use Transaction

SOLAR02. Within the transaction, choose the SCM Configuration Structure. There, you will find nodes about EWM called Basic Settings for EWM. These nodes contain the latest versions of the relevant guides.

8.2 Master Data Integration

The exchange and synchronization of *master data* between EWM and ERP is managed in a special implementation of the qRFC known as the SAP CIF. In this section, we will introduce the CIF, the different functions of the CIF, how it is used to initially transfer master data to EWM, and how it can be administered.

> **Note**
>
> As of SAP ECC 6.0, CIF is an integrated part of the ERP system. To install the relevant communication layers for earlier version of the ERP system, you must import the relevant SAP R/3 plug-in for APO.

In the following sections, we will describe the following features of the CIF with regard to the integration between ERP and EWM:

▶ Initial transfer of master data from ERP to EWM

▶ Transfer of changed master data from ERP to EWM

▶ Control over master data objects creation methods in EWM

▶ Tools for administering the data transfer

Initial Transfer of a Master Data Object

New master data (for example, a new material master record) created in ERP can be transferred automatically to EWM, without manual intervention. To trigger the automatic transfer of the master data, you can schedule a job to run periodically or you can set up the CIF to run based on the creation of change pointers in EWM, so that the changes are transferred immediately. Toward the end of this chapter, we will show how to create the batch job. In the meantime, we will begin by showing you how the *manual transfer* of master data works so that you understand the background for the automatic transfer.

To begin the master data integration, you should start with creation of a new MATERIAL (as seen in Figure 8.2). To create the material master from the ERP Easy Access menu, follow the LOGISTICS • MATERIALS MANAGEMENT • MATERIAL

MASTER • MATERIAL • CREATE (GENERAL) • IMMEDIATELY menu path, or use Transaction code MM01. The data fields used during the master data creation that are relevant to EWM are described in detail in Chapter 4, Product Master Data.

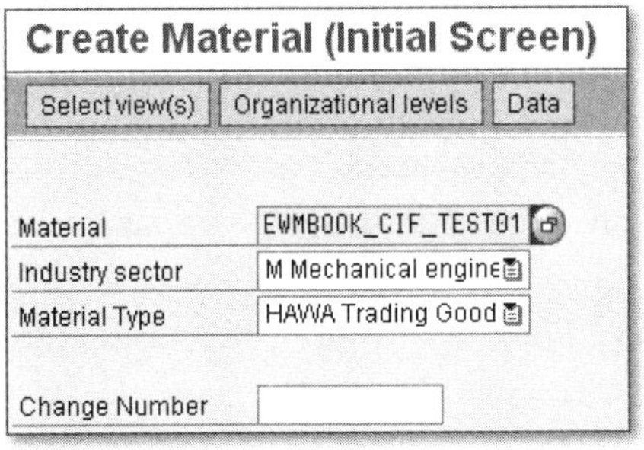

Figure 8.2 Creating a New Material Master in ERP

After the material is created and saved, you need to *create* and *activate* a CIF integration model to trigger the transfer to EWM. To create the integration model from the ERP Easy Access menu, follow the LOGISTICS • CENTRAL FUNCTIONS • SUPPLY CHAIN PLANNING INTERFACE • CORE INTERFACE ADVANCED PLANNER AND OPTIMIZER • INTEGRATION MODEL • CREATE menu path, or use Transaction code CFM1. To activate the integration model from the SAP Easy Access menu once it is created, follow the LOGISTICS • CENTRAL FUNCTIONS • SUPPLY CHAIN PLANNING INTERFACE • CORE INTERFACE ADVANCED PLANNER AND OPTIMIZER • INTEGRATION MODEL • ACTIVATE menu path, or use Transaction code CFM2.

The first step to using the CIF is to create a new integration model. In Transaction CFM1, you must enter a model name, an APO application (see the following note about the naming), and the logical system name of the EWM system. For the model name and APO application, you can use any string as long as they are unique. You will use these values again to later activate, change, or delete the model. Because you will likely reuse the model selections over and over again to create and activate the model, you should create an appropriately named selection variant for the transactions (both CFM1 and CFM2) with the model name, APO application, and logical system specified in the variant. You will also use this variant name if you automate the creation and activation of the models to capture new materials, as described later in this chapter.

> **Note**
>
> The CIF was originally developed for master data integration to SAP APO, and most references to the CIF within ERP will include the APO name in the title, even though the CIF is also used for integration of master data to EWM. Don't get confused — it's the same CIF!

The next step is to select the objects that you want to include into this integration model. In the left pane of the transaction screen, there are checkboxes and SELECT OPTION buttons. By selecting the checkboxes for object types, you include these types into the integration model. For example, if you check MATERIALS and PLANTS, you include both types into the model. Then, you select the SELECT OPTION buttons for the relevant object to display the selection data on the right pane of the screen. On the right side, you then enter the selection criteria for the objects that should be included. In Figure 8.3, you can see that we selected the MATERIALS checkbox and entered EWMBOOK_CIF_TEST* in the selection screen on the right. This specifies that every material that starts with EWMBOOK_CIF_TEST as a prefix for the material number will be included within this integration model when it is created.

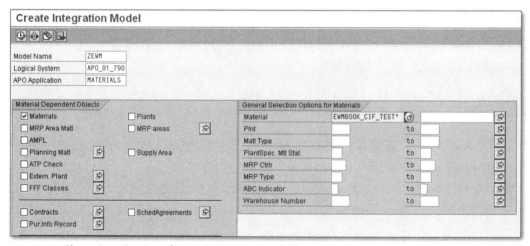

Figure 8.3 Creation of a New Integration Model for Material Master Data

Finally, to create the model, you select the EXECUTE button from the toolbar. The master data objects will be selected according to your selection criteria and the number of master data objects (per object name) will be shown on the resulting summary page. From the summary page, you can review the data that was selected (by clicking on the hot link in the NUMBER column) and decide if everything that you expected is included. If you find something is missing, you can still go back and change the selection. Otherwise, you can save the new integration model by clicking on the GENERATE IM button (as shown in Figure 8.4).

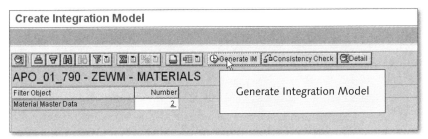

Figure 8.4 Creation of an Integration Model: Overview of the Selected Objects

Once you generate the integration model, the next step is to activate it. Activating the integration model triggers the distribution of the materials (the ones that were included when you created the integration model in the previous step) to EWM. To activate the integration model, start Transaction CFM2, enter the model data from earlier (model name, logical system, and APO application) in the selection screen and execute. (Here again, it makes sense to use a variant to save the selection criteria — a common method is to use the same name for the selection variant for the creation and the activation.) The result will be an overview screen that displays the selected models and the current status (as you can see in Figure 8.5). The status, which can be seen on the right part of the screen, shows both the PREVIOUS STATUS and the NEW STATUS. (If you are doing a new activation of an existing model, you will see multiple entries there, once for each model version — the objective here is to activate the version of the model that you most recently created.) To activate the model selection, select the line and click on the ACTIVE/ INACTIVE button — the NEW STATUS will change to a green checkmark. Then, click on the START button to initiate the transfer of the data. Now, the integration model is active for the selected materials, and the material has been transferred to EWM. Any changes to the material will now be transferred automatically and immediately to EWM.

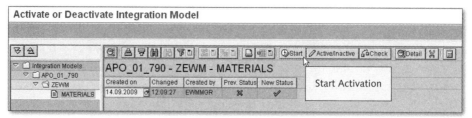

Figure 8.5 Starting the Activation of an Integration Model

Transferring Customers and Vendors to EWM

The transfer of customers and vendors to EWM works very similar to the material distribution described previously. You create an integration model using Transaction CFM1, check the Customers box and fill the selection criteria on the right. However, there is one important difference — during CIF transfer of customers and vendors, you can control if you only want to create a Business Partner (BP) in EWM or only a location — or both. EWM needs both objects. For that reason, when you set up an integration model containing customers and vendors, you have to set the Create Loc./BP field to the value 2 (Create Both), as seen in Figure 8.6).

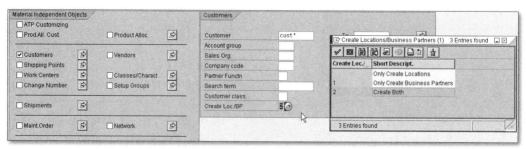

Figure 8.6 Customer Selection during Creation of an Integration Model. Note that you have to pay attention to the create Loc./BP checkbox

Administration of CIF

There are a number of tools and transactions available to administrate CIF. The most important transactions for managing the CIF include those shown in Table 8.1.

Transaction	Description
CFM1	Create Integration Model
CFM2	Activate Integration Models — for manual activation
CFM3	Activate Integration Models — for activation in the background
CFM4	Selection for and Display of Integration Models
CFM5	Integration Model Object Search — Lets you search in which integration model a master data object (e.g., material EWMBOOK_CIF_TEST01) is contained
CFM6	Modify Integration Model
CFM7	Delete Integration Models
CFG1	Display CIF Application Log
SMQ1	qRFC Monitor (Outbound Queue) — Called in the ERP system, CIF queues start with the prefix "CIF"
SMQ2	qRFC Monitor (Inbound Queue) — Called in the EWM system, CIF queues start with the prefix "CIF"

Table 8.1 Useful Transactions for CIF Administration

Automatically Transferring New Master Data Periodically to EWM

We have shown in the previous sections how to manually create and activate an integration model. However, when you have a lot of materials to manage, it is not often feasible to manually transfer all of the new master data. Therefore, it makes sense to automate these steps. To set up automatic transfer of the new master data to EWM, you should perform the following steps (which are described in more detail later):

1. Create a variant for integration model creation, using Transaction CFM1

2. Create a variant for the deletion of inactive integration models, using Transaction CFM7

3. Create a variant for activating integration models, using Transaction CFM3

4. Schedule a background job, using Transaction SM36

5. In the first step, you use Transaction CFM1 for integration model creation again and save the entered selection as a variant. This variant will be used later on, for the background job. In CFM1, you enter model name, logical system and APO application, and select the objects that you want to transfer (e.g., materials, customers, vendors, batches). For each of these object types, you can make special

selections with the selection options on the right side of the screen, to transfer only those objects into EWM with which you want to work. For example, if you work with batches, you should use the special restrictions ORG. AREA equal to A and CLASS TYPE equal to 023.

After you have specified the selection criteria, save them to a selection variant (using the Save button from the tool bar), and choose a name for the variant (recall the advice from earlier about naming the selection variants for the creation and activation similarly). Then, create the integration model as described previously.

In the next step, you create a variant for deletion of inactive integration models. Using Transaction CFM7, you may enter the model name, logical system, and APO application, check the checkbox SELECT INACTIVE IMS ONLY and save these selection criteria as a variant.

Then, you create a variant for activating the created Integration Model from the first step using Transaction CFM3. Once again, you enter model name, logical system and APO Application. In addition, you should check the checkboxes for the IGNORE FAULTY QUEUE ENTRIES and DO NOT ISSUE WARNING IN CASE OF PARALLEL CIF LOAD fields, and then save these selection criteria as a variant.

Finally, you schedule a new job, which executes the three steps in the following sequence:

1. Deletion of the existing integration model
2. Creation of a new integration model
3. Activation of the new integration model

To schedule the job from the SAP menu bar, follow the SYSTEM • SERVICES • JOBS • DEFINE JOBS menu path, or use Transaction code SM36. Assign a JOB name to the new job, and assign the three steps to the job by clicking the STEPS button. Create three steps for the job with the specified program names and in exactly the sequence seen in Table 8.2.

Background Job Step Number	ABAP Program Name	Variant
1	RIMODDEL	IM_EWM_01_DEL
2	RIMODGEN	IM_EWM_01_CRE
3	RIMODAC2	IM_EWM_01_ACT

Table 8.2 Steps for the Automatic Master Data Transfer Job

After the job steps are defined, specify the START CONDITION, where you can enter a specific date and time when the job should first be triggered and the periodic settings to run the job (e.g., every hour).

8.3 Delivery Integration

The main communication mechanism between ERP and EWM is the delivery interface. When an inbound delivery or outbound delivery (OD) is created in the ERP system, it is checked for the plant and storage location combination of the delivery items to determine whether a warehouse number is assigned (according to the customizing setting for the assignment of plants and storage locations to a warehouse number). If a warehouse number is relevant and the warehouse is EWM managed, ERP will trigger the distribution of the delivery document to EWM.

The distribution of deliveries to EWM requires an existing *distribution model* in ERP. You can create this distribution model manually, but we generally recommend for you to use the customizing activity that performs the setup for you automatically. The activity can be found in the ERP IMG by following the INTEGRATION WITH OTHER MYSAP.COM COMPONENTS • EXTENDED WAREHOUSE MANAGEMENT • BASIC SETTINGS FOR EWM LINKAGE • GENERATE DISTRIBUTION MODEL ERP => EWM menu path, or using Transaction code /SPE/OL19. To start the setup, enter the ERP warehouse number, the logical system name of the EWM system, and a name for the distribution model view, as seen in Figure 8.7. When you select the EXECUTE button, the required configuration settings for qRFC distribution are created.

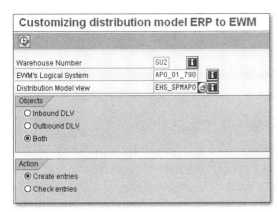

Figure 8.7 Creating the Distribution Model for Distribution of Transactional Data between ERP and EWM

To check the results, you can view the created DISTRIBUTION MODEL (as seen in Figure 8.8) in the ERP IMG by following the SAP NETWEAVER • APPLICATION SERVER • IDOC INTERFACE / APPLICATION LINK ENABLING (ALE) • MODELLING AND IMPLEMENTING BUSINESS PROCESSES • MAINTAIN DISTRIBUTION MODEL AND DISTRIBUTE VIEWS menu path, or using Transaction code BD64.

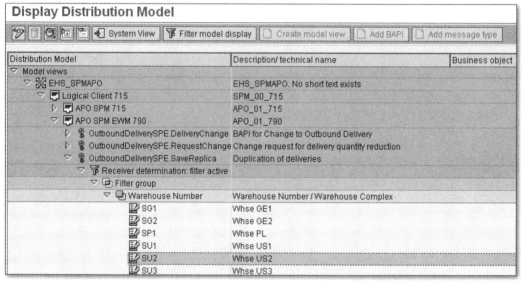

Figure 8.8 Generated Distribution Model with Assigned Warehouse Numbers

> **Note**
>
> Distribution model entries are not transported automatically. You can execute this customizing in all systems manually or use the model distribution of Transaction BD64. However, it is generally not recommended to distribute models from development or quality testing systems to production — you should set up the distribution model for your production landscape from scratch during the go-live preparation phase of your project.

It is not necessary to generate a distribution model for the communication from EWM to ERP. Because the reference documents hold the system name of the related ERP system for the inbound and outbound deliveries, EWM uses this system name to determine where to send the goods movement data. When posting a goods receipt or goods issue, EWM uses the actions of the Post-Processing Framework (PPF) to trigger the goods movement to be transferred to ERP. In Table 8.3, you can see the function modules use for the initiation of the transfer of data between EWM and ERP during delivery processing (on either ERP or EWM).

Direction	Process Step	Function Module	In System
Inbound	Create Inbound Delivery in EWM	/SCWM/INB_DLV_SAVEREPLICA	EWM
Inbound	Send Goods Receipt to EWM	/SPE/INB_DELIVERY_CONFIRM_DEC	ERP
Inbound	Send posting change (e.g., ROD->AFS) to ERP	/SPE/GOODSMVT_CREATE	ERP
Inbound	Send Delivery Completion Indicator to ERP	/SPE/INB_DELIVERY_CONFIRM_DEC	ERP
Outbound	Create Outbound Delivery in EWM	/SCWM/OUTB_DLV_SAVEREPLICA	EWM
Outbound	Send Goods Issue to ERP	/SPE/INB_DELIVERY_CONFIRM_DEC	ERP

Table 8.3 Important Process Steps and Function Modules Used during Delivery Processing in ERP and EWM

8.4   Purchase Order and Production Order Integration

Using the *Expected Goods Receipt* (*EGR*) in EWM allows you to receive and save data transferred from open purchase orders, scheduling agreements, or production orders and to generate EGR documents from them. The EGR documents can then be used as a template to create inbound delivery documents. This is particularly useful if you do not receive or create advance shipping notices (ASNs) or inbound deliveries for purchase orders.

To transfer open purchase orders, scheduling agreements, or production orders from ERP to EWM, there are reports available in both ERP and EWM. The ERP and EWM versions essentially perform the same function, so it does not matter which you use, except that the ERP report logs the purchasing document numbers that it sends to EWM on the ERP side, and the application log (error messages) also remains on the ERP side in this case. Both reports can also be scheduled to run in the background.

8.4.1 Pulling Expected Goods Receipts into EWM from ERP

To pull the EGR documents from ERP into EWM from the EWM Easy Access menu, follow the EXTENDED WAREHOUSE MANAGEMENT • DELIVERY PROCESSING • INBOUND DELIVERY • EXPECTED GOODS RECEIPT • GENERATE OR DELETE EXPECTED GOODS RECEIPT menu path, or use Transaction /SCWM/ERP_EGR_DELETE (which calls report /SCWM/ERP_DLV_DELETE). This report deletes existing expected goods receipts documents in EWM and requests new expected goods receipts from SAP ERP for the entered time period (normally determined by a scheduling horizon). You can use the LOGS button to view the creation and deletion logs of the background runs (see Figure 8.9).

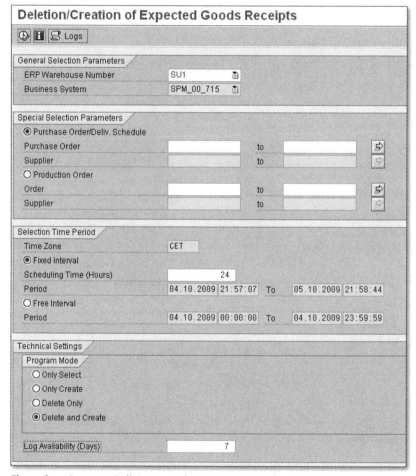

Figure 8.9 Report to Pull Open Purchasing Documents from ERP to EWM

8.4.2 Pushing Expected Goods Receipts from ERP to EWM

To push the EGR documents from ERP (as seen in Figure 8.10) via the ERP Easy Access menu, follow the LOGISTICS • LOGISTICS EXECUTION • INBOUND PROCESS • GOODS RECEIPT FOR INBOUND DELIVERY • EXTENDED INBOUND DELIVERY PROCESSING • SUBSEQUENT FUNCTIONS • MAINTENANCE OF EXPECTED GOODS RECEIPT menu path, or use Transaction /SPE/EGR (which calls report /SPE/INB_EGR_CREATE). This report works similarly to the EWM version. If you set the TEST MODE checkbox, the system doesn't actually make any changes in EWM, but only shows which data would be transferred.

Figure 8.10 Report to "Push" EGR Documents from ERP to EWM

8.5   Summary

In this chapter, we described the basic communication mechanisms between ERP and EWM, including both the master data and the transactional data. You should now understand how to manually transfer the master data and how to automate the transfer so that it occurs automatically. And you should understand how to set up the communication with regard to the transactional data, so that it is always communicated back and forth without additional manual effort. In the following chapters, we will begin to describe the functional processes supported by SAP EWM and how you may use them to manage your warehouse operations.

Inbound processing relates to all physical and system processes for incoming goods. The inbound process differs, depending on whether the goods are delivered from a supplier or from production.

9 Inbound Processing

Goods receipt and putaway processing includes all process steps that may be relevant for inbound processing, including unloading, goods receipt posting, deconsolidation, quality inspection, value-added services (VASs) (e.g., labeling for putaway preparation), and putaway execution to the final destination bin (as seen in Figure 9.1). Because there are many potential process steps involved, the inbound process may be somewhat complex. To avoid the goods receipt process becoming a bottleneck in your warehouse processes, Extended Warehouse Management (EWM) provides you with functionality to optimize and accelerate your inbound processes, including:

▸ Flexible modelling of inbound process steps, including consideration of the warehouse layout

▸ Integrated quality inspection procedures, including automation of follow-up activities based on the usage decision

▸ Dynamic determination of relevance of deconsolidation for efficient putaway execution

▸ Dynamic determination of relevance of VASs, such as oiling or labelling, including management of auxiliary products

▸ Complete transparency of inventory while executing the goods receipt process steps

▸ Overview of all relevant process steps, including the overall goods receipt status, in the warehouse monitor

EWM also supports various business environments, including those which primarily use Advance Shipping Notice (ASNs) for processing inbound receipts (which is common in the automotive, high-tech, and service parts industries) and also those that do not have ASN information available and use the purchase orders for processing inbound receipts (which is more common in the consumer products, retail, and fashion industries). In the latter case, your organizations may work directly with the purchase orders (represented in EWM as Expected Goods Receipts (EGRs) in EWM) or create inbound deliveries in ERP based on the purchase orders. In addition, you can also perform inbound receipts for production or process orders or inbound deliveries based on those orders. In short, there are many ways to initiate the inbound process, and we will attempt to describe them all in this chapter.

This chapter is divided into the following parts:

▶ Goods Receipt Notification (GRN), which acts as a basis for an efficient administrative goods receipt process

▶ Truck Arrival, including check-in, creation of the transportation unit (TU), and handling the TU inside the yard

▶ Administrative Goods Receipt, (which acts as a basis for an efficient goods receipt preparation process), including checking the delivery notes against the ASN and purchase order data and creating the inbound delivery

▶ Unloading and Goods Receipt, which includes unloading, visual inspection, and posting goods receipt

▶ Putaway Processing, which includes deconsolidation of mixed pallets, quality inspection (including counting), execution of VASs to prepare goods for putaway, and putaway

▶ Slotting, which is the process of determining the putaway strategies for a product based on the parameters of the product and the bins

▶ Quality Management, which is used for managing the inbound inspection and counting processes

9.1 Goods Receipt Notification

The warehouse can be notified of a pending goods receipt in many ways, including:

▶ Your vendor can notify you about the inbound delivery data in advance via Electronic Data Interchange (EDI) or Supplier Network Collaboration (SNC), which will generate an inbound delivery in ERP that will be transferred to the warehouse.

▸ The warehouse can be informed about expected incoming goods via replication of purchase order or production order data (as an EGR) from ERP to EWM.

9.1.1 Goods Receipt Notification Based on Advance Shipping Notice

You may be notified by your vendor about the incoming goods that they shipped to your warehouse, which can be submitted via EDI or initiated in SNC. In ERP, you can use the received data to create an inbound delivery to inform the warehouse about incoming products, quantities, batches, packaging information (such as handling unit (HU) types and HU numbers), expected goods receipt date, and additional inbound delivery data. Once the ASN is created in ERP, it can be transferred to EWM, where it is further processed. In the following section we'll further describe the detailed steps in the process.

ASN Creation

The primary benefits to the warehouse for using ASNs include:

▸ Inbound deliveries can be created in both ERP and EWM automatically, simplifying the administrative aspects of the goods receipt process.

▸ You can use the inbound delivery data to calculate expected workload (for more details, see Chapter 21, Labor Management) and use this data to plan your resources.

▸ You can assign the inbound delivery, using information supplied on the ASN, such as the tracking number, to a vehicle or TU when the truck driver arrives at the warehouse.

> **Note**
>
> To allow the creation of an inbound delivery document with reference to a purchase order, it is necessary to assign a confirmation control key to the relevant purchase order items. In the customizing settings for the confirmation control key, there is a setting that lets you include the line item of the purchase order in an inbound delivery document. You can also use the confirmation control keys to distinguish between those vendors who provide ASNs and those you manually create inbound deliveries for or use EGRs to perform the inbound processing.

An overview of the document flow for an inbound process using ASNs can be seen in Figure 9.1. To begin the process, you create a PO and send it to the VENDOR (which the vendor may confirm to acknowledge that he received it and plans to ship the requested product). Then when he ships the product, he sends the data for incoming goods (as discussed earlier, via EDI or SNC, or he could even send it manually) and then you create the follow-up steps manually). When SAP ERP receives these data, it validates them and then creates an inbound delivery for the ASN.

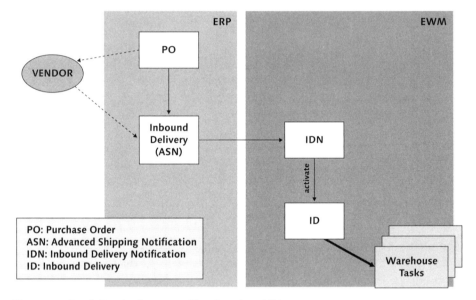

Figure 9.1 Goods Receipt Document Flow Based on ASN

Inbound Delivery Creation in ERP

When the inbound delivery is created in ERP and the inbound delivery is EWM relevant, the system calls EWM via a queued remote function call (qRFC)–enabled function module (via interface /SPE/INB_DELIVERY_SAVEREPLICA), which creates a document known as the inbound delivery notification (IDN) in EWM. The IDN replicates all of the relevant logistics data to support the inbound delivery process from the ERP delivery, including the shipping notification, purchase order number, and possible transportation information such as the carrier and container number. The IDN is the basis for the creation of an inbound delivery in EWM, and it is also the basis for after-the-fact confirmation messages back to the ERP system from EWM. The IDN document itself is not used for further processing within EWM.

If errors occur during ASN validation in ERP, then ERP assigns an error status to the incorrect delivery items before sending the details to EWM. In EWM, the IDN items are blocked for execution until the errors are resolved in ERP and the corrected inbound delivery is communicated to EWM.

Creation of the IDN in EWM

During the creation of the IDN in EWM, the system also validates whether the delivery document is complete and consistent so that it can be used for further processing in the system.

The following checks are executed automatically during IDN creation:

▶ Incompletion check — EWM determines whether all relevant fields in a delivery document are filled. Every input and output field that must be filled to further process a document is a mandatory field. Mandatory fields that need to be checked are assigned to an action. Every time this action is executed, the corresponding field is automatically checked for completeness. The settings for the incompleteness check are saved in an incompletion profile. When accessing the incompleteness check, the system determines the assigned completeness profile via the document and item types and therefore the corresponding settings for the mandatory fields.

▶ Consistency check — determines whether any data inconsistencies exists between the delivery document, Customizing, and master data. The consistency check contains the following checks, among others:

  ▶ Check whether the document type, document category, item type, and item category correspond to the settings in Customizing for delivery processing.

  ▶ Check whether the delivery date lies in the past

  ▶ Check whether the product data corresponds to the product master (for example, product ID and allowed units of measure)

  ▶ Check whether the location data corresponds to the location master

You can also execute the preceding checks manually in the EWM Easy Access menu by following the EXTENDED WAREHOUSE MANAGEMENT • DELIVERY PROCESSING • INBOUND DELIVERY • MAINTAIN INBOUND DELIVERY NOTIFICATION menu path, or using Transaction code /SCWM/IDN (as seen in Figure 9.2). You can also use this transaction to review the content of the IDN, or to manually activate the IDN if it is not done automatically. In the figure, you see that the CHECK, ACTIVATE, and REJECT buttons are circled.

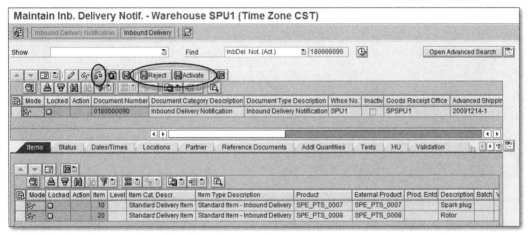

Figure 9.2 User Interface for Processing IDNs

If errors are found during the consistency check, the IDN is saved in error status and you must resolve the errors either in ERP or EWM. If you solve the errors in ERP, then ERP sends a change message to EWM (via interface /SCWM/INB_DELIVERY_REPLACE). EWM processes this change message as long as the inbound delivery is not yet being processed in EWM (i.e., as long as no warehouse task (WT) for the inbound delivery is created and as long as the goods receipt was not already explicitly posted).

If the errors are solved in EWM and the process continues in EWM with the inbound delivery creation and subsequent goods receipt, then EWM sends the changed data with the goods receipt confirmation to ERP (via interface /SPE/INB_DELIVERY_REPLACE). ERP then decides whether to accept the corrected data, or, if there are still errors according to ERP, you may need to manually process the inbound delivery again in ERP before the system will allow the goods receipt confirmation. If you subsequently manually correct the inbound delivery in ERP, then ERP returns the message that was originally sent by EWM to the qRFC inbound queue of ERP once again. Then you can restart the message processing, and ERP will continue processing accordingly.

Changes to ASNs after IDN Creation

Sometimes, your vendor will send a change to the ASN data or an ASN rejection for an existing inbound delivery. ERP will receive these messages and validates and forwards them to EWM. In EWM, the system will check whether the existing inbound delivery can be replaced with the changed or rejected data. EWM will allow the existing inbound delivery to be replaced as long as there are no WTs created for the appropriate inbound delivery and the goods receipt has not already been posted. If those conditions are not met, EWM will reject the change message from the ERP system (you must manually inform the vendor, if necessary). On the other hand, if EWM accepts the changes, it replaces the IDN and inbound delivery in EWM and sends a confirmation message to ERP (via interface /SPE/INB_DELIVERY_REPLACE).

Stock Type Determination during IDN Creation

EWM determines the relevant stock type for the line items during the creation of the IDN. Whereas the stock in ERP is tracked based on the combination of plant, storage location, and stock category, the stock in EWM is tracked according to party entitled (described further in Chapter 6, Warehouse Stock Management) and stock type, as seen in Figure 9.3.

The ERP plant is mapped to EWM as a party entitled. For each party entitled, you can maintain different stock types, which area defined as a combination of the availability group (which is mapped to the plant and storage location from ERP) and the non-location-dependent stock types (such as blocked stock, unrestricted-use stock, stock in quality inspection, and blocked stock returns). To set up the availability groups and the stock type mapping in the EWM Implementation Guide (IMG), follow the menu path EXTENDED WAREHOUSE MANAGEMENT • GOODS RECEIPT PROCESS • CONFIGURE AVAILABILITY GROUP FOR PUTAWAY.

You can set up different stock types for the goods receipt process (e.g., stock type F1 for unrestricted-use in Putaway and stock type F2 for unrestricted-use warehouse, as in the standard delivered configuration for EWM). Based on the different stock types, you can control whether stock is available for picking directly after posting goods receipt or whether it is only available for picking after confirmation of the putaway into the warehouse.

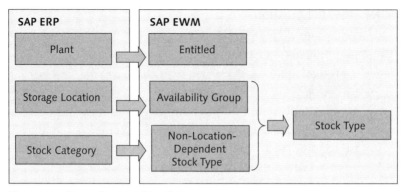

Figure 9.3 Determination of Stock Type in EWM

When the ERP inbound delivery is replicated in EWM, the availability group is determined from the PLANT and STORAGE LOCATION of the inbound delivery line item, and the NON-LOCATION-DEPENDENT STOCK TYPE is determined from the STOCK CATEGORY (for example, to indicate customs or scrap relevance). Then, based on the stock type role and availability group, EWM determines the stock type for the inbound delivery item. This stock type is saved in the IDN and is subsequently transferred to the EWM inbound delivery.

Creation of the Inbound Delivery by Activating the IDN

Once the IDN has been checked and saved, the inbound delivery can be created with reference to the IDN. You can use the Post-Processing Framework (PPF) to automatically create the inbound delivery by activating the IDN using PPF method /SCDL/IDR_TRANSFER. You can also generate the inbound delivery manually by activating the IDN using Transaction /SCWM/IDN (as seen in Figure 9.2).

The inbound delivery is the document that contains all of the data required for triggering and monitoring the complete inbound process, beginning with receipt of the goods in the yard and ending with storage of the goods at the final putaway bin. The inbound delivery is used as a reference object throughout the inbound process, including during execution of the following actions (among others):

- ▶ Registering the TU for the delivery in the yard
- ▶ Unloading the TU for the delivery
- ▶ Placing the products of the delivery into stock (putaway)
- ▶ Posting the goods receipt

▶ Adjusting the goods receipt quantity (in the case of discrepancies in the goods receipt, including overdelivery or underdelivery)

▶ Splitting an inbound delivery (an IDN can be split into several inbound deliveries based on partial quantity receipt, missing HUs, or other criteria)

▶ Creating and deleting inbound delivery items (deletion of an inbound delivery item can cause the creation of a split delivery)

Data Determined during Inbound Delivery Creation from the IDN

During the creation of the inbound delivery, the system determines the warehouse-specific data to save it within the inbound delivery in EWM, including the data described in the following text.

The warehouse process type is determined based on the document type, item type, and the priority of an inbound delivery (optional). The process type controls, for example, whether EWM should immediately confirm a WT, and is also used in determining the relevant steps during the process oriented storage control (POSC).

The warehouse door is determined based on the warehouse process type and staging area/door determination group (which can be used to differentiate between requirements during unloading at a door or staging area). The automatic door determination and assignment can be set up in the EWM Easy Access menu by following the EXTENDED WAREHOUSE MANAGEMENT • SETTINGS • SHIPPING AND RECEIVING • STAGING AREA AND DOOR DETERMINATION (INBOUND) menu path, or using Transaction code /SCWM/STADET_IN. You can also use Business Add-In (BAdI) /SCWM/EX_SR_STADET to define a customer-specific logic for automatic door determination.

If the supplier sends inbound delivery data that doesn't contain any packaging information, you can pack any unpacked items automatically in EWM. To enable the automatic packing, you must create and activate packaging specifications (pack specs) within EWM and set up the determination of the pack specs. The determination of the pack specs is set up based on the business characteristics (e.g., supplier, product, etc.). If the No AUTOMATIC PACKING indicator is set in Customizing for the document type, EWM does not perform automatic packing when it creates the inbound delivery.

If the PPF action for creating the WT for the initial process step is activated (e.g., unloading based on PPF using action /SCWM/PRD_IN_TO_CREATE in application /SCDL/DELIVERY and action profile /SCDL/PRD_IN), the creation of the HU WT for each inbound delivery item will be triggered when the inbound delivery is saved. For this, unloading must be active as the first step of the inbound process in the POSC (for details regarding storage control, see Chapter 13, Configuring Multistep Warehouse Movements).

The rough putaway bin is determined to plan the workload for the putaway activity areas of each inbound process step (e.g., the activity areas of the work centers and final putaway bin) using the preprocessing functions of Labor Management (LM). Rough putaway bin determination will only be executed if LM is activated. The putaway bin is determined based on the putaway bin determination (as described later in this chapter).

If batches or split valuations are assigned to the inbound delivery, the relevant master data is created in EWM, including the characteristic data for expiration date and country of origin.

The priority for inbound deliveries can be determined using priority points from Advanced Planning and Optimization (APO), which allows an optimal unloading sequence for multiple transportation units in the yard. APO calculates the priority points at the item level and communicates the calculated priority points to ERP, which then subsequently communicates them to EWM. EWM saves the priority points within the inbound delivery items. To calculate aggregated priorities at the header level, you may use the BAdI /SCWM/EX_DLV_DET_LOAD, and to aggregate the priority points at the TU level, you can use the BAdI /SCWM/EX_SR_PRIOP.

9.1.2 Goods Receipt Notification for Purchase Order/Production Order

If the warehouse cannot be informed via ASNs about incoming goods, you can replicate purchase order data and production order data from ERP. In EWM, these objects are translated to EGRs, and EGRs can be used to trigger the follow-up actions in the warehouse, including goods receipt and putaway. There are two mechanisms for transferring the expected goods receipt information. You can pull the data from ERP from within EWM (by scheduling report /SCWM/ERP_DLV_DELETE), or you can push the data from ERP to EWM. For more details about the integration of ERP with EGRs, see Chapter 8, Integration from ERP to EWM). The main advantages of using the EGR for inbound processing include:

▸ You can use the EGR data to plan the workload via LM (see Chapter 21, Labor Management, for more details). To view an aggregated overview of the expected incoming goods (including volume, weight, number of HUs and number of inbound delivery items based on selection criteria such as product, vendor, carrier, and time period), you can use Transaction /SCWM/GRWORK. Based on the results, you can plan activities in the warehouse, including, for example, scheduling appropriate resources or an appropriate number of doors for inbound processing during the defined time period.

▸ You can execute the goods receipt process steps in the warehouse even when the connection between EWM and ERP is temporarily unavailable.

In Figure 9.4, you can see an overview of the goods receipt process using EGR.

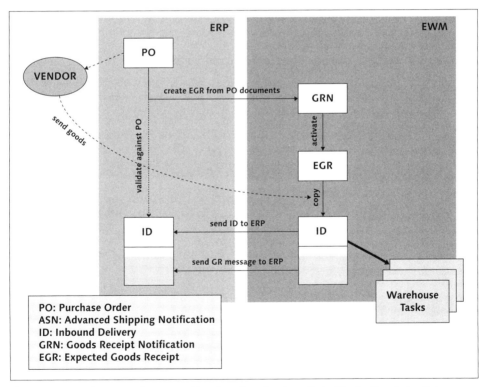

Figure 9.4 Goods Receipt Document Flow Based on Purchase Order/Production Order Data

When creating the GRN, EWM automatically validates whether the document is complete and consistent (in the same way as described for the IDN) so that it can be used for further processing in the system. In addition, you can perform the validation checks manually within the GRN processing transaction, which you can access in the EWM Easy Access menu by following the EXTENDED WAREHOUSE MANAGEMENT • DELIVERY PROCESSING • INBOUND DELIVERY • EXPECTED GOODS RECEIPT • MAINTAIN NOTIFICATION OF GOODS RECEIPT menu path, or using Transaction code /SCWM/GRN.

Once the GRN is validated, you can then create the EGR from the GRN either manually (from Transaction /SCWM/GRN) or automatically, in a way similar to the creation of the inbound delivery from the IDN as described previously in this chapter. You can automate the activation of the GRN, which will trigger the creation of the EGR, using the PPF method /SCDL/GRN_TRANSFER.

Once the EGR is created, you can access it for further processing from the EWM Easy Access menu by following the EXTENDED WAREHOUSE MANAGEMENT • DELIVERY PROCESSING • INBOUND DELIVERY • EXPECTED GOODS RECEIPT • MAINTAIN EXPECTED GOODS RECEIPT menu path, or using Transaction code /SCWM/EGR.

The EGR document contains data from an open purchase order or open production order and represents a template that enables you to create an inbound delivery. From the EGR, you can create the inbound delivery manually by following the EXTENDED WAREHOUSE MANAGEMENT • DELIVERY PROCESSING • INBOUND DELIVERY • GR PREPARATION - EXTERNAL PROCUREMENT menu path, or using Transaction code /SCWM/GRPE. You can also add additional items to an existing inbound delivery in the goods receipt preparation dialog by copying items from EGRs.

As the EGR only acts as a template for copying existing data, you can't change any of this data within the EGR. In the resulting inbound delivery created from the EGR, however, you can change the data, including the quantity of the delivery items. To access the resulting inbound delivery, use the normal inbound delivery processing transaction, Transaction /SCWM/PRDI.

> **Note**
>
> Splitting an inbound delivery is not possible when the inbound delivery was created based on an EGR. If the received quantity differs from the purchased quantity, you can't create follow-up inbound deliveries automatically using the process codes (in contrast to inbound deliveries that were created based on IDNs). Instead, you must simply change the delivery quantity manually in the inbound delivery or via the resulting WTs, and then you must create a new inbound delivery for subsequent goods receipts for the same EGR.

9.1.3 Setup for Inbound Delivery Processing

There are several settings that are important to understand with regard to inbound processing. In this section, we will describe several of the important customizing settings related to the inbound delivery processing and the goods receipt process. Like many documents in SAP systems, the inbound delivery consists of a document header and one or more document items. The inbound delivery header contains important data such as the goods receipt office, ASN number, various delivery statuses (e.g., unloading status, putaway status, goods receipt status), priority points, and many others.

The purpose of the inbound delivery is defined by a combination of the document category and the document type. The document category describes the fundamental business attributes of a document. The possible inbound document categories (which cannot be changed) include:

▶ GRN Goods Receipt Notification

▶ EGR Expected Goods Receipt

▶ IDR Inbound Delivery Notification

▶ PDI Inbound Delivery

The document type is also used to classify the document and define the primary business use of the document. Some example document types (which are configurable) for inbound delivery processing include:

▶ INB Inbound Delivery

▶ INBP Inbound Delivery from Production

To maintain the document types in the EWM IMG, follow the EXTENDED WARE-HOUSE MANAGEMENT • GOODS RECEIPT PROCESS • INBOUND DELIVERY • MANUAL SETTINGS • DEFINE DOCUMENT TYPES FOR INBOUND DELIVERY PROCESS) menu path, or you can use the available wizard by choosing the USE WIZARD TO DEFINE DOCUMENT TYPES FOR INBOUND DELIVERY PROCESS menu option on the same path.

In the customizing for the inbound delivery type, for example, you can specify the following attributes:

▶ Handling method for change documents

▶ Retention period

▸ Profile assignments, such as status profile, action profile, field control profile, partner profile, etc.

▸ Specification of allowed predecessor documents types.

Each combination of the document type and the document category (which are predefined and tied to the standard transactions and document flows) represents a document in an EWM business process. In Table 9.1, you can see an example of the document type and document category combinations and the resulting documents.

Document Type	Doc. Category	Document
INB	IDR	Inbound Delivery Notification
INB	PDI	Inbound Delivery

Table 9.1 Examples of Combinations of Inbound Delivery Type and Document Category to Define the Documents for Inbound Processing

The inbound delivery item contains data such as:

▸ Product data (e.g., product number, batch number, country of origin)

▸ Delivery quantity

▸ Movement data (e.g., warehouse process type, goods movement bin)

▸ Status and shipping conditions (e.g., goods receipt status, tolerance limits for overdelivery and underdelivery)

The inbound delivery item is defined by a combination of the item type, document category, and the item category. The item categories are defined by SAP and cannot be changed. They describe the fundamental business attributes of an item. For the standard delivery item, the item category is DLV.

The item type classifies the items for a document type with regard to the complete business process. The item type defines the business characteristics of the item in a delivery document. Examples of item types (which are configurable) for the inbound process include:

▸ IDLV — Standard Item — ID

▸ ICR — Customer Returns

You can maintain the item types in the EWM IMG by following the EXTENDED WAREHOUSE MANAGEMENT • GOODS RECEIPT PROCESS • INBOUND DELIVERY • MANUAL SETTINGS • DEFINE ITEM TYPES FOR INBOUND DELIVERY PROCESS menu path, or you can use the available wizard by selecting the USE WIZARD TO DEFINE ITEM TYPES FOR INBOUND DELIVERY PROCESS menu option on the same path.

In the customizing for the item type, you can define, for example:

► Profiles (such as status profile, field control profile, partner profile, etc.)

► Process management and control parameters (such as the requirement for documentary batch or triggering a warning message for required inspections for volume, weights, and measures for new products)

For both the document type and the item type, we mentioned that you can assign different types of profiles. The profiles that you can maintain and assign to the delivery type or item type include:

► Status profile, for assigning different status types to the document type (e.g., completion, goods receipt, quality inspection)

► Quantity offsetting profile, for calculating the open quantities for a document, or to calculate, for example, requested quantity and reduced quantity (the quantity offsetting profile is only relevant for the item type)

► Text profile, for assigning the possible long texts that can be stored on the document type and item type (typically used for maintaining notes, providing instructions, printing on documents, etc.)

► Field control profile, to determining which fields are displayed and changed during delivery document processing

► Incompletion profile, for ensure that all relevant fields in a delivery document are filled so that the document can be further processed

► Action profile, for determining the relevant PPF actions to trigger printing, WT creation, etc. (the action profile is only relevant for the document type). In Figure 9.5, you can see an example of the PPF actions used for inbound processing using the standard action profile /SCDL/PRD_IN, including the creation of putaway WTs and printing of unloading lists. For more details on PPF processing, see Chapter 24, Post-Processing Framework and Form Printing.

► Partner profile, for specifying the relevant partner roles (e.g., supplier, receiving office) to the header type or item type

▸ Reference document profile, for specifying allowed reference documents categories (e.g., purchase order, ERP document (i.e., delivery), etc.)

▸ Date profile, for flexibly defined date types for the delivery processing (e.g., such as start/end of goods receipt, start/end of unloading, start/end of putaway)

You can maintain all of these profiles in the EWM IMG by following the EXTENDED WAREHOUSE MANAGEMENT • CROSS-PROCESS SETTINGS • DELIVERY PROCESSING menu path, and then choosing the relevant profile configuration element (e.g., STATUS MANAGEMENT, QUANTITY OFFSETTING, ETC.).

When the inbound delivery is created, EWM determines the document type and item types based on the parameters of the source document (e.g., ERP inbound delivery) and the document category of the target document.

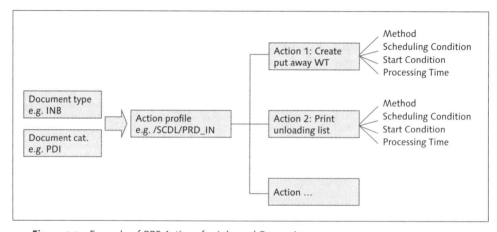

Figure 9.5 Example of PPF Actions for Inbound Processing

To determine the document type of the target document (e.g., INB), EWM uses the following parameters in the determination:

▸ Document category of the source document (e.g., IDR)

▸ Document type of the source document (e.g., INB)

▸ Document category of the target document (e.g., PDI)

To define the document type determination in the EWM IMG, follow the menu path EXTENDED WAREHOUSE MANAGEMENT • GOODS RECEIPT PROCESS • INBOUND

DELIVERY • DEFINE DOCUMENT TYPE DETERMINATION FOR INBOUND DELIVERY PROCESS.

To map the document types from ERP to EWM in the EWM IMG, follow the menu path EXTENDED WAREHOUSE MANAGEMENT • INTERFACES • ERP INTEGRATION • DELIVERY PROCESSING • MAP DOCUMENT TYPES FROM ERP SYSTEM TO EWM.

To determine the stock type of the inbound delivery item, EWM begins by determining the availability group. To customize the determination of the availability group in the EWM IMG, follow the menu path EXTENDED WAREHOUSE MANAGEMENT • INTERFACES • ERP INTEGRATION • GOODS MOVEMENTS • MAP STORAGE LOCATIONS FROM ERP SYSTEM TO EWM. Based on the availability group, the non-location-dependent stock type and the stock type role (normal stock, scrapping stock, customs blocked stock) from the ERP inbound delivery, EWM determines the stock type for the inbound delivery item. To configure the availability group in the EWM IMG, follow the menu path EXTENDED WAREHOUSE MANAGEMENT • GOODS RECEIPT PROCESS • CONFIGURE AVAILABILITY GROUP FOR PUTAWAY.

To determine the warehouse process type, EWM includes the following parameters in the determination:

▶ Document type (e.g., PDI), which is mandatory
▶ Item type, which is optional
▶ Delivery priority, which is optional
▶ Control indicator for process type determination, which is optional
▶ Process indicator for determination of the warheouse process, which is optional

Furthermore, because not every field is required in the determination table, the following logic is used for the warehouse process type determination:

▶ The item type is more specific than the document type
▶ The processing priority is more specific than the control indicator
▶ The control indicator for warehouse process type determination can be assigned on the WAREHOUSE DATA tab of the product master to enable product-specific determination of the warehouse process type

To configure the process type determination in the EWM IMG, follow the menu path EXTENDED WAREHOUSE MANAGEMENT • CROSS-PROCESS SETTINGS • WAREHOUSE TASK • DETERMINE WAREHOUSE PROCESS TYPE.

To define the relevant warehouse process types (which are assigned to the inbound delivery item) in the EWM IMG, follow the menu path EXTENDED WAREHOUSE MANAGEMENT • CROSS-PROCESS SETTINGS • WAREHOUSE TASK • DEFINE WAREHOUSE PROCESS TYPE.

In SAP applications, you can collect customizing settings into Business Configuration sets (BC Sets), which allow you to transfer the settings from one system to another. SAP also uses BC Sets to collect configuration settings and deliver them to customers together with the standard coding. This allows you to choose which processes you want to enable in your system by activating the relevant BC Sets. In Chapter 26, Deploying Extended Warehouse Management, you can find more information about accessing and activating BC Sets. In EWM, the following BC sets are delivered and are relevant to making settings related to the inbound processing:

▶ /SCWM/DLV_STANDARD, which creates settings for standard processes of delivery processing without catch weight management (you can also use this BC set to restore the sample Customizing)

▶ /SCWM/DLV_STANDARD_CW, which enables standard processes for delivery processing with support for catch weight management

▶ /SCWM/DLV_INBOUND_PROD, which creates document types and item types, required customer profiles, and ERP integration for the inbound delivery for the production order in EWM

▶ /SCWM/DLV_EXPGR, which creates document types and item types, required customer profiles, and ERP integration for EGR, and determination of document types and item types when creating an inbound delivery from an EGR

▶ /SCWM/DLV_EXPGR_PROD, which creates document types and item types, required customer profiles, and ERP integration for EGR for production, and determination of document types and item types when creating an inbound delivery from an EGR

9.2   Truck Arrival and Yard Management

Once the warehouse has been notified of a pending receipt, either via ASNs or EGRs, the next step in the inbound process is the arrival of the truck at the warehouse. When the truck arrives at the checkpoint of the warehouse, you can register the vehicles and TUs that arrive in the yard using the yard management functions of the Shipping and Receiving (S & R) component.

> **Note**
>
> Using yard management, including the creation of TUs and vehicles, is completely optional. It is not mandatory for inbound processing in EWM.

If you use yard management to manage the yard activities (including arrival and movement of the vehicles and TUs), registering the vehicles and TUs that arrive in the yard is a prerequisite for executing the yard activities.

The vehicle represents the means of transport (MTR), which specifies the class of the vehicle. The vehicle generally represents the physical entity of the transport vehicle, such as the truck that pulls the trailer, the engine that pulls the rail cars, or the ship that transports the containers — or the vehicle could also be an attached vehicle, such as a delivery van. To specify the MTR from the Easy Access menu of the EWM system, follow the menu path ADVANCED PLANNING AND OPTIMIZATION • MASTER DATA • TRANSPORTATION LANE • MAINTAIN MEANS OF TRANSPORT. A vehicle can comprise one or more TUs.

The TU acts as the container for the received inbound deliveries and therefore forms the basis for efficient goods receipt processing. A TU is the smallest loadable unit of a vehicle that is used to transport goods. The TU can be a fixed part of the vehicle or separate from the vehicle. TUs are logically tracked using the HU entities of EWM by assigning packaging materials to them. By linking these packaging materials to the MTR, you can define the construction rules for the vehicle. To assign the packaging materials to the MTR in the EWM Easy Access menu, follow the menu path EXTENDED WAREHOUSE MANAGEMENT • SETTINGS • SHIPPING AND RECEIVING • LINK BETWEEN PACKAGING MATERIAL (TU) AND MEANS OF TRANSPORT. Here, you can define how many TUs a vehicle is supposed to have and the order in which they should be arranged. You can also specify whether a TU is optional or obligatory. For example, if the TU is a fixed part of the vehicle, then it should be set up as an obligatory TU.

The steps that you execute at the checkpoint depend on whether the vehicle and TU data are provided in advance via the ASN or whether you first have to record this data when the vehicle has arrived. To check the vehicle and TU into the yard (as seen in Figure 9.6) from the EWM Easy Access menu, follow the EXTENDED WAREHOUSE MANAGEMENT • SHIPPING AND RECEIVING • YARD MANAGEMENT • ARRIVAL AT/DEPARTURE FROM CHECKPOINT menu path, or use Transaction code /SCWM/CICO.

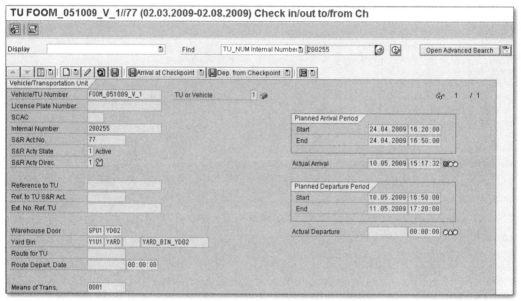

Figure 9.6 Check-in of TU with the Check-in/Check-out Transaction

If the transport information was provided on the ASN, then the TU can be automatically created when the inbound delivery is transferred from ERP to EWM. In this case, EWM will create a new planned S&R activity for the vehicle and the assigned TUs.

When the truck arrives at the warehouse, you can check the data and add additional information, such as the license plate, standard carrier alpha code (SCAC), driver name, and MTR, and then you can confirm the arrival of the truck. The status of the S&R activity then changes from PLANNED to ACTIVE for the vehicle and the assigned TUs when the status of the vehicle/TUs changes to ARRIVAL AT CHECKPOINT automatically. The actual arrival time is automatically captured by the system with the confirmation of the S&R activity. If the actual arrival time is outside of the planned arrival period, a warning or error message occurs, depending on the settings in customizing, which can be accessed in the EWM IMG via the menu path EXTENDED WAREHOUSE MANAGEMENT • MASTER DATA • CROSS-PROCESS SETTINGS • SHIPPING AND RECEIVING • MASTER DATA • GENERAL SETTINGS • GENERAL SETTINGS FOR SHIPPING AND RECEIVING.

After you create and check in the vehicle and TUs, you can then move the vehicle and associated TUs into the yard. To access the yard move transcations from the EWM Easy Access menu, follow the EXTENDED WAREHOUSE MANAGEMENT • SHIPPING AND RECEIVING • YARD MANAGEMENT • CREATE WAREHOUSE TASK IN YARD menu path, or use Transaction /SCWM/YMOVE.

You can create the yard move (which is a special kind of WT) to move the vehicle and TUs to either a parking place in the parking lot or directly to an empty door. When creating the yard move, you can create the yard move for a vehicle (which includes the yard movements for the assigned TUs automatically) or you can move the TUs individually.

Yard movements can also be executed by an operator in the yard in the radio frequency (RF) environment, as seen in Figure 9.7. To access the yard movements in the RF Transaction (/SCWM/RFUI), if you are using the standard delivered RF menu, follow the menu path 05 INTERNAL PROCESSES • 06 YARD MOVEMENTS • 01 CREATE ADHOC YARD WT.

Figure 9.7 RF Screen for Yard Movements

> **Note**
>
> For yard movements, the WTs are always HU WTs, and the HU for the TU always remains empty. That is, the contents of the TU (which includes the deliveries, with its associated HUs and unpacked products) is never packed into a TU-HU . If the TU-HU is moved in the yard, the system only considers the packaging material (that is, the HU) from a stock point of view, whereas the related stock (the delivery items and HUs) doesn't follow every movement of the TU-HU. In simpler terms, this means that the stock for the product is not visible on the TU in the reports of EWM, even thought they are indirectly linked.

9.2.1 Setting Up Yard Management

In Chapter 18, Yard Management, we will describe the details of yard management, including the setup of the yard, the organizational elements in the yard, TUs, and vehicles. In addition to the settings that we'll describe there, the following settings are specific to using yard management in the inbound process.

Staging Areas and Doors

To define the staging areas in the warehouse in the EWM IMG, follow the menu path EXTENDED WAREHOUSE MANAGEMENT • MASTER DATA • STAGING AREAS • DEFINE STAGING AREAS.

To define the staging area/door determination group in the warehouse in the EWM IMG, follow the menu path EXTENDED WAREHOUSE MANAGEMENT • MASTER DATA • STAGING AREAS • DEFINE STAGING AREA AND DOOR DETERMINATION GROUPS.

To assign the door to door determination groups in the EWM IMG, follow the menu path EXTENDED WAREHOUSE MANAGEMENT • MASTER DATA • STAGING AREAS • ASSIGN STAGING AREA/DOOR DETERMINATION GROUP TO DOOR.

To assign doors to staging areas in the EWM IMG, follow the menu path EXTENDED WAREHOUSE MANAGEMENT • MASTER DATA • STAGING AREAS • ASSIGN STAGING AREA TO WAREHOUSE DOOR.

To set up the door determination in the EWM Easy Access menu, follow the EXTENDED WAREHOUSE MANAGEMENT • SETTINGS • SHIPPING AND RECEIVING • STAGING AREA AND DOOR DETERMINATION (INBOUND) menu path, or use Transaction code /SCWM/STADET_IN.

TUs and Vehicles

To define the means of transport in the EWM IMG, follow the menu path EXTENDED WAREHOUSE MANAGEMENT • MASTER DATA • SHIPPING AND RECEIVING • DEFINE MEANS OF TRANSPORT.

To define the controlling parameters for forming vehicles/TUs (e.g., maximum number of seals, action profile for PPF) in the EWM IMG, follow the menu path EXTENDED WAREHOUSE MANAGEMENT • CROSS-PROCESS SETTINGS • SHIPPING AND RECEIVING • SHIPPING AND RECEIVING • GENERAL SETTINGS • DEFINE CONTROL PARAMETERS FOR FORMING VEHICLES/TRANSPORTATION UNITS.

To define packaging material type for the TU, which is basically a special HU type with the virtual HU indicator in the EWM IMG, folllow the menu path EXTENDED WAREHOUSE MANAGEMENT • CROSS-PROCESS SETTINGS • HANDLING UNITS • BASICS • DEFINE PACKAGING MATERIAL TYPES.

To assign the packaging material type to TU in the EWM Easy Access menu, follow the EXTENDED WAREHOUSE MANAGEMENT • SETTINGS • SHIPPING AND RECEIVING • LINK BETWEEN PACKAGING MATERIAL (TU) AND MEANS OF TRANSPORT menu path, or use Transaction code /SCWM/PM_MTR.

9.3   Goods Receipt Preparation

After the truck arrives at the warehouse, you can execute the administrative activities to prepare for the goods receipt. Once the driver delivers the necessary paperwork (sometimes known as delivery notes, inbound documentation, ASN paperwork, etc. — it usually consists of a bill of lading and packing list) to the receiving clerk in the goods receiving office, then the clerk will execute the administrative activities — namely to check the paperwork against inbound deliveries created for the ASN or, if an inbound delivery for the ASN doesn't already exist, to create the inbound deliveries based on the paperwork (starting in EWM by calling the inbound delivery creation directly from EWM).

9.3.1   Administrative Goods Receipt Based on ASNs

If the inbound delivery was created with reference to an ASN, the inbound delivery was transferred to EWM (as described earlier in this chapter), and you can use the EWM inbound delivery to execute the administrative tasks for the goods receipt process. To begin, the clerk in the goods receiving office may check the delivered paperwork against the inbound delivery documents in EWM. To access the inbound delivery information (as seen in Figure 9.8), from the EWM Easy Access menu, follow the EXTENDED WAREHOUSE MANAGEMENT • DELIVERY PROCESSING • INBOUND DELIVERY • MAINTAIN INBOUND DELIVERY menu path, or use Transaction /SCWM/PRDI. To begin processing, you can select the inbound delivery based on the appropriate search parameter (e.g., ASN tracking number, purchase order number, or the ERP inbound delivery number).

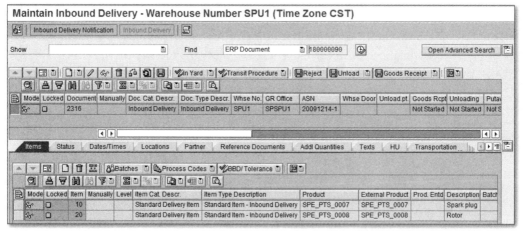

Figure 9.8 Processing an Inbound Delivery

You can also use the warehouse monitor to select the relevant inbound delivery based on various search criteria or using a user- or role-specific monitor node (that could, for instance, preselect inbound deliveries with a certain status for a specified date range). To access the warehouse monitor (as seen in Figure 9.9) from the EWM Easy Access menu, follow the EXTENDED WAREHOUSE MANAGEMENT • MONITORING • WAREHOUSE MANAGEMENT MONITOR menu path, or use Transaction code /SCWM/MON. For more information on setting up predefined selection criteria for a node of the warehouse monitor, see Chapter 15, Warehouse Monitoring and Reporting.

Once you validate the information on the inbound delivery with the delivered paperwork, you can continue with the WT creation for the inbound delivery. On the other hand, if you find discrepancies with the inbound delivery, you can adjust it with the correct information. In the inbound delivery processing, you can even create an additional inbound delivery item, if necessary.

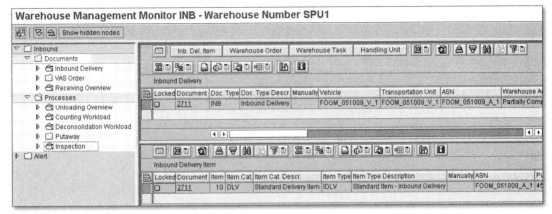

Figure 9.9 Displaying IDs in the Warehouse Monitor

In addition to verifying the materials, quantities, and HUs of the inbound delivery, you can also verify the assignment of the TU activity, if relevant. This assignment is necessary if you want to unload the truck with RF or by printing an unloading list based on WTs. If the TU activity assignment doesn't already exist, you can assign the inbound delivery to the TU activity from the check-in process. When assigning the TU activity, you can search based on various search parameters (e.g., TU activity number, license plate, carrier number, parking lot, etc.).

If the door was not determined and assigned automatically (as described earlier), you can assign the door manually to the TU activity from the EWM Easy Access menu by following the EXTENDED WAREHOUSE MANAGEMENT • SHIPPING AND RECEIVING • MAINTAIN DOOR ASSIGNMENT menu path, or using Transaction code /SCWM/DOOR. When manually assigning the door, you can search for doors based on the status of the doors (e.g., which doors are empty).

If WTs for unloading were not created automatically (as described earlier), you can create warehouse taks for unloading from the SAP Easy Access menu by following the EXTENDED WAREHOUSE MANAGEMENT • SHIPPING AND RECEIVING • UNLOAD menu path, or using Transaction code /SCWM/UNLOAD. To print unloading instructions, you can use PPF action /SCWM/PRD_IN_UNLOAD_LIST_PRINT in application /SCDL/DELIVERY and action profile /SCDL/PRD_IN. (For more information on using PPF actions for printing, see Chapter 24.)

If you have not received an ASN for the inbound shipment, you can create the inbound delivery manually in ERP using Transaction VL60. To create the inbound delivery in Transaction VL60, enter the items of the delivery note and pack these items with a manual creation of incomimg HUs. When you save the inbound delivery, it will be replicated to EWM automatically. In EWM, you can trigger the automatic activation of the IDN for the creation of the inbound delivery using the relevant PPF actions.

9.3.2 Administrative Goods Receipt Based on EGRs

If the inbound delivery hasn't been created already in ERP, you can also create the inbound delivery directly and manually in EWM based on EGRs, as long as the deliveries are created with reference to a purchase order or production order. To create inbound deliveries with reference to purchase orders (as you can see in Figure 9.10) from the EWM Easy Access menu, follow the EXTENDED WAREHOUSE MANAGEMENT • DELIVERY PROCESSING • INBOUND DELIVERY • GR PREPARATION - EXTERNAL PROCUREMENT menu path, or use Transaction code /SCWM/GRPE. To create inbound deliveries for production orders from the EWM Easy Access menu, follow the EXTENDED WAREHOUSE MANAGEMENT • DELIVERY PROCESSING • INBOUND DELIVERY • GR PREPARATION - PRODUCTION menu path, or use Transaction code /SCWM/GRPI. Prior to creating the inbound deliveries, you must download the EGR data using report /SCWM/ERP_DLV_DELETE, as described previously in this chapter.

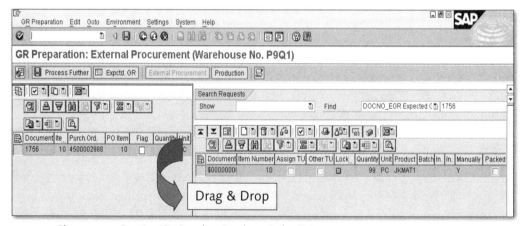

Figure 9.10 Creating IDs Based on Purchase Order Data

While creating the inbound delivery, you can enter the TU number, carrier, and the SCAC for the partner. If the TU number is unique, the carrier and SCAC code are optional entries, but you still may want to enter them to use some of the reporting features. Once the TU data is entered, you can search for the available EGRs based on the purchase order or production order data using the appropriate selection parameter. On the left pane, EWM will display the relevant EGRs, and you can flag the EGR items you want to create inbound deliveries for and then select the COPY FLAGGED ITEM function. EWM will then generate the inbound delivery, copy the relevant data from the EGR, and provide the resulting delivery header data in a dialog box. When you save the inbound delivery (which is automatically activated in EWM), it is replicated to ERP as an inbound delivery.

In the transactions for creating inbound deliveries from EGRs, you can also:

▸ Delete the newly created delivery headers and items

▸ Assign delivery items to a TU activity

▸ Create batches and perform batch item splits for delivery items

▸ Maintain serial numbers

▸ Navigate to the packing and unpacking transaction (Transaction /SCWM/PACK)

Once you have created the inbound delivery, you can assign doors or trigger door determination similar to the method described previously for inbound deliveries created for ASNs.

9.4 Unloading and Goods Receipt

Once the inbound deliveries have been created and verified, you may begin the physical goods receipt process, which includes unloading, visual inspection of the unloaded goods, and posting goods receipt. In the following sections, we will describe these processes further.

9.4.1 Unloading

In EWM, there are two variants for unloading — simple unloading and complex unloading. Simple unloading lets you mark the unloading status of the inbound delivery using the inbound delivery or TU user interfaces. Complex unloading is a process that occurs in the physical warehouse that requires the warehouse operator to execute WTs to unload the individual pallets from the TU. As you can imagine, the complex unloading process gives you more granular data and allows you to more closely control the business process. In the following sections, we will describe how to execute both simple and complex unloading.

Simple Unloading

In EWM, the simple unloading process allows you to set the unloading status of the inbound delivery manually. You can update the status in the inbound delivery interface in the EWM Easy Access menu by following the EXTENDED WAREHOUSE MANAGEMENT • DELIVERY PROCESSING • INBOUND DELIVERY • MAINTAIN INBOUND DELIVERY menu path, or using Transaction code /SCWM/PRDI. You can also set the status at the TU level using the desktop transaction for processing the TU activity. From the Easy Access menu, follow the EXTENDED WAREHOUSE MANAGEMENT • SHIPPING AND RECEIVING • PROCESS TRANSPORTATION UNIT menu path, or use Transaction code /SCWM/TU.

Complex Unloading

In EWM, the complex unloading process utilizes WTs to facilitate the unloading process. If WTs for unloading were already created (as described earlier in Section 9.3.1, Administrative Goods Receipt Based on ASNs), you can confirm these WTs using the mobile data entry (or RF) transactions, or you can use the desktop transactions. To confirm unloading WTs on the desktop, from the EWM Easy Access menu, follow the EXTENDED WAREHOUSE MANAGEMENT • SHIPPING AND RECEIVING • UNLOAD menu path, or use Transaction code /SCWM/UNLOAD.

For the WTs, the source bin corresponds to the goods movement bin in the inbound delivery item. For putaway-relevant delivery items, the goods movement bin is determined as follows:

- If goods receipt is posted for the TU, the goods movement bin is empty.
- If the door determination and assigment is done automatically or manually the goods movement bin is determined according to the assignment of the door storage bin and supply chain unit (SCU). To update the assignment, from the EWM Easy Access menu, follow the EXTENDED WAREHOUSE MANAGEMENT • MASTER DATA • SHIPPING AND RECEIVING • ASSIGN DOOR STORAGE BIN AND SUPPLY CHAIN UNIT menu path, or use Transaction code /SCWM/DOOR_SCU.
- If a door is not assigned, the goods movement bin is determined by the source bin of the determined warehouse process type.
- If no goods movement bin is found via the first or second option, the goods movement bin is copied from the staging area bin.

The destination bin of the unloading WT corresponds to the staging bay in the inbound delivery item. To maintain the staging area and door determination from

the EWM Easy Access menu, follow the EXTENDED WAREHOUSE MANAGEMENT •
SETTINGS • SHIPPING AND RECEIVING • STAGING AREA AND DOOR DETERMINATION
(INBOUND) menu path, or use Transaction code /SCWM/STADET_IN. In this case,
however, the system posts goods receipt automatically before the unloading WT
will be confirmed.

9.4.2   Visual Inspection and Completeness Check

After the goods are unloaded, you can perform a visual inspection and completeness check. If you determine a quantity difference during the completeness check,
you can correct the inbound delivery with the physical goods receipt transaction
(Transaction /SCWM/GR) or within the user interface for the inbound delivery
processing (Transaction /SCWM/PRDI). You can adjust the quantities on the item
level if they resulted from damage, loss, or expiration of the shelf-life data, for
example.

In delivery processing, you can use process codes to control particular exception
situations, for example, when the quantity delivery is more than or less than
the delivery quantity. EWM supports three possible options for managing these
exceptions:

▶ **No quantity adjustment**

In this case, EWM does not adjust the delivery quantity, but it saves a process
code in the delivery for documentation purposes.

▶ **Adjustment of delivery quantity**

In this case, EWM adjusts the delivery quantity and saves a process code in the
delivery but the transferred delivery quantity is not adjusted.

▶ **Adjustment of delivery quantity and delivery quantity transferred**

In this case, EWM adjusts both the delivery quantity and the transferred delivery quantity. The result is that the delivery is split, with the adjusted quantity
remaining on the original delivery and the remaining quantity being moved to
a new delivery, which is subsequently also transferred to ERP.

For example, EWM generates an IDN for 100 pieces. The document flow also
carries a quantity of 100 pieces. EWM generates an inbound delivery with an
inbound delivery quantity of 100 pieces. In inbound delivery it was specified by
the worker that EWM is to adjust the inbound delivery quantity to 90 pieces,
because 10 pieces are missing. In Customizing for the process code and the process

code profile, it is defined as an adjustment for both the delivery quantity and the transferred delivery quantity. EWM adjusts the inbound delivery quantity to 90 pieces. This triggers a quantity adjustment for the transferred delivery quantity in the document flow to 90 pieces, and a delivery split in the goods receipt process, meaning that EWM generates another inbound delivery using the difference quantity of 10 pieces, which is then replicated to ERP.

In addition to using the process codes to indicate quantity differences, you can also use exception codes to indicate exceptions such as damaged goods being received. The exception code can then trigger follow-up actions using the PPF, similar to using an exception code during a WT confirmation. For example, the exception code can trigger an inspection of the HU. To trigger the inspection, you would use inspection object type (IOT) preliminary inspection HU. The IOT defines the software component, the process, and the object for which inspection documents can be created in the quality inspection engine (QIE; which we will further describe later in this chapter). Following the inspection, you can decide how to proceed with the damaged product and trigger the appropriate follow-up actions from the inspection document processing.

9.4.3 Posting Goods Receipt

After you have checked and verified the inbound goods, you can post the goods receipt manually in Transaction /SCWM/PRDI or /SCWM/GR. When posting the goods receipt, you can either post for the entire inbound delivery, or you can perform a partial goods receipt.

If you prefer an automatic posting, you can let EWM post the goods receipt for the inbound delivery when the WT for putaway is confirmed. Unless the putaway is confirmed in a single WT, this will result in multiple partial goods receipts for the inbound delivery. Whether they are posted manually or automatically, you can see the individual partial goods receipts in the document flow for the inbound delivery. If you use putaway HUs, you can only post goods receipts for the complete HUs.

Once goods receipt is posted for the inbound delivery in EWM, the goods receipt posting is transferred to ERP using the PPF action /SCDL/MSG_PRD_IN_GR_SEND, which calls the Business Application Programming Interface (BAPI) /SPE/INB_DELIVERY_CONFIRM_DEC.

9.5   Putaway Processing

After the goods have been unloaded and verified and a goods receipt has been posted, you can put away into the warehouse. During the inbound process, there are often additional process steps that must take place in between the unloading of the products and the final putaway. For example, you may have to perform quality inspection, deconsolidation, or repacking before executing the final putaway. In EWM, the flow of the multistep process for inbound receiving and putaway is controlled using the storage control. In Chapter 13, we will describe in detail how to set up the POSC and layout-oriented storage control (LOSC), which are responsible for determining the routing of the products through the warehouse based on the processes required and physical layout of the warehouse, respectively. In the meantime, we will provide a brief description from a process perspective, so that you have a good understanding of how these are used within the inbound processing.

> **Note**
>
> POSC is only relevant when moving products on HUs.
>
> When POSC and LOSC are used together for multistep movement control, the POSC is always checked first; then the LOSC is checked to determine whether an intermediate location must be used in moving from one process step to another.

Figure 9.11, contains an example of a complex inbound process with multiple process steps, including UNLOADING, COUNTING, DECONSOLIDATION, and FINAL PUT AWAY.

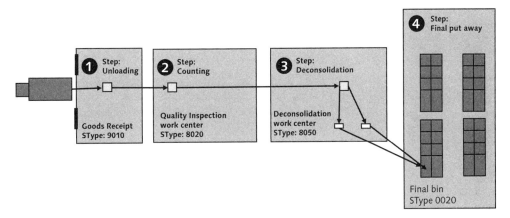

Figure 9.11 An Inbound Process with Multiple Process Steps

9.5.1 Process-Oriented Storage Control for Inbound Processes

The POSC is used to map complex putaway processes to determine the relevant process steps required and the sequence of the processes steps. This lets you track the overall process while having visibility to the execution of the individual process steps.

In the customizing for the storage control, you can flexibly define the necessary process steps to fulfill an overall process. In the example provided in Figure 9.12, you can see that the following process steps are defined as part of the POSC for the putaway process for HUs:

1. Unload the HUs at the door

2. Perform a quality inspection, including counting

3. Deconsolidate mixed pallets so that they can be put away separately into the warehouse

4. Put away the deconsolidated HUs to the final bin

EWM determines the relevant processes via the POSC according to the inbound delivery type and inbound delivery item type, and the warehouse process type (among other criteria). In Figure 9.12, you can see a graphical depiction of the decision process used by the POSC to determine the relevant processes. As mentioned earlier, the POSC requires HUs for managing the internal warehouse processes. One reason for this is that the POSC uses HUs to store process control information.

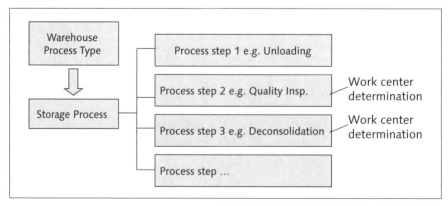

Figure 9.12 Determination of POSC in the Inbound Process

> **Note**
>
> HUs are more flexibly defined and more easily used in EWM than in ERP, and you do not necessarily need to use HU-managed HUs in ERP to use HUs in EWM (see Chapter 6 for more information about using HUs in EWM). Therefore, you should not necessarily be concerned just because the POSC only works with HUs.

9.5.2 Layout Oriented Storage Control for Inbound Processes

If you sometimes need to use an interim bin when transferring stock from one area of the warehouse to another (e.g., a pick-up/drop-off point, pick point, identification point, etc.), you can manage this requirement in EWM using the LOSC. The LOSC is described in detail in Chapter 13.

9.5.3 Combined Storage Control for Inbound Processing

As mentioned previously, if both the POSC and the LOSC are used together, the POSC is always checked first during execution of the storage control. An example of a warehouse storage process that includes both the POSC and LOSC could include the following process steps:

1. Unloading the HUs at the door (POSC)
2. Deconsolidating the HUs at the work center (POSC)
3. Identifying goods at the ID point (LOSC)
4. Putting away the HUs into the final destination bin (POSC)

In the following sections, we will describe the possible inbound activities, or process steps, in detail.

9.5.4 Quality Inspection in Inbound Processes

When products are received from external vendors, or even when products are received from other points in your own network, you may want to inspect or count the products to ensure compliance to your own requirements for storing the products in your warehouse. In EWM, the QIE is leveraged to facilitate these inspections. The QIE is a function of the Supply Chain Management (SCM) basis and can be used in various applications. In EWM, you can manage the quality inspections (including detailed counting) using the QIE on its own, or you can integrate the QIE with ERP Quality Management (QM) to facilitate the inspection of stock in the warehouse as requested by QM.

Quality Inspection Types

In EWM, if you need to inspect products, packaging materials, or transports during the inbound processes, you can perform the following types of inspections:

- Inspections for the goods receipt process
- Inspection of the entire inbound delivery
- Inspection of the delivered HUs
- Count the delivered products
- Inspect the delivered products for supplier inbound deliveries
- Inspect the delivered products for customer returns

Quality Inspection Process

When inspection is relevant for an inbound delivery, the system generates an inspection document that describes the inspection object and contains the main attributes such as inspection object type, inspection rule, quantities, and inspection status. The time that inspection documents are created can be defined in customizing. You can create the inspection documents during activation of the inbound delivery or when the inbound delivery is transferred to status IN YARD.

The defined IOT specifies the software component, process, and object in which inspection documents may be created in the QIE. In the case of an active inspection object type, EWM looks for an inspection rule. If the system finds an inspection rule, it creates an inspection document based on the inspection object type.

You can also create inspection documents manually, for example, for incoming HUs. To trigger the manual inspection document creation from the EWM Easy Access menu, follow the EXTENDED WAREHOUSE MANAGEMENT • WORK SCHEDULING • INSPECTION DOCUMENT • PROCESS PRODUCT INSPECTION DOCUMENT menu path (or use Transaction code /SCWM/QIDPR) or PROCESS HU INSPECTION DOCUMENT (or use Transaction code /SCWM/QIDHU) or PROCESS DELIVERY INSPECTION DOCUMENT (or use Transaction code /SCWM/QIDDH).

When you execute the goods receipt (or the first partial goods receipt for an item), EWM releases the inspection document. Once the inspection document is released, EWM determines the work center for quality inspection and creates the WT for movement to the work center (based on the relevant storage control).

If you trigger a sample inspection via the QIE (and if the sample is stock-relevant), EWM generates two WTs. The first WT is used to transport the sample to the work center, and the other is used to put away the remaining quantity that is not being checked. Once you check the sample, you document the result by setting the appropriate decision code in the inspection document. To update the inspection documents, as you can see in Figure 9.13), from the EWM Easy Access menu, follow the EXTENDED WAREHOUSE MANAGEMENT • EXECUTION • QUALITY INSPECTION AND COUNT menu path, or use Transaction code /SCWM/QINSP. You can also execute the inspections on the RF device using the relevant inspection transactions.

For inspection items, you must specify a decision code in the inspection document, however, this is optional for samples. In addition, you can also recording findings. Depending on the decision code specified, a follow-up action can be triggered via the PPF (e.g., creation of a WT for scrapping or follow-up action alerts, emails, and workflows to start manual follow-up actions, which are determined based on the exception code linked to the decision code).

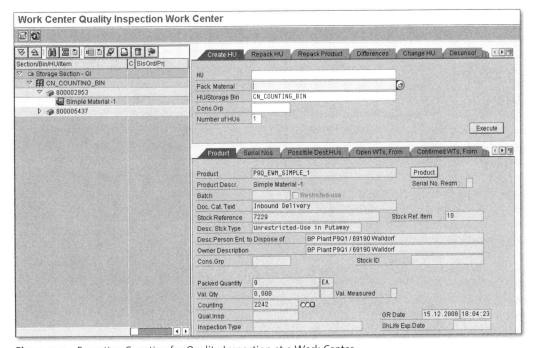

Figure 9.13 Executing Counting for Quality Inspection at a Work Center

> **Note**
>
> The layout for work centers in general can be defined in customizing. The work center layout is used in the work center, and controls which areas and tabs appear on the interface. Therefore, you can easily adapt the user interface to your own business needs.

Within the overall goods receipt process in EWM, you can conduct more than one quality inspection. As an example, Figure 9.14 shows a graphical depiction of a goods receipt process in which two inspections are performed. The first is a preliminary check when the truck arrives, which is an overall check of the goods as received on the truck. The second quality inspection occurs at the HU level during the unloading process.

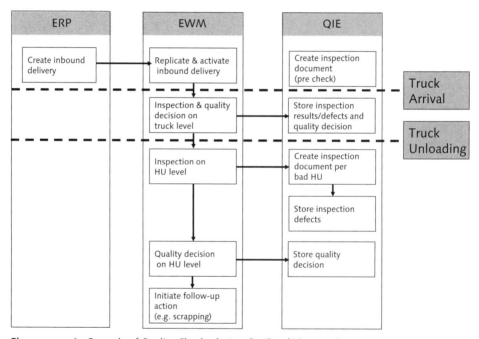

Figure 9.14 An Example of Quality Checks during the Goods Receipt Process

Later in this chapter we will discuss the QIE in more detail and provide further information regarding configuration and implementation of the quality inspection settings in EWM.

9.5.5   Deconsolidation

The deconsolidation process lets you break a mixed pallet that was received on an inbound delivery into multiple HUs for putaway. During the putaway task creation, EWM determines whether a received mixed pallet should be deconsolidated when it creates the inactive product putaway WT (which can be created automatically with the first active WT, according to the customizing settings of the POSC).

The final destination bin determined by the WT creation is assigned to an activity area according to the warehouse customizing (see Chapter 3, The Warehouse Structure, for more details), and each activity area has a consolidation group assigned to it. Consolidation groups are used in both the inbound and outbound processes. For inbound processing, a consolidation group is used to describe a collection of storage bins, and it is used specifically in determining deconsolidation.

When a mixed HU is received, EWM determines the relevant activity area and the assigned consolidation group for all included products during creation of the inactive product WTs. If different activity areas are determined, EWM creates a HU WT for the deconsolidation work center according to the defined storage control.

In Figure 9.15, you can see a graphical depiction of the checks performed during the putaway task creation for determining deconsolidation.

If the products in the mixed HU are assigned to be put away into the same activity area, then the attributes for deconsolidation can be defined in the EWM IMG by following the menu path EXTENDED WAREHOUSE MANAGEMENT • GOODS RECEIPT PROCESS • DECONSOLIDATION • DEFINE ATTRIBUTES FOR DECONSOLIDATION. There you can define the following deconsolidation attributes per activity area:

▶ Maximum number of WTs in the received mixed HU

▶ Maximum number of WTs in the putaway HU

If the number of WTs exceeds the maximum permitted number of WTs in the putaway HU, the putaway HU is directed to a deconsolidation station, where its contents can deconsolidated. For example, if you receive a mixed HU with fifteen different products where the products are stored in the same activity area, EWM checks the parameter for the maximum number of WT in the received mixed HU to determine if the mixed HU can be used directly for the putaway or whether the HU must be directed to the deconsolidation work center. If the parameter is set to ten, for example, then the HU will be deconsolidated before final putaway.

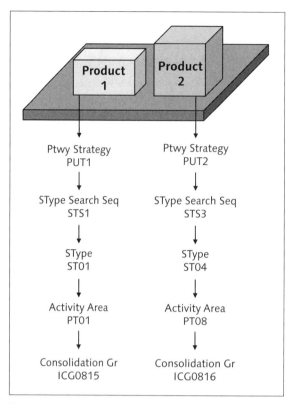

Figure 9.15 Logic to Determine the Necessity for Deconsolidation

To access the important customizing settings for deconsolidation in the EWM IMG, follow the menu path EXTENDED WAREHOUSE MANAGEMENT • GOODS RECEIPT PROCESS • DECONSOLIDATION. For example, you can specify:

▸ Definition of attributes for deconsolidaion

▸ Determination of the deconsolidation work center (note: the work center determined in POSC is more specific)

▸ Definition of deconsolidation work center

In Figure 9.16, you can see the desktop transaction for the deconsolidation work center, which can be reached via the EWM Easy Access menu by following the EXTENDED WAREHOUSE MANAGEMENT • EXECUTION • DECONSOLIDATION IN GOODS RECEIPT menu path, or using Transaction code /SCWM/DCONS. In the example shown in the figure, the work center has a separately defined inbound and outbound section, which helps to logically segregate the HUs similar to the physical layout of the work center.

In addition to the desktop transaction, you can also execute the deconsolidation using the relevant RF transaction. To access the deconsolidation functions of the RF Transaction (/SCWM/RFUI), if you are using the standard delivered RF menu, follow the menu path 03 INBOUND PROCESSES • 02 DECONSOLIDATION.

At the work center, you create putaway HUs during the course of executing the deconsolidation. The MAXIMUM NUMBER OF WTS IN THE PUTAWAY HU parameter is used to determine the maximum number of WTs (which is usually analogous to the number of product and destination bin combinations) that can be deconsolidated to the destination putaway HU before it suggested the HU be closed. When you close the HU, the putaway WTs will be activated and you can execute the WTs for putaway to the final destination bin (which would usually be executed on an RF device).

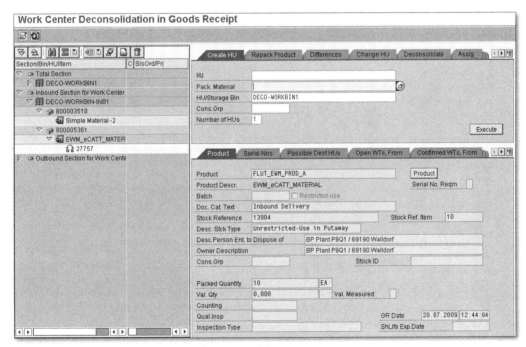

Figure 9.16 Example of a Work Center for Deconsolidation

To specify the settings for the work centers in the EWM IMG, follow the menu path EXTENDED WAREHOUSE MANAGEMENT • MASTER DATA • WORK CENTER. Here, you can specify:

▶ Work center layouts

▶ Definition of work centers (to which you assign the layout)

9.5.6 Value Added Services

During the inbound processing, you can choose to activate VASs for execution of certain activities such as repackaging, labeling, oiling (for preservation), or other activities that need to be performed before the product is put away into the destination bins. To trigger these activities, EWM checks (for example, during the inbound delivery creation or at the first goods receipt posting) the customizing and master data for a relevant VAS. If the VAS is relevant, EWM automatically creates the VAS order and then checks for the existence of the pack spec.

To set up the VAS relevance check in the EWM IMG, follow the menu path EXTENDED WAREHOUSE MANAGEMENT • CROSS-PROCESS SETTINGS • VALUE-ADDED SERVICES (VAS) • DEFINE RELEVANCE FOR VAS.

The determination of pack spec for the VAS order is based on the condition technique. To set up the configuration related to the condition check (including access sequences, condition types, and determination procedures) in the EWM IMG, follow the menu path SCM BASIS • PACKING • PACKAGING SPECIFICATION • DETERMINATION OF PACKAGING SPECIFICATIONS.

For more information regarding VAS orders and VAS processing, see Chapter 19, Value-Added Services.

9.5.7 Putaway

The putaway process step can be divided into two parts —the putaway preparation, in which the destination bin is determined based on various parameters, and the putaway execution, where the warehouse worker confirms the WT that was created in the preparation step.

During the putaway task creation, the physical storage bin for putaway is determined by selecting and applying the suitable putaway strategies according to the master data (which may have been determined manually, or via slotting, which is discussed later in this chapter) and the customizing.

Putaway Strategies

The putaway strategy is used to determine the bin location for a quantity of product based on the characteristics of the product, the physical nature of the storage type, and section in which the bins are located. In EWM, the following putaway strategies are available:

▶ Manual Entry: the destination storage bin is entered manually when the WT is created. Therefore, EWM does not determine a storage section or a storage bin. (The specified bin can be disallowed based on such validations as the storage section check, capacity check, etc.)

▶ Fixed Storage Bin: this strategy is used for puting away products in bins that are preassigned to the product. In EWM, the assignment of one or more fixed bins to a warehouse product is possible (even within the same storage type). On the STORAGE TYPE tab of the product master, you can specify the maximum number of allowed assigned bins to a warehouse product within the given storage type.

▶ Near Fixed Picking Bin: this strategy is used when you put away products in a reserve storage area when the reserve storage bins are located directly above the fixed storage bins of the picking storage type.

▶ General Storage: this strategy is used for a general storage area to which a putaway strategy is not relevant. A general storage is a type of warehouse organization in which one or more storage bins per storage section are defined that can be grouped to storage sections. In general storage, the storage bin will not be determined via a putaway strategy but will either be determined, for example, by the process type or storage control, or entered manually.

▶ Addition to Existing Stock: this strategy is used to put away stock in storage bins that already contain stock of the product, with the prerequisite that sufficient free capacity still exists in the relevant storage bin. If the system cannot find a storage bin with the same product, or if the storage bin does not have sufficient capacity, EWM searches for the next empty storage bin. *Note: This strategy may violate the first-in/first-out (FIFO) principle and should only be used in situations where capacity constraints or process effeciency override the need for managing the stock via FIFO.*

▶ Empty Storage Bin: this strategy is used to put away stock in empty storage bins and support warehouses that are organized "randomly" (i.e., the location of the bin does not matter as long as it is within the appropriate storage type, section, and bin type).

▶ Bulk Storage: this strategy is used for a warehouse area where similar pallets or containers are stacked one atop another to conserve space. *Note: This strategy also directly violates the FIFO principle, but you can mitigate this by specifying a window, in terms of days of putaway, within which you can place stock in the same bin, but after which you must begin putting stock in a new bin.*

▶ Pallet Storage: this putaway strategy is used for warehouse areas where pallets are stored in racks. EWM processes different HU types (e.g., pallets) and allocates them to a suitable storage bin section. In this strategy, only HUs with the same HU types can be put away in the same storage bin.

During the putaway preparation, the destination storage bin is determined (as you can also see in Figure 9.17) by evaluating the following sequences, in this order:

1. Determination of storage type sequence

2. Determination of storage section sequence

3. Determination of bin type sequence

4. Determination of storage bin

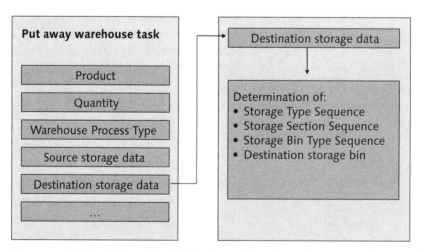

Figure 9.17 Determination of Destination Storage Data during Putaway Warehouse Task Creation

In the following sections, we will discuss each component of the destination bin determination.

Storage Type Search Sequence

To begin the determination of the relevant storage bin for putaway, EWM checks the storage type search sequence specified in customizing. The storage type search sequence is selected based on various criteria (as you can see in Figure 9.18), including the warehouse number, putaway control indicator (PACI; from the product master), warehouse process type, quantity classification (from the determined pack spec for the product or from the product master), stock type, party entitled, and the hazardous rating. From the storage type search sequence, the system then determines the sequence of the storage types it will use to find the destination bin.

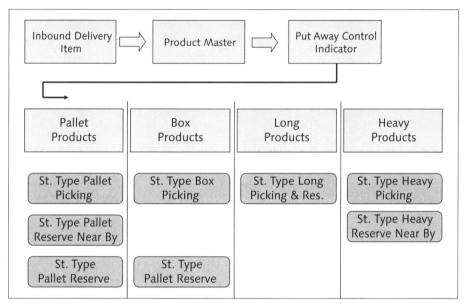

Figure 9.18 Example of Storage Type Search Sequence

The PACI controls that certain products (e.g., pallet products, box products, etc.) are put away in certain storage types in a preferential manner. The PACI is linked to a specific storage type search sequence. To define the storage type search sequence in the EWM IMG, follow the menu path EXTENDED WAREHOUSE MANAGEMENT • GOODS RECEIPT PROCESS • STRATEGIES • STORAGE TYPE SEARCH. Under this node, you can specify:

► Definition of storage type search sequence for putaway

▶ Assignment of storage types to storage type search sequence

▶ Definition of putaway control indicator

▶ Specification of storage type search sequence for putaway

▶ Optimization of access strategy for storage type search for putaway

In Figure 9.19, you can see an example for the storage type search sequence for various groups of products.

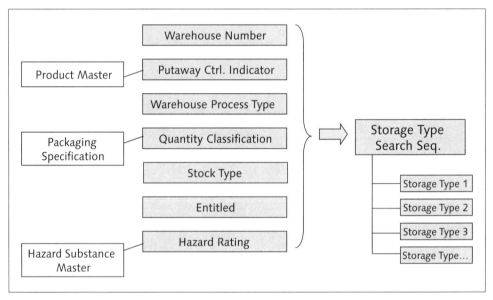

Figure 9.19 Determination of the Storage Type Search Sequence

Storage Section Search Sequence

In the next step, EWM determines the possible storage sections per storage type. For storage section determination, EWM uses the storage section search sequence. This sequence specifies in which storage sections the system searches for destination storage bins. On the product master, you can group the products using the storage section indicator (SSI), so that like products will be handled in a similar way from a storage section placement perspective (for example, slow-moving vs. fast-moving products). The storage section indicator is then used (along with other criteria, such as the warehouse number, storage type, and hazard rating) to determine the storage section search sequence, as shown in Figure 9.20.

To set up the storage section search in the EWM IMG, follow the menu path
EXTENDED WAREHOUSE MANAGEMENT • GOODS RECEIPT PROCESS • STRATEGIES •
STORAGE SECTION SEARCH. Under this node, you can specify:

▸ Storage section indicators

▸ Storage section search sequence

▸ Storage section check

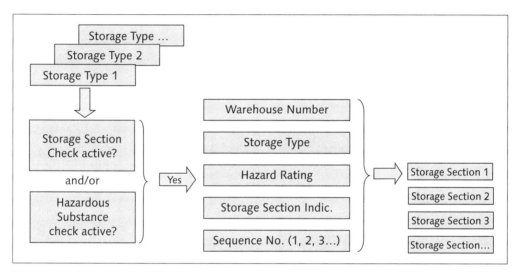

Figure 9.20 Determination of Storage Section Sequence per Storage Type

Storage Bin Type Sequence

In the next step, EWM determines the possible storage bin types per storage type.
A storage bin type groups bins according to their physical attributes (for example,
large bins vs. small bins). On the storage bin type settings, you specify whether the
HU type is checked during putaway. If it is checked, then the bin type sequence
is determined based on the warehouse number, storage bin type, and HU type (as
you can see in Figure 9.21).

To set up the storage bin type determination in the EWM IMG, follow the menu
path EXTENDED WAREHOUSE MANAGEMENT • GOODS RECEIPT PROCESS • STRATEGIES •
STORAGE BIN DETERMINATION. Under this node, you can specify:

▸ Storage bin types

▸ Assignment of storage bin types to storage types

▸ Definition of HU types for each storage type and storage bin type

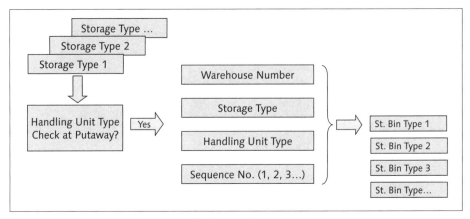

Figure 9.21 Determination of Storage Bin Type per Storage Type

Storage Bin Determination

The determination of sequences for storage type, storage section, and storage bin type leads to possible combinations for determining of storage bins. Figure 9.22, shows an example matrix of possible combinations.

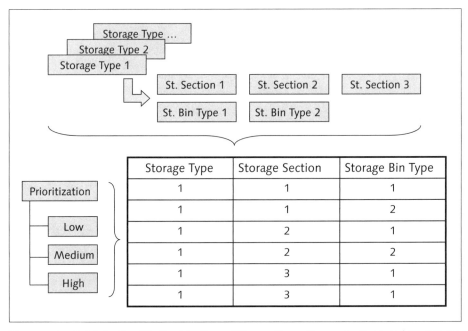

Figure 9.22 Matrix for Possible Combinations of Storage Types, Storage Sections, and Storage Bin Types

Priorities can be defined for storage type, storage section, and storage bin type to control the sequence in which alternatives are checked during the storage bin determination. If the priority of the storage bin type is a low number, for example, the alternative storage bin types are investigated before alternative storage sections or storage types are considered. EWM determines the destination storage bin based on the prioritization of the possible combinations (as you can see in Figure 9.23) and on the settings of the destination storage type as long as a suitable storage bin was determined.

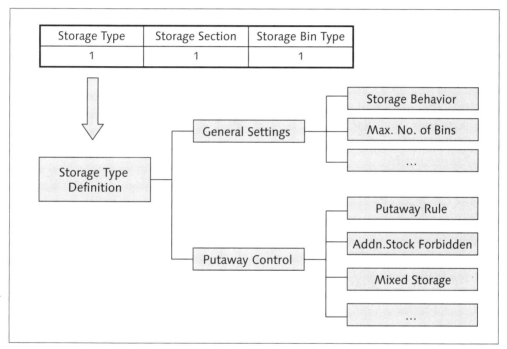

Figure 9.23 Determination of Storage Bin per Combination of Storage Type, Storage Section, Bin Type Based on Storage Type Settings

Settings on the Storage Type

The settings in the configuration of the storage type play an important role in the determination of the destination storage bin, as it determines the strategies used and the checks performed for determining the bin relevance. In Chapter 3, we discussed the storage type settings in detail. In particular, for the relevance to the putaway bin determination, you should pay special attention to the settings related to the following topics:

- Storage section check
- HU-type check
- Mixed storage check
- Addition to existing stock forbidden
- Search rule for empty bins (note that the value SORTING ACCORDING TO DEFINITION is relevant to cross-line stock putaway (CLSP) in which a special bin sorting can be defined)
- Capacity check
- Putaway rule

In many cases, the putaway strategies are dependent on the interplay between various settings in the storage type definition. For example, if you want to use the Addition To Existing Stock strategy , you must specify the following fields in the specified way:

- Storage Behavior: Define as a standard warehouse, which means the bins in the storage type do not have any special attributes.
- Putaway Rules: Set to ADDITION TO EXISTING STOCK/EMPTY BIN.
- Addition To Stock Forbidden: Means that a quant of a particular product with a particular attribute can be placed into storage in a storage bin with the same product and the same attribute as an addition to existing stock. If additions to existing stock are allowed, the appropriate entry is blank (addition to existing stock permitted).
- Mixed Storage: Specify the appropriate setting based on your requirements. If you specify that only one HU is allowed per bin, then you may limit addition to stock opportunities. Note that if you are storing loose material, the storage bin counts as an HU for the mixed storage check. As a result, packed and unpacked stock cannot be stored at the same time if you only allow one HU.

To take another example, if you want to use the Empty Bin strategy, you must specify the settings as:

- Storage Behavior: Define as a standard warehouse

▶ Putaway Rules: Set to Empty Bin

To further define the putaway rules (and to check the relevant documentatin for special rules) in the EWM IMG, follow the menu path EXTENDED WAREHOUSE MANAGEMENT • GOODS RECEIPT PROCESS • STRATEGIES • PUTAWAY RULES.

Queue Assignment

While creating the putaway WTs and respective WOs, the resulting WOs will be assigned to the appropriate queue based on the settings in the EWM Resource Management. For more details on Resource Management and the queue determination, see Chapter 5, Other Warehouse Master Data, and Chapter 22, Data Capture and Resource Optimization.

Putaway Execution

You can execute the putaway tasks and warehouse orders in the desktop transactions (for paper-based processes), including the warehouse monitor, or you can use the relevant RF transactions. For example, to confirm a WO in the EWM Easy Access menu, you can follow the EXTENDED WAREHOUSE MANAGEMENT • EXECUTION • CONFIRM WAREHOUSE TASK menu path, or you can use Transaction code /SCWM/TO_CONF. To confirm the WOs in the RF transactions (from Transaction code /SCWM/RFUI) if you are using the standard delivered menu, follow the menu path 03 INBOUND PROCESSES • 03 PUTAWAY • 03 PUTAWAY BY WO. You can also use the system-guided options, according to the queue determination as described earlier.

Exception Handling

One of the key challenges within a warehouse is dealing appropriately with exception situations as they occur. In EWM, you can use exception codes to describe exception situations in the different warehouse processes. Exception codes can be defined for different document types (such as for inbound deliveries or outbound deliveries), product shortages during goods receipt, product shortages during picking (pick denial), and other warehouse situations where processing abnormalities can exist. You can enter the exception codes in both RF and desktop transactions, and you can define which ones can be used in which context to be sure that they are used appropriately.

You can use the exception codes to not only track when exceptions occur but to also trigger follow-up actions for putaway execution (the follow-up actions can be defined in customizing). The exception codes are assigned to internal process codes, which control the triggering of the follow-up actions when an exception code is used.

For example, you can define an exception code that can be used during putaway if the destination storage bin is not accessible. By assigning the internal process code CHBD to the exception code, you can drive the user to a special screen to let them change the storage bin.

In Table 9.2, you can see some examples of the internal process codes delivered in the standard EWM customizing for both RF and desktop transactions, along with the resulting system behavior.

Internal Process Code	Description	System Behavior
CHBA	Change Batch	RF: start new screen Desktop: open corresponding field for input
CHBD	Change Destination Storage Bin (Location)	RF: start new screen changing destination bin Desktop: input of exception code necessary to change destination bin
CHHU	Change Destination HU	RF: start new screen changing destination HU Desktop: input of exception code necessary to change destination HU
DIFF	Specify Difference Quantity	Changes quantities of the WT, storage bin, and delivery item according to the difference category assigned to the exception code
SKFD	Skip Current Validation Field	RF: current validation field will be closed (e.g., barcode can't be read)
SKVA	Skip Complete Validation	RF: all verfication fields will be closed

Table 9.2 Examples of Internal Process Codes That Can Be Assigned to Exception Codes and Their Resulting System Behaviors

For more information regarding Exception Handling, see Chapter 16, Exception Handling.

Availability Group Mapping to ERP Storage Locations

When the putaway is confirmed, the stock can be transferred to the availability group as defined in the storage type settings for the destination storage type. As discussed in Chapter 6, the availability group is used in the mapping to the storage location of ERP, therefore the confirmation of the putaway may result in an immediate transfer of the stock from one storage location to another, and subsequently to APO to update the stock availability for global ATP checking. For example, the stock may be transferred from the received on dock (ROD) storage location to the available for sale (AFS) storage location when the stock is put away from the dock to the final storage bin.

9.6   Slotting

Slotting is the process of determining a storage concept for a product that ensures the most efficient storage and picking of goods. In EWM, you can trigger the slotting function in the EWM Easy Access menu by following the EXTENDED WARE-HOUSE MANAGEMENT • MASTER DATA • SLOTTING • SLOT PRODUCTS FOR WAREHOUSE menu path, or using Transaction code /SCWM/SLOT. You can also schedule the transaction periodically as a background job, to ensure that all of the products in the warehouse are periodically evaluated to ensure that they are optimally slotted.

In the inbound process, EWM evaluates the following storage parameters that are relevant to putaway and which are evaluated and updated by the slotting function on the basis of master data, such as product master data (e.g., weight, volume), packaging data, and requirement data:

► Putaway control indicator (which helps determine the storage type search sequence during the putaway bin determination)

► Maximum quantity in storage type

► Storage section indicator (which helps determine the storage section search sequence during the putaway bin determination)

▶ Storage bin types (which helps determine the storage bin type sequence during the putaway bin determination).

Note

To calculate parameters such as the maximum quantity in the storage type, slotting needs requirement data for the relevant product. This requirement data can be determined in SAP APO (Service Parts Planning) and transferred via RFC to EWM, as discussed in Chapter 23, Integration with Other Applications, or you can update the requirement data directly in the EWM product master.

When slotting is executed, it creates planned values in the EWM product master that can later be written to the actual values by activating them (which can be run as a separate process, using Transaction code /SCWM/SLOTACT). For example, you may determine during slotting that the putaway control indicator for a product should be changed from 0001 to 0002, but you don't want to change it immediately. Therefore, EWM will store the evaluated value in the PLANNED PUTAWAY CONTROL INDICATOR field in the product master, and when you activate the value, the new value will replace the old value and henceforth the new value will be used during the putaway bin determination. You can also specify during slotting that the results of the slotting should be saved immediately (which stores the results in the planned values), not saved (which allows you to check what the result could be before you save them), or saved and activated (which immediately updates the actual values rather than saving them to the planned values).

During slotting, the putaway control indicator, storage section indicator, and storage bin types are determined using the condition technique (or bin type determination rules). To support the evaluation by the system, you must create the appropriate condition records for these fields, which indicate the thresholds to use for making the evaluation and assigning the new values.

In the following sections, we will provide an example for the setup of slotting and describe the settings so that you have a good understanding of how to use them to support your own slotting implementation.

Using the Condition Technique in Slotting

The example shown in Figure 9.24 describes the determination of the putaway control indicator based on the requirement data setting in the SLOTTING tab of the product master. The product with demand of 50 PC should be stored in STORAGE TYPE MM (moderate moves), while the product with demand of 5 PC should be stored in STORAGE TYPE MS (slow moves). In the following text, we will describe how to make the settings to support this requirement.

To begin, you should define the STORAGE TYPE SEARCH SEQUENCE FOR PUTAWAY (as seen in Figure 9.25) in the EWM IMG by following the menu path EXTENDED WAREHOUSE MANAGEMENT • MASTER DATA • GOODS RECEIPT PROCESS • SLOTTING • MASTER DATA • STORAGE TYPE SEARCH SEQUENCE • DEFINE STORAGE TYPE SEARCH SEQUENCE FOR PUTAWAY AND ASSIGN STORAGE TYPES TO STORAGE TYPE SEARCH SEQUENCE.

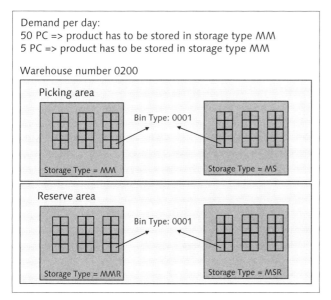

Figure 9.24 Example for Putaway Control Indicator Determination Based on Requirement Data

Change View "Storage Type Search Sequence for Putaway": Overview

New Entries

Storage Type Search Sequence for Putaway

WhN	Srch Seq.	Seq. No.	Typ	STG	EvtWhsItem	Description
0200	0A	2	666			Put Away in Storage Type OA
0200	PEC	1	PEC			Put Away in Storage Type PEC
0200	PEC	2	666			Put Away in Storage Type PEC
0200	PUMM	1	MM			Stor Type Srch Seq Med Size Moderate Mov
0200	PUMM	2	MMR		50	Stor Type Srch Seq Med Size Moderate Mov
0200	PUMS	1	MS			Stor Type Srch Seq Med Size Slow Moves
0200	PUMS	2	MSR		50	Stor Type Srch Seq Med Size Slow Moves

Figure 9.25 Example for Definition of Storage Type Search Sequence

Next, you should specify the PUTAWAY CONTROL INDICATOR (as you can see in Figure 9.26) in the EWM IMG by following the menu path EXTENDED WAREHOUSE MANAGEMENT • GOODS RECEIPT PROCESS • SLOTTING • MASTER DATA • DEFINE PUTAWAY CONTROL INDICATOR.

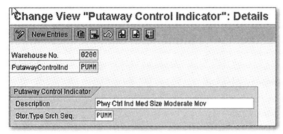

Figure 9.26 Example for Definition of Putaway Control Indicator

Next, you should define the possible REQUIREMENT CATEGORIES that can be used to influence the slotting. In the product master, you can assign three different requirements or demand data, namely: demand quantity, sales order items, and recommended storage quantity. To check or create the requirement types (as you can see in Figure 9.27) in the EWM IMG, follow the menu path EXTENDED WAREHOUSE MANAGEMENT • MASTER DATA • GOODS RECEIPT PROCESS • SLOTTING • INFLUENCING PARAMETERS • DEFINE REQUIREMENT TYPE.

Figure 9.27 Definition of the Different Requirement Types

Next, define the REQUIREMENT INDICATORS FOR SLOTTING and assign the INDICATORS (as seen in Figure 9.28) in the EWM IMG by following the menu path EXTENDED WAREHOUSE MANAGEMENT • MASTER DATA • GOODS RECEIPT PROCESS • SLOTTING • INFLUENCING PARAMETERS • INTERVALS • DEFINE REQUIREMENT INDICATORS and ASSIGN INTERVALS TO REQUIREMENT INDICATOR.

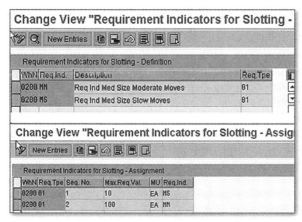

Figure 9.28 Example for Creating Requirement Indicators and Assigning the Quantity Intervals

To set up the condition technique, you must edit the CONDITION TABLE for the putaway control indicator based on the predefined determination procedure, condition type, and access sequence (as you can see in Figure 9.29) in the EWM IMG by following the menu path EXTENDED WAREHOUSE MANAGEMENT • MASTER DATA • GOODS RECEIPT PROCESS • SLOTTING • CONDITION TECHNIQUE • CONDITION TABLES • EDIT CONDITION TABLE FOR PUTAWAY CONTROL INDICATOR.

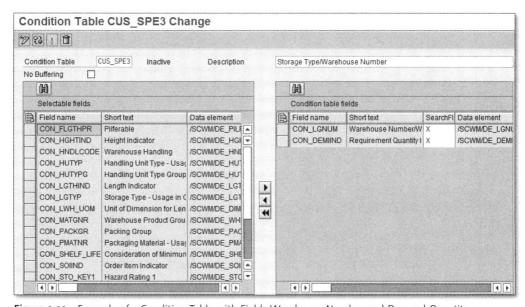

Figure 9.29 Example of a Condition Table with Fields Warehouse Number and Demand Quantity

To register and create the condition maintenance group (which bundles condition tables and types for condition maintenance) in the EWM IMG, follow the menu path EXTENDED WAREHOUSE MANAGEMENT • MASTER DATA • GOODS RECEIPT PROCESS • SLOTTING • CONDITION TECHNIQUE • SETTINGS FOR USER INTERFACE • REGISTER CONDITION MAINTENANCE GROUP and CREATE CONDITION MAINTENANCE GROUP.

Next, define the WAREHOUSE NUMBER PARAMETERS FOR SLOTTING (as seen in Figure 9.30) in the EWM IMG by following the menu path EXTENDED WAREHOUSE MANAGEMENT • MASTER DATA • GOODS RECEIPT PROCESS • SLOTTING • GENERAL SETTINGS • DEFINE WAREHOUSE NUMBER PARAMETERS FOR SLOTTING. In the definition of the parameters for slotting, you should pay special attention to the requirement types for calculating the default requirement indicators, particularly the REQUIREMENT TYPE FOR CALCULATING THE ORDER ITEM INDICATOR, REQUIREMENT TYPE FOR CALCULATING THE REQUIREMENT QUANTITY INDICATOR, and REQUIREMENT TYPE FOR CALCULATING THE TARGET STOCK INDICATOR.

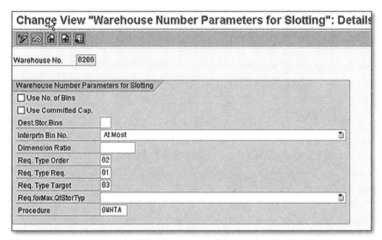

Figure 9.30 Assignment of the Requirement Types for the Warehouse

Finally, you can create the CONDITION RECORDS (assuming that the relevant condition table already exists) by following the EXTENDED WAREHOUSE MANAGEMENT • MASTER DATA • SLOTTING • CONDITION MAINTENANCE FOR SLOTTING menu path, or using Transaction code /SCWM/GCMC. As you can see in Figure 9.31, we assigned the putaway control indicators based on the requirements indicators.

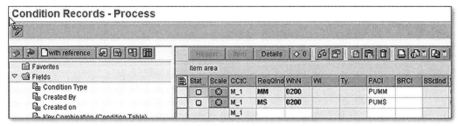

Figure 9.31 Example of a Condition Table for Putaway Control Indicator Determination Based on Requirement Indicator for Moderate and Slow Movers

Storage Bin Type Determination Rules

In addition to using the condition technique for determining the optimum bin type for slotting, you may alternatively use the storage bin determination rules to determine the optimum bin type. To specify which option you will use per storage type in the EWM IMG, follow the menu path EXTENDED WAREHOUSE MANAGEMENT • GOODS RECEIPT PROCESS • SLOTTING • GENERAL SETTINGS • DEFINE STORAGE TYPE PARAMETERS FOR SLOTTING. If you specify the BIN TYPE DETERMINATION as STORAGE BIN TYPE DETERMINATION RULES, then you should also specify the relevant DETERMINATION RULE. The options for the DETERMINATION RULE include:

- Maximum Weight
- Capacity Factor: Product
- Simple Volume Check
- Simple Dimensional Check
- Dimension Check with Z-Axis Rotation
- Dimension Check with Rotation and Tilt
- Weight Check and Simple Volume Check
- Weight Check and Simple Dimenstion Check
- Weight Check and Dimenstion Check with Z-Axis Rotation
- Weight Check and Dimenstion Check with Rotation and Tilt.

Executing Slotting

Once the settings are made, slotting can be executed manually using Transaction /SCWM/SLOT or periodically scheduled as a background job to update the planned indicators.

9.7 Quality Management in EWM

To support inspection processes for inbound receipts, EWM leverages the QIE from the SCM basis. The QIE generically enables integration of quality inspections for various SAP solutions and non-SAP applications.

9.7.1 Quality Inspection Engine Architecture

QIE is technically designed as an add-on for use in a heterogeneous system landscape. When the QIE was introduced to the SCM environment, execution of inspections within SCM could be supported. Figure 9.32, shows the QIE architecture for the EWM environment.

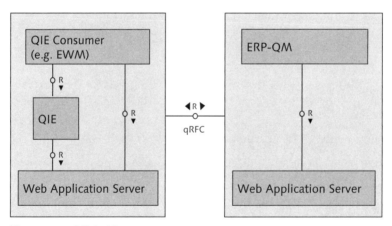

Figure 9.32 QIE Architecture

The QIE consumer as an independent system is linked to the QIE via a qRFC or PI interface and makes use of the QIE functionality. The QIE can also be part of the consumer system, as is the case for EWM. QIE is independent from the ERP system, but ERP can be linked to QIE via qRFC. The development platform for the QIE is the Web Application Server (WAS).

9.7.2 Quality Inspection Engine Data

The IOTs define the software component (e.g., EWM), the process that specifies the key of the business process in which the inspection is triggered, and the object type (e.g., product) in which inspection documents in the QIE can be created. The IOTs for EWM have been predefined by SAP. In the following sections, we will decsribe the IOTs in detail.

IOT Preliminary Inspection Inbound Delivery

Use of this IOT causes the system to automatically create an inspection document for checking complete deliveries.

If the IDN is activated, EWM automatically generates an inspection document for checking complete deliveries based on an inspection rule for the current version of the inspection object type and warehouse number, which can be defined in the EWM Easy Access menu by following the EXTENDED WAREHOUSE MANAGE-MENT • MASTER DATA • QUALITY MANAGEMENT • MAINTAIN INSPECTION RULE menu path, or using Transaction code /SCWM/QRSETUP. EWM automatically releases the inspection document when creating it, so that it is already available when the goods physically arrive. EWM stores the inspection document as a reference document for the delivery header in the delivery. This document cannot contain samples or items.

IOT Preliminary Inspection HU

Scheduling quality inspection for HUs in advance is not possible. The inspection document is created manually for the HU using the appropriate exception code in the RF transaction (Transaction /SCWM/RFUI).

For each delivery loaded in a TU (with multiple deliveries), all HUs can be classified as good or incorrect. After classification of all of the HUs, the system automatically creates the HU inspection document. In doing this, it generates one inspection document for each delivery and one item for each HU in this inspection document. Because this inspection document is created manually, it makes sense to only create one inspection rule for the warehouse number and version of the inspection object.

IOT Counting Inbound Delivery

The system creates this inspection document automatically, depending on the customizing for the inspection document creation within inbound delivery processing. The system releases it when it creates it. Counting is always a 100% inspection.

For counting and product inspections, the system checks the date/time of inspection document creation. If the date/time has been reached, EWM looks for an inspection rule and for any dynamic modification criteria that have been defined. Depending on the inspection rule it finds, EWM changes the stock type to blocked stock.

IOT Q-Inspection Returns Delivery

This IOT is used to direct the inspection of customer returns.

IOT Q-Inspection Product/Batch Inbound Delivery

This IOT drives the inspection of individual products/batches being received into EWM.

IOT Q-Inspection Product/Batch Warehouse — Internal

This IOT is used to generate the inspection of products/batches that are already present in the warehouse.

Inspection Rules

If the inspection object type is active, the system looks for an inspection rule. It can only generate inspection documents if an inspection rule exists. In the inspection rule, the following attributes can be specified:

- specifications for the creation of an inspection document (inspection procedure, for example, 100% inspection)
- type of determination of the inspection scope (inspection procedure, sampling procedure)

- specifications for the inspection frequency (dynamic modification)
- codes for the inspection decision

It is also possible to attach documents, such as an inspection instruction, to the inspection rule.

Results, Decisions, and Findings

When an object is selected for inspection, an inspection document is created. The purpose of the inspection document is to collect the data related to the inspection, such as specifications, results, and decision about the acceptance or rejection of the inspected object (e.g., the inspection document or the sample).

The inspection document also includes samples and items. An item is used to group units of the inspected product for further business processing. An inspection document can contain several items. If a code group for items was specified in the inspection rule, the items can be valuated individually in the inspection document.

A finding describes deviations from the requirements and can be created for inspection documents, inspection document items, or samples.

Based on the decision, follow-up actions can be defined, which trigger follow-up processes such as putaway, scrapping, stock transfer, and return delivery. Follow-up actions are only available for the quality inspection of products.

9.7.3 Counting

Counting is a quality inspection procedure in the goods receipt process used to ensure consistency between the quantity of the inbound delivery item and the actual quantities. There are two forms of counting — explicit counting and implicit counting.

In explicit counting, counting is performed at a special work center for counting. The system determines the location (storage type, section, bin) for the counting station on the basis of the POSC settings (for more details about the POSC, see Chapter 13).

> **Note**
>
> Explicit counting can only be used for HUs.

In implicit counting, counting is performed during confirmation of the putaway WT. If a difference is determined, the WT is confirmed with differences and an exception code must be entered.

In the following text, we will describe the main customizing settings for quality inspection, using the counting procedure as an example.

To begin, you must generate the IOT based on the process that must be supported (as you can see in Figure 9.33). To generate the IOT in the EWM IMG, follow the menu path EXTENDED WAREHOUSE MANAGEMENT • CROSS-PROCESS SETTINGS • QUALITY MANAGEMENT • BASICS •GENERATE INSPECTION OBJECT TYPES VERSION.

IOT	Description	Vers.	Software Component	Object Type	Process	
1	Preliminary Inspection Inbound Delivery	3	SCM_EWM	DLV	INBCK_VERSOE	▲
2	Counting Inbound Delivery	3	SCM_EWM	PROD	INBCT_VERSOE	▼
3	Q-Inspection Returns Delivery	1	SCM_EWM	PROD	INBCU_VERSOE	

Generation of Inspection Object Type Versions

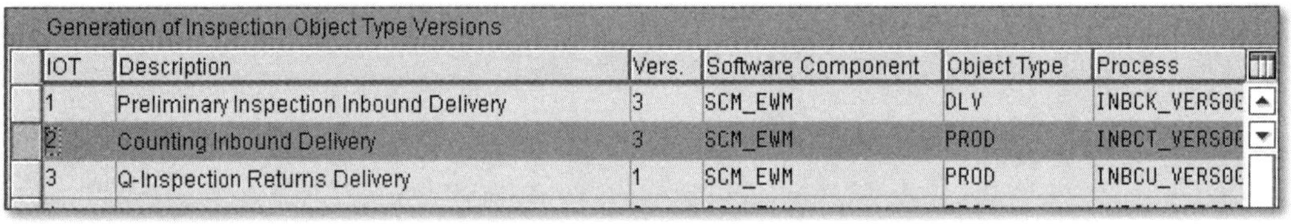

Figure 9.33 Example: Generate Inspection Object Type for Counting

Next, you must activate the general IOT (as you can see in Figure 9.34) in the EWM IMG by following the menu path EXTENDED WAREHOUSE MANAGEMENT • CROSS-PROCESS SETTINGS • QUALITY MANAGEMENT • BASICS • MAINTAIN INSPECTION OBJECT TYPES VERSION.

Change View "Maintain Inspection Object Type Version": Overview

New Entries

Dialog Structure
▽ ⬜ Maintain Inspection Obje
    ⬜ Maintain Properties

Maintain Inspection Object Type Version

Version	InspObjTyp		Act.InsObj	Changed By	
2	2 Counting Inbound Delivery		☑	BAUERFR	

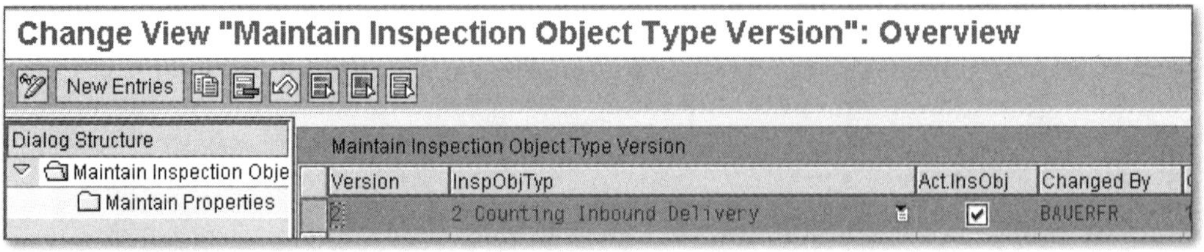

Figure 9.34 Example: Activation of Inspection Object Type for Counting

Next, you must define the properties that should be used to search for an inspection rule with a sequence relevant to inspection rule determination, as shown in Figure 9.35. To activate the properties in the EWM Easy Access menu, follow the

Extended Warehouse Management • Master Data • Quality Management •
Maintain Inspection Rule menu path, use Transaction code /SCWM/QRSETUP.

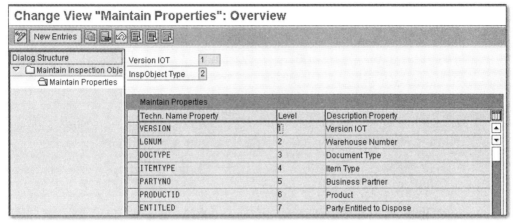

Figure 9.35 Example of the Definition of Properties to Search for Inspection Rules for Counting

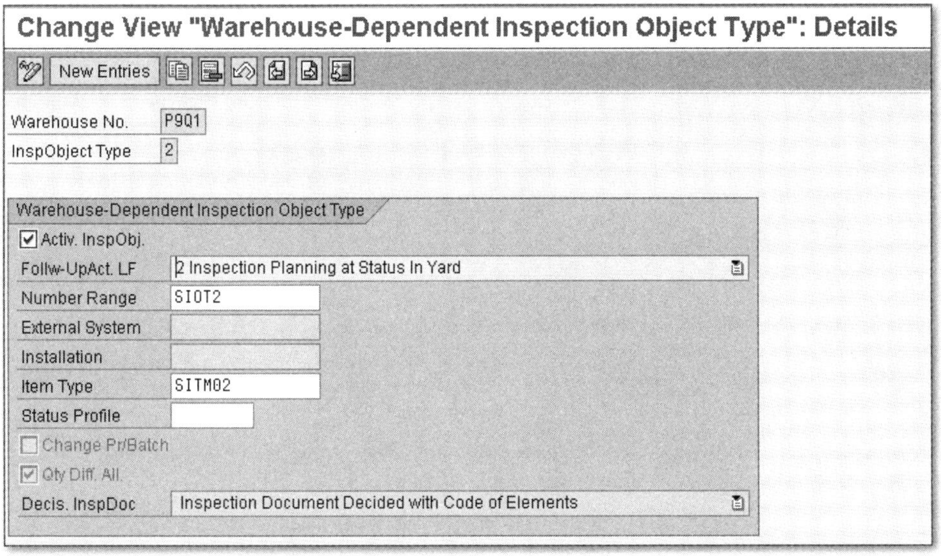

Change View "Warehouse-Dependent Inspection Object Type": Details

Warehouse No. P9Q1
InspObject Type 2

Warehouse-Dependent Inspection Object Type

☑ Activ. InspObj.
Follw-UpAct. LF 2 Inspection Planning at Status In Yard
Number Range SIOT2
External System
Installation
Item Type SITM02
Status Profile
☐ Change Pr/Batch
☑ Qty Diff. All
Decis. InspDoc Inspection Document Decided with Code of Elements

Figure 9.36 Example of Warehouse-dependent Settings for Inspection Object Type for Counting

Next, you must activate the IOT for your warehouse (as you can see in Figure
9.36) in the EWM IMG by following the menu path Extended Warehouse Management • Cross-Process Settings • Quality Management • Basics • Ware-

HOUSE-DEPENDENT ACTIVATION OF INSPECTION OBJECT TYPE. You can define when the inspection document will be created (e.g., when the inbound delivery has the status IN YARD).

Next, define the item types from type position, or from type sample, which are used to create the appropriate element in the inspection document. To define the item types (as you can see in Figure 9.37) in the EWM IMG, follow the menu path EXTENDED WAREHOUSE MANAGEMENT • CROSS-PROCESS SETTINGS • QUALITY MANAGEMENT • SETTINGS FOR INSPECTION RULES • DEFINE ITEM TYPES.

Next, define the follow-up actions based on an internal follow-up action code (as shown in Figure 9.38). The following action codes are available:

▶ Scrapping — the affected stock is posted in the next stock type marked as scrapping stock

▶ Detailed inspection — an internal warehouse inspection document is created for the affected stock

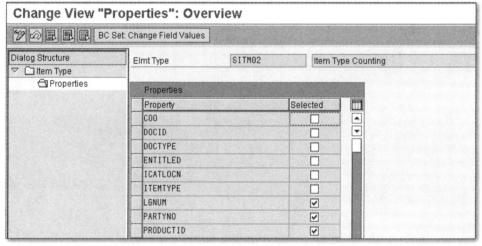

Figure 9.37 Definition of an Item Type for Counting

▶ Stock transfer to different warehouse — a stock transfer order is created in ERP for the affected stock

▶ Putaway for delivery — a putaway WT is created with the warehouse process type of the inbound delivery for the affected stock

▶ Follow-up action is determined externally — an externally controlled posting is expected (this action is only valid for returns)

To define the follow-up actions in the EWM IMG, follow the menu path EXTENDED WAREHOUSE MANAGEMENT • CROSS-PROCESS SETTINGS • QUALITY MANAGEMENT • RESULT• MAINTAIN FOLLOW-UP ACTION.

Figure 9.38 Example of a Follow-up Action Putaway

Next, define the DECISION CODES and assign them to a predefined CODE GROUP (as you can see in Figure 9.39). The decision code is relevant for closing the inspection document and follow-up actions can be defined per decision code. To define the decision codes in the EWM IMG, follow the menu path EXTENDED WAREHOUSE MANAGEMENT • CROSS-PROCESS SETTINGS • QUALITY MANAGEMENT • RESULT • DEFINE DECISION CODES. In the example shown in Figure 9.39, if the valuation is positive (accept) then follow-up action A (PUTAWAY) will be executed.

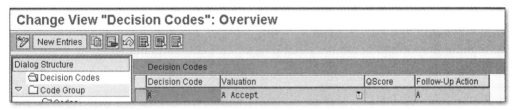

Figure 9.39 Example of the Creation of Decision Codes

You can optionally maintain the quantity interval for counting. In the quantity interval, you can define a maximum quantity. If the quantity of the inbound delivery item is lower than the defined quantity, a quality inspection document will be created. To maintain the quantity interval in the EWM IMG, follow the menu path EXTENDED WAREHOUSE MANAGEMENT • CROSS-PROCESS SETTINGS • QUALITY MANAGEMENT • SETTINGS FOR INSPECTION RULES • MAINTAIN QUANTITY INTERVAL FOR COUNTING.

You can also optionally maintain the value interval for counting. In the value interval, you can define a maximum value. If the value of the inbound delivery item is lower than the defined value, a quality inspection document will be created. To maintain the value interval in the EWM IMG, follow the menu path Extended Warehouse Management • Cross-Process Settings • Quality Management • Settings for Inspection Rules • Maintain Value Interval for Counting.

In the next step, you must create an inspection rule. To maintain the inspection rule from the EWM Easy Access menu, follow the Extended Warehouse Management • Master Data • Quality Management • Maintain Inspection Rule menu path, or use Transaction code /SCWM/QRSETUP. If explicit counting is used, a process step must be assigned to the inspection rule.

If counting will be executed explicitly, additional general settings have to be defined for the work center. Each work center has to be assigned to a warehouse number, storage type, and storage bin. Therefore, a storage type and a storage bin have to be defined. To create a storage bin for the work center, from the EWM Easy Access, follow the Extended Warehouse Management • Master Data • Storage Bin • Create Storage Bin menu path, or use Transaction code /SCWM/LS01.

You must also define a work center layout for quality inspection. The layout controls which areas and tab pages appear on the interface. To specify the work center layout in the EWM IMG, follow the menu path Extended Warehouse Management • Master Data • Work Center • Specify Work Center Layout.

When you define the work center in customizing, you assign the work center layout to it. For additional information about settings up the work center, see Chapter 3.

9.8 Summary

In this chapter, we described the different inbound process steps, including GRN, truck arrival, administrative goods receipt, unloading, and goods receipt and putaway processing, using ASNs and identification of incoming goods based on expected goods receipts. We described how the EWM functions can be used to support your warehouse requirements and also how to set them up in EWM.

In addition, we described the slotting and quality inspection processes, how they are used in the inbound process, and how to set them up. You should now have a good understanding of the entire inbound process and the main settings in customizing.

In the next chapter, we will discuss the outbound processing in detail.

One of the primary goals of a warehouse is to deliver the right products to the right place at the right time, therefore the outbound processing (which includes the picking, packing, staging, loading, and other related activities) plays an important role in Extended Warehouse Management (EWM).

10   Outbound Processing

The outbound processing usually starts with the creation of a sales order in a Customer Relationship Management (CRM) or ERP system. The integration of these orders in a warehouse management system (WMS) allows orders to be fulfilled by the warehouse, which is responsible for not only storing products efficiently but also for ensuring that the goods are delivered to their destination on time (thus the common mantra, "the right parts to the right place at the right time"). A secondary objective of the warehouse is that the products should be delivered efficiently — this not only supports the objective of delivering products to their destination on time, but also ensures the sustainability of warehouse operations.

To support efficient processing in the warehouse, EWM provides features and functions in the outbound process that allow efficient parallel processing of activities to get products to their destination faster and to optimize the utilization of the resources during the process.

In this chapter, we will discuss the business processes for outbound processing and the features and functions that support efficient processing in the warehouse, including delivery processing, wave picking, pick task creation, warehouse order (WO) creation, storage control, packing, staging, loading, goods issue, and special activities such as value-added services (VASs).

10.1   Outbound Delivery Creation

The outbound process starts with the creation of an outbound delivery, which is subsequently used to trigger the outbound processing in the warehouse. The outbound delivery can be created in ERP, based on a sales order from CRM or ERP (or manually created without reference to a preceding document), or it can be created in EWM directly. In the following sections, we will discuss the processes used to create the outbound deliveries.

10.1.1 Outbound Processing for Sales Orders

The basic objective of the outbound process is to deliver products to requested parties, which can be customers, other warehouses in the supply chain, or other internal customers, such as technicians. The role of the WMS is to execute the warehousing processes. The management of deliveries, orders, billing, and accounting are supported by the respective ERP and CRM systems.

In this section, we will provide an overview of the entire outbound business process, so that you have a basis for understanding the functions of the EWM. Figure 10.1 shows the overall ORDER TO CASH process, which starts with marketing and order management, availability checking and promising of order quantities, and then creation of the request for outbound delivery, which is transferred to the warehouse.

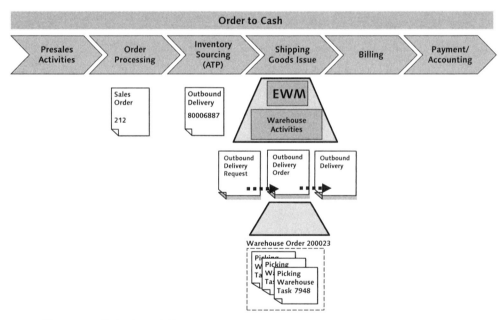

Figure 10.1 Order-to-cash Process

Sales orders are created in CRM or ERP, and subsequently, the outbound delivery document is created in ERP.

> **Note**
>
> For CRM orders, there is sometimes a special case for service parts management scenarios when the direct delivery distribution will result in unchecked deliveries being created in ERP as soon as the sales order is created, rather than replicating the sales orders to ERP, as is normally the case for CRM. This possibility is discussed further in Chapter 23, Integration with Other Applications.

If the products on the outbound delivery created in ERP are warehousing relevant (as discussed in Chapter 2, Organizational Structure), outbound deliveries are created and replicated to EWM, where an *outbound delivery request (ODR)* is created. Based on the ODR, the follow-up processing in the warehouse can be initiated, beginning with the creation of the *outbound delivery order (ODO)*. In EWM, the ODO serves as the starting point for the outbound processing within the warehouse. With reference to the ODO, the warehouse tasks (WTs) and WOs are created, and the physical processes for picking, packing, staging, and loading will be executed. At the end of the warehouse processing, the goods issue for the ODO is posted, and the *final outbound delivery* (simply called "outbound delivery" in EWM, but often referred to as the "final delivery" or "final outbound delivery") is created. This outbound delivery serves as the basis for communication back to ERP to trigger the post goods issue for the ERP outbound delivery and the subsequent follow-up steps, such as the billing and the update to the order (if relevant). In Figure 10.1, you can see the references to the document flow just described beneath the Shipping / Goods Issue chevron.

It's also possible for you to create an outbound delivery in ERP without reference to a sales order. Outbound deliveries created without reference are replicated to EWM in the same way and processed the same way in EWM. In EWM, there is no distinction made whether the delivery was created with or without reference — the only impact for EWM is that the delivery type in ERP may be different (or it could also be the same), which affects the determination in ERP of the document type for the ODR and subsequent ODO.

When the outbound delivery is received in the warehouse and the ODR is created, the document type and item type of the ODR are determined according to the mapping tables in the customizing. To maintain the mapping for the document types and item type for the interface in the EWM IMG, follow the menu path

EXTENDED WAREHOUSE MANAGEMENT • INTERFACES • ERP INTEGRATION • DELIVERY PROCESSING • MAP DOCUMENT TYPES FROM ERP SYSTEM TO EWM and MAP ITEM TYPES FROM ERP SYSTEM TO EWM.

We will discuss the warehouse operations part of the outbound process in subsequent sections, but first, we will discuss the outbound delivery process when it is triggered from EWM with the direct outbound delivery.

10.1.2 Direct Outbound Delivery Process

Aside from the sales order–driven process described earlier, there may also be circumstances in the warehouse when you must spontaneously create outbound deliveries. For example:

▶ you can "push" certain products (e.g., common consumable items or fresh produce) to a destination (for example, if you are shipping to your own retail stores) if there is space left over on the truck after fulfilling a customer's order

▶ you may be requested by the customer (i.e., "pulled") to add additional products to a truck in the case of urgent requirements (e.g., items forgotten on the order or urgent emergency customer needs)

▶ you can ship returnable packaging materials (e.g., reusable pallets or metal containers) to a supplier or another point in the supply chain that needs them

▶ you can sell products directly to an end customer from the warehouse (i.e., a direct sale or counter sale).

Therefore, EWM allows you to directly create an ODO in the EWM system and later replicate the delivery to ERP (for inventory update and to support billing). In Figure 10.2, you can see a graphical depiction of the processes involved during the creation of a direct delivery order. The Advanced Planning Optimizer (APO) and Global Trade Services (GTS) are optional systems for these scenarios, but are necessary if you want to check the availability of inventory for direct sales or to administer products in global trade scenarios (i.e., shipping across international borders, or shipping product from your warehouse that was received from an international location and is in bonded stock).

In EWM, when creating a direct ODO, EWM first checks if the quantity is deliverable from EWM before it optionally checks the availability of inventory according to Global ATP (gATP) in APO or according to ERP. If you must check export regulations, GTS can be called to perform the additional checks. If all checks are passed, EWM creates an ODO and subsequently creates the outbound delivery in ERP. In EWM, you would then execute the warehouse activities with reference to the ODO, just as in the processed described previously. For direct outbound deliveries, immediate invoicing (or invoice before goods issue (IBGI), which will be further described later in this chapter) is often required. Therefore, EWM triggers the invoice process in ERP and the printing is executed from there. When you post goods issue for the ODO, the confirmation is also sent to ERP, as in the sales order–related process. In ERP, the goods issue is posted for the ERP outbound delivery, and the subsequent delivery-related billing can be triggered (if the IBGI was not already executed).

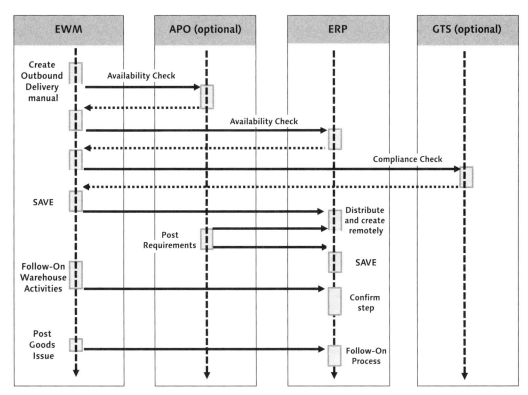

Figure 10.2 Direct ODO Process

10.2 Overview of Outbound Processing in the Warehouse

In the following paragraphs, we will provide an overview of the outbound process in EWM before going into depth on individual topics. During the overview, we will refer to Figures 10.3 through 10.6 to provide a visual reference so that you will gain a good understanding of the overall process, which will help you consume the subsequent detailed information.

As we discussed in the previous section, you can start the process with an outbound delivery in ERP that is transferred to EWM and results in creation of the ODR (which is a special kind of warehouse request). You can also start the process with the creation of the ODO if you create a direct outbound delivery, but the process in the warehouse beyond the ODO is the same regardless of how the ODO was created. In Figure 10.3, you can see the beginning of the process, starting with the creation of the ODR.

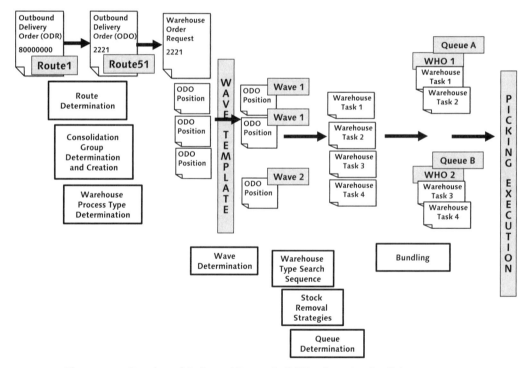

Figure 10.3 Overview of Outbound Process in EWM – Preparing the Picks

Once the ODR is created in EWM, you can create the ODO with reference to an ODR by activating the ODR (this can also be automated with a Post-Processing Framework (PPF) action; for more details on the PPF, see Chapter 24, Post-Processing Framework and Form Printing). To manually activate the ODR in the EWM Easy Access menu, follow the EXTENDED WAREHOUSE MANAGEMENT • DELIVERY PROCESSING • OUTBOUND DELIVERY • MAINTAIN OUTBOUND DELIVERY REQUEST menu path, or use Transaction code /SCWM/ODR. In the transaction, select the ODR based on the available search options or use the advanced search, then activate the ODR by selecting the ACTIVATE button (which you can see in Figure 10.4; note the ODR in the figure is locked and cannot be activated; to find the reason for when an ODR is locked, you can select the CHECK button). If the ODR is successfully activated, EWM will create the ODO.

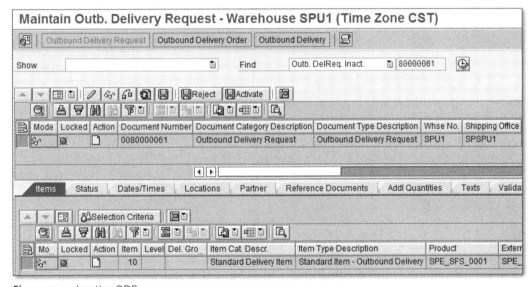

Figure 10.4 Inactive ODR

During the activation of the ODR and creation of the ODO, the following determinations are performed to assign the parameters to the ODO:

▶ Route determination (which we will discuss in more detail later)

▶ Consolidation group determination

▶ Warehouse process type determination

Once the ODO is created, you can opt to create the WTs directly, or you can group the request items (analogous to the ODO items) into waves and release the wave to trigger the WT creation. We will discuss wave processing later in this chapter. In the meantime, we will discuss the manual creation of the WTs so that we can continue with the process.

> **Note**
>
> Waves are created from the ODO items and not the ODO headers, so you can create waves such that the ODO is split across multiple waves. This is important, for example, for creating waves to group picks based on activity area, for example (and this is an important distinction between wave processing in EWM versus the wave concept used by ERP WM).

To maintain the ODO, from the EWM Easy Access menu, follow the EXTENDED WAREHOUSE MANAGEMENT • DELIVERY PROCESSING • OUTBOUND DELIVERY • MAINTAIN OUTBOUND DELIVERY ORDER menu path, or use Transaction code /SCWM/ PRDO. In Figure 10.5, you can see an ODO with items relevant to picking. To create the WTs for picking from the ODO maintenance (which you can see in Figure 10.5), follow the menu path OUTBOUND DELIVERY ORDER • FOLLOW-ON FUNCTIONS • WAREHOUSE TASK. Alternatively, you can use the transaction dedicated to creating WTs for ODOs from the EWM Easy Access menu by following the EXTENDED WAREHOUSE MANAGEMENT • WORK SCHEDULING • CREATE WAREHOUSE TASK FOR WAREHOUSE REQUEST • STOCK REMOVAL FOR OUTBOUND DELIVERY ORDER menu path, or using Transaction code /SCWM/TODLV_O.

During WT creation, EWM determines the relevant location for picking the stock and allocates the stock to the WT. It determines the picking location by checking the STOCK REMOVAL CONTROL INDICATOR from the master data of the product for the ODO item, then determining the storage type search sequence assigned to the control indicator and searching through the storage types based on the stock removal strategies of the storage types to find available stock according to the strategies. Once the appropriate stock has been found (from one or more bins), each pick from each bin is assigned to an individual WT and the parameters of the WT are determined, including the appropriate queue assignment, based on the warehouse process type and source and destination activity area (among other parameters).

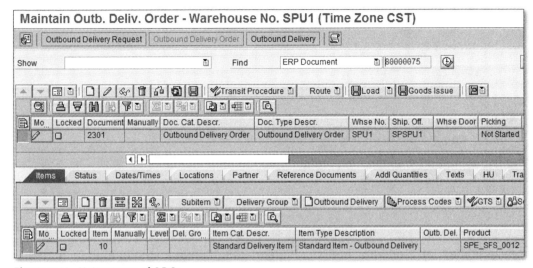

Figure 10.5 Maintenance of ODOs

During the WT creation and before the WTs are saved, the warehouse order (WO) creation process is also initiated. The purpose for creating the WOs at the same time as the WTs is to group the WTs into WOs in such a way that the WO represents a bundle of work that can be executed by a resource in the warehouse. Therefore, the Warehouse Order Creation Rules (WOCRs), which are applied during the creation of the WOs, are meant to parse and sort the WTs such that logical bundles of work are created to optimize the picking operations. Among the rules that are checked during the WO creation is the queue assignment; each WO must only be assigned to a single queue, therefore the WTs for which separate queues were determined will be automatically assigned to separate WOs. Later in this chapter, we will further discuss the WOCR and queue determination in detail.

Once the WTs and WOs are created, you can start the physical execution of the outbound processing in the warehouse (which is depicted in Figure 10.6). The pick execution can be done via paper pick tickets (printed from the WO via PPF actions) or via the radio frequency (RF) transactions (which use the queue assignment of the WO to manage the assignment of work to the resources). Later in this chapter, we will discuss how to execute the confirmations of the pick tasks.

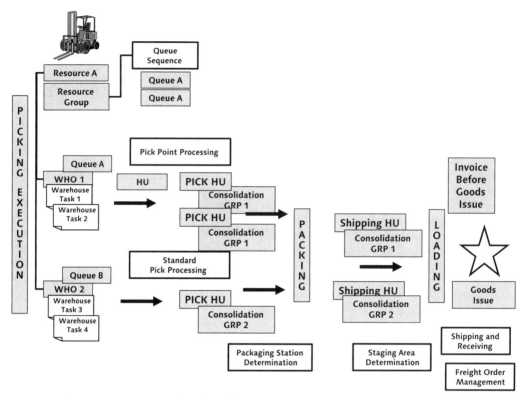

Figure 10.6 Overview of Outbound Process in EWM — Picking Execution

Depending on the settings in the process-oriented storage control (POSC), the following processes may be relevant during outbound processing:

▶ Picking

▶ Kitting

▶ Value-added services

▶ Packing

▶ Staging

▶ Loading

If packing is relevant to your outbound process, then once the picks are confirmed, the products will be delivered to the appropriate packing station (later in this chapter, we will discuss how the pack station is determined).

> **Note**
>
> You can execute packing during the picking process by assigning a pick handling unit (HU) during the confirmation of the WT. In the POSC, you specify whether the Pick HU is sufficient to use as the final HU or whether the Pick HU should be repacked or overpacked at the pack station by excluding or including the packing step as part of the storage control.

At the pack station (which is modeled as a work center), you execute the packing steps by using either the desktop transaction (which is suitable for work stations that have a PC) or using the RF transactions (which are more suitable for stations with only smaller portable devices or for mobile work stations). At the pack station, you can also generate customer labels for the outbound HUs as needed.

Once the packing is complete, you close the HUs at the pack station, which triggers the creation of the follow-up task according to the storage control. Based on the setup of the work center, the product can be moved to the outbound area of the work center, from which the next WT would be created. If the next step in the process is the staging step, then the appropriate staging area is determined and assigned as the destination for the WT (later in this chapter, we discuss how the staging area and door are determined). You could also create the WT manually if the PPF action for automatic creation is not enabled. Then you confirm the move from the work center to the staging area.

Once the product arrives at the staging area, the loading task would usually be the next relevant process step. As the loading tasks are generally created manually using the RF transactions, then the WT would not generally be automatically created when the WT to move stock to the staging area is confirmed. When the truck arrives to the outbound loading door and the products are ready to be loaded, you can create the loading WTs on the RF device, or you can execute a more simple loading process (later in this chapter we will discuss complex loading vs. simple loading).

Beginning with the loading process, the management of the trucks (and the respective products loaded on them) is executed using the EWM Shipping and Receiving (including Yard Management) and Freight Order Management functions. For more information about yard management, see Chapter 18, Yard Management.

You can elect to post goods issue for the ODO once you have loaded the products, or you can elect to automate the goods issue via the yard management check-out function. Once the goods issue is posted, the final outbound delivery document is created and the document is transferred to ERP. In ERP, the goods issue is posted for the outbound delivery and the follow-up actions, such as the accounting posting, update of sales orders in ERP or CRM, and the trigger of the billing are executed, if necessary.

In the following sections, we will discuss certain aspects of the outbound processing in more detail to help you understand how to set up the complete process. Certain topics, such as kitting and VASs, are covered in more detail in their respective chapters, so we will not cover them here.

10.3   Route Determination

Route determination is performed during various stages of the outbound process. The purpose of the route determination is to determine which transportation route will be used to transport the products to their destination. It is important to know the route that will be used even before the picking processes in the warehouse start so that the system can determine which products will be shipped together and from which doors and staging lanes. This information is then used to determine the grouping and routing within the warehouse.

10.3.1   Executing the Route Determination

Route determination is performed by the routing guide engine (RGE), which is a component of Supply Chain Management (SCM), and it can be used by various applications, including EWM. The general role of the route determination process is to select an optimal route from a group of available routes based on shipping-related data such as start and destination locations, delivery date, document type, delivery weight, and hazardous condition of the delivery items.

In general, route determination is an automated process that is executed in the background. However, you can also manually assign routes during the outbound process. While routes may be determined as early as the order creation in CRM or

ERP, the routes can also be redetermined in EWM based on the latest information available there as the ODO is being prepared for picking and shipping.

> **Note**
>
> While routes in ERP and EWM are similar in their purposes, there are differences between the routes set up in ERP versus those set up via the RGE. For example, the routes from RGE have legs and stops assigned, can be distributed between systems, are used in gATP checking, provide more functionality for managing routes and schedules of carriers, support cross-dock routes, and can be simulated in the RGE. In addition, the RGE can be activated in EWM by document type.

In Figure 10.7, you can see an example of a route created in EWM. You can see that the route contains three components — the route header, the route header details (LEGS, CD ROUTES, and the tabs used to specify the relevance — namely the REQUEST TYPES, LEAD TIMES, SHIPPING CONDITIONS, and TRANSP. GROUPS), and the route leg details (for each leg, the stops, carrier, and departure calendar).

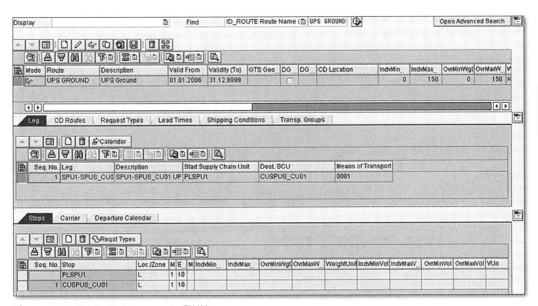

Figure 10.7 Route Maintenance in EWM

The route determination is called from various points in the outbound process, including:

► During order creation in CRM

► During ODR creation in EWM

► During ODO creation in EWM

In Figure 10.8, you can see when and from which system the RGE is called. The route determination is called in EWM when a document is created or incurs a change event.

If you use the CRM system for order creation, you can call the RGE while performing the gATP check to determine the route and assign it to the sales order. When the ODR is created in EWM from the outbound delivery received from ERP (which was created with reference to the CRM sales order), you can then call the RGE again to redetermine the route based on the latest information available.

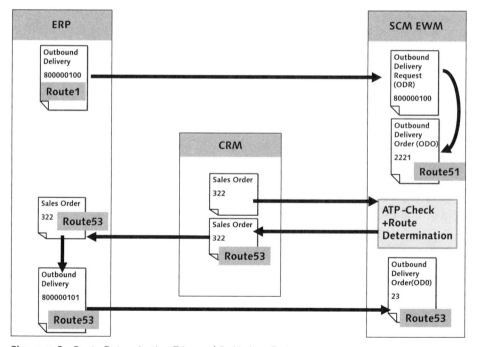

Figure 10.8 Route Determination Triggered By Various Systems

In EWM, you can call the RGE during the creation or change of ODRs, ODOs and outbound deliveries. The route can then be determined based on various parameters including dates, calendars, carrier, means of transport, and dangerous goods indicators. You can configure the route determination to be called automatically, or you can leave it to be called manually on demand. In that case, you could, for example, always use the route passed from the ERP outbound delivery (whether it was determined in CRM or in ERP, based on the route determination of ERP) but leave open the option to trigger the determination manually as needed.

In the document processing in EWM, certain checks can be performed (either triggered automatically or manually) to validate whether the document data is consistent with the assigned route. If they are inconsistent, the document will be locked and you must release the document manually after reassigning the route or otherwise resolving the issue. The validation checks are based on parameters such as dates, products, weight/volume, request type, dangerous goods, and more.

One of the reasons to have separate ODR and ODO documents is route determination. As separate items of the ODR can be assigned to different routes, the generation of the ODO from the ODR can result in a split of the ODR items onto separate ODOs (based on the separate routes). For example, if one of the ordered items is a dangerous good, which can't be shipped via a certain mode of transportation, then the route for the dangerous good could be different than the rest of the items and result in a separate ODO being created so that the picking, packing, and shipping of the item can be handled separately. This is especially useful, for instance, if the scheduling of shipment for the different carriers used for the different modes of transportation are separate.

In Figure 10.9, you can see when the RGE can be called during outbound processing in EWM.

During the route determination, the RGE calculates the transportation cost using a cost profile (based on fixed transportation costs, distance-dependent cost, time-dependent costs, and weight-dependent costs). The transportation cost can then be used as a factor in determining the best route.

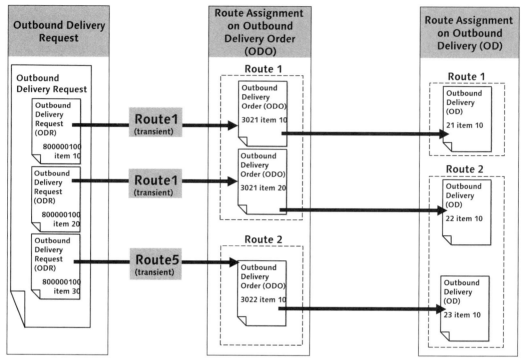

Figure 10.9 Route Determination on Outbound Documents

10.3.2 Setting Up Route Determination

To support route determination, you must set up and validate certain background information in the EWM master data using the transactions described in the paragraphs below.

To maintain the locations in the EWM Easy Access menu, follow menu path EXTENDED WAREHOUSE MANAGEMENT • MASTER DATA • SHIPPING AND RECEIVING • ROUTE DETERMINATION • LOCATION, or use Transaction code /SAPAPO/LOC3.

To maintain the calendars in the EWM IMG, follow the SCM BASIS • CONFIGURABLE PROCESS SCHEDULING • CALENDAR AND TIME ZONES • MAINTAIN PROCESS SCHEDULING CALENDAR (TIME STREAM) menu path, or use Transaction code /SCMB/SCHED_CAL.

To maintain the zones in the EWM Easy Access menu, follow the EXTENDED WARE-HOUSE MANAGEMENT • MASTER DATA • SHIPPING AND RECEIVING • ROUTE DETERMI-NATION • MAINTAIN ZONES FOR ROUTE menu path, or use Transaction code /SCTM/ZONE.

To maintain the routes in the EWM Easy Access menu, follow the EXTENDED WARE-HOUSE MANAGEMENT • MASTER DATA • SHIPPING AND RECEIVING • ROUTE DETERMI-NATION • MAINTAIN ROUTE menu path, or use Transaction code /SCTM/ROUTE.

To maintain the profiles for carriers in the EWM Easy Access menu, follow the EXTENDED WAREHOUSE MANAGEMENT • MASTER DATA • SHIPPING AND RECEIVING • ROUTE DETERMINATION • CARRIER PROFILE FOR ROUTING GUIDE menu path, or use Transaction code /SCTM/TSPP.

To maintain the transportation cost profiles in the EWM Easy Access menu, follow the EXTENDED WAREHOUSE MANAGEMENT • MASTER DATA • SHIPPING AND RECEIVING • ROUTE DETERMINATION • DEFINE GENERAL TRANSPORTATION COST PRO-FILE menu path, or use Transaction code /SAPAPO/TPK.

To simulate and test the routes in the EWM Easy Access menu, follow the EXTENDED WAREHOUSE MANAGEMENT • MASTER DATA • SHIPPING AND RECEIVING • ROUTE DETERMINATION • SIMULATE ROUTE DETERMINATION menu path, or use Transaction code /SCTM/RGINT.

10.4   Details of Warehouse Process Steps

In the following sections, we will describe in detail the various process steps and the setup (configuration and master data) in EWM relevant to support the overall outbound process, as described previously in this chapter.

10.4.1   Warehouse Process Type Determination

During the creation of the ODO, the system determines a warehouse process type for each delivery line item. This warehouse process type plays a major role in EWM in the determination of the relevant follow-up processes for the ODO. The warehouse process type specifies the type of the process and is used to specify the parameters of the process and to determine the relevance of certain aspects of the process (therefore, it is often found as a key field in the relevant customizing settings). For example, the process type is used in the determination of storage control, and therefore it is used to determine the relevant process steps (e.g., warehouse process type 2010 determines that only the activities pick and ship are relevant during the storage control). To define the warehouse process types in the EMG IMG, follow the menu path EXTENDED WAREHOUSE MANAGEMENT • CROSS-PROCESS SETTINGS • WAREHOUSE TASK • DEFINE WAREHOUSE PROCESS TYPES.

The warehouse process type is copied from the ODO into the WT for picking and the corresponding WO. From the WO, the process type is used to determine the queue, and it therefore influences the execution of the WOs in the warehouse. You can maintain the DETERMINATION OF THE WAREHOUSE PROCESS TYPE (shown in Figure 10.10) in the EWM IMG by following the menu path EXTENDED WAREHOUSE MANAGEMENT • CROSS-PROCESS SETTINGS • WAREHOUSE TASK • DETERMINE WAREHOUSE PROCESS TYPE.

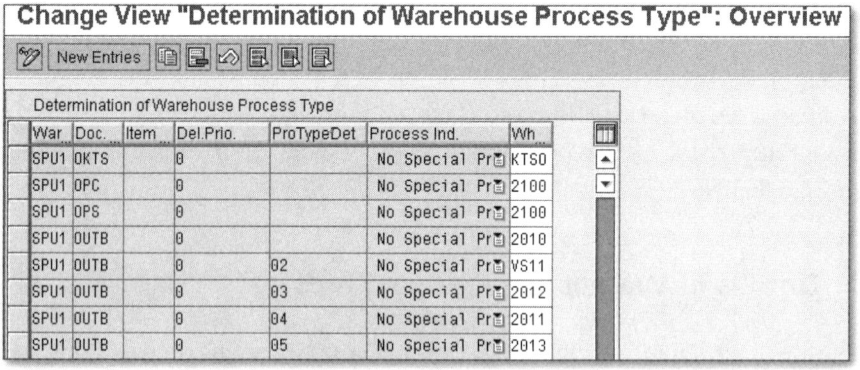

War	Doc.	Item	Del.Prio.	ProTypeDet	Process Ind.	Wh
SPU1	0KTS	0			No Special Pr	KTS0
SPU1	0PC	0			No Special Pr	2100
SPU1	0PS	0			No Special Pr	2100
SPU1	0UTB	0			No Special Pr	2010
SPU1	0UTB	0		02	No Special Pr	VS11
SPU1	0UTB	0		03	No Special Pr	2012
SPU1	0UTB	0		04	No Special Pr	2011
SPU1	0UTB	0		05	No Special Pr	2013

Figure 10.10 Determination of the Warehouse Process Type

The determination of the warehouse process type is based on warehouse number, document type, item type, process type determination, and process indicator. Among these, you can assign the process type determination indicator in the product master to influence the process type determination. To specify the possible entries for the WAREHOUSE PROCESS TYPE DETERMINATION indicator (as you can see in Figure 10.11) in the EWM IMG, follow the menu path EXTENDED WAREHOUSE MANAGEMENT • CROSS-PROCESS SETTINGS • WAREHOUSE TASK • DEFINE CONTROL INDICATORS FOR DETERMINING WAREHOUSE PROCESS TYPES.

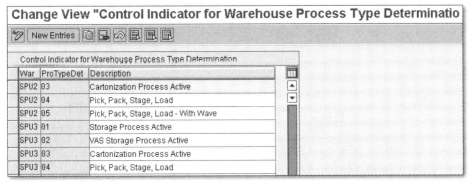

Figure 10.11 Define Control Indicators for Warehouse Process Type Determination

> **Note**
>
> In the ODO item type, you can specify an incompleteness profile, which checks that the ODO has a warehouse process type assigned and blocks the ODO one is not assigned.

10.4.2 Wave Management

In EWM, you can group the warehouse request items (such as the ODO items) into waves to manage the process and optimize the warehouse processing. The items assigned to a wave are generally similar in some respect, whether they are picked from a similar area or are picked in a similar way due to their size or shape, for example. The items of the wave are also generally processed together, beginning with the release of the wave and the resulting creation of the WTs. You can therefore use the waves to manage the timing of the processing in the warehouse. In the wave, the assigned time parameters are used to schedule execution of the wave and ensure that the products leave the warehouse on time to be received at the customer according to the promised schedule.

As you can see in Figure 10.12, the ODO items can be independently assigned to waves, regardless of the other items of the ODO. This provides the advantage that the items of the ODO can be independently processed based on the most efficient method for the warehouse (and represents a significant shift from the architecture of ERP WM, where the entire delivery is assigned to the wave at once).

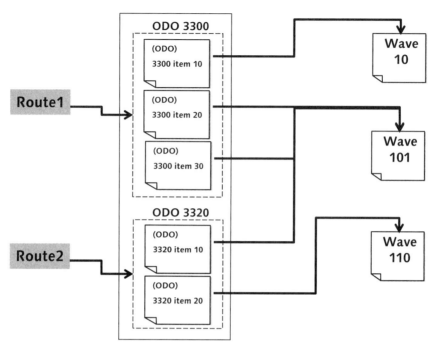

Figure 10.12 Assignment of Delivery Positions to Waves

To assign the items to the wave, you can set up the automatic determination of waves via the wave templates, or you can create or change waves manually. To maintain the waves in the EWM Easy Access menu, follow the EXTENDED WARE-HOUSE MANAGEMENT • WORK SCHEDULING • WAVE MANAGEMENT • MAINTAIN WAVES menu path, or use Transaction code /SCWM/WAVE. In Figure 10.13, you can see that we have created a wave with an item from multiple ODOs. In the top pane you can see the wave header information, and in the bottom pane you can see the assigned warehouse request items. To assign additional items, select the WAREHOUSE REQUESTS tab, use the selection criteria to select request items, select the appropriate ones from the list, and click the ASSIGN button. If you want the system to automatically assign a wave according to the wave template and conditions for determining wave templates, select the items and click the ASSIGN AUTO-MATICALLY button.

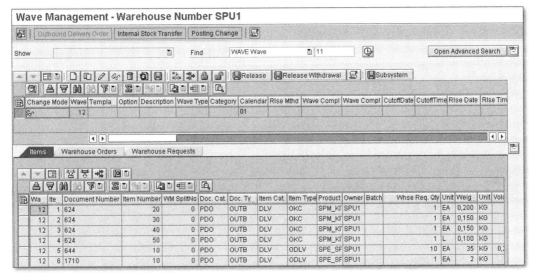

Figure 10.13 Wave Monitor Transaction

Managing Waves with Wave Templates

To more easily manage the creation, release, and execution of waves, you can use *wave templates* to group the warehouse request items together. The wave template serves two purposes in the process, namely:

▶ to facilitate the automatic assignment of warehouse request items to waves, which may be performed during the creation of the warehouse request or subsequent to the creation

▶ to consistently assign parameters to the wave that controls the wave processing (including the release method, wave type (for selecting waves in report), wave category (used as a filter in the WOCR), wave start time and wave completion time, capacity profile, and calendar assignment)

A common use for wave templates is to create them for certain time periods for certain days of the week (or every day of the week) so that the items that are scheduled to be picked during those time frames will be appropriately grouped together, assigned to waves, released, and processed in the warehouse according to the time requirement specified in the ODO based on the required delivery dates of the sales order and the possible routes determined in the ODO. If you want to segregate picks according to warehouse area for the type of pick (as described previously), then you would create separate wave templates and set up the wave template determination appropriately. For example, if you want to start picking bulk items four hours ahead of the shipping time but only start picking case pick items two hours ahead of the shipping time, then you would set up two wave templates with different release times based on the typical shipping windows. Then you would set up the wave template determination such that the bulk items are assigned to one wave, which is released at least four hours ahead of time and the case pick items are assigned to a separate wave, which is released two hours later.

Because the wave templates are master data, you can create or change the templates flexibly in the productive environment (as long as you have the proper authorization). To maintain the wave template in the EWM Easy Access menu, follow the EXTENDED WAREHOUSE MANAGEMENT • WORK SCHEDULING • WAVE MANAGEMENT • MAINTAIN WAVE TEMPLATES menu path, or use Transaction /SCWM/WAVETMP. In Figure 10.14, you can see a wave template with the associated parameters for the WAVE CUTOFF time, WAVE RELEASE time, and PICK COMPLETION time.

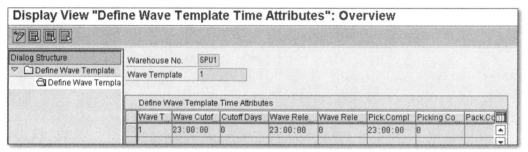

Figure 10.14 Maintain EWM Wave Template

In the header of the wave template (the DEFINE WAVE TEMPLATE level in Figure 10.14), you also assign the release strategy for the wave. The possible release strategies include AUTOMATIC (the release is triggered by a batch report), MANUAL, or IMMEDIATE.

In addition to creating the wave templates, you must also set up the PPF actions and conditions for automatically assigning the items to the waves, as described in the following section.

Automatic Wave Assignment

To determine wave templates automatically for warehouse request items (whether you want it to be triggered automatically or manually), you must use the condition technique. The determination checks which wave template corresponds to certain data from the header, item, or split item of a warehouse request. The wave template determination and wave creation are technically executed via a PPF action (for more information about the PPF, see Chapter 24). When the warehouse request is created, EWM checks to see if the assigned process type of the request is relevant for automatic wave creation. If it is relevant, then EWM schedules a PPF action that can be set to process immediately or to only process via the relevant report. To activate the process type for automatic wave creation (as you can see in Figure 10.15) in the EWM IMG, follow the menu path Warehouse Management • Goods Issue Process • Wave Management • General Settings • Set Automatic Wave Generation for Warehouse Process Type.

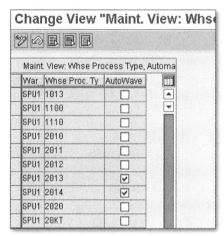

Figure 10.15 Activation of Automatic Wave Assignment over Warehouse Process Type

When the PPF action is executed (whether immediately or subsequently via Transaction SPPFP), it checks the condition tables to determine if the warehouse request items are relevant for a wave template. If a wave template is found, then it assigns the item to an existing wave or creates a new one (depending on the timing and the release status of the waves). An important aspect of the automatic wave assignment is the relationship of the warehouse request planned completion time and the wave completion time for the wave template. EWM schedules the waves based on the completion time of the calculated warehouse request item and the planned completion time from the wave template to ensure that the products are processed and leave the warehouse on time.

To maintain the CONDITION RECORDS for the wave template determination (as you can see in Figure 10.16) in the EWM Easy Access menu, follow the EXTENDED WAREHOUSE MANAGEMENT • WORK SCHEDULING • WAVE MANAGEMENT • MAINTAIN CONDITIONS FOR DETERMINING WAVE TEMPLATES menu path, or use Transaction code /SCWM/WDGCM.

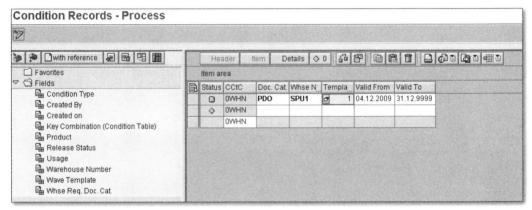

Figure 10.16 SAP Condition Technique Settings for Wave Management

> **Note**
>
> In the condition maintenance, to select existing records, select one of the key fields on the left and click the SELECT RECORDS button to generate the selection screen. To create a new record, switch to CHANGE mode, then simply enter data in the blank line on the right pane and press Enter once the data is entered. If a blank record is not already being displayed, select the dropdown box in the CONDITION TYPE field to assign a condition type, and then the screen will open up for maintenance.

Wave Processing

Once waves have been created, you can use the wave to further process the warehouse request items assigned to the wave. In the most common case, you would release the wave to create the WTs (and therefore also the WOs) for the wave request items. However, using the wave processing Transaction (/SCWM/WAVE) or warehouse monitor (/SCWM/MON), you can also block, unblock, split, or delete waves, merge waves, assign or unassigned items, or perform other activities for the wave. If the release strategy for the wave template is set to MANUAL, then you must use the monitor or wave processing transaction to release the wave as appropriate.

10.4.3 Warehouse Order Creation during Outbound Processes

As discussed in the previous sections, you can initiate the creation of the WTs by releasing waves or by manually creating the WTs for the ODO. When the WTs are created, the WOs are created at the same time to ensure that the created WTs are always assigned to an appropriate WO for execution. (While you can confirm the WTs directly, the most common method for executing the WTs is by executing the respective WOs.)

During the creation of the WOs, the WOCR are used to appropriately group WTs to bundle them logically for efficient processing by resources in the warehouse. In Figure 10.17, you can see the process of WO creation, including the various steps in the process that we'll describe in more detail in the following text.

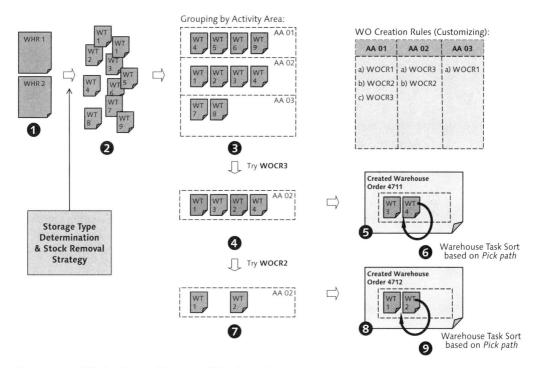

Figure 10.17 WO Creation and Sorting of Warehouse Tasks

1. In step 1, the warehouse request items for which the tasks will be created are selected (for example, for the ODO or for the wave) and the task generation is started.

2. In step 2, the WTs are created with the appropriate source and destination bin based on the storage type determination and stock removal strategy, and the activity area is determined for the WTs.

3. In step 3, the WTs are grouped by activity area. Only WTs with the same activity area and queue assignment will be grouped together into a WO.

4. In step 4, the WTs are filtered according to the item filter of the first WOCR in the sequence for the activity area (as seen in the customizing reflected in the top right of the diagram). The item filter may include, for example, minimum or maximum weight or volume, processing time, route, wave category, etc.). The items that do not meet the item filter criteria pass to the next WOCR.

5. In step 5, the WTs are sorted according to the sort rule (which groups the items and sorts them to optimize efficiency in the warehouse; note: the sorting rule must include sort field DSTGRP for the consolidation group). Once the tasks are sorted, they are subtotaled by consolidation group and then filtered according to the subtotal filter. Finally, the filtered items are evaluated according to the limit values of the WOCR (which checks the capacity of every single WO according to the WOCR).

6. In step 6, the items that passed the subtotal filter and limit value check are sorted according to the picking path (so that the items of the WO are in the appropriate pick sequence). The result of step 6 is a complete WO, which will be executed in the warehouse once the WO creation is complete. The remaining items go back to step 5 to check the subtotal filter and limit values once again, and the process continues until all of the items have been assigned to a WO or only items that do not pass the subtotal filter or limit values remain. Individual items that do not pass the subtotal filter are passed on to the next WOCR.

7. Before step 7, the next WOCR in the sequence for the activity area is selected. In steps 7, 8, and 9, the remaining items are processed similar to steps 4, 5, and 6 except according to the next WOCR.
8. The cycle will continue until the sequence of WOCRs assigned to the activity area has been exhausted. At that point, the remaining items are grouped according to a remainder rule, which groups the tasks according to activity area, queue, and consolidation group.

As mentioned for step 6, after the WTs are bundled together based on the customizing, WTs are sorted according to the sort rule, which allows sorting of the WO items according to a defined pick path to increase the productivity of the picker. The sort rule can be defined dynamically based on the various fields (including the defined bin sorting). To define the sort rules (as in Figure 10.18), which can be assigned to the WOCRs in the EWM IMG, follow the menu path EXTENDED WAREHOUSE MANAGEMENT • CROSS-PROCESS SETTINGS • WAREHOUSE ORDER • DEFINE SORT RULES FOR WAREHOUSE TASKS.

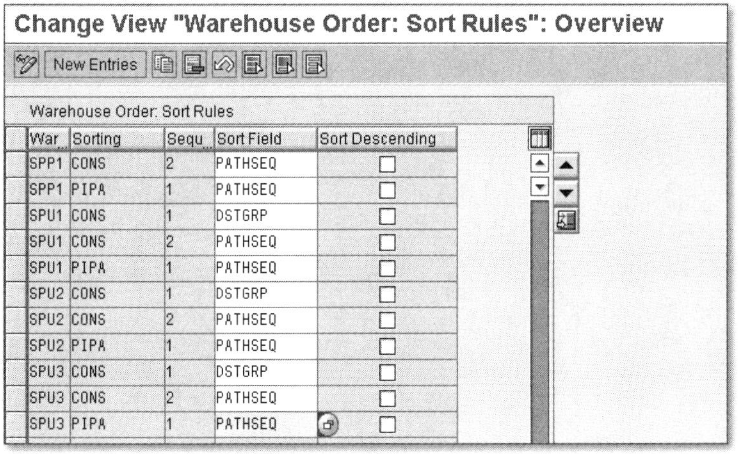
Change View "Warehouse Order: Sort Rules": Overview

New Entries

Warehouse Order: Sort Rules

War..	Sorting	Sequ..	Sort Field	Sort Descending
SPP1	CONS	2	PATHSEQ	☐
SPP1	PIPA	1	PATHSEQ	☐
SPU1	CONS	1	DSTGRP	☐
SPU1	CONS	2	PATHSEQ	☐
SPU1	PIPA	1	PATHSEQ	☐
SPU2	CONS	1	DSTGRP	☐
SPU2	CONS	2	PATHSEQ	☐
SPU2	PIPA	1	PATHSEQ	☐
SPU3	CONS	1	DSTGRP	☐
SPU3	CONS	2	PATHSEQ	☐
SPU3	PIPA	1	PATHSEQ	☐

Figure 10.18 Sorting Rules for Warehouse Tasks

To define the sort rule according to bin sorting, you can assign the sort field PATHSEQ in the sort rule. To use bin sorting in the sort rule, the bin sorting must be correctly executed for activity PICK (as described in detail in Chapter 3, The Warehouse Structure). To update the bin sorting, as you can see in Figure 10.19, in the EWM Easy Access menu, follow the EXTENDED WAREHOUSE MANAGEMENT • MASTER DATA • STORAGE BIN SORT STORAGE BINS menu path, or use Transaction code /SCWM/SBST.

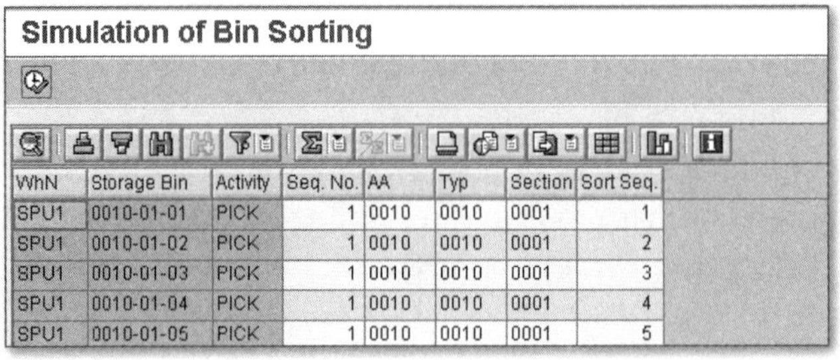

Simulation of Bin Sorting

WhN	Storage Bin	Activity	Seq. No.	AA	Typ	Section	Sort Seq.
SPU1	0010-01-01	PICK	1	0010	0010	0001	1
SPU1	0010-01-02	PICK	1	0010	0010	0001	2
SPU1	0010-01-03	PICK	1	0010	0010	0001	3
SPU1	0010-01-04	PICK	1	0010	0010	0001	4
SPU1	0010-01-05	PICK	1	0010	0010	0001	5

Figure 10.19 Bin Sorting over Activity Area

During the WT execution in the radio frequency (RF) device (which uses Transaction code /SCWM/RFUI), you may want to re-sort the WTs for the WO, as long as the option is allowed in the customizing. To update the setting to allow or disallow the re-sorting by activity area in the EWM IMG, follow the menu path EXTENDED WAREHOUSE MANAGEMENT • MASTER DATA • ACTIVITY AREA • DEFINE SORT SEQUENCE FOR ACTIVITY AREA.

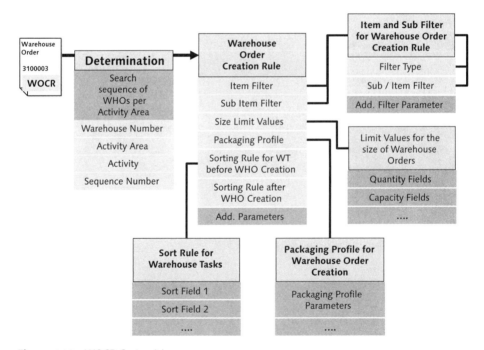

Figure 10.20 WOCR Customizing

As the customizing for the WO creation includes several dependent customizing activities, we have collected the relevant ones on the chart in Figure 10.20 and indicated the dependencies there so that you have a good understanding of the overall ways to control WO creation.

One of the most important settings is the creation of the WOCR itself. To define the WOCR (as you can see in Figure 10.21) in the EWM IMG, follow the menu path EXTENDED WAREHOUSE MANAGEMENT • CROSS-PROCESS SETTINGS • WAREHOUSE ORDER • DEFINE CREATION RULE FOR WAREHOUSE ORDERS.

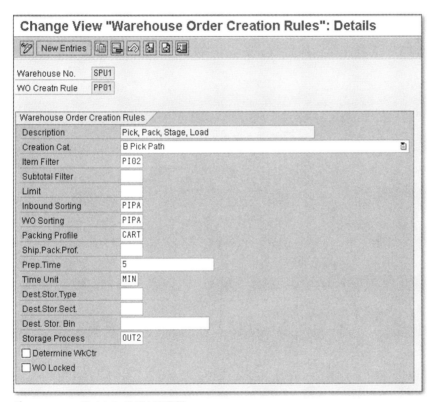

Figure 10.21 Maintain EWM WOCR

The settings for the filters and sort criteria that can be assigned to the WOCR can be found under the node in the EWM IMG at the menu path EXTENDED WARE-HOUSE MANAGEMENT • CROSS-PROCESS SETTINGS • WAREHOUSE ORDER.

10.4.4 Storage Type Determination

To begin the WO creation process, we first described the process for creating the WT, which included the source bin determination via the storage type search sequence and the stock removal rules. In this section, we will describe the storage type determination, which is used in the source bin determination.

To begin the source bin determination for the correct picking of products in the outbound process, EWM first determines the sequence of storage types in which it can search for the products and then determines for each storage type the stock removal rule that defines how it can pick stock within the given storage type. Figure 10.22 shows the STORAGE TYPE SEARCH SEQUENCE and the STOCK REMOVAL STRATEGY.

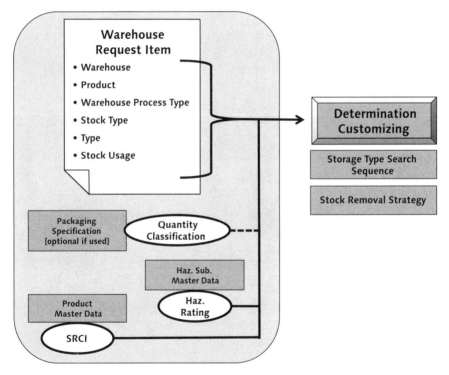

Figure 10.22 Picking Strategy Determination

The storage type search sequence, which defines which storage types can be searched and in which sequence they should be searched for available materials in the warehouse, is determined based on:

- the stock removal control indicator (SRCI), which is a parameter stored on the WAREHOUSE view of the product master (and can be determined by slotting)
- the hazardous material rating (HAZ. RATING), if applicable
- the QUANTITY CLASSIFICATION (which can be used, for example, to distinguish the profile of the storage type in terms of the quantities stored there (e.g., pallets, cases, eaches (or individual units))
- the PACKAGING SPECIFICATION

Based on the determined STORAGE TYPE SEARCH SEQUENCE, the storage types are assigned to the sequence, as you can see in Figure 10.23. To configure the storage type search sequence determination and the storage types assigned in the sequence in the EWM IMG, follow the menu path EXTENDED WAREHOUSE MANAGEMENT • GOODS ISSUE PROCESS • STRATEGIES • SPECIFY STORAGE TYPE SEARCH SEQUENCE. If you specify the Transportation Unit (TU) checkbox, EWM will also include the stock on TU when searching within the assigned storage type.

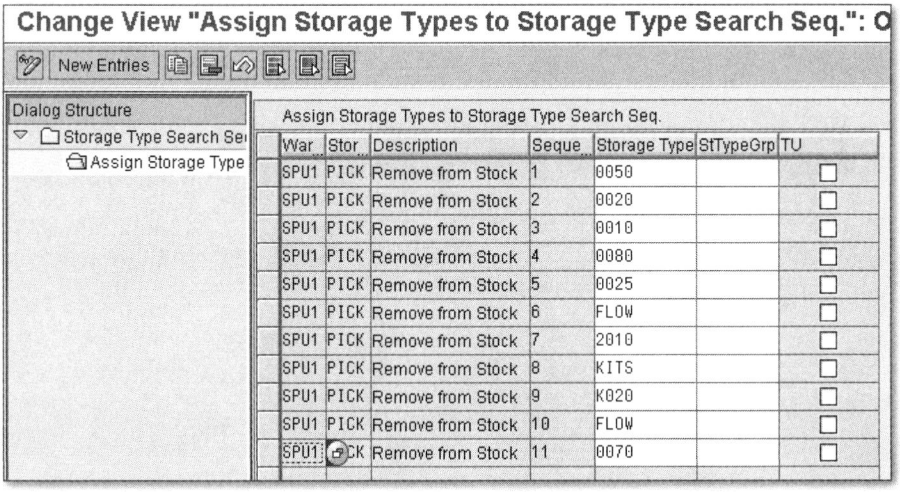

War	Stor	Description	Seque	Storage Type	StTypeGrp	TU
SPU1	PICK	Remove from Stock	1	0050		☐
SPU1	PICK	Remove from Stock	2	0020		☐
SPU1	PICK	Remove from Stock	3	0010		☐
SPU1	PICK	Remove from Stock	4	0080		☐
SPU1	PICK	Remove from Stock	5	0025		☐
SPU1	PICK	Remove from Stock	6	FLOW		☐
SPU1	PICK	Remove from Stock	7	2010		☐
SPU1	PICK	Remove from Stock	8	KITS		☐
SPU1	PICK	Remove from Stock	9	K020		☐
SPU1	PICK	Remove from Stock	10	FLOW		☐
SPU1	PICK	Remove from Stock	11	0070		☐

Figure 10.23 Assign Storage Types to Storage Type Search Sequence

To define the SRCIs that may be assigned to the products in the EWM IMG, follow the menu path EXTENDED WAREHOUSE MANAGEMENT • GOODS ISSUE PROCESS • STRATEGIES • DEFINE STOCK REMOVAL CONTROL INDICATOR.

To specify the determination for the STORAGE TYPE SEARCH SEQUENCE (as shown in Figure 10.24) in the EWM IMG, follow menu path EXTENDED WAREHOUSE MANAGEMENT • GOODS ISSUE PROCESS • STRATEGIES • DETERMINE STORAGE TYPE SEARCH SEQUENCE FOR STOCK REMOVAL.

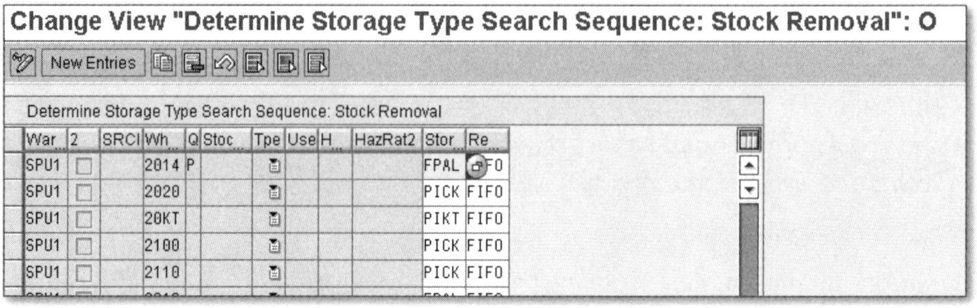

Figure 10.24 Determine Storage Type Search Sequence and Stock Removal Strategy

To optimize the access sequence for the storage type determination for stock removal, which allows you to decrease the size of the determination table and speed up access to the table by the programs, in the EWM IMG, follow the menu path EXTENDED WAREHOUSE MANAGEMENT • GOODS ISSUE PROCESS • STRATEGIES • OPTIMIZATION OF ACCESS STRATEGIES FOR STOR. TYPE DETERMINATION IN STCK RMVL. In Figure 10.25, you can see the typical settings for the optimization of the access sequence.

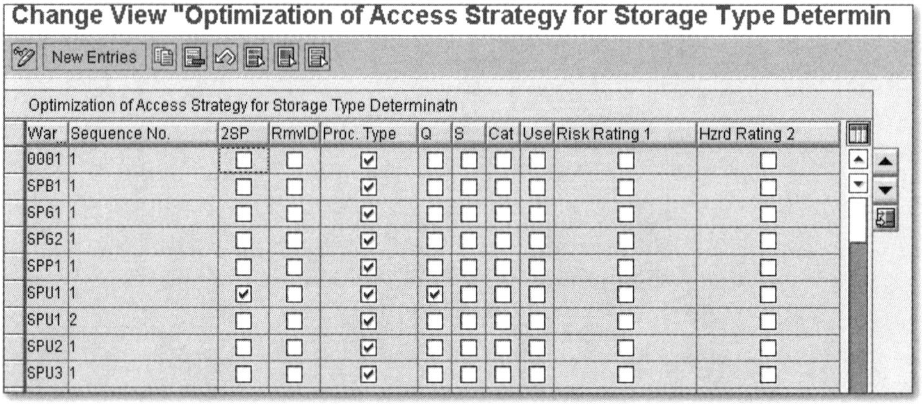

Figure 10.25 Optimization of Access Strategy for Storage Type Determination

10.4.5 Stock Removal Strategies

A stock removal strategy is a method used within an area of the warehouse to determine the bins from which to pick products from stock. Once the system has determined a storage type based on the storage type search process, the stock removal strategy is then applied to the given storage type. You map stock removal strategies in the system to a storage type or a storage type group.

SCM EWM and ERP Warehouse Management (WM) are similar in that they both use the stock removal strategy concept, but the methods for applying those strategies differ. In ERP WM, static and predefined stock removal strategies are specified as the allowed entries for the removal strategy. In EWM, you can flexibly define a sort template for the stock removal strategy that the system uses to order the quants for the selection process. The fields can be flexibly assigned, and you can create your own stock removal strategy based on your own requirements. The stock removal rule is then assigned to the storage types which are included in the storage type search sequence. In Figure 10.26, you can see a comparison of the static stock removal strategies of ERP WM vs. the flexible stock removal rules that can be created in SCM EWM.

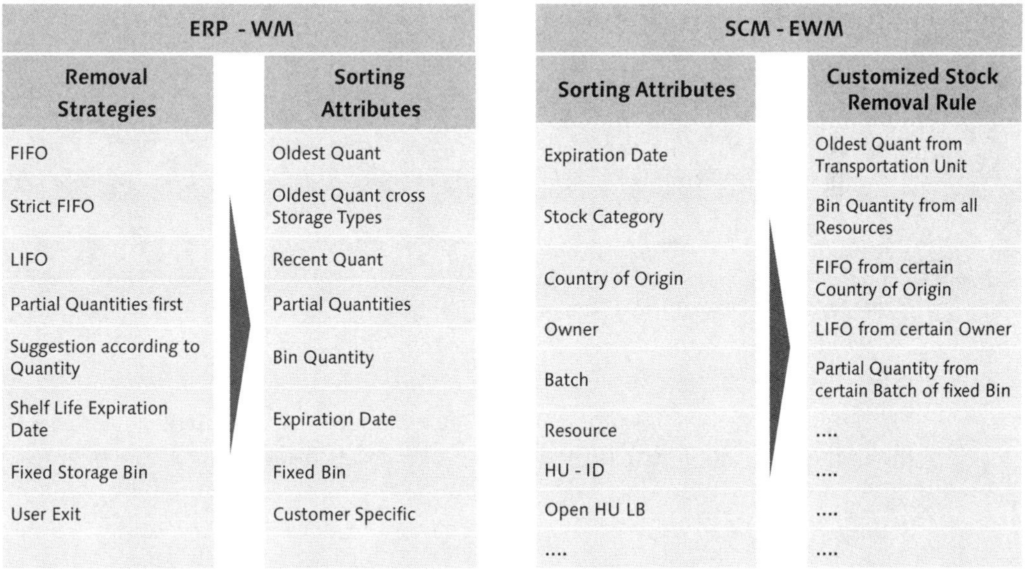

ERP - WM		SCM - EWM	
Removal Strategies	**Sorting Attributes**	**Sorting Attributes**	**Customized Stock Removal Rule**
FIFO	Oldest Quant	Expiration Date	Oldest Quant from Transportation Unit
Strict FIFO	Oldest Quant cross Storage Types	Stock Category	Bin Quantity from all Resources
LIFO	Recent Quant	Country of Origin	FIFO from certain Country of Origin
Partial Quantities first	Partial Quantities	Owner	LIFO from certain Owner
Suggestion according to Quantity	Bin Quantity	Batch	Partial Quantity from certain Batch of fixed Bin
Shelf Life Expiration Date	Expiration Date	Resource	....
Fixed Storage Bin	Fixed Bin	HU - ID	....
User Exit	Customer Specific	Open HU LB	....
		....	....

Figure 10.26 Difference of Stock Removal Strategy in ERP WM and EWM

In Figure 10.27, you can see the assignment of the sort fields to the STOCK REMOVAL RULE, including the list of fields available in the standard system for inclusion in the sorting for the rule. Based on the available fields, the strategies supported include the ones defined in the sections below, including first-in/first-out (FIFO), stringent FIFO (FIFO across all storage types), last-in/first-out (LIFO), partial quantities, large/small (a strategy that supports the separation of pallet, case, and each picks by area), shelf-life expiration date (SLED), fixed bin, and a custom strategy developed in the available Business Add-In (BAdI).

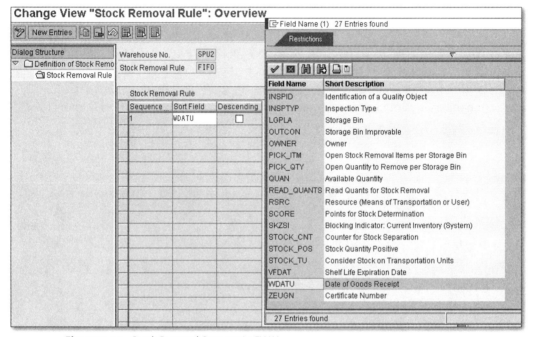

Figure 10.27 Stock Removal Strategy in EWM

FIFO

This removal strategy, like others that are date based, is implemented using the sorting in the STOCK REMOVAL RULE, based on the goods receipt date in the quant.

Stringent FIFO

This strategy ensures application of a FIFO rule across all picking areas, using storage type groups. The stock is sorted by the defined sort fields within a single storage type group. For each storage type search sequence, you can group the storage types differently.

LIFO

For some warehouse organizations, or within some industries, some products can't be removed using the FIFO principle. For example, in the building materials industry, products that are to be removed from stock, such as lumber, are stacked on top of products that are already stored in the warehouse. If you used the FIFO strategy for those products, the warehouse worker would first have to remove the products lying on top to get to the product with the oldest goods receipt date. The LIFO strategy is provided for such situations. When the system searches for a suitable quant to remove from stock, it always suggests the last quant that was placed into stock.

Partial Quantities First

With this strategy, the system overrides the FIFO principle for managing the stock to optimize the capacity utilization in the warehouse. It allows you to keep the number of partial HUs in a storage type as low as possible by preferentially picking stock from partial pallets before full pallets.

Fixed Bin

With this strategy, the system determines the assigned fixed bin as the source of the WT. Fixed bins are assigned to the products by storage type using Transaction code /SCWM/BINMAT, and multiple fixed bins can be assigned to the same product in the storage type (if, for instance, you need multiple bins to satisfy the volume of stock required to be picked in a given period).

If you allow negative available stock in the bin (according to the configuration of the storage type), then the fixed bin will be assigned even if there's no available stock in the bin at the time the WT is created. In this case, you must use replenishment control to ensure that products are available in the storage bin at the time of picking. The pick denial and picker directed replenishment processes (see Chapter 16, Exception Handling) can become especially pertinent in these cases.

SLED

With this strategy, the system ensures that the products with the oldest shelf-life expiration date are removed from stock first. This strategy is implemented similar to the other date-based removal strategies; in the stock removal rule, the SLED field is specified as the sort criteria.

Custom Strategy Developed in the Available BAdI

If the procedures for the stock removal rule do not provide enough flexibility to solve your requirement (for example, if you also need some decision tree heuristics enabled), SAP also provided a BAdI in EWM where you can specify your own stock removal strategy. To access in the BAdI in the EWM IMG, follow the menu path EXTENDED WAREHOUSE MANAGEMENT • BUSINESS ADD-INS (BADIS) FOR EXTENDED WAREHOUSE MANAGEMENT • GOODS ISSUE PROCESS • STRATEGIES • STOCK REMOVAL • STRATEGIES • BADI: DELETION OF QUANT BUFFER AND BADI: FILTERING AND/OR SORTING OF QUANTS.

10.4.6 Storage Control in the Outbound Processes

Because the outbound process contains multistep processing, which may include, for example, steps such as picking, packing, kitting, VASs, staging and loading, storage control plays an important role in the process. In Chapter 13, Configuring Multistep Warehouse Movements, we already described the storage control mechanisms (POSC and LOSC). In this section, we'll describe the specific points regarding storage control that are relevant to the outbound process.

In Figure 10.28, you can see an example of a multistep process for outbound processing that includes the steps for picking, packing, staging, and loading (a very typical process for nearly every warehouse).

Using the POSC, it is possible to set up this process such that the next step in the process is always determined at the creation of the previous step, and therefore the destination bin is always chosen appropriately to drive the efficient execution of the tasks in the warehouse. For example, when the picks are being executed from the source storage types, the destination bin of the WT is automatically determined, based on storage control, to be the inbound area of the appropriate packing work center.

It is also possible to use a combination of the POSC and LOSC in the outbound process. For example, referring once again to Figure 10.28, if the storage type of ACTIVITY AREA 0020 had a pick point assigned, where the product was dropped from the high-rack location to the pick point to remove the partial quantities necessary for the pick, and then replaced back in stock, then the storage control would take into account that the full quant quantity must be picked from the source storage bin and delivered to the ID point, then the partial quantities must be removed to the Pick HU at the ID point for the pick, and then the Pick HU would be delivered to the inbound area of the work center.

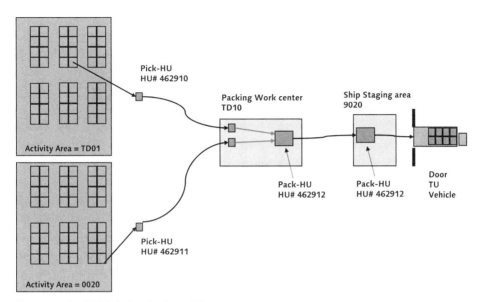

Figure 10.28 POSC during Outbound Process

10.4.7 Picking Execution — Optimization of Picking

Once the WOs have been created, you can begin executing the WOs in the warehouse. In the following sections, we will describe the process for manual picking using a picking list and the execution of the WOs using the mobile data entry (or RF) transactions.

10.4.8 Execution with Picking List

If you prefer to execute the WOs in your warehouse or just a portion of your warehouse using paper-based picking lists, you can manage this process using the features of EWM by executing the following steps:

1. Create the WOs, as described previously

2. Print the picking lists at your selected printer, with the aid of the PPF actions for the WO

3. Execute the picking in the warehouse and record the picking results on the paper pick list

4. Confirm the WO using the desktop graphical user interface (GUI) transactions

5. Manage the exceptions and trigger follow-up processes if necessary, such as the creation of new pick tasks to cover short picks

> **Note**
>
> While the paper-based process is not optimized during the pick execution (because the warehouse worker does not have the opportunity to interact in real time with the system), you can still use the features of the wave management and WO creation to help optimize the picking processes.

Printing the Picking List

The printing process is enabled in EWM using the PPF and the condition technique, which are described in detail in Chapter 24. In this section, we will describe the features for printing that are specific to outbound processing.

EWM delivers two standard forms for the printing of picking documents, however, it is very common in projects to create custom forms that are specific to the needs of your business (e.g., with a company logo, specific formatting, or additional fields to cover unique business requirements). To create your own forms, you can use the standard forms as a baseline, or you can just view them to check how they work before you start creating your own. The standard forms delivered are SmartForms (accessible via Transaction SMARTFORMS), and they include:

► /SCWM/WO_MULTIPLE — WO for multiple printing

► /SCWM/WO_SINGLE — WO for single printing

Confirming the Warehouse Orders

Once you have physically executed the picking tasks in the warehouse, you can confirm the WOs (as you can see in Figure 10.29) in the EWM Easy Access menu by following the EXTENDED WAREHOUSE MANAGEMENT • EXECUTION • CONFIRM WAREHOUSE TASK menu path, or using Transaction code /SCWM/TO_CONF. You can also confirm the tasks directly in the warehouse monitor (Transaction /SCWM/MON) via the standard methods available there for WOs and WTs.

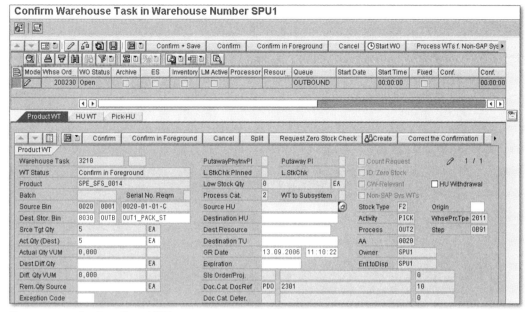

Figure 10.29 Confirmation of WTs

You can also confirm the WTs using the transaction for mobile data entry, which is accessible on the desktop user interface (UI) using Transaction code /SCWM/ RFUI. The simple UI of the transactions designed for mobile devices can sometimes be ideal for users to quickly enter the transactions that were executed on paper. However, if you plan to confirm the WOs this way on a regular basis, you may want to consider creating a special verification profile that limits the verification fields that need to be keyed by the users and assign the verification profile to the desktop users.

10.4.9 Execution with Mobile Devices

Execution of the WOs for outbound processing in the warehouse via mobile devices is generally preferred, because it allows for more efficient processing and also allows opportunities to reduce errors by verifying the data during the execution. It also lets users interact directly with the system in real time, which reduces the effort to enter the data into the system and also allows the user and the system to more appropriately react to unexpected issues in real time (e.g., short picks or validation errors). Finally, if you use the system-guided processes (described in more detail in the following sections), you can optimize your processes by the most appropriate activity to the warehouse operator based on his activity assignment and based on which activity he performed last (i.e., using interleaving).

To confirm the WOs you can start the mobile data entry transaction in the EWM Easy Access menu by following the EXTENDED WAREHOUSE MANAGEMENT • EXECUTION • LOG ON TO RF ENVIRONMENT menu path, or using Transaction code /SCWM/ RFUI. In actual practice, the mobile devices are often configured to call the transaction as soon as you log on so you don't have to manually select the transaction. Once you log on the RF Environment, then you can begin selecting the processing functions from the menu. For more details on RF transactions, see Chapter 22, Data Capture and Resource Optimization.

> **Note**
>
> While the RF menu is configurable and you can change it in your own implementation, we will refer to the menu paths for the remainder of this section assuming that you are using the standard delivered configuration for the menu. (In parentheses are the object IDs used in assigning the menu options to the menu structure in the configuration.)

After you log on and specify your resource, the RF menu offers various ways for you to confirm the WOs for picking. Among them are the options described in the following text, which you can select from the RF menu (the menu path is provided below the option).

There are two options for system-guided picking, namely:

▸ System-guided Selection: With this option, you are fully system guided according to your queue assignment, as determined by your resource and its resource group

  RF MENU: SYSTEM GUIDED • SYSTEM-GUIDED SELECTION (WKSYSG)

▸ System-guided by Queue: In the beginning of the transaction, you specifiy the queue in which you want to work, and the system only assigns you WOs from your specified queue

  RF MENU: SYSTEM GUIDED • SYSTEM-GUIDED BY QUEUE (WKSYSQ)

You can also specify which specific activity you want to perform in the warehouse by using the following options:

▸ Pick by Warehouse Order: You can use this option if you know the WO number that you will process. For example, you may have been handed a group of pallet labels for shipping upon which is printed the WO number. If the WO number is printed as a barcode, you can scan the barcode to start the process. (You can also use it to manually enter the confirmations on the desktop transaction for a printed WO.)

RF Menu: Manual Selection • Manual selection by WO (WKMNWO)

▶ Pick by Handling Unit: You can use this option if you pick the entire HU and the HU is already determined as the source HU on the WT.

RF Menu: Manual Selection • Manual selection by HU (WKMNHU)

▶ Pick by Warehouse Request: You can use this option if you know the number of the warehouse request (in the outbound case, this is the ODO number). This option can be useful, for example, in an emergency pick situation when you are supplied a specific order number to pick.

RF Menu: Manual Selection • Manual selection by WR (WKMNWR)

There are also picking transactions available under the Picking submenu, including RF Menu: Outbound Processes • Picking.

While the different transactions may look similar, they differ by object ID and by context. For example, the transactions under the Picking submenu, while they look like the options under the System-guided or Manual menu, they are assigned to a different context, therefore, you may be assigned to different orders, or you may not be allowed to process an order that you specify manually. As an example, if you select the Manual System-guided option, you may be assigned to a putaway WO, whereas if you select the System-guided Picking option, you will only be assigned to pick WOs.

On the mobile devices, you can also use exception codes which react differently than if you used the same exception code on a desktop transaction. For example, if you use a specific exception code during picking that indicates that the stock is not available in the bin, you can be triggered via the RF transaction to go directly to the source bin of a replenishment to move the stock to the picking bin (this is known as a picker-directed replenishment). On the desktop transaction, the same exception code would not trigger such a follow-up activity — it would simply update the confirmed quantity on the WTs, and perhaps send an alert to a supervisor or inventory control. For more details about exception codes, see Chapter 16.

On the mobile transaction, you can see a list of the possible exception codes in the current context by entering the code LIST to the exception code box (if the code

LIST is enabled for the context). In Figure 10.30, you can see the code entered on the exception code box and the resulting list of possible codes.

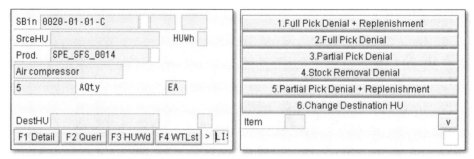

Figure 10.30 Exception Codes List Box during Picking

10.4.10 Cancelling Picking

If you need to cancel a pick even after the pick is already confirmed, you can cancel the pick (as seen in Figure 10.31) in the EWM Easy Access menu by following the menu path WAREHOUSE MANAGEMENT • EXECUTION • CANCEL PICKING, or using transaction code /SCWM/CANCPICK. When you cancel a pick, the warehouse request will be initialize and you can create a new pick WT, if necessary.

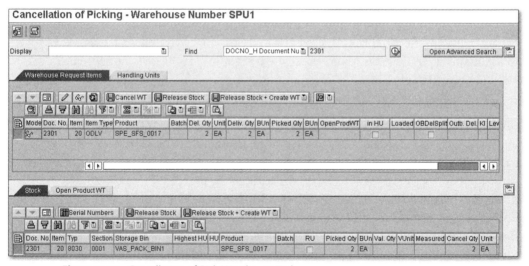

Figure 10.31 Cancellation of Pick Warehouse Task

10.4.11 Pick Denial

If insufficient warehouse stock exists to fulfill the warehouse request item, you can "deny" or "short" the pick to allow you to post goods issue for the ODO even without confirming all of the requested quantity. While the gATP check for the order usually takes care of determining the proper availability of stock and only sending requests to the warehouse for available stock, there are circumstances under which the stock may still not be available. For example, the stock quantities in inventory management may have been incorrect due to an incorrect count of the product in the storage bin, or the stock may have been lost in the warehouse and is currently being investigated (meanwhile the stock is only available in the difference analyzer and inventory management did not know that the stock was lost when the availability was checked), or the stock may only be available in an unpickable bin (for example, in a non-functioning material flow system (MFS)).

You may realize the shortage in inventory at different points in time. For example, you may realize while attempting to create the WTs that the system cannot find sufficient stock, or you may realize while picking that the stock quantity in the bin is not enough to fulfill the request on the WO.

In EWM, there are a couple of special features that help you manage the situation when it occurs. In the first case, when the system cannot find the requested quantity of an ODO in stock, you can configure the system to automatically execute a pick denial.

In the second case, when you discover a shortage at the bin and execute a bin denial via an exception code entered during picking, if no other stock can be found in the warehouse, then the system can execute a pick denial. Based on the configuration, the pick denial situation can be immediately transferred to ERP (even before the goods issue for the ODO) so that the open quantity for the product can be forwarded to another warehouse and the customer order can be fulfilled.

10.4.12 Pick, Pack, and Pass

In large warehouses that process large volumes of small-quantity orders, a multi-zone process of picking items to a container and then passing the container to the next zone for picking additional items can often be enabled (see the diagram in Figure 10.32 for an example). Sometimes, the process may be enabled by a manual or automatic conveyor system, and there may also be printers or pick-to-light systems in the various zones to support the picking processes within the zone. EWM provides the option to support this *Pick, Pack, and Pass* requirement with the standard functionality, including the option to directly control the conveyor system.

In the illustration in Figure 10.32, you can see that the HU is transported to two picking station. At the individual picking stations, warehouse workers pick the required product into the HU and place it on the conveyor system to be moved to the next station. To support this process, EWM creates two WOs — one for each zone — and then groups the WOs together into a *Top WO*. The HU that is used across the multiple picks zone to collect the products and which may be shipped to the customer in the end is assigned to the Top WO. Once all of the WOs are confirmed, the HU is moved to the final goods issue area.

In the illustration, you can also see the relationship between the objects (WT, WO, Top WO) on the left side, and the relationship between those objects and the physical process on the right side.

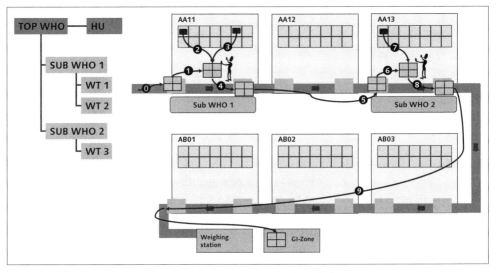

Figure 10.32 Pick, Pack, and Pass Process and Relationship of Objects

To support the Pick, Pack, and Pass process, you must map each picking zone as an activity area (as described in Chapter 3) and specify that the activity areas are joined. To maintain the activity areas in the EWM IMG, follow the menu path Extended Warehouse Management • Master Data • Activity Areas • Define Activity Area.

Next, you must join the activity areas together and specify the sequence of the activity areas for transport of the HU (as seen in Figure 10.33). To join the activity areas in the EWM IMG, follow the menu path EXTENDED WAREHOUSE MANAGEMENT • CROSS-PROCESS SETTINGS • WAREHOUSE ORDER • JOIN ACTIVITY AREAS TOGETHER.

New Entries: Overview of Added Entries

War	H.Act.Area	AA	Sort Sequence
SPU1	APPP	AA01	1
SPU1	APPP	AA02	2
SPU1	APPP	AA03	3
SPU1	APPP	AB01	4
SPU1	APPP	AB02	5
SPU1	APPP	AB03	6

Assign Activity Areas to Joined Activity Areas

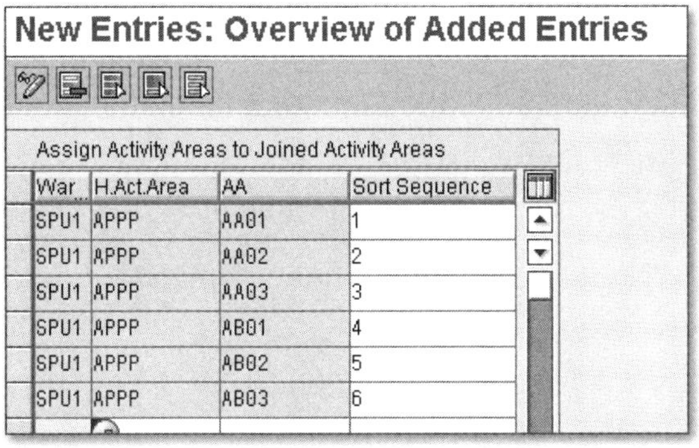

Figure 10.33 Assigning Activity Areas to Joined Activity Areas

For the Pick, Pack, and Pass scenario, you should also define the starting point and end point for each pick zone (which is defined as an activity area) (see Figure 10.34). To assign the bins as the starting points and end points of the activity areas in the EWM Easy Access menu, follow the EXTENDED WAREHOUSE MANAGEMENT • MASTER DATA • STORAGE • ASSIGN START/END STORAGE BIN FOR ACTIVITY AREA menu path, or use Transaction code /SCWM/SEBA. Before assigning them as starting point and ending points, the bins must be created, as described in Chapter 3 (using Transaction /SCWM/LS01).

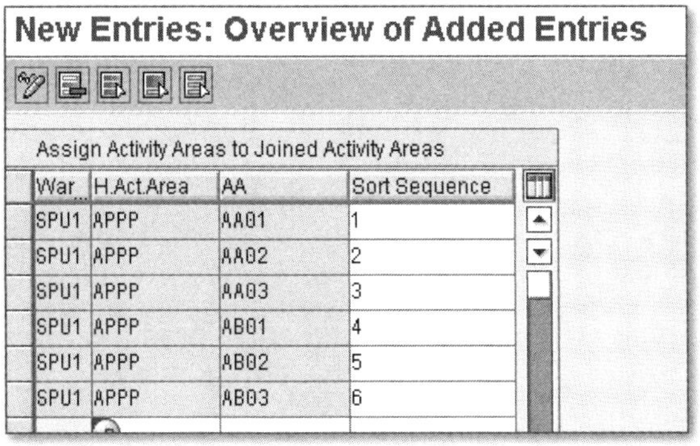

New Entries: Overview of Added Entries

War	H.Act.Area	AA	Sort Sequence
SPU1	APPP	AA01	1
SPU1	APPP	AA02	2
SPU1	APPP	AA03	3
SPU1	APPP	AB01	4
SPU1	APPP	AB02	5
SPU1	APPP	AB03	6

Assign Activity Areas to Joined Activity Areas

Figure 10.34 Assign Start/End Points to an Activity Area

You must also create the WAREHOUSE ORDER CREATION RULE (WOCR) to support the Top WO creation for the PICK, PACK, AND PASS process (as you can see in Figure 10.35). For PICK, PACK, AND PASS there are possible creation categories available, namely:

▶ PICK, PACK, AND PASS: SYSTEM-DRIVEN — for the system-driven option, the sequence of the WOs in the Top WO is determined according to the sort sequence assigned in the configuration settings for joining the activity areas (as you saw previously in Figure 10.33).

▶ PICK, PACK, AND PASS: USER-DRIVEN — for the user-driven option, the sequence is manually determined during the execution, for example, by the MFS.

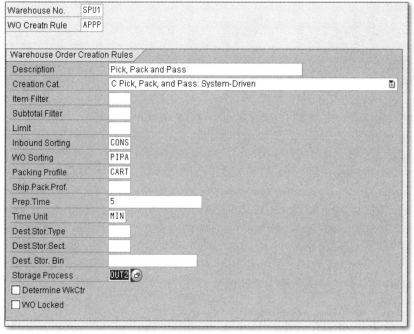

Figure 10.35 Pick, Pack and Pass WORC

10.4.13 Pick Point Handling

In certain areas of the warehouse, you may not be able to remove products from the HU directly at the picking bin. This could be due to the size or shape of the products, the type of equipment used for the removal of the products, or constraints at the picking bin. In this case, you may want to set up a pick point, where you can deliver the HU to remove the stock for picking (to a Ship HU) before returning the HU to the original source bin. In EWM, this *Pick Point* is modeled as a work center where you can perform the picking operations. To configure the pick point, create a pick point storage type for the pick point, specify that the HU-managed source storage type is pick point active, and assign the pick point to the storage type in the LOSC.

As you can see in Figure 10.36, when you generate the WTs for picking, the picking WT is created inactive and an HU WT is initially created to move the HU to the pick point. At the PICK POINT, you execute the picking from the source HU to a Ship HU, for example, via the available RF transactions. From there, the Ship HU is moved to the following area according to the POSC (which could be the goods issue zone, VAS work center, or a packing station), and the original HU is triggered to be moved back to the STORAGE BIN with an additional HU WT.

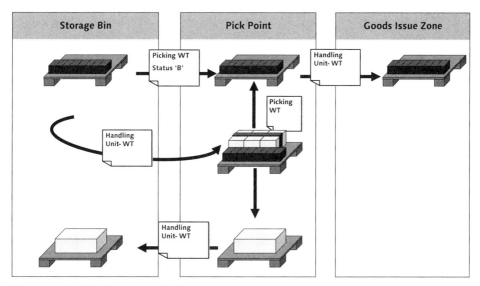

Figure 10.36 Pick Point Material Flow

The execution of the pick at the pick point can use a combination of mobile transactions (which are accessible via Transaction /SCWM/RFUI), because the pick point is technically modeled as a work center. The transactions include:

▶ Logon to Pick Point — used to log on to the work center
▶ Creation of Single HU — used to create the Ship HU

▶ Pick Point — used to execute the picking, print HU labels, or inquire about workload remaining on the wave or consolidation group

▶ HU Maintenance — used to close the Ship HU, which triggers the move of the HU to the next destination according to the POSC.

10.4.14 Packing

To consolidate products for shipment (which reduces effort handling and may also reduce freight charges), you can group the picked products into larger packages during picking (if supported by the consolidation of tasks into WOs by the WOCR) or at a packing work center (if the products, for example, are picked from different warehouse areas and cannot be consolidated during picking). In EWM, the products can be packed according to the assigned consolidation group, which is determined based on:

▶ Warehouse number

▶ Route (assigned to the ODO as described earlier in this chapter)

▶ Ship-to party (assigned to the ODO)

▶ Priority of the delivery item (transferred from the ERP delivery to the ODO)

Based on these criteria, the consolidation group is assigned to the ODO item and assigned to the corresponding WTs during the task creation. Depending on the setup of the WOCR, the warehouse may be created for only a single consolidation group (which may then be packed to a single Pick HU that can also be used for shipping) or for multiple consolidation groups (which need to be repackaged at the packing station).

In EWM, the packing station is modeled as a work center. You can therefore execute the packing at the work center on a desktop transaction or use the mobile transaction. To access the desktop transaction for packing (as you can see in Figure 10.37) in the EWM Easy Access menu, follow the EXTENDED WAREHOUSE MANAGEMENT • EXECUTION • PACKING - GENERAL menu path, or use Transaction code /SCWM/PACK.

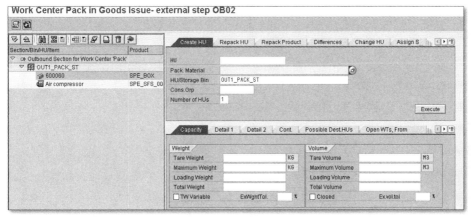

Figure 10.37 Desktop Transaction for Packing at the Packing Work Center

To access the mobile packing functions (which are accessible via Transaction code /SCWM/RFUI), if you are using the standard delivered RF menu, follow the menu path 04 OUTBOUND PROCESSES • 02 PACKING. There you will find the options for the functions that you can perform at the packing work station, similar to the ones defined earlier for the picking point work center (as you can see in Figure 10.38).

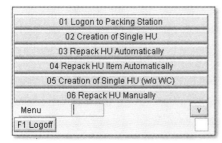

Figure 10.38 RF Menu for Packing at the Packing Work Center

To ensure that the products that need to be packed are moved to the appropriate packing station, you must include the packaging step in the appropriate process within the POSC (for more information on the POSC, see Chapter 13).

In addition, you must specify the appropriate determination of the work center for packaging. For the work center determination, you can use flexible determination or static determination. For static determination, you can directly specify the storage bin of the packing station work center to the WOCR. For flexible determination, you must specify in the WOCR that flexible determination should be used (by selecting the DETERMINE WORK CENTER option within the WOCR), and then you must configure the determination table (as you can see in Figure 10.39) in the EWM Easy Access menu by following the EXTENDED WAREHOUSE MANAGEMENT • MASTER DATA • WORK CENTER • DETERMINE WORK CENTER IN GOODS ISSUE menu path, or by using Transaction code /SCWM/PACKSTDT.

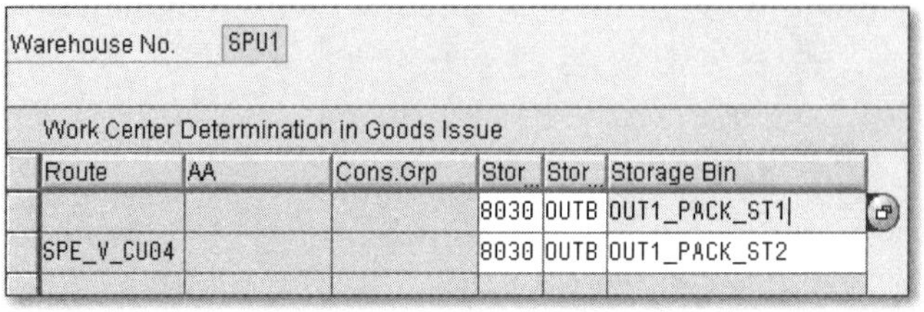

Warehouse No.	SPU1					
Work Center Determination in Goods Issue						
Route	AA	Cons.Grp	Stor	Stor	Storage Bin	
			8030	OUTB	OUT1_PACK_ST1	
SPE_V_CU04			8030	OUTB	OUT1_PACK_ST2	

Figure 10.39 Determination of Work Center for Packing

10.4.15 Door and Staging Area Determination

Once the materials are packed together correctly, the next stages in the process are typically the staging and shipping process steps. When you close the HU at the packaging station, the WT is created to move the HU to the next destination according to the storage control. If the staging process is next in the POSC, then EWM checks the staging area and door determination to determine the next destination. In Figure 10.40, you can see the determination table for the STAGING AREA, STAGING AREA GROUP, STAGING BAY, and WAREHOUSE DOOR. This table is used to determine, according to the route and warehouse process type (to separate, for example, the determination of inbound vs. outbound), which area of the warehouse should be used for staging and loading. To access the table in the EWM Easy Access menu, follow the EXTENDED WAREHOUSE MANAGEMENT • SETTINGS • SHIPPING AND RECEIVING • STAGING AREA AND DOOR DETERMINATION (OUTBOUND) menu path, or use Transaction code /SCWM/STADET_OUT.

To limit the size of the customizing table (and therefore your time commitment for maintaining it) and to improve the performance of the selections, you can specify the access sequence for determining the staging area and doors in the EWM Easy Access menu by following the EXTENDED WAREHOUSE MANAGEMENT • SETTINGS • SHIPPING AND RECEIVING • ACCESS SEQUENCE TO STAGING AREAS AND DOOR DETERMINATION menu path, or using Transaction code /SCWM/STADET_ASS.

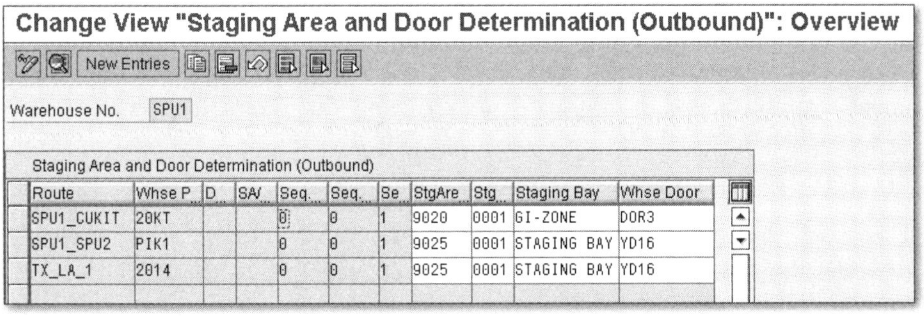

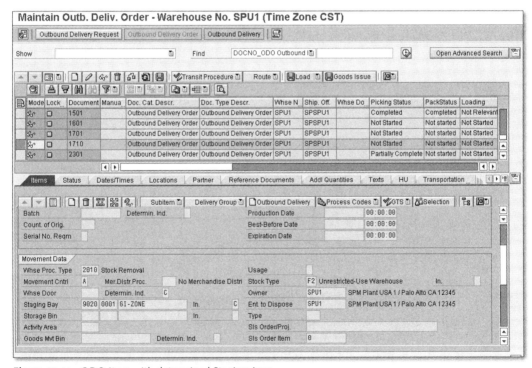

Figure 10.40 Staging Area and Door Determination in Outbound Processes

Once the determination is executed, you can find the STAGING BAY assigned to the ODO item, as shown in Figure 10.41 and in Transaction /SCWM/PRDO. The DOOR assignment, on the other hand, is made at the ODO header level (not shown in the figure).

Figure 10.41 ODO Item with determined Staging Area

10.4.16 Loading, Shipping, and Freight Order Management

Once the HUs have arrived to the staging area, the processing within the warehouse is complete, and the shipping and receiving (S&R) activities, which include loading, yard management, and transportation are used to manage the remaining processes.

To begin the loading process, you can create a loading list, which provides visibility to the items that are to be loaded and shipped together on the TU.

The TU is a special kind of HU that is used to reflect the truck, trailer, or container used for shipping (including the associated data like carrier, license plate, driver, etc.). It is used to manage the S&R and yard management functions and track the status and movement of the trucks on the premises. In EWM, you can assign HUs or delivery items to a TU to reflect which items were loaded onto the truck. You can also manage the vehicles separate from the TUs. For more information about managing vehicles and TUs in the yard, see Chapter 18. To maintain TUs, in the EWM Easy Access menu, follow the EXTENDED WAREHOUSE MANAGEMENT • SHIPPING AND RECEIVING • CREATE TRANSPORT UNIT menu path, or use Transaction code /SCWM/TU.

To properly track product movement, you may want to capture information about the truck arrival, start of loading, end of loading, and truck departure. To support the capture of this information, you can use the loading and yard management processes for the TUs.

To track the loading process, which reflects the movement of the products from the staging bay to the trailer at the dock door, you can use either the simple loading or complex loading process. Simple loading only results in the change of the loading status and captures the timestamp of the loading. The loading status can be changed and stored on the ODO level or on the TU level. You can execute the loading (as in Figure 10.42) in the EWM Easy Access menu by following the EXTENDED WAREHOUSE MANAGEMENT • SHIPPING AND RECEIVING • LOAD menu path, or using Transaction code /SCWM/LOAD.

If you prefer to track the loading of individual pallets to the TU, which is a closer modeling to the physical process, you can use the complex loading process by creating and confirming loading WTs. When you confirm the loading WTs, the HUs are assigned to the TU. In the loading transaction described previously (/SCWM/LOAD), you can manage the complex loading WTs.

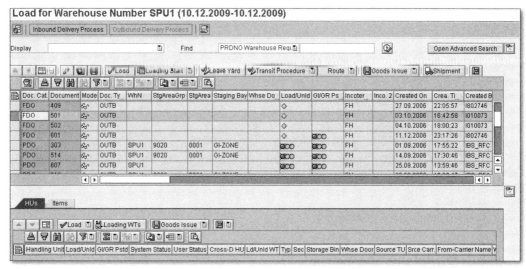

Figure 10.42 Desktop Transaction for Loading

You can also execute the complex loading by creating and confirming the WTs (in one step) via the mobile transactions (Transaction /SCWM/RFUI). To facilitate the loading process in various ways, EWM provides the following mobile transactions to manage the S&R process:

▶ Loading by Delivery

▶ Loading by Shipment

▶ Loading by TU

▶ Loading by Door

▶ Loading by HU

▶ Loading by Route

▶ Build Vehicle

Finally, you can trigger the automatic posting of the goods issue based on the completion of loading (when the final HU is loaded onto the TU, for example) via the PPF. You can also opt to automate the goods issue posting via the checkout from yard management, as we will discuss later in this chapter and which is also discussed in Chapter 18. For more information about PPF processing, see Chapter 24.

10.4.17 Freight Order Management

To solve basic requirements for transportation management related to your warehouse processes, including consolidation of orders onto shipments (with possible integration to external systems for transportation planning), printing the necessary paperwork for shipping, and communicating shipments to freight forwarders or subsystems for planning or execution, you can use the Freight Order Management component of EWM.

In Freight Order Management, the planning and execution of transportation is managed via shipments (which collect the ODOs shipped together from a source site to a destination site) and freight order documents (which collect shipments that are shipped together on a TU).

The shipments are defined by their document type. A shipment can be a:

▶ Planned shipment, which is created to group the ODOs and send the requests to the external transportation planning system

▶ Final shipment, which is created based on the final loading of the TU

▶ Bill of lading, which is created from the freight order document after the final loading of all of the shipments assigned to the freight order document.

Figure 10.43, shows a diagram of the outbound process, which includes:

▶ The assignment of the ODOs to PLANNED SHIPMENTS (step 1)

▶ Creation of the TRANSPORTATION REQUEST from the PLANNED SHIPMENT (step 2)

▶ Creation of the FREIGHT ORDER DOCUMENT based on the results of the planning with regard to the TRANSPORTATION REQUEST (step 3)

▶ Creation of the TU for LOADING (step 4)

▶ Creation of the FINAL SHIPMENT upon final LOADING of the shipment (step 5)

▶ Update of the FREIGHT ORDER DOCUMENT based on the creation of the FINAL SHIPMENT (step 6)

▶ Creation of the BILL OF LADING (a shipment type, not just a printed document) upon the final loading of the last shipment assigned to the FREIGHT ORDER DOCUMENT

▶ Update of the ODO with the BILL OF LADING reference number

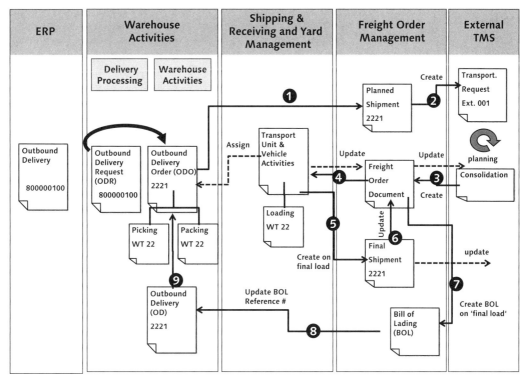

Figure 10.43 Freight Order Management Integration

10.4.18 Invoice Before Goods Issue

In the warehouse, you are sometimes required, based on customer demands or based on international shipping requirements, to include the actual invoice price on certain documents or even to include the actual invoice with the shipment when it is delivered from the warehouse. On the other hand, you may not want to post goods issue (which would normally trigger the billing) until after the products have left your facility. In these cases, you may want to use the invoice before goods issue (IBGI) process to create and print invoices even before the goods issue is posted. From EWM, you can trigger the IBGI process, which will result in the creation of the invoice in CRM or in ERP. If the printer determination is set up appropriately in CRM or ERP, the invoice can then be printed directly on a printer in the warehouse. In Figure 10.44, you can see a flow diagram for the IBGI process, which triggers the IBGI based on creation of the final outbound delivery (which

465

would otherwise be created only when the goods issue is posted, but which is created beforehand during the IBGI process).

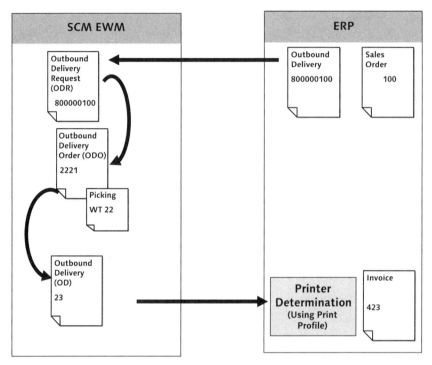

Figure 10.44 IBGI Process Flow Overview over ERP System

Once the picking for the ODO is complete, you can create the final outbound delivery from the ODO within the ODO maintenance transaction (Transaction /SCWM/PRDO). Once the outbound delivery is created, you can then trigger the creation of the invoice in the EWM Easy Access menu by following the EXTENDED WARE-HOUSE MANAGEMENT • DELIVERY PROCESSING • OUTBOUND DELIVERY • MAINTAIN OUTBOUND DELIVERY menu path, or using Transaction code /SCWM/FD. In EWM, you assign the relevant print profile for IBGI, which is then transferred to ERP (or CRM) to drive the printer determination for the invoice printing.

You can also trigger the creation and printing of the invoice from the TU maintenance transaction (Transaction /SCWM/TU), which would result in printing the invoice for all of the outbound deliveries assigned to the TU.

Once you have created the final outbound delivery, you can no longer adjust the pick quantities of the ODO. If you need to adjust the pick quantities, you must delete the outbound delivery.

Also, you can't change an invoice once it has been created. To overcome this restriction, you must first cancel the invoice (and usually destroy or mark and file the paper copies), then you can request the invoice creation again once you have adjusted the quantities.

> **Note**
>
> The configuration to enable the IBGI process is described in more detail in the online help (*http://help.sap.com*). You must update the configuration related to IBGI in both the ERP and EWM systems. If IBGI is activated in ERP, the IBGI Indicator is passed on the outbound delivery from ERP to EWM.
>
> If you use CRM for billing, you must also make the appropriate settings in CRM to enable IBGI (including the business partner status settings).

10.4.19 Posting Goods Issue

The goods issue can be posted in EWM in various ways, some of which we already mentioned (such as when the TU is loaded or when the check-out is performed for the TU from the yard). You can also manually post goods issue from the ODO (Transaction /SCWM/PRDO) or from the S&R transactions (for example, Transaction /SCWM/TU).

For the triggering of the goods issue posting in the background, the PPF is used, and it must be customized appropriately based on the requirements (for example, to only trigger the posting when a specific condition is reached). For more information on using the PPF, see Chapter 24.

EWM also supports partial goods issues, if all of the items can't be delivered at the same time. For example, if you are loading a truck and not all of the HUs or products will fit on the truck, you can post goods issue just for the items that were actually shipped on the truck. Once the goods issue is posted in EWM, the outbound delivery (only containing the posted items) is replicated to ERP, where the corresponding delivery (and the related documents) is updated.

You can also cancel the goods issue posting from EWM, as long as you are using a release of ERP that also supports the goods issue cancellation together with EWM. To cancel (or reverse) the post goods issue, use the outbound delivery maintenance transaction (Transaction /SCWM/FD) and select the dropdown box next to the GOODS ISSUE button to select the REVERSE GOODS ISSUE option.

10.5 Summary

In this chapter, we described the outbound processes within the warehouse, including picking, packing, staging, loading, invoice printing, and goods issue. We also provided some hints about how to optimize the outbound process using the WOCR and how to optimize the execution using the resource management functions. And we discussed the S&R processes used to manage transportation planning and the execution of both the warehouse and yard functions to manage the doors and the trucks and trailers.

In the next chapter, we will discuss a special outbound process used to supply materials to the production supply area (PSA) in support of production activities.

Raw materials or components used to make semifinished or finished materials can be managed via Extended Warehouse Management (EWM) and are supplied to the production floor via the production supply integration.

11   Production Supply

When a production or process order is created in ERP, the raw materials or components necessary to execute the production can be handled by Extended Warehouse Management (EWM). In these cases, it is necessary to integrate EWM directly with the ERP Production Planning (PP) module to support the production execution. The integration can be set up in various ways, depending on the organizational structure of the production area and the warehouse. In this chapter, we will describe the various ways that the organizational structure can be set up to support the production supply integration, and we will describe the transactional processes for executing the production supply.

11.1   Organizational Structure for Production Supply

The basic method of integration between EWM and PP is using the production supply area (PSA). The logical location of the PSA with regard to the products is dependent on the organizational structure of the warehouse and the production area. The three basic options for the organizational structure are described in the following sections.

11.1.1   Single EWM Warehouse

The most common scenario for handling the production supply is to manage the stocks, including the PSA, in a single warehouse. In this case, a separate storage location is used to manage the production area and the stocks in the PSA within the warehouse are also managed within this production storage location. Stocks are moved to the PSA based on a production staging request, which is generated from the production order (see Section 11.3, Executing the Production Supply, for more details on how to generate the production staging request). When the stocks are moved to the PSA in the warehouse, they are automatically moved to the storage location of production. When the stocks are issued to the production order, either directly or via backflushing, the stocks are automatically removed from the PSA in the warehouse. Figure 11.1 shows the relationships and links between the bins in the warehouse and the organizational areas in ERP, and the normal direction of the flow of goods for the single warehouse scenario. Note in the figure that the production storage location is assigned to the same warehouse as the Available For Sale (AFS) and Received On Dock (ROD) storage locations in ERP.

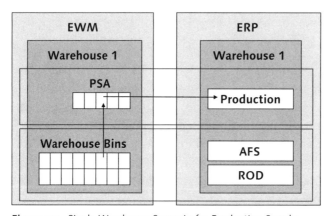

Figure 11.1   Single Warehouse Scenario for Production Supply

11.1.2   Separate EWM Warehouse

It is also possible to manage the stocks in separate warehouses, one for the stock of the warehouse and another for the stock of the production area, including production supply. In this case, the stocks moved from the warehouse to the PSA are actually moved in a multistep move, because they have to not only move from bin to bin but also from warehouse to warehouse. Once the stocks are in the PSA, the process of issuing the stocks to the production orders works the same as for the single warehouse scenario. Figure 11.2 shows the relationship and links between the bins in the warehouse and the organizational areas in ERP, and the normal direction of the flow of goods for the multiple warehouse scenario. Note in the figure that the production storage location is assigned to a separate warehouse from the AFS and ROD storage locations in ERP.

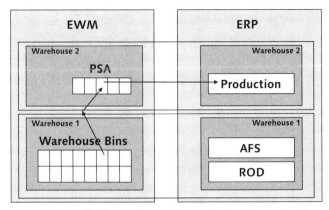

Figure 11.2 Multiple Warehouse Scenario for Production Supply

11.1.3 Non-EWM-Managed Storage Location

It is also possible to manage the stocks such that the stock in the PSA is not managed by the warehouse, but the stock is automatically transferred out of the warehouse and into the production storage location during the execution of the production staging. In this case, the issuance of stocks to the production order no longer require interaction with the EWM, because the stocks already exist at the production storage location and are no longer managed by EWM. Figure 11.3 shows the relationship and links between the bins in the warehouse and the organizational areas in ERP, and the normal direction of the flow of goods for the non-EWM-managed PSA scenario. Note in the figure that the production storage location is not assigned to an EWM-managed storage location.

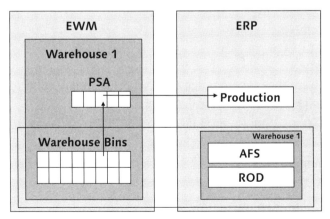

Figure 11.3 Non-EWM-Managed Production Supply Scenario

11.1.4 Configuring the Organizational Structure for Production Supply

The organizational structures described previously are configured the same way in ERP and in EWM as described in Chapter 2, Organizational Structure, and Chapter 3, The Warehouse Structure. The important distinction is the assignment of the production storage location to the warehouse in ERP and the creation of the PSA bins in EWM. In the singe warehouse scenario, the production storage location is assigned to the same warehouse as the AFS and ROD storage locations (recall that AFS and ROD are used here for examples and that your actual storage locations names may differ). In the scenario with multiple warehouses, the production storage location is assigned to the separate warehouse, and in EWM the PSA storage type and bins are set up in the separate warehouse as well. In the non-EWM-managed PSA scenario, the production storage location is not assigned to a warehouse at all, and in EWM the PSA storage types and bins are only created as interim storage types and bins within the single warehouse.

11.2 Setting Up the Integration to Production

In addition to setting up the organizational structure as described in the previous sections of this chapter, you must also set up several configuration settings and master data on both ERP and EWM to support the production supply scenario. In EWM, there are several Business Configuration Sets (BC Sets) that can be used to set up some of the basic settings for the scenario. These various BC Sets are collected into a couple of hierarchical BC Sets, including /SCWM/PROD_SUPPLY and the optional BC Set /SCWM/DLV_PROD_SUPPLY_FOR_TEST. To execute the BC Sets in EWM, follow the TOOLS • CUSTOMIZING • BUSINESS CONFIGURATION SETS menu path or use Transaction SCPR20.

The additional configuration settings that you must set up in ERP include:

▸ Movement type and delivery type configuration for production supply delivery creation, via the Implementation Guide (IMG) node: LOGISTICS EXECUTION • EXTENDED WAREHOUSE MANAGEMENT INTEGRATION • PRODUCTION PLANNING AND CONTROL • DEFINE DELIVERY TYPE DETERMINATION

▸ Automatic creation of inbound deliveries into the production storage location based on the posting of the outbound delivery from the supplying location (only for the multiple warehouse scenario) using the SPED output type for the outbound delivery, via the subcomponents of the IMG node: LOGISTICS EXECU-

TION • SHIPPING • BASIC SHIPPING FUNCTIONS • OUTPUT CONTROL • OUTPUT DETERMINATION • MAINTAIN OUTPUT DETERMINATION FOR OUTBOUND DELIVERIES

The additional configuration settings that you must set up in EWM include:

▸ Map ERP delivery types to the relevant EWM document types via the IMG node: EXTENDED WAREHOUSE MANAGEMENT • INTERFACES • ERP INTEGRATION • DELIVERY PROCESSING • MAP DOCUMENT TYPES FROM ERP SYSTEM TO EWM

▸ Map item types of ERP deliveries to the relevant EWM item types via the IMG node: EXTENDED WAREHOUSE MANAGEMENT • INTERFACES • ERP INTEGRATION • DELIVERY PROCESSING • MAP ITEM TYPES FROM ERP SYSTEM TO EWM

▸ Define the document type determination for outbound deliveries via the IMG node: EXTENDED WAREHOUSE MANAGEMENT • GOODS ISSUE PROCESS • OUTBOUND DELIVERY • DEFINE DOCUMENT TYPE DETERMINATION FOR OUTBOUND DELIVERY PROCESS

▸ Define the item type determination for outbound deliveries via the IMG node: EXTENDED WAREHOUSE MANAGEMENT • GOODS ISSUE PROCESS • OUTBOUND DELIVERY • DEFINE ITEM TYPE DETERMINATION FOR OUTBOUND DELIVERY PROCESS

▸ Define document type determination for posting changes via the IMG node: EXTENDED WAREHOUSE MANAGEMENT • INTERNAL WAREHOUSE PROCESSES • DELIVERY PROCESSING • DEFINE DOCUMENT TYPE DETERMINATION FOR THE POSTING CHANGE PROCESS

▸ Define item type determination for posting changes via the IMG node: EXTENDED WAREHOUSE MANAGEMENT • INTERNAL WAREHOUSE PROCESSES • DELIVERY PROCESSING • DEFINE ITEM TYPE DETERMINATION FOR THE POSTING CHANGE PROCESS

▸ Define document type determination for inbound deliveries via the IMG node: EXTENDED WAREHOUSE MANAGEMENT • GOODS RECEIPT PROCESS • INBOUND DELIVERY • DEFINE DOCUMENT TYPE DETERMINATION FOR INBOUND DELIVERY PROCESS

▸ Define item type determination for inbound deliveries via the IMG node: EXTENDED WAREHOUSE MANAGEMENT • GOODS RECEIPT PROCESS • INBOUND DELIVERY • DEFINE ITEM TYPE DETERMINATION FOR INBOUND DELIVERY PROCESS

▸ Assign storage locations to the appropriate availability groups (the same as the one assigned to the storage type in the following text) via the IMG node:

EXTENDED WAREHOUSE MANAGEMENT • INTERFACES • ERP INTEGRATION • GOODS MOVEMENTS • MAP STORAGE LOCATIONS FROM ERP SYSTEM TO EWM

▶ Configure relevant stock types for the production supply materials via the IMG node: EXTENDED WAREHOUSE MANAGEMENT • MASTER DATA • PRODUCT • DEFINE STOCK TYPES (note that the relevant stock types depend on which scenario you use)

▶ Configure the storage types to be used for production supply and assign the appropriate storage type roles (the role should be set to "K") and availability groups (the same as the availability group mapped to the storage location in the earlier steps) via the IMG node: EXTENDED WAREHOUSE MANAGEMENT • MASTER DATA • DEFINE STORAGE TYPE

▶ Configure the warehouse process types to be used for the production supply warehouse tasks (for both the production supply and consumption posting, deliveries commonly process types 2100 and 4100, respectively) via the IMG node: EXTENDED WAREHOUSE MANAGEMENT • CROSS-PROCESS SETTINGS • WAREHOUSE TASK • DEFINE WAREHOUSE PROCESS TYPE

▶ Configure the process type determination via the IMG node: EXTENDED WAREHOUSE MANAGEMENT • CROSS-PROCESS SETTINGS • WAREHOUSE TASK • DETERMINE WAREHOUSE PROCESS TYPE

▶ Configure automatic posting of goods issue for the consumption delivery posting, if necessary, via the IMG nodes: EXTENDED WAREHOUSE MANAGEMENT • GOODS ISSUE PROCESS • OUTBOUND DELIVERY • PRODUCTION SUPPLY • MAINTAIN SETTINGS FOR AUT. GOODS ISSUE FOR PRODUCTION SUPPLY and EXTENDED WAREHOUSE MANAGEMENT • GOODS ISSUE PROCESS • OUTBOUND DELIVERY • PRODUCTION SUPPLY • POST GOODS ISSUE FOR CONSUMPTION POSTING

The master data that you must set up to support the production supply scenario within ERP includes:

▶ Data to support the production processes, including Products, Bills of Material (BoM), Work Centers, and Routings

▶ PSA — to create the PSA from the ERP Easy Access menu, follow the LOGISTICS • LOGISTICS EXECUTION • MASTER DATA • WAREHOUSE • PRODUCTION SUPPLY • PRODUCTION SUPPLY AREA • CREATE/CHANGE menu path, or use Transaction code PK05

▶ Control Cycle Records — to create the control cycle records from the ERP Easy Access menu, follow the Logistics • Logistics Execution • Master Data • Warehouse • Production Supply • Control Cycle Production Supply • Create menu path, or use Transaction code LPK1. Within the control cycle record, you specify the method for determination of the production supply quantities, including the following options:

  ▶ Pick parts — individual components are picked and supplied to the PSA order by order

  ▶ Release order parts — allows requests of parts independent of individual orders; especially for using production supply with EWM to process orders

  ▶ Crate parts — used for materials stored in crates or other standard-size containers and allows requests for parts independent of individual orders, based on emptying of a container currently held in the PSA; replenishment for crate parts is generated directly in EWM using Transaction /SCWM/REPL

The master data that you must set up to support the production supply scenario within EWM includes:

▶ Products, as described in detail in Chapter 4, Product Master Data

▶ PSA — To create the PSA from the EWM Easy Access menu, follow the Extended Warehouse Management • Master Data • Production Supply Area (PSA) • Define PSA menu path, or use Transaction code /SCWM/PSA. If you manually create the PSAs, you must also create the mapping between the EWM PSA and the ERP PSA by following the Extended Warehouse Management • Interfaces • ERP Integration • Map Production Supply Area (PSA) menu path, or using Transaction code /SCWM/PSAMAP

▶ Alternatively, you can transfer the PSAs from ERP to EWM by following the Extended Warehouse Management • Interfaces • ERP Integration • Repli-

CATE PRODUCTION SUPPLY AREA (PSA) menu path, or using Transaction code /SCWM/PSA_REPLICATE

▸ Warehouse storage bins in the production staging storage type, as described in detail in Chapter 5, Other Warehouse Master Data

▸ Assignment of the bin to the product and the PSA — To assign the bins to the product, PSA, and party entitled from the EWM Easy Access menu, follow the EXTENDED WAREHOUSE MANAGEMENT • MASTER DATA • PRODUCTION SUPPLY AREA (PSA) • ASSIGN BIN TO PSA/PRODUCT/ENTITLED IN WAREHOUSE NUMBER menu path, or use Transaction code /SCWM/PSASTAGE. Alternatively, you can assign the bin to the product and party entitled for a PSA by following the EXTENDED WAREHOUSE MANAGEMENT • MASTER DATA • PRODUCTION SUPPLY AREA (PSA) • ASSIGN BIN TO PRODUCT/ENTITLED IN PSA menu path, or using Transaction code /SCWM/PSASTAGE2.

11.3 Executing the Production Supply

Now that you understand the setup necessary to support the production supply process, we will describe the business processes being supported in the following sections. The basic steps of the production supply execution include:

▸ Generation of the production (or process) order

▸ Release of the production order

▸ Initiation of production staging

▸ Executing the picks for production

▸ Confirming the production order

▸ Backflushing, or directly issuing, the components for production

▸ Closing and settling the production order

In this chapter, we will focus on the EWM-relevant portions of the production process, including the production staging, picking, and goods issuing or backflushing.

> **Note**
>
> In this chapter, we will focus primarily on the common production supply scenario for picking pick parts using a single warehouse. The scenarios using multiple warehouses, or where the PSA is not in the warehouse, will work similarly but with some differences, as indicated in the following sections.

11.3.1 Production Staging

Once the production order is created and released, it is ready for production staging, which is the process of requesting the products to be supplied from the warehouse to the PSA so that the production operators can access the necessary components for seamlessly continuing the production process. To execute the production staging, access the production order in ERP from the Easy Access menu by following the LOGISTICS • PRODUCTION • SHOP FLOOR CONTROL • ORDER • CHANGE menu path, or using Transaction code CO02 (note: it is also possible to execute the creation, release, and staging in a single step during the order creation). After entering the order number and pressing ⌗Enter⌗ to access the order information (as seen in Figure 11.4), follow the FUNCTIONS • WM MATERIAL STAGING• EXECUTE menu path, and save the order. The result will be the creation of an outbound delivery in ERP, which is distributed to EWM to pick the components for the order and deliver them to the PSA.

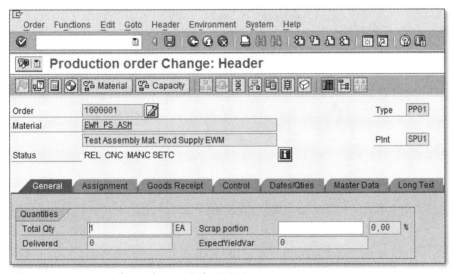

Figure 11.4 Creation of a Production Order in ERP

> **Note**
>
> You can also generate material staging for process orders using the *pull list* process for release order parts (using Transaction MF60).

To check the deliveries created for the production staging, view the outbound deliveries using the Outbound Delivery Monitor (from the SAP Easy Access menu, follow the LOGISTICS • LOGISTICS EXECUTION • OUTBOUND PROCESS • GOODS ISSUE FOR OUTBOUND DELIVERY • LISTS AND LOGS • OUTBOUND DELIVERY MONITOR menu path, or use Transaction code VL06O). As you can see in Figure 11.5, you can use the PSA or the production order number to find the relevant outbound delivery. You can then drill down into the delivery by double-clicking on the delivery number. Note that the production order number is not visible in the standard screens for the delivery display, however, the delivery line is tied to the production order (which is why you can select the delivery using the production order number as described earlier) — you can see the link between the ERP delivery line and the production order via Transaction SE16 on table LIPS, field AUFNR.

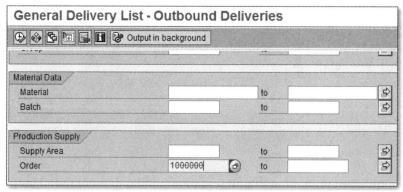

Figure 11.5 Selecting the Outbound Delivery for Production Supply on ERP Based on the Production Order Number

11.3.2 Executing the Picks for Production

Once the outbound delivery is created in ERP, it is transferred to EWM (the same as described in Chapter 10, Outbound Processing), and you can execute the picking for the outbound delivery. However, there is one significant difference to the outbound process for sales orders — namely, the outbound delivery for production supply is actually a *posting change* delivery (ahead of the posting change is the creation of a posting change request — just like with the Outbound Delivery Order (ODO) creation from the Outbound Delivery Request (ODR), the posting change creation from the posting change request is normally automated). Therefore, to start the process you must use the posting change maintenance transaction. To start the transaction from the EWM Easy Access menu, follow the EXTENDED

WAREHOUSE MANAGEMENT • DELIVERY PROCESSING • POSTING CHANGE • MAINTAIN POSTING CHANGE menu path, or use Transaction code /SCWM/IM_PC. From the delivery maintenance transaction, you can select the delivery according to the production order number or the ERP outbound delivery number. In Figure 11.6, you can see the selection of the POSTING CHANGE according to the production order number.

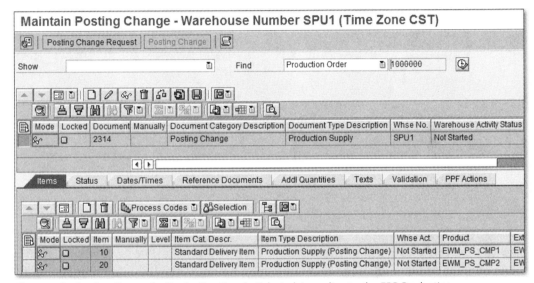

Figure 11.6 Posting Change for Production Supply, Selected According to the ERP Production Order Number

From the delivery maintenance transaction, you can generate the warehouse tasks by following the menu path POSTING CHANGE • FOLLOW-ON FUNCTIONS • WAREHOUSE TASK. From there, the normal picking and posting of the posting change delivery takes place in a way similar to the processing of ODOs as described in Chapter 10, Outbound Processing.

To access the relevant documents via the EWM Warehouse Monitor (Transaction /SCWM/MON), be sure to use the POSTING CHANGES node, via the DOCUMENTS • POSTING CHANGES menu path, as seen in Figure 11.7.

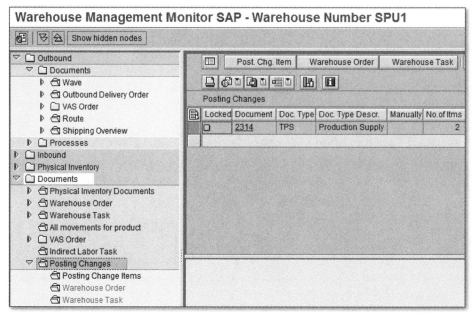

Figure 11.7 Selection of the Posting Change Deliveries for Production Supply, via the Posting Changes Node in the Warehouse Monitor

When the posting change delivery is posted and transferred to ERP, the stock will be moved in ERP from the warehouse storage location to the production storage location. If the production storage location is not in the warehouse, the stock will be removed from the warehouse entirely during the goods issue. And if the stock is being moved to another warehouse (as in the multiple warehouse scenario), the goods issue will also result in the creation of an inbound delivery to the receiving warehouse via the SPED output type in ERP, then the inbound delivery will be automatically processed in the receiving warehouse and the stock added to the PSA.

With the single warehouse scenario, it is also possible to configure the transfer of stock from the warehouse to the PSA using a two-step procedure, if you need to model a transportation process when moving from one to the other.

11.3.3 Goods Issue and Backflushing

Once you supply the products to the PSA and transmit the posting change delivery to ERP, ERP can see the inventory in the PSA. After the production operator physically executes the production, he may confirm the production (or process) order, which can trigger the backflushing of components from the PSA and issuance to the order (which triggers the inventory posting and financial postings related to the inventory movement, and provides an input to the settlement of the production order for costing). Alternatively, the operator can trigger the goods issue interactively via the inventory management transactions (e.g., Transaction MIGO). In either case, the goods issue does not occur immediately, but an outbound delivery is created and submitted to EWM (if the production storage location is warehouse managed), where it should be automatically processed and the EWM outbound delivery posted back to ERP. The posting of the outbound delivery from EWM and transfer of the goods issue to ERP results in the removal of the stock from the EWM PSA and posting of the inventory movement in inventory management. In the end, EWM and ERP should be consistent in terms of the stock remaining in the PSA.

If the production storage location is not EWM managed, the goods issue, or backflushing, does not need to be transmitted to the warehouse. Because the stock is already in the production storage location, it can be issued directly.

11.4   Summary

In this chapter, we described the setup and transactional processing for the supply of components from the warehouse to the production storage location for production supply to a production order (or process order). We described the process options, the configuration and master data required for setup, and the transactional process flow. You should now be able to set up the basic process and execute the production supply. In the coming chapters, we will describe the internal processes of EWM, monitoring and analytics, exception handling, and several special processes within the warehouse.

The use of internal movements such as replenishment, rearrangement, and internal transfers are an important aspect of ensuring efficient warehouse operations. Effective use of these activities can improve order fill times and warehouse space utilization.

12   Internal Warehouse Movements

In this chapter, we will discuss the configuration and use of internal warehouse movements, including:

- Replenishment (including the five basic replenishment strategies)
- Rearrangement (including alerts for monitoring the warehouse for possible rearrangement moves)
- Ad hoc movements
- Posting changes

Using internal warehouse movements effectively can contribute to improvements in warehouse operations by reducing order fill times, and reducing warehouse space requirements. At the end of this chapter, you should be able to use and understand the different options that EWM offers for internal warehouse movements.

12.1   Replenishment

During replenishment, a quantity of a material is moved from a reserve area to a primary or forward picking area. The forward picking area is filled according to the quantity requirements of the materials in that area. The required material quantity can either be determined for the storage type as a whole or, in the case of a fixed bin scenario, for each individual fixed bin in the primary area.

In EWM there are five basic replenishment strategies (each of which we will discuss in detail in this chapter), namely:

- Planned replenishment
- Order-related replenishment
- Crate part replenishment
- Direct replenishment
- Automatic replenishment

In the following sections, we will briefly explain the difference between planned and unplanned replenishment, then we will look at the basic configuration for replenishment and discuss each of the five replenishment strategies in more detail.

12.1.1 Planned and Unplanned Replenishment

In EWM, there are two basic categories of replenishment strategies — planned and unplanned. Planned replenishment, order-driven replenishment, and crate part replenishment are planned replenishment strategies, which means that they are executed at specific times. This can be executed manually by following the Extended Warehouse Management • work scheduling • Schedule Replenishment menu path, or using Transaction code /SCWM/REPL. You can also execute the report for the replenishment in batch mode, by scheduling the execution of program /SCWM/REPLENISHMENT using a variant (as seen later in this chapter in Figure 12.9).

The unplanned replenishment strategies include *direct replenishment* and *automatic replenishment*, which are triggered during the execution of transaction on an ad hoc basis. The replenishment can be triggered, for example, when a picker is directed to a fixed bin that doesn't have sufficient quantity, or, in the case of automatic replenishment, during the confirmation of a pick task when the quantity in the source bin falls below the minimum level. These unplanned replenishment activities are not performed in batch mode.

12.1.2 Configuration for Replenishment

In the following description of the required configuration for replenishment, we will refer to a simple scenario where a primary (or forward picking) Storage Type 0050 is replenished from a reserve storage type (as seen in Figure 12.1).

484

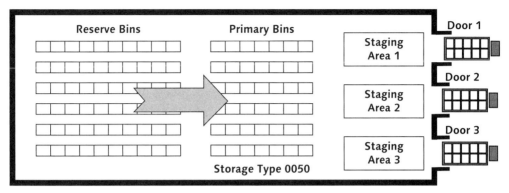

Figure 12.1 Replenishment from Reserve Bins to Primary Bins

Storage Type Configuration: Storage Type Level or Bin Level Replenishment

During the setup of the replenishment processes, you must first evaluate whether the replenishment in a storage type will be executed at a *storage type level* or *storage bin level for a fixed bin scenario*. On the storage type configuration (accessed in the EWM IMG via the EXTENDED WAREHOUSE MANAGEMENT • MASTER DATA • DEFINE STORAGE TYPE menu path), you use the REPL. LEVEL indicator to make this distinction. In Figure 12.2, you can see the storage type settings for replenishment.

You can choose to replenish a material based on the total quantity of a material in a storage type using the *replenishment at a storage type level* strategy. In that case, the minimum and maximum quantities from the material master are considered. You can also replenish individual fixed bins in a storage type using the *storage bin level for fixed bins strategy*. In that case, the minimum and maximum quantities are taken from the quantites specified in the fixed bin table (Transaction /SCWM/BINMAT, as also described in Chapter 5, Other Warehouse Master Data).

Basic Replenishment Configuration

The basic configuration for each type of replenishment can be found in the EWM Implementation Guide (IMG) by following the menu path EXTENDED WAREHOUSE MANAGEMENT • INTERNAL WAREHOUSE PROCESSES • REPLENISHMENT CONTROL. First, you can specify the EXECUTION TIME FOR REPLENISHMENT, as seen in Figure 12.3. By defining the execution time indicator and maintaining it on the replenishment strategy, the system calculates the planned completion time for the warehouse task or the replenishment warehouse request by adding the entered execution time to the current system time.

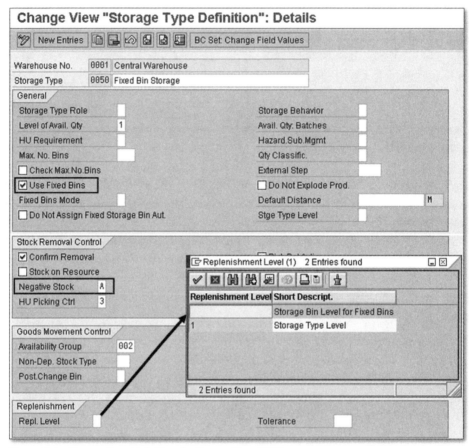

Figure 12.2 Storage Type Definition for Storage Type 0050

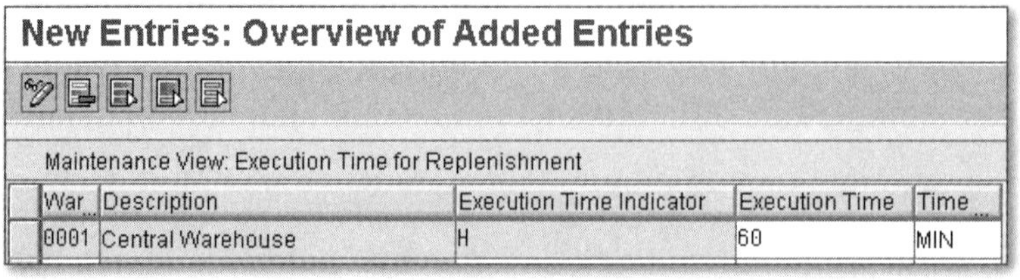

Figure 12.3 Execution Times for Replenishment

You can then configure the replenishment strategies that are intended to be used in a specific storage type in the EWM IMG by following the EXTENDED WAREHOUSE MANAGEMENT • INTERNAL WAREHOUSE PROCESSES • REPLENISHMENT CONTROL • ACTIVATE REPLENISHMENT STRATEGIES IN STORAGE TYPE menu path, as seen in Figure 12.4.

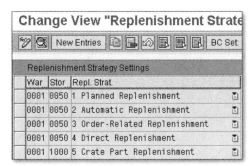

Figure 12.4 Activate Replenishment Strategies in Storage Type

For each replenishment strategy for each storage type, you can specify several settings (as seen in Figure 12.5), including the following:

▶ REPL. STRAT.

In this case, the replenishment strategy 1 PLANNED REPLENISHMENT has been activated.

▶ WHSE PROC. TYPE

When performing the planned replenishment the standard delivered warehouse process type 3010 can be used. This process type is also used to determine the reserve area from which the replenishment quantity is taken.

▶ QTY TYPE USED

For the calculation of the current stock in the bin, the physical quantity can be used (rather than the available quantity).

▶ WT IMMED.

When the replenishment is executed the warehouse task is created immediately (instead of a warehouse request being created).

Change View "Replenishment Strategy Settings": Details

New Entries | BC Set: Change Field Values

Warehouse No.   0001 Central Warehouse
Storage Type   0050 Fixed Bin Storage
Repl. Strat.   1 Planned Replenishment

Replenishment Strategy Settings

Whse Proc. Type   3010
Qty Type Used   Physical Quantity
Ind. Exec. Time   H

☐ Consider only unblocked stock
☐ Pckr-Drvn Repl.   ☑ WT Immed.
Storage Type   ☐ Do not consider putaway quantity
St. Type Group   ☐ New quantity at WT creation

Figure 12.5 Settings for a Replenishment Strategy for a Storage Type

Document/Item Categories for Replenishment Warehouse Requests

In the last basic customizing setting for replenishment, you can assign the document and item type for the creation of a warehouse request for replenishment (as seen in Figure 12.6). This customizing can be found in the EWM IMG by following the menu path EXTENDED WAREHOUSE MANAGEMENT • INTERNAL WAREHOUSE PROCESSES • REPLENISHMENT CONTROL • MAINTAIN DOCUMENT/ITEM CATEGORIES FOR REPLENISHMENT WAREHOUSE REQUEST. The advantage that the creation of a warehouse requests offers over creating the warehouse task immediately is that they can be assigned to a wave. The wave can then be released at a suitable time — for example, you can release the wave outside of the peak picking times.

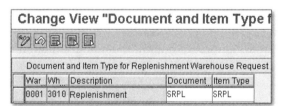

Change View "Document and Item Type f

Document and Item Type for Replenishment Warehouse Request

War	Wh	Description	Document	Item Type
0001	3010	Replenishment	SRPL	SRPL

Figure 12.6 Document and Item Categories for Creation of Replenishment Warehouse Requests

12.1.3   Planned Replenishment

During planned replenishment the system calculates the replenishment in accordance with the defined MIN. QTY and MAX. QTY. Replenishment control is triggered when the stock is less than the minimum quantity. The system then rounds down the replenishment quantity to a multiple of the minimum replenishment quantity. The replenishment quantity is the calculated quantity for which the warehouse task or the warehouse request is created.

As a prerequisite, you must assign a fixed bin on the fixed bin table from the EWM Easy Access menu by following the EXTENDED WAREHOUSE MANAGEMENT • MASTER DATA • STORAGE BIN • MAINTAIN FIXED STORAGE BIN menu path, or using Transaction code /SCWM/BINMAT. In Figure 12.7, you can see the assignment of a fixed bin within the primary picking storage type (0050, in our example).

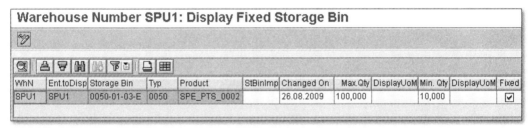

Figure 12.7   Maintenance of the Fixed Storage Bin for a Product

In addition to the configuration and fixed bin assignment, you can also specify the MIN. QTY and MAX. QTY and the replenishment quantities on the product master data (as described in detail in Chapter 4, Production Master Data). In Figure 12.8, you can see that the MIN. REPLENISH. QUANTITY for storage type 0050 for the given product is set to 4 EA.

To execute the planned replenishment from the EWM Easy Access menu, follow the EXTENDED WAREHOUSE MANAGEMENT • WORK SCHEDULING • SCHEDULE REPLENISHMENT menu path, or use Transaction code /SCWM/REPL. In the example seen in Figure 12.9, the planned replenishment is performed specifically for material SPE_PTS_0002 in bin 0050-01-03-E (in STORAGE TYPE 0050).

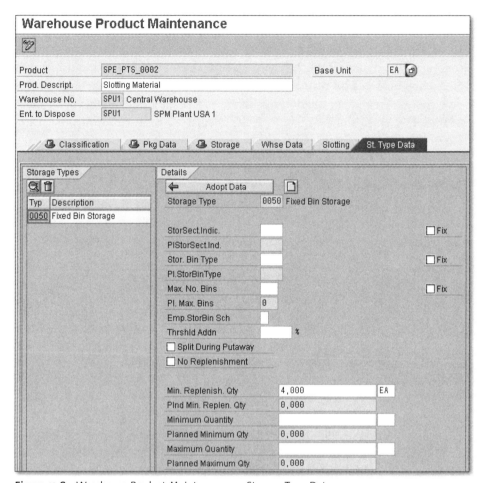

Figure 12.8 Warehouse Product Maintenance — Storage Type Data

The result of the replenishment calculation is that 92 EA will be replenished to the destination bin 0050-01-03-E and when saving the replenishment items the WT will be created immediately (as specified by selection of the WT IMMED. indicator). In Figure 12.10, you can see the resulting PLANNED REPLENISHMENT ITEMS, which resulted from the selections in Figure 12.9.

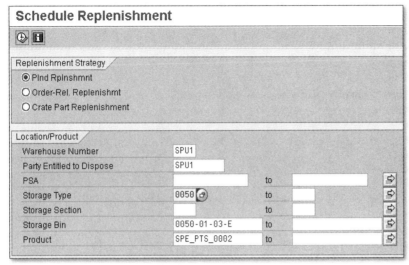

Figure 12.9 Replenishment Transaction Selection Screen

Figure 12.10 Planned Replenishment Items

Example

The calculations for the planned replenishment for the preceding example are shown here in additional detail.

Current bin quantity:	5 EA
Minimum quantity:	10 EA
Maximum quantity:	100 EA
Minimum replenishment quantity:	4 EA

The replenishment quantity is calculated as the difference between the maximum bin quantity and the current bin quantity, and then it is rounded to a multiple of the minimum replenishment.

> Maximum Qty – Current Bin Qty = 100 EA – 5 EA = 95 EA
>
> Rounding down 95 EA to the nearest multiple of the minimum replenishment quantity (4 EA) results in a calculated replenishment quantity of 92 EA.

12.1.4 Order-Related Replenishment

During order-related replenishment, the system calculates the replenishment in accordance with the quantity of the selected open outbound delivery orders (ODOs). To execute order-related replenishment, you must activate the order-related replenishment strategy for the storage type as described previously. In Figure 12.11, you can see the settings for the order-related replenishment for a storage type.

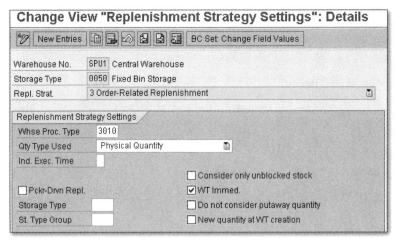

Figure 12.11 Activate Order-related Replenishment in Storage Type 0050

In order for order-related replenishment to consider an ODO, a Rough Bin Determination must be performed for the ODO item. To activate the Rough Bin Determination for the process type determined for the ODO item in the EWM IMG, follow the menu path Extended Warehouse Management • Cross-Process Settings • Warehouse Task • Define Warehouse Process Type (as seen in Figure 12.12).

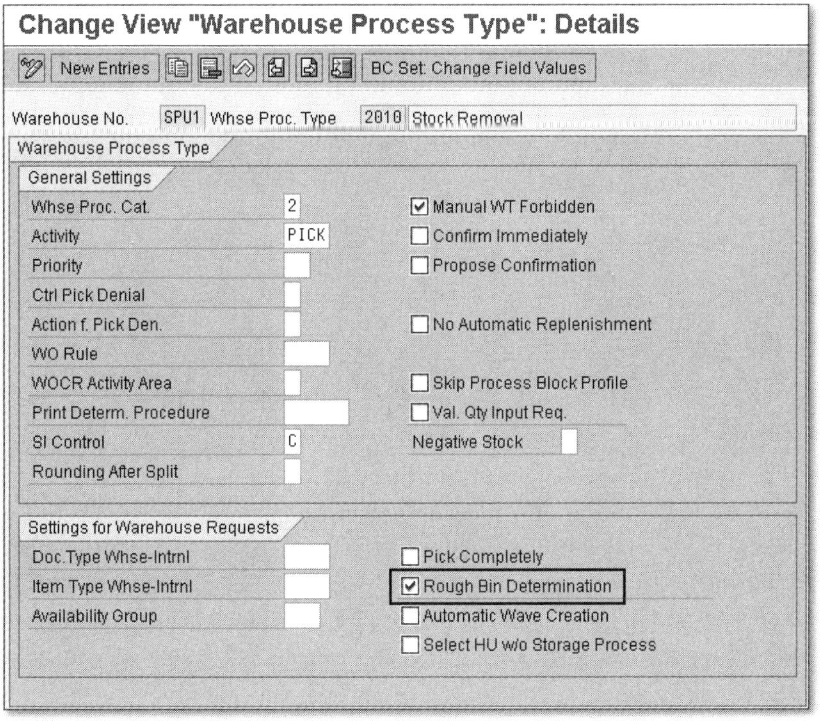

Figure 12.12 Switch on Rough Bin Determination on the Process Type

If the rough bin determination on the ODO was successful, the STORAGE BIN on the ODO item should be filled (as seen in Figure 12.13). If two or more bins are determined during the rough bin determination, the storage bin fields on the ODO item are empty, and entries for the individual bins are made in the table /SCWM/ DB_ITEMSPL.

Replenishment control is triggered when the stock in the bin is less than the required quantity, which is the total of all of the quantities of the ODOs. In order-related replenishment, the system *rounds up* the replenishment quantity to a multiple of the *minimum replenishment quantity* (as seen in Figure 12.9) to ensure that the replenishment quantity meets the demand of the open warehouse requests.

493

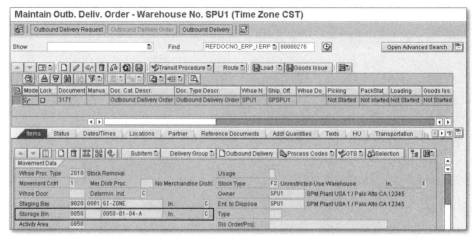

Figure 12.13 Rough Bin Determination on the ODO

To trigger the creation of the order-related replenishment tasks, you use the same transaction as for the planned replenishment task creation (Transaction /SCWM/ REPL). However, the selection criteria available on the screen with regard to open warehouse requests (e.g., GOODS ISSUE DATE, WAVE RELEASE TIME FROM, WAVE, WAVE TEMPLATE, etc.) are now relevant (as seen in Figure 12.14).

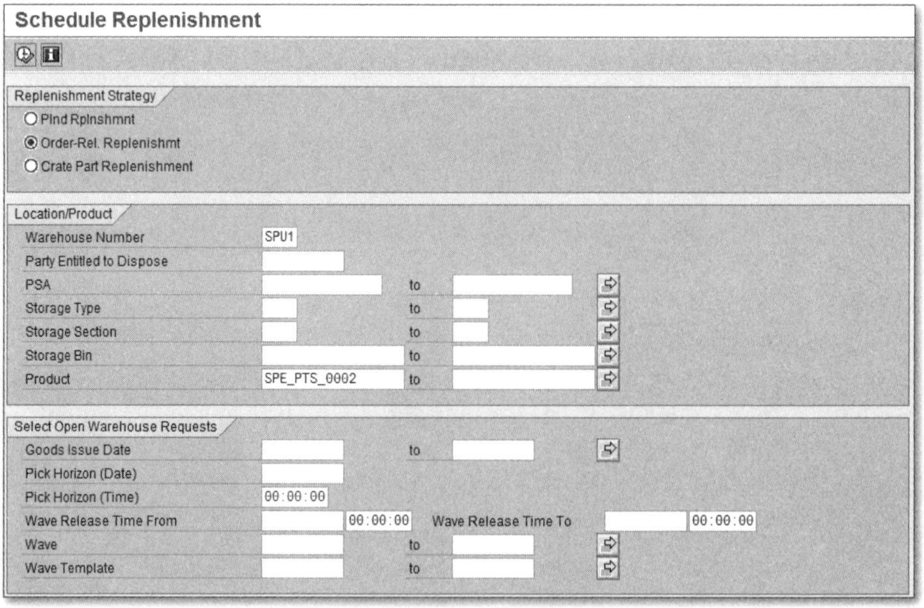

Figure 12.14 Selection Criteria for Order-related Replenishment

In our example, because the quantity of the open ODO was 20 EA and the minimum replenishment quantity on the material master was 3 EA, the calculated replenishment quantity is 21 EA (as seen in Figure 12.15).

Example
Current bin quantity: 0 EA
Minimum quantity: 10 EA
Maximum quantity: 100 EA
Minimum replenishment quantity: 3 EA
To calculate the replenishment quantity, take the difference between the maximum bin quantity and the current bin quantity to a multiple of the minimum replenishment quantity, and round it up to the nearest multiple of the replenishment quantity.
Total ODO quantities = 20 EA
Rounding up the total ODO quantity (20 EA) to the nearest multiple of the minimum replenishment quantity (3 EA) gives a replenishment quantity of 21 EA.

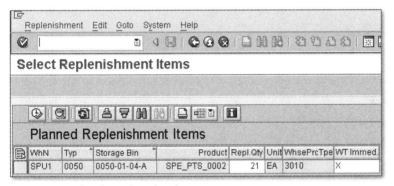

Figure 12.15 The Planned Replenishment Items

In order-related replenishment, the maximum quantity specified for the product or for the bin can be exceeded by selecting the EXCEED MAXIMUM QUANTITY indicator in the selection criteria (as shown in Figure 12.16). Even though the replenishment quantity can exceed the maximum quantity of the bin, during the WT creation the capacity of the bin is still considered (the capacity utilization of the total quantity of the bin is still not allowed to exceed the bin capacity).

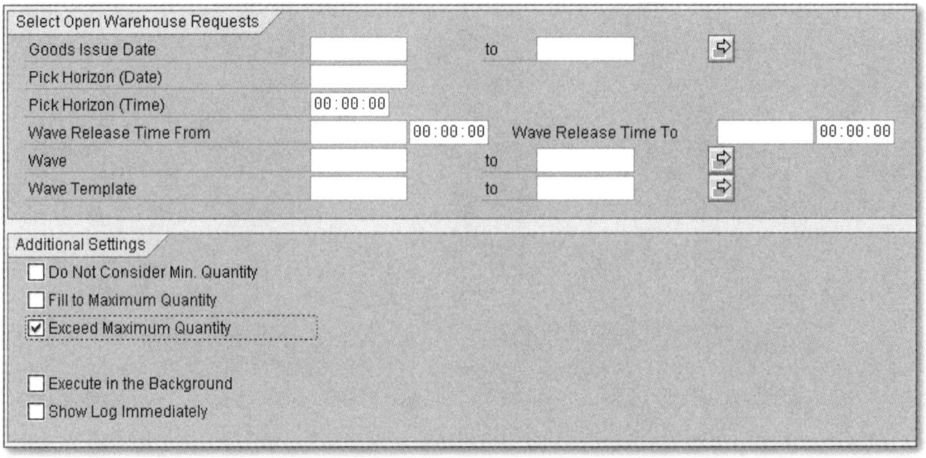

Figure 12.16 Specifying the Indicator to Exceed the Maximum Quantity during Order-related Replenishment

12.1.5 Crate Part Replenishment

Crate parts are parts that are typically replenished in fixed quantities, such as full pallets or other fixed-size containers, independent of the existing order quantities (such as in the kanban technique, for example). Crate part replenishment allows you to organize the replenishment of these crate parts to production supply areas (PSAs) for production supply. The crate part replenishment can be activated for a storage type in the same manner the other replenishment types described previously (in the EWM IMG by following the menu path EXTENDED WAREHOUSE MANAGEMENT • INTERNAL WAREHOUSE PROCESSES • REPLENISHMENT CONTROL • ACTIVATE REPLENISHMENT STRATEGIES IN STORAGE TYPE).

To enable the crate part replenishment, a PSA must be created via the EWM Easy Access menu by following the EXTENDED WAREHOUSE MANAGEMENT • MASTER DATA • PRODUCTION SUPPLY AREA (PSA) • DEFINE PSA menu path, or by using Transaction code /SCWM/PSA (as seen in Figure 12.17).

A storage bin also needs to be assigned to the PSA (as seen in figure 12.18) in the EWM Easy Access menu by following the EXTENDED WAREHOUSE MANAGEMENT • MASTER DATA • PRODUCTION SUPPLY AREA (PSA) • ASSIGN BIN TO PSA/PRODUCT/ ENTITLED IN WAREHOUSE NUMBER menu path, or using Transaction code /SCWM/ PSASTAGE.

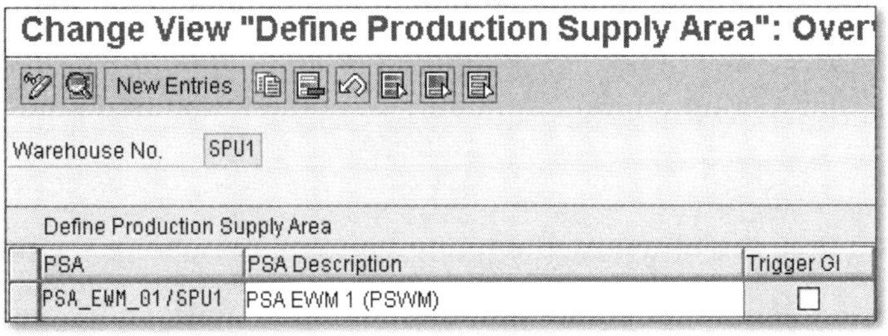

Figure 12.17 Define PSA

In addition, you can also specify for the entitled to dispose and PSA (as also seen in Figure 12.18), the minimum production quantity (the replenishment starts as soon as the storage bin quantity falls below this minimum quantity), and the crate part replenishment quantity (which determines the REPLENISHMENT QUANTITY, which will be calculated as the multiple of this crate quantity).

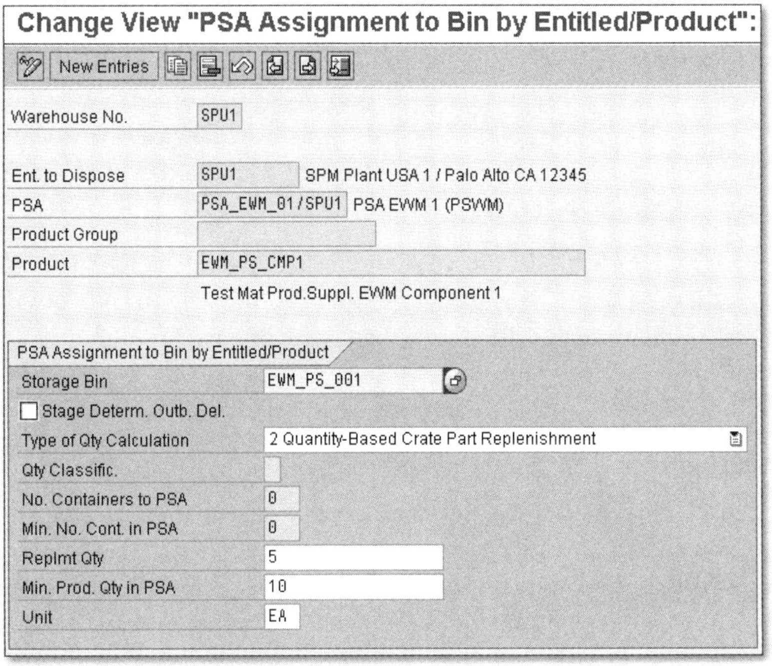

Figure 12.18 Assigning a Storage Bin to the PSA

In Figure 12.19, you can see the replenishment items created for this example. The REPL. QTY is calculated as 10 EA, because the crate part replenishment quantity is 5

EA and the MIN. PROD. QTY IN PSA is 10 EA (as specified in the PSA assignment for the product in Figure 12.18). Therefore, 2 crates of 5 EA will equal the minimum quantity of 10 EA, which results in the REPL. QTY of 10 EA.

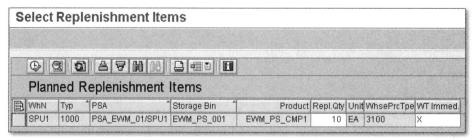

Figure 12.19 Create Replenishment Items Created for a PSA

12.1.6 Direct Replenishment

Direct replenishment is only possible in fixed storage bin scenarios. It is started during a bin denial when an exception code refers to the internal process code REPLENISHMENT. The system calculates the replenishment in accordance with the maximum and minimum quantity, and it assumes that the quantity at the storage bin is zero. The system rounds down the replenishment quantity to a multiple of the minimum replenishment quantity.

When a picker goes to a pick bin and discovers that there is not enough material available, he can trigger a direct replenishment through an exception code in the radio frequency (RF) environment. There are then two options:

▸ A replenishment can be created in the background for a different resource (which is often beneficial if the reserve area is further away from the bin that needs to be replenished).

▸ The picker himself can replenish the bin (which may be useful if the reserve bin is very close to the fixed bin and easily accessible to the picker). This strategy is known as a picker-driven replenishment. In this case, a warehouse task is displayed in RF for the replenishment as the next item to be processed in the picker's warehouse order (WO). As a prerequisite, the system must have found stock in the permitted storage types (as you can see in the configuration displayed in Figure 12.20). *Picker-driven replenishment* is only possible in RF scenarios.

In order for direct replenishment to work, the replenishment strategy for the storage type must be activated (as described earlier).

In the replenishment strategy settings, in addition to activating the PCKR-DRVN REPL., you can also specify either the STORAGE TYPE as the source ST. TYPE GROUP for the replenishment task, or you can specify a storage type group for the source bin determination.

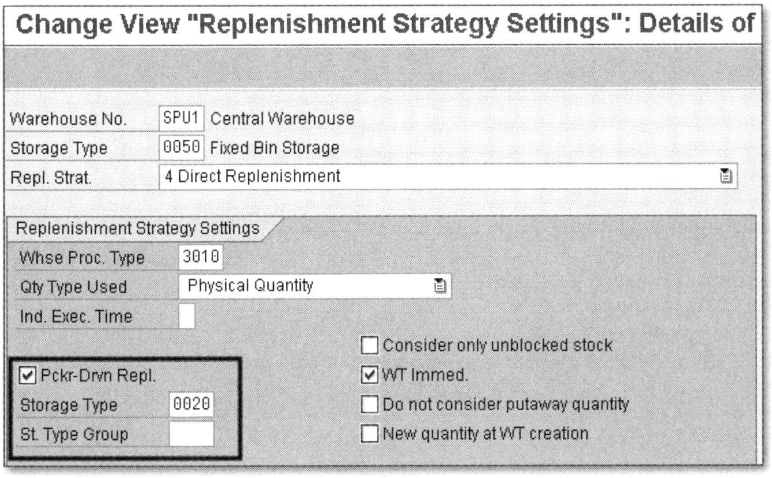

Figure 12.20 Activate Direct Replenishment in Storage Type 0050

In Figure 12.21, you can see an example of the process for a picker-driven direct replenishment. When the picker arrives at the storage bin and sees that insufficient quantity is available in the bin, he can enter the exception code REPL (which has been assigned to the internal exception code REPLENISHMENT). The system would then start the direct replenishment and find the material in the reserve area (as specified in the setup seen in Figure 12.20). The next screen displayed to the picker would then be the replenishment task (in the example, the determined quantity was 100 EA). After the replenishment is completed, the original pick (which could now be executed) would be displayed to the picker.

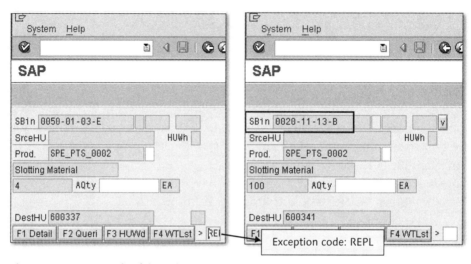

Figure 12.21 An Example of the Picker-driven Replenishment

12.1.7 Automatic Replenishment

Automatic replenishment is another unplanned replenishment technique. When this replenishment strategy is activated in the configuration (in the EWM IMG via the EXTENDED WAREHOUSE MANAGEMENT • INTERNAL WAREHOUSE PROCESSES • REPLENISHMENT CONTROL • ACTIVATE REPLENISHMENT STRATEGIES IN STORAGE TYPE menu path), it automatically triggers a replenishment of a particular bin in the background when you confirm a warehouse task and the quantity in the *source bin* falls below the minimum quantity specified for the bin or storage type. Automatic replenishment calculates the replenishment quantity in accordance with the maximum and minimum quantity, and always *rounds down* the replenishment quantity to a multiple of the minimum replenishment quantity.

12.2 Rearrangement

During rearrangement, the original storage concepts in the warehouse, as determined during the slotting process, are compared with the actual location of products in the warehouse. To determine which products are in the least optimal current location versus their optimal location, rearrangement uses evaluation points that can be maintained in the configuration.

A typical case for rearrangement is a material that previously did not have a high demand or has a seasonal demand (for example, umbrellas) and was therefore stored in a slow mover area. After the latest slotting run (which occurred, for example, in September), the product was identified as having a much higher demand in the coming months and was therefore slotted to a section for fast movers and also to a bin type of a larger size (as seen in the example in Figure 12.22).

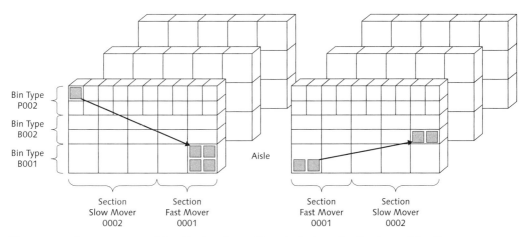

Figure 12.22 Rearrangement of One Product from a Slow- to Fast-moving Section and Another from a Fast- to Slow-moving Section

In the example shown in Figure 12.22, you can see on the left side of the diagram a rearrangement move for a material moving from a slow mover section to a fast mover section nearer the aisle. The bin type also has to change to be suitable for the larger quantity required of the material in the coming months.

On the other hand, you can also see on the right side of the diagram a previously fast moving part (which is currently not fully occupying its bin due to reduced demand) that can be moved to the section for slower moving parts further away from the aisle and put in a smaller bin type to optimize overall bin space.

12.2.1 Additional General Configuration for Rearrangement

The general configuration for rearrangement is similar to the setup for replenishment described previously (see Figures 12.3 - 12.6 and the related text). In the following sections, we focus on the setup for the warehouse process type related to rearrangement (process type 3020 in the standard delivered configuration).

Rearrangement General Configuration

The general customizing for rearrangement can be found in the EWM IMG by following the menu path EXTENDED WAREHOUSE MANAGEMENT • INTERNAL WARE-HOUSE PROCESSES • WAREHOUSE OPTIMIZATION. Here, you can execute the DEFAULT VALUES FOR REARRANGEMENT activity, as seen in Figure 12.23. For each warehouse, you specify a default process type and specify whether the material needs to be moved to the global optimal storage type or to the optimal storage type in that storage type group during creation of a rearrangement task. Here, you can also specify the execution times for the rearrangement.

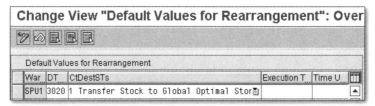

Figure 12.23 Customizing for Default Values for Rearrangement

To specify the document type and item type for the warehouse requests for rearrangement in the EWM IMG, follow the menu path EXTENDED WAREHOUSE MANAGEMENT • INTERNAL WAREHOUSE PROCESSES • WAREHOUSE OPTIMIZATION • SPECIFY DOCUMENT TYPE AND ITEM TYPE FOR REARRANGEMENT. These documents and item types are used when a warehouse request for rearrangement should be created instead of immediately creating a warehouse task (see Figure 12.24). Warehouse requests have the advantage that the rearrangement tasks can be released at suitable times to smooth the workflow in the warehouse.

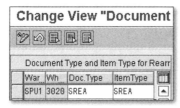

Figure 12.24 Customizing of Document and Item Type for Rearrangement

Evaluation Points

During the creation of rearrangement tasks, the system can suggest to you which rearrangements provide the most benefit to execute. This evaluation is based on the setup of evaluation points, or what is called the slotting index.

In order for rearrangement to determine which of the current suboptimal material locations are the worst compared to their optimal locations, these evaluation points are used. The evaluation points can be maintained in customizing in three different areas in the IMG (one each for storage type, storage section, and bin type search strategies). They can be found in the EWM IMG by following the EXTENDED WAREHOUSE MANAGEMENT • GOODS RECEIPT PROCESS • STRATEGIES menu path, then following:

- STORAGE TYPE SEARCH • ASSIGN STORAGE TYPES TO STORAGE TYPE SEARCH SEQUENCE
- STORAGE SECTION SEARCH • MAINTAIN STORAGE SECTION SEARCH SEQUENCE
- STORAGE BIN DETERMINATION • ALTERNATIVE STORAGE BIN TYPE SEQUENCE

During rearrangement, the evaluation points for storage type, storage section, and bin type are added together from the three customizing tables to calculate the overall evaluation for each current bin. In this evaluation, *higher numbers indicate a worse position* compared to the optimal location.

The configuration for STORAGE TYPE SEARCH SEQUENCE FOR PUTAWAY (as seen in Figure 12.25) specifies a *point value per storage type* in the search sequence for putaway. In this example, the first storage type in the search sequence (0020) receives no evaluation points, but the second storage type in the sequence (0050) receives a "penalty" of 100 POINTS.

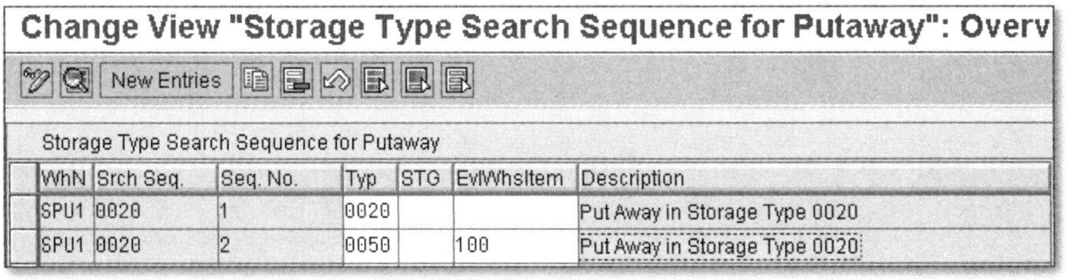
Change View "Storage Type Search Sequence for Putaway": Overv

New Entries

Storage Type Search Sequence for Putaway

WhN	Srch Seq.	Seq. No.	Typ	STG	EvlWhsItem	Description
SPU1	0020	1	0020			Put Away in Storage Type 0020
SPU1	0020	2	0050		100	Put Away in Storage Type 0020

Figure 12.25 Evaluation Points for Storage Types

Similar to the evaluation point assignment in the storage type search sequence, the Storage Section Search Sequence No. (as shown in Figure 12.26) assigns points according to the section in the storage section search sequence for putaway. In this example, for storage type 0020 and section indicator FAST, the first storage section in the sequence (0001) doesn't receive any evaluation points, whereas the second storage section in the sequence (0002) receives 10 "penalty" points, and so on.

> **Note**
>
> The evaluation points of the slotting index are additive within the sequence. In other words, the total slotting index for the third sequence number in the given sequence is the sum of the evaluation points for the first and second and third sequence numbers. In the example provided in Figure 12.26, an item in section 0003 would be given a total of 20 (0 + 10 + 10) evaluation points for the storage section.

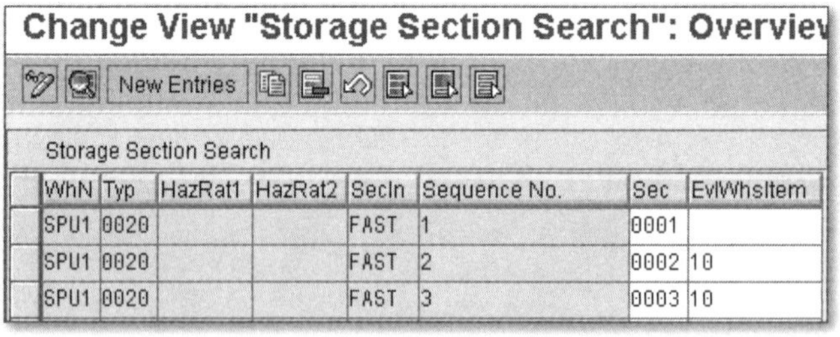

Change View "Storage Section Search": Overview

New Entries

Storage Section Search

WhN	Typ	HazRat1	HazRat2	SecIn	Sequence No.	Sec	EvlWhsItem
SPU1	0020			FAST	1	0001	
SPU1	0020			FAST	2	0002	10
SPU1	0020			FAST	3	0003	10

Figure 12.26 Evaluation Points for Storage Sections

For storage bin types, evaluation points can also be assigned in the Alternative Storage Bin Type Sequence (as seen in Figure 12.27). A product that is currently in a given storage type 0020 with an optimum bin type, but which is actually in a suboptimal bin type, will be assigned evaluation points according to the actual bin type in which the product is located. In the example provided, a product that is assigned bin type B001, but is actually in bin type P002, would be assigned 6 evaluation points (3 + 3), according to the sum of the evaluation points in each step of the sequence (see the previous note regarding the additive nature of the summation of the evaluation points).

504

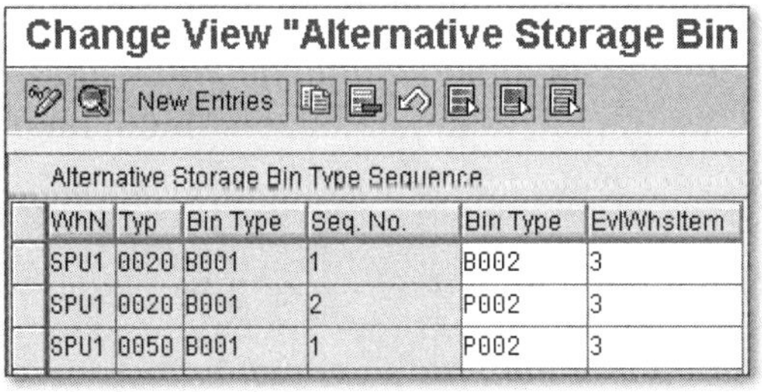

WhN	Typ	Bin Type	Seq. No.	Bin Type	EvlWhsItem
SPU1	0020	B001	1	B002	3
SPU1	0020	B001	2	P002	3
SPU1	0050	B001	1	P002	3

Figure 12.27 Evaluation Points for Alternative Atorage Bin Types

12.2.2 Master Data for Determination of Optimal Storage Bins

You must specify the rearrangement-related data in the product master in order for the system to determine the optimal storage bin during the rearrangement analysis. This product master data can be maintained manually or as part of a slotting run (see Chapter 9, Inbound Processing, for more details regarding slotting). As described previously, rearrangement compares the current bin locations against the optimum storage locations for that material in the warehouse.

To determine the optimal storage type, storage section, and storage bin type, the product master must specify the relevant settings for determination of the storage type sequence, storage section sequence, and alternate bin type sequence to be used during putaway. This can be specified manually in the material master or determined during slotting. Depending on the demand of a product, slotting might change the putaway control indicator (PACI), section indicator, and bin type.

In the product master, you can specify the PACI for the product (either manually or via slotting). The PACI is, in turn, used to determine the storage type sequence used during putaway (see Chapter 9 for more details). According to the storage type sequence, the first storage type in the sequence is defined as the optimal storage type for the product (and is usually assigned zero evaluation points, as seen in Figure 12.25). The subsequent storage types in the sequence are considered suboptimal and are assigned evaluation points for the calculation of the slotting index during rearrangement.

In the example shown, the PACI assigned is 0020, which is assigned to storage type search sequence 0020. This storage type search sequence (seen in Figure 12.28) has first storage type 0020 and then 0050 assigned. Because STORAGE TYPE 0020 is the first storage type in the sequence it is the *optimal storage type*, and the subsequent suboptimal storage types are assigned evaluation points.

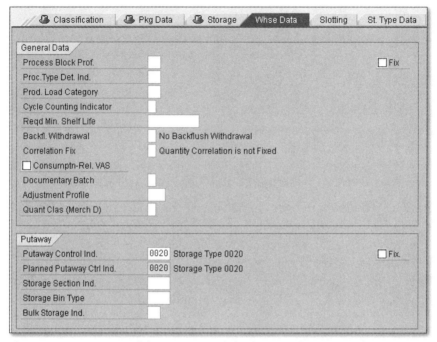

Figure 12.28 Assignment of the putaway control indicator in the EWM product master

When you then look at the storage type data view for the optimal storage type, the storage section indicator (which is used to determine the storage section search sequence) and the optimal storage bin type (which is also used to determine the alternate bin types) are assigned there.

In the example shown in Figure 12.29, the STORSECT.INDIC. FAST is assigned (the storage section sequence can be seen in Figure 12.26). In this case, slotting has determined that the material is currently a fast-moving product and that, for an optimal storage, the product needs to be stored in section 0001 (according to the search sequence assigned to the FAST indicator). Section 0001 is therefore the *optimal section*. In the example, the storage bin type B001 is the *optimal bin type* for storing the material in that storage type (and the alternate bin types are specified as seen in Figure 12.27).

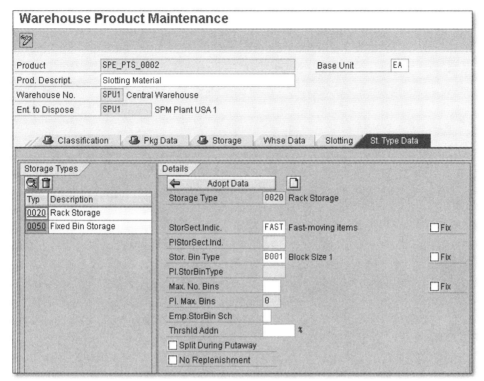

Figure 12.29 Assignment of the Storage Section Indicator and Storage Bin Type for the Storage Type on the Storage Type Data View of the EWM Product Master

12.2.3 Execution of Rearrangement

You can execute the rearrangement in the foreground from the EWM Easy Access menu by following the EXTENDED WAREHOUSE MANAGEMENT • WORK SCHEDULING • REARRANGEMENT menu path, or using Transaction code /SCWM/REAR. Or you can execute it in the background (and there is a special background version of the program that can be accessed via Transaction code /SCWM/REAR_BATCH). You can evaluate the proposed rearrangement within the foreground transaction using the different views for analyzing the situation in the warehouse. You can review the analysis by STORAGE BIN TYPE, STORAGE SECTION, or a combination STORAGE BIN TYPES/STORAGE SECTION can be made (as seen in Figure 12.30).

In the transaction, you can also use the EMPTY BINS tab to view how many bins of each bin type exist in each storage type and storage bin type combination. You can

507

use this view to see if it is possible to rearrange a material to a new more optimal bin or if there are no bins available of that bin type and section.

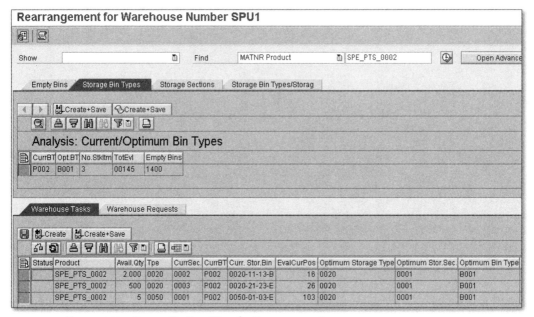

Figure 12.30 Storage Bin Type View for Rearrangement

In the example in Figure 12.30, you can see on the STORAGE BIN TYPES tab one entry for current bin type P002. You can also see that the optimal bin type for that material is B001 and that we have 3 items in suboptimal locations.

When you highlight the entry and click the DETAILS button, you can see the information on the WAREHOUSE TASKS tab in the lower half of the screen. Here, you can see the individual quantities in their current storage bin locations. For each of these bin positions the evaluation points have been calculated. For example, the material in bin 0020-11-13-E is in the optimal STORAGE TYPE 0020 and doesn't get any penalty points, but because it is in section 0003 it gets 20 points. And for being in a suboptimal BIN TYPE P002 in storage type 0020, 6 points are added. Therefore, the total number of penalty points is 26.

In the suggested task list, you can determine, based on the evaluation points calculated, which moves would be most beneficial to get the products closer to the opti-

508

mum storage concept. In the example, the product in STORAGE BIN 0050-01-03-E is the most relevant product to move, as it has the highest evaluation points.

The same evaluation of suggested moves can also be evaluated on the STORAGE SECTIONS tab, but the summary is performed according to the current storage section in this view (as seen in Figure 12.31). Note that the evaluation points are the same. In this view, the section is the first value in the column, and the value in parentheses in the same column is the storage type in which the product is located.

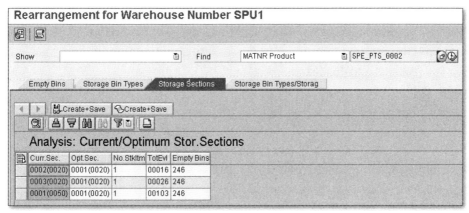

Figure 12.31 Storage Section View for Rearrangement

12.2.4 Alerts for Rearrangement

Rearrangement can be particularly relevant when the capacity utilization of a particular area is too high. To monitor the warehouse and identify rearrangement opportunities based on the capacity utilization, you can create alerts for the stock situation in the warehouse. To specify the threshold values for the alerts in the EWM IMG, follow the menu path EXTENDED WAREHOUSE MANAGEMENT • INTERNAL WAREHOUSE PROCESSES • WAREHOUSE OPTIMIZATION • DEFINE THRESHOLD VALUES FOR STOCK SITUATION. For example, as you can see in Figure 12.32, you can specify a lower threshold and upper threshold and an alert priority for the relevant threshold levels.

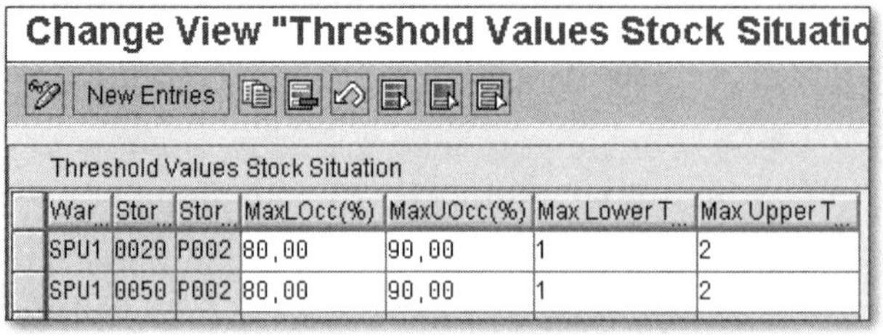

Change View "Threshold Values Stock Situatio

War	Stor	Stor	MaxLOcc(%)	MaxUOcc(%)	Max Lower T	Max Upper T
SPU1	0020	P002	80,00	90,00	1	2
SPU1	0050	P002	80,00	90,00	1	2

Figure 12.32 Threshold Values for Stock Situation

Once you have maintained the threshold values and alert levels, you can use Transaction /SCWM/WM_ANA (which you can also access via the menu path EXTENDED WAREHOUSE MANAGEMENT • WORK SCHEDULING • ANALYZE STOCK SITUATION) to EVALUATE THE STOCK SITUATION AND TRIGGER THE ALERTS. You can also schedule a job (report /SCWM/RWM_ANALYSIS) to periodically evaluate the criteria and trigger the alerts.

To view the ALERTS (as seen in Figure 12.33 for both a low threshold and high threshold being exceeded), access the ALERT MONITOR in the EWM Easy Access menu by following the SCM BASIS • ALERT MONITOR • ALERT MONITOR menu path, or using Transaction code /SAPAPO/AMON1.

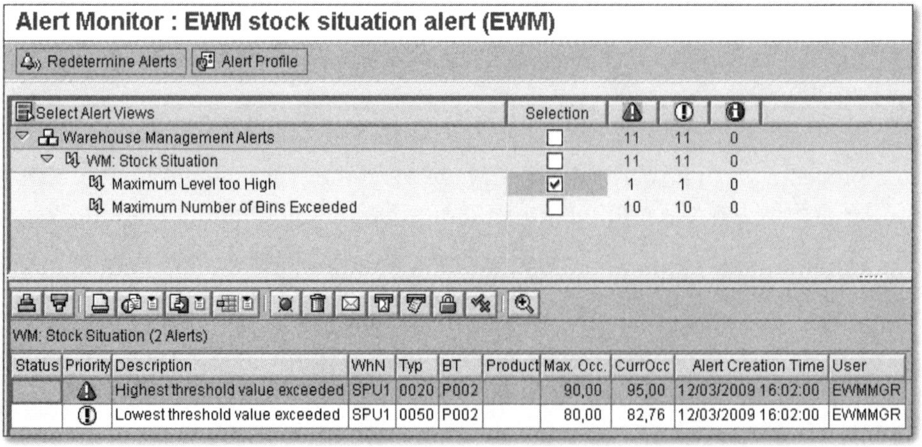

Alert Monitor : EWM stock situation alert (EWM)

Select Alert Views	Selection	⚠	ⓘ	ⓘ	
▽ Warehouse Management Alerts	☐	11	11	0	
▽ WM: Stock Situation	☐	11	11	0	
Maximum Level too High	☑	1	1	0	
Maximum Number of Bins Exceeded	☐	10	10	0	

WM: Stock Situation (2 Alerts)

Status	Priority	Description	WhN	Typ	BT	Product	Max. Occ.	CurrOcc	Alert Creation Time	User
	⚠	Highest threshold value exceeded	SPU1	0020	P002		90,00	95,00	12/03/2009 16:02:00	EWMMGR
	ⓘ	Lowest threshold value exceeded	SPU1	0050	P002		80,00	82,76	12/03/2009 16:02:00	EWMMGR

Figure 12.33 EWM Stock Situation Alerts — Maximum Level too High

You can also evaluate the stock situation to check to see if the maximum number of occupied bins has been exceeded (as seen in Figure 12.34). In this case, alerts have been triggered because the product occupies too many bins of a specific bin type. For example, product SPE_SFS_0021 occupies 4 bins of bin type P002 and the specified upper maximum level of occupied bins of bin type P002 is 2, therefore a PRIORITY 1 alert (the red-colored one) is created. Product SPE_PTS_0002 only occupies 2 bins, but the lower maximum level is one bin of bin type P002, therefore an alert with PRIORITY 2 is generated.

Alert Monitor : EWM stock situation alert (EWM)

Redetermine Alerts | Alert Profile

Select Alert Views	Selection	⚠	❶	❶	
▽ Warehouse Management Alerts	☐	7	2	0	
▽ WM: Stock Situation	☐	7	2	0	
Maximum Level too High	☐	2	0	0	
Maximum Number of Bins Exceeded	☑	5	2	0	

WM: Stock Situation (7 Alerts)

Status	Priority	Description	WhN	Typ	BT	Product	Max. Occ.	CurrO	Alert Creation Time	User
	⚠	Highest threshold value exceeded	SPU1	0020	P002	SPE_SFS_0014	2,00	3,00	26.10.2009 06:02:59	EWMMGR
	⚠	Highest threshold value exceeded	SPU1	0020	P002	SPE_PI_0001	2,00	3,00	26.10.2009 06:02:59	EWMMGR
	⚠	Highest threshold value exceeded	SPU1	0020	P002	SPE_SFS_0021	2,00	4,00	26.10.2009 06:02:59	EWMMGR
	⚠	Highest threshold value exceeded	SPU1	0020	P002	NWP-110	2,00	3,00	26.10.2009 06:02:59	EWMMGR
	⚠	Highest threshold value exceeded	SPU1	0020	P002	NWP-112	2,00	3,00	26.10.2009 06:02:59	EWMMGR
	❶	Lowest threshold value exceeded	SPU1	0020	P002	SPE_PTS_0002	1,00	2,00	26.10.2009 06:02:59	EWMMGR
	❶	Lowest threshold value exceeded	SPU1	0020	P002	SPE_SFS_0011	1,00	2,00	26.10.2009 06:02:59	EWMMGR

Figure 12.34 EWM Stock Situation Alerts — Maximum Number of Bins Exceeded

12.3 Ad Hoc Moves

An ad hoc move is a transfer of a product or an HU from one location to another. EWM provides two main transactions for this type of warehouse move. Both can be reached from the EWM Easy Access menu by following the menu path EXTENDED WAREHOUSE MANAGEMENT • WORK SCHEDULING • CREATE WAREHOUSE TASK WITHOUT REFERENCE. To move a single quantity of a product, you then select menu path MOVE PRODUCT (or use Transaction code /SCWM/ADPROD), or to move an HU with its complete contents, select the menu path MOVE HANDLING UNIT (or use Transaction code /SCWM/ADHU).

In Figure 12.35, you can see the form view for Transaction /SCWM/ADHU. To move an HU, you must simply specify the HU to move, the destination bin, and the warehouse process type (9999, in this case). From the destination bin, the storage type and section can be determined automatically, so you don't have to enter those on your own. Then you simply click the CREATE button (which provides a preview which you can review before saving), or click the CREATE + SAVE button.

You can elect to confirm the warehouse task immediately using the CONFIRM checkbox, if the immediate confirmation is allowed for the specified warehouse process type.

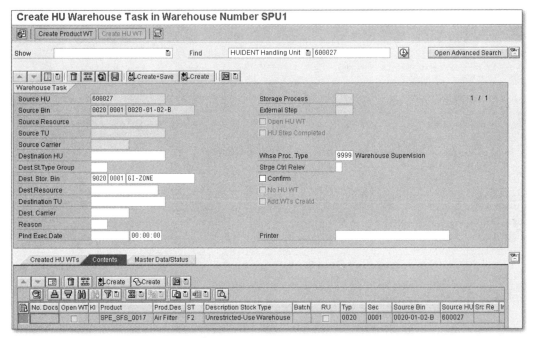

Figure 12.35 Ad hoc Moves for an HU

12.3.1 RF Creation and Execution of Ad Hoc Warehouse Tasks

You can also create and confirm ad hoc warehouse tasks via RF devices. As you can see in Figure 12.36, the warehouse worker moves 4 EA of product SPE_SFS_0001 from bin 0020-10-01-A to the bin GI-ZONE. To access the transaction for ad hoc moves if you are using the standard delivered menu for mobile data entry, follow the menu path 05 INTERNAL PROCESSES • 04 CREATE ADHOC PRODUCT WT. To create the product warehouse task, on the source bin screen, specify the source bin and product, then specify the quantity and the destination bin. If you want to specify an HU number at the destination bin, specify the destination HU or you can leave it blank (if the storage type allows). Once you have verified the information on the final screen and press ⌈Enter⌉, the warehouse task will be saved. If the warehouse process type allows immediate confirmation and proposes immediate confirmation, then the warehouse task will be immediately created and confirmed — therefore, you should consider creating a process type for use in the warehouse RF transaction that allows and proposes immediate confirmation.

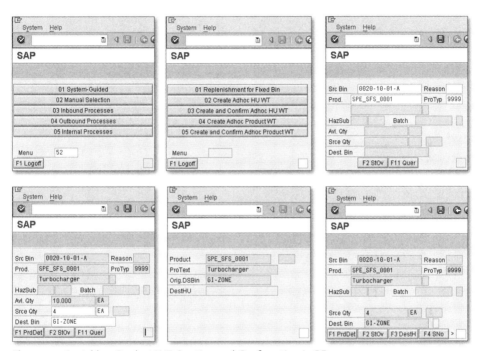

Figure 12.36 Ad hoc Product WT Creation and Confirmation in RF

12.4 Posting Changes

Posting changes can be driven from ERP or initiated within Extended Warehouse Management (EWM). When posting changes are initiated via ERP, a posting change document is created in ERP and transferred to EWM as a posting change request. The posting change in the warehouse is generated from the posting change request when the request is activated, and the warehouse tasks are generated with reference to the posting changes. The warehouse tasks for execution of the posting change can be created automatically by EWM via the Post-Processing Framework (PPF) action, according to the relevant configuration.

Posting changes can also be generated directly in EWM (as seen in Figure 12.37) via the EWM Easy Access menu by following the EXTENDED WAREHOUSE MANAGEMENT • WORK SCHEDULING • MAKE POSTING CHANGE FOR PRODUCT menu path, or using Transaction code /SCWM/POST.

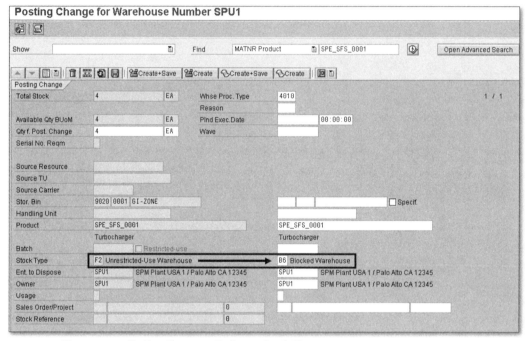

Figure 12.37 Posting Change — Perform a Stock Change

During the creation of the EWM Posting Change, you can select a material based on several criteria, including product number, storage bin, HU, or owner. You can then enter a process type and an attribute that should be changed for this material. In the example shown, the product is posted from UNRESTRICTED-USE WAREHOUSE (STOCK TYPE F2) to BLOCKED WAREHOUSE (STOCK TYPE B5). For more information regarding stock types in EWM, see Chapter 6, Warehouse Stock Management.

You can decide when creating the posting change whether the posting change should be created immediately or whether a warehouse request should be created, from which a subsequent posting change may then be created.

12.5   Summary

In this chapter, we reviewed the use and setup of internal warehouse movements in EWM, including replenishment, rearrangement, ad hoc moves, and posting changes. For replenishment, we reviewed each of the replenishment strategies. For rearrangement, we discussed the execution and configuration of movements for rearrangement and the use of alerts for analyzing the stock situation in the warehouse. And, finally, we discussed the use and execution of ad hoc moves and posting changes.

In the next chapter, we will discuss the use of and configuration of multistep moves in the warehouse using the process-oriented storage control (POSC) and layout-oriented storage control (LOSC).

Storage control lets you set up, control, and display complex warehouse processes in inbound, outbound, and internal warehouse processing. Based on settings in the storage control, Extended Warehouse Management (EWM) decides how multi-step movements will be carried out within the warehouse.

13   Configuring Multistep Warehouse Movements

To manage multistep movements in the warehouse, EWM utilizes a process known as storage control to control the product movements. The storage control is based on the processes being performed in the warehouse and the layout of the warehouse, and it enables the traceability and stock visibility for each of the process steps in the warehouse. In this chapter, we will describe the two methods for controlling multistep movements in the warehouse and how to set them up.

13.1   Introduction

There are two types of storage control used in the warehouse. *Process-oriented storage control (POSC)* is used to set up and control the processes in the warehouse in which different process steps (such as unloading, quality inspection, picking, etc.) can be flexibly defined. *Layout-oriented storage control (LOSC)* is used to consider the warehouse layout in the product movements (e.g., moving the product to an identification point before putting it away into a high rack or moving the product to an interim location or conveyor when going from one area of the warehouse to another where different equipment is used).

> **Note**
>
> POSC only operates with handling units (HUs).

13.1.1 Storage Control in Inbound

In Figure 13.1, you can see a couple of typical inbound process variants. In the first example (starting at door 1), which utilizes the POSC, the inbound process includes the following process steps:

1. The truck is unloaded at the door using HU warehouse tasks.

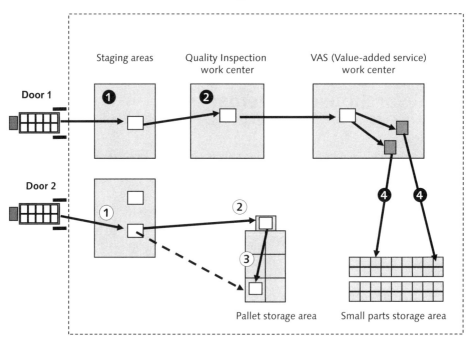

Figure 13.1 Examples of Inbound Processes Exhibiting Storage Control

2. EWM determines that the product must be inspected based on a quality inspection rule. Therefore, EWM creates the HU warehouse task to move the HU to the quality inspection work center automatically upon confirmation of the unloading warehouse task. At the work center, the quality inspection is performed.

3. EWM determines that the pallet needs to be repacked based on determination of a relevant packaging specification and the relevance for a value-added service (VAS) order. Therefore, EWM creates the HU warehouse task to the VAS work center automatically when the HU is closed at the quality work center. At the

VAS work center, the goods are repacked into appropriately sized HUs based on the VAS order.

4. After repacking is executed, EWM creates an HU warehouse task to move the HU to the final destination bin.

The second example (which begins at door 2) uses a combination of POSC and LOSC. In this example, the inbound process includes the following steps:

1. The truck is unloaded at the door using HU warehouse tasks.

2. EWM determines that the area where the HU is to be put away utilizes a pick-up/drop-off point. When the unloading warehouse task is confirmed, EWM immediately creates the HU warehouse task to the pick-up/drop-off bin based on the LOSC settings. EWM also creates an inactive HU warehouse task for put-away (shown with a dashed line) to the final destination bin based on the put-away strategy. This inactive task will be activated and utilized in the next step. (Alternatively, you can also define an intermediate storage bin assigned to the activity area. In this case, EWM would create an inactive product warehouse task based on the settings in the POSC.)

3. When the HU warehouse task is confirmed to the pick-up/drop-off bin, EWM automatically activates the HU warehouse task for putaway (and the source bin of the warehouse task is updated to the current bin of the HU). This task can then be executed by the warehouse worker responsible for putaway to that area.

In this example, steps 1 and 3 are defined using the POSC, while step 2 is set up via the LOSC. Note that EWM always checks the POSC first, and then it checks the LOSC and, if required, adjusts the flow of the process based on the layout.

In inbound processing, the storage process used for determining POSC (as seen in Figure 13.2) is assigned to the warehouse process type in customizing (for more details regarding inbound processing, see Chapter 9, Inbound Processing). To define the process type in the EWM Implementation Guide (IMG), follow the menu path SCM EXTENDED WAREHOUSE MANAGEMENT • CROSS-PROCESS SETTINGS • WAREHOUSE TASK • DEFINE WAREHOUSE PROCESS TYPE.

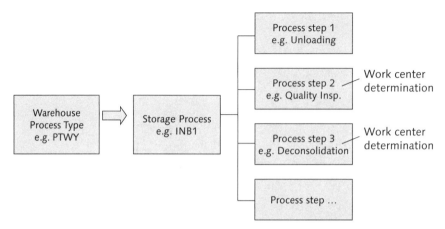

Figure 13.2 Storage Process Determination in Inbound Processing

13.1.2 Storage Control in Outbound

In Figure 13.3, you can see outbound processing variants based on different process steps. In the first example (shown with the numbers in the dark circles), the outbound process includes the following process steps:

1. Pick warehouse tasks are executed, and the products are picked into a Pick HU. At confirmation of the last warehouse task for picking, EWM determines that the products must be consolidated (based on the consolidation group settings), and it automatically creates the warehouse task for the Pick HU to the packing work center.

2. At the PACKING WORK CENTER, the warehouse operator packs the goods from the Pick HUs into Ship HUs. In the background, EWM creates product warehouse tasks for the moves from one HU to another.

3. When the ship HUs are closed at the packing work center, EWM determines that the next process step is the Staging step, and it automatically creates the warehouse task to move the Ship HU to the correct STAGING AREA.

4. When the HU warehouse task is confirmed at the staging area, EWM determines that the last process step is the Loading step. Because the HU warehouse tasks for loading the truck are normaly created manually when the truck arrives at the door, EWM does not automatically create the loading tasks.

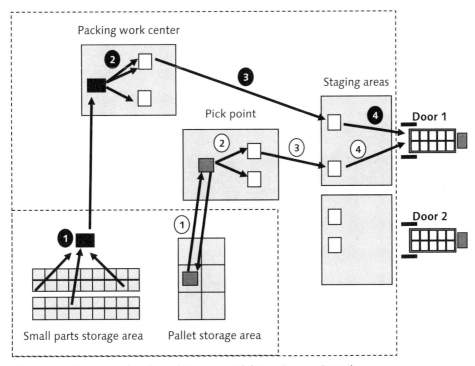

Figure 13.3 Examples of Outbound Processes Exhibiting Storage Control

In the second example from Figure 13.3 (shown with the numbers in the light colored circles), you can see a combination of POSC and LOSC. In this case, the outbound process includes the following steps:

❶ The pick warehouse tasks are created at the PALLET STORAGE AREA based on the determined stock removal strategy. EWM determines that a PICK POINT is assigned to the pallet storage area and creates an HU warehouse task to move the full HU to the PICK POINT.

❷ The warehouse operator executes picking at the HU-managed PICK POINT and confirms the warehouse tasks for picking.

❸ When the pick HU is closed, EWM determines that the next process step is the Staging step and automatically creates the warehouse task for the Pick HU to the correct STAGING AREA. When the original HU from the storage area is closed (with the remaining stock still on the HU), EWM automatically creates the HU warehouse task to move the HU back to the PALLET STORAGE AREA.

❹ When the HU warehouse task is confirmed at the staging area, EWM determines the next process step is the Loading step. Because the HU warehouse tasks for loading the truck are normaly created manually when the truck arrives at the door, EWM does not automatically create the loading tasks.

In the preceding example, steps 2, 3, and 4 are defined using the POSC, while step 1 (the movement to the pick point) is set up using the LOSC.

For the outbound scenario, the storage process is assigned to the warehouse order creation rule (WOCR) in customizing (as seen in Figure 13.4; for more details on outbound processing, see Chapter 10, Outbound Processing). To define the WOCR in the EWM IMG, follow the menu path SCM EXTENDED WAREHOUSE MANAGEMENT • CROSS-PROCESS SETTINGS • WAREHOUSE ORDER • DEFINE CREATION RULE FOR WAREHOUSE ORDERS.

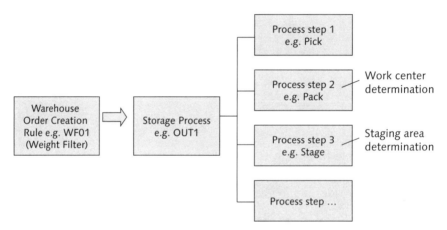

Figure 13.4 Storage Process Determination in Outbound Processing

13.1.3 Storage Control for Warehouse Internal Movements

Figure 13.5 shows an example of an internal movement (in this case, replenishment) that utilizes storage control.

The following process steps are executed in the example from Figure 13.5:

❶ EWM creates an inactive replenishment product warehouse tasks from the PALLET STORAGE AREA to the SMALL PARTS STORAGE AREA based on the determined replenishment strategy. EWM determines that the product must be repacked based on the consolidation group of the replenishment warehouse task and automatically creates an HU warehouse task from the PALLET STORAGE AREA to the DECONSOLIDATION WORK CENTER.

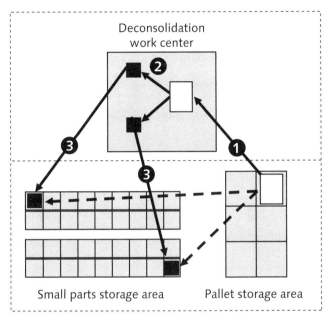

Figure 13.5 Example of an Internal Process Exhibiting Storage Control

❷ The warehouse worker repacks the products from the pick HUs into replenishment HUs.

❸ When the replenishment HUs for the small parts area is closed, EWM activates the replenishment product warehouse tasks.

The storage process determination for warehouse internal movements depends on which processes are being controlled. In the case of the replenishment scenario described in the previous example, the storage process is linked to the WOCR. Another example of a warehouse internal process is the cancellation of picking (Transaction /SCWM/CANCPICK); in this example, the storage process is linked to the warehouse process type.

In the following sections, we will further describe, in detail, both the POSC and LOSC.

13.2 Process-Oriented Storage Control

POSC is used to map complex processes in the warehouse, including putaway, stock removal, and internal movements. Based on a product's processing requirements, it could be necessary to carry out different process steps. Therefore, the configuration of the POSC starts first with a definition of the storage processes that products, depending on their physical and storage characteristics (among others), must use to move through the warehouse.

13.2.1 Definition of Storage Process

The storage process is set up by defining external process steps and then assigning those process steps to a storage process in customizing. External process steps can be defined flexibly by assigning internal process steps, which are predefined by SAP and cannot be changed. To assign the internal process steps in the EWM IMG (as seen in Figure 13.6), follow the menu path SCM EXTENDED WAREHOUSE MANAGEMENT • CROSS-PROCESS SETTINGS • WAREHOUSE TASK • DEFINE PROCESS-ORIENTED STORAGE CONTROL.

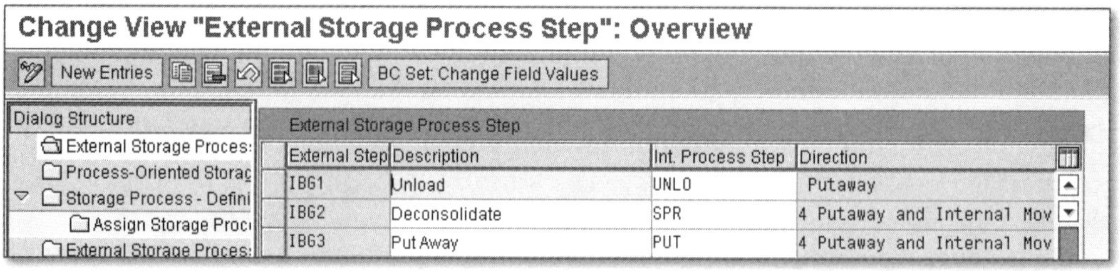

Figure 13.6 Definition of External Process Steps in Customizing

For each process, you can only assign certain internal process steps. For internal processing, for example, you can assign the internal process step as Picking, Packing, Unloading, Counting, VAS, or Quality Inspection. For the putaway process, you can assign the internal process step Deconsolidation, Packing, Putaway, or VAS. For stock removal, you can assign internal process steps Picking, Packing, VAS, Staging, or Loading.

Note

The internal process steps Count, VAS, Deconsolidate, and Quality are predefined by SAP and are dynamic process steps. EWM automatically determines dynamically if these process steps need to be executed, and they do not need to be included in the defined storage processes to be executed.

Once you have assigned the internal process steps to the external steps, you can then assign the external process steps to a storage process. These assigned process steps represent possible product movements. In Figure 13.7, you can see an example of inbound storage process.

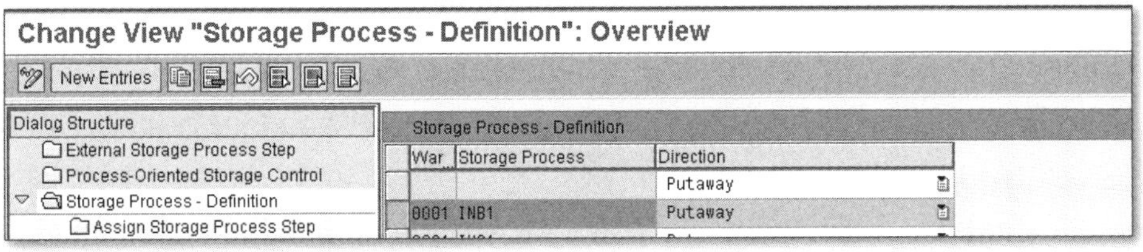

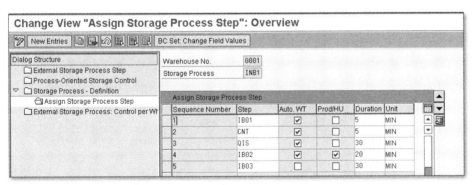

Figure 13.7 Definition of an Inbound Storage Process as an Example

For the storage process, you can assign the storage process steps (as seen in Figure 13.8) by selecting the storage process and then double-clicking on the Assign Storage Process Step folder.

Figure 13.8 Assignment of Process Steps to the Storage Process

In the example from Figure 13.8, the inbound storage process consists of five process steps. For each process step, you also specify the following settings:

▶ Automatic Creation of Subsequent Warehouse Task (Auto.WT): If you select this flag, EWM creates the subsequent warehouse task automatically.

▶ Product/HU Warehouse Task: This indicator is used to specify which process step should be used for the creation of the putaway warehouse task during inbound processing (whether it is a product warehouse task or HU warehouse task) and also to specify the process step after which the HU warehouse task should be created in the case of transportation cross-docking and merchandise distribution (for more details on these cross-docking scenarios, see Chapter 17, Cross-Docking). In the example, the process step IB02 (Deconsolidate) has the indicator set, which specifies that the putaway warehouse task should be created (which determines the final putaway bin) when the deconsolidation warehouse tasks are created in the work center. (Note that there are several dependencies for this field that are well documented in the help field for the field on the table.)

▶ The time-related settings in the process step are used by the system to estimate the total processing time for labor planning.

Once the storage processes have been set up, you can configure the destination location for process steps in the storage control customizing. To do so, select the PROCESS-ORIENTED STORAGE CONTROL folder and specify the relevant parameters for each external step (e.g., the destination bin for the HU), as seen in Figure 13.9.

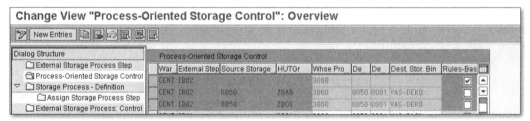

Figure 13.9 Determination of Warehouse Process Type and Destination Location in POSC

In the example shown in Figure 13.9, for process step IB02 (Deconsolidation), different destination locations are possible, depending on the HU type group. If the received HU is a pallet, the HU type group is not a box (ZBOX) or a bag (ZBAG). In that case, the destination bin will be determined using the rule-based method, which will result in the deconsolidation work center being determined based on the deconsolidation settings. In contrast to the destination location determination for POSC, in the rule-based determination, the source data can be specified in more detail (e.g., a specific work center should be determined for a specific staging area). To configure the deconsolidation location determination in the EWM IMG, follow the menu path SCM Extended Warehouse Management • Goods Receipt Process • Deconsolidation • Specify Deconsolidation Station. On the other hand, if the received pallet is a box (HU type group ZBOX) or a bag (HU type group ZBAG) then the destination bin of the HU warehouse task is VAS-DEKO (as specified for the HU type group).

In addition, you can specify the warehouse process type used to create the corresponding HU warehouse task for the external process step.

13.3 Layout-Oriented Storage Control

The LOSC is used to control the movements in the warehouse based on the physical restrictions of the warehouse layout. For example, EWM can determine automatically that a warehouse movement from storage bin A to storage bin B cannot be executed directly but must pass storage bin C. The LOSC is used by EWM, for example, during the use of identification points, intermediate zones, and pick points. In Figure 13.10, you can see an example in which the LOSC is used to determine the destination for the warehouse tasks.

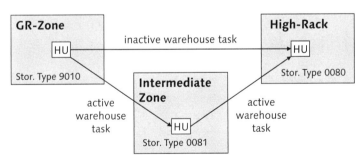

Figure 13.10 Example of LOSC

In the example shown in Figure 13.10, a homogeneous HU was received at the goods receipt (GR) zone. EWM determines the destination bin in the HU-managed storage type 0080 (high-rack) based on the putaway strategy. EWM also determines that the HU can be put away to the final destination bin only via an intermediate zone. Therefore, EWM creates an inactive HU warehouse task from the

GR zone to the final destination bin and an active HU warehouse task from the GR zone to the intermediate zone. When the active HU warehouse task is confirmed at the intermediate zone, EWM changes the source bin of the inactive HU warehouse task based on the new location of the HU and activates the warehouse task. You can then confirm the activate HU warehouse task to the destination bin.

If the destination storage type is not HU managed, EWM would then create an inactive product warehouse task to the final destination bin and an active HU WT to the intermediate zone. When the active HU WT is confirmed, EWM would change and activate the inactive product WT for execution.

To set up this example, you must define the intermediate zone as an intermediate location by configuring the storage type for the intermediate zone and creating the storage bin (see Figure 13.11). To configure the storage type in the EWM IMG, follow the menu path SCM EXTENDED WAREHOUSE MANAGEMENT • MASTER DATA • DEFINE STORAGE TYPE. For more information on setting up the storage type and storage bin, see Chapter 3, The Warehouse Structure.

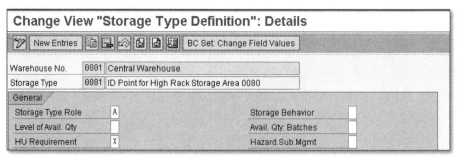

Figure 13.11 Storage Type Definition for an ID Point

Once you have created the interim storage type and a storage bin for the storage type, you can specify the interim storage type and bin for the LOSC (as seen in Figure 13.12). To define the LOSC in the EWM IMG, follow the menu path SCM EXTENDED WAREHOUSE MANAGEMENT • CROSS-PROCESS SETTINGS • WAREHOUSE TASK • DEFINE LAYOUT-ORIENTED STORAGE PROCESS CONTROL.

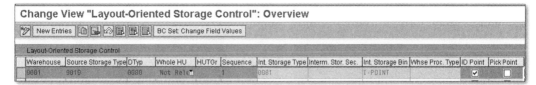

Figure 13.12 LOSC Configuration

In the setup for the LOSC, you can specify the following settings:

▶ Source and destination storage type

▶ Storage group

▶ Whole HU indicator: The Whole HU indicator is used to specify whether a withdrawal of a complete HU, an empty HU, or simply a partial withdrawal should be performed.

▶ HU Type Group: The HU type group can be used to specify that only specific HUs are to be moved to the intermediate storage location.

▶ Intermediate storage type, section, and bin

▶ Warehouse process type: The warehouse process type is the process type used to create the warehouse task to the intermediate storage location.

13.4 Summary

In this chapter, we described the different possibilities to set up warehouse processes for inbound, outbound, and warehouse internal processes in EWM using POSC and LOSC, and we provided examples to help clarify the relevant customizing settings. You should now have a good understanding of the POSC and LOSC mechanisms and how they are used in EWM.

In the next chapter, we will discuss the physical inventory (PI) processes in the warehouse.

Whether it is mandatory by law (as in many countries) or just a Best Practice, physical inventory (PI) is an absolute necessity in every warehouse management solution. By offering several methods of PI, SAP Extended Warehouse Management (EWM) supports you in examining the stock situation in your warehouse in an efficient way and helps to reduce inventory losses in the warehouse.

14   Physical Inventory

In this chapter, we will provide an overview of the capabilities of SAP EWM to support Physical Inventory (PI). We will discuss the main objects used by PI, the supported procedures of PI, and the integration with Resource Management.

14.1   Introduction

In the chapter, we will discuss both *storage bin–specific* PI and *product-specific* PI. Storage bin specific refers to a dedicated position in the warehouse where all products and handling units (HUs) have to be counted. In this case, the system will provide a PI document for counting in the area (e.g., a whole storage type or separate bins for different storage types). The user counts all of the different products in these areas. For example, this counting procedure would be used during an annual inventory to ensure that every bin is counted (as is often required on an annual basis by law).

Product-specific PI is only driven by the chosen product that must be counted; this can include one or more single storage bins or HUs in the warehouse. This procedure is used to sort through the current stock in the warehouse for a specific product and is often used, for example, for products with a higher value.

You can also execute PI for different stock categories in the warehouse, such as whether the stock is blocked, in quality inspection, or ordinary stock for unrestricted use.

Because SAP EWM can manage several warehouses using different warehouse numbers, there are specific PI settings on the warehouse number level (as you can see in Figure 14.1). To access the warehouse-specific settings in the EWM Implementation (IMG), follow the menu path EXTENDED WAREHOUSE MANAGEMENT • INTERNAL WAREHOUSE PROCESSES • PHYSICAL INVENTORY • WAREHOUSE-NUMBER-SPECIFIC SETTINGS • SPECIFY PHYSICAL-INVENTORY-SPECIFIC SETTINGS IN THE WAREHOUSE.

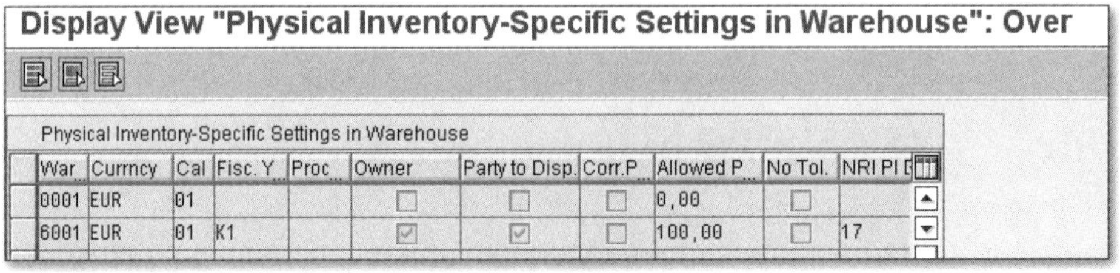

Display View "Physical Inventory-Specific Settings in Warehouse": Over

Physical Inventory-Specific Settings in Warehouse

War	Currncy	Cal	Fisc. Y	Proc	Owner	Party to Disp.	Corr.P	Allowed P	No Tol.	NRI PI
0001	EUR	01			☐	☐	☐	0,00	☐	
6001	EUR	01	K1		☑	☑	☐	100,00	☐	17

Figure 14.1 PI Settings at the Warehouse Number Level

In the PI settings at the warehouse level, you can specify, for example, the following settings:

▶ **Factory Calendar**

The factory calendar is used to distinguish between working days and non-working days. For cycle counting, it is necessary to calculate the intervals in working days to determine when the next count is scheduled.

▶ **Currency Unit**

The currency unit is used in the calculation of the product value. The product values are used in the tolerance level checking during inventory counting and clearing and can also be used to determine items relevant to counting. To transfer the product values from ERP to EWM from the EWM Easy Access menu, follow the EXTENDED WAREHOUSE MANAGEMENT • PHYSICAL INVENTORY • PERIODIC PROCESSING • DETERMINE AND SET PRICES FROM ERP menu path, or use Transaction code /SCWM/VALUATION_SET. The values will be stored in the EWM system, and if the price changes in ERP, the updated values in EWM must be manually triggered again.

▶ **Fiscal Year**

The fiscal year assignment can be used to assign your own specific fiscal year variants, which could change based on government or company regulations. To maintain the FISCAL YEAR VARIANTS, as seen in Figure 14.2, from the EWM IMG, follow the menu path ADVANCED PLANNING AND OPTIMIZATION • SUPPLY CHAIN PLANNING • DEMAND PLANNING (DP) • BASIC SETTINGS • MAINTAIN FISCAL YEAR VARIANTS.

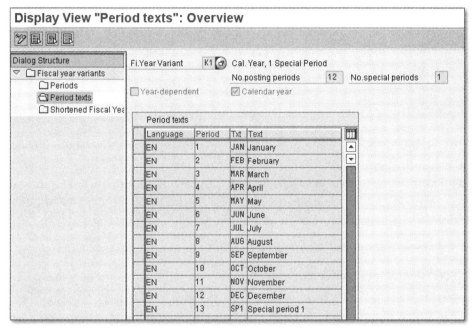

Figure 14.2 Definition of the Fiscal Year Variants

▸ **Procedure**

The procedure refers to the condition procedure for printing (which is described further in Chapter 22, Data Capture and Resource Optimization) if you don't use the mobile data entry option for PI (which is also described further in Chapter 22).

▸ **Owner / Party Entitled to Dispose**

If these parameters are selected, EWM will propose an owner and party entitled to dispose based on the defaults for the warehouse.

▸ **Correction Permitted**

If this indicator is selected, you can use the difference analyzer to correct a PI document for which an inventory count has already been entered. The difference analyzer is used to manage the differences found in the warehouse (during PI or other processes) and integrate them into the inventory in ERP.

▶ **Allowed Percentage and No Tolerance Check**

A tolerance check is performed during the count entry to help ensure accurate counting and data entry. If you want to specify a percent change allowed, you can specify the allowed percentage here, or you can completely deactivate the tolerance check. The tolerance check only provides a warning message to the user to prompt the user to validate the entered count.

14.2 Physical Inventory Process

The purpose of the PI is to ensure an accurate accounting of the inventory in the warehouse. To ensure a stable and secure process for accounting for the inventory, the PI process is modeled in EWM in steps. This helps control, for example, that a warehouse worker cannot increase or decrease the stock without an additional control and without having the approval of a warehouse supervisor.

The defined steps of the PI include:

▶ **Creation of an inactive PI document**

Inactive PI documents are useed to plan the phsical inventory. As long as the documents are not activated, you can't execute the inventory count, but you can use the inactive documents, for example, to plan the workload for counting.

▶ **Activation of the PI documents**

The activation of the PI documents starts the real execution of the counting. With the activation of the documents, EWM automatically creates warehouse orders (WO) for the PI counting, which can be used for execution on mobile devices.

▶ **Counting and recounting**

After the documents are created and activated, the warehouse user must count the stock. The count result is saved to the document, and if the count result is approved, the stock of the bin is automatically updated. If a recounting is triggered, a new PI document is created and the user must count the bin or the product again.

▶ **Stock posting for stock differences**

When the counting (and recounting) is complete, the invnetory document is completed or "posted," and the counting results are booked. Differences between the counted quantities and the book quantities are posted to a difference area and are visible in the difference analyzer.

Once all of the steps of the PI have been executed successfully, the PI document will include the details of the count, including the count result, difference quantities, count date, and counter.

There are different PI procedures in EWM, and for each of these, you create the PI documents differently. Later in this chapter, we'll describe these difference procedures further. In the meantime, we'll describe the PI objects and how to use them to process the PI.

14.3 Physical Inventory Objects

There are specific objects in EWM that support the PI process — namely, these are the PI document, PI areas, and the difference analyzer. In the following sections, we will describe these objects and their attributes in more detail.

14.3.1 Physical Inventory Documents

The PI process always starts with the creation of the PI documents. These documents represent the items to be counted, and the follow-up process is always documented on this object. Therefore, the PI document forms the basis for the execution of the counting activities in the warehouse. As it serves as the major instruction object for the resource that executes the count, the document includes all of the information about the count, including the planned count date, the inventory procedure (e.g., ad hoc, cycle count, etc.), the reason for the count and the priority, the product to be counted and its bin position, the status of the document, and whether the storage bin should be blocked during the inventory counting.

Figure 14.3 illustrates the possible statuses of a PI document, including at which points in the process the tolerance checks can be carried out.

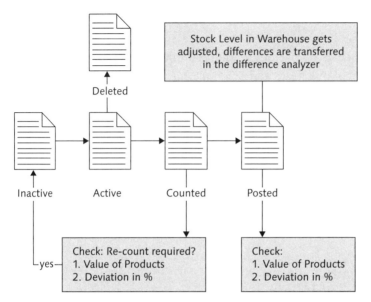

Figure 14.3 Process Overview of the PI Document

Tolerance Checks

A common business requirement within PI is to include tolerance checks at different points in the process. Particularly when counting high value products, you may want to control the count results and final postings that adjust the stock situation in the warehouse management system. Therefore, SAP EWM supports the assignment of tolerance groups to individual users. These tolerance groups can be used while entering the count results and during the posting (which is used to adjust the system quantities).

The tolerance checks are executed without any user interaction in the background and can include a check of both the value of the product and the deviation in the count from the book quantity (as a percentage). The tolerance checks are performed based on tolerance groups (which allows for a more efficient process for managing the various tolerances). The tolerance groups can be assigned to the following processes:

- Tolerance Groups for Difference Analyzer
- Tolerance Groups for Posting Differences
- Tolerance Groups for Recounting

To manage the tolerance groups in the EWM IMG, follow the menu path Extended Warehouse Management • Internal Warehouse Processes • Physical Inventory • Warehouse-Number-Specific Settings • Specify Physical-Inventory-Specific Settings in the Warehouse • Define Tolerance Groups. In the underlying folders, you can maintain the different tolerance groups described previously. For example, in Figure 14.4, you can see the tolerance groups for posting differences.

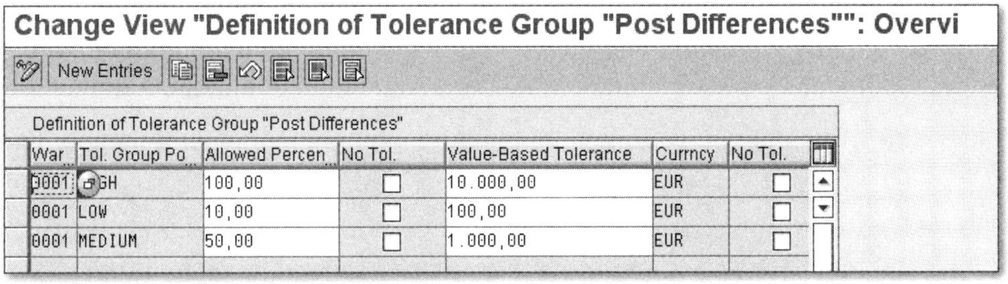

War	Tol. Group Po	Allowed Percen	No Tol.	Value-Based Tolerance	Currncy	No Tol.
0001	HIGH	100,00	☐	10.000,00	EUR	☐
0001	LOW	10,00	☐	100,00	EUR	☐
0001	MEDIUM	50,00	☐	1.000,00	EUR	☐

Figure 14.4 Configuration of Tolerance Groups for Posting Differences

Using the tolerances, you can, for example, trigger an immediate recount document to be created when the count results are entered, thereby prohibiting the immediate stock adjustment if the count difference is too high. The stock could only be adjusted following a recount confirmation.

Creating the Physical Inventory Document

SAP EWM supports the manual and automatic creation of a PI request (inactive PI documents) and the manual and automatic creation of executable PI documents (active PI documents) based either on the product or on the bin location. In Figure 14.5, you can see an example for creating a PI request. To create the PI document from the EWM Easy Access menu, follow the Extended Warehouse Management • Physical Inventory • Create Physical Inventory Document menu path, or use Transaction code /SCWM/PI_CREATE.

The priority of a PI document is directly linked to a *PI reason*. Therefore, you assign the priority when you create the PI document and assign a Reason code (as seen in Figure 14.5). Often, you can use the reason code as a direct indication of the priority. You can configure the reasons and priorities independently based on the activity. To set up the reasons and priorities (as seen in Figure 14.6) in the

EWM IMG, follow the menu path EXTENDED WAREHOUSE MANAGEMENT • INTERNAL WAREHOUSE PROCESSES • PHYSICAL INVENTORY • REASON AND PRIORITY.

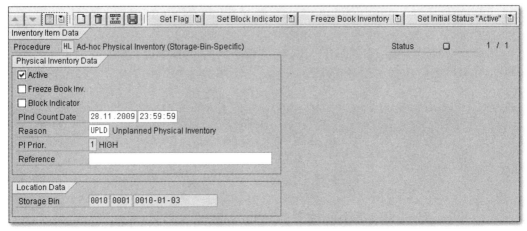

Figure 14.5   Creation of PI Document

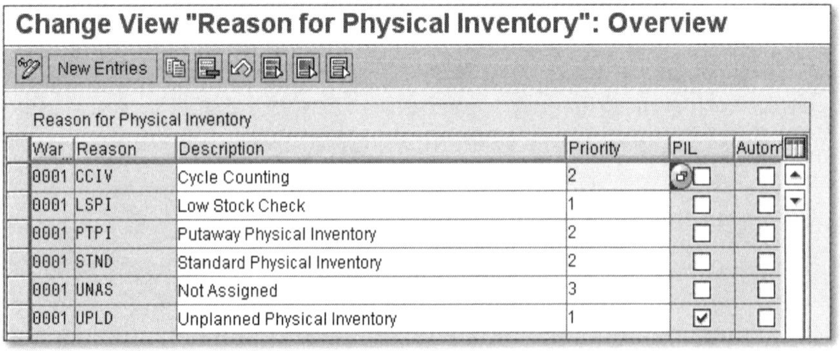

Change View "Reason for Physical Inventory": Overview

War	Reason	Description	Priority	PIL	Autom
0001	CCIV	Cycle Counting	2	☐	☐
0001	LSPI	Low Stock Check	1	☐	☐
0001	PTPI	Putaway Physical Inventory	2	☐	☐
0001	STND	Standard Physical Inventory	2	☐	☐
0001	UNAS	Not Assigned	3	☐	☐
0001	UPLD	Unplanned Physical Inventory	1	☑	☐

Figure 14.6   Configuration of Reasons for PI

The possible values for the priority are only single-character numeric and include the values 1 to 9. In addition, you can assign other attributes to the reason code (e.g., to immediately activate the request so that an executable PI is automatically created).

You can assign the different PI reasons to the available *PI procedures*. Depending on the inventory procedure, you can change the reason to affect the behavior of the PI process. To assign the reasons to the individual PI process in the EWM IMG, follow the menu path EXTENDED WAREHOUSE MANAGEMENT • INTERNAL WAREHOUSE PROCESSES • PHYSICAL INVENTORY • REASON AND PRIORITY.

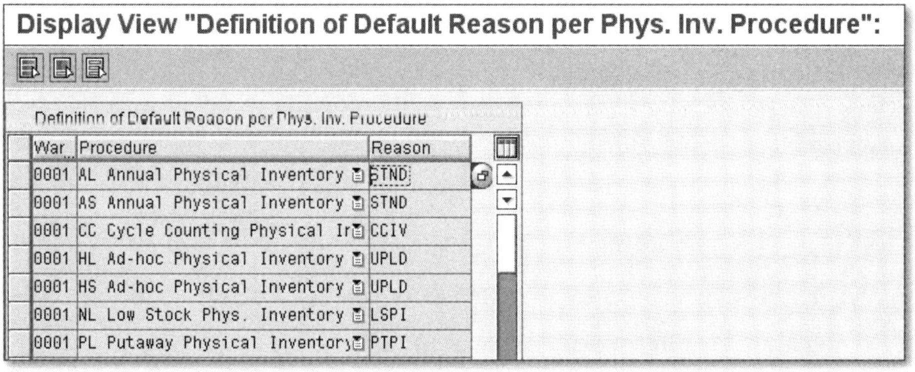

Figure 14.7 Definition of the Reasons per PI procedure

The PI processing transaction offers you the transparency of all processed PI documents, regardless of status. To process the PI documents (as seen in Figure 14.8) from the EWM Easy Access menu, follow the EXTENDED WAREHOUSE MANAGEMENT • PHYSICAL INVENTORY • PROCESS PHYSICAL INVENTORY DOCUMENT menu path, or use Transaction code /SCWM/PI_PROCESS. In the figure, you can see the different process statuses in the PI document as it is counted and posted.

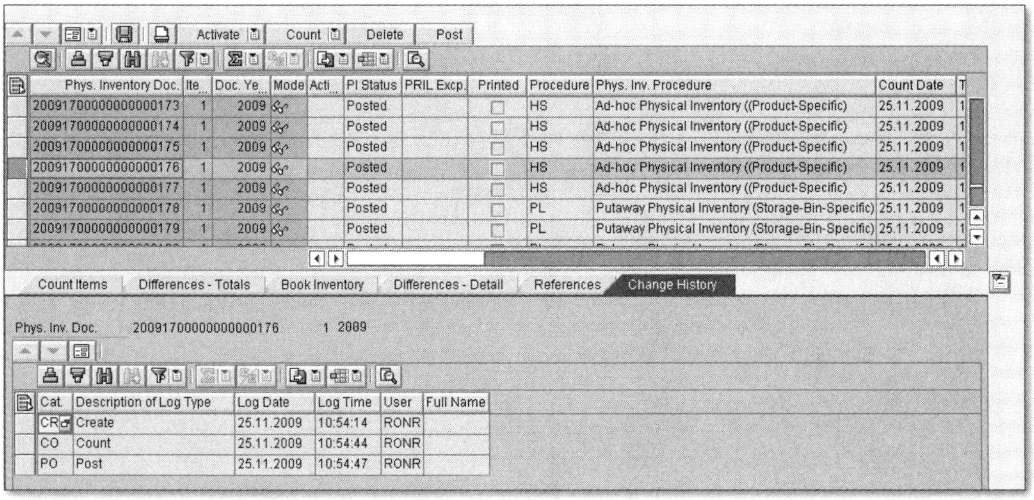

Figure 14.8 Processing the PI Documents

14.3.2 Physical Inventory Areas

With the use of PI areas, you can structure your warehouse in different groupings of bins according to your PI requirements. When you define the PI areas, you can assign certain attributes, including:

- Whether a putaway PI is allowed
- Whether a low-stock/zero-stock PI is allowed
- Whether the document is to be posted automatically after the count
- Whether the book inventory is to be proposed in the printout
- Whether it is allowed to count an HU as complete
- Whether the product data is included in printouts
- The threshold value for the low-stock PI or check

Once the PI areas are created, they are assigned to an activity area. The bin sorting for the activity area is performed according to the same method as described in Chapter 3, The Warehouse Structure, for activity INVE. To assign the ACTIVITY AREA to a PHYSICAL INVENTORY AREA (as seen in Figure 14.9) in the EWM IMG, follow the menu path EXTENDED WAREHOUSE MANAGEMENT • INTERNAL WAREHOUSE PROCESSES • PHYSICAL INVENTORY • WAREHOUSE-NUMBER-SPECIFIC SETTINGS • ASSIGN PHYSICAL INVENTORY AREA TO ACTIVITY AREA.

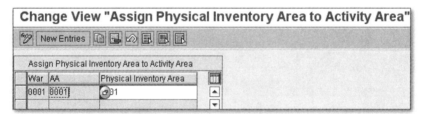

Figure 14.9 Assignment of PI Areas to Activity Areas

You can also specify which PI procedures (e.g., continuous inventory, cycle counting, annual inventory) can be used per PI area. To specify the allowed procedures (as seen in figure 14.10) in the EWM IMG, follow the menu path EXTENDED WAREHOUSE MANAGEMENT • INTERNAL WAREHOUSE PROCESSES • PHYSICAL INVENTORY • PHYSICAL-INVENTORY-AREA-SPECIFIC SETTINGS • DEFINE PHYSICAL INVENTORY AREA.

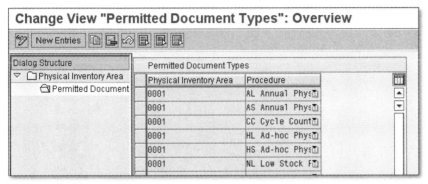

Figure 14.10 Permitted PI Procedures per Area

14.3.3 Difference Analyzer

The difference analyzer is a tool that enables you to analyze any differences that have occurred in the warehouse before they get posted to the ERP system (when they would also make adjustments to Finance (FI) and Controlling (CO)). This review of apparent deviations found, for example, during picking or PI, may help you find the reason for the differences in your warehouse and to reconcile the stock situation in your ERP system, or it may even help you identify reconciling differences, which would allow you to avoid posting differences to ERP. When you do post differences to ERP, the summarized differences are posted to the corresponding ERP storage location as inventory differences, and material documents are created in ERP (which, as normal, would be visible in Transaction MB51, among others) Financial documents are also posted as a result. In Figure 14.11, you can see the interactions of EWM and ERP with the DIFFERENCE ANALYZER.

Differences incurred can be displayed in the difference analyzer on a single level or on a cumulative level. The single-level view is driven by the business process where a certain deviation for a single product has occurred. Hence, a link to the involved document, for example, a picking task or PI document, is included. The cumulative display shows the amount of product involved in any deviations and displays them in a summarized view without having a link to the business process from which these deviations have been triggered. The summarized inventory difference is displayed in the difference analyzer as an inventory bucket that must be synchronized with the ERP system. In Figure 14.12, you can see the single-level differences displayed in the difference analyzer.

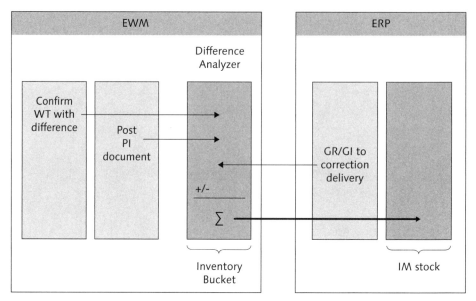

Figure 14.11 Using the Difference Analyzer with PI

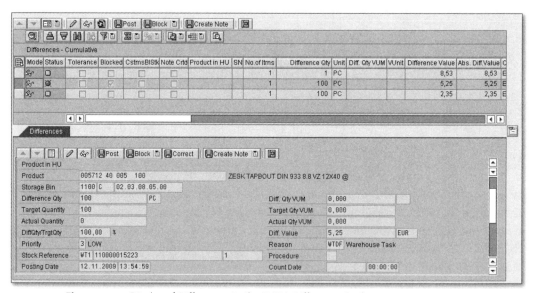

Figure 14.12 Display of Differences in the EWM Difference Analyzer

To start the difference analyzer from the EWM Easy Access menu, follow the EXTENDED WAREHOUSE MANAGEMENT • PHYSICAL INVENTORY • DIFFERENCE ANALYZER menu path, or use Transaction code /SCWM/DIFF_ANALYZE.

When posting differences from the difference analyzer, the tolerance checks are performed to prevent users from making unauthorized inventory postings to ERP. To assign users to the tolerance groups for the difference analyzer from the EWM Easy Access menu, follow the EXTENDED WAREHOUSE MANAGEMENT • SETTINGS • PHYSICAL INVENTORY • ASSIGN USER TO TOLERANCE GROUP FOR DIFFERENCE ANALYZE menu path, or use Transaction code /SCWM/PI_USER_DIFF.

In Figure 14.13, you can see the integration of the difference analyzer in the process flow of PI.

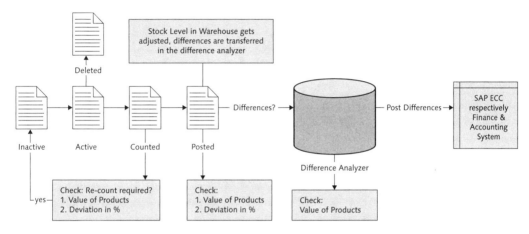

Figure 14.13 PI Process and Use of the Difference Analyzer

14.3.4 Physical Inventory Using External Systems

You can also perform the inventory counting using an external system, therefore EWM provides transactions for uploading the storage bin (Transaction /SCWM/PI_UPLOAD) and count data (Transaction /SCWM/PI_DOWNLOAD).

Currently, EWM doesn't provide a function for sample-based PI counting. Therefore, if you need these inventory procedures, you must use a third-party system to determine which bins must be counted. In sample-based counting, a system uses a formula to determine which bins must be counted. Therefore, you might need to download the storage bin and stock data, using the preceding transactions. Then you can determine the sample in the external system and carry out the sample-based PI in EWM.

In addition, you can develop additional logic in EWM and use the available Business Application Programming Interfaces (BAPIs) for creating, deleting, counting, or posting the inventory documents:

▶ /SCWM/BAPI_PI_DOCUMENT_CREATE

▶ /SCWM/BAPI_PI_DOCUMENT_DELETE

▶ /SCWM/BAPI_PI_DOCUMENT_COUNT

▶ /SCWM/BAPI_PI_DOCUMENT_POST

These functions can be used, for example, if the counting should be triggered automatically in the background for processes such as empty pallet handling or, in special cases, when you use a material flow system (MFS) and the system should determine an empty bin when a user sets an empty pallet or carton onto the conveyor.

14.3.5 Stock Comparison to ERP

If stock inconsistencies occur between ERP and EWM, you can identify and correct the inconsistencies from the EWM Easy Access menu by following the EXTENDED WAREHOUSE MANAGEMENT • PHYSICAL INVENTORY • PERIODIC PROCESSING • STOCK COMPARISON ERP menu path, or using Transaction code /SCWM/ERP_STOCKCHECK.

In ERP, stock is accumulated on the storage location level. Because EWM tracks the inventory at a more granular level, the transaction assumes that the EWM stock level is correct and adjusts the stock situation in ERP based on the EWM stock numbers.

14.3.6 Posting Differences Automatically

You can post differences to ERP from the EWM Easy Access menu by following the EXTENDED WAREHOUSE MANAGEMENT • PHYSICAL INVENTORY • PERIODIC PROCESSING • POST DIFFERENCES TO ERP SYSTEM menu path, or using Transaction code /SCWM/WM_ADJUST. You can also schedule the correspondent report to automatically post the differences to the ERP system. You may use this report, for example, for differences with a low value to decrease the administrative overhead of managing the PI processes. To ensure that only appropriate differences are posted in the background, the background user that is used to execute the report must be assigned to the appropriate tolerance group — then only differences up to the allowed tolerance will be posted automatically.

14.4   Supported Methods for Physical Inventory

To reflect different business process requirements with regard to PI in a warehouse, EWM offers several PI methods. In the following sections, we will describe each of the supported methods in detail.

14.4.1   Ad Hoc Physical Inventory

Ad hoc PI is used to carry out the counting for a storage bin or product at any time during a fiscal year. The trigger for the creation for ad hoc PI documents is usually done manually. It is also possible to link the creation to an exception code. For example, if a resource encounters a stock difference during picking and confirms the warehouse tasks using an exception code, the exception code can be linked to the immediate creation of an unplanned PI document.

14.4.2   Annual Physical Inventory

The objective of the annual PI method is to count and record all stocks within a defined time frame, usually once per year. During the annual PI, you may prohibit stock movements. You typically perform the PI for every bin in the warehouse, and you may even execute the PI for storage bins that are subject to continuous inventory but for which no stock movements have occurred during the current fiscal year.

14.4.3   Low Stock Check (Storage Bin Specific)

The low stock check is a procedure that can be performed during the confirmation of a warehouse task. It is used when a storage bin only contains a small quantity of a product after a stock removal. Usually, the picker can quickly establish the stock level, and you save the time to separately send a counter to the bin to verify the count. The intent of the low stock count is to verify the availability of inventory, which is especially critical when stock levels of low — this helps you maintain high service levels with your customers.

When confirming the warehouse task, SAP EWM automatically generates a PI document in background. The low stock (or limit) value for the quantity of products on a certain bin is freely defined. A variant of the low stock check is the *zero stock check*; where the limit value is zero. The additional value of the zero stock check is that the picker confirms that the bin is empty and that it can be used for a putaway — this benefits the putaway operator, who can be assured that the product will fit into the bin when he arrives for a confirmation of a putaway task.

14.4.4 Putaway Physical Inventory

You can also perform a PI for a storage bin at the time of the first putaway in a bin in the fiscal year. During the first putaway, the warehouse employee confirms that the stock in the warehouse matches the confirmed quantity in the warehouse task after the putaway.

Once the putaway PI is successfully executed, no further PI is performed for this storage bin during the same fiscal year (even if a new quant is entered or the bin is emptied).

14.4.5 Cycle Counting

Cycle counting is used to count products at regular intervals during a fiscal year. To distinguish the products (e.g., fast movers vs. slow movers), you can set up counting intervals based on the cycle count (CC) indicators. For each CC indicator, you specify the interval between counts in *work days* (see Figure 14.14). You then allocate the products (in the EWM product master) to the different CC indicators. This lets you schedule the PI of fast-moving products in your warehouse more frequently than slow-moving ones. The use of the factory calendar (assigned to the warehouse is the warehouse-specific settings for PI, as described earlier in this chapter) is necessary in this area for the relevant calculation of the work days for the warehouse. To configure the cycle count indicators in the EWM IMG, follow the menu path EXTENDED WAREHOUSE MANAGEMENT • INTERNAL WAREHOUSE PROCESSES • PHYSICAL INVENTORY • WAREHOUSE-NUMBER-SPECIFIC SETTINGS • CONFIGURE CYCLE COUNTING.

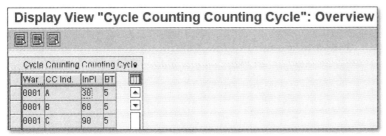

Figure 14.14 Set Counting Cycles per CC Indicator

To create the PI documents for cycle counting, you can schedule the creation transaction with a variant as a background job. This helps to relieve the administrative burden of creating the documents periodically (which is usually done daily or weekly).

14.4.6 Storage Bin Check

The storage bin check is a procedure you can use to check whether a product is actually stored in the storage bin in which it is supposed to be located, without having to do a detailed count. The quantity of the product in the storage bin is immaterial in this case, thus the storage bin check is not a real PI procedure; it is simply a verification of a product position.

You can maintain the periodicity of the STORAGE BIN CHECK on the ACTIVITY AREA and you can also influence it in the customizing with the interval assignment in working days (see Figure 14.15). To configure the periodicity of the storage bin check per PI area in the EWM IMG, follow the menu path EXTENDED WAREHOUSE MANAGEMENT • INTERNAL WAREHOUSE PROCESSES • PHYSICAL INVENTORY • PHYSICAL-INVENTORY-AREA-SPECIFIC SETTINGS • PERIODICITY OF STORAGE BIN CHECK.

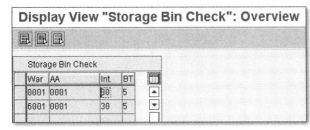

Figure 14.15 Maintaining the Periodicity of the Storage Bin Check

14.5 Integration to Resource Management

In addition to the paper-driven execution of PI documents, EWM also supports counting within the radio frequency (RF) environment (which is described further in Chapter 22). There are several benefits to executing the PI counts in RF, including:

▶ Printing of PI documents is not required

▶ Manual entry of count results is not required

▶ Real-time recording of results in the system

▶ Correct and accurate data entry (by avoiding possible key entry errors during manual entry)

Once a PI document is activated, the PI task(s) get bundled in a WO with the category assignment of "Physical Inventory." This WO for PI represents the executable work package for the PI counting.

In the EWM RF environment, you can choose to execute the counting documents via system-guided processes or manually. In the system-guided processing, the system assigns the WO and PI document to a user. Based on the area in the warehouse where the PI has to be performed, a queue can be determined by the system. The automatic determination is based on customizing but can be changed to manual afterward by the administrator in the EWM monitor. A resource group (which can be assigned to the resource users log on to when accessing the RF transactions via Transaction /SCWM/RFUI, described further in Chapter 22) can be assigned to a queue, allowing a single employee assigned to the resource group to request work for counting using a mobile device.

If you use system-guided processing for executing the PI counts, additional settings are required for managing the queue assignment. This is similar to managing the queues for other warehouse processes, for example, you might want to manage which resources perform which counts based on the physical parameters of the area and the resources. For more information on managing the workload via queues, see Chapter 22.

The warehouse operator can also choose (if authorizations allow) manual processing by specifying a WO (and therefore indirectly the PI document) in the RF transactions. Figure 14.16 illustrates the basic process for creating and executing PI (or "stock take" documents) in the RF environment. Note that the supervisor can control the process by managing the workload for the resources via the warehouse monitor, including direct assignment, reassignment, and prioritization of PI documents in the queues.

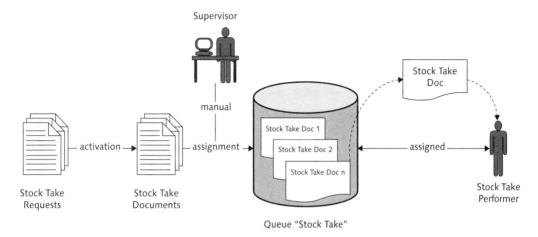

Figure 14.16 PI Process and the Integration into the Resource Management

When an employee executes the PI using a mobile device, EWM automatically captures the time and the counter to the PI document. In Figure 14.17, you can see an example of the mobile data entry screen that could be used on the RF device to capture the count information.

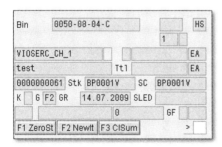

Figure 14.17 PI via Mobile Data Entry Transactions

Similar to the additional mobile data entry transaction (as described further in Chapter 22), the transactions performed via the RF framework can be configured with regard to screen flow, validation fields, and other characteristics.

Once a storage bin is counted, the count data is also stored on the bin and is visible via the storage bin display transactions (including Transaction /SCWM/LS03), as seen in Figure 14.18.

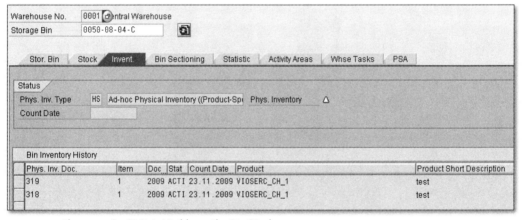

Figure 14.18 PI Data Visible on the Bin Display

14.6 Monitoring the Physical Inventory Progress

Knowing the quantity of warehouse positions and products that have still not been inventoried at the end of a fiscal year can be very important for planning to have a complete inventoried warehouse. A PI area can be considered completely inventoried when you have inventoried all storage bins that are assigned to the PI area. A warehouse is completely inventoried when you have completely inventoried all of the relevant PI areas. A product can be considered completely inventoried when you have counted the whole amount of stocks of the product per fiscal year and the entitled to dispose.

SAP EWM solves the requirement of ensuring a complete inventoried warehouse with monitoring functions in the EWM monitor. To access the EWM monitor from the EWM Easy Access menu, follow the EXTENDED WAREHOUSE MANAGEMENT • MONITORING • WAREHOUSE MANAGEMENT MONITOR menu path, or use Transaction /SCWM/MON.

The queries available in the EWM monitor with regard to the PI progress include:

▶ Product-related queries (as seen in Figure 14.19)

▶ PI area–related queries

▶ CC-related queries

To access the queries in the monitor, select the nodes below the folder via the menu path PHYSICAL INVENTORY • PHYSICAL INVENTORY PROGRESS.

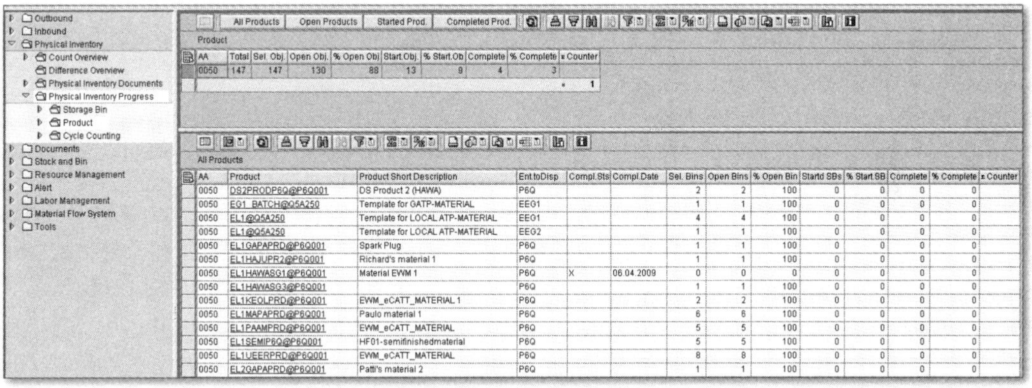

Figure 14.19 PI Progress Reports in the EWM Monitor

In the warehouse monitor, you can display the status of a PI area in an aggregated view or in a detailed view. The aggregated view contains the overall number of positions in the warehouse area and the absolute level and percentage level of both the positions already counted and the positions still to be counted. In the detailed view, you can determine which particular storage bins have not been counted and which have already been counted as well other information about the storage bins. You can also directly trigger the creation of a PI document to complete the relevant counts for a warehouse area.

Additional queries in the warehouse monitor allow you to display the count overview (as seen in Figure 14.20) and difference overview. And a summary of all registered differences can be queried in the warehouse management monitor based on a time horizon specified in the selection criteria.

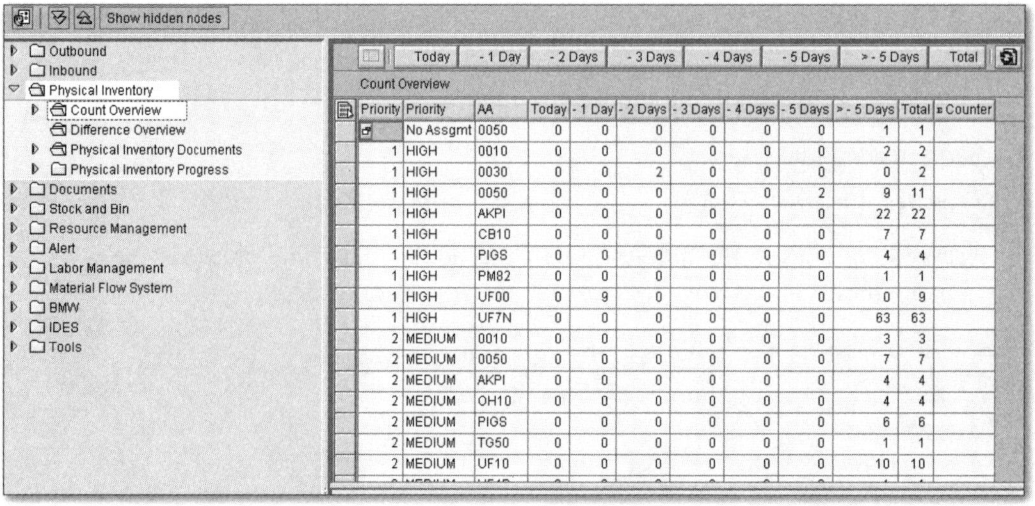

Figure 14.20 PI Count Overview in EWM Monitor

An overview of all PI documents grouped or sorted by inventory procedure or other criteria that can also be displayed in the EWM monitor. For each of the documents selected, you can perform various processes (including displaying, activating, deactivating, reassigning, printing, and changing priority of the inventory documents) by selecting the appropriate method in the monitor (accessed by selecting the relevant document and then using the dropdown selection next to the METHOD button, as shown in Figure 14.21).

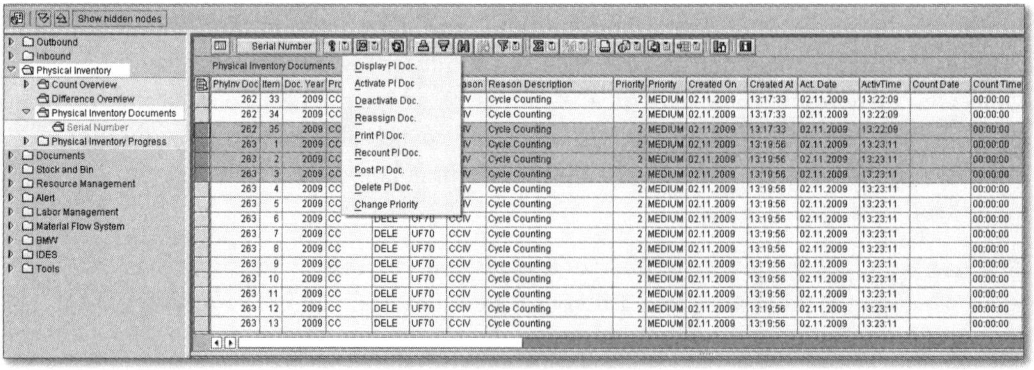

Figure 14.21 PI Document Overview in EWM Monitor

14.7   Summary

In this chapter, we described the objects related to the PI, the PI methods, and the processes for executing and monitoring the PI to help you ensure regulatory compliance and maintain an accurate inventory in the warehouse. In the following chapters, we will further discuss the methods for monitoring the warehouse using the warehouse monitor and analyzing the execution of the warehouse processing using the monitor and the SAP Netweaver Business Warehouse (BW).

SAP provides various tools for monitoring and reporting on warehouse activities, including the Warehouse Management Monitor (which collects reports on the objects of the warehouse into a single user interface), the Easy Graphics Framework (EGF), the Graphical Warehouse Layout (GWL), and SAP Netweaver Business Warehouse (BW)(with delivered extractors and content for Extended Warehouse Management (EWM)).

15 Warehouse Monitoring and Reporting

In EWM, there are different options available to keep warehouse supervisors constantly up to date regarding the current situation in the warehouse, including:

- Warehouse Management Monitor, for displaying information about warehouse documents and processes
- Easy Graphics Framework, for graphically displaying important warehouse figures in real time with autorefresh functionality
- Graphical Warehouse Layout, for displaying the warehouse (including storage bins, resources, and stock) as a two-dimensional graphic

In addition to the warehouse monitor functionalities, data can be extracted from EWM to SAP BW based on predefined DataSources (including executed workload, value-added services (VASs), and warehouse orders (WOs)). In BW, you can analyze the replicated data to help you improve the efficiency of the warehouse and to execute long-term planning of labor requirements based on business forecasts.

In the following sections, we'll describe, in detail, the different warehouse monitor and reporting functionalities of SAP EWM and BW.

15.1 Warehouse Management Monitor

The Warehouse Management Monitor (often simply referred to as the warehouse monitor) is a central tool in EWM that enables a supervisor to monitor the warehouse processes. In the case of overdue activities, the monitor raises alerts and, if necessary, the supervisor can take corrective actions. In addition to its monitoring capabilities, the warehouse monitor can be used to execute work in EWM.

15.1.1 Overview of the Warehouse Monitor

The warehouse monitor lets the supervisor control and monitor the warehouse activities. SAP delivers a standard monitor, which offers a comprehensive view of inbound, outbound, and internal processes, and their related documents. The monitor also contains alert monitoring capabilities, which highlight actual and potential problematic situations such has overdue waves or overdue inbound delivery and outbound delivery activities.

SAP delivers several predefined reports in the warehouse monitor for processes like inbound, outbound, and physical inventory (PI), for resource management, for stock and bin visibility, or labor management (LM), and methods to execute work in the warehouse such as confirmation of warehouse tasks, changing queues for resources, merging or releasing waves, and many more.

In addition, SAP designed the warehouse monitor so that you can adapt it very flexibly for your own requirements. The monitor is based on a framework that allows customer-specific adoptions and enhancements to create your own monitor with your own reports and methods. You can create or hide nodes for a user-specific view of the warehouse activities.

The warehouse management monitor consists primarily of a document and a process view. In Figure 15.1, you can see the basic screen layout of the warehouse monitor, with an example for the display of warehouse orders. As you can see in the figure, the warehouse management monitor is comprised of three subscreens. The left sub-screen displays the hierarchical tree which holds all relevant object classes (e.g., WOs, VAS orders, resources, etc.) that are assigned to predefined nodes. The nodes are presented like a folder structure. To expand a node, select the arrow to the left of the folder.

To open a selection screen for entering the selection criteria for a report, double-click on any node that looks like an open folder. The resulting selection criteria (an example of which you can see in Figure 15.2) only apply to the node and its related object classes.

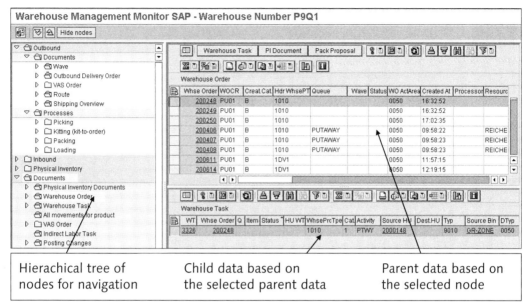

Figure 15.1 Layout of the Warehouse Management Monitor

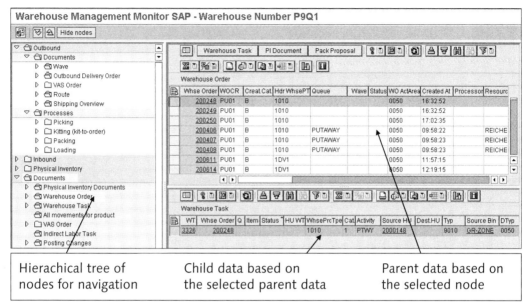

Figure 15.2 Example of a Selection Screen for Warehouse Orders

The right area of the monitor (as seen in Figure 15.1) is divided into two sub-screens — one to display parent data (e.g., all open WOs for activity area 0050) based on your defined selection criteria and one beneath to display child data (e.g., all warehouse tasks that are included in the selected WO). In both subscreens you can toggle between the list and the form view (which provides a focused view of one selected object). From these subscreens, you can perform various activities, including:

▸ Navigate directly to transactions to display detailed data (for example, you can navigate to wave management or to WO confirmation)

▸ Utilize one of several available methods (see Figure 15.3) to perform actions for the selected objects (for example, for WOs)

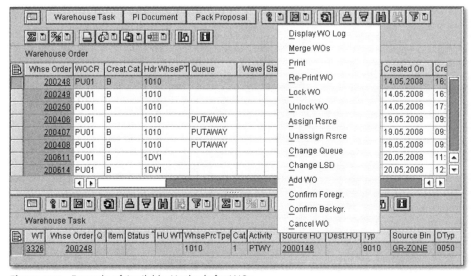

Figure 15.3 Example of Available Methods for WOs

▸ Utilize ABAP List Viewer (ALV) functions such as sorting, filtering, printing, changing layout, saving display variants, and more

▸ Resize the subscreens (using drag-and-drop functions similar to other windowing applications)

▸ View alerts of various types, including:

  ▸ Alerts raised due to overdue situations

  ▸ Alerts raised due to exceptions during execution (as seen in figure 15.4, which displays an exception entered on a radio frequency (RF) device during unloading when a handling unit (HU) was missing from the load)

In the following sections, we will describe various ways to personalize and adapt the warehouse monitor.

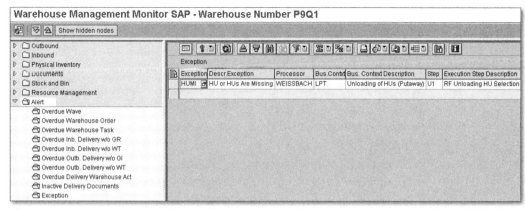

Figure 15.4 Alert Monitoring in the Warehouse Management Monitor

15.1.2   Personalizing the Warehouse Monitor

The warehouse management monitor framework can enhance the monitor to fit your needs. You could, for example, create a completely new monitor with your own content, or you could enhance the SAP standard monitor, and you can choose to make the changes available for all users or only for specific users. For example, you can tailor the SAP standard monitor by:

- Hiding nodes or branches that are irrelevant
- Creating selection criteria variants for standard nodes
- Creating variants of standard nodes
- Creating your own variant nodes based on standard nodes
- Creating new methods to execute work based on your business needs

In the following sections, we will describe these options in detail and describe how you can perform the changes.

Hiding Nodes or Branches

To hide a node or branch, simply right-click on the folder and select the HIDE NODE option. To reactivate the node, select the SHOW HIDDEN NODES button from the menu bar. Once the node is hidden, you will no longer see it again for the same monitor view, but other users will continue to see the node — that is, your specification of hidden nodes is specific to your user ID and does not affect other users.

If you want to permanently hide nodes for all users, you need to disable the node in the configuration, which we will describe later in this chapter.

Creating Selection Variants for Standard Nodes

Using selection variants allows you to specify selection criteria so that you don't need to reenter them every time you run the report. To create a selection criteria variant for standard nodes, you begin by right-clicking on a reporting node (which looks like an open folder) and select the SET SELECTION CRITERIA option (as seen in Figure 15.5). In the following example, we'll create a selection variant for selecting open WOs assigned to a specific queue that was created today. Therefore, we begin by right-clicking on the WAREHOUSE ORDERS folder.

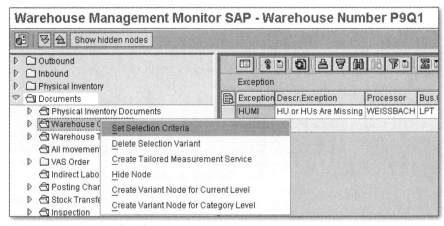

Figure 15.5 Creation of a Selection Variant

Once we select the SET SELECTION CRITERIA option, the selection screen pops up and we can specify the selection criteria, as shown in Figure 15.6.

On the selection screen, you should specify the selection criteria, and then save the selection criteria as a selection variant using the SAVE button at the bottom of the screen. On the resulting VARIANT ATTRIBUTES screen, you can specify dynamic selection criteria (such as today's date; as seen in Figure 15.7) and you can assign the name and description for the selection variant.

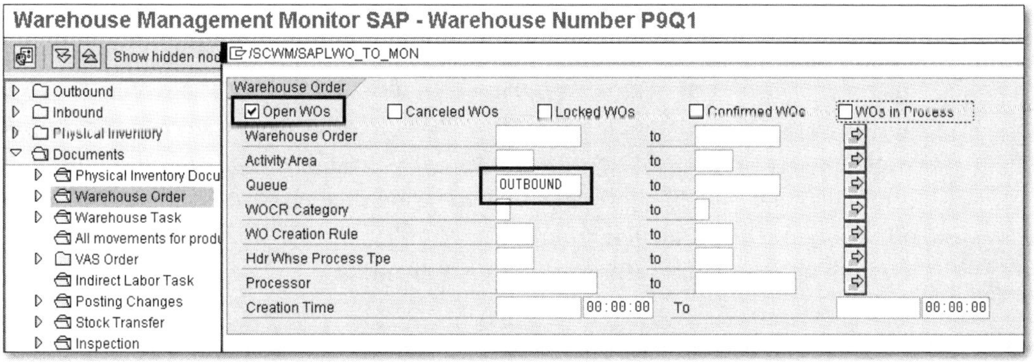

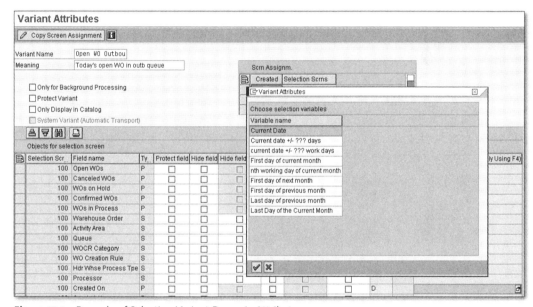

Figure 15.6 Definition of Selection Variant Attributes

Figure 15.7 Example of Selection Variant Dynamic Attributes

Once you save the selection variant, the variant will be available and you can select the selection variant on the selection screen using the GET VARIANT... button at the bottom of the screen.

Creating Nodes for Selection Variants

Once you have created a selection variant, as described previously, you can create a node in the warehouse monitor specifically for calling the report using the selection variant. This can be very helpful if you have a specific report with specific selection criteria that you use very frequently (for example, inventory for certain material or for a certain area, or open warehouse tasks for a certain area, activity, or time period). To create the node, right-click on the node you already created the selection variant for and select one of the CREATE VARIANT NODE options. This will result in a new code being created that you can execute simply by double-clicking on the node — the selection criteria will be pulled directly from the selection variant without requiring you to verify it once again.

Creating a New Node in the Warehouse Monitor

In addition to creating variant nodes, you can also create new nodes by configuring the warehouse monitor. For example, you could create a new node based on an existing one but with different or additional data available in the display variant. Here, we provide a simple example where we create a new node similar to an existing one so that we can describe the relevant structures and processes for creating the new node. Once the new node is created, you can adjust the assigned function module, for example, to adjust the selection criteria, data selected, or data displayed to the screen in the display variant. Once you understand the basic settings involved, you could enhance the standard SAP monitor or even create a completely new monitor based on your own business requirements.

In our example, we want to create a new node IDES on the first level in the hierarchy tree and a subnode based on the standard node OUTBOUND DELIVERY ORDER. In the following figures, we provide an example of how to create your own variant nodes. To access the setup for the monitor nodes in the EWM IMG, follow the menu path EXTENDED WAREHOUSE MANAGEMENT • MONITORING • WAREHOUSE MANAGEMENT MONITOR • DEFINE NODES.

In the first step, you define the OBJECT CLASS. The object class (e.g., WHRO — OUTBOUND DELIVERY ORDER) categorizes objects for management and control purposes. You would only need to create your own object class if you need to use custom methods. In our example, we use the standard object class WHRO, as you can see in Figure 15.8.

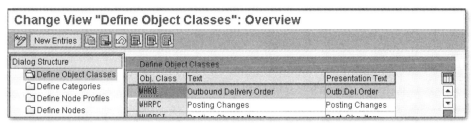

Figure 15.8 Definition of Object Class

In the second step, you define the CATEGORIES. The category enables logical grouping of nodes. In our example (seen in Figure 15.9), we create a new category called IDES.

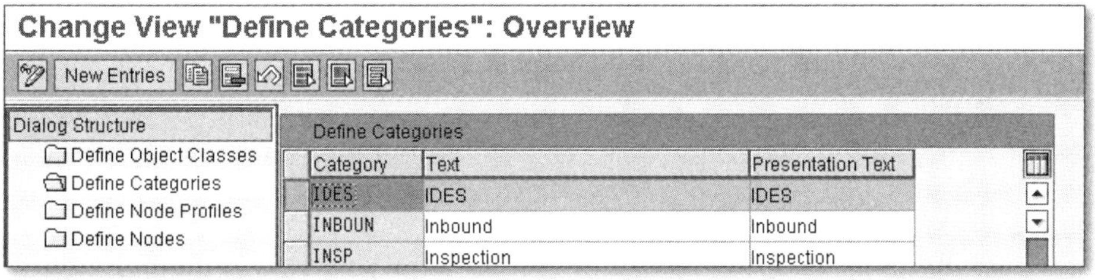

Figure 15.9 Definition of Category

In the third step, you define the NODE PROFILE. The node profile defines the node characteristics, such as object class association, function modules for selection, structures for list and form view, etc. A new node profile is only necessary if you need to define new structures and content for list and form views. In on our example (seen in Figure 15.10), we use the standard node profile for ODOs.

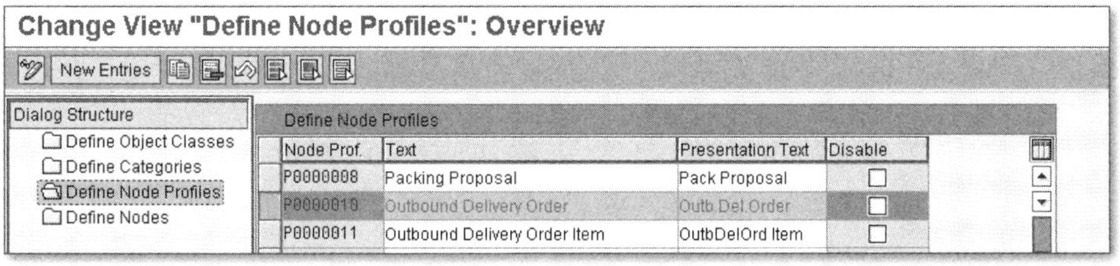

Figure 15.10 Definition of a node profile

In the fourth step, you define the NODE. The node defines a folder in the monitor hierarchy tree. The node can be added to an existing node or can be displayed solely on the first level of the hierarchy tree (category node). In our example, we

563

define two nodes — one for the first level of the hierarchy tree (as seen in figure 15.11) and one as a subnode where the node profile for ODO will be assigned.

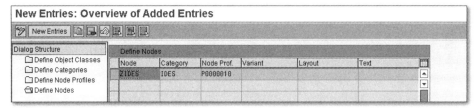

Figure 15.11   Example of a Node Definition

In the fifth and final step, you define the MONITOR and the NODE HIERARCHY. In the warehouse monitor, you can create your own monitors with your own hierarchy tree. For example, you may want to create separate monitors only for outbound processes or inbound processes. To set up the monitor and the hierarchy in the EWM IMG, follow the menu path EXTENDED WAREHOUSE MANAGEMENT • MONITORING • WAREHOUSE MANAGEMENT MONITOR • DEFINE MONITORS. In our example, we'll simply assign our new node (IDES) to the standard SAP monitor.

To assign the node hierarchy, we first assign the node (IDES) to the subnode (which includes the node profile for ODOs), as you can see in Figure 15.12.

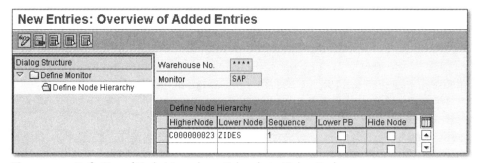

Figure 15.12   Definition of Node Hierarchy — Subnode to Higher Node

Next, we assign the node (IDES) to the higher node ROOT (as you can see in Figure 15.13), which causes our new node to be displayed on the first level of the hierarchy tree.

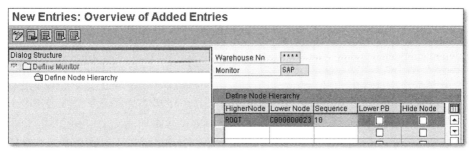

Figure 15.13 Definition of Node Hierarchy — Higher Node to the Root Node

Once we have set up the customizing settings, our new node is displayed in the warehouse monitor, as you can see in Figure 15.14.

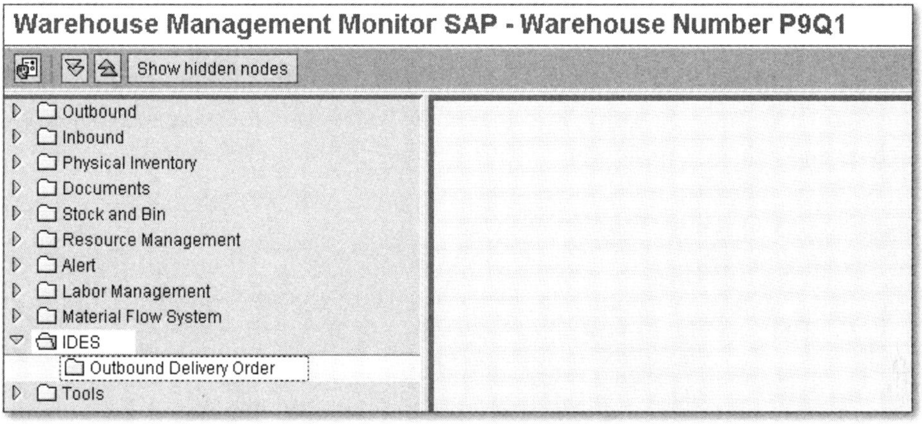

Figure 15.14 Display of a New Node in the Warehouse Monitor

Creating New Methods

You can manage WOs and processes in the warehouse monitor using methods. While there are several standard methods provided, you can also create and assign your own methods to enhance the capabilities of the monitor. Once you have defined the methods, you can assign them to the relevant object class in the EWM IMG, by following the menu path EXTENDED WAREHOUSE MANAGEMENT • MONITORING • WAREHOUSE MANAGEMENT MONITOR • DEFINE OBJECT CLASS METHODS.

15.2 Easy Graphics Framework

The Easy Graphics Framework (EGF) is a generic tool intended to provide a central framework for various applications to develop cockpits that can display vital information in an easy-to-understand and easy-to-use graphic format. The EGF offers real-time graphical display or automatic refresh that enables instant access to an overview of how processes are running within an application. In addition, the EGF provides tools for applications to display graphics in a cockpit or integrated within application screens (subscreens or pop-ups). The EGF layout can be defined as user specific or across users.

EWM offers a warehouse cockpit that is an example implementation of the EGF. The warehouse cockpit can be started by Transaction /SCWM/EGF and lets you display warehouse key figures and defined EGF objects graphically, and to evaluate or monitor them using defined chart types, including speedometers, GANTT charts, pie charts, traffic lights, etc. In Figure 15.15, you can see an example of the warehouse cockpit, which is displaying overdue warehouse tasks grouped by queues and defined thresholds (30 minutes overdue and 60 minutes overdue).

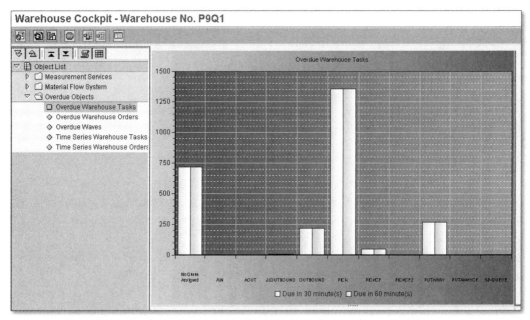

Figure 15.15 Displaying Overdue Warehouse Tasks in the Warehouse Cockpit

15.2.1 Enhancing the Warehouse Cockpit

In addition to the standard delivered warehouse cockpit, you can also enhance the cockpit implementation using the EGF. To start, you create your own key figures using measurement services. Then you can assign the key figures in the setup of the warehouse cockpit navigation.

Creating Your Own Key Figures

You can create your own key figures to display in the warehouse cockpit. To create the key figures, you can utilize basic measurement services and tailored measurement services. In the example provided in the following figures, we'll create a new key figure using a tailored measurement service to calculate the number of open WOs that were created in an activity area in the last few days. Then we'll assign the key figure to the warehouse cockpit and view the results.

To begin, we start the creation of a tailored measurement service (TMS) using the wizard (via Transaction /SCWM/TLR_WIZARD), as seen in Figure 15.16.

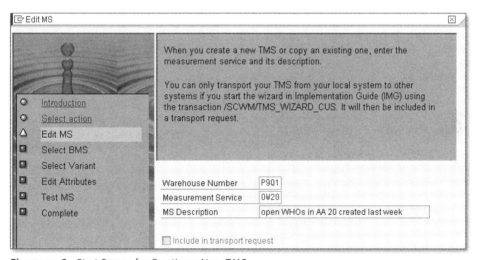

Figure 15.16 Start Screen for Creating a New TMS

A TMS is based on a basic measurement service (BMS), which acts as the building blocks of the warehouse key figures. In the second step, we specify the relevant BMS for calculating the TMS. In our example, we leverage the BMS for the number of WOs, as you can see in Figure 15.17.

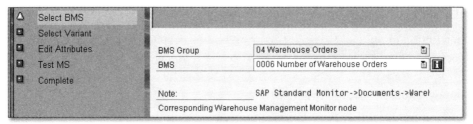

Figure 15.17 Selection of the Right Basic Measurement Service

In the third step, you create your own selection variant. In our example, we specified the static selection criteria for OPEN WAREHOUSE ORDERS, ACTIVITY AREA 0020, and we assigned the DYNAMIC SELECTION CRITERIA for CREATED IN LAST 5 WORKING DAYS. Then we assigned a name to the variant and save it (see Figure 15.18).

Variant Attributes

Copy Screen Assignment

| Variant Name | OW20 |
| Meaning | open WHOs in AA 20 last week |

☐ Only for Background Processing
☐ Protect Variant
☐ Only Display in Catalog
☐ System Variant (Automatic Transport)

Scrn Assignm.

Created	Selection Scrns
☑	0100
☐	0200
☐	0300

Objects for selection screen

Selection Scr	Field name	Ty	Protect field	Hide field	Hide field 'BIS'	Save fi	Switch GPA off	Required field	Selection variable	O	Name of Variable (Input Only Us
100	Open WOs	P	☐	☐	☐	☐	☐	☐			
100	Canceled WOs	P	☐	☐	☐	☐	☐	☐			
100	WOs on Hold	P	☐	☐	☐	☐	☐	☐			
100	Confirmed WOs	P	☐	☐	☐	☐	☐	☐			
100	WOs in Process	P	☐	☐	☐	☐	☐	☐			
100	Warehouse Order	S	☐	☐	☐	☐	☐	☐			
100	Activity Area	S	☐	☐	☐	☐	☐	☐			
100	Queue	S	☐	☐	☐	☐	☐	☐			
100	WOCR Category	S	☐	☐	☐	☐	☐	☐			
100	WO Creation Rule	S	☐	☐	☐	☐	☐	☐			
100	Hdr Whse Process Tpe	S	☐	☐	☐	☐	☐	☐			
100	Processor	S	☐	☐	☐	☐	☐	☐			
100	Created On	P	☐	☐	☐	☐	☐	☐	D		current date - 5 work days

Figure 15.18 Defining the Variant Attributes for the TMS

In the fourth step, you define the thresholds and exception codes. Thresholds can be used to control the key figures and provide visual clues when a parameter is beyond the defined threshold. In our example, if there are more than three open WOs, then the color on the graphic is changed from green to red.

Exception codes are used to trigger subsequent activities. If any of the thresholds are violated, the exception code is triggered and the follow-up activities can be initiated using the Post-Processing Framework (PPF) (described in detail in Chapter 24, Post-Processing Framework and Form Printing).

In the fifth and final step, you assign the new object to the navigation tree of the warehouse cockpit, as you can see in Figure 15.19.

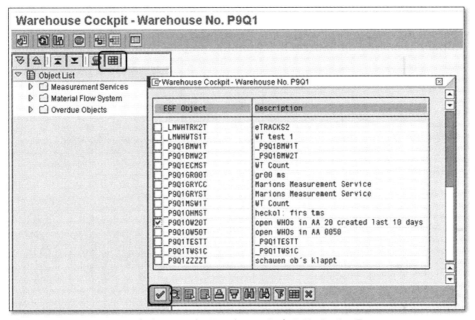

Figure 15.19 Assignment of Object to the Warehouse Cockpit Navigation Tree

Once the new TMS is assigned to the navigation tree, the new EGF object can be graphically displayed in the warehouse cockpit, as you can see in Figure 15.20.

Defining the Warehouse Cockpit Layout

You can define your own layout for the warehouse cockpit, either on an individual user basis or across users. This enables you, for instance, to group objects in the navigation tree or to define the number of rows and columns of the display grid and the layout of the grid. You can also define different layout options only for the navigation tree; the navigation tree and the grid layout; or the navigation tree, grid layout, and the input data (e.g., warehouse number).

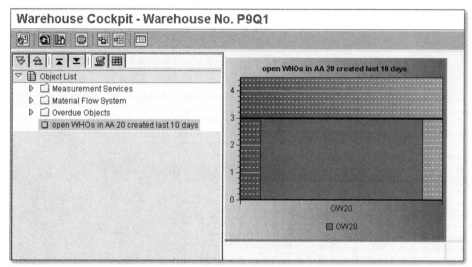

Figure 15.20 Display of the TMS for Open WOs Displayed in the Warehouse Cockpit

Customizing the Warehouse Cockpit Objects

In customizing, you can assign your own chart types aside from the chart types delivered by SAP. To define the chart types in the EWM IMG, follow the menu path EXTENDED WAREHOUSE MANAGEMENT • MONITORING • EASY GRAPHICS FRAMEWORK • DEFINE CHART TYPES. Once the chart types are created, you can assign them to the EGF objects.

Defining the EGF Objects

You can also create your own objects aside from the objects delivered by SAP for the warehouse cockpit. Several steps are necessary to create your own object with your own data. To illustrate the possibilities, we'll show an example where we integrate a web page in the warehouse cockpit.

In the first step, we define the service provider the EGF receives data from. For each EGF object, you must assign a service provider in the customizing. The service provider implements an ABAP object-oriented interface provided by the EGF. Via the interface methods, EGF retrieves data from the application at runtime. In Figure 15.21, you can see a graphical depiction of how the service provider works.

Figure 15.21 Overview of the Simplified Data Flow in the EGF

To begin creating the service provider, you must first create the object type using Transaction SE24.

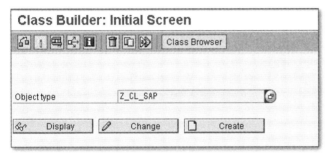

Figure 15.22 Creation of an Object Type for the Service Provider

The EGF can work with various interfaces, methods, and function modules. In our example, the service provider interface /SCWM/IF_EGF_SP has been assigned.

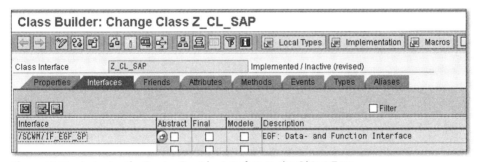

Figure 15.23 Assigning the Service Provider Interface to the Object Type

Once the interface is assigned to the object type, the GET_URL method must be implemented. This method gets a URL from the application. This URL forms the link to the graphic that the EGF will display. For on our example, the implementation looks like the method definition shown in Figure 15.24.

```
Class Builder: Class Z_CL_SAP Change
```

Ty.	Parameter	Type spec.	Description
▶□	IV_OBJECT_ID	TYPE /SCWM/DE_EGF_OBJECT_ID	EGF Object
▶□	IV_CELL_ID	TYPE /SCWM/DE_EGF_CELL_ID	Cell Identifier
▶□	IV_CHART_TYPE	TYPE /SCWM/DE_EGF_CHART_TYPE	EGF Chart Type
▶□	IV_REFRESH	TYPE ABAP_BOOL	Flag: Call Through Refresh
▶□	IV_CHART_ONLY	TYPE ABAP_BOOL	Flag: Refresh Graphic Only
▶□	IV_HEIGHT	TYPE INT4	Height
▶□	IV_WIDTH	TYPE INT4	Width
▶□	IT_COCKPIT_INPUT	TYPE /SCWM/TT_DS_SELOPT_TABLE OPTIONAL	Selection Parameter
▶□	IT_OBJECT_INPUT	TYPE /SCWM/TT_DS_SELOPT_TABLE OPTIONAL	Selection Parameter
□▶	EV_URL	TYPE W3URL	URL
□▶	ET_MSG	TYPE /SCWM/TT_EGF_MESSAGES	EGF: Messages

Method	/SCWM/IF_EGF_SP~GET_URL	Inactive (revised)

```
1  ⊟ method /SCWM/IF_EGF_SP~GET_URL.
2▶
3▶     ev_url = 'http://www.sap.com/index.epx'.
4▶
5  └ endmethod.
```

Figure 15.24   Implementation of Service Provider Method GET_URL

Once the object type is activated, we'll assign it to the new defined object (as shown in Figure 15.25) in the EWM IMG via the menu path SCM EXTENDED WAREHOUSE MANAGEMENT • MONITORING • EASY GRAPHICS FRAMEWORK • DEFINE OBJECTS.

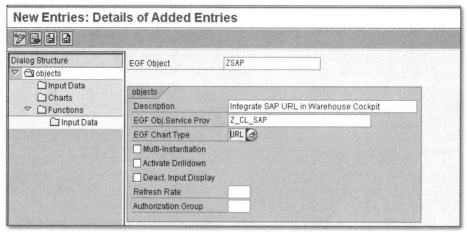

Figure 15.25   Example of an Object Definition in EGF

In the third step, you assign the new object to a cockpit. In our example, we enhance the objects delivered by SAP with our new object in the warehouse cockpit (as in Figure 15.26). To define the cockpit in the EWM IMG, follow the menu path Extended Warehouse Management • Monitoring • Easy Graphics Framework • Define Cockpits.

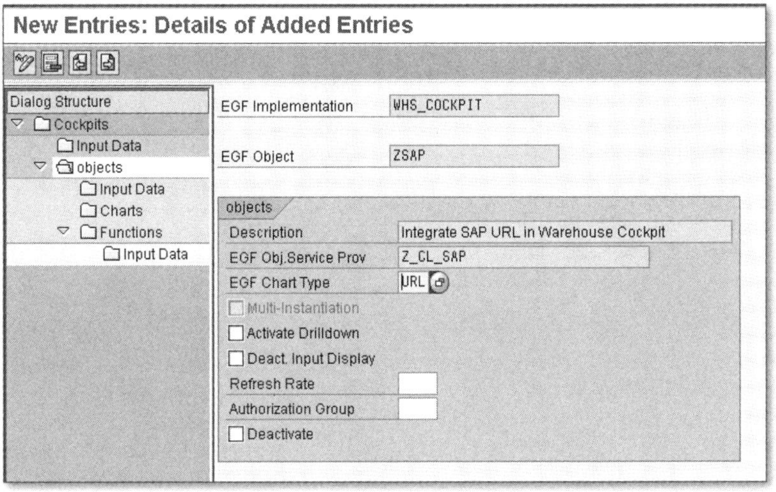

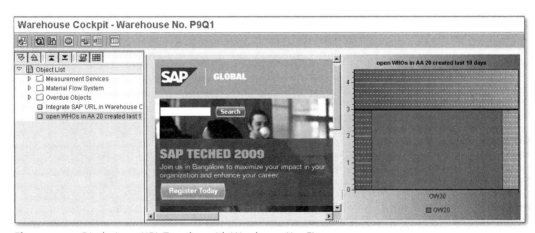

Figure 15.26 Assigning the New EGF Object to the Warehouse Cockpit

Once the new object has been assigned to the cockpit, you can assign the object to the navigation tree of the warehouse cockpit, as described previously in this chapter. In Figure 15.27, you can see the final result of the assignment.

Figure 15.27 Displaying a URL Together with Warehouse Key Figures

15.3   Graphical Warehouse Layout

The Graphical Warehouse Layout (GWL) lets you display the warehouse as a two-dimensional graphic. Using the GWL, you can get graphical information about the stock situation, empty bins, resources working in the warehouse, location of HUs, and nodes and conveyors of the material flow system (MFS). The GWL displays the warehouse data per warehouse number.

The GWL lets you check the warehouse coordinates for travel distance calculations (used in LM), and to get an overview of empty bins or blocked bins to see if your warehouse is optimally distributed. In Figure 15.28, you can see an example of a warehouse layout using the GWL.

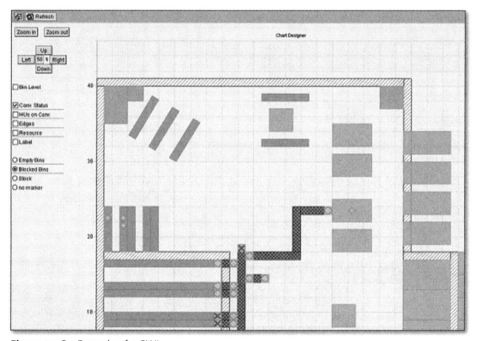

Figure 15.28   Example of a GWL

In addition to the previously described objects, you can also define warehouse objects such as conveyor segments, walls, and offices in the EWM IMG by following the menu path EXTENDED WAREHOUSE MANAGEMENT • MONITORING • GRAPHICAL WAREHOUSE LAYOUT • DEFINE GWL OBJECT. In the example, different objects are displayed in different colors (e.g., walls are grey lined, single bins are visualized in green, shelves are shown in brown and determined from the bin data). Bin dimensions shown in the GWL are determined by the bin type definition from the customizing, and the bin position is determined by the XYZ coordinates maintained in the bin master data. Bin status is shown in the display using a star — for example, in the display, we selected to show a blocked bin on the left side, and the blocked bins were then marked in the display. SAP delivers four standard statuses for selection: empty bins, blocked bins, stock and no marker. You can also enhance the WGL with your own statuses using the available Business Add-In (BAdIs).

You can also define and visualize the control points of the MFS. These control points are visualized with a red cross or a green circle, depending on the actual status — a red cross indicates that the control point is in status Error and a green circle indicates that the status is OK.

You can use the Zoom In and Zoom Out pushbuttons to change the scale and display either the entire warehouse or individual objects in the warehouse. To navigate up, down, left, and right, use the buttons in the top left. The percentage value in the middle of the buttons indicates how far the current display will shift in the respective direction compared to the total warehouse size.

15.4 Warehouse Reporting

To drive improvements in warehouse operations and plan appropriately based on labor requirements, it is important to get an aggregated but detailed view on key figures and attributes. To facilitate this sort of analysis, EWM distributes actual and executed data to BW so that the data can be analyzed there. In the following sections we'll give an overview of the EWM BW integration and reporting approaches using the standard content.

15.4.1 Overview of EWM BW integration

To support the integration between EWM and BW, SAP provides standard extractors in EWM and standard content in BW. In this section, we will provide a high-level overview to the integration between EWM and BW.

In BW terms, EWM is a source system, as it provides data to the BW system. To facilitate the communication between the two systems, you must first set up the technical connectivity between the systems. Once the systems are connected properly and reporting content is activated, reporting relevant data can be requested and uploaded from EWM to BW. These data are passing from EWM to BW via the extract transform load (ETL) process, which uploads and harmonizes the data and loads it to content-specific tables in BW, namely the Persistent Staging Area (PSA). From the PSA, data flows throughout the BW system and are provided to queries, the basis of BW reports. Because performance is an important requirement, the uploaded EWM data are aggregated and partitioned for specific reporting purposes in BW.

BW harmonizes the data coming from multiple source systems so that they can be integrated in a single reporting approach. This harmonization and normalization is done in BW during the upload of extracted data from the PSA to InfoProviders such as Data Store Objects (DSOs) and InfoCubes, which store the data. The Info-Providers are responsible for the aggregation and partitioning of the reporting-relevant data.

When EWM reporting-relevant data are extracted, transformed, and uploaded to InfoProviders, queries can request data directly from the InfoProviders and provide them to frontend systems for visualization in the reporting tools.

In Figure 15.29, you can see a graphical overview of this process.

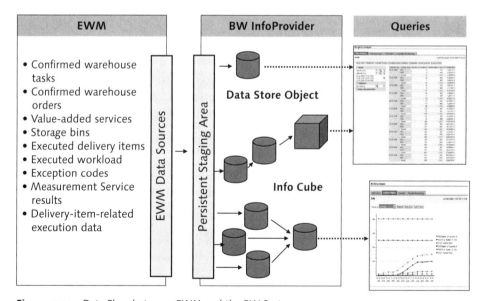

Figure 15.29 Data Flow between EWM and the BW System

15.4.2 EWM-Specific Reporting Content

The upload of the data from EWM is performed by the DataSources located in EWM. A DataSource determines which fields of business events are to be transferred to BW, and these fields are included in the extract structure. The DataSource also describes the properties of the extractor.

A DataSource contains an extract structure (a data dictionary (DDIC) structure) and information about the kind of data that is provided. These data are replicated to the InfoSources in the PSA on the BW side. In Table 15.1, you can see a list of the DataSources available in EWM.

DataSource	Description
0WM_LGNUM_ATTR	Attributes of a Warehouse
0WM_MS_TEXT	Measurement Service Names
0WM_LGNUM_TEXT	Warehouse Number Descriptions
0WM_DLVI	Delivery Items
0WM_PL_DLVI	Delivery-item-related Execution Data
0WM_EXCCODES	Exceptions
0WM_EWL	Executed Workload
0WM_MS_RESULT	Measurement Service Results
0WM_BIN	Storage Bin
0WM_VAS	Value-Added Services
0WM_WO	Warehouse Orders
0WM_WT	Warehouse Tasks
0WM_WT_WO	Warehouse Orders and Warehouse Tasks

Table 15.1 List of DataSources Available for EWM

15.4.3 BW Objects for Reporting

In this section, we'll introduce the most important BW objects that are used for uploading and using the reporting relevant data from a source system such as EWM. In Figure 15.30, you can see a graphical representation of the data flow from a source system (such as EWM) to BW.

InfoPackages

To access DataSource content data and provide them to BW, the corresponding metadata of the InfoPackage must be transferred to the BW system (a process known as *replication*). This InfoPackage is responsible for uploading data from a source system such as EWM, to the BW DataSource.

InfoProvider

InfoProviders (including DSOs, InfoCubes and MultiProviders) are BW objects that show logical views of data relevant to reporting purposes. InfoProviders represent physical and logical databases providing reporting-relevant data for other InfoProviders or queries.

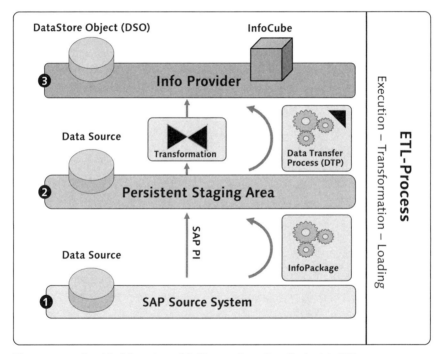

Figure 15.30   Graphical Overview of Setting-up Reporting Content in BW

DSO

The DSO is the basis of the data flow in BW. All data uploaded to BW are stored in this database. In Table 15.2, you can see the DSOs that are delivered standard by SAP for storing warehouse-relevant data.

Data Store Object	Description
0WM_DS01	Results Measurement Services
0WM_DS02	Executed Workload
0WM_DS03	Exception Log
0WM_DS04	Warehouse Orders
0WM_DS05	Warehouse Tasks
0WM_DS06	Delivery Items
0WM_DS07	Storage Bin
0WM_DS08	Value-Added Services
0WM_DS09	Strategic Planning

Table 15.2 Warehouse-specific DSOs Delivered By SAP

InfoCubes

InfoCubes (similar to the DSO) contain persistent transactional data from a certain source system like EWM in a homogenous business context. In Table 15.3, you can see the InfoCubes that are delivered standard by SAP for storing warehouse-relevant data.

InfoCube	Description	Details
0WM_C01	InfoCube Aggregated Executed Workload	This InfoCube aggregates the executed workload from DSO *Executed Workload* (0WM_DS02)
0WM_C02	InfoCube Exceptions	This InfoCube is assigned to DSO *Exceptions* (0WM_DS03)
0WM_C04	InfoCube WO	This InfoCube contains information about WOs
0WM_C05	InfoCube WT	This InfoCube contains information about warehouse tasks

Table 15.3 Warehouse-specific InfoCubes Delivered By SAP

InfoCube	Description	Details
0WM_C06	InfoCube DLVI	This InfoCube aggregates the delivery items from DSO *Delivery item* (0WM_DS06) according to different criteria
0WM_C07	InfoCube BIN	Analysis of storage bins
0WM_C09	InfoCube strategic planning — basic	Aggregation of delivery items (real time)
0WM_C10	InfoCube strategic planning — real time	Data from InfoCube *Strategic Planning – Evaluation Data* (0WM_C09) is loaded, and can be viewed as historical data via planning version 0

Table 15.3 Warehouse-specific InfoCubes Delivered By SAP (Cont.)

MultiProvider

MultiProviders can merge data from multiple InfoProviders to provide a set of data to queries. They only hold data transiently to offer them to downstream queries. In Table 15.4, you can see the MultiProviders that are delivered standard by SAP to transfer warehouse-relevant data.

MultiProvider	Description
0WM_MP01	Results of Measurement Services
0WM_MP02	Executed Workload
0WM_MP03	Aggregated Executed Workload
0WM_MP04	Exceptions
0WM_MP05	WOs and Warehouse Tasks
0WM_MP06	Aggregated Delivery Items
0WM_MP07	Aggregated Storage Bins

Table 15.4 Warehouse-specific MultiProviders Delivered By SAP

Transformation

The transformation is used to harmonize and standardize fields from a source to a target BW object. Transformations are always used during data upload to persistent data targets. The main areas of operation are editing replicated data during upload form the BW PSA to the DSOs and during the data upload from DSOs to InfoCubes.

Data Transfer Process

The Data Transfer Process (DTP) is the BW object that manages the dataflow (filter, full, or delta update) for a certain transformation. According to the dataflow model, it may be necessary to create more than one DTP (e.g., if multiple transformation are in use).

15.4.4 Extraction Process

The extraction process is responsible for the retrieval of reporting-relevant application data from the source system, such as EWM. The extraction process is divided into two parts — the initial extraction and the delta extraction.

The initial extraction is the first extraction process. It is designed to be executed once and export all data captured up to a certain point in time. The delta process is scheduled to run periodically multiple times in the lifetime of a DataSource to supply the BW system with any new or changed reporting-relevant application data.

There are also two types of data extraction — *push extraction* and *pull extraction*. The main difference between push and pull extraction is the way delta data is determined during the initial and delta extraction process. In the following sections, we'll explain these two methods in detail. In describing them, we will consider two key questions that will help you understand the overall extraction concept, namely:

▶ Where are the data taken from?

▶ How are the delta data determined?

Pull Extraction

During online transactional processing, reporting-relevant application data are written to database tables. Those database tables are the source for data taken during both the initial and delta extraction.

While the initial extraction takes all data stored at the point of extraction in the corresponding database tables, the delta extraction only considers data that has not yet been extracted to BW. Data are *pulled* directly from the database tables in both extraction processes (initial extraction and delta extraction) at the request of BW. This request is sent via intermediate document (IDoc) from BW to EWM. It is triggered by an InfoPackage, and normally scheduled for a specific interval.

To determine delta data, extractors check the database tables against a specific value — the *delta-relevant field* — which could, for example, be represented by a timestamp containing the last extraction time. This delta-relevant field is stored and taken from the BW Delta Queue, where it is updated during every delta data extraction.

In EWM, the following DataSources are preconfigured for pull data extraction:

- Executed Workload (DataSource 0WM_EWL)
- Warehouse Tasks and WOs (DataSource 0WM_WT_WO)

Push Extraction

In the push extraction process, the initial and delta extractions are strongly differentiated from one another. During initial extraction, data are not taken from database tables, but from DataSource-specific setup tables. Before the initial extraction can be processed these setup tables must be maintained to provide the reporting-relevant data. The InfoPackage then accesses the data from the setup tables and extracts them to BW.

Using DataSources that are set up for the push data extraction, the delta data determination is managed by the update processing of the application. The update program of the application called during online postings (e.g., confirmation of warehouse tasks) *pushes* reporting-relevant data to the BW Delta Queue. This process has to be activated before delta extraction is executed. As soon as BW requests data from EWM via the corresponding InfoPackage, data are taken from the BW Delta Queue and transferred to BW.

In EWM, the following DataSources are preconfigured for push data extraction:

- Storage Bins (DataSource 0WM_BIN)
- Delivery Items (DataSource 0WM_DLVI)
- Value-Added Services (DataSource 0WM_VAS)
- Warehouse Orders (DataSource 0WM_WO)
- Warehouse Tasks (DataSource 0WM_WT)

15.4.5 Reporting Tools

SAP provides various reporting and analysis tools to display queries in BW. One option is the Business Explorer (BEx). These tools allow business experts to create and distribute the necessary reports and analyses. The tools are integrated with each other and have user-friendly, intuitive interfaces. A detailed analysis of BW information can be performed both on the Web and in Microsoft® Excel. You can also define formatted reports optimized for presentation and printing. Additional web applications and formatted reports can easily be converted into PDF files and printed.

In addition, there are also reporting and analysis tools in the SAP Business Objects suite. One example is Crystal Reports, which allows you to create reports and publish them in a variety of formats, including Microsoft® Word and Excel, email, or as HTML, which can be published over the Web. Another tool from the Business Objects suite is xCelsius, which allows you to transform data into insightful dashboards. These dashboards enable decision makers to monitor business performance, identify critical data relationships, and use what-if scenarios to understand potential performance. Multiple reports and data can be consolidated from various locations into a single dashboard — giving you a holistic view of your company's warehouse data. Figure 15.31 shows an example of a dashboard with a focus on LM data from EWM.

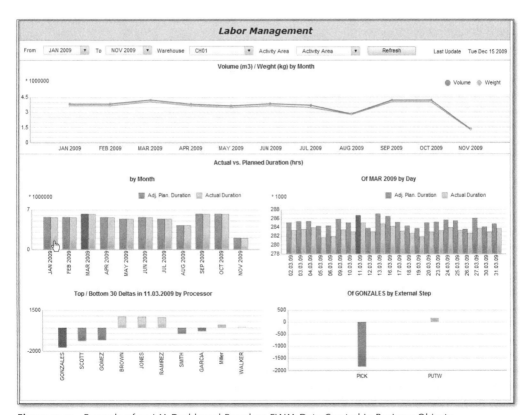

Figure 15.31 Example of an LM Dashboard Based on EWM Data Created in Business Objects

15.5 Summary

In this chapter, we described the warehouse monitoring and reporting functions in EWM, including the Warehouse Management Monitor, EGF, warehouse cockpit, and GWL. We also described the warehouse reporting possibilities based on extracting data from EWM to SAP BW and BW specific reporting content. You should now have a good understanding of the EWM monitoring and reporting capabilities.

In this chapter, we will discuss how to effectively use exception codes to manage exceptions found during the warehouse business processes.

16   Exception Handling

To keep the gap between the real world (physical warehouse) and the system data small over time, detected inconsistencies must be entered into the warehouse management system as soon as possible. Extended Warehouse Management (EWM) provides advanced functionality to record and manage exceptions that occur during warehouse processing in real time.

For example, if a warehouse employee is assigned to a picking warehouse task, the system tells him the pick quantity and the storage bin from which the stock should be picked. When the warehouse employee arrives at the bin, he notices that the bin is empty or that the entire requested quantity is not available in the bin (or the bin is "short"). With EWM exception handling, the employee is able to describe the problem by entering an appropriate *exception code* via the mobile data entry transaction. The system can then react in the way that you specified in the customizing — for example, it can block the storage bin for further processing, create a physical inventory (PI) document for the bin, trigger replenishment, or direct the employee to another bin for the same product.

Exception handling is fully integrated into EWM. You can enter exception codes in every goods movement transaction and for nearly every process step. SAP delivers around 40 exception codes in the standard delivered settings for EWM, and you can create as many new ones as you want (within the theoretical limits defined by the field size, which is four characters). Every exception code has a clearly defined business implication — for example, changing a warehouse task quantity, blocking a storage bin, change of a delivery quantity, creation of PI documents, start of a workflow, or triggering of an alert in the SAP Alert Framework. These business implications are configurable.

In the following sections, we will provide more information about exception handling. First, we explain how exception codes are configured, and we will provide an example. After that, we will demonstrate how the new exception code can be used in the application. Then we will also describe exceptions for Stock Transfer Orders (STOs), and, finally, we will describe how EWM lets you change the quantity for a putaway task using exception codes (even when it has already been confirmed).

16.1 Configuring Exception Codes

In this section, we will explain how you can define exception codes in Customizing and how follow-up actions like business impact, workflow processing, or alert triggering are assigned. We will start with some technical background information, in order for you to understand the basics of EWM exception codes. Then, we will show you an example of how to create a new exception code that will reduce the delivery quantity based on an exception found at putaway confirmation.

16.1.1 Technical Information about EWM Exception Codes

There are several concepts of exception processing that are important for understanding the discussion; therefore we will explain them in the following sections. These terms include *internal process code*, *business context*, *execution step*, and *exception code profile*.

Internal Process Code

You can use an internal process code to define how EWM should react upon assignment of an exception code to the warehouse task during confirmation. You can define the exception code itself freely (which is up to four characters long, as seen later in this chapter in Figure 16.2), and you can give it any name you want (free-form text). But in order for EWM to know what it should do when the exception code is used, you must assign an internal process code to the exception code. Examples of some commonly used internal process codes are shown in Table 16.1.

Internal Process Code	Description
BIDF	Pick Denial (Entire Quantity)
BIDP	Pick Denial (Partial Quantity)
CHBD	Change Destination Storage Bin (Location)
COCO	Confirmation Correction
DIFF	Post with Difference

Table 16.1 Examples for Internal Process Codes in EWM

Business Context and Execution Steps

Exception codes and internal process codes are organized into business contexts and execution steps. The contexts and steps are defined by SAP and all internal process codes are assigned to one or more business contexts and execution steps. Examples for business contexts include Confirm Warehouse Task (Intern. Movemnt), Confirm Warehouse Task (Stock Removal), Confirm Warehouse Task (Putaway), Follow-Up Action After Quality Inspection, and MFS — Communication Point. Possible execution steps for assignment to the exception code are also delivered by SAP, including some commonly used ones shown in Table 16.2.

Execution Step	Description
02	Desktop Product Warehouse Task
05	RF Product WT Action on Source Data
06	RF Product WT Action on Target Data
16	Desktop Differences at Work Center
17	RF Packing

Table 16.2 Examples of Execution Steps in EWM

To view the business contexts and execution steps in the EWM Implementation Guide (IMG), follow the menu path EXTENDED WAREHOUSE MANAGEMENT • CROSS-PROCESS SETTINGS • EXCEPTION HANDLING • MAINTAIN BUSINESS CONTEXT FOR EXCEPTION CODES.

Exception Code Profile

The availability of exception codes can be restricted to certain users based on profiles assigned to the users. For example, you could assign certain exception codes with extensive follow-up actions to more qualified warehouse employees. By linking the user ID with the *exception code profile*, you can ensure that only this group of persons can execute special exception codes. To assign user IDs to exception code profiles in the EWM Easy Access menu, follow the menu path EXTENDED WAREHOUSE MANAGEMENT • SETTINGS • ASSIGN USER TO EXCEPTION CODE PROFILE, or use Transaction code /SCWM/EXCUSERID.

16.1.2 Defining a New Exception Code

To create a new exception code in the EWM IMG, follow the menu path EXTENDED WAREHOUSE MANAGEMENT • CROSS-PROCESS SETTINGS • EXCEPTION HANDLING • DEFINE EXCEPTION CODES (as seen in Figure 16.1). In the example from the figure, we want to create a new exception code for managing putaway discrepancies. If a received product is unusable, we want to confirm the putaway warehouse task with a quantity difference and also reduce the inbound delivery quantity. (Note: Whether you allow the operators to reduce the delivery quantity for unusable product versus missing product depends on your company's business policies, and the example in Figure 16.1 may not be relevant in every case.)

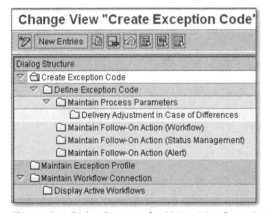

Figure 16.1 Dialog Structure for Maintaining Exception Codes in the IMG

To create a new exception code, you must start with the first activity — CREATE EXCEPTION CODE. First, enter the name of the EXCEPTION CODE and a DESCRIPTION, as seen in Figure 16.2. To the right of the description, we selected the WITH HIST. checkbox. Selecting this indicator will let you evaluate the processed exceptions in the EWM monitor (Transaction /SCWM/MON) according to criteria such as Business Context, Execution Step, and Date (via the node: ALERT • EXCEPTION).

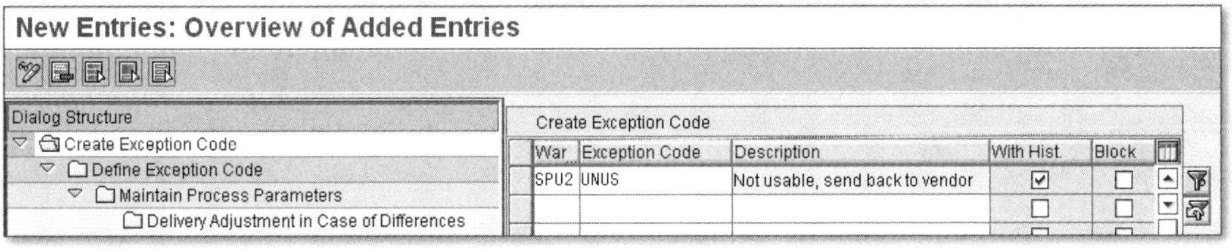

New Entries: Overview of Added Entries

Dialog Structure	Create Exception Code					
▽ 🗁 Create Exception Code	War	Exception Code	Description	With Hist.	Block	
▽ 🗀 Define Exception Code	SPU2	UNUS	Not usable, send back to vendor	☑	☐	
▽ 🗀 Maintain Process Parameters				☐	☐	
🗀 Delivery Adjustment in Case of Differences				☐	☐	

Figure 16.2 Creation of a New Exception Code

Next, you define the exception code by selecting the line and double-clicking on the next activity in the dialog structure — DEFINE EXCEPTION CODE. In this node, you define in what context the new exception code will be valid, for example, for which business contexts. To create a new entry (as seen in Figure 16.3), select the NEW ENTRIES button. In the example, we have already chosen the BUSINESS CONTEXT: TPT CONFIRM WAREHOUSE TASK (PUTAWAY). The pop-up window on the bottom right of the screen shows which execution steps are available within this business context. For the first entry, we will select STEP 02 (DESKTOP PRODUCT WAREHOUSE TASK) to make the exception code usable on the desktop transaction when confirming a product warehouse task.

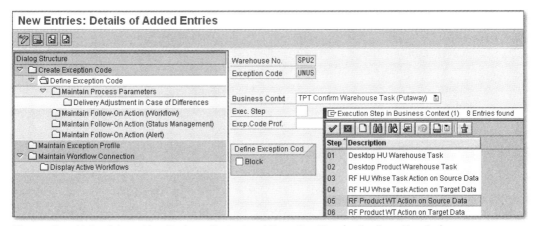

Figure 16.3 Maintaining a New Business Context and Execution Step for the Exception Code

You can also define multiple business contexts and execution steps for which the exception code is relevant. For example, in Figure 16.4, you can see that we specified that the exception code is not only usable in the desktop transaction, but also in the RF transaction, STEP 05 (RF PRODUCT WT ACTION ON SOURCE DATA).

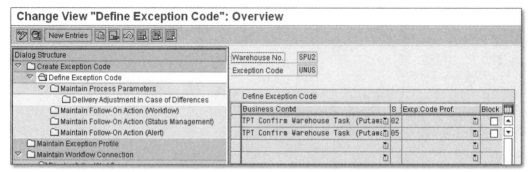

Figure 16.4 Exception Code UNUS is Now Assigned to Two Execution Steps

After you have defined the contexts in which exception code UNUS is valid, you must define how the system should react when the exception code is used within the context by maintaining the process parameters (use the next activity in the dialog structure — MAINTAIN PROCESS PARAMETERS). This activity has to be executed for every defined business context/execution step combination. To start, select the line (such as, in our case, TPT 02), double-click on the MAINTAIN PROCESS PARAMETERS folder, and then select the NEW ENTRIES button — there you can maintain the internal process code.

The internal process code describes what business implications are associated with the exception code. To check the possible entries, you can use the value help to see what entries are allowed. In Figure 16.5, you can see the possible entries defined by the SAP standard delivered configuration. The exception code we are creating in the example is intended to reduce the delivery quantity and confirm the warehouse task with a difference, so we would choose the code DIFF – POST WITH DIFFERENCE.

After choosing the code and pressing ⌊Enter⌋, *additional process parameters,* which are used to capture more details about the internal process code, may show up on the screen. In our case, for INT. PROC. CODE — DIFF, we have to maintain a *difference category*, as seen in Figure 16.6. In our case, we want to change the delivery quantity, so we would assign DIFF. CAT. 3 – DIFFERENCE AS CHARGES FOR INBOUND DELIVERY.

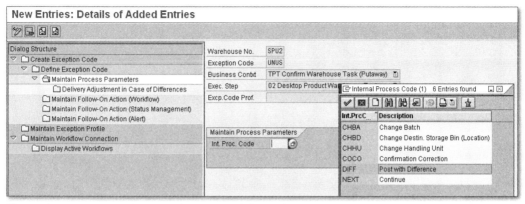

Figure 16.5 Maintaining the Internal Process Code for Each Execution Step

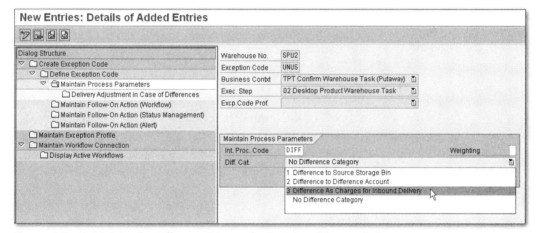

Figure 16.6 Maintaining the Difference Category for the Internal Process Code

If it is necessary to change the delivery quantity (as is the case in our example), you also need to specify the relevant parameters in the DELIVERY ADJUSTMENT IN CASE OF DIFFERENCES activity in the dialog structure. With the relevant entry selected in the preceding node (or while creating the entry), double-click on the activity and select the NEW ENTRIES button. In this customizing activity, you define what the system should do with the differences. You can, for example, define for all delivery item types ("****", as we did in our example in Figure 16.7) that the delivery should be adjusted with the difference quantity using the assigned process code.

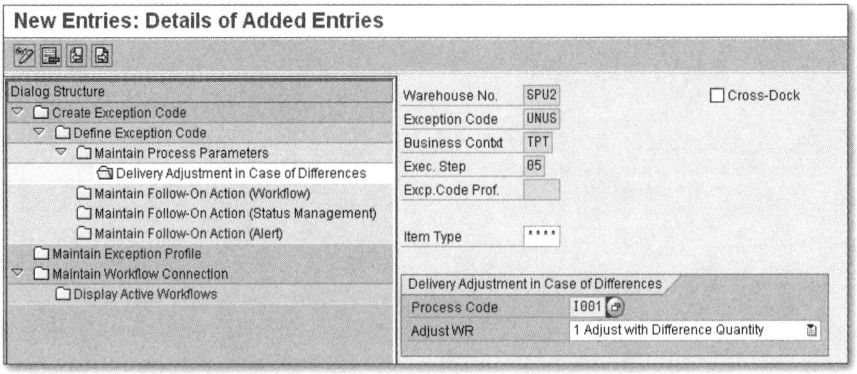

Figure 16.7 Configuring Delivery Quantity Adjustment in Cases of Differences

Once you have set up the exception code on EXEC. STEP 05, you must then repeat the process for the additional execution steps, and then the exception code is ready for use (in our case, both on the desktop and the RF transactions).

You can also assign follow-up actions such as triggering a workflow, setting statuses via SAP Status Management, or triggering alerts using SAP Alert Management. To assign the follow-up actions, select the exception codes within the DEFINE EXCEPTION CODE folder and select the appropriate folder for generating a follow-up action (for example, Workflow, Status Management, or Alert) at the next level of the hierarchy in the dialog structure. As this was not required for our exception code UNUS, we stopped after assigning of the delivery adjustment parameters.

16.2 Using Exception Codes

Exception codes may be used when confirming tasks in the desktop or RF transactions, according to the configuration defined in the previous sections of this chapter. In this section, we will describe how to use the exception codes, and we will illustrate by providing examples using exception code UNUS, which we created in the previous section. Recall that the purpose of our new exception code UNUS was to confirm a warehouse task with a difference quantity and to reduce the delivery quantity accordingly, if a product is determined to be unusable during putaway.

Exception Codes on Desktop Transactions

Exception codes can be used on desktop transactions, for example, during task confirmation. In Figure 16.8, you can see that we have assigned an exception code to the warehouse task while confirming it in the foreground in Transaction /SCWM/TODLV. In this example, we have selected the Warehouse Order (WO), which contains one warehouse task with a planned quantity of 3 EA. To confirm the warehouse task with a difference, we selected the CONFIRM IN FOREGROUND button, adjusted the quantities (reduced ACT.QTY (DEST) to 2 EA and set DEST.DIFF. QTY to 1 EA (or we could specify one or the other and let the system calculate the other for us), and entered exception code UNUS. When we saved the confirmation, the delivery quantity was adjusted from 3 EA to 1 EA. If the Goods Receipt had been posted already, it would have been corrected by a Goods Receipt Cancellation of 1 EA.

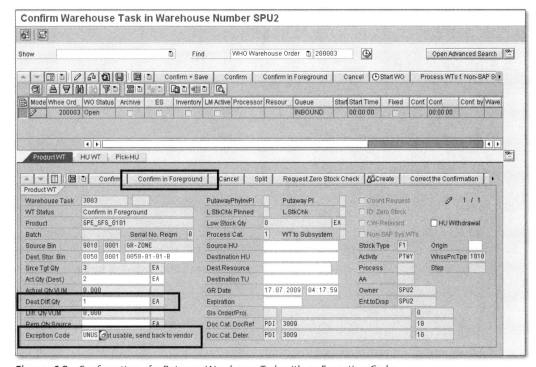

Figure 16.8 Confirmation of a Putaway Warehouse Task with an Exception Code

Exception Codes in RF (Mobile Data Entry) Transactions

When warehouse operators use mobile devices, they can enter their work in real time to the warehouse management system and get a direct response from the system. Also, inconsistencies can be entered and handled in real time. For example, if the operator encounters an unforeseen situation during a picking or putaway process, he can use EWM Exception Handling to tell the system what kind of exception has occurred and give EWM the chance to directly react to the situation in the best possible way.

To illustrate this, we will once again refer to our earlier example. In our example, we are in the process of putting away the product and we detect that 1 EA is not usable. On the RF screen for PUTAWAY BY HU, we see the source data of the first warehouse task (source bin, product and quantity). The requested quantity is 3 EA — and we want to reduce it to 2 EA. If we try to reduce the quantity without entering an exception code, we get an error message, as seen in Figure 16.9. The system reminds us that we have to use an exception code to specify the difference quantity.

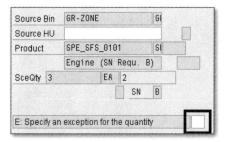

Figure 16.9 Exception Codes Need to Be Entered in RF in Cases of Quantity Differences

On the RF screen, we can specify the exception code in the exception code box on the bottom right of the screen if we know it, or we can use a special exception code (LIST) to call up a list of the possible exception codes depending on the business context.

Our exception code (NOT USABLE, SEND BACK TO VENDOR) does not appear on this page, so we press the Page Down key on the keyboard or use the DOWN ARROW pushbutton on the right side to see the additional entries, as you can see in Figure 16.10 (we knew that there were more entries by the fact that the Page Down button showed up on the page – if there were no additional entries, it would not have been there, as you can see in Figure 16.11).

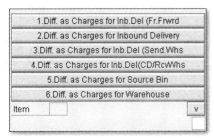

Figure 16.10 A List of Allowed Exception Codes Can Be Displayed Using Exception Code LIST

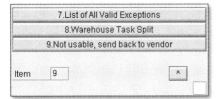

Figure 16.11 Second Page of Exception Codes. The code can be selected by entering its number in the item field.

Our exception code (NOT USABLE, SEND BACK TO VENDOR) now appears in position 9 on the list. We can select the exception code directly from the list either by pressing the pushbutton directly on the screen (if you use a mobile device with a touch screen) or by entering the position number in the ITEM field.

> **Note**
>
> The exception code LIST also needs to be defined in the Exception Handling customizing, as described in the previous section. However, in the standard delivered EWM customizing, this has already been done for most RF business contexts and execution steps. If you define your own business contexts or execution steps, be sure to include the LIST exception code as an allowed entry, otherwise users will not be able to use it in that context.

Once we select the exception code from the list, it is now assigned to the transaction and we can continue processing with the difference quantity assigned. Because the exception code was tied to the internal process code DIFF, the system knows that we want to enter a difference quantity, so we are presented with a new screen to enter the quantities, as seen in Figure 16.12. After the quantities have been entered, you can press F1 SAVE to return to the previous screen. Or, if you are processing products that are managed by serial number, you enter the unus-

able serial number (the one for which the difference was entered) by clicking the
F2 SNo button (or pressing the [F2] function key on the keyboard).

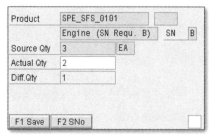

Figure 16.12 Exception Handling Screen in RF for Specifying Quantity Differences during
Warehouse Task Confirmation

Once the warehouse task has been confirmed, you can see the used exception code
and the quantity adjustments in the respective user transaction or in the Warehouse Monitor (Transaction /SCWM/MON, for example, using the node: DOCU-
MENTS • WAREHOUSE TASKS). If there is also a delivery quantity adjustment, the
delivery quantity is reduced by the difference quantity, and the assigned PROCESS
CODE is visible in the delivery, as you can see in Figure 16.13.

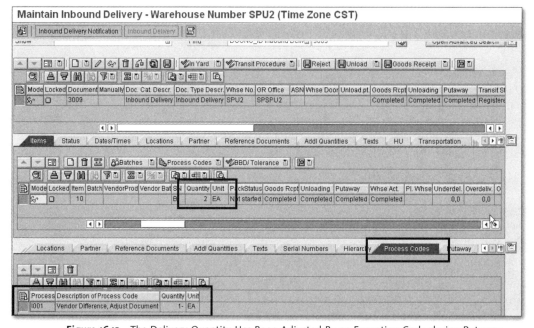

Figure 16.13 The Delivery Quantity Has Been Adjusted By an Exception Code during Putaway

When you configure exception codes in EWM, you can test your exception codes for validity in the EWM IMG by following the menu path EXTENDED WAREHOUSE MANAGEMENT • CROSS-PROCESS SETTINGS • EXCEPTION HANDLING • TEST CONFIGURATION OF EXCEPTION CODES. This tool allows you to test the execution of your follow-up actions (business workflow and alerts) with application data without the need to create objects for testing (e.g., open warehouse tasks, PI documents, etc.). It also lets you display all exception codes that have been defined for a business context and execution step.

> **Note**
>
> When you are using an EWM transaction that lets you enter exception codes, and you want to derive the appropriate business context and execution step to configure the relevant exception codes, you can easily verify it as long as you have some basic debugging skills (or work with an ABAP developer who does). To begin, set a breakpoint in class /SCWM/CL_EXCEPTION_APPL and method VERIFY_EXCEPTION_CODE (there are various ways to do that), then proceed with the transaction and enter an exception code. Once the system enters the debugger at the breakpoint you have just set, you can see the current business context in variable IV_BUSCON and the current execution step in variable IV_EXECSTEP.

16.3   Managing Stock Transport Order (STO) Exceptions

An STO is a document in the ERP system that is used to order and ship stock from one warehouse to another. While the stock is being processed in the sending and receiving warehouse and shipped, quantity exceptions can occur, and products can get broken or lost. EWM Exception Handling provides functionality for processing the quantity differences in these cases.

16.3.1   Background and Overview of STOs

When an STO is created in the ERP system, for example, from warehouse WH1 to warehouse WH2, ERP first creates an outbound delivery document for the shipping warehouse (WH1) and sends it to the assigned EWM system. In EWM, this outbound delivery behaves the same way as any other outbound delivery — the main difference is that the ship-to party is not a customer but a plant (although the plant business partner is updated in such a way that it looks like a customer to EWM in certain ways). In the simplest scenario, you pick the stock and post goods issue for the outbound delivery order (ODO) in EWM. Based on the goods issue in EWM, the outbound delivery is transferred to ERP, where the goods issue is posted for the outbound delivery. Depending on the configuration in ERP, an inbound delivery for the receiving warehouse "WH2" can be created automatically (if you use the SPED output condition on the outbound delivery), or you can create it manually with reference to the STO. If it is automatically created, the inbound delivery can replicate all data (including handling units (HU), serial numbers, batches, stock IDs, etc.) from the outbound delivery, and the inbound delivery is sent to the assigned EWM system, where the goods receipt is posted and the putaway is executed. However, during execution of the putaway in the receiving warehouse WH2, the warehouse employee may detect a quantity difference, and he can report and resolve the differences using STO Exception Handling.

16.3.2 General Customizing for STO Discrepancies

When the employee in the receiving warehouse recognizes the exception, he can decide who is responsible for the discrepancy — the shipping warehouse ("shipper") or the carrier (also known as the freight forwarder). This decision is reflected in the exception code, which he enters during the confirmation of the putaway warehouse task. In the standard delivered configuration, EWM provides the two exception codes for quantity differences during inbound processing for STOs, as shown in Table 16.3.

Exception Codes	SAP Description	Process Code (for adjusting delivery)
DIFC	Diff. as Charges for Inb.Del (Fr.Frwrdr)	CARR
DIFE	Diff. as Charges for Inb.Del (Send.Whse)	SHIP

Table 16.3 Exception Codes for STO Discrepancies with Delivery Adjustment

16.3.3 General Customizing for STO Discrepancies

Before we start with the preceding exception codes, first some words about the general customizing that has to be done. In ERP, the EWM exception code for differences in stock transport orders must be mapped to a *reason code*. To map the exception codes in the EWM IMG, follow the menu path LOGISTICS EXECUTION • SERVICE PARTS MANAGEMENT (SPM) • CROSS-PROCESS SETTINGS (SPM) • PROOF OF DELIVERY • DEFINE MAPPING FOR WAREHOUSE EXCEPTION CODE. As you can see in Figure 16.14, the exception code can be mapped to a responsible party and to reason codes for overdelivery (DFG1) and underdelivery (DFG2).

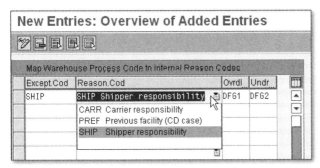

Figure 16.14 Mapping the EWM Exception Codes to ERP Reason Codes

Maintaining this customizing table is required for ERP to interpret the exception situation correctly. Note that the column EXCEPT.COD is not the exception code that the user enters in EWM, but the process code for adjusting the delivery, which is transferred from EWM to ERP on delivery.

16.3.4 Carrier Responsibility

By choosing exception code DIFC, the employee in the receiving warehouse defines that the *carrier* is responsible for the difference. In this case, the shipping warehouse will not be involved in the process.

If you use "stock in transit" (which is configurable, but often used at STO processing) the difference quantity will be first posted to stock in transit of the receiving plant. However, this is only temporary, because the quantity difference is posted from transit stock into consumption when the inbound delivery is completed (i.e., when the delivery completed indicator is set by EWM).

To follow up on the process with the carrier, you must manually create a debit/ credit note and communicate it to the carrier. The quantity adjustment (and the subsequent financial adjustments) will only affect the receiving warehouse (and plant/storage location in ERP), as the stock ownership for the products is now essentially transferred to the carrier.

16.3.5 Shipper Responsibility

If the *shipping warehouse* is responsible for the difference, you use exception code DIFE in the receiving warehouse. When you complete the inbound delivery (i.e., the delivery completed indicator is set by EWM), the difference quantity is posted from the "stock in transit" of the receiving plant into a special storage location of the shipping plant. In the standard delivered customizing for this process, the storage location is named Proof of Delivery (POD).

In Figure 16.15, you can see an example organizational structure for entities involved in the handling of a shipper discrepancy. The example shows an STO from WAREHOUSE A to WAREHOUSE B. In the ERP system, WAREHOUSE A is assigned to PLANT A with storage locations Received on Deck (ROD) and Available for Sale (AFS). For handling the STO discrepancies, the POD storage location is assigned to PLANT A as well. Correspondingly, WAREHOUSE B is assigned to PLANT B, again with storage locations ROD and AFS. If there are also STOs from WAREHOUSE B to WAREHOUSE A, there should be an additional POD storage location also assigned to PLANT B, to handle potential discrepancies.

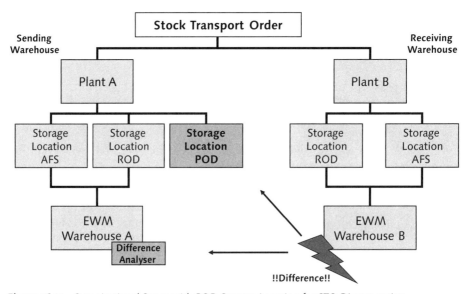

Figure 16.15 Organizational Setup with POD Storage Location for STO Discrepancies

To define the POD storage location for STO differences in the ERP system within the ERP IMG (as shown in Figure 16.16), follow the menu path LOGISTICS EXECUTION • SERVICE PARTS MANAGEMENT (SPM) • CROSS-PROCESS SETTINGS (SPM) • PROOF OF DELIVERY • DEFINE POD STORAGE LOCATION FOR SHIPPER DISCREPANCIES.

The POD storage location should not be assigned to the EWM warehouse number in the ERP customizing. The stock remains purely in ERP Inventory Management (IM) and is no longer managed by the warehouse as long as it remains in this logical POD storage location.

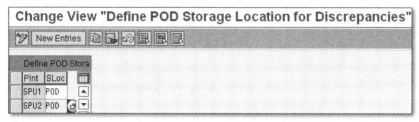

Figure 16.16 Assignment of POD Storage Location to Plants

16.3.6 Correction Delivery for the Shipping Warehouse to Clear Difference

When you post the stock from "in transit stock" into the POD storage location, a special *correction delivery* is also created for the shipping warehouse at the same time. This correction delivery is either an inbound delivery or an outbound delivery, depending on the sign of the difference quantity (overage or shortage). Once it is created in ERP, the correction delivery is transferred to EWM, where it can be manually accepted or rejected by the responsible employee.

If the correction delivery is rejected, the difference quantity will stay in the POD storage location in ERP and has to be cleared manually. If the correction delivery is accepted in EWM, the difference quantity will be posted to the *EWM Difference Analyzer*, where it can be reviewed and posted.

Note

You can also configure the system to automatically accept incoming correction deliveries in EWM by setting up the respective Post-Processing Framework (PPF) actions to post GR and GI. You can set up the PPF action for GI by activating the action /SCWM/PRD_OUT_POST_GI_ODIS for application /SCDL/DELIVERY and action profile /SCDL/PRD_OUT_ODIS. For GR, you can activate action /SCWM/PRD_IN_POST_GR_IDIS of action profile /SCDL/PRD_IN_IDIS.

In the EWM Difference Analyzer, the STO discrepancies can be shown by switching on the PENDING CLAIM checkbox in the default values of the transaction, as seen in Figure 16.17.

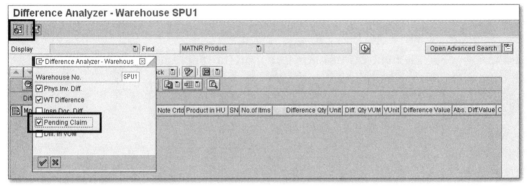

Figure 16.17 STO Differences in the EWM Difference Analyzer

If you find that the missing stock is found somewhere in the shipping warehouse, then there will be a second entry in the EWM Difference Analyzer — Physical Inventory Difference — but with the opposite sign. If the differences are then posted together to the ERP system, because the net effect to inventory is zero, there will also be no net financial impact.

In EWM, the STO discrepancy quantity is sometimes called *Pending Claims Quantity* (PCQ) or *Unassigned Bin Quantity* (UBQ). For more information about managing stock discrepancies, including the PCQ in the EWM Difference Analyzer, see Chapter 14, Physical Inventory.

> **Note**
>
> To perform the necessary settings for correction deliveries in EWM (document types, item types, etc.), you can activate Business Configuration (BC) Set /SCWM/DLV_COR-RECTION via Transaction SCPR20, and the correct settings will be updated automatically. For more information about activating BC Sets, see Chapter 26, Deploying Extended Warehouse Management.

16.4 Managing Exceptions at Cross-Docking

Cross-docking is a method used to speed up processing in the warehouse by moving stock directly from the goods receipt area directly to the goods issue area, without first executing a putaway into the warehouse. There are different methods of cross-docking, which are explained in detail in Chapter 17, Cross-Docking.

Discrepancy handling for the transportation cross-docking case is similar to the discrepancy processing for STOs. The warehouse employee in the receiving warehouse decides to whom the quantity difference shall be posted. In this case, the responsibility can be assigned to the carrier, to the shipping warehouse, or to the previous warehouse (which may differ from the shipping warehouse in the case of multiple cross-docking steps). Table 16.4 lists exception codes for managing exceptions during cross-docking.

Exception Codes	Description	Process Code (for adjusting delivery)
DIFC	Diff. as Charges for Inb.Del (Fr.Frwrdr)	CARR
DIFE	Diff. as Charges for Inb.Del (Send.Whse)	SHIP
DIFP	Diff. as Charges for Inb.Del(CD/RcvWhse)	PREF

Table 16.4 Exception Codes for Managing Quantity Exceptions during Cross-docking

Discrepancies for carrier and shipper differences are handled in the same way as described in the previous section for STOs. On the other hand, if the *previous warehouse* is responsible for the discrepancy, the stock difference is posted to the POD storage location of the plant that is assigned to the previous warehouse and the stock shows up in the EWM Difference Analyzer of the defined previous warehouse.

If you define your own exception codes for processing cross-docking quantity discrepancies, you must ensure that you heed the following information about the exception processing for cross-docking. EWM manages cross-dock stock as if it belongs to an inbound delivery and to an outbound delivery at the *same time*. Therefore, to allow an exception code to update the outbound delivery and inbound delivery at the same time, you must set up the customizing appropriately, including the following requirements for the setup:

▶ You must define an exception code using the internal process code DIFF

▶ You must assign the delivery update methods to the internal process code (similar to Figure 16.7). For cross-docking, you assign both the inbound delivery item type and the outbound delivery item type to the internal process code

▸ You assign a process code to the inbound delivery and outbound delivery item type

▸ You must activate the Cross-Dock flag (as seen in Figure 16.7)

This Cross-Dock flag must be activated to allow EWM Exception Handling to update the delivery quantity, even if the exception itself happens in the wrong business context. For example, you confirm a picking warehouse task for a transportation cross-docking HU and detect an exception, which you enter in the business context TPI Whse Task: Confirm (Stock Removal). The inbound delivery item type, however, does not belong to this business context, but rather to TPT Whse Task: Confirm (Putaway). Yet, the exception is allowed to be posted there because the Cross-Dock flag is activated for the delivery adjustment.

16.5 Confirmation Corrections

Normally, when you confirm a warehouse task in EWM, it is not possible to subsequently perform any changes to the warehouse task. The cancellation of a warehouse task is only possible before confirmation, and quantity changes can only be performed during confirmation of a warehouse task.

However, there is one exception to this general rule — you can change the quantity of confirmed putaway warehouse tasks in EWM via a *confirmation correction*. Confirmation corrections can be used if the warehouse employee has already confirmed the putaway warehouse task and determines afterward that there is something wrong with the stock (for example, there is a piece broken or missing). Using the confirmation correction, you can correct the warehouse task and, at the same time, adjust the quantity of the inbound delivery item and the goods receipt quantity to charge the missing quantity to the vendor.

Confirmation corrections can be performed using a desktop transaction or using an RF transaction. The RF transaction for confirmation, if you are using the standard delivered customizing for the RF menu, can be found in the RF transactions (Transaction code /SCWM/RFUI) via the menu path 03 Inbound Processes • 03 Putaway • 04 Confirmation Correction • 02 Confirmation Correction by WT / SI / WO / Bin. The desktop confirmation correction can be accessed by selecting the Correct the Confirmation button on the Product WT tab within the warehouse task confirmation (Transaction code /SCWM/TO_CONF).

To use the confirmation correction, the following prerequisites apply:

1. The putaway warehouse task must be a product warehouse task.

2. The putaway warehouse task must be linked to an inbound delivery item.

3. The destination storage type of the putaway warehouse task must be a final storage type.

4. You must have defined a Delay for completing inbound deliveries in customizing in the EWM IMG via the menu path EXTENDED WAREHOUSE MANAGEMENT • GOODS RECEIPT PROCESS • INBOUND DELIVERY • DEFINE DELAY IN COMPLETING INBOUND DELIVERIES.

5. The ID must use a document type and item type with a status profile for which the status DWM is activated in the EWM IMG via the menu path EXTENDED WAREHOUSE MANAGEMENT • CROSS-PROCESS SETTINGS • DELIVERY PROCESSING • STATUS MANAGEMENT • DEFINE STATUS PROFILES.

6. The inbound delivery item must not yet be completed.

7. You must have defined an exception code with the internal process code COCO (Confirmation Correction) and assigned it to the business context TPT (Confirm Warehouse Task (Putaway)) and both the 06 RF PRODUCT WT ACTION ON TARGET DATA and 02 DESKTOP PRODUCT WAREHOUSE TASK steps (in the EWM IMG, via the menu path EXTENDED WAREHOUSE MANAGEMENT • CROSS-PROCESS SETTINGS • EXCEPTION HANDLING • DEFINE EXCEPTION CODES).

You can perform multiple confirmation corrections to the putaway warehouse task, but only until the delivery delay time is completed.

> **Note**
>
> When the completion delay has passed, EWM sets the Decentralized Warehouse Management (DWM) status of the delivery item to COMPLETED. Because all other statuses are also COMPLETED, EWM calculates the overall status DCO of the inbound delivery to COMPLETED, which triggers the sending of the *closing indicator* to the ERP system. Once the closing indicator has been sent, the delivery can no longer be changed in any way.
>
> If you do not specify a completion delay for inbound deliveries in Customizing, EWM immediately sets the status DWM for sending the completion indicator to COMPLETED, and you may no longer make any confirmation corrections.
>
> When you confirm a warehouse task for putaway, EWM checks if this warehouse task needs confirmation correction. If it does, it calculates the exact time when the delivery should no longer be changed using the completion delay time specified in customizing. EWM then schedules a job at this time, which then will close the delivery. This job uses report /SCWM/R_PRDI_SET_DWM, and the job name created follows the naming convention "PRDI_SET_DWM_xxx" (where xxx is the document number of the inbound delivery). You can view the jobs using the background job monitor (Transaction SM37).

16.6 Summary

In this chapter, we described the methods that you can use in EWM for managing exceptions discovered in the warehouse, including how to configure and use exception codes, manage STO exceptions, manage cross-docking exceptions, and process confirmation corrections for putaways. You should now have a good understanding of how to configure and use these exception processing methods to manage unexpected or unintended occurrences in your warehouse operations. In the following chapters, we will continue describing the details for special processes in the warehouse, including Cross-Docking, Yard Management, Value Added Services, Kitting, and Labor Management.

In this chapter, we will discuss the various cross-docking methods and how to configure and implement each method.

17 Cross-Docking

Cross-docking is a method used to optimize the processing of goods in a warehouse by using incoming stock (from production or from external suppliers) directly for outbound processing without storing them in the warehouse. Cross-docking (as shown in Figure 17.1) has several benefits from a warehousing perspective, including:

▶ It reduces the handling of materials in the warehouse, potentially avoiding damage and additional labor requirements

▶ It speeds up the flow of the material through the warehouse, potentially reducing lead times

▶ It can reduce storage space requirements and stock keeping costs

▶ It can reduce transportation costs by consolidating cross-dock materials and materials from storage

Generally speaking, there are two types of cross-docking: *planned cross-docking* and *opportunistic (or unplanned) cross-docking*. When you use planned cross-docking, the decision to cross-dock specific goods is already made before the goods physically arrive in the warehouse. When you use opportunistic cross-docking, the decision is made at the time when the goods arrive in the warehouse based on the actual situation with regard to demand, including open customer orders or deliveries or requirements for transfer of stock to other locations within your supply chain.

Extended Warehouse Management (EWM) supports five different methods of cross-docking, including:

▶ Transportation cross-docking (TCD)

▶ Merchandise distribution

▶ Opportunistic cross-docking (triggered by EWM)

▶ Push deployment (PD)

▶ Pick from goods receipt (PFGR)

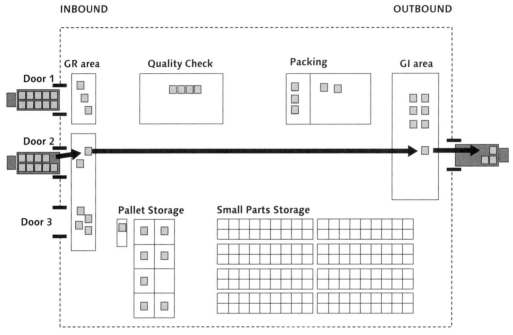

Figure 17.1 Cross-docking Visualization

TCD and merchandise distribution are planned cross-docking methods. The others are opportunistic methods for cross-docking.

The decision on whether cross-docking will be performed or not is made in different systems, depending on the cross-docking method (see Figure 17.2). For TCD, the decision is made in EWM based on the EWM route determination in the sending EWM warehouse. For merchandise distribution, the decision is made in ERP based on the purchase order. EWM-triggered opportunistic cross-docking is decided in EWM directly (as the name implies). And decisions related to PD and PFGR are made in the Advanced Planning and Optimization (APO) system.

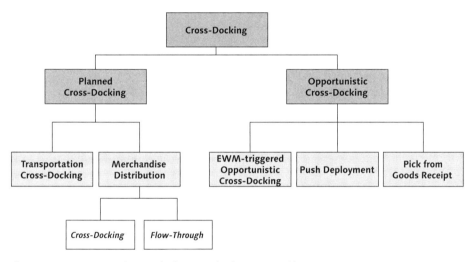

Figure 17.2 Overview of Cross-docking Methods Supported by EWM

In this chapter, we will further describe each of the cross-docking methods that EWM supports, describe the business function, and inform you of how to set them up to make use of them in your warehouse.

> **Note**
>
> The ability to use cross-docking processes in the warehouse is not just dependent on the system capabilities but also the warehouse layout and your business requirements. Not every warehouse can implement cross-docking process due to requirements such as strict first-in/first-out (FIFO) or first-expired/first-out (FEFO), and even for those warehouses where it is technically possible to implement cross-docking, it doesn't make sense for one reason or another. Before you embark on a new implementation of cross-docking, we strongly encourage you to consult with logistics experts within your organization or even industry experts or consultants.

17.1   Transportation Cross-Docking (TCD)

In this section, we will describe the TCD process in EWM. As described previously, TCD is one of the planned cross-docking methods. The decision on whether TCD is relevant for a warehouse process is made by EWM at the original sending warehouse during the route determination of the outbound delivery order (ODO). If the route determination indicates that it is better to send the goods first to another warehouse and then (possibly together with other goods) to the final location instead of sending it directly to the final location, then the system will assign a *cross-docking route* and change the ship-to party of the ODO to the cross-dock warehouse. In addition, the original ship-to party is assigned to the partner role *final ship-to party* during the route determination so that it can track the final destination through the interim documents.

Once the goods issue is posted by EWM for the ODO and transferred to ERP (with the cross-docking route and final ship-to party assigned), ERP determines that cross-docking is relevant and creates a pair of deliveries — an inbound delivery into the cross-dock warehouse and an outbound delivery from the cross-dock warehouse to the final location. The deliveries are linked together, which means that the stock from the cross-docking inbound delivery is "reserved" for the cross-docking outbound delivery (therefore the transportation cross-docking is "planned" at the cross-dock warehouse). When the goods arrive in the cross-docking warehouse, the handling units (HUs) are unloaded from the truck (only packed products are relevant for TCD, so all of the items will technically be on HUs, even if it is only a single logical HU for the shipment) and can be moved directly from the inbound dock to the outbound dock.

The TCD process can be monitored in the ERP system using the *TCD monitor*. You can start the monitor from the SAP Easy Access menu by following the Logistics • Logistics Execution • Transportation Cross-Docking • Transportation Cross-Docking Monitor menu path, or using Transaction code /SPE/CDMON. Figure 17.3 shows the cross-docking monitor for a TCD process, including the OD from the original sending location (plant SPU1), and the pair of deliveries at the cross-dock location (plant SPU2). When the TCD documents are selected, you can see more details about the delivery header on the right side and details about the items on the delivery in the bottom pane.

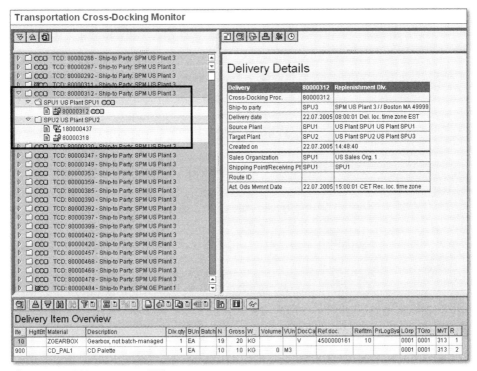

Figure 17.3 TCD Monitor in ERP

In the following sections, we will discuss cross-docking routes and their impact on route determination, the required organizational setup and customizing in the ERP system to support cross-docking, and the impact of TCD on EWM internal stock processing.

17.1.1 Cross-Docking Routes

To support the TCD process in EWM, you create special routes called *cross-docking routes*. When an ODO is created, the EWM route determination determines all suitable routes between the source (current warehouse) and the destination (ship-to party). The result can be either a direct route from source to destination (also called a *linear route*) or a cross-docking route. Using a cross-docking route to ship goods to a customer, in some cases, may be faster than using a linear route — for example, the linear route may depart very rarely, whereas the cross-docking route and the subsequent shipments from the cross-dock facility to the destination may depart more often. And another reason for using the cross-docking route may be that it is more cost-efficient, as it allows you to consolidate goods from one warehouse with goods from other warehouses in an intermediate warehouse to ship to the destination in a single shipment.

A cross-docking route in EWM is a route that consists of at least two linear routes — an incoming linear route and an outgoing linear route. In Figure 17.4, you can see an example that includes two warehouses — SPU1 and SPU2. In our example, you can ship stock from SPU1 to customer CUST_SPU2, and you want to perform cross-docking in warehouse SPU2. To trigger the cross-docking, you have created a cross-docking route called CD_SPU2 for warehouse SPU2. (Note that cross-docking routes are always created *for one specific cross-docking location*, which makes them fundamentally different from linear routes.) You then assign the incoming linear route SPU1_SPU2 to the cross-docking route (which leads from warehouse SPU1 to SPU2) and the outgoing linear route SPU2_CUST (which leads from warehouse SPU2 to the customer).

When the route determination for the OD runs for warehouse SPU1, there is no direct route found from SPU1 to CUST_SPU2. However, the system examines the cross-docking route, by checking its incoming and outgoing linear routes, and decides that it is a valid route to ship from SPU1 to CUST_SPU2.

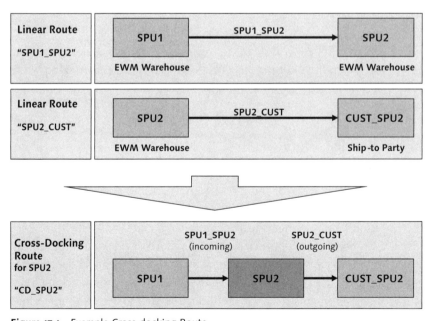

Figure 17.4 Example Cross-docking Route

In Figure 17.5, you can see how this cross-docking route looks in the EWM system, with the cross-docking location and cross-docking routes assigned.

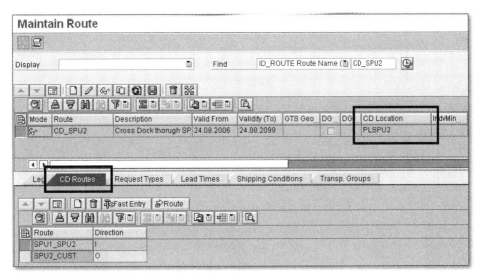

Figure 17.5 Cross-docking Route in EWM Route Maintenance

Once a *cross-docking route* is determined, the ship-to party of the outbound delivery is changed to the cross-dock location, and the original ship-to party is assigned to the partner role final ship-to party. During subsequent goods issue posting of this outbound delivery in ERP, the system triggers the creation of the delivery pair (inbound delivery and outbound delivery) for the cross-docking warehouse (SPU2 in our example).

17.1.2 TCD Storage Locations

During TCD, the in-transit stock remains in the ownership of the sending warehouse and never changes ownership while in the cross-docking warehouse. This means that during the TCD process, the stock in the ERP system always remains in the plant that triggered the TCD (SPU1 in our example). Only the final goods issue posting from the last cross-docking warehouse (as there could be multiple cross-docking warehouses in the chain), removes the stock from the triggering plant. Therefore, TCD requires a special organizational setup in ERP. You need to define special *cross-docking storage locations* for each plant that can trigger a TCD process, as seen in Figure 17.6. In the figure, you can see that there is one additional cross-docking storage location CDU2 assigned to plant SPU1, and this storage location is assigned to warehouse SPU2 (whereas all other storage locations of plant SPU1 are assigned to warehouse SPU1).

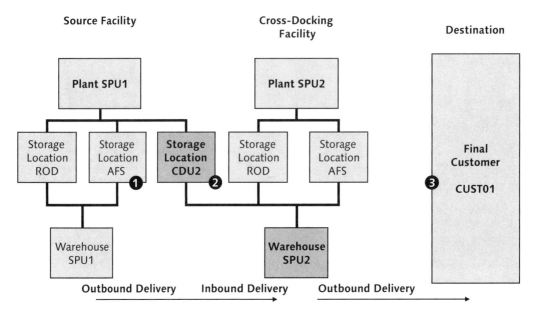

Figure 17.6 Define Special Cross-docking Storage Locations

To maintain cross-docking storage locations in the ERP Implementation Guide (IMG) (as seen in Figure 17.7), follow the menu path LOGISTICS EXECUTION • SERVICE PARTS MANAGEMENT (SPM) • TRANSPORTATION CROSS-DOCKING (SPM) • MAINTAIN STORAGE LOCATIONS AND SHIPPING POINTS FOR CD WAREHOUSES.

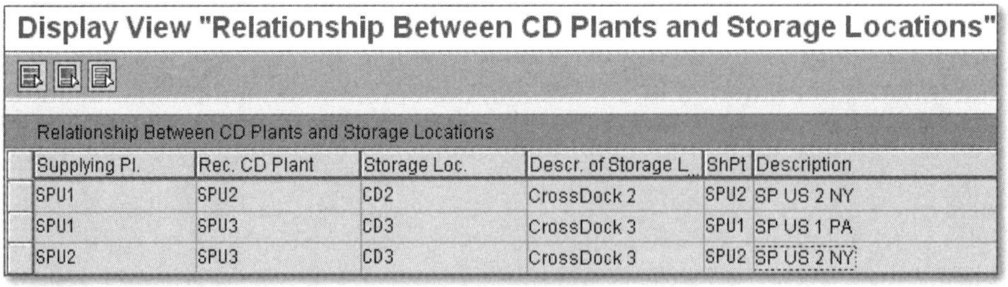

Display View "Relationship Between CD Plants and Storage Locations"

Relationship Between CD Plants and Storage Locations

Supplying Pl.	Rec. CD Plant	Storage Loc.	Descr. of Storage L.	ShPt	Description
SPU1	SPU2	CD2	CrossDock 2	SPU2	SP US 2 NY
SPU1	SPU3	CD3	CrossDock 3	SPU1	SP US 1 PA
SPU2	SPU3	CD3	CrossDock 3	SPU2	SP US 2 NY

Figure 17.7 Setup of Cross-docking Storage Locations in ERP

For the TCD storage locations in ERP, you have to define availability groups and stock types, as described in Chapter 6, Warehouse Stock Management. In the previous example, we assigned availability group CD2 to storage location CDU2, and we created a new stock type, also called CD2, for this availability group.

17.1.3 Integration of TCD into EWM Stock Processing

TCD can be used with or without *storage control* (multistep movements of HUs, as described in Chapter 13, Configuring Multistep Warehouse Movements). In other words, you can execute the stock processing in the cross-docking warehouse, for which the inbound delivery and outbound delivery pair has been created, either with or without using a storage process consisting of multiple steps. In either case, the criteria for linking the cross-docking inbound delivery and outbound delivery together is the TCD process number. In Figure 17.8, you can see the TCD PROCESS NUMBER in the REF. DOCUMENT CAT. of the inbound delivery at the cross-docking facility.

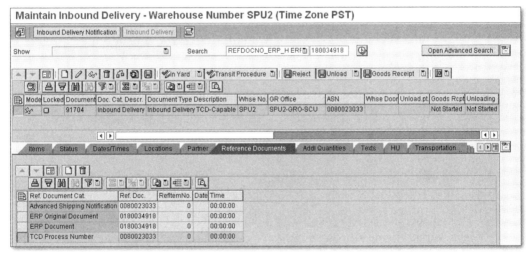

Figure 17.8 TCD Process Number in a Cross-docking ID

The TCD PROCESS NUMBER is the number of the original outbound delivery in the sending warehouse that triggered the cross-docking process. In Figure 17.9, you can see the TCD PROCESS NUMBER and the assigned ERP INBOUND DELIVERY REFERENCE in the REFERENCE DOCUMENTS tab of the ODO from the cross-docking facility.

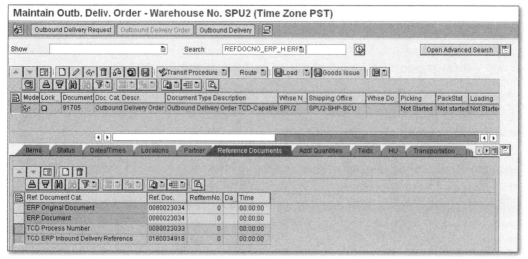

Figure 17.9 TCD Process Number in the Cross-docking ODO

In the following sections, we'll compare the process when not using storage control with the process when using storage control.

TCD Scenario without Storage Control

If you use TCD without storage control, EWM will create an active *HU pick warehouse task* for the ODO at the cross-docking warehouse. Because only packed products are relevant in TCD, you will always pick the entire TCD HU. If you attempt to create an active putaway warehouse task for an inbound delivery, EWM will display an error message, because the stock is only intended for cross-docking.

When the Picking HU warehouse task is created for the ODO, the system will determine the destination storage bin — for TCD without storage control, this will most commonly be the staging area in the goods issue zone. When you pick a TCD-relevant HU, EWM uses the HU warehouse tasks for picking to update both the corresponding inbound delivery and ODO simultaneously.

TCD Scenario with Storage Control

If you use TCD with storage control, EWM will first determine the putaway steps for the highest-level HU of the inbound delivery at the cross-docking warehouse — for example, the inbound delivery may be relevant for unloading and deconsolidation, according to the process-oriented storage control (POSC) (see Chapter 13 for more details about how to use the process control).

After the goods receipt posting, you can create the HU pick warehouse task for the TCD HU, either by releasing the corresponding wave (if the ODO line is assigned to a wave), creating the HU warehouse task manually for the ODO, or if you have set the Prod/HU WT indicator in the Customizing settings for the current process step (for example, unloading), EWM will create the pick HU warehouse task automatically.

If the highest-level HU is still in inbound processing (for example, if the unloading or the deconsolidation has not yet been completed), EWM creates the Picking HU warehouse task with an *inactive* status. Once the inbound steps of the highest-level HU have been completed, EWM activates the picking warehouse task automatically.

17.1.4 TCD for Contract Packagers

A contract packager is an organization that is responsible for packaging inbound product (for more information on contract packagers, see Chapter 9, Inbound Processing) and forwarding it to the warehouse for storage and distribution. The contract packager can be modeled in your supply chain in various ways, including as EWM warehouses. If the TCD process starts at a *contract packager warehouse* and the contract packager is not assigned to its own plant, then you need to define the plant that physically represents its warehouse. This setting is necessary because the plant to which the contract packager is assigned doesn't normally model his geographical location. To maintain the plant in the ERP IMG, follow the menu path LOGISTICS EXECUTION • SERVICE PARTS MANAGEMENT (SPM) • TRANSPORTATION CROSS-DOCKING (SPM) • DEFINE SOURCE PLANTS FOR CONTRACT PACKAGERS.

17.1.5 Additional Remarks about TCD

The following comments also apply to the TCD process and are worth mentioning in any discussion about TCD:

▸ SAP delivers a BC Set (/SCWM/DLV_TCD) with the standard delivered content for EWM that automatically performs customizing settings for the delivery of TCD.

- When using TCD, the final destination must be located domestically (i.e., in the same company code as the plants of the warehouses involved in the TCD process).
- TCD does not support return processes.
- If you use nested mixed HUs with TCD, in a lower level HU you can include either only TCD materials or only non-TCD materials (in other words, you can't mix both TCD relevant and non-TCD relevant materials in the lower level HU).

17.2   EWM-Triggered Opportunistic Cross-Docking

In contrast to the other cross-dock methods, *EWM-triggered opportunistic cross-docking* is a process that works entirely within a single EWM instance and does not need support from other applications or systems. When EWM generates warehouse tasks for putaway or picking, it determines at that moment in time whether opportunistic cross-docking will take place. You can activate this cross-docking procedure for the inbound delivery and outbound delivery process separately at the warehouse or product level. However, the coding for opportunistic cross-docking is implemented within example implementations of BAdIs, so to activate the functionality you must also activate these BAdIs.

> **Note**
>
> For easier reading, we will refer to EWM-triggered opportunistic cross-docking as simply "opportunistic cross-docking" in the remainder of this section.

17.2.1   Variants of Opportunistic Cross-Docking

Opportunistic cross-docking can either be initiated from the inbound processing or from the outbound processing. In the following sections, we will describe the features of the inbound- and outbound-driven processes.

Inbound Driven

When you create warehouse tasks for putaway, EWM checks whether *ODO items* exist that match the task items with regard to quantity and expiration date. Then, instead of creating the putaway warehouse task, EWM creates a cross-docking warehouse task with reference to the ODO item.

EWM also checks during the putaway warehouse task creation to see if the *stock in open pick* warehouse task is less adequate (in terms of FIFO or FEFO) for the ODO item than the stock to be put away (unless the warehouse task is relevant for a material flow system). If so, EWM cancels the open pick warehouse tasks and creates a new cross-docking warehouse task with reference to the same ODO item.

Outbound Driven

During the creation of warehouse tasks for picking, EWM checks to see if stock in the goods receipt area exists that is more adequate for the ODO item than stock from within the warehouse. Then, instead of creating the pick warehouse task, a cross-docking warehouse task with reference to the ODO item is created. For the outbound-driven opportunistic cross-docking to create the cross-docking warehouse tasks, the stock must already be posted for goods receipt, the goods receipt area must be part of the picking location determination, the stock determination must be active, the picking strategy must *not* be FIFO, and the inbound delivery items must not be relevant for quality inspection. In addition, stock in HUs is skipped when a HU quantity split would be required to fulfill the pick warehouse task, and stock in mixed HUs is skipped entirely.

17.2.2 Activating Opportunistic Cross-Docking

The opportunistic cross-docking functionality is coded within *example BAdI implementations*. This means that you have to implement these BAdIs by copying the example class to activate the functionality. To activate the opportunistic cross-docking, you must perform the steps described in this section.

Creating Implementations for Cross-Docking BAdIs

The BAdI for opportunistic cross-docking inbound can be activated in the EWM IMG by following the menu path EXTENDED WAREHOUSE MANAGEMENT • BUSINESS ADD-INS (BADIS) FOR EXTENDED WAREHOUSE MANAGEMENT • CROSS PROCESS SETTINGS • CROSS-DOCKING (CD) • OPPORTUNISTIC CROSS-DOCKING • EWM-TRIGGERED OPPORTUNISTIC CROSS-DOCKING • OPPORTUNISTIC CROSS DOCKING INBOUND. There you must create an implementation of this BAdI using example class /SCWM/ CL_EI_CD_OPP_INBOUND and activate the implementation.

The BAdI for opportunistic cross-docking outbound can be activated in the EWM IMG via the menu path EXTENDED WAREHOUSE MANAGEMENT • BUSINESS ADD-INS (BADIS) FOR EXTENDED WAREHOUSE MANAGEMENT • CROSS PROCESS SETTINGS •

CROSS-DOCKING (CD) • OPPORTUNISTIC CROSS-DOCKING • EWM-TRIGGERED OPPOR-TUNISTIC CROSS-DOCKING • OPPORTUNISTIC CROSS DOCKING OUTBOUND. There you must create an implementation of this BAdI using example class /SCWM/CL_EI_CD_OPP_OUTBOUND and activate the implementation.

Creating a Product Type Group and Product Group

To activate opportunistic cross-docking, you must define PRODUCT GROUPS that you can later assign to the products (as you can see in Figure 17.10). To define the PRODUCT GROUPS in the EWM IMG, follow the menu path SCM BASIS • MASTER DATA • PRODUCT • PRODUCT GROUPS • DEFINE PRODUCT GROUPS.

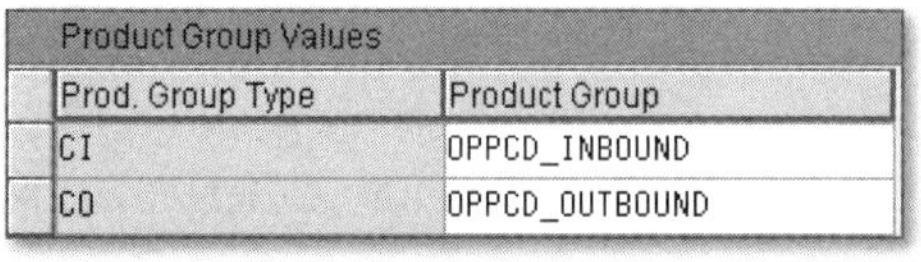

Product Group Values	
Prod. Group Type	Product Group
CI	OPPCD_INBOUND
CO	OPPCD_OUTBOUND

Figure 17.10 Define Product Group

Before you create the PRODUCT GROUPS, you may need to define the PROD. GROUP TYPES within the EWM IMG by following the menu path SCM BASIS • MASTER DATA • PRODUCT • PRODUCT GROUPS • DEFINE PRODUCT GROUP TYPES.

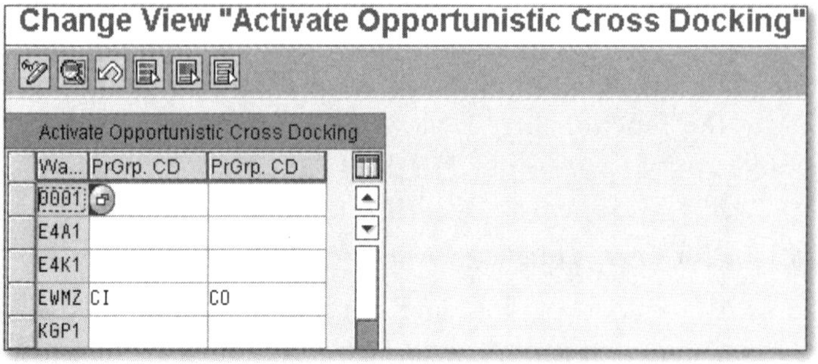

Change View "Activate Opportunistic Cross Docking"

Wa...	PrGrp. CD	PrGrp. CD	
0001			
E4A1			
E4K1			
EWMZ	CI	CO	
KGP1			

Figure 17.11 Activation of Opportunistic Cross-docking for the Warehouse

Activating Opportunistic Cross-Docking at the Warehouse Level

You must also activate the EWM-triggered opportunistic cross-docking for the warehouse (as shown in Figure 17.11) in order for the checks and activities described previously to be performed. To activate it for the warehouse in the EWM IMG, follow the menu path EXTENDED WAREHOUSE MANAGEMENT • CROSS-PROCESS SETTINGS • CROSS-DOCKING (CD) • OPPORTUNISTIC CROSS-DOCKING • EWM-TRIGGERED

OPPORTUNISTIC CROSS-DOCKING • ACTIVATE EWM-TRIGGERED OPPORTUNISTIC CROSS-DOCKING.

Maintaining the Stock Removal Strategy to include the Goods Receipt Area

For opportunistic cross-docking, the picking warehouse task of the ODO item will be created to pick stock from an inbound storage type. Therefore, you must assign the relevant inbound storage types in the stock removal strategies in the EWM IMG via the menu path EXTENDED WAREHOUSE MANAGEMENT • GOODS ISSUE PROCESS • STRATEGIES • SPECIFY STORAGE TYPE SEARCH SEQUENCE.

Maintaining Stock Determination

Because the picking warehouse task for opportunistic cross-docking will be created for inbound stock that is still assigned the stock type for stock received on dock but not yet put away (e.g., stock type F1), you need to maintain the EWM stock determination (for more details about the stock determination, see Chapter 6). Whereas the ODO item usually searches for free stock (e.g., of stock type F2), the inbound stock (e.g., stock type F1) needs to be maintained within the stock determination for the relevant stock determination group for cross-docking.

To start, you must first maintain a new stock determination group for cross-docking (as seen in Figure 17.12) in the EWM IMG by following the menu path EXTENDED WAREHOUSE MANAGEMENT • CROSS-PROCESS SETTINGS • STOCK DETERMINATION • MAINTAIN STOCK DETERMINATION GROUPS.

Maintain Stock Determination Groups			
Wa...	StkDetGrp	Description	WM Handling
EWMZ	CD	OPPCD	1 WM has priority

Figure 17.12 Creation of a New Stock Determination Group for Opportunistic Cross-docking

Next, you must permit the inbound stock type (e.g., F1) for an ODO item that has the normal stock type assigned (e.g., F2), as you can see in Figure 17.13. To specify the stock determination in the EWM IMG, follow the menu path EXTENDED WAREHOUSE MANAGEMENT • CROSS-PROCESS SETTINGS • STOCK DETERMINATION • CONFIGURE STOCK DETERMINATION.

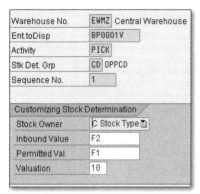

Figure 17.13 Stock Determination for Outbound Deliveries to Support Opportunistic Cross-docking

Switching on the Assignment of Warehouse Tasks to RF Queues

Inbound-driven cross-docking will take appropriate ODO items into consideration even if open pick warehouse tasks exist. Those warehouse tasks will only be cancelled and replaced by cross-docking warehouse tasks if execution takes place within the radio frequency (RF) environment (i.e., not if the picks are intended to be paper-based or sent to a material flow system). Therefore, if you want to use the inbound-driven opportunistic cross-docking, you must set up the RF queue determination in the EWM IMG by following the menu path EXTENDED WAREHOUSE MANAGEMENT • CROSS-PROCESS SETTINGS • RESOURCE MANAGEMENT • DEFINE QUEUES.

Maintaining Master Data for Opportunistic Cross-Docking

Finally, to activate opportunistic cross-docking for products, you must assign the product group (the one that you created in the previous steps) to the products in the PROPERTIES 2 tab of the SAP APO view of the product master. To access this view of the product master from the EWM Easy Access menu, follow the EXTENDED WAREHOUSE MANAGEMENT • MASTER DATA • PRODUCT • MAINTAIN PRODUCT menu path, or use Transaction code /SAPAPO/MAT1. Enter the material number and select the GLOBAL DATA radio button.

If you have configured the stock determination as described previously, you also need to assign the STOCK DETERMINATION GROUP in the WAREHOUSE DATA tab of the warehouse product. To access the warehouse product from the EWM Easy Access menu, follow the menu path EXTENDED WAREHOUSE MANAGEMENT •

MASTER DATA • PRODUCT • MAINTAIN WAREHOUSE PRODUCT, OR use Transaction code /SCWM/MAT1.

17.3 Merchandise Distribution

Merchandise distribution is a retail-specific function that can be used to plan the flow of trading goods through a warehouse or distribution center. Merchandise distribution is essential for logistic processes in the retail industry. The retailers plan, control, and manage their flow of merchandise from vendors via distribution centers to the stores or customers. The merchandise can pass through one distribution center or, as is the case with multilevel merchandise distribution, several distribution centers. The recipient is known at the time of procurement.

Merchandise distribution is planned either by using an allocation table (push) or a collective purchase order (pull) in SAP ERP. Based on the purchase orders, inbound deliveries and outbound deliveries are created. Once the inbound delivery and outbound delivery documents are sent to EWM, it performs the merchandise distribution, which influences the internal processing within EWM.

The interface to EWM also contains information about which inbound deliveries and outbound deliveries are assigned to each other. During goods receipt, EWM determines the relationship between inbound deliveries and ODOs based on the purchase order item reference and the merchandise distribution process. If the quantity at goods receipt is different from the expected quantity, it is possible to perform a quantity adjustment in the ODO at this point.

After the goods receipt has been posted, the goods are distributed to the recipients using different processing methods. Based on decision made in ERP, EWM uses either merchandise distribution cross-docking or merchandise distribution using flow-through (which may be product driven or recipient driven). For merchandise distribution cross-docking, the merchandise is brought directly from goods receipt to goods issue without being put away. For flow-through, the merchandise is transported to a zone for repackaging and then brought to the goods issue area. In this case, there is no placement into storage between the receipt and issue from the distribution center. This extra repackaging step differentiates the flow-through process from the merchandise distribution cross-docking.

> **Note**
>
> To use EWM merchandise distribution in SAP ERP 6.0, your system must be configured as an SAP Retail system, you must have implemented Enhancement Package 4, and you must have activated business function Retail, CD/FT_EWM Integration.

Basic Customizing in ERP and EWM

To activate merchandise distribution in ERP, you must make the relevant settings in the ERP IMG at the following menu paths:

▶ LOGISTICS – GENERAL • MERCHANDISE DISTRIBUTION

▶ INTEGRATION WITH OTHER SAP COMPONENTS • EXTENDED WAREHOUSE MANAGEMENT • ADDITIONAL MATERIAL ATTRIBUTES • ATTRIBUTE VALUES FOR ADDITIONAL MATERIAL MASTER FIELDS • DEFINE ADJUSTMENT PROFILE

To support merchandise distribution with EWM, you must enable merchandise distribution in the EWM IMG by following the menu path EXTENDED WARE-HOUSE MANAGEMENT • CROSS-PROCESS SETTINGS • CROSS-DOCKING (CD) • PLANNED CROSS-DOCKING • MERCHANDISE DISTRIBUTION • BASIC SETTINGS FOR MERCHANDISE DISTRIBUTION.

Merchandise Distribution Cross-Docking

As described earlier, for merchandise distribution cross-docking, the merchandise is brought directly from the goods receipt area to the goods issue area without being put away. The inbound deliveries and outbound deliveries are linked to each other.

Recipient-Driven Flow-Through

For recipient-driven flow-through, the stock is picked from the goods receipt area and brought to a cross-docking staging area. From there, warehouse tasks for picking are created with homogenous consolidation groups. A single consolidation group can't be used for more than one customer for flow-through, so the picking warehouse order (WO) is created *per customer* (thus the name "recipient driven," or "customer-driven"). From the cross-docking staging area, the stock is picked into Pick HUs via the confirmation of the relevant WOs. For more details about consolidation groups and Pick HUs, see Chapter 10, Outbound Processing.

Merchandise-Driven Flow-Through

In the merchandise-driven flow-through, the stock is brought from the goods receipt area to a pick point workstation. (A pick point is an area where stock is delivered to be redistributed to individual orders via picking.) At the pick point workstation, the stock is repacked into Pick HUs based on product. From these Pick HUs, the final picking warehouse tasks for the customers are confirmed.

17.4 Push Deployment and Pick From Goods Receipt

PD and PFGR are opportunistic cross-docking processes that are triggered from an APO system via the event-driven quantity assignment (see Figure 17.14). As described in the beginning of the chapter, for opportunistic cross-docking processes you work with standard inbound deliveries using a standard goods receipt process. During the goods receipt, EWM decides whether the arriving goods will be cross-docked or not.

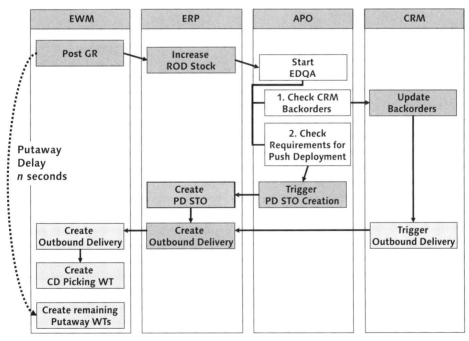

Figure 17.14 Event-driven Quantity Assignment in SAP APO

During goods receipt posting of an inbound delivery in EWM, the creation of the putaway warehouse task in EWM may be delayed (according to the configuration for the putaway delay defined in the EWM IMG via the menu path EXTENDED WAREHOUSE MANAGEMENT • CROSS-PROCESS SETTINGS • WAREHOUSE TASK • DEFINE PUTAWAY DELAY). At the same time, the goods receipt posting is interfaced to ERP and subsequently from ERP to APO. In APO, a workflow called Event Driven Quantity Assignment (EDQA) is started to perform checks to see if the stock should be put away or used to fulfill open customer orders (PFGR) or demands from other warehouses (PD).

The first check is for customer orders. If there are open customer orders (backorders) available in CRM, the EDQA will create an outbound delilvery for them in ERP. This delivery is sent to EWM, where the pick warehouse task for crossdocking is created, and the stock is picked directly from the goods receipt area.

If there are open demands for other warehouses, the APO system will create a Stock Transfer Order (STO) in the ERP system, and an outbound delivery for the STO will be created. This outbound delilvery is sent to EWM, where the crossdocking warehouse task is created, and the stock is once again picked from the goods receipt area.

If the EDQA workflow determines that no cross-docking will take place, the putaway delay in EWM will expire without an outbound delilvery having been created in the interim, and then a "normal" putaway warehouse task can be created within EWM.

For more information about push deployment in APO, see the help application in the SAP Online Help (*http://help.sap.com*) for SAP SCM via the menu path SAP SUPPLY CHAIN MANAGEMENT (SAP SCM) • SAP ADVANCED PLANNING AND OPTIMIZATION (SAP APO) • SERVICE PARTS PLANNING (SPP) • DEPLOYMENT.

For more information about push deployment in SAP ERP, see the SAP Online Help for SAP ERP Central Component (ECC) via the menu path SAP ERP CENTRAL COMPONENT • LOGISTICS • LOGISTICS - GENERAL (LO) • SERVICE PARTS MANAGEMENT (LO-SPM) • TRANSPORTATION CROSS-DOCKING • PUSH-DEPLOYMENT.

For more information about picking from goods receipt in SAP ERP, see the SAP Online Help for SAP ECC via the menu path SAP ERP CENTRAL COMPONENT • LOGISTICS • LOGISTICS - GENERAL (LO) • SERVICE PARTS MANAGEMENT (LO-SPM) • TRANSPORTATION CROSS-DOCKING • PICK FROM GOODS RECEIPT.

17.4.1 Putaway Delay at Goods Receipt in EWM

When you post goods receipt in EWM for an inbound delivery, the system checks to see if the warehouse process type (WPT) and stock type are relevant for *putaway delay*. To set up the putaway delay in the EWM IMG, follow the menu path EXTENDED WAREHOUSE MANAGEMENT • CROSS-PROCESS SETTINGS • WAREHOUSE TASK • DEFINE PUTAWAY DELAY. The PUTAWAY DELAY is defined in seconds (see Figure 17.15).

If you defined automatic putaway warehouse task creation, the task creation is only triggered after the expiration of the putaway delay automatically by a job, which is scheduled in the background. You can review these jobs or check their status via Transaction SM37.

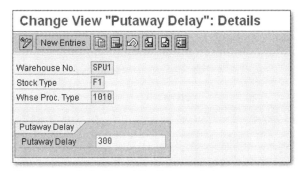

Figure 17.15 Definition of the Putaway Delay

If an inbound delivery item has the same stock type and WPT as the entry in the customizing, EWM starts the putaway delay and therefore delays the generation of the warehouse tasks for putaway. If the WPT and stock type are not relevant, EWM generates the warehouse tasks for putaway without delay (which means that it will not perform PD or PFGR).

On the other hand, if the putaway delay is relevant, no putaway warehouse tasks should be created for the inbound delivery item until the putaway time has elapsed (and none will be automatically created until the job described previously is executed). If you try to create the putaway warehouse tasks manually for an inbound delivery, the system triggers an appropriate message to warn you about this situation. However, the message is only a warning message, so users can bypass it, but if the message is bypassed and the stock is put away, opportunities for cross-docking may be missed.

17.4.2 Integration of PD and PFGR into the EWM Storage Control

PD and PFGR are integrated into the EWM POSC. To show how this is done, let's take a look at an example (as shown in Figure 17.16). In our example, you receive an inbound delivery that contains three products. PD or PFGR is necessary for one of these products. The other two products are for putaway. Accordingly, you can unload the HU from the truck (the first step of the storage process) and bring it to a deconsolidation work center (the second step of the storage process).

In the work center, you perform deconsolidation for the HU. You unpack the HU and you repack the product that requires PD or PFGR into another HU. If EWM also determines an *outbound storage process* for this HU after deconsolidation, EWM will process all of the respective outbound steps according to the warehouse process. The other two products will be packed into a putaway HU, for which you execute the additional steps until it is put away into the final storage bins.

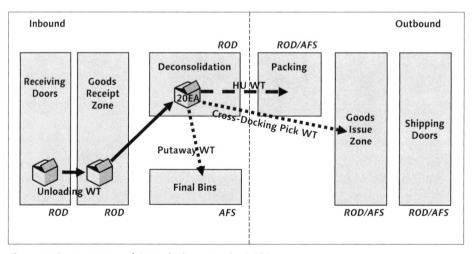

Figure 17.16 Integration of Cross-docking into the POSC

For the first product of the HU, EWM determines that the WPT and the stock type are relevant for the putaway delay. By doing so, EWM delays the creation of the unload warehouse task and the putaway product warehouse tasks for the entire inbound delivery. Subsequently, SAP APO determines that PD or a PFGR is necessary for one product and informs SAP ERP of this. SAP ERP creates an outbound delivery and sends it to EWM. EWM then creates an *inactive product warehouse task for picking* to take the HU from the goods receipt zone to the goods issue zone. This warehouse task reserves the stock for cross-docking. After the putaway delay has expired, EWM creates the corresponding *inactive product warehouse tasks for putaway* for the other products.

After the unloading is completed, EWM checks to see if *deconsolidation* is necessary. EWM determines that deconsolidation is necessary for the HU because the inactive picking warehouse task has a different consolidation group than the inactive putaway warehouse task. Remember that for putaway warehouse tasks, the consolidation group comes from the activity area of the destination bin, whereas for picking warehouse tasks it comes from the ODO item, based on the ship-to party.

Accordingly, EWM creates a warehouse task to bring the HU from the goods receipt zone to the deconsolidation work center. EWM simultaneously updates the inactive pick and putaway product warehouse tasks. These inactive warehouse tasks now lead from the deconsolidation work center to the final bins (for putaway) and to an outbound area (for cross-docking).

17.5 Summary

In this chapter, we described the various methods for cross-docking used by EWM. You should now have a good understanding about these processes, how they might apply in your warehouse, and how to set them up if you want to enable them for your operations. In the following chapters, we will continue describing the special processes within the warehouse, continuing now with Yard Management.

Extending the management of the warehouse to the shipping and receiving yard, where the trailers are stored, is becoming increasingly common and useful for tracking and controlling inventory.

18   Yard Management

The "yard" can be loosely defined as the area outside of the warehouse that is used to store inbound and outbound trailers and may be used by vehicles that bring the trailers in or out. Systems for managing the trailers and vehicles in the yard, known commonly as yard management systems, have become increasingly popular in the last several years. From an inventory management (IM) perspective, manufacturers and distributors are increasingly interested to know where the inventory is located within their entire supply chain, not just within the warehouse. A natural extension of the warehouse management system, therefore, is to track the materials that are stored in the area directly outside of the warehouse itself, namely the yard.

In SAP Extended Warehouse Management (EWM), yard management capability has been built natively into the warehouse management system as part of the shipping and receiving functions — it is not an add-on or extension or otherwise decoupled from the warehouse management system. Having the yard management system directly incorporated into the warehouse management system provides the advantage that the systems can share structures and processes (therefore the topics that we discuss in the following sections will sound very familiar), and you can design integrated processes that cover the end-to-end business processes for inbound and outbound distribution. In addition, you can use the same reporting tools within the warehouse monitor to view the yard management activities and the warehouse activities (which we will discuss later in this chapter).

Yard management in EWM is completely an optional process step. If you want to activate yard management for your warehouse from the EWM Implementation Guide (IMG), follow the menu path EXTENDED WAREHOUSE MANAGEMENT • CROSS-PROCESS SETTINGS • SHIPPING AND RECEIVING • YARD MANAGEMENT • ACTIVATE YARD MANAGEMENT FOR WAREHOUSE.

18.1   Yard Management Structure

The basic element of the yard management structure is the yard. The yard is modeled in the EWM system as a storage type. This storage type can be within the same logical warehouse as the storage types and bins within the physical warehouse, or you can create a separate logical warehouse to use for the yard. For example, if the yard is shared with other warehouses, it might make sense to create a separate logical warehouse for the yard. To create the warehouse and storage type, use the same methods as described in Chapter 3, The Warehouse Structure. To assign a warehouse and storage type to control the yard in the EWM IMG, follow the menu path Extended Warehouse Management • Master Data • Shipping and Receiving • Yard Management • Define Yard Using Storage Type.

You can optionally define storage sections within the yard storage type to segregate the storage areas of the yard. To create the storage sections for the yard storage type from the EWM IMG, follow the menu path Extended Warehouse Management • Master Data • Shipping and Receiving • Yard Management • Structure Yard Using Storage Areas.

The structural elements that are used within the yard to move and store the transportation units (TUs) and vehicles include:

▶ **Checkpoints**

Checkpoints are used to check the TUs and vehicles in and out of the yard. To create the checkpoints from the EWM IMG, follow the menu path Extended Warehouse Management • Master Data • Shipping and Receiving • Yard Management • Define Checkpoints.

Once the checkpoints are created, they should be assigned to relevant yard bins and supply chain units. To make this assignment from the ERP Easy Access menu, follow the Extended Warehouse Management • Master Data • Shipping and Receiving • Yard Management • Assign Checkpoint to Yard Bin and SCU menu path, or use Transaction /SCWM/YM_CHKPT_BIN.

▶ **Warehouse doors**

Warehouse doors represent the physical doors in the warehouse that are used for loading and unloading, and to connect the yard to the warehouse. The TUs are assigned to doors to unload or load the transporation units to or from the warehouse. To create warehouse doors from the EWM IMG, follow the menu path EXTENDED WAREHOUSE MANAGEMENT • MASTER DATA • WAREHOUSE DOOR • DEFINE WAREHOUSE DOOR.

Warehouse doors are also assigned to yard bins so that the stock can be visible in the yard bin via the warehouse monitor while the TU is situated at the warehouse door. To assign yard bins to the warehouse door from the EWM Easy Access menu, follow the EXTENDED WAREHOUSE MANAGEMENT • MASTER DATA • SHIPPING AND RECEIVING • YARD MANAGEMENT • ASSIGN WAREHOUSE DOOR TO YARD BIN menu path, or use Transaction code /SCWM/YM_DOOR_BIN.

▶ **Parking spaces**

Parking spaces are used to store trailers or vehicles while they are in the yard. To create the parking spaces from the EWM Easy Access menu, follow the EXTENDED WAREHOUSE MANAGEMENT • MASTER DATA • SHIPPING AND RECEIVING • YARD MANAGEMENT • CREATE STORAGE BIN menu path, or use Transaction code /SCWM/LS01. For more details on how to create storage bins, refer to the section on creating storage bins for the warehouse in Chapter 3.

In Figure 18.1, you can see a graphical representation of the yard and its structural elements.

Each of the structural elements of the yard is assigned to a storage bin within the yard storage type. This allows the EWM inventory management engine to track the location of the inventory using the same methods that are used within the warehouse, and it also allows EWM to use the same methods to track movements of the inventory between bins using WTs (which will be discussed further in the following sections).

To assign the warehouse doors to yard bins from the EWM IMG, follow the EXTENDED WAREHOUSE MANAGEMENT • MASTER DATA • SHIPPING AND RECEIVING • YARD MANAGEMENT • ASSIGN WAREHOUSE DOOR TO YARD BIN menu path, or use Transaction code /SCWM/YM_DOOR_BIN.

To assign the checkpoints to yard bins from the EWM IMG, follow the EXTENDED WAREHOUSE MANAGEMENT • MASTER DATA • SHIPPING AND RECEIVING • YARD MANAGEMENT • ASSIGN CHECKPOINT TO YARD BIN AND SCU menu path, or use Transaction code /SCWM/YM_CHKPT_BIN.

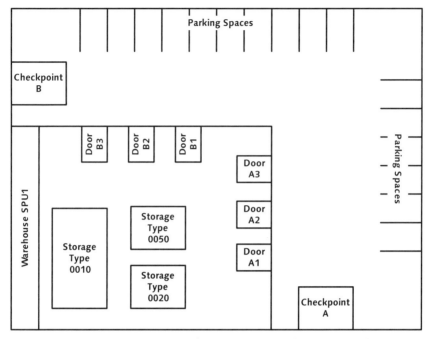

Figure 18.1 Graphical Representation of an Example Yard and Its Structural Elements

18.2   Transportation Units and Vehicles

The trucks, trailers, containers, canisters, and other vehicles and conveyances used to move the products into and out of the warehouse via the yard are managed using the yard management and shipping and receiving capabilities of EWM. Conveyances, including trailers, canisters (often simply called "cans"), and other types of containers are managed using objects known as TUs. The trucks, rail engines, and other vehicles that are used to transport the conveyances are managed using objects known as vehicles. Together, these vehicles and TUs can be flexibly used to manage all of the inbound and outbound product that arrives or departs on any type of conveyance transported by any type of vehicle.

18.2.1 Creating Transportation Units

You can use one of three methods to create TUs. First, you can create them from the TU user interface (UI). Second, you can create them from the check-in/check-out UI (described further in the following sections). And finally, you can have the TUs created automatically during the interface with Advance Shipping Notice (ASN) or inbound delivery data from ERP. Regardless of the method that you choose, the creation of the TUs can be quick and easy and can be used to hold the important data about the conveyance used to transport the products to and from the warehouse. It is also a prerequisite for assigning the deliveries to the TU to track which products are held inside.

To create TUs from the TU UI, from the EWM Easy Access menu, follow the EXTENDED WAREHOUSE MANAGEMENT • SHIPPING AND RECEIVING • PROCESS TRANSPORTATION UNIT menu path, or use Transaction code /SCWM/TU. This same transaction can be used to create or change TUs; assign deliveries, handling units (HUs), or vehicles to the TU; assign doors to the TU; or to read or process other information about the TUs. To create a TU, select the CREATE button, or follow the TRANSPORTATION UNIT • CREATE menu path, and enter the required data on the pop-up screen (as seen in Figure 18.2).

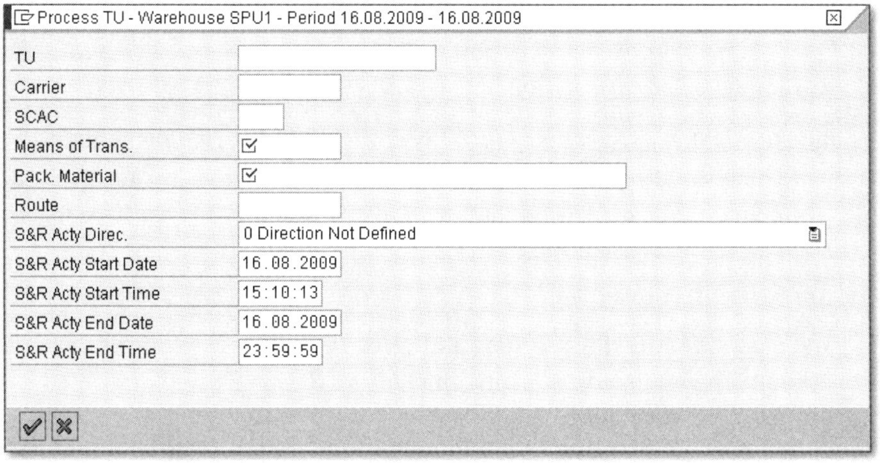

Process TU - Warehouse SPU1 - Period 16.08.2009 - 16.08.2009	⊠
TU	
Carrier	
SCAC	
Means of Trans.	☑
Pack. Material	☑
Route	
S&R Acty Direc.	0 Direction Not Defined
S&R Acty Start Date	16.08.2009
S&R Acty Start Time	15:10:13
S&R Acty End Date	16.08.2009
S&R Acty End Time	23:59:59

Figure 18.2 Creation of a TU

On the TU creation screen, the follow data can be entered:

▶ TU

The external TU number is used to track the TU throughout the yard. It should usually represent some indicator, which can be found on the TU itself, so that the data can be matched up to the physical TU. (An internal TU number is also created for each TU, but is often not functionally used by end users.)

▶ CARRIER

The carrier can be assigned here and should be set up in EWM as a business partner with the role CARRIER

▶ SCAC

The Standard Carrier Alpha Code (SCAC) is a unique code used to identify carriers in certain regions

▶ MEANS OF TRANS.

The means of transport is intended to identify the method used to transport the TU

▶ PACK. MATERIAL

The packaging material identifies the packaging material defined within EWM used to package the products within TU. Certain data, for example, the capacity of the TU, are derived from the packaging material

▶ ROUTE

The transportation route can be assigned to the TU

▶ S&R ACTY DIRECT.

The direction indicates whether the TU is intended to be used for inbound or outbound activity. If it is not known at the time of creation, it can be left as value Undefined, and it will be automatically assigned when an inbound or outbound delivery is assigned to the TU

▶ S&R ACTY START DATE and START TIME

The intended start time for shipping and receiving activities related to the TU (for example, the intended unloading time for a TU)

▸ S&R Acty End Date and End Time

  The intended end time for shipping and receicing activities related to the TU
  (for example, the time by which the unloading must be performed in order for
  the warehouse to avoid demurrage charges)

Once you create the TU, you can select the TU and read the data associated with
it by entering the selection criteria in the selection field and executing the search
function to select the TUs. You can also select multiple TUs at once, as seen in
Figure 18.3.

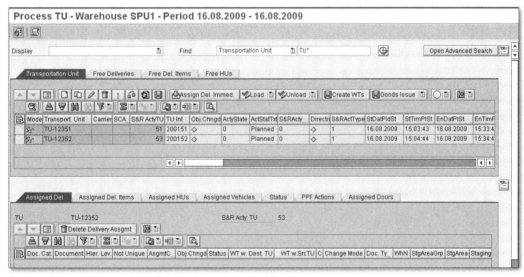

Figure 18.3 TU Selection and Maintenance within the TU UI

> **Note**
>
> It is not necessary to recreate TUs for conveyances that have already been in the yard
> before. You can reuse the TU that already existed. For example, if a carrier runs a regular
> route to your warehouse and you want to check it into the yard each day, you can reuse
> the TU from the previous days rather than creating it new each day. This helps to elimi-
> nate unnecessary data entry, data maintenance, and duplicate table entries.

18.2.2   Other Functions of the Transportation Unit UI

Once the TU is created, you can perform the following activities for the TU within
the TU maintenance transaction:

- Change certain data on the TU header, including route, license plate, additional identification numbers for the TU, planned start and end time, total weight, and seal numbers

- Assign deliveries or delivery items (inbound or outbound)

- Assign HUs

- Assign vehicles

- Assign doors

- Start and finish loading or unloading the TU (for simple loading or unloading, described further in the following sections)

- Create loading or unloading WTs (for complex loading or unloading, described further in the following sections)

- Block or unblock TUs and assign reason codes

- Arrive the TU to the door or depart from the door

- Arrive the TU to or depart the TU from the checkpoint

- Perform goods receipt or goods issue for the TU (which performs the relevant activity for all of the assigned deliveries)

- Copy, delete, or archive the TU or perform various other maintenance functions

Checking in the Transportation Unit

The most common use for checking in a TU via the TU UI would be to create an inbound TU, assign the inbound deliveries, and then check in the TU at the same time, which would be a common business practice for a warehouse clerk who is checking in a trailer that was not previously scheduled. Similar functions can be performed in the check-in/check-out UI, except that you cannot assign the deliveries in that UI, so if the delivery assignment is required and you want to perform all of the activities in one transaction, you should use the TU UI.

> **Note**
>
> Before checking in or checking out a TU or vehicle from the TU UI, you must define the default values for your user by selecting the DEFAULT VALUES button in the top right on the button bar and enter the default data in the pop-up box (as seen in Figure 18.4).

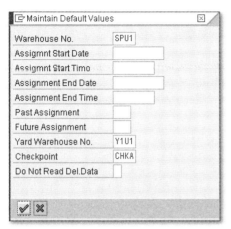

Figure 18.4 Default Values for the User, as Assigned in the TU UI

Simple vs. Complex Loading and Unloading

The simple loading and unloading functions can best be described as a one-step procedure that assigns the loading or unloading status without requiring detailed input of the individual products or HUs. Complex loading and unloading, in contrast, requires the creation of WTs to track the activities for each HU as it is being loaded onto or unloaded from the TU. Whether you use the simple or complex unloading and unloading may depend on various criteria and can be driven by the setup of the process-oriented storage control (POSC). If checks on the loading and unloading status are not for the goods issue or goods receipt posting, then the loading and unloading processes are completely optional, therefore you should consider whether you want to make them mandatory steps or not. The simple and complex unloading and loading processes are described further in Chapter 9, Inbound Processing, and Chapter 10, Outbound Processing.

18.2.3 Creating Vehicles

Vehicles are the trucks, locomotive engines, ships, or other equipment used to convey the TUs from one place to another. Often, the vehicle will arrive together with the TU to the yard and you will want to track the vehicles as they arrive to and depart from the yard.

To create or maintain a vehicle, you can use either the vehicle UI or the check-in/check-out transaction. To use the vehicle UI, from the SAP Easy Access menu, follow the SMALL CAPS: EXTENDED WAREHOUSE MANAGEMENT • SHIPPING AND RECEIVING • PROCESS VEHICLE menu path, or use Transaction code /SCWM/VEH.

From the vehicle UI, to create a new vehicle, select the CREATE button or follow the menu path VEHICLE • CREATE. In the resulting pop-up screen (as seen in Figure 18.5), enter the relevant data for the vehicle, which can include:

► Vehicle Number

► Carrier

► SCAC

► Means of Transport

► S&R Activity Start Date and Time

► S&R Activity End Date and Time

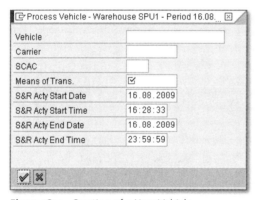

Figure 18.5 Creation of a New Vehicle

18.2.4 Other Functions of the Vehicle UI

Once the vehicle is created, you can select the vehicle once again to maintain it (as seen in Figure 18.6) by using the selection box in the top right of the screen (or click the OPEN ADVANCED SEARCH button to enter additional selection criteria).

For the resulting vehicles, you can select a vehicle and perform the following functions:

► Change certain data on the vehicle header, including license plate number, driver, language, additional vehicle identification, total weight of the vehicle, and planned start arrival and departure

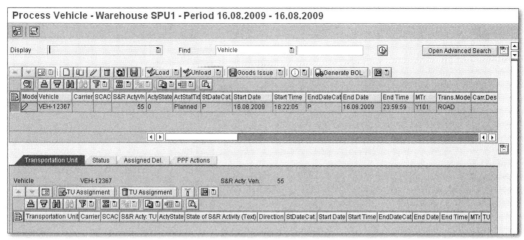

Figure 18.6 Vehicle Maintenance

▸ Assign (or delete assignment of) TUs

▸ View the assigned deliveries (according to the deliveries assigned to the TUs, which are assigned to the vehicle)

▸ Perform simple loading or unloading (or reverese loading or unloading)

▸ Perform (or reverse) goods issue or goods receipt for the deliveries that are assigned to the TUs assigned to the vehicle

▸ Generate a bill of lading for the assigned objects

▸ Block or unblock a vehicle and assign reason codes

▸ Arrive the vehicle to the door or depart from the door (together with assigned TUs)

▸ Arrive the vehicle to or depart the vehicle from the checkpoint (together with assigned TUs)

▸ Perform goods receipt or goods issue for the TUs assigned to the vehicle (which performs the relevant activity for all of the assigned deliveries)

▸ Copy, delete, or archive the vehicle or perform various other maintenance functions

18.3 Check-In and Check-Out

Often, warehouse yards are enclosed within a gated area with a guard station or other check-in/check-out facility at the entry/exit gate. In other cases, the yard is open and the truck drivers will go to a central point to check-in or check-out their loads. Either way, the same system processes can be used for the check-in and check-out of the trailers and vehicles.

When a physical vehicle or trailer arrives at the warehouse, it is checked into the yard at the checkpoint (either physically or virtually, as described earlier). If the TU or vehicle already exists, it can be directly processed in the check-in/check-out transaction. The TUs may have been previously created in at least one of two ways:

▶ Assignment of the trailer number on the ASN, which automatically generates the TU in EWM when the inbound delivery is interfaced from the ERP system

▶ Manual creation of the TU, often based on appointment scheduling by the carrier for the inbound drop-off or unloading

To access the check-in/check-out transaction from the EWM Easy Access menu, follow the Extended Warehouse Management • Shipping and Receiving • Yard Management • Arrival at/Departure from Checkpoint menu path, or use Transaction code /SCWM/CICO. To check in a trailer or vehicle, select the relevant TU or vehicle number using the selection criteria in the top right of the screen (or click the Open Advanced Search button to find more selection options), then select the TU or vehicle on the screen and click the Arrival at Checkpoint button (circled in Figure 18.7). You can also cancel an arrival if you make a mistake (up to the point of the next process step being completed) by selecting the dropdown box next to the Arrival at Checkpoint button and selecting the Cancel Arrival at CHKPT + Save option.

Similarly, if you want to check out a trailer that is departing from the yard (typically an empty trailer or trailer that has just been loaded at the warehouse, but could also be an inbound trailer that has to depart the yard again for some reason), search for the TU or vehicle, select it on the screen, and press the Dep. from Checkpoint button. You can also cancel a departure by selecting the drop-down box from beside the Dep. from Checkpoint button and selecting the Cancel Dep. From CHKPT + Save option.

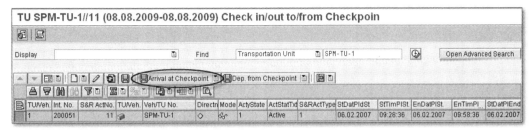

Figure 18.7 Yard Management Check-in/Check-out UI

> **Note**
>
> You can also check in or check out the TUs and vehicles from their respective UIs (Transactions /SCWM/TU and /SCWM/VEH) as described in the previous sections.

18.4   Yard Movements

After the vehicles and TUs arrive to the yard and are checked in at the checkpoint, they need to be moved within the yard, either to a yard parking position or to a warehouse door. To move the vehicle or TUs, you can either use the yard movement UI or you can use the RF-enabled mobile data entry transactions (described further in Chapter 22, Data Capture and Resource Optimization). To create a yard move via the graphical user interface (GUI) transaction, from the EWM Easy Access menu, follow the EXTENDED WAREHOUSE MANAGEMENT • SHIPPING AND RECEIVING • YARD MANAGEMENT • CREATE WT IN YARD menu path, or use Transaction code /SCWM/YMOVE.

Selecting the Objects for Movement

To select the object to move, use the selection box in the top right of the screen (as seen in Figure 18.8), or click the OPEN ADVANCED SEARCH button to use additional criteria for the selection.

Creating the Yard Move Task

To create the WT, either enter the relevant data for the WT directly on the header view in the top pane (you may have to scroll to the right to get to the data, depending on your assigned layout) or switch to the FORM VIEW by selecting the SWITCH TO FORM VIEW button to enter the relevant data there (as seen in figure 18.9).

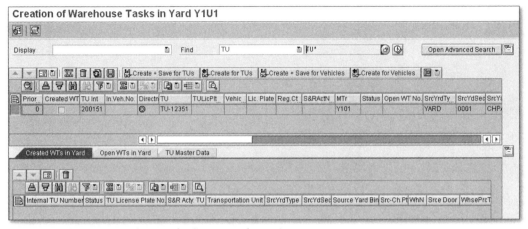

Figure 18.8 Selection of Relevant TUs for Yard Movement

> **Note**
>
> If you want to enter the data for the WT, before entering the FORM view, be sure to
> select the object that you want to view in the FORM view, otherwise you will be taken
> to a blank form view.

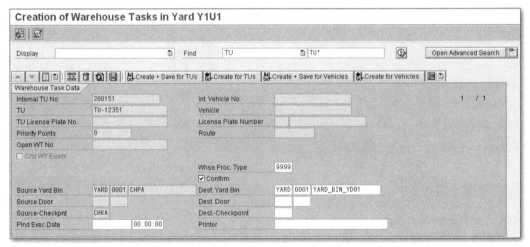

Figure 18.9 Assignment of Destination Data for the Yard Move in the Form View

When entering the data for the WT, you must at least enter the process type and
the destination, whether it is a destination yard bin (such as a parking place), a
destination door, or a destination checkpoint.

If you are going to assign a destination door or a destination yard bin, you only need to input the yard bin or the door (not the storage type or section) and the rest of the data will be filled automatically.

If you want to confirm the task immediately (indicating that the object has already been moved or will be moved immediately), select the CONFIRM checkbox. Otherwise, the WT will be created and then must be confirmed in a separate step. This could be useful if, for instance, you want to create the WTs on the GUI and then have the yard workers execute the tasks on the RF device. Once you have entered the data, click the relevant CREATE + SAVE button (or CREATE, and then save it in a separate step), and the task will be created.

Once the WT is created, if it requires separate confirmation, you can confirm it with the Yard Move UI by selecting the object and selecting the OPEN WTs IN YARD tab on the bottom pane (as seen in Figure 18.8). From this tab, you can confirm the task in the background, confirm in the foreground, or cancel the WT. Alternatively, you can select the warehouse task in the WT confirmation UI (Transaction /SCWM/ TO_CONF) and confirm it there, or you can use the RF transaction for confirming WTs (further described in Chapter 22).

Common Yard Flows

Common flows of TUs or vehicle through the yard may include:

▶ Check in full TU • Move to yard • Move to door for unloading • Depart empty from door • Move to checkpoint • Check out

▶ Check in full TU • Move to door for "live" unload • Depart from door • Move to checkpoint • Check out

▶ Check in full TU• Move to yard • Move to door for unloading • Depart from door • Move empty to yard • Move empty to checkpoint • Check out

▶ Check in full TU • Move to yard • Move to door for unloading • Depart from door • Move empty to yard • Move empty to door for loading • Depart full trailer from door • Move full trailer to yard • Move full trailer to checkpoint • Check out

▶ Check in empty trailer • Move to yard • Move to door for loading • Depart from door • Move full trailer to yard • Move full trailer to checkpoint • Check out

There are several other possible variations, but this will give you a sense of how the movements through the yard typically occur.

18.5   Monitoring the Yard

To monitor the activities or the objects in the yard, you can use the warehouse monitor for the yard warehouse (recall from the introduction to this chapter that you can assign the yard to the warehouse or create a separate warehouse). To access the warehouse monitor from the EWM Easy Access menu, follow the EXTENDED WAREHOUSE MANAGEMENT • MONITORING • WAREHOUSE MANAGEMENT MONITOR menu path, or use Transaction code /SCWM/MON.

For example, from within the warehouse monitor, by following the STOCK AND BIN • YARD MANAGEMENT • YARD BINS • YARD MOVES menu path, and selecting the OPEN WTs ONLY checkbox, you can select the open WTs, or "yard moves," within the yard (as seen in Figure 18.10). Note that you can also perform certain actions related to the WTs (for example, confirming the WT, cancelling the WT, assigning the WT) by selecting the WT and clicking the MORE METHODS button.

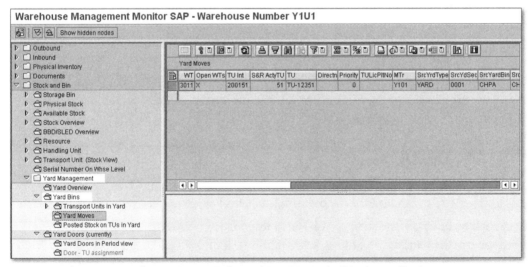

Figure 18.10   Selecting Open WTs for Yard Activities in the Warehouse Monitor

From the warehouse monitor, you can also view (via the menu path specified in parentheses):

▶ Stocks in the yard (STOCK AND BIN • YARD MANAGEMENT • YARD BINS • POSTED STOCK ON TUS IN YARD)

▶ Empty parrking places in the yard (STOCK AND BIN • YARD MANAGEMENT • YARD BINS — select the LIMIT RESULT TO FREE OBJECTS checkbox)

▶ TUs in the yard and the stock on the TUs (STOCK AND BIN • YARD MANAGEMENT • YARD BINS • TRANSPORT UNITS IN YARD — select the TUs and click the DELIVERY ITEM button)

▶ Status of doors and list of TUs in the doors (STOCK AND BIN • YARD MANAGEMENT • YARD DOORS (CURRENTLY))

▶ Yard overview (STOCK AND BIN • YARD MANAGEMENT • YARD OVERVIEW)

Note

The preceding nodes specifically provide information about the yard and can also be accessed when you are viewing information about the main warehouse (i.e., when you specified the main warehouse in the defaults when you first entered the transaction or by selecting the DEFAULT VALUES button). Just be sure to specify the warehouse number for the yard warehouse on the selection screen when you access the report for the node.

You can also find information about the yard bins, yard doors, and yard moves by using the nodes from the other sections in the yard monitor. For example, to find the list of yard moves, you can follow the DOCUMENTS • WT menu path and select the option to search for OPEN WTs.

18.6   Interfacing Yard Data to ERP

In addition to information about which products are on the deliveries and the status changes that occur at goods receipt and goods issue, the yard-relevant data is also passed back and forth between EWM and ERP via the delivery documents.

On inbound deliveries, the TU number can be passed to EWM from ERP if the TU number is received from the vendor or carrier on the ASN. When this TU number is passed to EWM on the inbound delivery, EWM automatically creates a TU if it does not exist already.

In addition, when the TU is checked into the yard (and even before goods receipt), the check-in status is transferred to ERP, which subsequently transfers the data to global available to promise (global ATP, or gATP) about which stocks are in the yard. Global ATP uses this information to check the availability of the yard stock when a request for availability of the material is received from CRM or ERP, and if the yard stock is set as relevant according to the ATP rule set, availability may be confirmed based on the stock that is in the yard.

18.7   Summary

In this chapter, you learned about the capabilities of EWM to support yard management and how to set it up, including setup of the yard and creation, check-in, check-out, and movement of TUs and vehicles. In the following chapters, we will discuss additional special processes within EWM, including Value Added Services (VAS), Kitting, and Labor Management.

In this chapter, we will introduce the topic of value-added services (VAS) and discuss how to configure and implement VAS for various warehouse business processes.

19 Value-Added Services (VAS)

VAS activities are activities that enhance the value of a product in the warehouse. These activities are generally performed by warehouse operators at a work center in the warehouse. Examples of VAS activities include packaging, oiling (or other preservation activities), assembly, kitting, tagging, and price marking. For example, a VAS could be an activity for packing a material in a specific customer-requested box and applying a label, as shown in Figure 19.1.

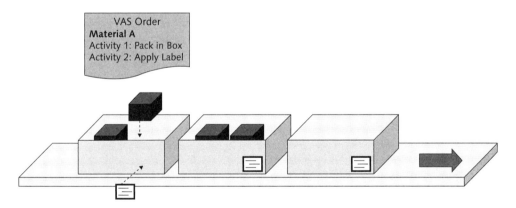

Figure 19.1 Example of a VAS Activity — Packing and Labeling

To manage the VAS activities in the warehouse, Extended Warehouse Management (EWM) uses VAS orders. VAS orders are documents in EWM that specify the VAS activities that need to be performed and the auxiliary materials used. They are also used to track the time spent on the VAS activity.

Execution of VAS activities are billed to the customer for whom the VAS was performed. For example, if a customer requests packaging according to a specific configuration, it could be offered as a VAS activity, which is then billed to this customer. The amount of time and materials used for the VAS will therefore be important to support the billing.

In this chapter, we will review VAS in EWM. First, we will look at the configuration and master data setup for VAS. Then we will look at the use of the work center during the VAS execution. And, finally, we will review how the VAS orders can be executed together with the other logistical processes of the warehouse.

19.1 Configuration and Master Data for VAS

There are several configuration and master data elements used to support VAS that are important to understand if you are going to set up VAS for your warehouse. In this section, we will describe those in detail.

19.1.1 Configuration for VAS

In the following sections, we will review the support configurations for VAS in EWM.

Product Group Types and Product Groups

In EWM, you can create VAS orders for materials automatically during inbound or outbound processing, or you can create them manually. When you know that a specific material always requires some VAS activities before it is put away or before it is shipped, you can set up the customizing to automatically generate the VAS order.

To create a VAS order for a material automatically, it needs to be assigned to a VAS-specific product group type and product group. To create the possible group types (as seen in Figure 19.2) in the EWM Implementation Guide (IMG), follow the menu path SCM BASIS • MASTER DATA • PRODUCT • PRODUCT GROUPS • DEFINE PRODUCT GROUP TYPES.

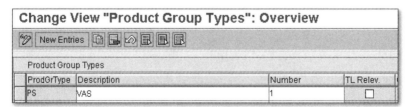

Figure 19.2 Maintaining the Product Group Type for VAS

For each product group type, you can create one or more product groups. This way, you could, for example, make a material only relevant to inbound VAS order creation, only for outbound VAS order, or for both inbound and outbound (see Figure 19.3). To create the product groups in EWM IMG, follow the menu path SCM BASIS • MASTER DATA • PRODUCT • PRODUCT GROUPS • DEFINE PRODUCT GROUPS.

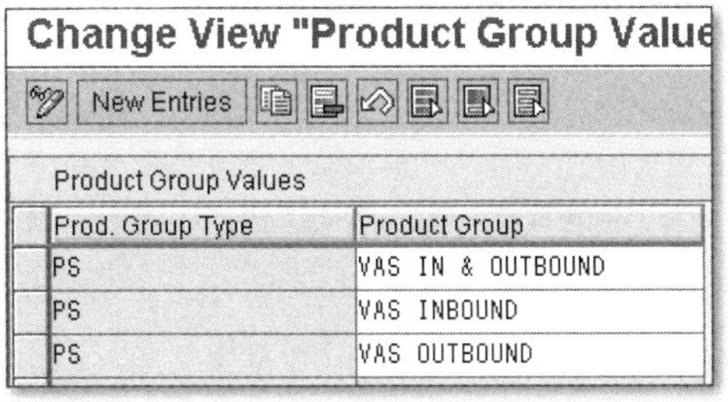

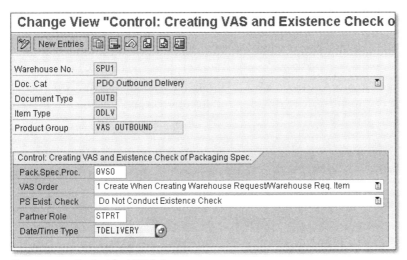

Figure 19.3 Maintaining the Product Groups for VAS

Figure 19.4 Control for VAS Relevance

Maintaining the VAS Relevance

To maintain VAS in the EWM IMG menu, follow the menu path EXTENDED WAREHOUSE MANAGEMENT • CROSS-PROCESS SETTINGS • VALUE-ADDED SERVICES (VAS) • DEFINE RELEVANCE FOR VAS. Here, you can maintain for which document types and item types VAS can be relevant. In Figure 19.4, you can see that we specified that VAS is relevant for an outbound delivery order (ODO) item with the document type OUTB, item type ODLV, and a material for which product group VAS OUTBOUND has been maintained.

The following fields in the VAS relevance are also important for driving the VAS process:

▶ Packaging Specification Procedure: This setting specifies the determination procedure that will be used to determine the packaging specification (pack spec), which is required for VAS order creation.

▶ VAS Order: This parameter determines whether a VAS order can be created automatically when receiving the Warehouse Request (Item) (i.e., when the ODO is created).

▶ Pack Spec Existence Check: This parameter is used to determine whether a pack spec existence check needs to be performed. It's possible that an ODO is VAS order relevant, but no VAS order can be created unless the pack spec can be determined. This setting lets you check whether the pack spec exists and to specify whether a warning or error message should result if one is not found.

▶ Partner Role: The specified partner role will be used from the requirements document to find the correct pack spec. In the example seen in Figure 19.4, the PARTNER ROLE STPRT (ship-to-party) is used for determining the pack spec, because the document type is an outbound document type (document category PDO).

▶ Date/Time Type: This field specifies which date/time type from the document will be used to determine the pack spec.

VAS Settings for the Warehouse

There are also some specific settings for VAS at the warehouse level, as shown in Figure 19.5. They can be maintained in the EWM IMG by following the menu path EXTENDED WAREHOUSE MANAGEMENT • CROSS-PROCESS SETTINGS • VALUE-ADDED SERVICES (VAS) • WAREHOUSE NUMBER-DEPENDENT VAS SETTINGS.

In the VAS settings for the warehouse, you can specify the following:

▶ VAS NO. RANGE

▶ PERFORMING ENT. (Performing Entity) of the warehouse

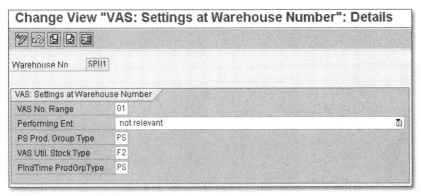

Figure 19.5 VAS Settings at the Warehouse Number Level

▶ PS PROD. GROUP TYPE (Pack Spec Product Group Type) from the product master used to determine the VAS relevance

▶ VAS UTIL.STOCK TYPE (VAS Utilities Stock Type) for specifying the stock type ofVAS consumption posting for auxiliary products

▶ PlndTime ProdGrpType (Planned Time Product Group Type) used for determining the planned times for Process Step Duration.

19.1.2   Master Data for VAS

In the following sections, we will review the master data required for VAS order creation. The master data comes from both the product master and the packaging specification.

Maintaining the Material Master

The VAS relevance, as seen previously, is based on the product group assignment for the product. The product group is assigned on the PROPERTIES 2 tab of the Advanced Planning and Optimization (APO) view of the product master (see Figure 19.6), which can be accessed from the EWM Easy Access menu by following the menu path EXTENDED WAREHOUSE MANAGEMENT • MASTER DATA • PRODUCT • MAINTAIN PRODUCT, or using Transaction code /SAPAPO/MAT1.

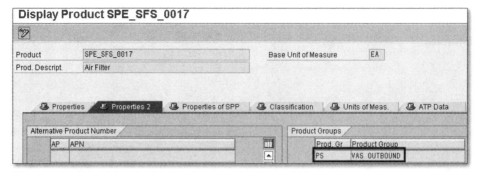

Figure 19.6 Maintaining the Product Group on the Material Master

Creation of the Packaging Specification for VAS

In Chapter 5, Other Warehouse Master Data, we already discussed the creation of pack specs in detail. In this section, we will look specifically at creating a pack spec for a VAS. To create a packaging specification or maintain existing packaging specifications from the EWM Easy Access menu, follow the EXTENDED WAREHOUSE MANAGEMENT • MASTER DATA • PACKAGING SPECIFICATION • MAINTAIN PACKAGING SPECIFICATION menu path, or use Transaction code /SCWM/PACKSPEC.

To determine the correct pack spec for VAS order creation, a condition record must be maintained for the condition determination procedure maintained in configuration (as described earlier in this chapter). This condition record can be assigned to the pack spec on the DETERMINATION tab (as you can see in figure 19.7).

Figure 19.7 Assignment of the Condition Record for Pack Spec Determination

In Figure 19.8, you can see the LEVEL detail of the pack spec. A level of the pack spec corresponds to an activity or a set of activities that need to be performed during the VAS execution. During the creation of the VAS order, the levels of the pack spec will be adopted into the VAS order as activities. For the pack spec shown in the example, 2 EA of product SPE_SFS_0017 will be packed into a packaging material SPE_BOX at the VAS work center. In a subsequent step, a label will be applied to the box.

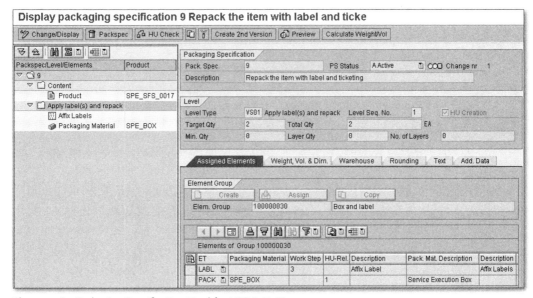

Figure 19.8 Packaging Specification Used for VAS Activities

On the WAREHOUSE tab for the level, you must assign an external step. The external step corresponds to the VAS process step, which is used to determine the work center where the VAS activity for this pack spec level will be performed, as shown in Figure 19.9.

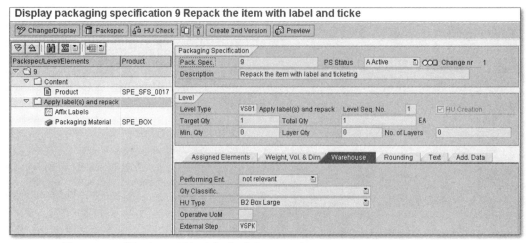

Figure 19.9 Warehouse Tab of the Pack Spec Level

19.2 VAS Order Creation

As mentioned earlier, when a VAS order is created, the levels of the pack spec get copied to the VAS order as activities, and the quantities of the reference document (e.g., outbound delivery order (ODO) or inbound delivery) will be taken over.

In EWM, you can create the VAS order manually or automatically. When creating a VAS order manually or displaying a VAS order, you can use the following transactions, depending on which source document is used for creating the VAS order:

▶ /SCWM/VAS_I — VAS in Goods Receipt Process

▶ /SCWM/VAS_O — VAS in Goods Issue Process

▶ /SCWM/VAS_KTS — VAS for Kit Creation on Stock

▶ /SCWM/VAS_KTR — VAS for Reverse Kitting

▶ /SCWM/VAS_INT — VAS for Internal Warehouse Operations

19.3 VAS Integration in Warehouse Processes

The VAS functionality in EWM is tightly integrated with the inbound and outbound warehouse processes. When a material requires VAS activities before putaway or before shipping, it can be automatically routed to a VAS work center via the process-oriented storage control. At the work center, the VAS activities can be performed and then the process can continue, for example, by creating the putaway warehouse tasks to final storage or by creating an outbound warehouse task to the staging area for shipping.

19.3.1 VAS for Outbound Process

VAS can be used during outbound processing. For example, a material may need to be shipped to a customer who wants the material labeled and packed in a specific carton. An integrated outbound process with VAS activity might include the following steps:

▶ The ODO for the customer is received and the system may determine that the product for this customer requires a VAS activity, and it automatically creates a VAS order.

▶ The picker withdraws the product from the source bin, and the product is routed to the VAS work center, where the picker confirms the destination bin.

▶ At the work center, the packer repacks the product and labels the carton according to the customer's specification. Upon completion of all VAS activities, the VAS order is marked as completed, and the auxiliary materials are consumed.

▶ After the VAS execution, the outbound process continues as normal with the creation of a warehouse task to the staging area for shipping.

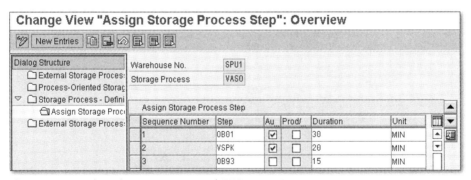

Figure 19.10 Outbound Storage Process with VAS Integration

In Figure 19.10, you can see the configuration for the storage process to support the process described previously. You can find the configuration for the process-oriented routing in the EWM IMG by following the menu path EXTENDED WARE-

HOUSE MANAGEMENT • CROSS-PROCESS SETTINGS • WAREHOUSE TASK • DEFINE PRO-
CESS-ORIENTED STORAGE CONTROL. The described process contains the picking step
(OB01), the VAS step (VSPK), and the staging step (OB93).

In Figure 19.11, you can see the ODO for the described process. On the DOCUMENT
FLOW tab for the item, you can see VAS order 77 with document category VAS.

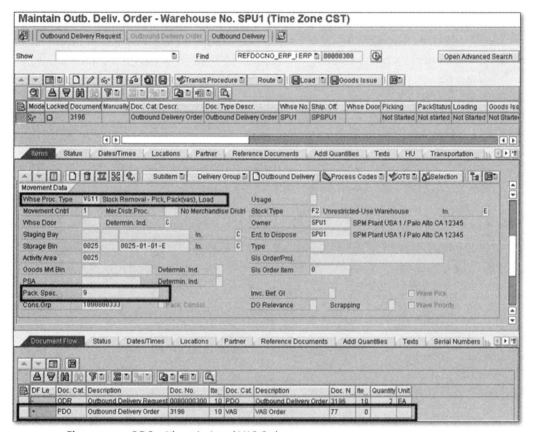

Figure 19.11 ODO with an Assigned VAS Order

In the figure, you can also see that WHSE PROC. TYPE VS11 is determined, and is
responsible for the determination of the storage process. In Chapter 10, Outbound
Processing, we provided more detail about the role the process type plays in the
storage process determination for outbound processing. You can also see in the
figure that the packaging specification (pack spec 9) has been determined for the
material and this pack spec will be used to perform the VAS order.

The next step in the process is the creation of the pick warehouse task for the ODO, which can be performed, for example, in Transaction /SCWM/TODLV_O (as seen in Figure 19.12). You can see in the figure that the material is picked from the source bin (0025-01-01-E) and that the destination bin (VAS_PACK_BIN1) has been determined.

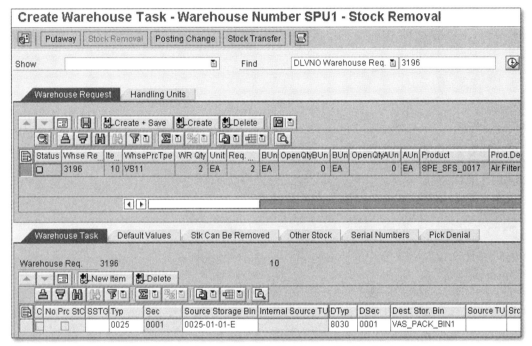

Figure 19.12 Creation of the Pick Warehouse Task (Note that the destination bin is in the VAS Work Center.)

As explained in Chapter 10, a Pick handling unit (HU) must be used when using the process-oriented routing. The existence of the HU lets the storage process pass from one HU to another during the repacking for the VAS order.

When the pick task has been confirmed and the product on the pick HU has been delivered to the work center, you can start the VAS activity using the work center processing transactions.

19.3.2 Using the VAS Work Center and VAS Execution

In the work center, the work for the VAS order can be performed. To display the work center for VAS execution (as seen in Figure 19.13) via the EWM Easy Access menu, follow the EXTENDED WAREHOUSE MANAGEMENT • EXECUTION • CREATE CONFIRMATION FOR VAS menu path, or use Transaction code /SCWM/VASEXEC.

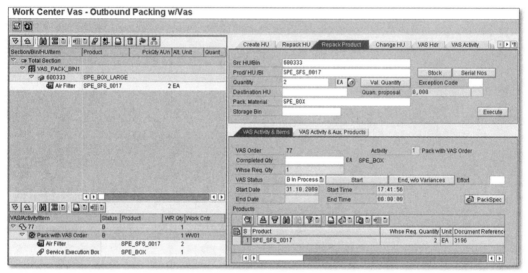

Figure 19.13 Processing the VAS Order in the Work Center

By pressing the PACKSPEC button in the work center, you can view or print the packaging specification to obtain details about the activities for the VAS that needs to be performed. In Figure 19.14, you can see a print preview of the pack spec. From the printout, you can see that 2 EA of product SPM_SFS_0017 should be packed in a packaging material called SPE_BOX, and then a label should be applied.

VAS Execution

To execute the VAS order, as shown in Figure 19.13, you first press the START button on the VAS ACTIVITY & ITEMS tab of the VAS order. This enters the start date and time for the VAS order, based on the current date and time (but you can also change it manually). Next, you perform the activities of the VAS order, as determined by the pack spec (as seen in Figure 19.14), including:

▶ Creating the HU with packaging material SPE_BOX (which can be performed in the REPACK PRODUCT tab in the scanner area of the work center, as you can see in Figure 19.13)

▶ Packing 2 EA of material SPE_SFS_0017 into the box (which can also be done in the same REPACK PRODUCT tab; when the data is entered, as shown in figure 19.13, press the EXECUTE button)

▶ Applying a label to the box, which in this case is only shown as a work step on the pack spec

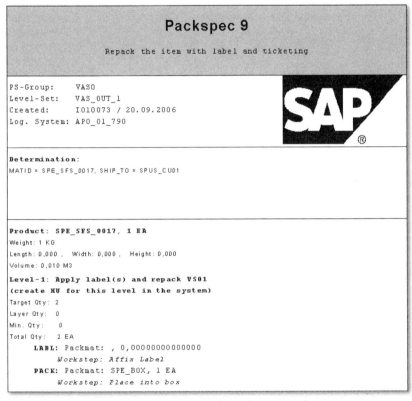

Figure 19.14 Print Preview of the Pack Spec from the VAS Work Center

At the end of the VAS execution the end date and time can be entered and then the VAS order status can be completed either with or without variances. You can also select the END, W/O VARIANCES button to automatically update the end time and complete the order without variances.

For larger quantities or longer activities, you can also update the completed quantities as the activity is executed (for example, when a shift is finished) and not just at the end of a completed VAS order.

19.3.3 Effort Codes and Consumption of Auxiliary Materials

During VAS processing, you can also capture additional work or efforts using effort codes. In Figure 19.15, you can see the effort code being maintained at the VAS work center. In this example, you can see that an additional clean-up effort was required during VAS execution, and the effort code EF1A was selected. The effort code is captured on the VAS order and can be evaluated at a later time (for example, for billing).

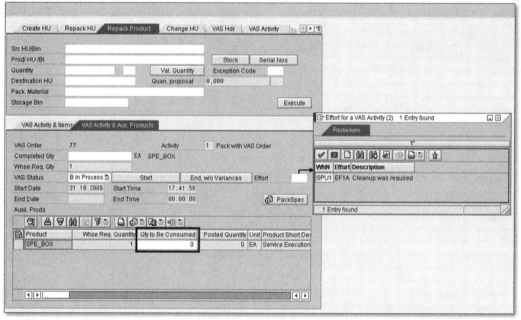

Figure 19.15 Effort Codes and Consumption of Auxiliary Materials

In Figure 19.15, you can also see QTY TO BE CONSUMED, which can be maintained for the auxiliary packaging material SPE_BOX. If the auxiliary packaging material is specified as CONSUMPTN-REL. VAS on the product master (as you can see in Figure 19.16), the goods issue for the specified quantity will be automatically posted upon completion of the VAS order.

For the auxiliary material to be goods issued, the requested quantity must be available in the goods movement bin for the work center. This bin can be assigned in the EWM Easy Access menu by following the EXTENDED WAREHOUSE MANAGEMENT • MASTER DATA • ASSIGN STORAGE BINS FOR VAS CONSUMPTION POSTING menu path, or using Transaction code /SCWM/73000001.

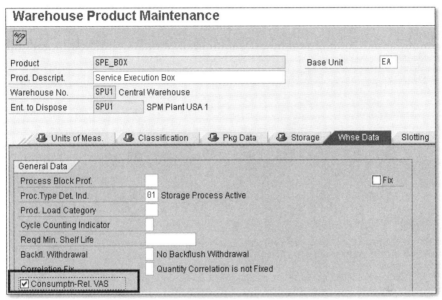

Figure 19.16 Consumption Relevance for VAS in the Product Master for the Auxiliary Packaging Material

Storage Process Continuation after the VAS Order Execution

Once you complete the VAS activity, you can continue the process by creating a warehouse task to move the product to the work center of the next VAS activity. This may be the case, for example, if multiple VAS activities need to be performed at different work centers. You can create the subsequent warehouse task by selecting the CREATE VAS WAREHOUSE TASK button as shown in Figure 19.17.

In our example, no other VAS activities need to be performed. Therefore, we can simply press the COMPLETE PROCESS STEP FOR HU button. As you can see in Figure 19.17, the HU step is completed and an HU warehouse task for the next step in the storage process is created. In the example, the next warehouse task is for a move to the outbound staging area for shipping.

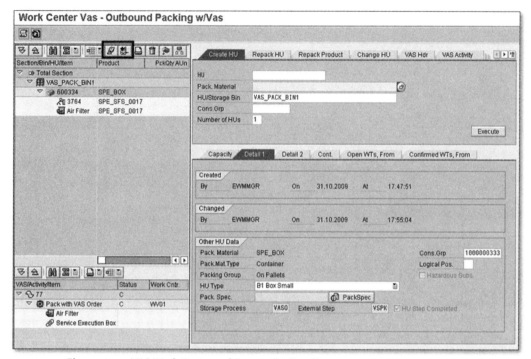

Figure 19.17 VAS Work Center and Process Continuation

19.3.4 VAS for Inbound Processes

Similar to the outbound process, VAS orders can be used during the inbound process as well. For example, you can create an activity in which a material is repacked before being put away to the final bin. You would perform the repacking according to the packaging specification found via the determination procedure assigned to the inbound delivery document type and item type in the configuration for VAS relevance (for more details about the setup, see the section earlier in this chapter regarding configuration for VAS).

An example of an inbound process with VAS might include the process steps for unloading, VAS, and then putaway. In this example, once you have completed the unloading step, the system checks to see if a VAS order exists for the inbound delivery item, and if so, the HU is automatically routed to the VAS work center. If no VAS order exists for the delivery item, the VAS step will be skipped and the putaway step is immediately performed for the HU.

19.3.5 VAS for Internal Processes

You can also create a VAS order for a particular material with reference to an internal warehouse request, rather than an inbound delivery or outbound delivery. In that case, you must first define an order type for internal VAS (as seen in Figure 19.18). To define the order types for VAS in the EWM IMG, follow the menu path EXTENDED WAREHOUSE MANAGEMENT • CROSS-PROCESS SETTINGS • VALUE-ADDED SERVICES (VAS) • DEFINE ORDER TYPES FOR VAS FOR INTERNAL WAREHOUSE PROCESSES.

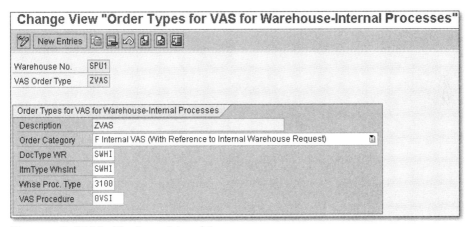

Figure 19.18 VAS for Warehouse-internal Processes

As you can see in Figure 19.18, you can specify the document type and item type, and you can also specify which warehouse process type should be used for the pick task and which determination procedure should be used for determining the packaging specification.

To create the VAS for internal processes from the EWM Easy Access menu, follow the EXTENDED WAREHOUSE MANAGEMENT • WORK SCHEDULING • VALUE-ADDED SERVICES (VAS) • VAS FOR INTERNAL WAREHOUSE OPERATIONS menu path, or use Transaction code /SCWM/VAS_INT.

When you create the VAS order for internal processes, the internal warehouse request is created in the background. To display the internal warehouse request via the EWM Easy Access menu, follow the EXTENDED WAREHOUSE MANAGEMENT • WORK SCHEDULING • MAINTAIN INTERNAL STOCK TRANSFER menu path, or use Transaction code /SCWM/IM_ST. In the document flow for the created item, you can see the corresponding VAS order.

19.4   Summary

In this chapter, we reviewed the use, setup, and execution of VAS in EWM. First, we discussed the configuration and master data required for using VAS, then we looked at how the VAS can be integrated in the outbound processes, inbound processes, and internal processes. We also reviewed how the VAS order is executed in the work center, how to use effort codes for VAS orders, and how to use consumption-relevant materials for auxiliary packaging materials.

In the following chapters, we will continue discussing the special processes in the warehouse by describing kitting, Labor Management (LM), and mobile data capture with mobile devices.

In this chapter, we will discuss the various kitting methods, how they are triggered, and how kitting is executed in Extended Warehouse Management (EWM).

20 Kitting

A kit is a set of products that is defined by a bill of material (or component list) and which is always shipped to a customer in a complete and assembled form. The customer orders the kit; in the warehouse, they either pick an existing kit or pick the component and build the kit; the warehouse ships the kit to the customer; and customer service bills the customer for the complete kit (based on kit pricing, not the pricing of the individual components).

EWM supports various kitting functions that may take place in a warehouse, including:

▶ Kit to Order: Using the Kit to Order process, kits are created when requested by a sales order. If you do not have a certain kit in stock when the order is placed, or you don't typically stock this kit, you can use the Kit to Order process to assemble the kit at a kitting work center during outbound delivery processing. EWM supports Kit to Order processes that are initiated either from an SAP ERP sales order or an SAP Customer Relationship Management (CRM) sales order.

▶ Kit to Stock: Using the Kit to Stock functionality, you can create kits and stock them in the warehouse to speed up subsequent outbound delivery processing. Kit to Stock can be triggered from ERP (based on requirements from Advanced Planning and Optimization (APO) or Material Requirements Planning (MRP), or manually generated) or locally in EWM.

▶ Reverse Kitting: The Reverse Kitting functionality is used to split a kit into its components.

A kit consists of a *kit header material* and *kit components*. The kit header material is what the customer orders and what he will be shipped and billed. The kit components are materials that are used to assemble the kit. In Figure 20.1, we show an example of a kit. In this case, it is a simple BRAKE KIT, which consists of 2 BRAKE ROTOR DISKS and 4 CARBON-METALLIC PADS.

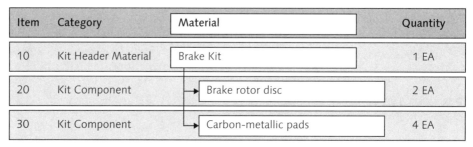

Item	Category	Material	Quantity
10	Kit Header Material	Brake Kit	1 EA
20	Kit Component	Brake rotor disc	2 EA
30	Kit Component	Carbon-metallic pads	4 EA

Figure 20.1 An Example Kit Structure of a Brake Kit

EWM does not save the kit structure as master data. Instead, it receives the information in the form of items and subitems of a delivery from the ERP system. This allows flexibility for the kit to be adjusted in the originating sales order, if, for example, the customer doesn't need every component of the kit or if the customer needs an additional component packaged together with the kit.

> **Note**
>
> EWM does not support nested kitting, that is, a kit within a kit.

20.1   Kit to Order using ERP Sales Orders

You can use the Kit to Order process in EWM to assemble kits during OD processing and to ship and bill the kit to the customer. Because, in most scenarios, the kit was requested by a sales order, this process is known as Kit to Order. In this section, we will cover the Kit to Order process for Sales Orders created in the Sales and Distribution (SD) component in the ERP system. EWM also supports Kit to Order using CRM sales orders, which we will cover in the next section.

If a sales order is created in ERP, the system checks to see if there is a sales bill of material (BoM) assigned to the material that the user enters. If it finds a sales BoM, the system performs a BoM explosion and creates a subitem for every component of the kit in the sales order. After the sales order is saved, an outbound delivery can be created that contains the kit information from the sales order, and the delivery is transferred to the EWM system.

In EWM, the kit components are relevant for picking, but the kit header material is not, as determined by the item type determination based on the ERP delivery item types. During creation of the picking warehouse tasks, the system therefore only creates tasks for the kit components.

The assembly of the kit components can be performed using three different methods (these will be described further in the following sections):

▸ At a work center, using value-added service (VAS) orders

▸ At a work center, but without using VAS orders

▸ During picking (without VAS orders).

The following rules are relevant to the Kit to Order process in EWM:

▸ The kit header and kit components always retain the fixed quantity ratio to each other, defined by the kit structure. The quantity ratio always describes a *linear correlation*. When the quantities are changed during warehouse processing, at kit header level or at kit component level (for example, by a pick denial), the quantites are recalculated based on the fixed quantity ratio.

▸ A kit is always fully delivered to a customer

▸ The kit header and the kit components are always scheduled for the same date

▸ All components of a kit must come from the same warehouse

▸ All components of one kit must be packed into the same handling unit (HU)

▸ An assembled kit is not represented as its own, "dedicated" object in EWM — there is no "single kit ID"

▸ Pricing is only performed at kit header level

20.1.1 Kit to Order at a Work Center Using VAS Orders

In this variant, the kit is assembled in a work center and a VAS order is used to document the assembly. With the VAS order it is possible to monitor the kitting progress and to report on the duration of the kitting activities, and the operator who performed the activities. In the following sections, we will describe the detailed process steps required to support the process of kitting at a work center using a VAS order.

Creating the Sales Order for Kitting

The first step in the kitting process is to create the sales order in ERP (using Transaction VA01). After the kit header material number is entered, the system determines the BoM and performs the BoM explosion, creating the subitems in the sales order (as seen in Figure 20.2). In this example, the quantity structure of the kit is simple — there is one piece of the kit header material that contains one piece of each kit component. The HL Itm column (which is an abbreviation for Higher Level Item) shows the relationship between the items (for example, items 20 and 30 belong to item 10).

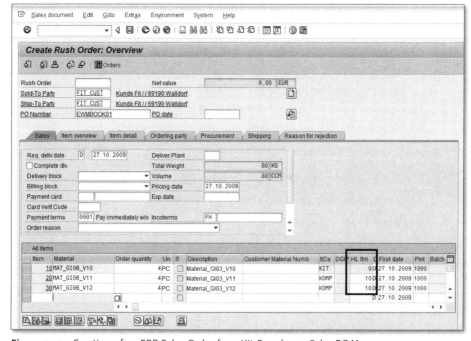

Figure 20.2 Creation of an ERP Sales Order for a Kit Based on a Sales BOM

> **Note**
>
> During sales order creation, it is possible to adjust the kit structure that was read from the sales BOM. If you adjust the kit structure in the sales order, the subsequent documents also reflect the changed kit structure. If the sales order is for multiple quantities, each of the kits for which the structure was changed will be built the same in the warehouse.

Creating the Delivery for Kitting in ERP

After the sales order is saved, an outbound delivery is created in ERP (as seen in Figure 20.3). The outbound delivery takes over the entire kit structure from the sales order, including the item category (as determined by the copy control in the configuration of ERP Logistics Execution) and the HL ITM column, which shows the relationship of the structure.

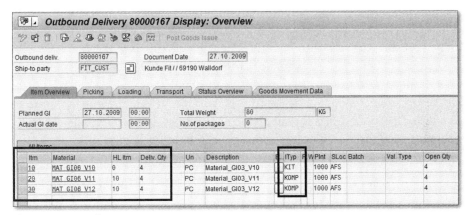

Figure 20.3 OD for Kitting

Creating the Kitting Master Data — The Sales BoM

The sales BOM, which was used by the sales order, can be maintained in the ERP Easy Access menu via the menu path LOGISTICS • SALES AND DISTRIBUTION • MASTER DATA • PRODUCTS • BILLS OF MATERIAL • BILL OF MATERIAL • MATERIAL BOM. In Figure 20.4, you can see the sales BOM for the example that we use here. As you can see, the quantity of each item on the sales BOM is 1 piece.

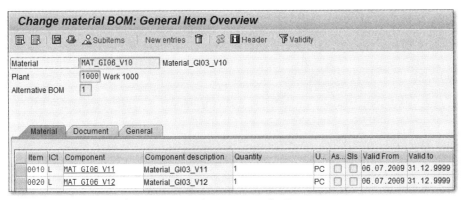

Figure 20.4 Sales BoM for Maintaining the Structure of a Kit

Transferring the Delivery for Kitting to EWM

Once the outbound delivery is saved in ERP, it is transferred to EWM, creating an outbound delivery request (ODR) and, subsequently, an outbound delivery order (ODO). The kit structure is replicated from the ERP delivery to the ODR and the ODO. Although EWM does not contain master data for the kit, it uses the kit structure contained in the outbound delivery and its quantity relationships for further processing.

In our example, EWM derives from the quantities for the header material and the components that the relationship between header and items is 1:1. EWM will not allow goods issue for the outbound delivery if this relationship is not maintained — for example, because one of the components could not be fully picked. In this case, the missing component has to be repicked again (from the same or a different location) or the other components also have to be shorted from the order (by unpicking them), to reestablish the correct quantity relationship.

The item hierarchy in the EWM ODO (which can be accessed via Transaction /SCWM/PRDO, as seen in Figure 20.5) is noted by a "+" sign in the LEVEL column. As described previously, the kit header item isn't picking relevant or goods movement relevant, whereas the kit component items are both picking relevant and goods movement relevant.

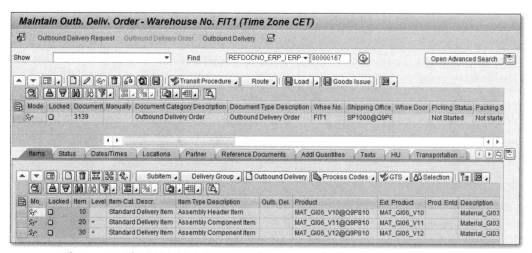

Figure 20.5 The EWM ODO Containing the Kit Hierarchy

Creating the VAS Order in EWM

To use VAS for documenting the kitting activity, the *VAS relevance* for the delivery item type of the *kit header item* must be set in the EWM Implementation Guide (IMG) via the menu path EXTENDED WAREHOUSE MANAGEMENT • CROSS-PROCESS SETTINGS • VALUE-ADDED SERVICES (VAS) • DEFINE RELEVANCE FOR VAS. When necessary, a VAS order for the kit header item is created (as seen in Figure 20.4). EWM saves the number of the VAS order in the document flow for all kit items of the warehouse request.

A VAS order for the kit header item has some special features related to kitting, including:

▶ All activities *prior* to the kitting activity (such as oiling) and the kitting activity itself have the *kit component items*. This is based on the assumption that you perform all activities prior to assembling the kits and the kitting activity itself using the kit components.

▶ All activities *after* the kitting activity (such as packing) have the kit header item. This is based on the assumption that you perform all activities after assembling the kits

During the creation of the EWM ODO, the VAS order is created using the data from the packaging specification (which we will describe in the next section).

Creating Packaging Specifications for the VAS Order

The VAS order in the previous example only contains one activity for the assembly of the kits. If you have more activities (for example, oiling or packing), the kitting activity can always be identified easily, because it has the KITTINGACT flag checked (as seen in Figure 20.6). As we described in Chapter 19, Value-Added Services, VAS uses packaging specifications as master data. The KITTINGACT flag in the VAS order shown in Figure 20.6 is checked because the *level type* of the level of the assigned *packaging specification* is defined as a kitting level type. To define the level type as a kitting level type in the EWM IMG (as seen in Figure 20.7), follow the menu path EXTENDED WAREHOUSE MANAGEMENT • MASTER DATA • PACKAGING SPECIFICATION • MAINTAIN STRUCTURE OF PACKAGING SPECIFICATION • DEFINE LEVEL TYPE.

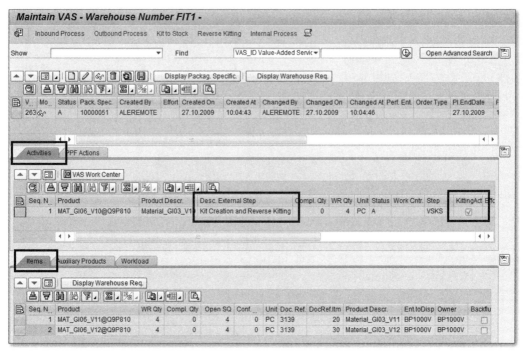

Figure 20.6 The VAS Order for Kitting

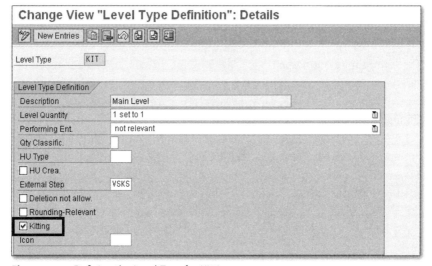

Figure 20.7 Defining the Level Type for Kitting

As described previously, if there are multiple activities in the kitting VAS order, the kitting indicator specifies which activity is the kitting activity. For example, let's describe a packaging specification that has three levels, including:

▶ Oiling the components

▶ Assembling the kit, and

▶ Packing of the kit

In this example, the oiling is done for kit components, so you want the warehouse worker to record the first activity in the VAS order on the *kit component level*. The second VAS activity (assembling) results in the kit. You therefore set the kitting indicator for this level. In the third VAS activity (packing), the warehouse worker records how many kits he has packed.

Figure 20.8 shows the packaging specification from which the VAS order (shown in Figure 20.6) was created. As you can see, the KIT CREATION level (which is selected in the tree on the left-hand side) is based on the level type KIT (which we created in Figure 20.7).

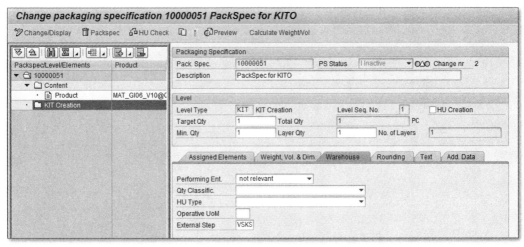

Figure 20.8 Packaging Specification for Creating a VAS Order

Picking the Kit Components and Kit Creation in the EWM Work Center

Once the picking warehouse tasks have been created in the warehouse and the items are confirmed into a Pick HU, the Pick HU is delivered to a kitting work center. (Note: You can also configure EWM to create kits during picking, which we will describe later in this chapter.)

To access the transaction for processing the kits at the work center from the SAP Easy Access menu, follow the EXTENDED WAREHOUSE MANAGEMENT • EXECUTION • CREATE CONFIRMATION FOR VAS menu path, or use Transaction code /SCWM/VASEXEC. In this transaction (as you can see in Figure 20.9), you can see the Pick HU containing the picked items in a tree view on the top left side of the screen. You can see the VAS order containing the kitting activity in a second tree view, on the bottom left side. On the top of the tree views, there is a button for kit creation. You use this button to inform the system that you have assembled the kit. The system then creates a kit header item and calculates its quantity based on the item quantities. The generated kit header item is then inserted as a new node into the tree, between the Pick HU and the items.

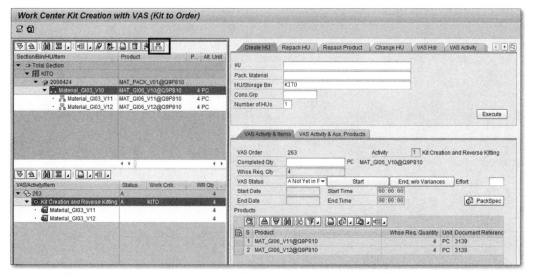

Figure 20.9 Kit Creation and VAS Order Processing in a Kitting Work Center

Note that the generated kit header is a "virtual" or "dummy" item of the HU at this point. This HU item is then displayed, for example, in the packing and VAS work centers. This item is also used by the system in goods issue posting, to check whether packed kits are complete so that the goods issue can be posted. These HU items can also be printed when printing the HU details.

Using the VAS order (which you can access by selecting the VAS order on the bottom-left pane of the work center screen, and then the VAS processing tabs will become available on the bottom right pane), you can record the kitting progress by using the button to capture the start and end date and time of the kitting, and entering an effort code (which can be used, for example, to capture the level of effort required to execute the VAS order). You can also display or print the kitting instructions by clicking the PACKSPEC button.

Once the kit is assembled, you can release the HU from the work center by clicking the COMPLETE PROCESS STEP FOR HU button. Then, the warehouse task for the next process step, according to the process-oriented storage control is created (for example, to transport the HU to the goods issue zone). Finally, you post the goods issue for the ODO, and the goods issue is replicated into the ERP system.

You can define the movement type used for the goods receipt of the kit header material (as seen in Figure 20.10) in the EWM IMG by following the menu path LOGISTICS EXECUTION • SERVICE PARTS MANAGEMENT (SPM) • OUTBOUND PROCESS (SPM) • KIT TO ORDER • SET GOODS RECEIPT MOVEMENT TYPE FOR KIT HEADERS.

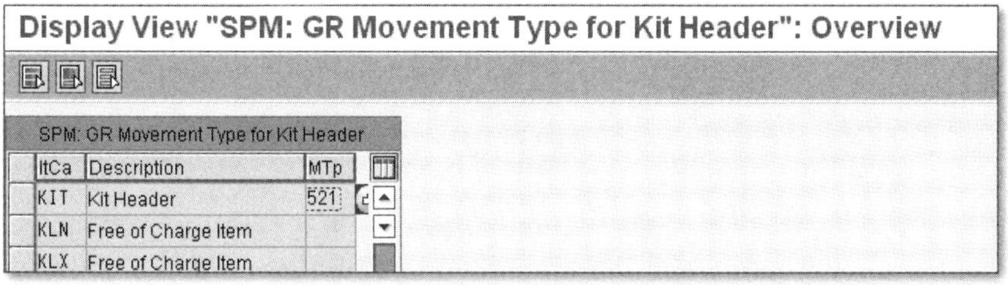

Display View "SPM: GR Movement Type for Kit Header": Overview		
SPM: GR Movement Type for Kit Header		
ItCa	Description	MTp
KIT	Kit Header	521
KLN	Free of Charge Item	
KLX	Free of Charge Item	

Figure 20.10 Assigning Movement Type for Goods Receipt Posting of Kit Headers to the Item Category

In the standard delivered configuration for kitting, movement type 521 (Receipt w/o order) is assigned to item category KIT. If you use other item categories or want to use another movement type, then you have to maintain this table for the additional item category or to assign the new movement type.

20.1.2 Kit to Order at a Work Center without VAS Orders

You can also process kits at a work center, but without using a VAS order to capture the workload data. This process is very similar to the process described earlier, and you can use kitting without a VAS order as long as:

▸ You don't need detailed documentation of the kitting procedure in EWM. Because there is no VAS order, you can neither document the start and end time of the assembly, nor its effort. It is not possible to display or print assembly instructions from the packaging specification. You can only store information for the kit in the outbound delivery in the form of free text. You can display this text in the work center as additional information.

▸ You are not performing kitting in a special *kitting work center*, but at a generic work center that is also suitable for packing (although you can still use separate work centers for general packing functions vs. kitting).

From a configuration perspective, the setup for this process is also very similar to the setup for the process with VAS orders as described previously, with the following exceptions:

▸ To avoid creating VAS orders, deactivate the need for VAS in the EWM IMG via the menu path EXTENDED WAREHOUSE MANAGEMENT • CROSS-PROCESS SETTINGS • VALUE-ADDED SERVICES (VAS) • DEFINE RELEVANCE FOR VAS (for example, by using a different document type, item type, or product group).

▸ If you use process-oriented storage control, assign a storage process containing a *packing step* (for packing in a work center).

▸ Configure the layout of the work center to allow the creation of kits in the EWM IMG via the menu path EXTENDED WAREHOUSE MANAGEMENT • MASTER DATA • WORK CENTER • SPECIFY WORK CENTER LAYOUT.

20.1.3 Kit to Order During Picking

You can also create a kit without a VAS order during the execution of a picking warehouse order (WO) by using the Kit to Order During Picking process. This means that you do not process the kits in a special work center, but you simply confirm the kit components to a Pick HU during the WO confirmation. You can create kits this way under the following circumstances:

▶ You do not need detailed documentation of the kitting procedure in EWM. As before, because there is no VAS order and no packaging specification for assembly, you cannot document the start and end time of the kitting nor show nor print assembly instructions.

▶ You do not perform kitting in a *work center*, but instead you create the kit during the picking execution.

To enable Kit to Order During Picking, you must set up the system to automatically generate an HU item for the kit header in the Pick HU at the time when the Pick HU is created. To make this setting in the EWM IMG, follow the EXTENDED WAREHOUSE MANAGEMENT • GOODS ISSUE PROCESS • OUTBOUND DELIVERY • MANUAL SETTINGS • DEFINE ITEM TYPES FOR OUTBOUND DELIVERY PROCESS menu path, and activate the CREATE KIT ITEM AUTOMATICALLY indicator in the PROCESS MANAGEMENT AND CONTROL block (as seen in Figure 20.11) for the relevant item type (for example, item type OKM for document category PDO).

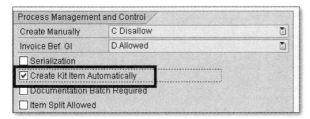

Figure 20.11 Specifying the Creation of the Kit Header Item Kit to Order Using CRM Sales Orders

Kit to Order is also supported using sales orders from SAP CRM. While the steps within EWM remain exactly the same, the start of the process differs. When creating a sales order in CRM, you enter a kit header material number and quantity in the sales order and CRM triggers the rule-based Global ATP check in SAP Supply Chain Management (SCM). If there is stock of the kit in the warehouse (due to a Kit to Stock process being performed or a kit being returned to the warehouse), Global ATP will confirm the availability of the kit to CRM, just like a normal material.

If there is no stock of the kit in the warehouse, Global ATP determines the kit structure, which contains the kit header material and the components required to assemble the kit, by calling the SCM Integrated Product and Process Engineering (iPPE) , which contains the kit structures. Global ATP then performs the availability check for the kit components and, assuming the components are available, confirms the quantities for the sales order item. After the ATP check has been performed, you can see the kit structure in the CRM sales order (as shown in Figure 20.12).

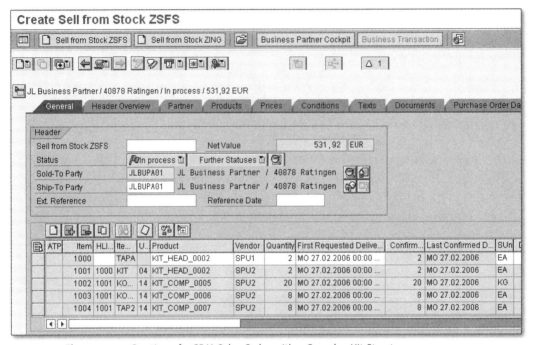

Figure 20.12 Creation of a CRM Sales Order with a Complex Kit Structure

After the CRM sales order is saved, it is transferred to the ERP system as an *unchecked delivery* (assuming that you use the direct delivery distribution method for integration to ERP by activating the system configuration for Service Parts Management in CRM). In ERP, the unchecked deliveries are processed and *checked deliveries* are created via Transaction VL10UC. The checked deliveries are transferred to EWM, where EWM creates an ODR and, subsequently, an ODO based on the checked delivery from the ERP system.

From this point forward, the remaining process steps are identical to the process for using ERP sales orders. At the end, when the goods issue for the ODO is posted in EWM and the OD is transferred to ERP (where the OD is subsequently post goods issued), the CRM sales order is updated and the CRM billing can be performed.

20.2   Kit to Stock

In addition to kitting specifically for outbound orders, you can also execute the kitting ahead of orders being received from customers based on prior knowledge of or anticipation of the orders (for example, based on forecasts or sales promotions) using the *Kit to Stock* process in EWM. The Kit to Stock process is a simple, streamlined kit creation process that is executed and documented in the warehouse management system.

Kit creation can be triggered in the ERP system based on a production order (which could have been created manually or automatically based on requirements from planning, for example, using the Kit to Stock process from SAP Service Parts Planning), or it can be triggered in the EWM system directly using a VAS order.

20.2.1   Kit to Stock Using an ERP Production Order

You can start the Kit to Stock process in the ERP system by creating a production order, either manually or automatically, as described previously. From the production order, you can then trigger the creation of an inbound delivery for the kit header and an outbound delivery for the kit components by releasing the production order.

The created deliveries are sent to EWM and converted to the ODR and inbound delivery notification (IDN) to an ODO and an inbound delivery, respectively. For the inbound delivery, a VAS order will be automatically created (as seen in Figure 20.13). After you confirm the VAS order at the kitting work station (as described earlier), then you goods issue the kit components via the outbound delivery and perform goods receipt of the kit header via the inbound delivery, and goods receipt and goods issue will be transferred to the ERP system. As a result of the update of the deliveries, the production order in the ERP system will update accordingly.

Based on the VAS order, you can execute and document the process in the EWM system, as described in the previous sections. You could also process the deliveries in the delivery Transactions /SCWM/PRDI and /SCWM/PRDO, if required. However, only basic functions such as posting goods movements are available to you here. You cannot use functions such as loading or unloading, route determination, GTS checks, and customs processing. Figure 20.13 shows an example of a Kit to Stock VAS order.

20 | Kitting

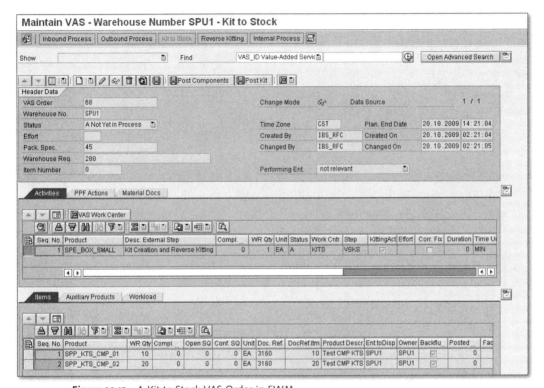

Figure 20.13 A Kit to Stock VAS Order in EWM

20.2.2 Kit to Stock Initiated from VAS Orders in EWM

You can also initiate the Kit to Stock process in the EWM system by manually creating a VAS order for Kit to Stock. To start the Kit to Stock processing EWM from the Easy Access menu, follow the EXTENDED WAREHOUSE MANAGEMENT • WORK SCHEDULING • VALUE-ADDED SERVICES (VAS) • VAS FOR KIT CREATION ON STOCK menu path, or use Transaction code /SCWM/VAS_KTS.

The VAS order can be created with or without a BoM. Figure 20.14 shows the creation of a VAS order with a BoM.

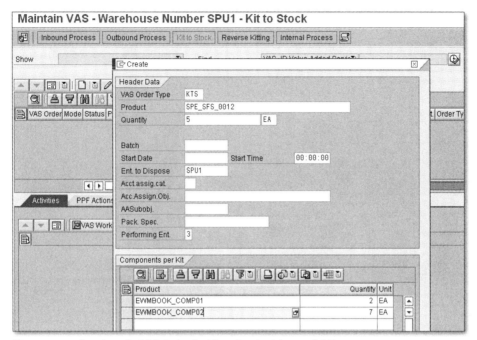

Figure 20.14 Creation of a VAS Order for Kit to Stock without a BOM

To configure the VAS order types in the EWM IMG, follow the menu path
Extended Warehouse Management • Cross-Process Settings • Value-Added
Services (VAS) • Define Order Types for VAS for Kit to Stock. In the standard
delivered EWM configuration, VAS Order Type KTS is defined, as you can see in
Figure 20.15.

In the configuration table for the VAS order type, you must specify which inbound
and outbound document and item types the system should use, which stock types
are relevant, and whether *backflush withdrawal* should be performed for the items.
You also assign the VAS procedure, which is used for determining the packaging
specifications during VAS order creation.

Change View "Document Types for VAS for Kit to Stock": Details

New Entries ▧ ▨ ⬧ ▨ ▨ ▨ BC Set: Change Field Values

Warehouse No. SPU1
VAS Order Type KTS

Document Types for VAS for Kit to Stock

Description	Document Type Kit Creation for Stock
Order Category	D VAS for Creating Kits for Stock (Kit to Stock)
Doc.Type Outb.	OKTS
Outb. Item Type	OKSR
Stock Type	F2
Doc. Type Inb.	IKTS
InbDel.ItemType	IKSR
Stock Type	F2
☑ Backfl. Withdrawal	
VAS Procedure	0VSK

Figure 20.15 Definition of VAS Order Type KTS

20.3 Reverse Kitting

If you no longer need a kit that is in stock, but you instead need the components of the kit, you can use the *Reverse Kitting* functionality to disassemble the kits back into their component parts. The process is initiated by creating a *VAS order for reverse kitting* manually in EWM (you can't trigger Reverse Kitting from ERP or CRM). To start Reverse Kitting from the EWM Easy Access menu, follow the EXTENDED WAREHOUSE MANAGEMENT • WORK SCHEDULING • VALUE-ADDED SERVICES (VAS) • VAS FOR REVERSE KITTING menu path, or use Transaction code /SCWM/VAS_KTR. As you can see in the dropdown selection in Figure 20.16, you can create the VAS order with or without a BoM.

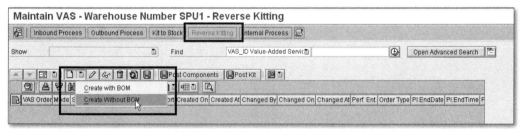

Figure 20.16 Creating a VAS Order for Reverse Kitting

If you create the VAS order *with* a BoM, EWM will attempt to find and explode a BoM from the ERP system. Based on the BoM, the system will automatically determine the quantities of the kit components using the number of kits entered. If you create the VAS order *without* a BoM, you must manually specify the kit components and the kit header material.

You must also specify a packaging specification in the VAS order for reverse kitting (as we have already shown in the Kit to Order process). The packaging specification acts as the master data for creating a VAS order. For reverse kitting, the VAS order can only have one activity. If the packaging specification has other levels aside from the kitting level, the system will not consider the other levels.

You can also configure EWM to perform an availability check for the kit. If availability is checked and the system is unable to confirm the kit availability completely, it will reduce the quantities of the components and the kit header material automatically.

To maintain the order types for Reverse Kitting in the EWM IMG, follow the menu path EXTENDED WAREHOUSE MANAGEMENT • CROSS-PROCESS SETTINGS • VALUE-ADDED SERVICES (VAS) • DEFINE ORDER TYPES FOR VAS FOR REVERSE KITTING. In the standard delivered EWM configuration, the VAS ORDER TYPE KTR (seen in Figure 20.17) has been defined specifically for reverse kitting.

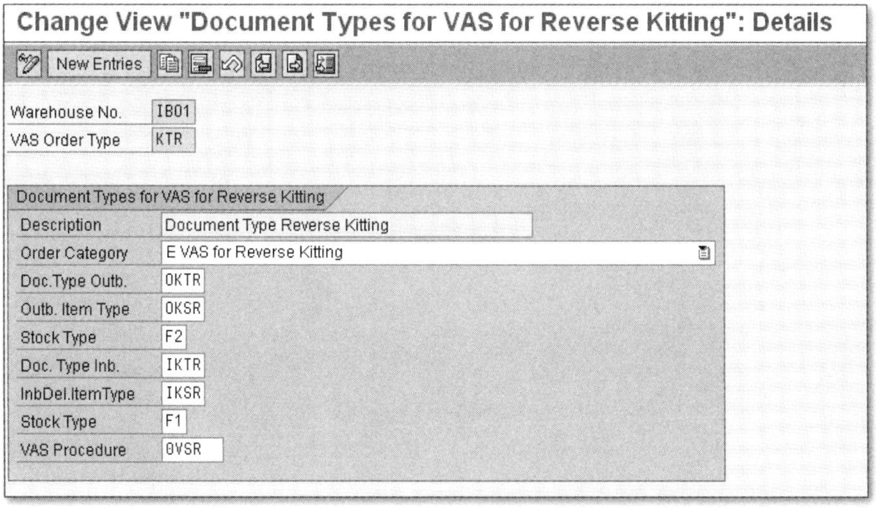

Figure 20.17 Settings for the Reverse Kitting Order Types in EWM

When you save the VAS order, an ODO is created for the kit header, and an inbound delivery is created for the kit components. Both deliveries are transferred to ERP when the respective goods issue or goods receipt is posted for the delivery.

> **Note**
>
> In the case of Reverse Kitting, where the ODO and the inbound delivery are created locally in EWM, the system does not create or use an ODR or an IDN.

20.4 Summary

In this chapter, we described the kitting processes and the configuration required to support it. You should now understand how to set up and use the Kit-to-Order, Kit-to-Stock, and Reverse Kitting processes. In the next chapters, we will finalize the discussion of the process topics with Labor Management (LM) and data capture, and then we will move on to the technical topics (Post-Processing Framework (PPF), authorizations and roles, and deployment options).

Labor Management provides a basis for measuring and evaluating the effectiveness of employees and processes in the warehouse and allows organizations to continuously improve their warehouse labor costs.

21 Labor Management

The driving engine of most warehouse operations is its employee labor force. The employees provide the energy and force to move most of the products around in the typical warehouse (aided by the proper equipment, either manually driven or automated). On the other hand, employee labor makes up the majority of costs in most warehouses, up to 60% or more of total operating costs according to Modern Material Handling Online (*mmhonline.com*, September 2005). Therefore, warehouse managers are often extremely conscientious about the effect of productivity on their overall cost structure. One of the most important tools introduced in recent years is the advent of Labor Management (LM) software, which helps to track and report employee productivity compared to established standards (which may include utilization of engineered labor standards (ELS), and industry Best Practices for establishing standards for manual tasks in the warehouse), and comparing productive time versus unproductive time for warehouse workers. In actual practice, labor management often adheres to the old rule of "what gets measured gets improved," and many warehouse managers find that implementing an effective labor management program (which does not just include software, but also an effective feedback mechanism and often a system of rewards and penalties) can help them to significantly reduce labor costs.

In version 5.1, SAP introduced an LM system within SAP Extended Warehouse Management (EWM), including the ability to use engineered labor standards (ELS) as the baseline for predicting the anticipated time that a particular task should take to execute in the warehouse. In addition to the ability to upload and store the ELS (or other labor standards based on simpler criteria), SAP provided the ability to:

▶ Automatically capture the actual execution time for direct activities

▶ Capture (via manual data entry) the indirect activities

- Calculate the planned workload based on the standards

- Report the comparison between the calculated planned workload and the actual workload

- Perform operational planning based on future workload

- Report employee performance over a period of time, within EWM, or by transferring data to ERP Human Resources (HR)

In this chapter, we will describe the methods that are used to perform the preceding activities, how to configure and set them up, how to use measurement services to calculate and report employee performance results, and how to support an effective labor management program by reporting the results or transferring them to HR.

21.1 Activating Labor Management

EWM LM is not active by default for any warehouse or activity. To activate LM, you must first activate it at the warehouse level, then you must activate the relevant internal storage process steps, and then you can deactivate the external process steps that are not relevant — in other words, you manage deactivation of the external process steps for each active internal process step by exception. To activate LM for the warehouse in the EWM Implementation Guide (IMG) (as seen in Figure 21.1), follow the EXTENDED WAREHOUSE MANAGEMENT • LABOR MANAGEMENT • ACTIVATE LABOR MANAGEMENT menu path, and then select the ACTIVATE LM FOR WAREHOUSE NUMBER node (it is already selected by default when you enter the transaction).

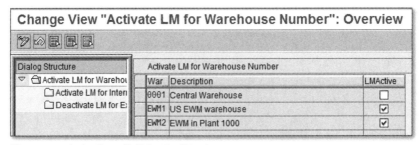

Figure 21.1 Activation of LM for the Warehouse

Once you have activated LM for the warehouse, you must also activate LM for the internal process step (as seen in Figure 21.2). To access the activation for the internal process step in the EWM IMG, follow the same menu path specified previously, select the warehouse, and then select the ACTIVATE LM FOR INTERNAL PROCESS STEP node.

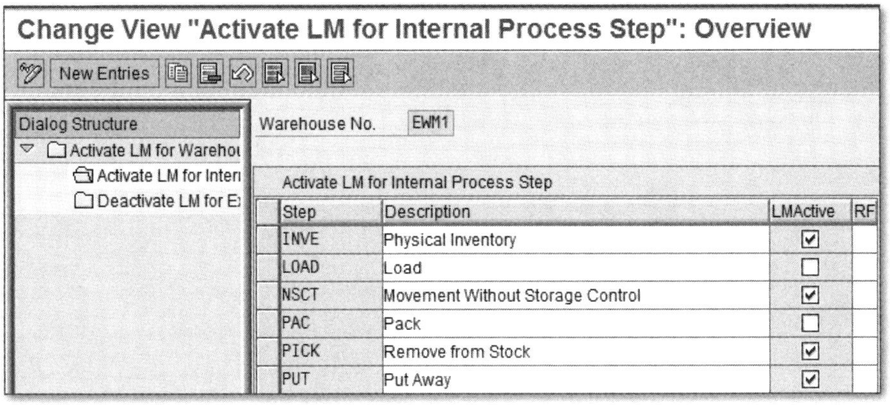

Change View "Activate LM for Internal Process Step": Overview

Step	Description	LMActive	RF
INVE	Physical Inventory	☑	
LOAD	Load	☐	
NSCT	Movement Without Storage Control	☑	
PAC	Pack	☐	
PICK	Remove from Stock	☑	
PUT	Put Away	☑	

Figure 21.2 Activation of LM for the Internal Process Step

For each internal process step, there may be one or more external process steps assigned (as seen in figure 21.3). To assign the external process steps relevant to each internal process step in the EWM IMG, follow the menu path EXTENDED WAREHOUSE MANAGEMENT • LABOR MANAGEMENT • DEFINE EXTERNAL PROCESS STEPS.

Change View "External Storage Process Step": Overview

External Step	Description	Int. Process Step	Direction
INVE	Inventory	INVE	Not Relevant
OB01	Pick	PICK	Stock Remova
OB02	Pack	PAC	Putaway; Sto
OB03	Prepare for Loading	STAG	Stock Remova
OB04	Load	LOAD	Stock Remova

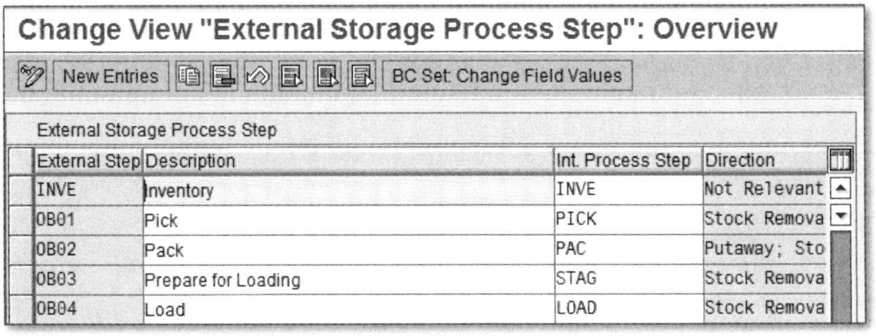

Figure 21.3 Creation of External Process Steps and Assignment to Internal Process Steps

You can deactivate LM for any external process step assigned to any internal process step for which LM is already active. If an external process step is not deactivated explicitly, then it is implicitly active as long as the assigned internal process step is active for LM. To specify the external process steps for which LM is not active (as seen in Figure 21.4), follow the EXTENDED WAREHOUSE MANAGEMENT • LABOR MANAGEMENT • ACTIVATE LABOR MANAGEMENT menu path and then select the DEACTIVATE LM FOR EXTERNAL PROCESS STEP node.

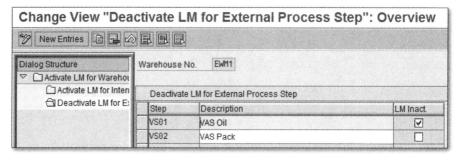

Figure 21.4 Deactivation of External Process Steps, By Exception

21.2   Master Data for Labor Management

To enable the LM processes, certain master data must be created specifically for use by the LM module. Specifically, you must create processors to assign and track the labor activities, and you must also create formulas and conditions to drive the calculations for reporting the results.

21.2.1   Processors

A processor correlates to an employee who is responsible for performing warehouse activities and is assigned to execute warehouse orders (WOs) or other activities in the warehouse (including certain indirect activities that are further defined in later sections in this chapter). The processor is created in the EWM Easy Access menu by following the EXTENDED WAREHOUSE MANAGEMENT • MASTER DATA • RESOURCE MANAGEMENT • PROCESSOR • CREATE PROCESSOR menu path, or using Transaction code /SCMB/PRR1. On the Identification tab for the processor, you assign the employee's USER NAME, which correlates the activity for the processor to the employee's SAP logon, and you also assign the PERSONNEL NUMBER, which allows the data to be passed to HR (as discussed later in this chapter and in Chapter 23, Integration to Other Applications).

The processor creation interface (as seen in Figure 21.5, in edit mode) is the same as the business partner (BP) interface, but the processor creation transaction only allows the BP role PROCESSOR to be maintained there. You can also create the Processor role in the generic BP transaction. For more details on BP creation and maintenance, and the BP roles, see Chapter 5, Other Warehouse Master Data.

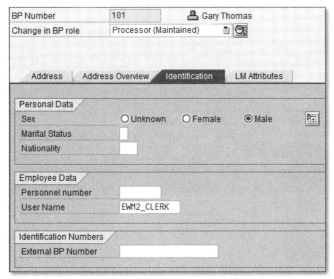

Figure 21.5 Maintaining the Processor Master Data, as BP Role "Processor" and with the Assigned User Name

21.2.2 Formulas and Conditions

Formulas and conditions are used for evaluating and calculating both actual workloads, according to the ELS, and expected workloads for planning. Conditions are used in the evaluation of the standard time for each work step (as further defined in the following Conditions section) and are applied using the conceptual algorithm *if* condition, *then* standard time = formula. The formula, therefore, is used to calculate the standard time for the work step if the condition is met.

Formulas

To create a formula from the EWM Easy Access menu, follow the EXTENDED WAREHOUSE MANAGEMENT • SETTINGS • LABOR MANAGEMENT • FORMULA EDITOR menu path, or use Transaction code /SCWM/LM_FE. As you can see in Figure 21.6, you can create separate formulas for the calculation of the standard time (FORMU-

LAS FOR ENGINEERED LABOR STANDARDS) and for planning goals. Each formula is assigned units of measure for weight, length, volume, and time, in case the input variable is calculated in a different unit of measure, so that the evaluation of the standard time is consistent for all activities.

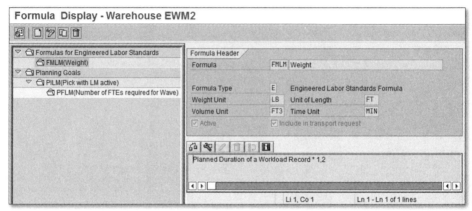

Figure 21.6 Formula Maintenance for LM

When you create a new formula, you can use the predefined fields and functions from the list below the formula editor (as seen in Figure 21.7). As mentioned previously, the formula is used to calculate the standard time for the work step, so you will use the variables available from the work step as operands, including fields from the WO, product, packaging specification, and workload. You can also reuse other formulas that you already created as operands in the new formula, meaning that you can create complex formulas (however, you may not create a recursive formula where you use, for example, formula ABC as an operand within formula ABC). In addition, you can use calculated measurement services in your formula — for example, you may want to use the average picks per hour from an area to calculate the expected workload for a group of picks, and average picks per hour may already be evaluated as a calculated measurement service. Measurement services are further explained in Chapter 15, Warehouse Monitoring and Reporting.

Using the formula, you can blend fixed times and variable times into your calculation for the standard time. For example, for a pick from activity area 0020, you can indicate that the standard time is calculated as the travel time plus 15 seconds for each unit picked plus a fixed time of 10 seconds for arriving at the bin and validating the bin data.

While creating the formula, you can add a new field by double-clicking on the field in the bottom left pane. You can search for fields within the pane by entering some text in the search box and pressing the FIND button. You can also filter and sort the fields to narrow down the list. You can also add a function by double-clicking on the function in the bottom right pane, or you can single-click on the function and press the INSERT WITH INPUT HELP button to use the function with some guided assistance. The FIND, FILTER, and SORT functions are also available there.

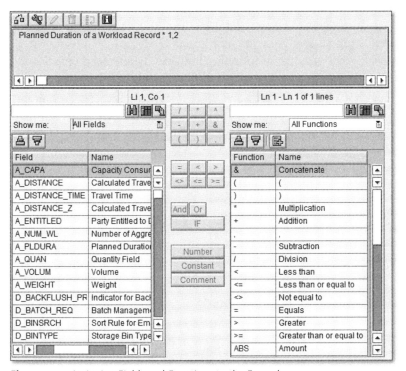

Figure 21.7 Assigning Fields and Functions to the Formula

While editing the formula, you must use the selections at the bottom and the functions above the editor (e.g., CHANGE, DELETE, INSERT LINE BREAK) to update the formula (place the cursor in front of the target that you want to process). If you prefer to enter the formula in free text mode, select the EXPERT MODE button above the editor. To save the formula, it must be free of syntax errors. To check the syntax without saving, select the CHECK button above the edit area. If you want to transport the formula to a target system (for example, from your development system to a quality assurance environment or production), you can select the INCLUDE IN

TRANSPORT REQUEST checkbox. After you include the formula in a transport, you may not delete the formula, but you can control whether it is active or not using the ACTIVE indicator.

Conditions

To create a condition from the EWM Easy Access menu, follow the EXTENDED WAREHOUSE MANAGEMENT • SETTINGS • LABOR MANAGEMENT • CONDITION EDITOR menu path, or use Transaction code /SCWM/LM_CE. As you can see in Figure 21.8, you can create conditions for standard calculations (ELS), preprocessing items, or preprocessing headers. The method for creating, editing, and transporting the conditions are the same as for formulas, however, when creating the conditions, remember that they are evaluated as conditions and therefore should have a conditional operator within them (e.g., >, <, =). If they do not, and they simply calculate a value, the condition would always be evaluated as True. Therefore, if you have a condition without a conditional operator and you perform a syntax check, the system will tell you that the condition does not have syntax errors, but it is incomplete.

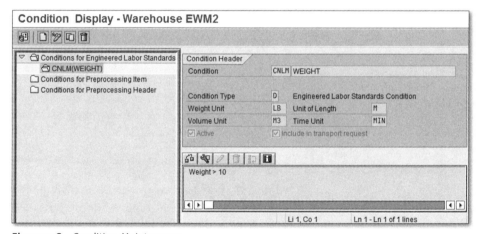

Figure 21.8 Condition Maintenance

The fields that you can use to build the conditions for preprocessing headers and preprocessing items include fields from the product, delivery item, packaging specification, and other conditions for the same level (i.e., header versus item). The fields that you can use to build the conditions for the ELS include fields from the product, WO, packaging specification, workload, and other conditions for ELS.

21.3   Engineered Labor Standards

Engineered Labor Standards is a generic industry term used to mean labor standards that are calculated by adding up the individual standards for components of a task. For example, if a picking task is made of the individual processes of travelling to the location, confirming the bin, removing the item to be picked from the bin, placing the item in the proper container on the material handling equipment, then boarding the equipment and preparing to travel to the next location, then the ELS for that particular picking task can be calculated by adding up the times that it should take to travel to the location to perform each of those individual steps. The standard may be comprised of a constant time (for example, the total times to confirm the bin, board the equipment, and prepare to travel to the next location), which should take the same amount of time regardless of the quantity to be picked, and a variable time, which may depend, for example, on how many units of the product are being picked from the location, as each individual pick requires the operator to bend over to retrieve the item, verify it, and place it in the container. The ELS is therefore best represented by a formula that takes into account the constant time and the multiple variables.

At the same time, the labor standard may be determined in different ways under different circumstances. For example, if the items to be picked are very small, the operator may be able to pick several at a time, which takes more time for the individual pick, but less time per item. On the other hand, if the items to be picked are very large, the operator must pick one at a time, which may take less time per unit, but more time overall. Therefore, you might want to apply conditions under which the labor standard is calculated one way, versus other conditions under which it is calculated a different way.

21.3.1   Determining Engineered Labor Standards

To accommodate these requirements, EWM allows you to create ELS that may be comprised of multiple steps, each of which may have various conditions and formulas applied to calculate the total labor standard for the activity. To create the ELS in the EWM IMG, follow the menu path EXTENDED WAREHOUSE MANAGEMENT • LABOR MANAGEMENT • DETERMINE ENGINEERED LABOR STANDARDS. As seen in Figure 21.9, you can:

- ▸ Define the work steps
- ▸ Define the standard times for the work steps
- ▸ Define and assign the work step sequence

Or, if your work step sequence consists of only one work step and it only occurs in one active assignment, you can use the DIRECT ELS DEFINITION node to create the ELS. If you use the DIRECT ELS DEFINITION, the work steps and work step sequence (including standard time assignment) are created automatically.

Change View "Direct ELS Definition": Overview

New Entries

Dialog Structure		Direct ELS Definition										
☐ Define Work Step		Whse No.	Step	AA	Obj.-Typ	Seq. No.	Condition	Constant	Time Unit	Formula	Active	
☐ Work Step: Define Standard Time		EWM1			Warehouse 1			8,000	SEC		☑	
☐ Define Work Step Sequence		EWM2	PILM		Warehouse 1			1,000	MIN		☑	
☐ Assign Work Step Sequence		EWM2	PILM		Warehouse 1		CNLM			FMLM	☑	
☐ Direct ELS Definition												

Figure 21.9 Using the Direct ELS Definition to Create the Work Steps, Sequences, and Assigned Standard Times (or Formulas)

When assigning the standard times to the work steps, you can either assign a constant time, or you can assign a formula. If you assign a formula, you can view the formula by selecting the line and pressing the FORMULA button on the right side of the table. As the conditions and formulas are assigned here in the configuration table, you must create the conditions and formulas, which are considered master data but are transportable, before updating this configuration table. If you plan to transport the configuration table, you must also ensure that the conditions and formulas exist in the target system, either by transporting them or creating them manually.

21.3.2 Uploading Engineered Labor Standards

In addition to creating the standards in the configuration table as described previously, you can also upload standards from an external system. For example, some industrial engineering consulting firms provide software or services to help companies calculate their ELS. If you consult with one of these organizations, or if you create the standards on your own somehow outside of the EWM system, you may want to upload the standards in SAP to reduce the effort to manually create or maintain the standards (especially as the standards will probably change over time as your processes and procedures, product mix, or labor skills change over time).

To upload your ELS from the EWM Easy Access menu, follow the EXTENDED WARE-HOUSE MANAGEMENT • SETTINGS • LABOR MANAGEMENT • UPLOAD ENGINEERED LABOR STANDARDS menu path, or use Transaction code /SCWM/ELS_UPLOAD. As you can see in Figure 21.10, via this transaction you can upload not only ELS, but also formulas and conditions, work steps, work step sequences, and assignment of work step sequences.

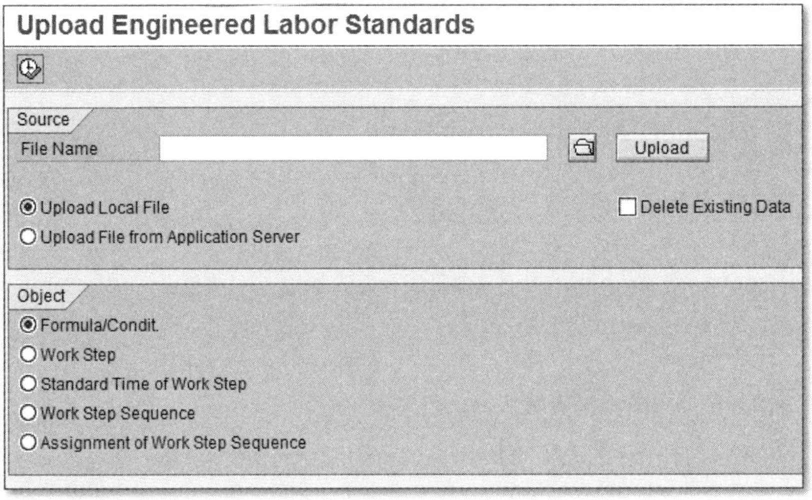

Figure 21.10 Upload of ELS or Other Data to Support the Calculation of the ELS

You can choose to upload the data file from your personal computer using the UPLOAD LOCAL FILE option, or you can upload the file from the SAP Application Server (AS) (which is generally better for very large data files; to get the data file transferred to the AS, contact your local SAP Basis or SAP NetWeaver contact). The input file must be created in comma-delimited or semi-colon-delimited format. The first row of the file is ignored, as it usually contains the header information (such as field names). The structure of the data for each row of the input file depends on the type of data being uploaded, as indicated in Table 21.1.

Data Type	Structure
Formulas and conditions	/scwm/s_els_up_frml
Work step	/scwm/s_els_up_st
Standard Times	/scwm/s_els_up_ste
Work Step Sequence	/scwm/s_els_up_seq
Assignment of Work Step Sequence	/scwm/s_els_up_ass

Table 21.1 Structures of Upload of Different Data Types in the ELS Upload Program

21.4 Direct Labor Activities

Direct labor activities are labor activities that generally support some value-added activity of the warehouse, including picking, packing, putaway, replenishment, execution of physical inventory (PI) counting, execution of value-added services, yard management moves, and many others.

21.4.1 Capturing Start and End Times

When an operator performs a direct labor activity that is LM relevant, you should capture the start and end time of the execution of the activity to compare them to the labor standard calculated for that activity. When the operator performs the activities via mobile data entry transactions on an RF-enabled device, the start and end times are captured automatically and there is nothing more for you to do to capture the execution times. When an operator performs the activities without support of the mobile data entry transactions and the warehouse activities are subsequently entered into the system via the Graphical User Interface (GUI) transactions (for example, a pick or putaway task that is performed with a paper-printed form, or a PI count that is performed on paper), then you must request the operator to capture the start and end time and to enter them when they enter the transactions in the GUI (as seen in Figure 21.11). Note in the figure that the LM ACTIVE flag is activated, indicating that the start and end time should be entered. Error messages will occur when you save the confirmation of the LM-relevant WO if you do not assign the processor and execution times.

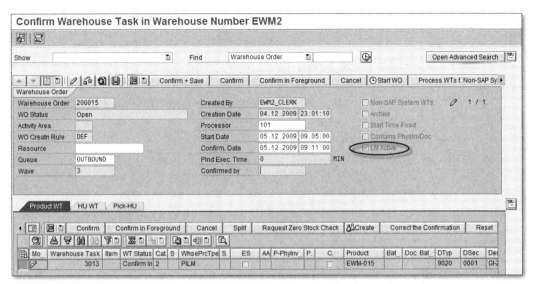

Figure 21.11 Manual Entry of the Start and End Time to the WO Header during the Confirmation of the WO

When an LM-relevant activity is executed in the warehouse, an executed workload document is created to capture the LM-related information. These executed workload documents can be viewed in the warehouse monitor (Transaction /SCWM/ MON, via the LABOR MANAGEMENT • EXECUTED WORKLOAD node, as seen in Figure 21.12).

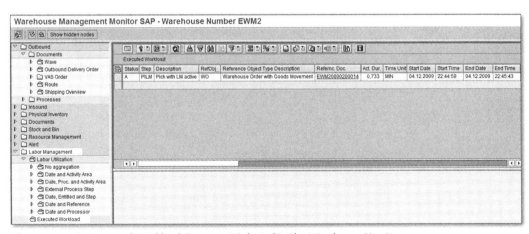

Figure 21.12 An Executed Workload Document Selected in the Warehouse Monitor

21.4.2 Travel Distance and Travel Time

The total execution time for an employee on a given resource to execute a warehouse activity includes the distance traveled between bins assigned to the activity and the distance travelled from the last position of the resource prior to starting execution of the new activity. In a large warehouse, or even in a large activity area, the travel time can be a significant portion of the total execution time for WOs. Therefore, EWM constantly maintains the location of the resource and calculates the total travel distance that the resource travels as it goes from bin to bin to execute the total activity (for example, individual tasks of a WO or individual bins of a PI), including the distance from the last position of the prior activity to the new one. This travel distance is captured on the executed workload document so that it can be used to calculate the labor standard for the employee.

To calculate the travel time based on the travel distance, the average speed of the resource assigned is used in the standard formula (time = distance/speed). Acceleration and deceleration of the resource, and average stop times in the warehouse are not considered, so you must take these into account when you calculate the average speed of the resources in the warehouse.

To enable EWM to calculate the travel distances for the planned and executed workload, you must populate the XYZ coordinates of the bins and specify the settings for the travel distance calculation in the EWM Easy Access menu (via the EXTENDED WAREHOUSE MANAGEMENT • SETTINGS • TRAVEL DISTANCE CALCULATION • SETTINGS FOR THE TRAVEL DISTANCE CALCULATION menu path, or Transaction code /SCWM/TDC_SETUP). Here, you define the average distance of the resource to the storage type (for use in calculating the travel distances for the planning workload), define the edges, and specify resource types that are excluded per edge (if, for example, a small piece of equipment can travel under an overhead rack that the other equipment cannot travel under). You also specify the network validity of the resource type per storage type (where a network is a group of valid routes within an area, from node to node and avoiding edges, unless the resource is excepted from the edge as described previously).

In addition to the settings to describe the networks, you should also specify a default bin for the resources. This is the bin that is used as the start bin for the travel distance calculation if the last bin of the resource is not known. If the last bin of the resource is known, it is stored on the resource table and is visible in the warehouse monitor on the resource view (Transaction /SCWM/MON). Due to the complexity of describing completely how to set up the resources, networks, and travel distance calculation, we will not describe them completely here. They are described well in the online help (*http://help.sap.com*).

There are also Business Add-Ins (BAdIs) for the travel distance calculation if you need to enhance the methods for calculating the travel distance for the execution of direct labor activities. There are BAdIs for changing the storage bin list in the travel distance calculation and for influencing the travel distance calculation using the storage bins in the list. To access the BAdIs in the EWM IMG, follow the menu path EXTENDED WAREHOUSE MANAGEMENT • BUSINESS ADD-INS (BADIS) FOR EXTENDED WAREHOUSE MANAGEMENT • CROSS-PROCESS SETTINGS • TRAVEL DISTANCE CALCULATION.

21.5 Indirect Labor Activities

In addition to the direct activities of the warehouse, there may be various indirect activities that are performed that you want to track and report as well. Indirect activities may include certain administrative activities or other activities involved with the operation of the warehouse that are not directly related to the products. Examples of indirect activities include administrative tasks such as creating WOs or managing the activities of the warehouse workers, cleaning the warehouse, performing preventive maintenance or battery changes on material handling equipment, taking paid breaks of any type, auditing warehouse activities, checking in or checking out loads, or any number of other activities. To track the time that is spent on these activities, EWM lets you create different indirect activity types and lets warehouse workers enter their indirect activities via GUI or RF transactions.

21.5.1 Creating Indirect Activity Types

To create the indirect activity types in the EWM IMG, follow the menu path EXTENDED WAREHOUSE MANAGEMENT • LABOR MANAGEMENT • DEFINE EXTERNAL PROCESS STEPS. As you can see in Figure 21.13, the EXTERNAL STORAGE PROCESS STEPS are not created by warehouse, so you can reuse them across warehouses to map to different internal process steps. Also note that not only are the indirect activity types created here, but also the other external storage process steps, so be cautious about changing or deleting existing ones. The related internal storage process steps are defined on the cross-client table /SCWM/TIPROCS, for which there is not an existing configuration node in the IMG.

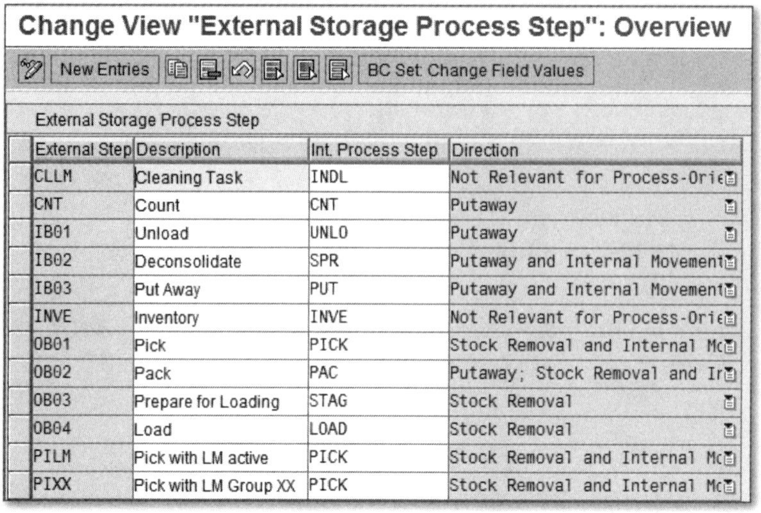
Change View "External Storage Process Step": Overview

New Entries | BC Set: Change Field Values

External Storage Process Step

External Step	Description	Int. Process Step	Direction
CLLM	Cleaning Task	INDL	Not Relevant for Process-Orie
CNT	Count	CNT	Putaway
IB01	Unload	UNLO	Putaway
IB02	Deconsolidate	SPR	Putaway and Internal Movement
IB03	Put Away	PUT	Putaway and Internal Movement
INVE	Inventory	INVE	Not Relevant for Process-Orie
OB01	Pick	PICK	Stock Removal and Internal Mc
OB02	Pack	PAC	Putaway; Stock Removal and Ir
OB03	Prepare for Loading	STAG	Stock Removal
OB04	Load	LOAD	Stock Removal
PILM	Pick with LM active	PICK	Stock Removal and Internal Mc
PIXX	Pick with LM Group XX	PICK	Stock Removal and Internal Mc

Figure 21.13 Creation of External Storage Process Steps

21.5.2 Entering Indirect Activities on the GUI

When a warehouse operator begins an indirect labor task or when they have finished the task and are ready to enter the start and end times in the EWM system (or when an administrator is tasked to enter the indirect labor tasks for other employees), they can enter the task either via the GUI or a mobile device. To enter the indirect labor task on the GUI from the EWM Easy Access menu, follow the Extended Warehouse Management • Labor Management • Maintain Indirect Labor Task menu path, or use Transaction code /SCWM/ILT. As you see in Figure 21.14, you can use the Set Start Time and Set Stop Time buttons at the top of the screen to automatically capture the start and stop times, or you can enter them manually.

21.5.3 Entering Indirect Activities on a Mobile Device

You can also use a mobile device to capture the start and end times of an indirect labor task. To enter the transaction from a mobile device (or from the GUI via Transaction /SCWM/RFUI), from the standard delivered menu, follow the 05 Internal Processes • 08 Labor Management • 01 Indirect Labor Task Reporting menu path. As you can see in Figure 21.15, the same Set Start Time and Set Stop Time buttons also exist there, or you can enter the times manually. When the operator uses an RF device to enter the transaction, they can only enter an indirect labor task for their own processor and not for another processor. If an administrator needs to enter indirect labor tasks for another user, they should use the GUI transaction described earlier.

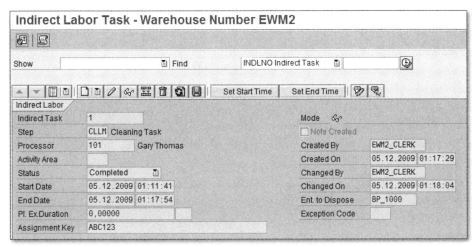

Figure 21.14 Entering an Indirect Labor Task on the GUI

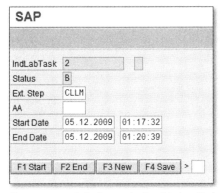

Figure 21.15 Entering an Indirect Labor Task on a Mobile Device

21.6 Calculating Workload for Planning

Prior to the activities in the warehouse being executed, you may want to estimate the workload necessary to execute the activities to plan your labor for a certain time period. This process is facilitated in EWM by calculating the planned workload. To begin this process, you must first set up the workload planning by assigning the planning activity area, and then you can execute the workload calculation.

21.6.1 Assigning the Planning Activity Area

If an activity area cannot be determined for the warehouse task via the work center, storage section, or storage type, then the planned workload is calculated without a planning activity area assigned. To assign the relevant planning activity area to the work centers, storage sections, and storage types from the EWM IMG, follow the menu path EXTENDED WAREHOUSE MANAGEMENT • LABOR MANAGEMENT • ASSIGN PLANNING ACTIVITY AREAS (as you can see in Figure 21.16). The rules and sequences that are used in the activity area determination are well defined in the IMG help for the node.

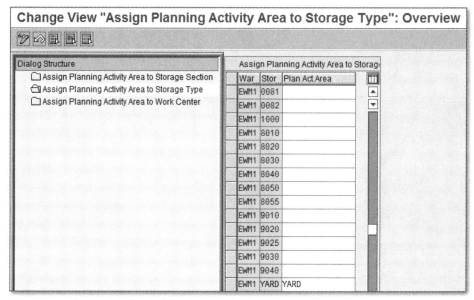

Figure 21.16 Assign Planning Activity Areas to the Storage Types

21.6.2 Calculating the Planned Workload

Once WOs are created for a given activity, you can generate the planned workload from the EWM Easy Access menu by following the EXTENDED WAREHOUSE MANAGEMENT • LABOR MANAGEMENT • PLANNING • PLANNING AND SIMULATION menu path, or using Transaction code /SCWM/PL. To generate the planned workload (as seen in Figure 21.17), enter an external step or activity area in the FIND box, or use the OPEN ADVANCED SEARCH button, enter additional criteria, and execute; then select the objects from the top pane and select the EVALUATE PLANNING FORMULA button. To check or change the formula used in the calculation, select the DISPLAY/CHANGE FORMULA button (circled in Figure 21.17). The resource required to execute the activities (in this case, the WOs for a given wave) are shown in the top pane after the planning formula is evaluated. If you use the ADVANCED SEARCH option, you can also select the AUTOMATIC PLANNING checkbox, which triggers the planning to be evaluated at the same time as the selections are made.

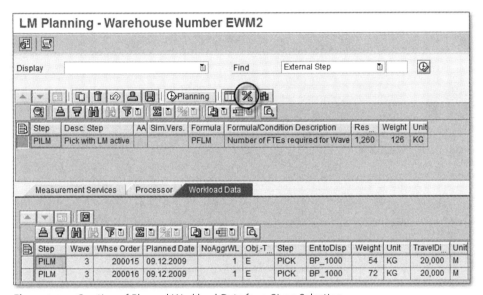

Figure 21.17 Creation of Planned Workload Data for a Given Selection

21.6.3 Preprocessing

You can also use the planning and simulation for evaluating deliveries or cycle counts for which no WOs have been generated in the system. To evaluate items for preprocessing, use the advanced search and select the USE PREPROCESSING checkbox to trigger the system to evaluate the unprocessed items for planned workload evaluation. You can also specify a percentage completion, to be taken into account during the evaluation, if you have not yet created all of the expected workload yet. For example, if you have only created 50% of the deliveries for the wave, you can specify this percentage so that the system can evaluate it and estimate the total workload.

Before you execute the planning and simulation for preprocessing, you must configure the PREPROCESSING HEADER and items in the EWM IMG, as seen in Figure 21.18, by following the menu path EXTENDED WAREHOUSE MANAGEMENT • LABOR MANAGEMENT • SET PREPROCESSING. You can also make the settings with the help of a wizard by following the menu path EXTENDED WAREHOUSE MANAGEMENT • LABOR MANAGEMENT • PREPROCESSING WITH ASSISTANT.

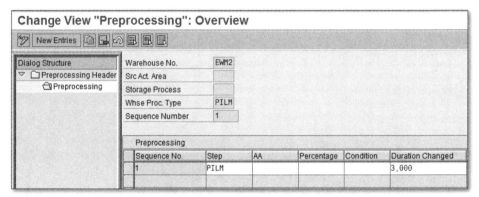

Figure 21.18 Settings for the Preprocessing Header and Items

To specify the delivery data and time used for preprocessing for both inbound deliveries and outbound deliveries in the EWM IMG, follow the menu path EXTENDED WAREHOUSE MANAGEMENT • LABOR MANAGEMENT • DEFINE DELIVERY DATE/TIME FOR PREPROCESSING (as seen in Figure 21.19).

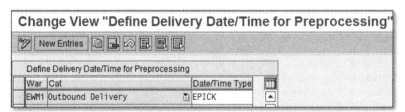

Figure 21.19 Assignment of Delivery Data and Time for Preprocessing

21.6.4 Viewing Planned Workload in the Warehouse Monitor

When you make the selections and generate the planned workload, the data is saved so that you can view it later. For example, once the planned workload is created and evaluated, you can view the planned workload in the warehouse monitor (as seen in Figure 21.20).

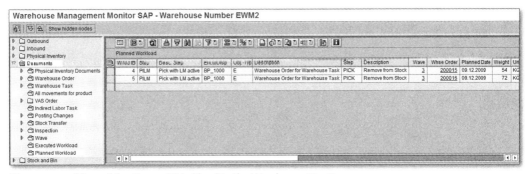

Figure 21.20 View of the Planned Workload in the Warehouse Monitor

21.6.5 Operational Planning

Operational planning can be performed within the planning and simulation transaction as well (Transaction /SCWM/PL, see menu path above). In the planning and simulation transaction, you can utilize the combination of the planned workload (based on active documents), planned workload from pre-processing, information about available processors, and the calculated measurement services to calculate and report the total planned workload. Formulas used for the operational planning can be created and utilized in the same ways as described in the previous sections — the only difference here is that you are utilizing the various sources of information described earlier in one combined view of the workload of the warehouse (rather than, for example, viewing the workload, preprocessing workload, resources, and results of the calculated measurement services separately).

Once you have combined these sources and calculated the total workload, you can simulate the results of changing various parameters in the warehouse, (e.g., the number of warehouse processors, and which specific processors, are available for executing the planned workload) by copying the planning workload (using the GENERATE SIMULATION LINES button) and changing parameters within the simulation. For example, as you can see in Figure 21.21, you can change the aggregate workload or the total weight being processed. In this case, because the formula included the weight as an input parameter, the planned workload in the simulation was changed after the parameters were changed and the planned workload was recalculated. The significant advantage to this feature is that it allows you to simulate and plan possible outcomes given various scenarios.

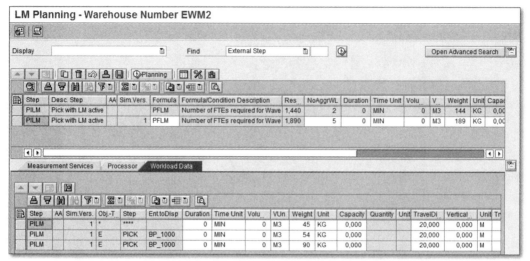

Figure 21.21 Simulation of the Planned Workload with Changed Parameters and Changed Results

21.6.6 Loading Planning and Simulation Results

You can also load the planning and simulation results from a file, if they are created in a separate system. To load the planning and simulation results from the
EWM Easy Access menu, follow the EXTENDED WAREHOUSE MANAGEMENT • LABOR
MANAGEMENT • PLANNING • LOAD PLANNING AND SIMULATION RESULTS menu path,
or use Transaction code /SCWM/PL_LOAD.

21.7   Employee Performance

Being able to evaluate employee performance is one of the key reasons that many
companies undertake an LM implementation. In EWM, you can create employee
performance documents that measure and rate an employee's performance by
comparing the executed workload with the expected duration of the activities
performed, and employees and supervisors can view the executed workload
documents so that they can evaluate the employee's performance for a given
timeframe.

21.7.1   Creating the Employee Performance Documents

To create the employee performance documents from the EWM Easy Access menu,
follow the EXTENDED WAREHOUSE MANAGEMENT • LABOR MANAGEMENT • EMPLOYEE

PERFORMANCE • EMPLOYEE PERFORMANCE OVERVIEW menu path, or use Transaction code /SCWM/EPERF. As you can see in Figure 21.22, you can select the processor and create the employee performance documents by processor. Once the performance documents are created, they must then be approved by the appropriate person before they can be transferred to HR (via the same transaction). The PERF. DOC. STATUS indicates the current status of the document (Created, For approval, Approved, Transferred, To delete, or Deleted).

Once the performance documents are created and approved, they can be transferred to HR (as described in Chapter 23). To trigger the data to be sent to HR from the EWM Easy Access menu, follow the EXTENDED WAREHOUSE MANAGEMENT • LABOR MANAGEMENT • EMPLOYEE PERFORMANCE • SEND PERFORMANCE DOCUMENT TO HR menu path, or use Transaction code /SCWM/EPD_TRANSFER.

Once you have created the document or it has been approved, you can only delete the document by accessing the SEND PERFORMANCE DOCUMENT TO HR function.

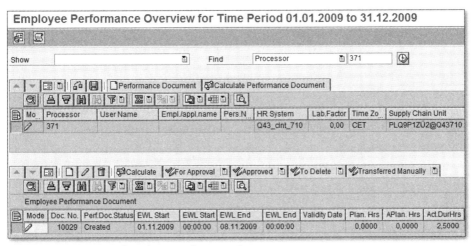

Figure 21.22 Creation of Employee Performance Documents

21.7.2   Efficiency versus Utilization

When evaluating an employee's performance, there are two calculations whose meaning are important to understand. These two measurements are *efficiency* and *utilization*. An employee's total effectiveness is optimal when both efficiency and utilization are high.

Efficiency

Efficiency is a measure of comparison of an employee's actual performance to the expected performance, as calculated in the expected workload. Efficiency is reported as a percentage and is calculated as actual time divided by expected time.

Utilization

Utilization is a measure of how much of an employee's total work time is spent working on direct activities. Utilization is calculated as actual time divided by total work time. The total work time can be evaluated by importing data from ERP HR, via the available BAdI. For example, in the BAdI, you could call the HR Business Application Programming Interface (BAPI) BAPI_TIMEAVAILSCHEDULE_BUILD to determine an employee's work hours. To access the BAdI in the EWM IMG, follow the menu path EXTENDED WAREHOUSE MANAGEMENT • BUSINESS ADD-INS (BADIS) FOR EXTENDED WAREHOUSE MANAGEMENT • LABOR MANAGEMENT • TIMES AT WHICH PROCESSOR IS AVAILABLE • BADI: DETERMINE AVAILABLE TIME OF PROCESSOR.

21.7.3 Viewing Calculated Results on Mobile Devices

Employees can view their own performance on a mobile device, as seen in Figure 21.23, to track their personal productivity during a given time period. They can access the results for the current day, previous day, current week, current month, or other time period (which allows manual date selection criteria to be entered). To access the transaction on the standard menu on a mobile device (which you can also access on the GUI via Transaction code /SCWM/RFUI), follow the menu path 05 INTERNAL PROCESSES • 08 LABOR MANAGEMENT • 02 DISPLAY EMPLOYEE SELF SERVICE.

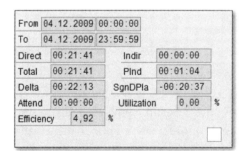

Figure 21.23 Employee Performance as Viewed By the Employee on an RF Device

21.7.4 Viewing Employee Performance in the Warehouse Monitor

A supervisor can view executed workload documents for employees on the warehouse monitor (Transaction /SCWM/MON) to gauge their performance for a selected time period, as shown in Figure 21.12. In addition, warehouse managers or supervisors (or anyone with the correct authorization) can view various labor utilization reports in the warehouse monitor based on various selection criteria, including:

- Date and activity area
- Date, processor, and activity area
- External process step
- Date, entitled, and step
- Date and reference
- Date and processor

21.8 Summary

In this chapter, we described the basic functionality to support LM. While we did not explain every detail about how to effectively manage your employee workforce using the capabilities of the EWM LM functionality, you should now understand the basic capabilities of the system and how to get started implementing your own LM program. For more details on particular functions supported by EWM LM and how to implement them, refer to the SAP Online Help (*http://help.sap.com*). In the coming chapters, we will continue to describe the features of EWM and then we will discuss how to implement the EWM functions in your SAP landscape.

With integrated Resource Management, Extended Warehouse Management (EWM) helps to optimize warehouse execution. When implemented together with an appropriate radio frequency (RF) framework, EWM provides significant flexibility and solves well-known problems with mobile device integration.

22 Data Capture and Resource Optimization

In this chapter, we'll provide a technical overview of several data capture methods and mobile device integration. We'll give details on the relevant business functions, including, for example, how to optimize the resources inside the warehouse using EWM Resource Management. With the detailed explanation of the RF Framework, we'll also provide an overview of how to enhance, change, configure and personalize existing transactions. We'll also discuss the technical details, for example, how to connect mobile devices to an SAP system.

We'll discuss the following technical possibilities for implementing mobile solutions in SAP projects, so that you can make an informed decision about how to implement mobile data capture in your warehouse:

▶ SAP Graphical User Interface (GUI) for GUI-based workstations and devices

▶ SAP Console for text-based devices

▶ Web SAPConsole, SAP Web Dynpro Java and SAP ITSmobile for web-based devices

▶ Third-party integration using Web Services or remote function calls (RFCs)

And, finally, we'll discuss additional topics of integration, including pick-by-voice and radio frequency identification (RFID) integration.

To begin, we'll provide an overall understanding of the data capture methods.

22.1   Overview of Data Capture Methods for Warehousing

A common logistics and warehousing business requirement is to optimize warehouse processing to save effort, resources, and money — and in the end, to increase margins. And the common challenges include the need to reduce additional work caused by paper-based systems and to reduce human error that occurs during the business process. A paper-driven warehouse process has the following disadvantages:

▶ Double the work to enter data into the system after the business process is finished

▶ Lack of guidance and additional information for warehouse operators using the paper-based warehouse process (e.g., a picking list)

▶ Lack of validation for the correctness of the work and the data (e.g., confirmation of the destination bin at putaway)

▶ Time lag between execution and data entry, which results in inaccurate data in the system

Workstations on the other hand, provide the warehouse worker with direct access to the system for real-time updates, validation of data entry, etc. But workstations can't be used everywhere in the warehouse, for various reasons. Therefore, the use of mobile devices is increasing. When all workers are connected to the warehouse management system in real time, there are significant benefits that can be leveraged. Processes can be executed more efficiently, in a standardized way, and with less wasted or duplicated effort. The system can help the operator improve warehouse execution and allow the operator to react appropriately when something unexpected happens.

In EWM, SAP has provided a flexible framework to integrate mobile devices very quickly, allowing you to quickly deploy mobile devices to your warehouse to achieve these benefits.

22.2   Technical Mobile Data Capture Integration

There are different methods of integrating mobile devices to an SAP system. The key challenge of integrating mobile devices into the SAP system landscape is that many mobile devices don't run on the same platform or operating system as a desktop PC, and SAP doesn't deliver the full SAP GUI for these mobile platforms. The standard solution that SAP provides uses a different frontend technology on such devices (which is driven by the often limited processing and visualizaton capabilities of the devices). The common methods for real-time connection between a mobile device and SAP are to use a thin client method, such as a telnet client or a web browser. For more details on SAP's mobile strategy, see the SAP mobile strategy topic at the SAP Service Marketplace at *http://service.sap.com*.

For more details on common connection options for mobile devices and how the thin client method compares, see the report entitled "Choosing Between the Six Mobile Application Architecture Styles" (Gartner 09/01/2006). According to Gartner, the six possible architectures for mobile applications include:

▸ Thick Client — data and code is stored on the device

▸ Rich Client — code is stored on the device, either a small amount of client data or none at all

▸ Streaming — streaming client on the device

▸ Thin Client — browser or similar generic client

▸ Messaging — email, mobile text message (via short messaging system, or SMS), instant messaging is used as data transport

▸ No Client — uses native device features, such as voice recognition

The use of the other options, aside from thin client, can also be achieved using SAP NetWeaver, the technology basis of the SAP System. We won't discuss the No Client and Streaming integration — these options are not often used in warehousing applications. With SAP Workflow you could easily send emails or text messages, however, this is also not the common method for processing on mobile devices in the warehouse. The most common methods used are the Rich, Thick, and Thin clients, so we will focus our discussion on those options.

In Figure 22.1, you can see the architecture of the common RF integration technologies and offline integration required for Rich and Thick Clients. This diagram could also be relevant to other SAP NetWeaver systems — only the EWM RF Framework component is unique to the SAP EWM system.

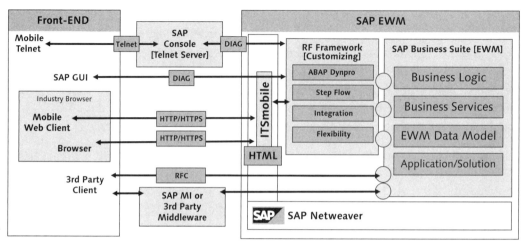

Figure 22.1 Common SAP System Landscape for Integration of a Mobile Client

Offline implementation of mobile device support is totally different and more complex, and therefore more investment is generally required during implementation. Our experience indicates that it requires roughly six to ten times more effort to implement the same process offline as online. For offline processes, SAP NetWeaver Mobile can be used as the standard technology. The major components required include an additional middleware server and an additional developed mobile client. Often, this client device logic needs to be developed specifically for your individual requirements, as each warehouse has different requirements. The key challenge of offline implementation is that data must be stored on the client and replicated into the system afterward. However, this client device needs additional business logic, so if something changes in the business logic, a deployment to all of the mobile devices may be required and a new version must be installed on all of the mobile clients. Furthermore, when a mobile process is finished, synchronization with the backend system is required. Therefore, this method is becoming less prevalent in the warehouse, but is still used in certain situations.

You can also use third-party clients that communicate directly with the SAP system. However, this also requires additional effort and custom development (which limits standard support possibilities from SAP). Additional developments on both the mobile client and the interfaces must be prepared, and every operation must be encapsulated and made available via an interface (e.g., RFC). This effort to put the logic on the client device and on the backend system will often have a negative effect on the total cost of ownership (TCO) for the solution.

Often, every warehouse looks physically different, and every company and every industry handles their business processes a little bit differently. When execution of the business processes is handled on mobile devices, the screens and the step flow to support those processes are often different. Therefore, the integration of mobile devices often requires you to change, enhance, or replace the logic of the mobile transactions. When logic and data are stored on the device, you must then make special consideration for:

▶ **Deployment**

When the logic must be changed, as often occurs during the lifecycle of your warehouse management system deployment, all of the logic must be redeployed or reinstalled onto the clients of the mobile devices

▶ **Tools and Development**

Many tools are not available on the operating systems that run on mobile devices. If you need them on the device itself you might need to develop them.

▶ **Performance and Stability**

The most common point of failure in this paradigm is often the mobile device, therefore, the coding and the development must be very good. Everything that can be handled by the backend server will improve performance.

▶ **Device Independence**

The support of the application can't be guaranteed when the device must be replaced or when the operating system changes. If one of your devices must be replaced after some time, the original operating system might not be available any longer. On the other hand, the use of a standard, such as HTML, can help solve this problem.

In Table 22.1, we've captured the parameters of each of the methods:

Condition	Online (fully connected)	Rich-client or Occasionally Disconnected	Offline or Occasionally Connected
Native user interface	No	Yes	Yes
Browser or telnet based	Yes	No	No

Table 22.1 Parameters Related to Common Mobile Client Integration Methods

Condition	Online (fully connected)	Rich-client or Occasionally Disconnected	Offline or Occasionally Connected
Business logic on client	Yes	Yes	No
Local data	All — synchronization required	Some synchronization required	No
Out of signal operation	No — limited if no system communication is required	Full or limited	Full
Peripheral support	Yes	Yes	Only when the browser provides the interface
Multidevice support	Limited	Limited	Full, with browser
TCO	Low	Medium	High

Table 22.1 Parameters Related to Common Mobile Client Integration Methods (Cont.)

EWM currently only supports online methods of communication via thin client architectures for mobile devices. The standard methods to make the transaction visible on the client are to use SAP Console for character-based devices and ITSmobile for Web-based representation. As the methods are generic and not specific to the application, they can also be used for other systems aside from EWM.

Each of the mobile data transactions for EWM is developed inside the EWM RF Framework, which allows the transactions to leverage the functions of EWM. While the screen may look simple, several things must be considered to ensure productive usage of the transactions. For example, the size and format restrictions of the devices don't allow for the same type of processing as could be allowed with a desktop PC with a large monitor and a mouse. The RF Framework allows you to manage the logic while effectively dealing with the restrictions at the same time.

At the same time, effective *data capture integration* requires optimization of warehouse task execution, integration to different hardware devices, a user-friendly interface to assist the warehouse workers (e.g., with colors or sounds), and support for various data sources, including barcodes, RFID tags, and pick-by-voice capability.

In EWM, SAP improved the mobile integration based on lessons learned from previous SAP products (e.g., ERP warehouse management) and implementation projects. In the mobile transactions of ERP WM, for example, enhancements were somewhat difficult to manage for standard ABAP developers who didn't already have SAP mobile development experience. Often, during implementation projects, the developer would rather create a new development or copy and enhance the standard programs. This has some significant disadvantages. With the additional copy of the standard objects, the application is no longer supported by the SAP standard support, the additional logic must be further tested in detail, and the transaction must continue to be supported as a custom object in future — all of which increase the TCO.

This was one of the reasons SAP developed the RF Framework, which gives you enough flexibility to change some system and business logic without creating modifications. The EWM RF Framework even provides a solution for managing the resizing of screens, which requires creation of a new dynpro for each additional screen size.

EWM uses the RF Framework as a technical integration component and develops all mobile transactions within the RF Framework. More than 110 mobile transactions were delivered in the latest release.

The EWM Resource Management is interwoven in the RF Framework, and the business requirements for warehouse optimization are solved by the effective combination of the RF Framework and by Resource Management. In the following sections, we'll explain the components of both the Resource Management and the RF Framework in more detail.

22.3 Resource Management and Warehouse Optimization

A resource is an employee or a piece of equipment used in the warehouse to execute the warehouse functions. In the following sections, we will discuss the components of Resource Management, the system-guided processing option that utilizes Resource Management, and monitoring of the resources.

EWM Resource Management is integrated directly into the EWM system (unlike ERP Task and Resource Management, which was developed as an add-on to ERP warehouse management). The objective of Resource Management is to optimize the execution of the warehouse activities utilizing the available resources. Resource Management consists of different business objects that require creation of certain master data and customizing. In the following sections, we'll describe the master data and customizing required to support Resource Management.

22.3.1 Users

The EWM *user* is the same as the SAP system user, and for each user, you can maintain certain default values related to Resource Management (including the personalization profile, warehouse, and resource number), so that the user doesn't have to enter them every time they log on to a mobile device. In Figure 22.2, you can see the setup of EWM user, which can be accessed via the EWM Easy Access menu by following the EXTENDED WAREHOUSE MANAGEMENT • MASTER DATA • RESOURCE MANAGEMENT • MAINTAIN USERS menu path, or using Transaction code /SCWM/USER.

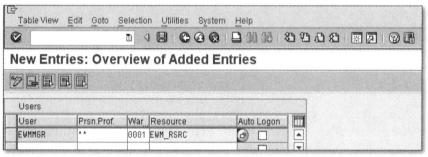

Figure 22.2 Creation of the Master Data Record for an EWM User. Entries Are Used as Default Values and for the Assignment of the RF Menu

The *personalization profile* is created in the customizing and lets you assign the user to an RF menu so that only specific transactions are available to the user. You can create these menus in the EWM Implementation Guide (IMG) in the menu manager. To create the personalization profile in the EWM IMG, follow the EXTENDED WAREHOUSE MANAGEMENT • MOBILE DATA ENTRY • RADIO FREQUENCY (RF) FRAMEWORK • DEFINE STEPS IN LOGICAL TRANSACTIONS menu path, then select the node DEFINE PRESENTATION PROFILES, and then node DEFINE PERSONALIZATION PROFILES. To access the RF Menu Manager in the EWM IMG, follow the menu path

EXTENDED WAREHOUSE MANAGEMENT • MOBILE DATA ENTRY • RADIO FREQUENCY (RF) FRAMEWORK • RF MENU MANAGER.

The AUTO LOGON indicator allows you to specify whether each user should be prompted for additional logon information. If the parameter is selected, the user will be automatically forwarded directly to the RF menu without being prompted to validate additional data on the logon screen.

22.3.2 Resources

The *resource* generally refers to the equipment being used by the warehouse operator, or it could also refer to a piece of automated equipment, or even the operator himself if he's not using any equipment. To create the resources in the EWM Easy Access menu (as seen in Figure 22.3), follow the EXTENDED WAREHOUSE MANAGEMENT • MASTER DATA • RESOURCE MANAGEMENT • MAINTAIN RESOURCE menu path, or use Transaction code /SCWM/RSRC.

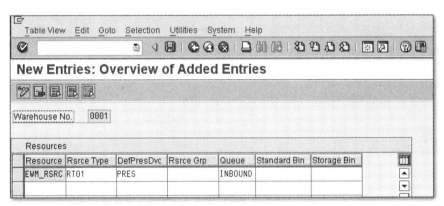

Figure 22.3 Creating Resources

For each resource, you can assign the following parameters:

▶ Resource group — used for system-guided processing (described later in this chapter)

▶ Resource type — used for the physical classification of the resources

▶ Default presentation device — used to affect the layout of the screens (EWM delivers a screen layout with 8 rows and 40 columns, which is a common screen size for vehicle-mounted devices, but you can specify a different screen size for the presentation device and drive the use of different screens based on the screen size)

▶ Queue — used as the default queue for system-guided processing (you can update the queue assignment in the warehouse monitor after the user logs on to the resource)

▶ Standard bin — bin used in the travel distance calculation if the current storage bin is not known

▶ Storage bin — represents the current storage bin of the resource and is automatically updated by the system, therefore, it's not much use to assign something here

22.3.3 Queues

The queue represents a container where all open WOs are waiting to be processed. During WO creation the correct queue is determined. The settings for the queue management are made in the EWM IMG via the menu path EXTENDED WAREHOUSE MANAGEMENT • CROSS-PROCESS SETTINGS • RESOURCE MANAGEMENT.

Once the queue has been defined, you must also set up the queue determination in the EWM IMG by following the menu path EXTENDED WAREHOUSE MANAGEMENT • CROSS-PROCESS SETTINGS • RESOURCE MANAGEMENT • DEFINE QUEUES • DEFINE QUEUE DETERMINATION CRITERIA. The queue determination is based on the source and destination activity area, bin access type, warehouse process type, and the activity (see Figure 22.4).

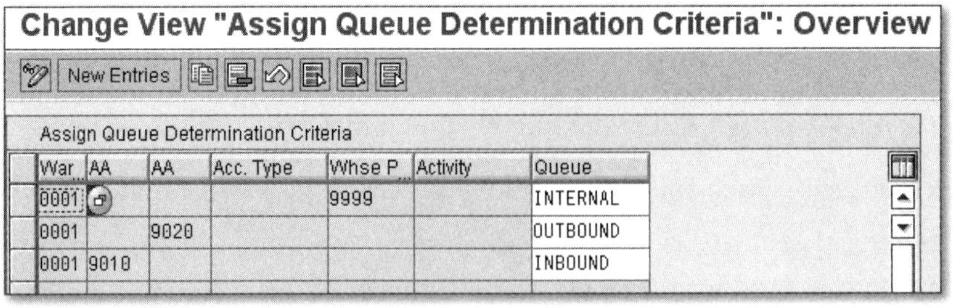

Change View "Assign Queue Determination Criteria": Overview

New Entries

Assign Queue Determination Criteria

War	AA	AA	Acc. Type	Whse P	Activity	Queue
0001				9999		INTERNAL
0001		9020				OUTBOUND
0001	9010					INBOUND

Figure 22.4 Queue Determination for WOs

> **Note**
>
> To confirm the tasks from the queues in the RF transaction, you must assign operation environment 3 (RF, Resource Management) active. You can only confirm the tasks in the RF if a valid queue is found and assigned to the WO. To check the correct determination of the queue, you may sometimes need to debug function module /SCWM/QUEUE_DET during WO creation. In addition, you can search the resource index (table /SCWM/WO_RSRC_TY), where all of the open WOs are stored.

22.3.4 Resource Groups

The RESOURCE GROUP is used to group resources for determining the queue sequence (see Figure 22.5). To create the resource groups in the EWM Easy Access menu, follow the EXTENDED WAREHOUSE MANAGEMENT • MASTER DATA • RESOURCE MANAGEMENT • MAINTAIN RESOURCE GROUP menu path, or use Transaction code /SCWM/RGRP.

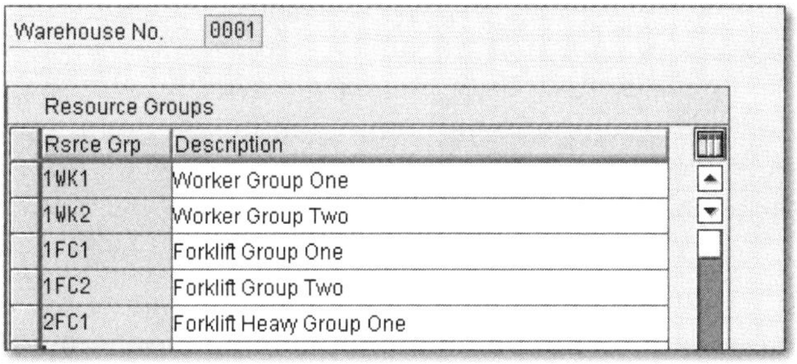

| Warehouse No. | 0001 |

Resource Groups

Rsrce Grp	Description
1WK1	Worker Group One
1WK2	Worker Group Two
1FC1	Forklift Group One
1FC2	Forklift Group Two
2FC1	Forklift Heavy Group One

Figure 22.5 Define Resource Groups to Cluster Different Resources

To use system-guided processing, the queues must be assigned to the resource groups in the appropriate sequence (as seen in Figure 22.6). To maintain the queue sequence via the EWM Easy Access menu, follow the EXTENDED WAREHOUSE MANAGEMENT • MASTER DATA • RESOURCE MANAGEMENT • MAINTAIN QUEUE SEQUENCE FOR RESOURCE GROUP menu path, or use Transaction code /SCWM/QSEC. Because the WOs are selected from the queues according to the queue sequence, this represents a sort of prioritization of the WOs by resource type, according to queue assignment (which is based in part on the source and destination activity area and warehouse process type).

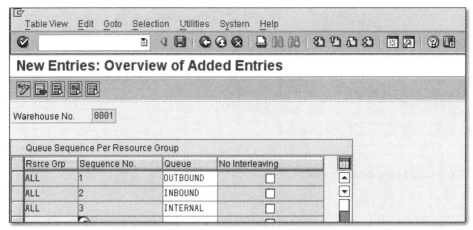

Figure 22.6 Queue Sequence per Resource Group

Note

This sequence is also used when a user wants to move a handling unit (HU) via a mobile transaction (e.g., picking or putaway). After the HU is entered in the first screen, the system selects the corresponding WO for processing. However, EWM only allows processing the WO if the corresponding queue is stored in the resource group prioritization sequence. In other words, you can manage the allowed activities of the resource types in the resource group by specifying the allowed queues in the prioritization sequence.

22.3.5 Resource Types

The resource type indicates the physical features of the resource (as you can see in Figure 22.7). For example, in the customizing for the resource type, you can specify the resource velocity, and you can specify the allowed BIN ACCESS TYPES and allowed HU TYPE GROUPS. To create the resource types in the EWM IMG, follow the menu path EXTENDED WAREHOUSE MANAGEMENT • CROSS-PROCESS SETTINGS • RESOURCE MANAGEMENT • DEFINE RESOURCE TYPES.

Once you have created the resource groups and the resource types, you can assign them to the resources as discussed previously in this chapter.

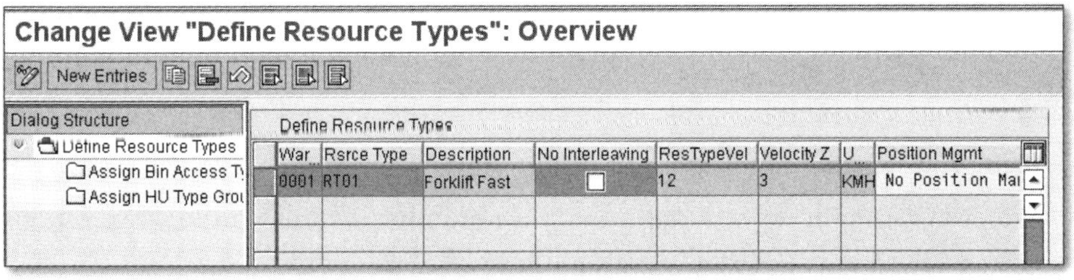

Change View "Define Resource Types": Overview
New Entries
Dialog Structure
Define Resource Types
Assign Bin Access T
Assign HU Type Grou
Define Resource Types
War
Rsrce Type
Description
No Interleaving
ResTypeVel
Velocity Z
U
Position Mgmt
0001
RT01
Forklift Fast
12
3
KMH
No Position Ma

Figure 22.7 Defining Resource Types and Their Access Properties

22.4 System-Guided Processing

System-guided processing works via the pull principle. In other words, when a resource asks for a new WO in a system-guided transaction, EWM searches for the next optimal WO based on the configuration. As you can see in Figure 22.8, EWM provides two options for system-guided processing in the standard delivered RF menu (accessed via Transaction /SCWM/RFUI), including:

- System-guided Selection — the system first searches for the next queue and then searches in the determined queue for the optimal WO.
- System-guided by Queue — the user specifies a queue and the system only searches for the next optimal WO in the specified queue.

Whse No.
0001
Resource
DefPresDvc
01 System-Guided
02 Manual Selection
01 System-guided Selection
02 System-guided by Queue
Menu
F1 Logoff
Menu
F1 Logoff

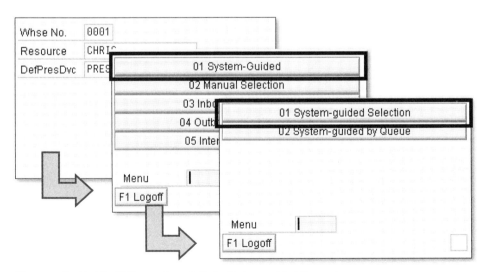

Figure 22.8 Mobile RF Transactions Path for System-guided Processing

When the user requests the next WO via the system-guided selection, the system performs the determination of the relevant WO according to the following sequence:

1. Assigned warehouse orders

   You can assign the WO in the warehouse monitor, and all additional selections will be overridden by this assignment.

2. Default queue

   The default queue is stored on the resource and is used if the system-guided option is selected without a queue being specified

3. Next optimal queue

   If there are no WOs in the default queue (and if the user didn't select the SYSTEM GUIDED BY QUEUE option from the RF menu), the next queue is determined according to the queue sequence, as described earlier in this chapter and seen in Figure 22.6. Note: If you change the queue sequence, all resources assigned to the queue sequence will be affected during the next WO selection.

4. Optimal WO within the determined queue

   The WOs assigned to the determined queue are sorted and evaluated according to various criteria, including priority and, if relevant, the Latest Start Date (LSD) and Time, which is calculated for the WO from the expected shipping time for outbound delivery orders (ODOs) and based on the expected activities according to the storage control (e.g., picking, packing, loading).

Figure 22.9, is a diagram describing EWM queue management. In the example, resource FM2 is only assigned to the outbound queue and so is only assigned to WOs from that queue. Resource SM3, on the other hand, is assigned first to the queue sequence for inbound, then replenishment, then outbound. If there are WOs in the inbound queue, resource SM3 would be assigned to those first before the other queues are checked.

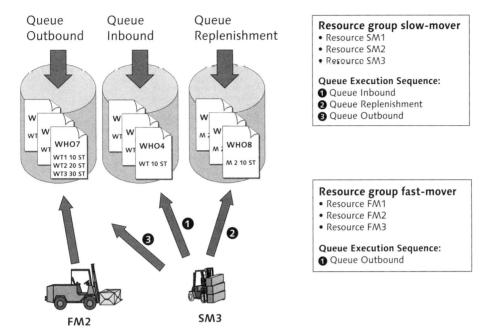

Figure 22.9 SAP EWM Queue Management

The priority index is also used in sorting WOs that have the same LSD. You can help ensure that WOs that are close to each other in LSD are grouped together as the same LSD by using rounding (thus bringing the priority index into play for orders with similar LSDs). This rounding is triggered via determination of the mode to the WO. You can set up the modes in the customizing to trigger a rounding of the LSD time, as you can see in Figure 22.10. To set up the modes in the EWM IMG, follow the menu path EXTENDED WAREHOUSE MANAGEMENT • CROSS-PROCESS SETTINGS • RESOURCE MANAGEMENT • DEFINE MODES.

If an LSD is not relevant, the system sorts the WOs according to the WO number to prioritize the selection. The calculation of the index is based on the execution priorities set up for the resource type (in Transaction /SCWM/EXECPR). You can also use the available Business Add-In (BAdI) to specify your own logic for prioritization of the WOs — for example, you can add your own heuristics for further optimization of the prioritization.

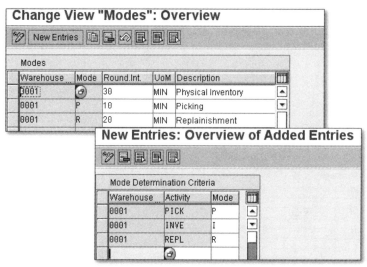

Figure 22.10 Definition of Modes to Ensure an Equal LSD via Rounding

As of EWM release 7.0, you can also use the following additional features related to resource management:

▸ **Interleaving**

Interleaving tasks of different types (e.g., inbound putaway and replenishment) allows you to reduce "deadheading," or transporting of the resource without stock on the equipment. After a WO is confirmed, the next queue in the sequence can be assigned to the resource and assignment of the next WO will be made from the next queue. To activate interleaving, group the queues to queue types in the EWM IMG by following the EXTENDED WAREHOUSE MANAGEMENT • CROSS-PROCESS SETTINGS • RESOURCE MANAGEMENT • DEFINE QUEUES menu path, then define the queue index in the EWM Easy Access menu by following the EXTENDED WAREHOUSE MANAGEMENT • MASTER DATA • RESOURCE

MANAGEMENT • MAINTAIN QUEUE TYPE SEQUENCE menu path, or using Transaction /SCWM/QTSQ.

▶ **Semi-system-guided processing**

Semi-system-guided processing allows the system (in system-guided mode) to send the warehouse operator to an area without specifying the HU for the operator to process, allowing him to specify which HU he wants to transport based on the physical availability of the HUs (which can be very useful, for example, during putaway from a staging area that has many pallets stacked up in a row).

▶ **Resource Execution Constraints (REC)**

The REC allows you to limit the resources working in a given area to avoid congestion. The system can calculate the time for the execution of the WOs assigned to the area, and during that time period, additional resources are not allowed to enter the area (i.e., no additional tasks for that area will be assigned) as long as the predefined number of resources are already assigned. To specify the number and type of resources allowed in the EWM IMG, follow the menu path EXTENDED WAREHOUSE MANAGEMENT • CROSS-PROCESS SETTINGS • RESOURCE MANAGEMENT • CONTROL DATA • DEFINE RESOURCE EXECUTION CONSTRAINTS (REC). (To calculate the REC based on your own algorithm, use BAdI /SCWM/ EX_RECGRP_LEAVETIME_CALC; and if the REC Storage Group is not free, you can also use BAdI /SCWM/EX_RECGRP_ENGAGED_HANDL.)

System-guided processing of EWM resource management is based on the rules established in customizing. The system doesn't react on its own when something changes in the warehouse (e.g., an accident). You can interact with the system and change the evaluated priorities in the warehouse monitor, but EWM does not, for example, calculate the route of every resource and determine the optimal WOs to be processed. If you want to further optimize the selections, you can use the BAdIs mentioned earlier for the WO selection via system-guided processing.

22.4.1 Monitoring of the Resources

You can visualize the EWM resource management data via the EWM monitor. After selecting the resources in the monitor (see Figure 22.11), you can perform various activities related to the resources by selecting the methods, including:

▶ Send a message to the operator (the operator will see the message when he presses the next button on the mobile device)

▶ Log on or log off the resource (this is especially useful to log off a resource if the user forgot to log off, because the resource can't be assigned as long as another user is already logged on)

▶ Maintain the resource to change its parameters

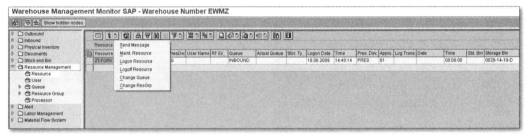

Figure 22.11 Selecting and Maintaining Resources in the Warehouse Monitor

In the warehouse monitor, you can also use the QUEUE selection to see the actual warehouse workload by queue. Every queue represents a work pool, allowing you to interact and plan the workload of the resources (see Figure 22.12). You can change the existing WOs via the provided methods, including:

▶ Lock or unlock the WOs

▶ Confirm or cancel the WOs in the foreground (which triggers the desktop transaction) or in the background

▶ Change the queue of the WO (if warehouse operators are using system-guided transactions, you can change the prioritization of the work by changing the queue of the WOs)

▶ Assign (or unassign) WOs to a specific resource (if it's not being processed already)

▶ Change the LSD (by changing the LSD, you can affect the prioritization within the queue)

In the EWM monitor, you can maintain your own user selection criteria and save them as selection variants, and you can create and save your own display variants as well. You can also use the table functions to make a graphical visualization, but to ensure an automatic refresh, you must use the Easy Graphics Framework (EGF) (as seen in Figure 22.13). For more details on the warehouse monitor and the EGF, see Chapter 15, Warehouse Monitoring and Reporting.

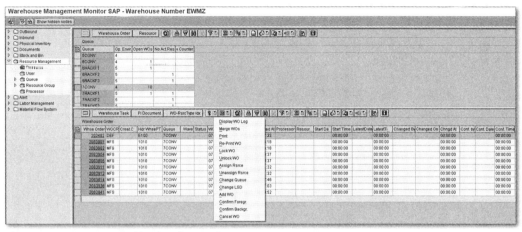

Figure 22.12 Resource Workload in the Warehouse Monitor

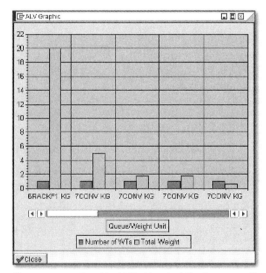

Figure 22.13 Graphical Workload of the Resource Management via the EWM Monitor

22.5 RF Framework

We already mentioned the flexibility and the advantages of the EWM Framework, but now we'll discuss those benefits in more detail in the following sections. Then, we'll continue to describe the features and setup of the RF Framework.

22.5.1 Advantages of the EWM RF Framework

The major advantages of the RF Framework include integration, management, and flexibility.

Integration of different device types

The RF Framework allows you to encapsulate the business logic from the user interface. You can generate the user interface based on the mobile device screen sizes, as described earlier when we discussed user profiles. We'll discuss these further in the later sections of this chapter.

Transaction Management Using Templates

The use of the RF Framework allows you to customize the RF transactions for different locations, as is often required during the rollout of the EWM implementation to multiple sites, as each site often has its own set of unique requirements. Using the RF Framework, you can specify that a different set of coding or different screens can be used per warehouse or even based on the screen size, minimizing the time and effort to create, test, deploy, and support the different logic per site (as opposed to, for instance, creating separate transactions or separate logic within the same transaction).

Flexibility of the RF Template

The customizing of the RF Framework allows you to flexibly enhance the available logic and the screen layout without developing new logic. The EWM standard business logic can be easily replaced using the RF Framework, allowing you to deploy your own business logic and change the business logic per warehouse.

Guides for Best Practices on using the RF Framework are available at the SAP Service Marketplace (*http://service.sap.com*), and you and your development team should review them if you intend to enhance the RF transactions in any way. Despite the initial learning curve of the RF Framework, using the framework appropriately to enhance your solution (as opposed to a pure ABAP development) will help you reduce the TCO for your system over time.

22.5.2 Setup of the RF Framework

In the following sections, we'll describe the technical setup for the RF Framework (which is geared more toward technical readers). Nearly all of the settings mentioned here can be accessed in the EWM IMG, starting at menu path EXTENDED WAREHOUSE MANAGEMENT • MOBILE DATA ENTRY.

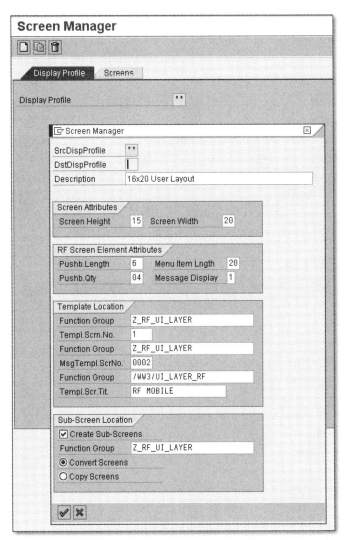

Figure 22.14 EWM RF Screen Manager — Generation of New Display Profiles

Screen Sizes and Presentation Profiles

To generate different screen sizes (which may be required to support different device types), you use the screen manager to create a DISPLAY PROFILE, which you can access in the EWM IMG via the EXTENDED WAREHOUSE MANAGEMENT • MOBILE DATA ENTRY • RADIO FREQUENCY (RF) FRAMEWORK RF • SCREEN MANAGER menu path, or using Transaction code /SCWM/RFSCR. Here, you can copy a display profile and change the screen size (see Figure 22.14). The system will generate the new ABAP screen and calculate the position of the elements. Afterward, if the screen is smaller than the original one, you may need to change some of the screen elements by manually adjusting the screen in the screen editor (via Transaction SE51).

When logging on to the RF device, you can specify the relevant PRESENTATION DEVICE (or it can be defaulted per resource, as described previously). To maintain the presentation devices (as seen in Figure 22.15) in the EWM Easy Access menu, follow the EXTENDED WAREHOUSE MANAGEMENT • MASTER DATA • MAINTAIN PRESENTATION DEVICES menu path, or use Transaction code /SCWM/PRDVC. The additional layer of logic for determining the screen is used to separate the frontend from the business logic. Once you create the presentation device, you assign the DISPLAY PROFILE, which defines which screen is used (as described earlier).

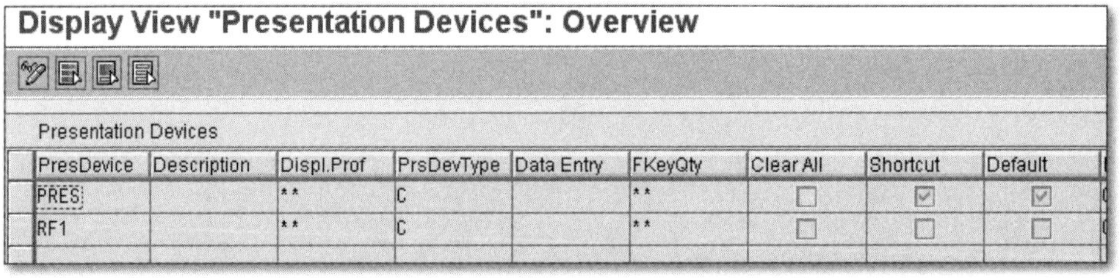

Display View "Presentation Devices": Overview

Presentation Devices

PresDevice	Description	Displ.Prof	PrsDevType	Data Entry	FKeyQty	Clear All	Shortcut	Default	
PRES		**	C		**	☐	☑	☑	
RF1		**	C		**	☐	☐	☐	

Figure 22.15 Presentation Devices Maintenance

For the presentation device, you also specify whether shortcut fields are used (via the SHORTCUT checkbox). The shortcut field is used to enter exception codes or the function key for devices that don't have function keys available. If the shortcut field is enabled the cursor always jumps to this field before leaving the screen. When devices types with physical available function keys are used, you may want to disable this function to reduce the steps of the user interaction.

You must also specify the *presentation profile* for the warehouse (as seen in Figure 22.16). This setting creates the 1:1 link between the RF Framework and the EWM warehouse number. The presentation profile is a key field used in several of the tables related to the RF Framework, allowing you, for example, to use different transactions in different warehouse locations. To assign the presentation profile in the EWM IMG, follow the menu path EXTENDED WAREHOUSE MANAGEMENT • MOBILE DATA ENTRY • ASSIGN PRESENTATION PROFILE TO WAREHOUSE.

Figure 22.16 Assigning the Presentation Profile to the Warehouse

The RF Menu

You can create menus using drag-and-drop functionality via the RF Framework Menu Manager (as seen in Figure 22.17). To access the Menu Manager in the EWM IMG, follow the EXTENDED WAREHOUSE MANAGEMENT • MOBILE DATA ENTRY • RADIO FREQUENCY (RF) FRAMEWORK •RF SCREEN MANAGER menu path, or use Transaction code /SCWM/RFMENU. The menu table includes the key fields PRESENTATION PROFILE and PERSONALIZATION PROFILE (which is also assigned to the EWM user, making the menu dependent on the user).

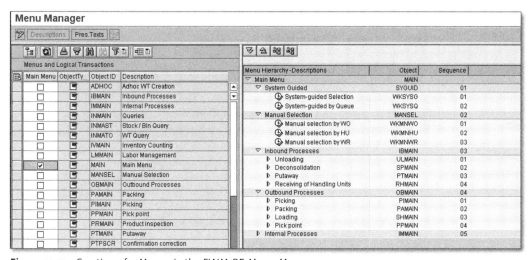

Figure 22.17 Creation of a Menu via the EWM RF Menu Manager

22.5.3 Enhancing the EWM RF Transactions

With the EWM RF Framework, the business logic is separate from the user interface and everything is maintained in the customizing. The EWM RF Framework is responsible for this flexibility and it allows you to enhance the existing EWM RF transactions. However, before we begin, we should caution you to be careful in this area, as you are affecting the standard business logic. At first, the complexity of the RF Framework may be daunting, but soon you'll realize that this provides you with the ability to flexibly enhance transactions in a consistent and sustainable way.

> **Note**
>
> As a reminder, a standard Best Practice is to always change as little as necessary. All changes that you make to the existing customizing are evaluated during runtime and can therefore impact the business logic of the transactions.

The heart of the EWM RF Framework is a huge view cluster for defining the process steps for the logical transaction. To access this view cluster in the EWM IMG, follow the menu path EXTENDED WAREHOUSE MANAGEMENT • MOBILE DATA ENTRY • RADIO FREQUENCY (RF) FRAMEWORK • DEFINE STEPS IN LOGICAL TRANSACTIONS. You can also view the tables of the view cluster in Transaction SE54 — the object name is /SCWM/RF_CUSTOM.

> **Note**
>
> In this text, in the interest of brevity, we won't explain every detail of the customizing, but provide a rough overview of the RF Framework.
>
> Additional information is available in the online help, the field help for the fields of the table, and in the RF Cookbook, which is accessible in the SAP Service Marketplace (*http://service.sap.com*). This RF Cookbook is specifically for developers who use the RF Framework to enhance existing transactions or create new ones.

All of the delivered RF transactions are customized in this view cluster (they are not accessible via a separate transaction code as in ERP WM). The definition of the logical transactions is customized in the nodes under the parent node (as you can see in Figure 22.18). For example, you can define the following:

- **Presentation profiles and personalization profiles**

  These are required to separate the logic from the screens for different warehouse numbers or different user groups.

- **Steps and states**

  These are required to divide the processes into various steps, assign the sequence of the steps, and assign the screens to the steps.

▶ **Function codes and function code texts**

These are required to create function buttons and allow you to trigger various functions from the screens.

▶ **Validation profiles**

These are required to drive the validation of the input values on the RF screens.

▶ **Logical transaction step flow**

The business logic is configured here; you can change the logic by changing the assignment of the follow-up step or by changing the function module assigned for the process step. In the assigned function module, all business logic is implemented in ABAP.

▶ **Map the logical transaction step to the subscreen**

During runtime, if a step is specified as a foreground step, the screen assigned in this table is displayed. To change the screen, you can copy and change the screen and assign the new screen in this table as a new row.

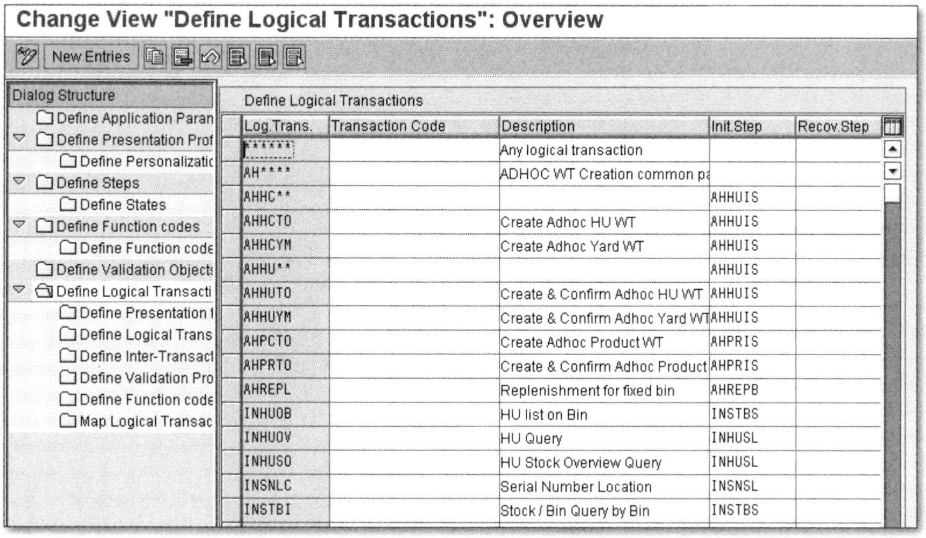

Change View "Define Logical Transactions": Overview

New Entries

Dialog Structure
☐ Define Application Param
▽ ☐ Define Presentation Prof
☐ Define Personalizatic
▽ ☐ Define Steps
☐ Define States
▽ ☐ Define Function codes
☐ Define Function code
☐ Define Validation Objects
▽ ☐ Define Logical Transacti
☐ Define Presentation f
☐ Define Logical Trans
☐ Define Inter-Transact
☐ Define Validation Pro
☐ Define Function code
☐ Map Logical Transac

Define Logical Transactions

Log.Trans.	Transaction Code	Description	Init.Step	Recov.Step	
******		Any logical transaction			
AH****		ADHOC WT Creation common pa			
AHHC**			AHHUIS		
AHHCTO		Create Adhoc HU WT	AHHUIS		
AHHCYM		Create Adhoc Yard WT	AHHUIS		
AHHU**			AHHUIS		
AHHUTO		Create & Confirm Adhoc HU WT	AHHUIS		
AHHUYM		Create & Confirm Adhoc Yard WT	AHHUIS		
AHPCTO		Create Adhoc Product WT	AHPRIS		
AHPRTO		Create & Confirm Adhoc Product	AHPRIS		
AHREPL		Replenishment for fixed bin	AHREPB		
INHUOB		HU list on Bin	INSTBS		
INHUOV		HU Query	INHUSL		
INHUSO		HU Stock Overview Query	INHUSL		
INSNLC		Serial Number Location	INSNSL		
INSTBI		Stock / Bin Query by Bin	INSTBS		

Figure 22.18 RF Framework Enhancement View Cluster

In Figure 22.19, you can see the assignment of the mapping of the logical transaction step to the subscreen.

> **Note**
>
> If you simply change the existing customizing, you would no longer have to see how the standard works. Therefore, we recommend you always copy existing entries to a new entry for a different presentation profile or personalization profile.

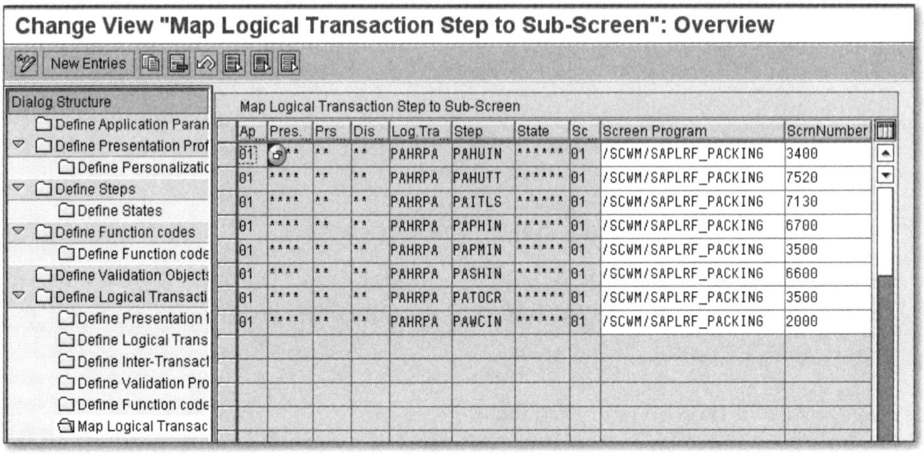

Figure 22.19 EWM RF Framework — Mapping the Subscreens to the Transaction Steps

Sometimes EWM delivers generic transactions. For example, the PI**** transactions are a good example of where we can enhance the delivered functionality. You could, for example, create a transaction, such as PIZZZZ. This allows you to use your custom transaction to enhance the functionality of the transaction while maintaining the standard transactions for the default profiles if you need to continue to use them (or copy the standard once again to a different one). However, SAP doesn't deliver such generic transactions in EWM for every business process.

22.5.4 Personalization of the EWM RF Transaction

EWM provides significant opportunities to personalize the mobile transactions, which are driven by the personalization profile (which can be created per presentation profile). As we described earlier in this chapter, you can assign the personalization profile to the EWM User via Transaction /SCWM/USER.

To personalize the mobile transactions, you can perform the following activities:

▶ Create personalized menus in the menu manager per user group and personalization profile. This allows you to control which users have access to which transactions or business functions.

▶ Use different screens per user group and personalization profile (specified in the central view cluster). For each user group, you can customize the different screens. For example, different data can be selected in the function modules and displayed to the screen.

▶ Use of different verification profiles per user group. Based on the user group and personalization profile, you can specify a different verification profile to ensure that a user must scan and verify objects on the screen (for example, verifying the quantity at the destination bin during a putaway process, which may only be required for novice users and not experienced ones).

22.6 Comparison of the Mobile Online User Interface Technologies

SAP EWM delivers the business logic and the ability to enhance and personalize mobile transactions with EWM and the RF Framework. Execution of these transactions depends on an appropriate user interface for the user on the mobile device. The selection of the technology to support the presentation of the user interface is often dependent on the hardware and software on the mobile device. In the following sections, we will describe the possible technolgies to support the mobile devices.

22.6.1 SAP Console

SAP Console is used to support text-based devices (as you can see in Figure 22.20). It's a very stable solution and already widely deployed to integrate mobile clients into the system architecture.

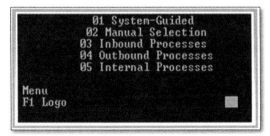

Figure 22.20 User Interface for SAP Console

In Figure 22.21, you can see a graphical representation of the architecture used to support the SAP Console. SAP Console and the required telnet server are running on an additional server. SAP Console translates the SAP User Interface Protocol DIAG to the Telnet protocol and transfers the data to the device. The client on the mobile device then presents a character-based user interface such as the one seen in Figure 22.20. The primary requirement of the telnet client is that it must support VT220 terminal emulation.

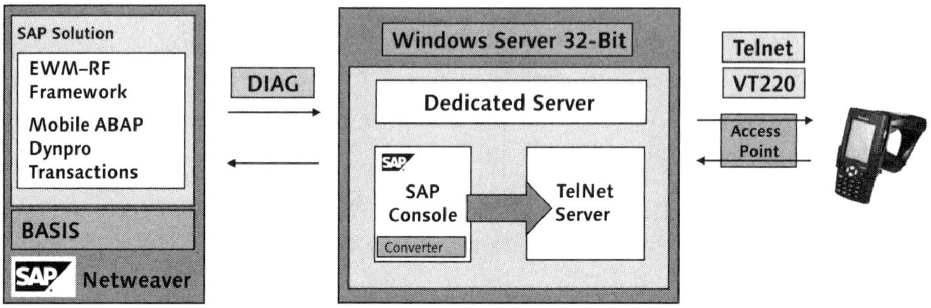

Figure 22.21 Detailed SAP Console System Landscape

SAP Console itself is just a converter without a database and therefore it doesn't save additional data somewhere. It just acts like a black box that converts the user interface during runtime. For more information and recommendations on using the SAP Console, see online support system (OSS) note 540469.

Since 2009, SAP Console also supports UTF-8 and not just a dedicated codepage. In the past, the Korean and Cyrillic font could not be used in parallel with the same SAP Console instance, but SAP now delivers a solution for that issue (for more information, see OSS note 1316470).

22.6.2 SAP Web SAPConsole

In previous years, a special version of the SAPConsole, known as the Web SAPConsole, was used to support browser-based devices, but it has since been replaced by ITSmobile. Because we no longer recommend Web SAPConsole, we will not describe the technology in detail. The defined SAP strategy for this technology is documented in OSS note 1046184.

The system landscape for Web SAPConsole is similar to SAPConsole, but requires both a browser-based client and a web server (such as IIS or Apache) to support the integration of the data to the web browser. Web SAPConsole is also designed as a black box, but Web SAPConsole converts the data to HTML instead of text-based telnet protocol. While the HTML could be changed to improve the screen, it is fairly complex to do and requires regular maintenance following system changes. ITSmobile, on the other hand, provides a much easier means for enhancing the screens presented by the browser.

22.6.3 SAP ITSmobile

The SAP Internet Transaction Server (SAP ITS) was the first approach used by SAP to enable SAP transactions for use on a web browser or the Internet. In the past, it has been used in Human Resources (HR) and Supplier Relationship Management (SRM) applications. The technology is very stable, and installations with thousands of users are common.

With ITSmobile, SAP has further enhanced the ITS to integrate optimally to mobile devices. ITSmobile is simply a user interface technology, and the business logic is implemented fully in ABAP. No data is stored in the ITSmobile application (i.e., it supports a thin client paradigm). ITSmobile is not a middleware. It runs on the same server as EWM, as it is a component of SAP NetWeaver (the underlying technical architecture for EWM).

Figure 22.22, you can see an example of an EWM screen displayed in a browser via ITSmobile.

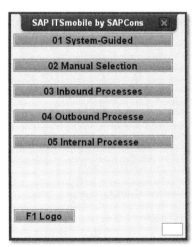

Figure 22.22 Enhanced SAP EWM ITSmobile Screen with New Layout

The first version of the ITS was a standalone deployment (as in the SAP Console architecture, an additional server was required between the backend system and the client). With SAP NetWeaver 6.40 (ERP2004), SAP brought the ITS into the backend and into the SAP kernel. In SAP NetWeaver 7.00, only an integrated version exists. As the first EWM release was delivered SAP NetWeaver NW7.00 (EWM 5.0 and EWM 5.10), only the integrated version can be used for EWM.

> **Note**
>
> Customers that use ERP warehouse management can also use the ITSmobile technology and the standalone version can be implemented there. The minimum version required is R/3 4.6C. The standalone version requires a bit more effort to implement, but the migration to the integrated version afterward can be done very quickly. Starting with ERP2005, the integrated version of ITSmobile can also be used for EWM WM.

ITSmobile can be deployed in two different ways:

▶ **Generation of HTML during execution**

  SAP provides a SAP GUI for HTML, in which the layout looks very similar to the native SAP GUI (as you can see in Figure 22.23), but it runs in a web browser.

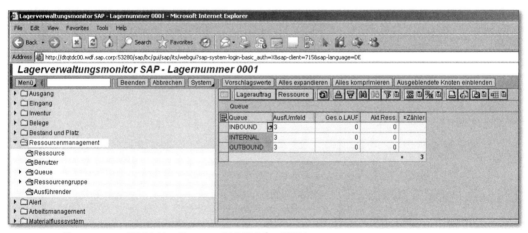

Figure 22.23 EWM Monitor over SAP GUI for HTML

▶ **Creation of business HTML template via a generator during design time**

  This option provides the basis for ITSmobile. SAP delivers a generator for integrating mobile devices. Because using the Web GUI on the mobile device provides suboptimal performance (because the ITS generates HTML and JavaScript that is optimal for a desktop PC but not for a mobile device), ITSmobile generates light HTML, which is optimal for mobile devices (with only the required HTML and JavaScript being included).

> **Note**
>
> A common bottleneck for displaying user interfaces for business functions on mobile devices is the mobile device itself. Therefore, the success of the project may depend on the selection of an appropriate device and operating system that provides sufficient throughput. Proper performance testing in a sufficient lab is highly recommended for your project.

ITSmobile is a web-based HTML technology and therefore relies on the web browser as the presentation mechanism to the user. There are two common operating system used with mobile devices — Windows Mobile and Windows CE. Windows CE generally has a newer browser than Windows Mobile. In today's market, the common versions for the OS are Windows CE 5.0 and Windows Mobile 6.1. However, the browser has its own separate version number (even thought the icon of the browser on the newest Windows Mobile platform looks like IE 7.0). There are also industrial browsers on the market, but nearly all use the standard rendering engine from Microsoft. Therefore the major decision criterion for the software of the mobile device is the operating system. SAP ITSmobile also supports Windows Mobile but there are limitations in performance, functions, and layout that you must consider.

In Figure 22.24, you can see a visual description of the process to enable an ABAP transaction via ITSmobile.

SAP has continuously improved the ITSmobile technology and generator. Therefore, we recommend that you always use the latest possible release and support packages available in your implementation project. Before starting the integration, implementing any additional relevant notes can also help prevent further issues. While there are generators provided by software and implementation partners of SAP, you should consider the capabilities and limitations of the various solutions before deciding which one to use in your implementation.

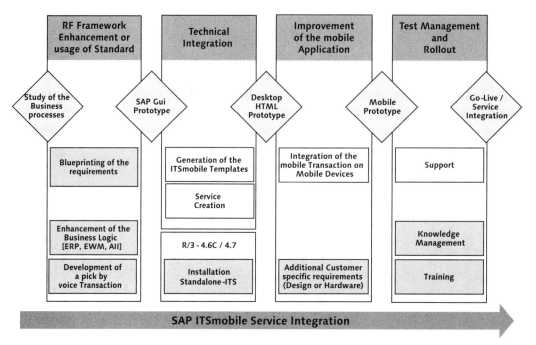

Figure 22.24 ITSmobile Service Implementation Process

Figure 22.25, shows the path of the ITSmobile technology and its display of HTML on mobile devices. A good understanding of the technology represented in the figure is important for implementing ITSmobile for mobile devices.

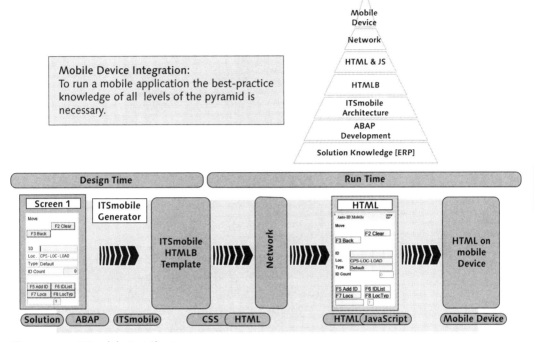

Figure 22.25 ITSmobile Fact Sheet

22.6.4 SAP ABAP and Java Web Dynpro

The Web Dynpro technology is a new SAP development approach provided by SAP NetWeaver. Web Dynpro is delivered for both Java and ABAP. However, the ABAP Web Dynpro variant currently doesn't provide support for integration with mobile devices — only Web Dynpro for Java does. In Figure 22.26, you can see the system landscape of the Java Web Dynpro technology.

With Web Dynpro, the developer only creates metadata and the server creates the correct HTML based on the client (via client recognition) during runtime. For different clients, the HTML Generator must be enhanced and changed, which can increase the maintenance and requires detailed knowledge of the clients. Web Dynpro also only allows the use of special HTML commands provided by SAP – additional standard HTML commands can't be used. Additional peripheral integration requires you to add additional HTML and JavaScript into the generated

HTML. While ITSmobile and Java Web Dynpro are similar, the primary difference is how HTML and JavaScript are created and how easy it is to enhance them.

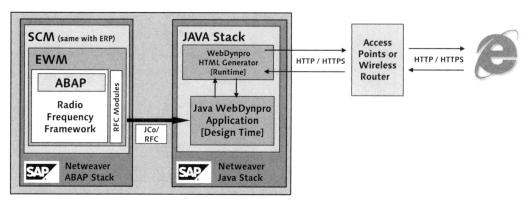

Figure 22.26 Java Web Dynpro Architecture

The RF Framework doesn't communicate directly with the Java Web Dynpro technology, and all of the standard delivered mobile transactions are only developed in ABAP and can't be used with Java Web Dynpro. Furthermore, if you use Java Web Dynpro, you would not be able to use the EWM RF Framework, and you would have to implement the mobile data transactions on your own in Java Web Dynpro. Therefore, Java Web Dynpro is not commonly used in EWM projects. Based on the effort and the TCO, it usually doesn't make sense to implement both ITSmobile and Java Web Dynpro, therefore, ITSmobile is most often chosen for the deployment on browser-based devices.

22.6.5 Third-Party Integration

The third-party integration of other mobile clients or software is also possible via the available interfaces provided by SAP. In most cases, the integration works directly via RFC or an additional server (for example, when an offline scenario is required). However, this development is not directly supported by SAP, and only the interfaces are provided within EWM. The delivered functions modules can be used, but they must be RFC enabled (which can be done by creating an RFC-enabled wrapper program), and in some cases they must be enhanced to provide the required functionality. During your implementation project, you must analyze, in detail, which functions you need to support your business processes. Even if additional client development is not required, for instance, you may still need to make some enhancements on the server side to provide the correct data in a way that the client will understand.

22.6.6 Windows Terminal Server and Citrix Integration

In mobile applications, you may want to use a Windows Terminal Server (WTS) client (such as Citrix) to run the full SAP GUI on mobile devices. Even if the full GUI would run on the device, you can choose this option, for example, if you want to avoid dropping the connection if you enter a "dead zone" in the RF coverage in the warehouse. While you can maintain connectivity using a direct connection with the SAP GUI for some time, the capability to manage the dropped connections is better with a WTS.

The WTS integration is an example of Thin Client integration. The SAP GUI session runs on the multi-client server. When using a WTS connection, you can, for example, trigger an automatic logon when your equipment goes out of range of the RF network. With this integration technique, you don't need to consider additional efforts on the SAP system if you are only using barcode scanning (which acts just like a keyboard entry). On the other hand, if you require RFID integration, additional hardware and peripheral integration may require additional effort.

22.7 Integration of the Other Technologies

In addition to mobile data entry methods for key entry and barcode scanning, you can also use other input methods, such as pick-by-voice or RFID input. In the following sections, we'll describe the various methods that you can use to utilize these input methods for EWM.

22.7.1 Pick-by-Voice Integration

Pick-by-voice is a method used to communicate with a system that allows the operator to speak into a microphone to confirm the warehouse tasks. For example, he may speak the pick quantity or the bin verification data when prompted by a screen or by a voice command via a speaker (which may be on a device with a loudspeaker or in an earpiece). To support this execution method, there are various software solutions on the market. And there are various integration methods deployed by those solution partners that are feasible for integration with EWM. In some cases, the partners may use a separate server to capture the voice interactions and integrate the data back to SAP, and in other cases, the vendor may provide direct integration to SAP via the Web SAPConsole or ITSmobile. (In Chapter 23, Integration with Other Applications, we describe some of these other options for voice integration). However, in this chapter, we'll focus on the method that is closest to the SAP standard delivered solution.

SAP delivers within ITSmobile a pick-by-voice integration based on the W3C Voice-XML standards. With SAP ITSmobile, users communicate directly with the SAP system and no additional server or middleware is required. In Figure 22.27, you can see a diagram of the system architecture for the pick-by-voice using the voice XML browser together with ITSmobile.

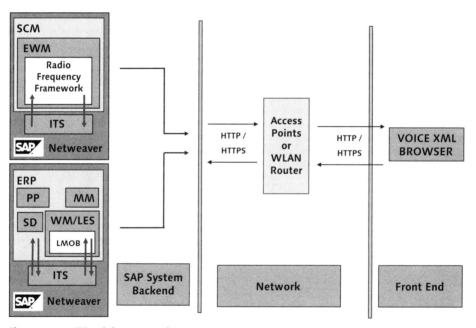

Figure 22.27 ITSmobile Voice Architecture

Communication with the SAP system works in both directions over Voice XML (a common standard defined by the W3C standards body). If the system sends a voice command to a user, an XML data stream is sent to a client running on the mobile device. This client must understand Voice XML and transform it to speech. In the opposite direction, the client must translate the speech using voice recognition to a string and send this data back to the SAP system.

Generally, the voice client is specifically "trained" and only understands specific commands or words. Additional logic can be implemented to improve and increase the efficiency of a pick-by-voice process. This additional logic could be stored in the mobile transactions. For example, in the ABAP Workbench (Transaction SE80), the ABAP developer can add information to the screen properties. On the other hand, implementing these changes to the transaction to support a mobile voice process would require developing a special mobile transaction that stores the special voice commands.

SAP EWM currently doesn't deliver voice transactions that can be used directly in the EWM standard. The current mobile picking transaction can't be used, because the screen flow is not optimized for a voice process. One reason that SAP doesn't deliver such standard processes is that voice processes are often very customer specific. Experience with customers who implement voice processes indicates that each customer specifically designs their voice-driven processes to optimize that process in the warehouse, as they are often high-volume processes.

Implementing a mobile voice solution on your own would require you to:

▸ Develop an ABAP transaction (for example, a simple transaction developed without using the RF Framework is still possible)

▸ Create and development an ITSmobile service with the voice HTMLB generator

▸ Deploy a mobile browser on a device that understands Voice XML and can transfer speech into a string (via voice recognition)

Because of the special skill sets involved and the need to use special hardware, implementing a voice solution in the warehouse often involves engaging an implementation partner and a hardware partner (if the implementation partner does not resell the hardware).

22.7.2   RFID Integration

RFID is a technology that allows a reader to read information from a specifically formatted tag (or Electronic Product Code (EPC) tag) without having direct line of sight to the tag. The data is transmitted through the air using radio frequency signals. SAP supports RFID integration into business processes within the warehouse using the Auto-ID Infrastructure (AII) solution. In this chapter, we won't cover every detail about RFID, but we'll briefly describe the business processes that support the use of RFID scanning and the methods used to integrate the data.

In the warehouse, there are at least three business processes for which RFID provides some benefits, including:

▶ Collective processing — To avoid scanning each carton individually, you can use gates or mobile devices to read all of the objects and transfer the data to the system. Additional checks, which are dependent on the business process, may be required to synchronize the data.

▶ Validation of data — To ensure that all of the necessary items are included within a container, you can use a gate to read the objects and let the system evaluate if all of the necessary products are on the container. A visual display, such as a light, can indicate that the data is correct.

▶ Automatic tracking of the objects — Data related to the product movements is automatically stored and the data repository may be used for reporting. For example, SAP Event Manager or the Auto-ID Object Event Repository can be used to report product movements, status, or current locations.

System Integration Using SAP Auto-ID Infrastructure

In a barcode enabled process, you can scan the barcode with a scanner and the data is immediately passed to the field where the curser is positioned. The technical integration for this scenario is not so complex. However, when using RFID, the process management and integration are a bit more complex.

To manage these scenarios, EWM relies on the SAP AII to capture and report (via RFC interface) the information that it needs to support the business processes. AII runs on the SAP NetWeaver stack and supports the following functions:

▶ Integration and management of hardware (such as mobile RFID devices and gate readers)

▶ Interface to integrate hardware that runs in the background without a user interface (such as RFID gates and RFID printers)

▶ Rule engine to manage different processes

▶ Flexible definition of ID types to manage different RFID standards

▶ Integration of mobile devices, including mobile transactions supported by ITSmobile

▸ Documents management for the integration of the ERP documents

▸ Web Dynpro user interfaces to display documents, objects, and events

There are two methods of integration for RFID, namely:

▸ Background-specific integration of gates

▸ Front-end driven integration of mobile devices

The frontend (or foreground) integration of mobile devices can be enabled by ITSmobile, however, this integration is more complex than the simple integration for barcode scanning. The ITSmobile technology generates HTML coding, and only runs in a browser. Therefore, the device manufacturers must provide drivers that can be called from the web browser and that can communicate with an RFID antenna and the hardware. (Today, only a few device manufacturers support this requirement.) As long as such a driver is provided, ITSmobile delivers a framework to capture and integrate the RFID data.

RFID Integration in SAP EWM

The following RFID-enabled processes are supported within EWM:

▸ Unloading

▸ Loading

▸ Warehouse task confirmation

▸ Packing

▸ "Tag and ship" (or "slap and ship") process

You can also implement other process with RFID, but you must specifically code the integration to these other processes.

Figure 22.28, is a graphical representation of the inbound process with RFID support. The RFID process starts with the recognition of the RFID tags during unloading. AII sends the message to EWM and the unloading and goods receipt posting is triggered. The confirmation of the HU warehouse task can also be performed automatically if the destination bin has a stationary reader.

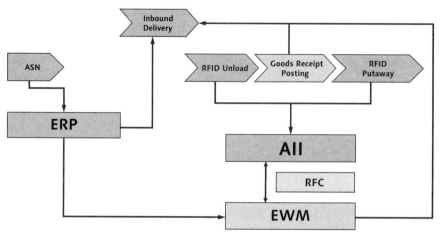

Figure 22.28 RFID-enabled Inbound Process in EWM

Figure 22.29, is a graphical representation of the outbound process with RFID support. Once the OUTBOUND DELIVERY is replicated from ERP to EWM the picking is started (which is not commonly an RFID-enabled process). When the picking label is set to be printed, the *tag commissioning* (which writes the EPC data to the RFID tag) of AII can be initiated, and instead of a picking label being printed, an RFID tag can be created. The loading is performed with AII functions, and after the loading is finished, a goods issue is triggered in EWM.

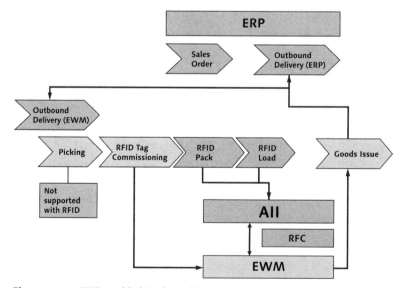

Figure 22.29 RFID-enabled Outbound Process in EWM

EWM and AII both support the printing of RFID HU labels.

In Figure 22.30, you can see the technical integration architecture for the integration between AII and EWM. This integration occurs via RFC. Mobile devices may be integrated via AII or EWM, because both systems are running on SAP NetWeaver and ITSmobile can be used with both. Because EWM offers a better integration with the RF Framework, it is often beneficial to integrate the mobile devices directly with EWM.

The integration of gates occurs in the background via AII. When the RFID tags are read, the device controller creates XML messages to send to AII. Based on the commands included within the XML message and the device ID, various processes can be triggered in AII via the RULE ENGINE, including sending the data to EWM for confirmation of the business process steps. When the data is received in EWM via the RFC interface, the relevant processes are executed (e.g., loading, unloading, task confirmation).

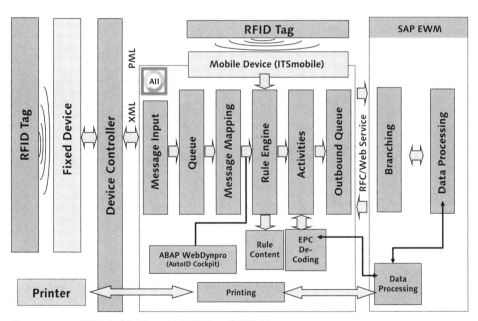

Figure 22.30 RFID Architecture SAP EWM and SAP AII

22.8 Summary

In this chapter, we described the various methods of mobile data capture for EWM, including mobile device integration and how EWM handles the challenges specific to mobile devices via the RF Framework. We also provided an overview of the different user interface technologies and the different possibilities you can integrate mobile devices into EWM. And, finally, we described the integration of pick-by-voice and RFID.

In the following chapters, we'll discuss the integration of EWM to other components, the Post-Processing Framework (PPF), and authorizations, roles, and archiving.

Extended Warehouse Management (EWM) is directly and indirectly integrated with several other SAP components and other applications to create a holistic solution for supporting warehouse processes.

23   Integration with Other Applications

To enable certain processes in the warehouse, the SAP EWM solution is integrated directly or indirectly with various functions of other SAP components, including:

- Customer Relationship Management (CRM)
- Supplier Network Collaboration (SNC)
- Service Parts Planning (SPP)
- Global Available to Promise (gATP)
- Global Trade Services (GTS)
- Environment, Health, and Safety (EHS)
- Business Intelligence (BI)
- Various component of ERP, including:
  - Master Data
  - Inventory Management (IM)
  - Purchasing
  - Sales and Distribution (SD)
  - Production Planning (PP)
  - Finance (FI), and
  - Human Resources (HR)
- Material Flow Systems (MFS)
- Warehouse Subsystems

In this chapter, we will describe the interaction with these other applications, the functional purpose, and, in some cases, briefly describe the integration. In other cases, we may refer to the chapter(s) where the full description and details of the setup are described.

23.1 Integration with CRM

The integration between CRM and EWM is indirect — the data that is required by one system is passed from the other to ERP and then ERP passes the needed data to the target system. For example, business partners (BPs) (customer, vendors, employees, etc.) can be created in CRM and transmitted to ERP, and then the BPs are replicated from ERP to EWM. On the flip side, information that is needed by CRM, for example, outbound delivery status data or items that were picked for a kit, are passed from EWM to ERP and then ERP passes the status and line item data to CRM.

It is important to understand how this integration works so that you can make the correct settings and perform the correct tests to ensure the entire end-to-end business process works correctly. Therefore, the following sections describe the methods for integrating data from CRM to EWM and from EWM to CRM.

It is not a requirement to have a CRM system in your SAP landscape, and there are many processes that support using EWM without CRM, but CRM does provide some unique capabilities. For more information regarding scenarios that are supported by the various deployment options, see Chapter 26, Deploying Extended Warehouse Management.

23.1.1 Business Partners

If a CRM system is used for order management, you must have the BP data (which includes customers, vendors, third-party suppliers, carriers, freight forwarders, plants, and employees) in the CRM system and the ERP system, and the BP data must also be integrated with the EWM system. You can either choose to use CRM as the leading system for BP data, in which case the data is then integrated to ERP and subsequently to EWM, or you can use ERP as the leading system for BP data, in which case the data is then integrated to both CRM and EWM. Either way, the data in EWM comes directly from ERP, and only indirectly from CRM. In Chapter 5, Other Warehouse Master Data, we describe in more detail how the BP data is integrated from ERP to EWM. The integration between CRM and ERP is not described in detail there, as it is not relevant to EWM integration.

23.1.2   Outbound Orders and Deliveries

Outbound orders (or sales orders) and deliveries are integrated from CRM to EWM indirectly through ERP. Outbound orders created in CRM are integrated with ERP as either sales orders or unchecked deliveries. Which of these integration methods is used is dependent on the direct delivery distribution flag in CRM. In earlier releases of CRM and ERP, there was also a service parts management flag that played a role in this distribution as well, but in later releases of ERP, the dependency on the service parts management flag has been significantly decreased and the direct delivery distribution flag in CRM has become the only relevant one for controlling the interface.

If the direct delivery distribution flag is activated in CRM, the sales order creation in CRM results in the creation of an unchecked outbound delivery in ERP. The unchecked outbound delivery is converted to a checked outbound delivery via the Logistics • Logistics Execution • Outbound Process • Outbound Delivery • Create • Collective Processing of Documents Due for Delivery • Check and Combine Unchecked Outbound Deliveries ERP Easy Access menu path, or by using Transaction VL10UC. Once the unchecked outbound delivery is created, the delivery is interfaced with EWM and creates an outbound delivery request (ODR). In EWM, the ODR is then converted to an outbound delivery order (ODO). Once the ODO is picked and goods issued in EWM, an EWM outbound delivery is created, and the outboard delivery is interfaced back with ERP. In ERP, the status update to the outbound delivery via the integration from EWM is subsequently integrated to the sales order in CRM. The method and the setup for the integration between ERP and EWM are described in detail in Chapter 10, Outbound Processing.

If the direct delivery distribution flag is not activated in CRM, the sales order creation in CRM results in replication of the sales order to ERP. The creation of the outbound delivery in ERP occurs via the delivery due list (for example, via Transaction VL10A, which can be accessed via the ERP Easy Access menu path Logistics • Logistics Execution • Outbound Process • Outbound Delivery • Create • Collective Processing of Documents Due for Delivery • Sales Orders). The integration of the outbound delivery and the processing in EWM takes place in the same manner as described in the previous paragraph. When the goods issued outboard delivery is posted from EWM to ERP, the status and document flow of the sales order in ERP is updated, and the CRM sales order is subsequently updated via the ERP-CRM interface.

23.1.3   CRM Sales Order Status Updates

Once the outbound delivery for the sales order is created in ERP and distributed to EWM, the status of the sales order item on CRM is updated to Completely Delivered. When the warehouse tasks are created and confirmed and the ODO is post goods issued from EWM, the final outbound delivery is created and transferred to ERP, where it updates the ERP outbound delivery. From ERP, the update to the outbound delivery subsequently updates the CRM sales order. Once the CRM sales order is confirmed, the billing may be executed in CRM.

23.1.4   Returns Order Processing

A return order created in CRM is transferred to ERP as a returns delivery, and the confirmed inbound delivery is subsequently created in ERP (either based on a return Advance Shipping Notice (ASN) from the customer submitted via Electronic Data Interchange (EDI) or received from SNC or manually created in ERP). The resulting inbound delivery is subsequently transferred to EWM in much the same way as an inbound delivery for an inbound purchase order, as described in detail in Chapter 9, Inbound Processing. In EWM, an inspection is performed (optionally) and goods receipt is posted for the delivery. The inspection results are transferred from EWM to ERP via the inspection document and subsequently transferred to CRM by ERP in an inspection confirmation. In CRM, you can then perform the pricing and billing (for credit to the customer) based on the inspection outcome, including the codes assigned within EWM during the detailed inspection. Figure 23.1 shows the detailed steps involved in the returns order processing using CRM and SNC.

If CRM is not involved in the return order process, the return order can be created in ERP and the return delivery transferred to EWM. In EWM, the return order can be received and the goods receipt transferred to ERP via the inbound delivery. Subsequent billing in ERP would provide credit to the customer. Inspection results from EWM do not affect the billing when using ERP sales order or ERP billing, as of release ERP 6.0 Enhancement Package 4.

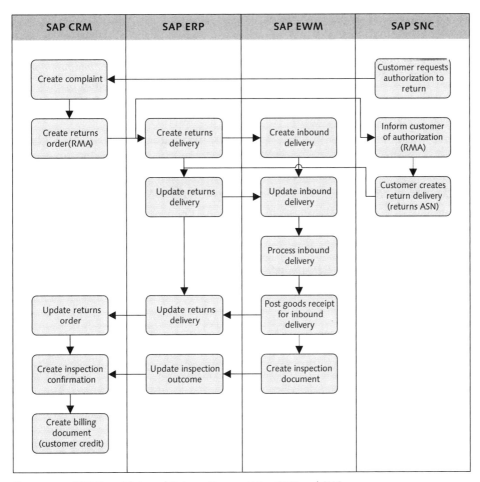

Figure 23.1 SAP Complaints and Returns Process Using CRM and SNC

23.2 Integration with SNC

SNC can be used to collaborate with both suppliers and customers via the Internet. For SNC scenarios that include logistics processes, the data relevant to EWM will be interfaced with EWM through ERP. In this section, we will describe the SNC scenarios that include EWM integration.

23.2.1 Integration with ASNs

When you create a purchase order in ERP, you can submit the purchase order to the vendor, either via EDI or SNC. When the vendor prepares the order for shipment and physically ships the product to your warehouse, he may submit the notification of the shipment (the ASN) to you via your SNC system. If so, the ASN created in SNC will result in the creation of an inbound delivery in ERP, including the relevant packing information, if it was included on the ASN. This inbound delivery is subsequently integrated to EWM and creates an inbound delivery notification (IDN). The IDN is converted by EWM to an inbound delivery, either automatically or manually, depending on the settings in EWM. The integration of the inbound delivery to EWM and the processing of the inbound delivery in EWM are described in detail in Chapter 9.

23.2.2 Integration of Return ASNs

When a customer wants to return a product for any reason, you can create a return sales order and provide them a return material authorization (RMA) number. When the customer receives the RMA, prepares the product for return, and physically ships the product, they can inform you through the SNC by sending a shipment notification. The shipment notification results in the creation of an inbound delivery in ERP, including any relevant packaging information that was included in the shipment notification. The inbound delivery is distributed to EWM, where an IDN is created.

From the IDN, the EWM inbound delivery is created, and the relevant inspection document for inspection of the returned product is also tied to the inbound delivery. Once the product is received and inspected, the inspection results and the inbound delivery statuses are relayed to ERP where the inspection outcome is updated, and the inspection confirmation is subsequently transferred to CRM to support the customer billing for credit. Figure 23.1 shows this process in more detail.

The inbound delivery processing for returns in EWM, including setup of the quality inspection engine to support the inbound inspection of the returned products, is also described in detail in Chapter 9.

23.3 Integration with SPP

EWM is integrated both directly and indirectly with SPP), a component of SCM used for planning service parts or other similar products in lieu of Advanced Planning and Optimization (APO)), for both master data and transactional business processes. In this section, we will describe how SPP demand data is read directly from EWM to support slotting plus how SPP processes for procurement and internal transfers are integrated indirectly to EWM.

23.3.1 Demand and Forecast Data for Slotting

During slotting, EWM can use the demand and sales order item data directly from the EWM product master (which can be uploaded to the product master from an external source), or it can read the demand and forecast data directly from the SPP system during the slotting run. If EWM reads the data from SPP, it does not need to (and, in fact, does not) store the data in EWM — instead, it simply reads the data directly and then uses that data during the slotting run. In Figure 23.2, you can see the forecast data that has been entered in SPP (in this case it was created manually, but it could also be generated by SPP).

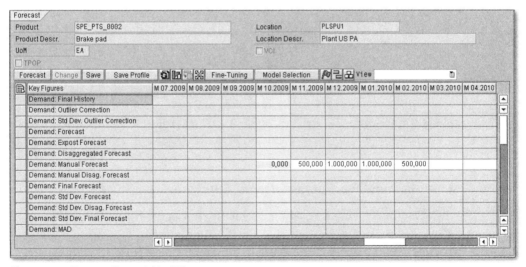

Figure 23.2 Forecast Data within SPP

In Figure 23.3, you can see that the forecast data for the current month and the next four months was read during slotting and was used in the determination of the slotting parameters.

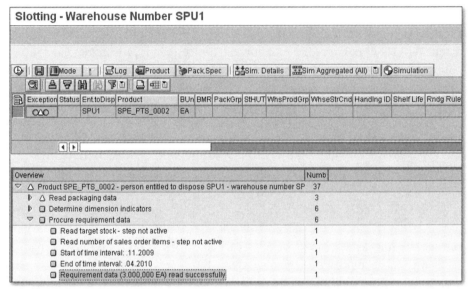

Figure 23.3 Requirement Data Is Read Directly from SPP and Used By the Slotting Algorithm to Determine the Slotting Results

---

Note

Between versions 5.0 and 5.1 of EWM, there was a change in the transaction data layer (TDL) setup for the EWM connection to SPP. To ensure that you have the correct settings in the TDL, or if you have trouble with the connection between EWM and SPP, review OSS note 836899 (TDL: Setup of customizing for EWM slotting — SPP data access).

23.3.2 Inbound Receipts for Vendor Purchases

When SPP (or APO or material requirements planning (MRP)) determines a need for procuring parts, it will generate a planned order in ERP. Within the ERP system, this planned order is converted to either a production order, if the material is produced in-house, or a purchase order, if the material is externally procured. If a purchase order is created, the expected receipt can be transferred to EWM in one of three ways.

The preferred method is to create an inbound delivery based on the ASN received from a vendor, as this reduces the data entry and validation required within the warehouse. Another method is to manually create an inbound delivery within ERP (using Transaction VL60 or VL31N) based on the expected materials and quantities to be received on a particular date. Often, this is a best guess based on the available information, or it can be created based on specific information provided by the vendor, for example, via phone, fax, or email. Finally, you can also elect to integrate the purchase orders directly to EWM as expected goods receipts (EGRs) and perform the goods receipt in the warehouse directly against the EGR.

More details on the integration of purchase orders are provided later in this chapter, and inbound processing is also covered in Chapter 9.

23.3.3 Inbound and Outbound Deliveries for Stock Transfers

If SPP (or APO) identifies a need to transfer stock within your own network, it will create a stock transfer requisition in SCM. Once the stock transfer requisition is approved in SCM, a stock transport order (STO) is created and transferred to ERP via the core interface (CIF).

When the STO is created, the first step in the transfer of the inventory is to create an outbound delivery for the sending location. If the sending location is controlled by an EWM-managed warehouse, the outbound delivery will be distributed to the relevant EWM system. Once the resulting ODO is picked, packed, and shipped, the completed ODO is post goods issued and the resulting outbound delivery is interfaced back to the ERP system.

In ERP, you can elect to automatically create the inbound delivery at the receiving location, or you can create the inbound delivery manually, or, if the receiving location is not EWM managed, you could elect to receive the stock manually via the STO (using Transaction MB1A or MIGO). To create the inbound delivery automatically, you should use the SPED output condition on the outbound delivery with the relevant determination and requirements assigned to the output type. This output condition, when processed, will result in the creation of the inbound delivery and will automatically transfer any handling units (HUs) assigned to the outbound delivery to the inbound delivery so that the receiving location can use the HUs for receiving the products.

23.3.4 Kit to Stock

When SPP identifies a need for stock of a particular kit, it will generate a planned order in ERP. In ERP, the planned order may be converted to a production order. If the production order is created for an EWM managed storage location, with both the issuing location for the components and the receiving location for the finished product (the kit) assigned to the EWM location, then the Kit to Stock process may be triggered in EWM.

To start the process, you must create and release the production order and then trigger the warehouse management staging from the production order. The warehouse management staging will result in the creation of an outbound delivery, which will then be distributed to EWM. In EWM, the components for the kit are picked and packed (either during the picking process or separately at a kitting work center, depending on the settings in EWM), and delivered to the production staging area for the work center of the production order. The inbound delivery for goods receipt of the kit stock is created at the same time as the outbound delivery indicated earlier and can also be found in EWM. Based on the inbound delivery, you can perform the goods receipt for the kits in EWM, just as described in Chapter 9.

23.4 Integration with Global ATP

In addition to relying on Global ATP to confirm availability for items on sales orders in CRM or ERP, the EWM also integrates indirectly with Global ATP to support the cross-docking processes. Specifically, the event-driven quantity assignment (EDQA) within Global ATP checks for open backorders and requirements for STOs when a goods receipt is performed within the warehouse, and if a backorder can be confirmed or an STO can be created, the resulting outbound delivery is then created and transferred to EWM. In Figure 23.4, you can see the flow of the process.

Cross-docking processes, including those dependent on the Global ATP, are described in detail in Chapter 17, Cross-Docking.

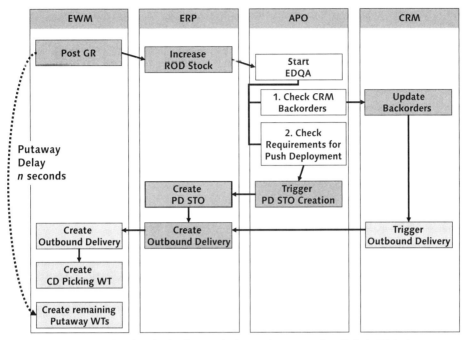

Figure 23.4 Process Flow for Check of Cross-docking Relevance within Global ATP, Using the EDQA

23.5 Integration with Global Trade Services (GTS)

EWM is also indirectly integrated with SAP GTS for tracking bonded ware-house stock and creating intrastate declarations for transfers of stock between countries.

The concept of bonded warehouse stock is that certain stock that arrives from a foreign country may only be relevant for import duties to be paid on the stock if it is consumed within the same country, and only at the time of consumption (not while it is sitting in the warehouse awaiting disposition). If the stock is redistrib-uted out of the stock before the import duties are paid, then the duty payment can be avoided entirely. The tracking of the stock levels for duty paid and duty unpaid stock (also known as bonded warehouse stock) is a function of GTS and is dependent on the real-time updates of both the inventory movements and the related duty payments.

To enable the bonded warehouse stock functionality, the inventory transferred in and out of the warehouse is transmitted from EWM to ERP and from ERP to GTS. In GTS, the determination of whether the outbound movements are taken from the duty paid stock or duty unpaid stock is made depending on the source and destination location (i.e., whether the products are shipped in country or out of country) — for domestic shipments, duty paid stock is consumed first (and duties are scheduled for payment for any quantities taken from duty unpaid stock), and for stock shipped internationally, duty unpaid stock is consumed first (and therefore the duties to be paid are avoided, though there may be duties relevant to the consumption at the receiving country).

Internal processes such as inventory adjustments and scrapping procedures in EWM are also integrated with GTS. For inventory adjustments, the inventory adjustment to the stock in ERP for materials labeled as bonded stock results in a work list entry being created in GTS, which will result in a bonded warehouse stock adjustment. When you generate planned scrapping, a customs declaration and scrapping list will be generated in GTS to support the authorization by customs authorities. Once the scrapping of duty unpaid goods is approved, then you can execute the transport order and outbound delivery for delivering the materials to be scrapped, including the picking in EWM.

GTS also supports the creation of intrastat documentation for STO movements between countries. The mode of transport and route assigned to the OD coming back to ERP from EWM is used in GTS to determine whether an intrastat declaration is required. If so, the intrastat declaration is created with GTS.

23.6 Integration with Other Applications

EWM is integrated with SAP ERP EHS (also called EH&S) for:

▶ Determining route compatibility of dangerous goods to be shipped with other materials

▶ Providing appropriate texts for printing of dangerous goods information on shipping documents

▶ Performing storage checks for hazardous substances for putaway in the warehouse

▶ Providing appropriate texts for warehouse workers via RF-enabled devices

▶ Providing inventory lists of hazardous substances in the warehouse

To support the preceding processes, the EHS dangerous goods master data, the hazardous substance master data, and the phrase management data is transferred from ERP to EWM and stored on EWM for use during route determination, putaway bin determination, document printing, and RF processing.

> **Note**
>
> The EHS data is transferred from ERP to EWM via Application Link and Enabling (ALE) separately and subsequent to the CIF integration of the product master data.

23.7 Integration with BW

SAP provides delivered content within SAP BW and delivered extractors for transferring data from EWM to BW to further analyze warehouse-related data. The connection to BW and the use of BW for warehouse analysis are described further in Chapter 15, Warehouse Monitoring and Reporting.

23.8 Master Data Integration

Certain master data within EWM is initiated in other systems, for example, in CRM, ERP, SCM, other EWM systems, or even in legacy systems. For example, material master data originates in ERP and is then enhanced with the warehouse-specific data within the EWM system; BPs are initiated either in CRM or ERP; packaging specifications can be created in one EWM system and then transferred to other relevant EWM systems; and demand data for products, if it is not captured directly from SPP; can be integrated from legacy demand capture or forecasting systems.

These master data are described in detail in this text, especially in Chapter 4, Product Master Data, and Chapter 5.

23.9   Integration with Inventory Management (IM)

To enable processes such as Global ATP and FI, which are dependent on real-time inventory updates in ERP and integration of the inventory to other systems, EWM must constantly inform ERP about changes in the inventory of the warehouse. Sometimes the inventory is adjusted via transactional business processes, such as goods receipts for inbound deliverys or goods issues for outbound deliveries; sometimes the inventory is updated via posting changes, which can be initiated in ERP or in EWM; and sometimes adjustments to the inventory must be made to the inventory based on discrepancies found during physical inventory (PI), differences in stock quantities found during placement or removal, differences on inbound receipts or stock transfers, or other out-of-sync situations that result from any number of system or process failures. In this section, we will briefly describe the methods for integration and update of inventory values between EWM and ERP.

23.9.1   Adjustments from Inbound and Outbound Deliveries

When inbound deliveries or ODOs are posted for goods receipt or goods issue in EWM, the corresponding document (inbound delivery or final outbound delivery) is transferred to ERP and the delivery document in ERP is subsequently posted. During the posting of the delivery in ERP, the material document is posted in ERP Materials Management (MM) and the relevant financial postings also occur in ERP FI. The document flow of the delivery displays the material document, and from the material document, you can directly access the financial documents. These processes are covered in detail in Chapters 9 and 10.

23.9.2   Posting Changes

Posting changes can be driven from ERP or initiated within EWM. When posting changes are initiated via ERP, a posting change document is created in ERP and transferred to EWM as a posting change request. The posting change in the warehouse is generated from the posting change request when the request is activated, and the warehouse tasks are generated with reference to the posting changes. The warehouse tasks for execution of the posting change may be created automatically by EWM via the post--processing framework (PPF) action, according to the relevant configuration.

Posting changes can also be generated directly in EWM by creating a posting change and specifying the source and destination stock type appropriately (for more information regarding stock types in EWM, see Chapter 6, Warehouse Stock Management). For these manually generated posting changes, the PPF actions automatically create the warehouse tasks as all of the necessary data has already been provided in the posting change document.

Posting changes are described further in Chapter 12, Internal Warehouse Movements.

23.9.3 Physical Inventory Adjustments

Inventory adjustments as a result of discrepancies found during warehouse transactions and during warehouse PI counts are transferred to ERP via the difference analyzer, which can be accessed from the EWM Easy Access menu via the EXTENDED WAREHOUSE MANAGEMENT • PHYSICAL INVENTORY • DIFFERENCE ANALYZER menu path, or using Transaction code /SCWM/DIFF_ANALYZER. PI adjustments are discussed in detail in Chapter 14, Physical Inventory.

Inventory adjustments driven from ERP are transferred to ERP via the respective integration documents, including transfer posting requests for requested scrap adjustments or changes in stock type, outbound deliveries for goods issues to cost centers or other goods issues, and inbound deliveries for receipts from vendors or returns from customers. These topics are covered in detail in Chapters 9, 10, and 12.

23.9.4 Comparing and Synchronizing Inventory

In general, the inventory between EWM and ERP should be kept in sync via the standard integration of transactions such as inbound deliveries and outbound deliveries, transfer posting, and PI adjustments. However, there may be situations where the inventories are out of sync for some reason. In these cases, it can be useful to compare the inventories between EWM and ERP. This can be accomplished via the STOCK COMPARISON transaction available in EWM, which can be accessed from the EWM Easy Access menu via the EXTENDED WAREHOUSE MANAGEMENT • PHYSICAL INVENTORY • PERIODIC PROCESSING • STOCK COMPARISON ERP menu path, or using Transaction code /SCWM/ERP_STOCKCHECK.

In the STOCK COMPARISON transaction, you can compare inventory of all products or for selected products, and you can specify whether you want to view the results for all comparisons or only for products that contain differences between ERP and EWM. You can also specify whether or not to consider unprocessed queues or intermediate documents (IDocs) in the evaluation of stock differences. If there are unprocessed queues, you would want to consider these, however, there may be situations where you do not — for instance, if you are trying to reconcile inventory in case there are unprocessed queues that cannot be processed due to some legitimate irreconcilable cause.

In Figure 23.5, you can see the selection screen for the comparison. Note that we included a specific material number and deselected the default selection to DISPLAY DIFFERENCES ONLY to show the actual results of the comparison.

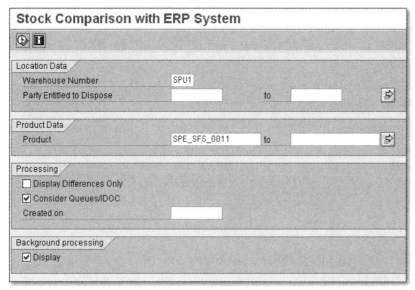

Figure 23.5 Selection Screen for the Stock Comparison between EWM and ERP

In Figure 23.6, you can see the actual results. Note that the quantities of the total stock for ERP and EWM match in this case.

Status	Product	Plant	SLoc	Prod.Desc.	Batch	Ent.toDisp	Owner	Tpe	Use	RU	NST	Description	CW-Relev.	No ERP Stk	Unit	Stock WM	Stock ERP
☐	SPE_SFS_0011	SPU1	AFS	Tire		SPU1	SPU1				FF	Unrestricted-Use Stock	☐	☐	EA	2.997	2.997
☐	SPE_SFS_0011	SPU1	ROD	Tire		SPU1	SPU1				FF	Unrestricted-Use Stock	☐	☐	EA	0	0

Figure 23.6 Results for the Stock Comparison between ERP and EWM

23.10   Integration with Purchasing

EWM is integrated with the Purchasing functions of ERP both indirectly and directly. On one hand, ASNs are created for purchase orders and the resulting inbound deliveries are transferred to EWM. On the other hand, purchase orders can be directly transferred from ERP to EWM and the resulting EGRs can be used to perform the goods receipt in EWM without relying on the creation of an inbound delivery. In the following sections, we will describe these methods of integration between EWM and Purchasing, and an additional method of creating an inbound receipt that doesn't rely on creating a purchase order ahead of time.

Inbound processing, including processing of inbound deliveries and EGRs, is described in further detail in Chapter 9.

23.10.1   Transfer of ASNs and Inbound Deliveries

When you create a purchase order in ERP, you may often transfer the purchase order to the vendor via EDI or other electronic means, or you can inform the vendor in other various ways (fax, email, etc.). Similarly, the vendor may provide purchase order confirmations and ASNs via EDI, other electronic means, email, fax, phone, or in other various ways. If the ASN is received electronically, you can automatically create an inbound delivery in ERP, or you can create the inbound delivery manually via Transactions VL31N or VL60. Subsequently, the inbound delivery is transferred automatically to EWM. In EWM, you can use the inbound delivery to process the goods receipt when the product arrives at the warehouse.

23.10.2 Downloading Expected Receipts for Purchase Orders

If the vendor does not provide ASNs or you do not otherwise create inbound deliveries for purchase orders, you can also choose to download the purchase orders to EWM as EGRs and process the inbound receipt of goods based on the EGRs. You can also use EGRs to add additional items to an existing inbound delivery, if, for instance, the vendor provides additional products in the same container as the product on the inbound delivery because there was additional space available, but the vendor did not inform you ahead of time. To download the EGR, you can schedule report /SCWM/ERP_DLV_DELETE in EWM, or you can execute report /SPE/INB_EGR_CREATE within SAP ERP to generate the EGR in the EWM system.

23.10.3 Inbound Delivery Creation in EWM

If an inbound delivery doesn't exist and an EGR doesn't exist, you can create an inbound delivery within EWM. Within the inbound delivery processing transaction (/SCWM/PRDI), you can create an inbound delivery. Selecting the CREATE INBOUND DELIVERY button results in calling the ERP inbound delivery creation transaction (VL60) directly. Once the inbound delivery is created, the delivery is immediately available in ERP and EWM. You may then continue to use the inbound delivery for processing in EWM as in the steps described previously.

23.11 Integration with ERP Sales and Distribution

EWM is indirectly integrated with ERP SD via outbound deliveries for sales orders and inbound deliveries for return orders.

23.11.1 Integrating Deliveries from ERP to EWM

Once you create sales orders for the fulfillment of products to a customer in ERP, you can then create an outbound delivery with reference to the sales order. When the outbound delivery is created for a plant and storage location that maps to a warehouse that is controlled by EWM (see Chapter 2, Organizational Structure, for more details regarding the mapping of the plant and storage location to the warehouse), then the delivery is transferred to the relevant EWM system where it creates an ODR. Once you create the ODO with reference to the ODR in EWM and the ODO is processed and the goods issue is posted, the final outbound delivery is created. The outbound delivery is transferred to ERP and the goods issue for the outbound delivery occurs there (and the subsequent updates to IM and FI also take place).

See Chapter 8, Integration from ERP to EWM, and Chapter 10 for more details regarding the integration of outbound deliveries.

23.11.2 Processes Supported Using ERP SD

There are some differences in the supported functions when using EWM with ERP SD versus CRM. The following functions are supported with ERP SD:

- Direct sales for service parts orders (including serial number requirements)
- Goods issues for internal consumption (e.g., for counter sales)

- Invoice before goods issue

- Cancellation of goods issue for outbound deliveries

- Kit to order (using sales bills of materials (BoMs)); though sales BoMs can't be used for other scenarios with EWM

- Outbound consolidation with STO to shipping facility (Global ATP is required)

- Bonded stock (GTS is required)

- Returns to vendor (RTV)

- Returns to plant

23.12   Integration with PP

EWM is integrated with PP for inbound processing (production receiving), outbound processing (production supply of raw materials or components), and Kit to Stock processes.

23.12.1 Production Receiving

EWM can be directly integrated with PP by downloading production orders for performing goods receipts with reference to the production orders. When you create the production orders in ERP, you can extract the production orders to EWM as EGRs in the same way as described previously for purchase orders. These EGRs can then be used in EWM to execute the goods receipt when the product arrives from production. For more information on using the EGRs for production orders, see Chapter 9.

23.12.2 Production Supply

When you create a production order for which raw materials or components must be provided by the warehouse, you can integrate the EWM by specifying or determining the warehouse controlled by EWM as the supplying location for the components (either automatically or manually). For more information on using EWM as the source of supply for production orders, see Chapter 11, Production Supply.

23.12.3 Kit to Stock

If you have demand for supplying kits to customers on a regular basis, you can choose to kit the stock ahead of time using a Kit to Stock scenario. The Kit to Stock requirement may be generated by APO (or SPP) and transferred to ERP, or it can be generated directly in ERP. In ERP, a production order is created for the requirement, or you can generate the production order manually. Inbound deliveries and outbound deliveries to support the goods issue of the items and the goods receipt of the kit are subsequently transferred to EWM, and in EWM the execution of the kitting process is performed via a value-added service (VAS). For more information on Kit to Stock, see Chapter 20, Kitting.

> **Note**
>
> The Kit to Stock process can also be originated in EWM as a VAS without requiring integration to ERP PP.

23.13 Integration with Finance

EWM is indirectly integrated with FI in some obvious and nonobvious ways. First, material movements are obviously integrated with FI via the account assignment of MM. This applies to goods receipts and goods issues of deliveries, and inventory adjustments from PIs, transfer postings, etc. In addition, EWM is integrated to ERP for transfer of material valuation and also for support of billing processes (in the obvious example for outbound deliveries for customer orders and cross-company billing for STOs, but also for billing of VAS to internal or external parties).

23.13.1 Goods Movements

Goods movements result in updates to FI via the standard account assignment determination of MM and creation of the accounting documents during the goods movement, whether the movement is initiated by posting of an inbound delivery or outbound delivery, PI adjustment, transfer posting, or other goods movement initiated by EWM.

> **Note**
>
> If your materials are valued according to moving average price, the value in the accounting document for the goods movement is always according to the most recent purchase order price.

23.13.2 Material Valuation

The valuation of materials is used during the PI processes to compare the valuation of the difference posting to the tolerances allowed for the user (see Chapter 14, Physical Inventory, for more details regarding PI processes, including the clearing of differences). The material valuation is extracted from ERP periodically via a report (/SCWM/R_VALUATION_SET), which can be scheduled as a batch job or run manually. The valuation is stored on tables /SCWM/T_VALUATE and /SCWM/T_VAL_SPLT (for split valuation), but it is not visible in the standard product master views. You can see the difference values during the clearing of differences in the difference analyzer (Transaction /SCWM/DIFF_ANALYZER).

23.13.3 VAS Billing

The data captured during the execution of VAS orders, including the quantity executed and the actual duration of execution of the order, can be used as a basis for the billing of the VAS, either internally or externally. While the billing execution is not provided in the standard implementation, you can create the billing situation on your own based on the actual results in various ways, including providing the information to ERP on the inbound deliveries or outbound deliveries or reading the data directly from EWM during the billing execution.

23.14 Integration with HR

EWM supports the capture of Labor Management (LM) data and the transfer of that data to the ERP HR module (SAP Human Capital Management (HCM)) to support pay-for-performance or other performance evaluation processes within HR.

23.14.1 Employee Data

The employee number of HR is assigned manually to the employee BP in EWM. As described in Chapter 5, the employee BP can be created initially in CRM or in ERP and is then transferred to EWM as a BP of type Employee. Once the BP is created in EWM, you can update the HR employee number directly in EWM. This employee number assignment is a prerequisite for sending the performance data from EWM to HR. In Figure 23.7, you can see the assignment of the employee number to the employee BP in EWM. Note that the employee number (and logon username) is assigned on the IDENTIFICATION tab of the Employee BP role.

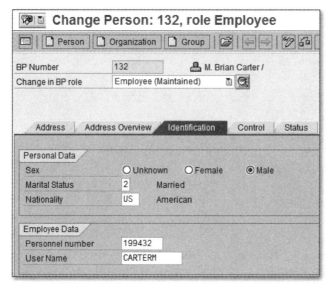

Figure 23.7 Assignment of the Personnel Number and Other Data to the Employee Business Partner in EWM

23.14.2 Performance Data

In EWM, you can review the employee performance data by following the EXTENDED WAREHOUSE MANAGEMENT • LABOR MANAGEMENT • EMPLOYEE PERFORMANCE • EMPLOYEE PERFORMANCE OVERVIEW menu path, or by using Transaction /SCWM/EPERF. For more information on performance data reporting within LM, see Chapter 21, Labor Management.

You can subsequently transfer the performance data from EWM to HR by following the EXTENDED WAREHOUSE MANAGEMENT • LABOR MANAGEMENT • EMPLOYEE PERFORMANCE • SEND PERFORMANCE DOCUMENT TO HR menu path, or using Transaction code /SCWM/EPD_TRANSFER. The data is transferred to HR using a direct remote function call (RFC) to a business application programming interface (BAPI) in ERP for an update of wage compensation. The performance data can then be used within HR to support pay-for-performance or other performance evaluation processes.

23.15   Integration with Material Flow Systems

In the first release of EWM, the EWM system connected to Material Flow Systems (MFSs) via a warehouse control unit (WCU), also known as a material flow unit (MFU)). EWM communicated to the WCU in the same way that it would communicate to other warehouse subsystems, via the RFC connection (see Section 23.16, Integration with Warehouse Subsystems for more details). Then the WCU would communicate to the programmable logic controllers (PLCs) of the MFS via TCP/IP communication.

In later releases (as of EWM 5.1), EWM communicates directly to the PLCs of the MFSs via TCP/IP. The communication container for the PLC communication is commonly known as a telegram. The telegrams are passed back and forth between EWM and the MFS to send movement requests or confirmations. In the EWM system, warehouse tasks are sent to the MFS via a telegram and the confirmation of the warehouse task from the MFS also occurs via a telegram. The warehouse tasks are used to reflect the movement from one communication point to another or between a communication point and a bin. The communication points are generally linked via conveyor segments or other automated equipment designed to move some type of container from one point to another, as seen in Figure 23.8.

The basic components of the MFSs include PLCs, communication channels, communication points, conveyor segments, and resources. The communication channel is the connection used for transmission of messages. The communication points are the points on the path of the equipment at which EWM and the PLC exchange messages. Conveyor segments are lengths of conveyor along which product can progress when travelling through the MFS. Conveyor segments are used to visualize the status of stock moves and to check capacity. To configure these items in the EWM Implementation Guide (IMG), follow the menu path EXTENDED WAREHOUSE MANAGEMENT • MATERIAL FLOW SYSTEM (MFS) • MASTER DATA. Once you have configured the relevant settings, you must also perform the master data updates for the communication points, PLCs, communication channels, and resources. To update the master data, follow the menu path EXTENDED WAREHOUSE MANAGEMENT • MASTER DATA • MATERIAL FLOW SYSTEM (MFS).

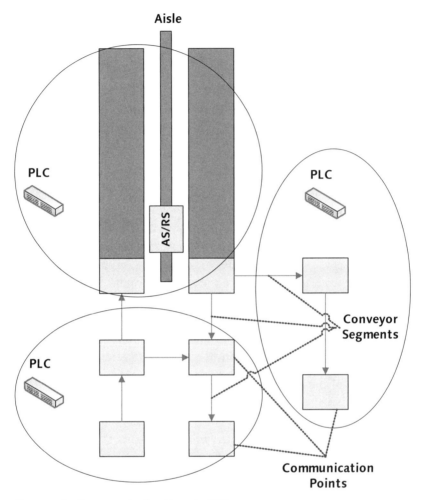

Figure 23.8 Components of an Example MFS

You must also configure the MFS actions. These actions are used to trigger follow-up activities when a particular telegram type is received from a particular communication point type. To configure the MFS actions, and to specify the structure for the telegram per PLC or per PLC interface type in the EWM IMG, follow the menu path EXTENDED WAREHOUSE MANAGEMENT • MATERIAL FLOW SYSTEM (MFS) • TELEGRAM PROCESSING.

Finally, you must configure how the EWM system should handle PLC errors reported by the telegrams returning from the MFS. To configure the relevant EWM exception codes to be used for each of the PLC error types in the EWM IMG, follow the menu path Extended Warehouse Management • Material Flow System (MFS) • Exception Handling.

For more details regarding the setup and use of the MFS, access the online help (*http://www.help.sap.com*) or the IMG documentation.

23.16 Integration with Warehouse Subsystems

It is often necessary in complex warehouse scenarios to integrate the warehouse system with various warehouse subsystems (in addition to the direct connection to MFSs described previously). For example, you may need to send requests to a WCU, or integrate with a voice picking system. The connections to warehouse subsystems are described in the following sections.

23.16.1 Integration with Warehouse Control Units

To integrate with WCUs or other warehouse subsystems that are responsible for managing warehouse tasks within a particular region in the warehouse, you can make use of the IDoc technology to send the warehouse tasks to the WCU or perform other activities. The IDocs available in EWM include:

▶ Create Warehouse Task

▶ Confirm Warehouse Task

▶ Move HU

▶ Complete Wave

▶ Create and Send Pick HUs

▶ Cancellation Request for Warehouse Order

▶ Block Storage Bin

The triggers for sending outbound IDocs are coded within the application (within function group /SCWM/LSUB in function modules with names starting with /SCWM/SUB_INITIATION_FOR_xxxx; to find the relevant triggers in the application, perform a where used list on the relevant function module). Inbound IDocs are processed within the ALE layer, according to the settings for the inbound IDoc type.

23.16.2 Integration with Voice Picking Systems

SAP EWM does not provide native capability to execute warehouse orders via what is commonly known as "voice picking," however, EWM can integrate voice picking systems in multiple ways. Different partners can use these various integration methods.

One method of integration that these partners use is the direct integration of their voice engine with the Web SAPConsole or ITSmobile mobile engine. This multimodal method uses the standard capabilities of EWM, which are supported via the mobile data transactions (see Chapter 22, Data Capture and Resource Optimization, for more details on the capabilities of EWM for mobile data capture), including picker-directed replenishment or other processes driven by the use of appropriate exception codes during the warehouse order execution.

Another method commonly used by voice picking partners is a store-and-forward processing technique, which works in a way similar to integration to other warehouse subsystems (described previously in this chapter). Via this method, the warehouse orders are transferred to the vendor's subsystem and the vendor communicates via a voice interface to the warehouse operators to manage the execution of these tasks. This method does not necessarily support all of the functionality of the native EWM mobile data transactions, however, these functions are not necessarily required in every circumstance. On the other hand, this method provides certain advantages, including the ability to operate the system on simpler voice-only devices. Some vendors even execute the voice execution via low-cost devices, such as a standard cell phone, providing a possible cost advantage.

23.17 Summary

In this chapter, we described the integration methods, both direct and indirect, between EWM and other applications, including both SAP and non-SAP applications. Providing a good understanding of the integration capabilities should help you understand the full capabilities of EWM working with the other applications in your information technology landscape and help you understand which end-to-end business processes can be supported with EWM.

The triggering of follow-up actions, such as printing and creating warehouse tasks, is managed in Extended Warehouse Management (EWM) with the Post-Processing Framework (PPF). With correct implementation of the PPF, you can solve many warehouse requirements and reduce administrative effort.

24   Post-Processing Framework (PPF) and Form Printing

In this chapter, we will discuss the use of the PPF in various areas of the EWM system. The PPF is a flexible framework that is part of the SAP Application Platform (and therefore can be used by other SAP products, and various areas within EWM). PPF was developed to process actions for different output types, such as printing, emailing, or faxing using smart forms. For EWM, it is also used for triggering follow-up actions, such as creating warehouse tasks. For printing in EWM, the PPF replaces the output control that is used, for example, in ERP Warehouse Management.

The basic purpose of the PPF is to trigger actions in the background (such as workflow or customer-specific user exits). The actions themselves should only be triggered when special conditions are met; therefore, the PPF provides the flexibility to configure system behavior based on business requirements. PPF provides tools for managing, scheduling, starting, and monitoring actions. The flexibility of the framework is its great strength, and due to its flexibility, SAP EWM uses the PPF to perform various functions. In the following sections, we will describe the details of PPF as it is used by EWM.

24.1   Overview of the PPF

In EWM, the PPF is used within various applications, including delivery processing, shipping and receiving, and printing in warehouse management (e.g., handling units (HU), warehouse orders (WOs), physical inventory (PI) documents, value-added service (VAS) orders, etc.). Aside from printing forms, labels, and other documents, the PPF is also used for such functions as the creation of warehouse tasks, posting goods receipt, and goods issue. In Figure 24.1, you can see a graphical depiction of some of the applications, actions, and logic checks that are involved with triggering the PPF actions.

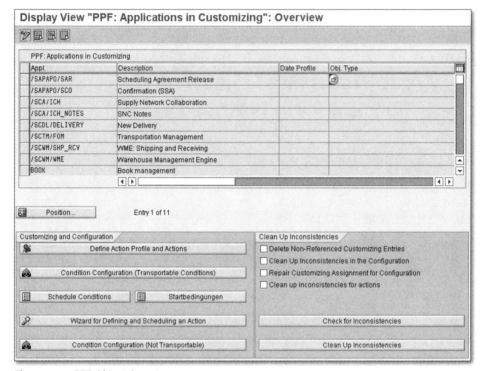

Figure 24.1 PPF Object Overview

When a PPF action is triggered (as long as the scheduling conditions are met), the action is scheduled. After the action is scheduled, it is selected and executed via a background process. This is important to understand, as it can potentially impact design for any custom activities, and provide a basis for understanding how to troubleshoot the application when issues arise.

24.2 Administration of the PPF

You can access the generic PPF customizing via Transaction code SPPFCADM (you can also access the action profiles and conditions within the EWM Implementation Guide (IMG) for each of the relevant applications). Using the generic administration transaction, you can change all of the settings related to the PPF. In the application customizing (as you can see in Figure 24.2), you can see the various applications that use the PPF. For EWM, the relevant application areas include:

▸ /SCDL/DELIVERY — delivery processing

▸ /SCWM/SHP_RCV — shipping and receiving

▸ /SCWM/WME — warehouse management engine

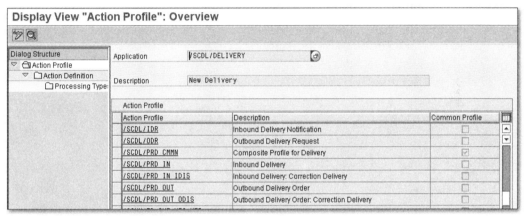

Figure 24.2 PPF Administration

The primary areas of consideration that are important for you to understand include the definition of the profiles and the action, the condition configuration, and the configuration of the schedule conditions and start conditions. In the following sections, we will describe these areas in further detail.

24.2.1 Defining Action Profiles and Actions

If you select the DEFINE ACTION PROFILES AND ACTIONS option in the PPF Administration, you will see the functions delivered by SAP. In EWM, there is a separate ACTION PROFILE for each type of delivery document (e.g., Inbound Delivery Notification (IDN), Inbound Delivery, Outbound Delivery Request (ODR), Outbound Delivery Order (ODO), etc.), as you can see in Figure 24.3. For each of the delivery types, when the delivery is created or changed, the PPF actions are checked and triggered, if relevant. The same is true for Shipping and Receiving, and the Warehouse Management Engine.

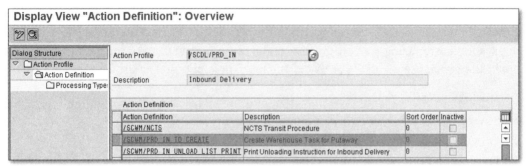

Figure 24.3 Action Profiles for all EWM Delivery Types

To check the ACTION DEFINITIONS for each ACTION PROFILE (as you can see in Figure 24.4), simply select the action profile from the list and double-click on the ACTION DEFINITION folder.

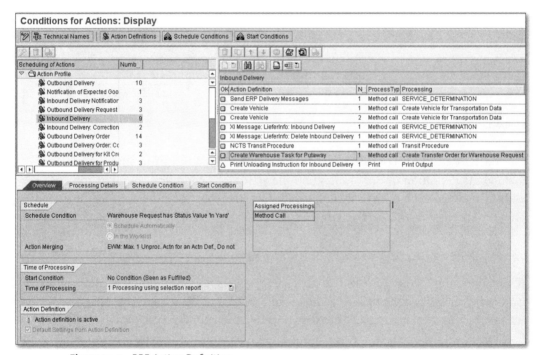

Figure 24.4 PPF Action Definition

For each ACTION DEFINITION, there is a method or a function where business logic is included. If you don't need the action definition checked, you can deactivate it (by selecting the INACTIVE checkbox). This will save on performance, but you should be sure that you don't need the check before you deactivate it.

> **Note**
>
> If you want to post goods receipt automatically via a PPF action, you can add a new action and assign the PPF method /SCWM/GM_POSTING. This PPF method is a Business Add-In (BAdI) that EWM delivers.

24.2.2 Condition Configuration

In the Condition Configuration (also accessible from the PPF Administration shown in Figure 24.2), you can see an overview of all of the functions of the PPF, including ACTION PROFILES, ACTION DEFINITIONS, scheduling details, etc. In Figure 24.5, you can see the condition configuration overview.

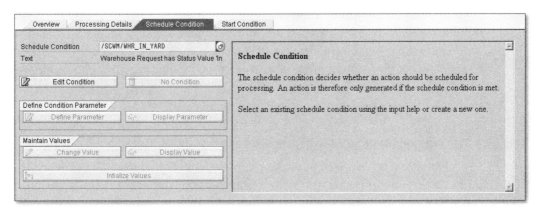

Figure 24.5 PPF Condition Configuration Overview

You can create or change actions based on the actions you defined previously in the action definition customizing. For example, you can overwrite the existing actions and choose your own settings. In the action definition, you can choose if the default should be used or if you want to define your own settings.

You also have the option of changing the SCHEDULE CONDITION and START CONDITION settings.

Time of Processing

If you want to change the system's behavior, for example, to create warehouse tasks when the inbound delivery is created, you must change the time of processing to IMMEDIATE PROCESSING and check if the schedule condition meets your needs. The time of processing allows the following settings:

- Processing when saving documents
- Immediate processing
- Processing using selection report

If the latter option is chosen, the selection report (RSPPFPROCESS) is used to determine when the PPF action should be processed. This report can be scheduled in the background, or you can execute it manually via Transaction code SPPFP. You should also use this transaction if you need to reprocess failed PPF actions.

Schedule Condition for Scheduling PPF Actions

The scheduling of the different actions can be maintained via the schedule conditions, which are accessed via the action definitions, as seen in Figure 24.5. For example, the schedule condition /SCWM/WHR_IN_YARD is responsible for the scheduling of the creation of the warehouse tasks. The business logic is developed within a BAdI, so if the business logic does not fit your requirements, you can replace the standard schedule condition with a custom one.

Starting Condition for Starting the Execution of PPF Actions

After an action is scheduled, it must be executed, but before the action is executed, the start condition is checked. If the start condition is not met, then the action is not executed. A blank start condition indicates that the action can be started.

> **Note**
>
> There is more information available for the PPF on the SAP Developer Network (SDN) (*http://sdn.sap.com*). There you can find a Modeling Guide and Implementation Guide that give you more detailed information on the PPF and additional examples for use.

24.3   Printing in EWM Using PPF

Printing relevance in EWM is determined using the flexible condition technique. Printing is initiated via the PPF, as already described previously, but to get additional flexibility the EWM uses the condition technique for determining the print relevance. This gives you the flexibility to define, based on your own requirements, which fields should be used for the printing determination without developing additional ABAP logic. The condition tables and access sequence can be created by you in the customizing, and the condition records can be created by the warehouse administrators directly in the productive system as master data. This allows you significant flexibility in managing your determination for printing.

We will not describe the condition technique or how to configure it in detail here — there are many sources to get that information. Instead, we will provide an example that will give you an idea how it should work.

Our example, in this case, is for printing a paper picking list. A picking list may be a WO, for example, with several warehouse tasks. For the WO object, there are actions in the PPF customizing. The determination of when a WO should be printed is performed according to the schedule condition. EWM checks for the condition table entries any time the WO is changed to determine if printing should be executed.

To enable the printing, certain printing parameters must also be maintained, such as the form, the printer, printing parameters, and other fields. These parameters are grouped together in the Print Warehouse Order (PWO) application, which you can access via Transaction code /SAPCND/GCM.

But you can further influence the determination. You can use the delivered fields, or you can change the determination by creating your own table with new fields. To check the available fields, you can use Transaction /SCWM/PRWO0. Via the customizing, you can create your own access rules to determine which parameters should be checked and how the printer determination should work. For example, you could use parameters such as warehouse number, warehouse process type, and activity area in the determination to let you select the printer based on the activity area where the picking will be performed. In Figure 24.6, you can see an example of the creation of the condition records based on the available fields for selection.

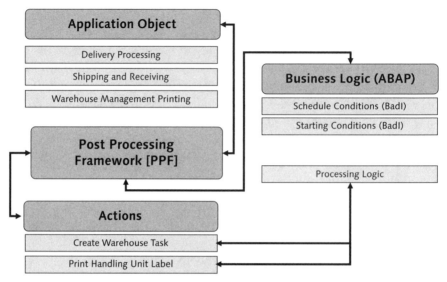

Figure 24.6 Setting Up the Condition Technique for Printing WOs

24.4 Summary

In this chapter, we discussed the PPF and how to use it to flexibly determine the relevance for follow-up actions on WOs, including printing. While we did not cover every technical detail in this chapter, you should have a basic understanding of how the functions work and how to get started setting them up.

In the following chapters, we will cover authorizations, roles, and archiving, and then we will discuss deployment options and techniques for getting started with your implementation.

Proper control of authorizations and roles in your warehousing application allows you to protect your business by ensuring that the correct people have access to perform the activities necessary for their job. Archiving helps you keep your system running at full speed by getting rid of old data that may slow it down.

25 Authorizations and Roles and Data Archiving

There are some concepts that apply to Extended Warehouse Management (EWM) that can be applied equally to other aspects of SAP Supply Chain Management (SCM) or other applications, such as SAP ERP or SAP Customer Relationship Management (CRM). Among those concepts are authorizations and archiving. While there are specific applications of these concepts that apply to EWM, the general concepts and methods of implementation are the same for EWM as they are for other applications. For this reason, we will not cover these topics in detail in this text. In this chapter, we will briefly discuss these topics and focus our attention on the aspects that are applicable to EWM, and what you should know to make informed decisions about the topics during your implementation. This information will help you set up these components.

25.1 Authorizations and Roles

The same concepts utilized by ERP, SCM, and other applications and components for controlling authorizations and roles are also applied to SAP EWM. These concepts let you control which transactions each individual can access, and which organizational elements each individual can perform. This control allows you to ensure that each individual in the organization has enough access to perform the activities necessary to do their job, but not the authorization to perform activities for which they are not authorized. This control also lets you ensure proper segregation of duties can be enforced throughout the organization (an important tenet of financial and accounting control legislation in various regions of the world).

25.1.1 The Authorization Concept

Authorizations are controlled by concepts in SAP known as roles (which can be single roles or composite roles, which are collections of single roles), authorization profiles (which can be generated from a role or created manually; there are also composite profiles), authorizations, authorization objects, and authorization fields. These objects work together to define which transactions a user may perform and for which organizational elements or object types within the transaction the user may perform the activity. These objects are created per client, and they can be transported from one client to another (or one system to another) using the change and transport system.

User Master Record

Each user in the SAP system has an assigned user ID and should use it to log on to the system and perform transactions. The user controls their own password and certain other data associated with their user ID, but the system administrators control other data associated with the user master record, including authorization and role assignments.

Single Roles

A role allows the assignment of authorizations and logon menus to multiple users who share similar job profiles. Roles are assigned to individual user IDs, or you can combine single roles into composite roles and assign the composite roles to users. You can also assign multiple single roles to a single user, in case the user has multiple job roles but other users do not share a similar job profile.

Composite Roles

A composite role is a collection of single roles and can be assigned to individual users to assign multiple roles to multiple users using the single composite role. For example, so-called "power users" who need to have access to multiple activities may be assigned a composite role.

Authorization Profiles

Authorization profiles are generated for roles. Until the authorization profile is generated, the role assignment to the user is ineffective.

Authorizations

Authorizations allow you to perform a particular activity in an SAP system, based on a set of authorization object field values. Authorizations are conferred on the user by assigning active roles whose authorization profile has been generated.

Authorization Objects

An authorization object is a collection of fields whose allowed value can be assigned when creating the authorizations. Authorization objects are used to check complex authorizations based on multiple conditions (joined by AND conditions).

Authorization Fields

The authorization fields are the individual fields whose values are checked within the check of the authorization object.

25.1.2 Control of Authorizations for EWM

The simplest way to control authorizations for users within EWM would be to assign one or more of the existing simple roles to the individual users (see the list in Section 25.1.3, Standard Roles Delivered with EWM). But more than likely, you will want to mix and match the roles into composite roles or adjust the simple roles based on the activities performed by individuals in your organization. To do so, you should either copy the existing roles and adjust them accordingly, or you should create your own simple or composite roles. When creating the roles, you can choose to control authorizations down to the organizational level (e.g., warehouse number) or specific field value (e.g., outbound delivery (OD) type) and assign them to the authorization profile for the role.

You should work with your authorization team to define what roles should exist, how the authorizations should be determined, and to which users those roles should be assigned.

25.1.3   Standard Roles Delivered with EWM

There are several standard roles that are delivered with EWM that can be used out of the box, or you can copy them and create your own roles to make them relevant to your organization. The following roles are delivered standard with EWM (note that these are equivalent to the role name texts, not the technical role names):

▸ EWM: Warehouse Supervisor

▸ EWM: Warehouse Expert

▸ EWM: Warehouse Specialist for Goods Receipt

▸ EWM: Warehouse Specialist for Goods Issue

▸ EWM: Warehouse Specialist for Yard Management

▸ EWM: Warehouse Worker

▸ EWM: Inventory Planner

▸ EWM: Physical Inventory Counter

▸ EWM: Display of Warehouse Information

▸ EWM: ERP Integration

▸ EWM: Labor Planner

▸ EWM: Labor Specialist

▸ EWM: Warehouse Analyst

▸ EWM: Identity Management Integration

To check which authorizations belong to the roles from the SAP Easy Access Menu, follow the TOOLS • ADMINISTRATION • USER MAINTENANCE • ROLE ADMINISTRATION • ROLES menu path, or use Transaction code PFCG. To see which transactions are allowed for the role, enter or select the role name, then go to the menu tab (as seen in Figure 25.1). To see the possible roles, either use the dropdown selection from the ROLE field in Transaction PFCG (see the previous menu path), or you can use the information system reports to find relevant roles. For example, you can use various selection criteria, including transaction codes, to find a role by following the TOOLS • ADMINISTRATION • USER MAINTENANCE • INFORMATION SYSTEM • ROLES • ROLES BY COMPLEX SELECTION CRITERIA menu path, or using Transaction code S_BCE_68001425.

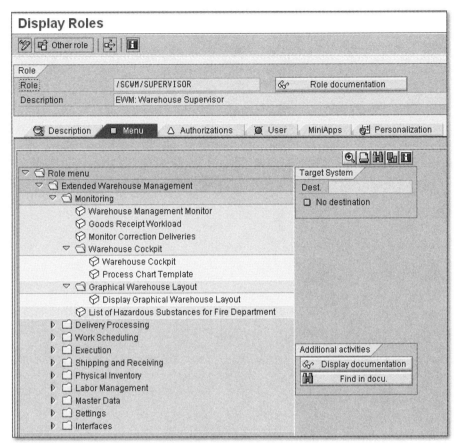

Figure 25.1 Menu Tab within the Role Maintenance, which Shows the Transaction Codes Allowed for the Role

While viewing the role, to see the detailed authorization objects, go to the Autho-rizations tab and select the Display Authorization Data button (circled in Fig-ure 25.2). Note that there aren't any assignments for the organizational elements within the standard roles. If you want to control authorizations to the organiza-tional element level, you should copy the standard roles to a new one and update the new roles.

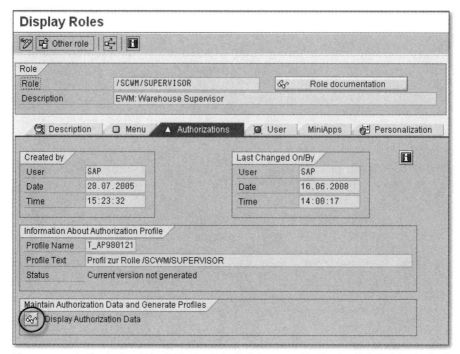

Figure 25.2 Authorization Tab within the Role Maintenance. To See the Detailed Authorizations, Select the Display Authorization Data Button

25.2 Data Archiving

Archiving lets you to remove data that is no longer needed and store it on another medium in case it must be accessed at some point in the future. To ensure that all of the relevant data is removed from the correct tables when a document is archived, the SAP NetWeaver system provides methods for archiving the data via archiving objects, which are correlated to functional processes or data objects.

When the objects are archived, there are three basic steps involved. First, the data objects are written to an archive file, then they are removed from the database, then the archive file is stored on another storage medium (e.g., copied to a storage system or to tape). In addition, for individual objects, there may be pre-processing steps involved. For example, you may need to set a deletion indicator or archiving indicator, which indicates that the data object is relevant to be archived from the online database to the offline archive. For example, for deliveries, the archiving indicator is set for deliveries whose expiry has passed by calling Transaction /SCDL/ BO_ARCHIVE, where you can specify the document category and other parameters relevant to the data selection. You can also schedule these preparation activities so that the data is ready for archiving during the next archiving run.

Several standard archive objects are provided within SAP EWM for archiving the major sources of database growth. For example, warehouse orders, warehouse tasks, inbound delivery requests, inbound deliveries, outbound delivery requests (ODRs), outbound delivery orders (ODOs), outbound deliveries, value-added services (VASs) orders, and other transactional activity objects are included within the standard archive objects. To find the list of available standard objects, you can check the relevant sections of the SAP Online Help (*http://help.sap.com*), or you can call up Transaction SARA and use the dropdown selection box for the ARCHIVING OBJECT field.

As part of your implementation project, you should have the implementation team and the business users define the expected lifetime of the data in the online database. This will let you define the archiving strategy for the EWM system with your archiving team.

25.3 Summary

In this chapter, we briefly introduced the topics of authorizations and archiving, and we provided information on these topics, which is specifically relevant for an EWM implementation. Because the topics are generic to SCM, or even to other SAP applications, we did not discuss them in detail. If you need more information on authorizations, roles, or archiving, we suggest consulting the SAP Online Help (*http://help.sap.com*) or the relevant texts available from SAP Press.

In the penultimate chapter of this text, we will describe some concepts relevant to deploying an EWM instance, including architecture options, automatic configuration, and data loading mechanisms. And, finally, we will conclude the text in the final chapter.

Understanding the options for deploying SAP Extended Warehouse Management (EWM) is important for making decisions before getting started with the implementation, and knowing how to use automated configuration methods and data load programs can help you get started quickly.

26 Deploying Extended Warehouse Management

One of the first important decisions that you will make after you decide to implement SAP EWM is how you will deploy the solution architecturally. For instance, you will need to make decisions about whether you will deploy the application on an Supply Chain Management (SCM) server or on an ERP server, whether you will connect the applications to a modern release of SAP ERP or an older one, whether you will put all of your warehouses on a single database server or on multiple servers, where you will physically position the servers, and how you will ensure the permanency of the data.

Once you have decided how you will deploy EWM, you will then need to know how to make use of automated programs for configuring the system for specific processes using the Extended Computer Aid Test Tools (eCATTs) and for loading certain master data.

In this chapter, we will describe the deployment options for EWM; introduce you to eCATTS and tell you how you can use them to automate your configuration; and describe methods for automating the loading of various master data and the current bin stock situation.

26.1 Deployment Options for EWM

In the following sections, we will discuss the various architectural deployment options available for implementing EWM.

26.1.1 Deploying EWM on SCM

As described in Chapter 1, Introduction, when EWM was released in 2005, it was released on the SAP SCM platform. The most common deployment option for customers today is still the SCM deployment option (the ERP option will be described in the following sections). The major advantages to deploying EWM on the SCM platform include performance and flexibility. On the performance side, the major advantage is the ability to decouple the warehouse functions from the functions of the rest of the enterprise, including sales, financials, production, and even supply chain planning.

When deploying EWM on SCM, you have the additional decision of whether to deploy EWM in the same instance as the Advanced Planning Optimization (APO), Service Parts Planning (SPP), and the Global Available to Promise (gATP) modules. While SAP generally encourages customers to consider implementing EWM on a separate instance from their other applications, more advanced server technologies and technologies for shared hosting of applications on common servers (e.g., public and private clouds) are making it easier for customers to reduce the number of instances that they need to maintain by hosting multiple applications on the same SCM instance. There are several important considerations to carefully understand before making the decision to host multiple applications on the same server, including:

- **Sizing**
  One of the most important considerations to weigh is whether the sizing of the server(s) is sufficient to handle both the average and peak volumes of the various applications, taking into account the timing of the peaks for each application. It is important to work closely with SAP and with your hardware vendor or host to perform the proper sizing of the applications, taking into account potential future growth, upgrade path for the applications and for the hardware, and other technical considerations. SAP provides the Quicksizer tool in the SAP Service Marketplace (*http://service.sap.com/quicksizer*) and services for performing customer-specific sizing for more complex cases. The major hardware vendors will also provide services and support for hardware sizing according to the customer's needs.

- **Availability**
  You should carefully consider the dates and times the applications are available to end users and batch program runs to ensure the business is not affected by

planned downtime of the hardware or applications. This is especially critical for global or multinational businesses and supply chains that employ 24-hour or 7-day distribution operations.

▶ **Version control**

Because the applications that are deployed on the same instance will always be tied to the same version, you should carefully consider whether your upgrade plans for the various applications will allow you to keep the versions in sync. For instance, if you need to be more responsive in your planning module than in your warehousing module (or vice versa) and you will upgrade more frequently, you need to consider the impacts on the other applications of the frequent upgrades.

▶ **Support pack and note application**

Similar to the considerations regarding version control, you must also consider whether your plan for applying support packs and online support system (OSS) notes for one of the applications will also impact the other applications.

26.1.2 Deploying EWM on ERP

In addition to the SCM deployment option, in 2007 SAP introduced implementing EWM as an add-on to ERP (also described in detail in Chapter 1). When EWM is installed as an add-on to ERP, the entire application, including the configuration tables, Implementation Guide (IMG) nodes, programs, transaction codes, Easy Access menu structure, and other necessary technical components are installed directly on the ERP server (along with sufficient components from the SCM basis to execute EWM on ERP). To minimize the development for creating the add-on application and consistent with other add-ons, the interface between ERP functions (such as Sales and Distribution (SD), Production Planning (PP), and other modules) and EWM remains technically the same.

The primary reason for SAP to allow such an ERP add-on implementation of EWM is to allow the installed base of ERP customers to enjoy the functionality of SCM without having to deploy an SCM instance. However, the same considerations described earlier for having multiple applications on the same instance also apply to deploying EWM as an add-on to ERP.

In this book, we primarily focus on the deployment option of EWM on an SCM server, but because the concepts for integration are primarily the same (and even the menu paths for the configuration and Easy Access menu transactions are the same), we do not make a distinction in most cases.

26.1.3 The Standard Connection to ERP

The standard method for connecting EWM to ERP is via the core interface (CIF) technology for master data and queued remote function call (qRFC) for transactional data. The standard technologies are covered in detail in Chapter 8, Integration from ERP to EWM, so we will not cover them again here.

26.1.4 Connecting EWM to Older Releases of ERP

The standard connection between EWM and ERP works fine as long as the ERP version is Release ERP 2005 or higher. For earlier releases of ERP (as early as SAP ERP 4.6C, which was the first release with CIF technology in ERP), a combination of CIF for master data and intermediate documents (IDocs) for transactional data can be used. This interface is very similar to the interface already used for connecting ERP to a decentralized warehouse management (DWM) system (which is basically a separate ERP system that is configured to act as a stand-alone warehouse management system, with similar capabilities for warehouse management as the ERP warehouse management application).

It is not a highly popular option at the moment, and with more customers upgrading their ERP instances to ERP 2005 to take advantage of the enhancement pack model (further described in Chapter 1), it will continue to become less popular over time, but any customer who chooses to connect EWM to an instance of ERP prior to ERP 2005 should contact SAP for more information on making the proper settings in EWM to enable this option.

Once you upgrade an earlier release of SAP to ERP 2005 or higher, you can then start using the qRFC instead of IDocs for integrating the transactional data (although it is not technically a requirement —you can continue using IDocs after the upgrade).

26.1.5 Connecting EWM to a Non-SAP ERP

Many customers inquire about connecting SAP EWM to a non-SAP ERP system. While SAP doesn't provide connection kits or pre-configured options for connecting directly to another ERP system, it is technically possible with the right amount of effort and as long as the customer accepts or can somehow work around the relevant restrictions. Probably the easiest way to enable this option is to set up the EWM system as if it is connecting to an older SAP ERP system so that it will use the IDoc methodology for passing transactional data back and forth. This allows the data to be passed asynchronously via containers, which can be easily passed through the SAP Process Integration (PI) layer (previously called SAP Exchange Infrastructure or SAP XI). For exchanging master data, you can either use CIF technology for exchanging master data, which probably requires coding in the legacy system for emulating the CIF integration, or you can enhance the existing IDocs (which were used in the past by APO) for inbound processing of master data.

As this option is also not a popular way to deploy EWM at the moment, we will not cover the details in this book, but if your company is considering deploying EWM and wants to connect it to a non-SAP ERP, you should contact your SAP representative to get more advice on how to proceed based on your specific circumstances.

26.1.6   Deploying EWM in a Mixed Warehousing Environment

EWM can be deployed in many situations where other warehousing technologies (both SAP and non-SAP) are used to manage the warehouses within your supply chain. Because the warehouse number is assigned at the plant and storage location level (as described in Chapter 2, Organizational Structure) and because the decision about how to manage the warehouse is made at the warehouse level, you can choose to use ERP warehouse management for one or more warehouses, ERP DWM for one or more warehouses, SCM EWM for one or more warehouses, the EWM add-on for ERP for one or more warehouses, and one or more non-SAP Warehouse Management Systems for one or more warehouses — or you can use any combination of the various warehouse technologies.

26.1.7   EWM Sizing and Deciding How Many Servers to Deploy

Appropriate sizing of your EWM server is an important aspect of ensuring the responsiveness of the applications for your end users. To help you with appropriate sizing, SAP provides tools (including the SAP Quicksizer, available at *http://service.sap.com/quicksizer*) and services (available from your SAP representative) to help you understand how much processing power is required to run your EWM application.

The SAP Quicksizer is a tool that allows you to input information about your anticipated data volumes, both on average and at peak volumes. Once you input this information, the tool can calculate the anticipated number of SAPs, or application-independent processing units, necessary to run your application. You can then compare the SAPs measurement to the capacity of your hardware, for both the database and application servers, to determine whether your existing hardware is sufficient or if you need to upgrade or procure new hardware (or perhaps configure the existing hardware differently). Your hardware vendor can help you acquire the necessary hardware based on the assessment of how many SAPs are required. The Quicksizer tool is designed based on various tests performed by SAP and its hardware partners of the SAP applications, including EWM. To input data about EWM in the Quicksizer, even if you will deploy EWM as an add-on to ERP, make sure to input all of the relevant data into the EWM sections, both EWM INBOUND and EWM OUTBOUND, of the SCM application area (as seen in Figure 26.1).

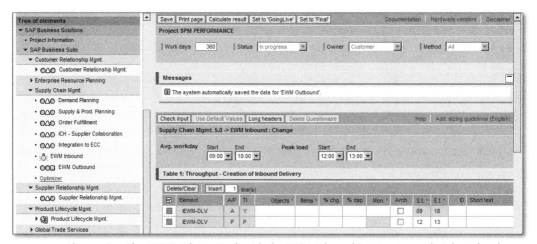

Figure 26.1 The SAP Quicksizer Tool, with the EWM Inbound Section Currently Selected and EWM Outbound Section Already Filled

In more complex cases or with very large volumes, you may need more sizing assistance due to the invalidity of the constraints and assumptions that are built into the SAP Quicksizer. In these cases, you should consult with SAP or with your hardware partner for additional assistance in calculating your requirements for sizing. For example, if the number of total SAPs output from the Quicksizer is close to or exceeds 30,000 SAPs, you may want to consider getting additional assistance to evaluate the hardware requirements.

Based on the output of the Quicksizer or your individual assessment regarding hardware requirements, you can then determine if you need one or more servers for your database and application servers. However, there may be other factors which may lead you to deploy on multiple instances, including:

▶ Physical proximity of the servers to the warehouses

▶ Requirements of the local operations to have onsite vs. central or regional support

▶ Your strategy (or your hosting partner's strategy) for deploying regional vs. regional support

▶ Availability and uptime of the servers, especially for global supply chains

26.1.8 Deciding Where to Position Your EWM Servers

Whether you have one or multiple EWM instances, you must next decide where, geographically, to deploy the servers. For some companies, this is an easy decision, as they have a strategy for central deployment of all applications, local deployment for warehousing applications, regional deployment at data centers, or a hosted environment where the host decided where to deploy the applications. In other circumstances, there may be a change to existing paradigms for availability or support. For example, many companies have legacy applications deployed locally at individual warehouses, but as they transition their environment to SAP applications, including EWM, they may choose to deploy them centrally or regionally at collective data centers. While this usually reduces support costs by leveraging experts at centralized locations, it also decreases the flexibility of the local warehouses to control the availability of the system and may introduce the risk of Wide Area Network (WAN) outages, which can affect availability of the system.

When considering a centralized strategy for deployment of the servers that host the EWM application, you should carefully consider whether adequate measures have been taken to ensure that the warehouses can access the application when they need it, including redundancy of communication lines and adequate service level agreements (SLAs) with vendors for bandwidth, speed, and availability of communications. In particular, speed of transmission is important to consider, especially for real-time communication during critical processes such as picking using radio frequency (RF)–enabled mobile devices.

26.1.9 High Availability for EWM

Due to the critical nature of the warehousing functions for ensuring customer satisfaction, companies that deploy EWM often inquire about ensuring the stability and availability of their warehousing applications. Because EWM is based on the SCM application, the same techniques for managing a high availability environment with mirroring and proper backups can be applied to EWM as to any other SCM environment (which is also similar to techniques used for ERP or other applications). Even companies which have not considered high availability (generally defined as providing at least 99.9% uptime for a given time period) for their ERP environments may want to consider high availability with appropriate SLAs (with their vendor or even internally) for their EWM applications. If your company doesn't consider implementing high availability, you should consider appropriate contingency plans for possible system outages and design your processes accordingly.

26.2 Automatic Configuration

SAP has provided methods for automatically configuring certain business processes within EWM using business configuration sets (BC Sets). BC Sets are containers for collecting configuration settings for transfer to another system or for repeated updates (if entries get regularly wiped out for some reason, for example, in test systems that are repeatedly refreshed).

BC Sets are a general technology provided by SAP within its various applications and details on them are widely covered. For more information on BC Sets in general, or on building or enhancing BC Sets, we suggest you review the documentation in the SAP Online Help (*http://help.sap.com*) and OSS note number 669542.

26.2.1 BC Sets for EWM Configuration

There are over 400 available BC Sets for configuring EWM business processes. To access the BC Sets relevant to EWM from the SAP Easy Access menu, follow the TOOLS • CUSTOMIZING • BUSINESS CONFIGURATION SETS • ACTIVATION OF BC SETS menu path, or use Transaction code SCPR20. Within the transaction, for the BC SET field, enter the text "/SCWM/*" and press F4 or select the dropdown box next to the field. To see more than the default number of entries in the dropdown selection list, change the MAXIMUM NO. OF HITS field to a larger number, then press

Enter . The resulting list, as partially seen in Figure 26.2, displays the full list of BC Sets relevant to EWM.

BC Set ID	BC Set description	Changed by	Changed on	Software Compone	Release	Release
/SCWM/ACT_AREA	Activity Areas	SAP	16.04.2008	SCMEWM	500	*
/SCWM/ACT_AREA_BIN	Assign Storage Bins to Activity Areas	SAP	06.05.2008	SCMEWM	500	*
/SCWM/ACT_AREA_SORT	Sort Sequence for Activity Area	SAP	16.04.2008	SCMEWM	500	*
/SCWM/ACT_CATEGORY	Activity Categories	SAP	08.12.2006	SCMEWM	500	*
/SCWM/AVAIL_GROUP	Availability Group: Putaway	SAP	05.02.2008	SCMEWM	500	*
/SCWM/BASIC_CREATION_RULE	Warehouse Order: Basics Creation Rule	SAP	29.09.2006	SCMEWM	500	*
/SCWM/BASIC_LIME	LIME Basic Settings for EWM	SAP	09.07.2008	SCMEWM	700	*
/SCWM/BASIC_NUMBER_RANGES	Number Ranges Warehouse-Number-Dependent	SAP	07.02.2007	SCMEWM	500	*
/SCWM/BASIC_PRODUCT_WC	Basic Data - Product, Work Center	SAP	29.09.2006	SCMEWM	500	*
/SCWM/BASIC_WHS_HU	Basic Data - Handling Units	SAP	29.09.2006	SCMEWM	500	*
/SCWM/BASIC_WHS_INDEP	Basic Data - Warehouse Number-Independent	SAP	09.07.2008	SCMEWM	500	*
/SCWM/BASIC_WHS_INDEP_BASIS	Basic Data - Warehouse-Number-Independent	SAP	12.12.2006	SCM_BASIS	510	*
/SCWM/BASIC_WHS_STRUCTURE	Basic Data - Structure	SAP	07.03.2007	SCMEWM	500	*
/SCWM/BASICS	Basic Data - Warehouse Number-Dependent	SAP	07.02.2007	SCMEWM	500	*
/SCWM/BULK_STOR_IND	Define Bulk Storage Indicators	SAP	29.09.2006	SCMEWM	500	*
/SCWM/BULK_STOR_TYPE_CONTR	Storage Type Control for Bulk Storage	SAP	29.09.2006	SCMEWM	500	*
/SCWM/BULK_STRUCTURE	Define Bulk Structures	SAP	29.09.2006	SCMEWM	500	*
/SCWM/CONS_GROUP	Define Consolidation Group	SAP	29.09.2006	SCMEWM	500	*

Figure 26.2 Partial List of BC Sets Relevant to EWM as Selected from the BC Set Activation Transaction

To determine which of these BC Sets are relevant for individual business processes, you can check the relevant sections of this text, you can check the relevant content from the solution manager, which described the business processes and how to set them up (see the Appendix for more details on accessing solution manager content), or you can work with your consultant or your SAP representative to understand which BC Sets are relevant for your processes.

> **Note**
>
> Some of the BC Sets are collective BC Sets that contain other BC Sets, so it may not be necessary to implement every BC Set individually, as it may be included within another BC Set. Also, in some cases there are dependencies that require that one BC Set is executed before another one. When these situations occur, the BC Sets are often included within another BC Set that also includes the dependent ones and executes them in the correct order.

26.2.2 Executing and Troubleshooting BC Sets

To execute the BC Sets, from the BC Set activation transaction (Transaction SCPR20, see the previous menu path), enter or select the name of the BC Set and then click the ACTIVATE BC SET button (as seen circled in Figure 26.3).

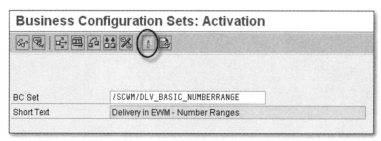

Business Configuration Sets: Activation

| BC Set | /SCWM/DLV_BASIC_NUMBERRANGE |
| Short Text | Delivery in EWM - Number Ranges |

Figure 26.3 Activation of a BC Set

Once you click the ACTIVATE BC SET button, if requested, create or assign a transport request number, then specify the requested variable field data (for example, the warehouse number or other input data which will be changed from the default data to your customized input data), and click the COPY VALUES button. On the Activation Options screen, select the relevant options for running the BC set and then press ⌴Enter⌴. Once the BC Set has been activated, you will see the activation log, which includes a list of messages that indicate whether each entry in the BC Set was successful (green light) or not successful (red light) and whether any warning messages (yellow light) or information messages (blue circle with an I inside) occurred, as seen in Figure 26.4). If errors occurred, there may be more information available by selecting the question mark within in the INFORMATION column. To drill down to a particular object to see the related messages, select the object in the right pane by double-clicking on it, or select the top level again to see all of the messages.

Resolving errors in the BC Set may require validation of the existing data in the prerequisite tables or even manual entry in one or more tables, depending on which dependencies exist and which entries failed, or there may have been a BC Set that should have been run as a prerequisite to the BC Set. If this is the case, you may simply run the prerequisite BC Set and then run your BC Set again to ensure that all of the relevant entries are created in the configuration tables.

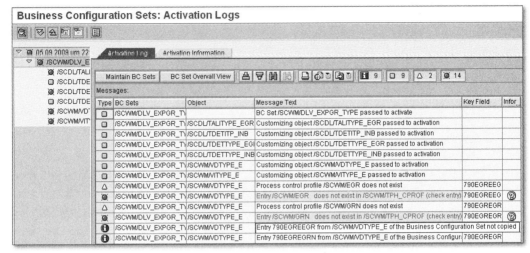

Figure 26.4 Activation Log from the Activation of a Business Configuration Set

> **Note**
>
> There are situations where the BC Sets have been created in such a way that errors may occur when you execute the BC Set the first time but not if you execute it again, possibly due to dependent entries. Therefore, it is advisable, if you encounter errors when executing the BC Set the first time, that you execute the BC Set again before spending additional time and effort to resolve the errors.

26.3 Data Loads

In this section, we'll discuss the various methods used to load master data and transactional data in preparation for a go-live or during the normal course of business.

26.3.1 Loading Business Partners

When EWM was initially released, SAP recommended that business partners (BPs) should be created in CRM and distributed to other systems via the CIF. Since then, SAP has decreased reliance on CRM for EWM and now recommends that BPs be created either in CRM and distributed to EWM, CRM, APO/SPP, gATP, and others, or they may be created in ERP and distributed to the relevant target systems, which may include EWM (and could even include CRM, if you want to distribute the data from ERP instead of CRM). Traditionally, the methods for automating an update of the BPs in CRM and ERP include:

- Legacy System Migration Workbench (LSMW)
- eCATTs
- Batch Data Communication (BDC)
- Custom programs

For more details on creating BPs in CRM or ERP, you should consult the SAP Online Help (*http://help.sap.com*) or the relevant texts from SAP Press.

Once you have created the BPs in CRM or ERP, the BPs should be integrated to EWM as described in detail in Chapter 5, Other Warehouse Master Data, and then they should be updated within EWM using the standard BP update tools (Transaction BP), or you can elect to perform mass updates on the BPs using Transaction MASSD (note that the technical object type, if it is not spelled out as "Business Partner," is BUS1006).

26.3.2 Loading Products

The process used for loading products manually is well described in Chapter 4, Product Master Data. However, during an initial data load it can often be cumbersome to perform each of these steps manually. It can be beneficial to use certain automation methods to speed up this process during the initial data load.

The first step to loading the products is to create the material master data with the correct parameters in the ERP system, if they do not already exist there. There are several tried and true methods that have been used over the years for loading material master data to ERP, including the LSMW, eCATTs/CATTs, BDC, or custom load programs. Once the materials are created in ERP, you then transfer the materials to EWM using the CIF technology. Once the material master data is transferred to EWM, the EWM material master record must be created and the data entered (which can be performed in one step or two).

To create the EWM product master data record, you must simply enter the product master data creation transaction (Transaction /SCWM/MAT1), enter the product, warehouse, and entitled to dispose, click the Create button, and save the transaction. You can also enter the data at the same time if you want to perform the creation and update in the same step, but you may also choose to use other methods to update the data, so in some cases it could be beneficial to perform the updates in two steps.

Options for automating the creation of the product master data record while also entering the data at the same time include eCATTs, BDCs, or custom programs. Options for automating the creation of the product master data record without entering the data at the same time include eCATTs, BDCs, Business Add-In (BAdI) (BAdI SMOD_APOCF005 is called at the end of the CIF integration), or custom programs. Options for automating the update of the product master data after the record has already been created include eCATTs, BDCs, mass change (via the SCM BASIS • MASTER DATA • GENERAL MASTER DATA FUNCTIONS • MASS MAINTENANCE menu path, or use Transaction code MASSD), the LSMW (which is provided as a toolset but without specific delivered content for the EWM product master), and custom programs.

26.3.3 Loading Storage Bins

In addition to the manual methods for creating storage bins one by one (Transaction /SCWM/LS01) and the method for generating storage bins from a template (Transaction /SCWM/LS10), you can also create storage bins from a data file. To upload the storage bins from the EWM Easy Access menu, follow the EXTENDED WAREHOUSE MANAGEMENT • INTERFACES • DATA UPLOAD • LOAD STORAGE BINS menu path, or use Transaction code /SCWM/SBUP. You can choose to upload the data file from your personal computer using the UPLOAD LOCAL FILE option, or you can upload the file from the SAP Application Server (which is generally better for very large data files; to get the data file transferred to the Application Server, contact your local basis or SAP NetWeaver contact). The input file must be created in comma-delimited format, and the structure must correspond to the /SCWM/S_LAGP_LSMW structure from EWM. The first row of the file is ignored, as it usually contains the header information (such as field names).

> **Note**
>
> One simple way to create a comma delimited file is to create a spreadsheet using your favorite spreadsheet program, and then save the spreadsheet with a.csv extension. In the spreadsheet, the field names for the fields of the structure should be aligned in the first row and the respective data should be aligned in the subsequent rows. The first row is generally ignored when using a comma-delimited file to upload data, which allows you to use this row to make sure that you have the data aligned correctly. Note that you must include all of the fields of the structure — even the ones for which you don't plan to upload any data.

You can also use the LSMW to upload the bins, using object 0215 (Storage Bin (EWM)). To start the LSMW, use Transaction code LSMW.

26.3.4 Loading Storage Bin Sorting

In addition to the manual method for updating the storage bin sorting (Transaction /SCWM/SBST), you can also automate the storage bin sorting update by uploading it from a data file. To upload the storage bins sorting from the EWM Easy Access menu, follow the Extended Warehouse Management • Interfaces • Data Upload • Load Storage Bin Sorting menu path, or use Transaction code /SCWM/SRTUP. You can choose to upload the data file from your personal computer using the Upload Local File option, or you can upload the file from the SAP Application Server (which is generally better for very large data files; to get the data file transferred to the application server, contact your local basis or SAP NetWeaver contact). The input file must be created in comma-delimited format, and the structure must correspond to the /SCWM/S_LAGPS_LSMW structure from EWM. The first row of the file is ignored, as it usually contains the header information (such as field names).

You can also use the LSMW to upload the bin sorting, using object 0216 (Storage Bin Sorting). To start the LSMW, use Transaction code LSMW.

26.3.5 Loading Packaging Specifications

In addition to the manual method for updating the packaging specifications (pack specs) via Transaction /SCWM/PACKSPEC, you can also automate the pack spec creation by uploading them from a data file. To upload the pack specs from the EWM Easy Access menu, follow the Extended Warehouse Management • Master Data • Packaging Specification • Initial Data Transfer of Packaging Specifications (or menu path Extended Warehouse Management • Interfaces • Data Upload • Initial Data Transfer of Packaging Specifications) menu path, or use Transaction code /SCWM/IPU. You can choose to upload the data file from your personal computer using the Physical file name option, or you can upload the file from the SAP Application Server (which is generally better for very large data files) by specifying the Logical file name option (to get the data file transferred to the Application Server, contact your local basis or SAP NetWeaver contact). You can elect to transfer the data or upload the data using the radio button on the right side of the screen, and via the options at the bottom of the screen, you may choose to resubmit an input file, see the details in the list, display a history of all logs, or only see the log of the update (without updating the database during the current run). See Figure 26.5 for a view of the selection screen for the update.

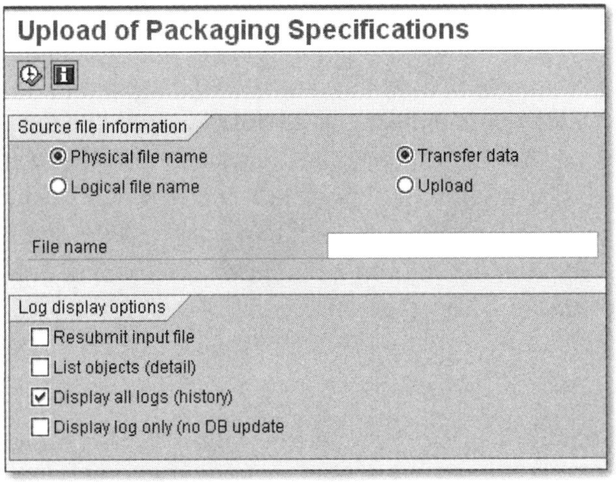

Figure 26.5 Selection Screen for Upload of Pack Specs

The input file must be a text file created in comma-delimited format. The text file should contain records for the different levels of the structure of the pack spec, and the record type should be identified in the first data field of the record, according to the following criteria:

▶ " " — records with a blank in the first field are ignored (for example, you can use this on the header row or in comments rows that are not to be printed)

▶ "*" — contains a comment that will be printed in the output

▶ "H" — header data, formatted like structure /SCWM/S_PS_DL_HEADER

▶ "C" — content data, formatted like structure /SCWM/S_PS_DL_CONTENT

▶ "L" — level data, formatted like structure /SCWM/S_PS_DL_LEVEL

▶ "E" — level element data, formatted like structure /SCWM/S_PS_DL_LEVEL_ ELEMENT

▶ "R" – condition record, formatted like structure /SCWM/S_PS_DL_CONDITION

The elements of a single pack spec must be consecutive and sequentially numbered according to the structure /SCWM/S_PS_DL_KEY, which is included at the beginning of each of the structures indicated previously. For more information about the file format, check the comments at the head of the program /SCWM/R_PS_DATA_ LOAD via Transaction SE38.

26.3.6 Loading Stock

When implementing EWM at a warehouse, one of the tasks that must be performed at cutover to the new solution is the loading of stock value to the bins. While there are methods for performing the stock updates using the standard functionality (for example, perform a goods receipt in ERP, which would create an inbound delivery and pass it to EWM, then process the putaway in EWM with reference to the inbound delivery), this is not a very efficient way for loading large quantities of stock. Therefore, SAP provides a method within EWM for uploading the stock values into EWM directly, including the storage bin level data, batch data, serialization data, and more.

To load the stock data from the EWM Easy Access menu, follow the EXTENDED WAREHOUSE MANAGEMENT • INTERFACES • DATA UPLOAD • STOCK DATA TRANSFER menu path, or use Transaction code /SCWM/ISU. You can choose to upload the data file from your personal computer using the LOCAL FILE option, or you can upload the file from the SAP Application Server (which is generally better for very large data files) by using the APPLICATION SERVER option (to get the data file transferred to the application server, contact your local basis or SAP NetWeaver contact). The input file must be created in comma-delimited format, and the structure must correspond to the /SCWM/S_STOCK_UPLOAD_EXT structure from EWM (removing the client number from the beginning). The first row of the file is ignored, as it usually contains the header information (such as field names).

Once you have created the file appropriately and specified the warehouse number and file name (along with the other relevant parameters), click the UPLOAD button (circled in Figure 26.6), which will upload the data from the data file, perform some data validations, and provide a list of the records that were uploaded from the file (with an indicator whether the data validations were passed or not in the STATUS column). When the data validations are passed, click the START STOCK DATA TRANSFER button (the EXECUTE icon on the left side of the button bar, also circled in Figure 26.6), and the data will be uploaded to EWM. If you do not select the DO NOT POST DATA in ERP checkbox, the inventory data will also be passed to ERP to update the stock quantities and financials in ERP.

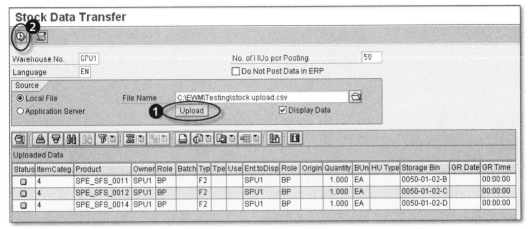

Figure 26.6 Stock Data Transfer Transaction, after Upload of the Input Data File and Correct Data Validations

You can also use the LSMW to upload the stock. In Transaction LSMW, use object 0225 WAREHOUSE STOCK EWM to upload the stock to the warehouse.

26.3.7 Loading Labor Management (LM) Data

You can also upload certain LM data to support the calculation of Engineered Labor Standards. See Chapter 21, Labor Management, for more details on loading the LM data.

26.4 Summary

In this chapter, we described the deployment options for EWM, introduced you to eCATTS, and described some methods for automating the loading of various master data and the current bin stock situation. You should be able to use these tools to significantly decrease the time necessary to deploy your EWM application.

Now that you have been introduced to SAP Extended Warehouse Management (EWM) and its many features and functions, we now encourage you to move forward and put the knowledge to good use.

27 Conclusion

In the introduction to this text, we said that we intended to provide knowledge, information, and reference material for project leads, implementation consultants, project team members, business analysts, and business users who are responsible for implementing, maintaining, or problem solving for the SAP EWM solution. To that end, we structured the book in sections and chapters so that you could easily consume information about the many features, functions, and capabilities, while at the same time get a deeper understanding of the business processes that the system was designed to support.

27.1 What We Covered

In section 1 (Chapter 1), we introduced the application, the background and history of warehouse management for SAP, and the purpose and intent of this text. In section 2 (Chapters 2 through 7), we described the basic warehouse setup, including the organizational structure, warehouse structure, product master data and other master data, the concepts of warehouse stock management, and the warehouse document types. In section 3 (Chapters 8 through 14), we described the different types of warehouse movements — inbound processing, outbound processing, internal movements, the setup of multistep warehouse movements, and physical inventory (PI). In section 4 (Chapters 15 through 25), we covered various special topics in warehouse processing, including warehouse monitoring, exception handling, cross-docking, yard management, value-added services (VAS), kitting, Labor Management (LM), data capture, integration to other applications, form printing and other applications of the post-processing framework (PPF), authorization, roles, and archiving. In section 5 (Chapter 26), we covered the various components for deploying EWM, including deployment options, methods for automatic configuration, and loading data.

27.2 Key Learnings

Hopefully, you have taken away from this text as much as we intended to provide and you are now more empowered than before to lead or work on an EWM implementation project or make a decision about whether EWM is right for your business. Whether you read the text from cover to cover, jumped from one topic of interest to another, or simply used it as a reference guide, we hope that the contents within it provided the details that you needed to move your project forward or make the right business decisions.

As you can imagine, however, even with the extensive length of this text, we could not cover every topic in enough detail to answer every question that you may have. What we intended to provide was a baseline understanding of the application so that you can continue to extend your own knowledge in the areas that make sense for you, leveraging the other resources for knowledge sharing that are available from SAP, SAP Press, and the extensive SAP partners network.

27.3 The Future of EWM

As SAP EWM represents the strategic platform for SAP warehousing applications, we fully anticipate that SAP will continue to invest in the application and continue to support the needs and requirements of various types of distribution operations in a wide range of industries, to effectively compete in the highly competitive supply chain software market. As the application expands and evolves, we hope to provide you additional information on the topics covered by the application in subsequent texts.

27.4 Next Steps

Now that you have reached the conclusion, we hope that do not simply close the book and put it away on the shelf, but that you always keep it at arm's reach, ready to quickly access it in case you have any questions about the EWM application and its utilization to support your warehouse processes.

If you have additional questions about SAP EWM, we encourage you to also explore the various resources provided by SAP, including the following:

- SAP online help: *http://help.sap.com* • SAP BUSINESS SUITE • SAP EXTENDED WAREHOUSE MANAGEMENT
- Service Marketplace: *http://service.sap.com/scm* • WAREHOUSING
- SAP Community Network: *http://sdn.sap.com*

There are various forums, wikis, blogs, articles, eLearning opportunities, and other resources available for all SAP applications, including EWM. The EWM wiki can be found at: *http://wiki.sdn.sap.com/wiki/display/SCM/SAP+Extended+Warehouse+Management*

Abbreviations

AA	Activity Area
AII	Auto ID Infrastructure
ALV	ABAP List Viewer
APO	Advanced Planning and Optimizer
ASN	Advance Shipping Notice
ATP	Available To Promise
BAdI	Business Add-In
BAPI	Business Application Programming Interface
BBD	Best Before Date
BC Set	Business Configuration Set
BI	Business Intelligence (now "BW")
BIW	Business Information Warehouse (now "BW")
BP	Business Partner
BW	Business Warehousing (formerly "BI")
CATT	Computer Aided Test Tool
CC	Cycle Count
CCI	Cycle Count Indicator
CD	Cross-Docking
CICO	Check-In / Check-Out
CIF	Core Interface
CMS	Calculated Measurement Service
CO	Controlling
CRM	Customer Relationship Management
DSO	Data Store Object
DWM	Decentralized Warehouse Management
eCATT	Extended Computer Aided Test Tool
EGF	Easy Graphics Framework
EGR	Expected Goods Receipt

EH&S	Environment Health and Safety
ELS	Engineered Labor Standards
EM	Event Management (formerly SCEM)
EPC	Electronic Product Code
ERP	Enterprise Resource Planning
ETL	Extract Transform Load
EWM	Extended Warehouse Management
FEFO	First-Expiration / First-Out
FI	Finance
FIFO	First-In / First-Out
GI	Goods Issue
GR	Goods Receipt
GRN	Goods Receipt Notification
GWL	Graphical Warehouse Layout
HU	Handling Unit
IBGI	Invoice Before Goods Issue
ID	Inbound Delivery (EWM)
ID	Identification
IDN	Inbound Delivery Notification
IM	Inventory Management
IOT	Inspection Object Type
iPPE	Integrated Product and Process Engineering
KTO	Kit-to-Order
KTR	Reverse Kitting
KTS	Kit-to-Stock
LIME	Lean Inventory Management Engine
LM	Labor Management
LOSC	Layout-Oriented Storage Control
LSMW	Legacy System Migration Workbench
MFS	Material Flow System
OD	(Final) Outbound Delivery (EWM)

ODO	Outbound Delivery Order
ODR	Outbound Delivery Request
PACI	Putaway Control Indicator
Pack Spec	Packaging Specification
PC	Posting Change
PCR	Posting Change Request
PD	Push Deployment
PFGR	Pick From Goods Receipt
PGI	Post Goods Issue
PI	Physical Inventory
PI	Process Integration (formerly XI)
PLC	Programmable Logic Controller
PO	Purchase Order
POSC	Process-Oriented Storage Control
PPF	Post-Processing Framework
PS	Project Systems
PSA	Production Supply Area
PSA	Persistent Staging Area
QI	Quality Inspection
QIE	Quality Inspection Engine
qRFC	Queued Remore Function Call
RF	Radio Frequency
RFC	Remote Function Call
RFID	Radio Frequency Identification
RFUI	Radio Frequency User Interface (transaction /SCWM/RFUI)
RGE	Routing Guide Engine
S&R	Shipping and Receiving
SCAC	Standard Carrier Alpha Code
SCEM	Supply Chain Event Manager (now "EM")
SCM	Supply Chain Management

SCU	Supply Chain Unit
SLED	Shelf-Life Expiration Date
SNC	Supplier Network Collaboration
SOS	Sales Order Stock
SPP	Service Parts Planning
SSI	Storage Section Indicator
STO	Stock Transport Order
TCD	Transportation Cross-Docking
TCO	Total Cost of Ownership
TLB	Tranport Load Builder
TMS	Tailored Measurement Service
TU	Transportation Unit
UI	User Interface
VAS	Value-Added Service
WAN	Wide Area Network
WBS	Work Breakdown Structure
WCU	Warehouse Control Unit
WME	Warehouse Management Engine
WO	Warehouse Order
WOCR	Warehouse Order Creation Rule
WR	Warehouse Request
WT	Warehouse Task
XSI	eXpress Ship Interface
YM	Yard Management

The Authors

M. Brian Carter has worked with SAP, focusing on warehousing and distribution, since 1997. He is currently a solution manager in the Business Unit Service and Asset Management focusing on warehousing and reverse logistics business processes for the SAP solution for service parts management. Before working with SAP, Brian worked in operations for a third party logistics firm in the U.S. Brian lives in the Philadelphia, PA area with his wife, Teresa, and their two children, Evan and Meredith.

Joerg Lange has worked since 2002 for SAP Deutschland AG & Co. KG as Senior Consultant and Project Manager, working with customers mainly in the logistics area, especially warehouse management. In 2004, he participated in the development phases of SAP Extended Warehouse Management and since then has worked on implementation projects in Germany, France, Italy and the U.S. Joerg currently lives in Ratingen, Germany with his wife, Rebecca, and his son, Jonas.

Frank-Peter Bauer has worked with SAP Extended Warehouse Management since 2002, first as a developer in the EWM development team and then as a solution manager for the SAP solution for service parts management, focusing on EWM. Since 2007, he has worked in the consulting department for supply chain management as a principal consultant, project lead, and business development manager for EWM. Before joining SAP, Frank-Peter worked for six years as a supply chain consultant focusing on logistics and warehousing. He has worked on implementation of EWM with companies in Germany, the United Kingdom, and Sweden.

Christoph Persich is a solution consultant and project lead in the SAP field services department, where he leads customer projects for warehousing. His focus is the online mobile device integration with radio frequency technologies, which he successfully implemented in several customer projects. He is also responsible for implementing SAP RFID solutions and integrating them into the SAP solutions for warehouse processes.

Tim Dalm is a Principal Consultant with SAP America, Inc., with eight years of experience with SAP logistics and warehouse management solutions. He has worked on several SAP Extended Warehouse Management projects in the US and Europe. Tim currently lives in Philadelphia, PA.

Index

A

Interested in reading more?

Please visit our website for all
new book releases from SAP PRESS.

www.sap-press.com